WARSHIPS
OF
WORLD WAR II

Published by Ian Allan Ltd., Shepperton-on-Thames, Surrey, and printed in the United Kingdom by R. J. Acford Ltd., Chichester, Sussex.

WARSHIPS OF WORLD WAR II

H. T. LENTON
&
J. J. COLLEDGE

LONDON

IAN ALLAN

H.M.S. Warspite in Malta Harbour.
[*P. A. Vicary*

CONTENTS

Part 1 — Capital Ships 9

Part 2 — Destroyers and Submarines . 77

Part 3 — Sloops and Frigates . . . 157

Part 4 — Auxiliary Fighting Vessels . . 253

Part 5 — Auxiliary Support Vessels . 331

Part 6 — Trawlers, Whalers and Drifters . 401

Part 7 — Coastal Forces 481

Part 8 — Landing Craft 553

INTRODUCTION

THIS volume contains details of the ships of the British and Dominion Navies dealt with in the separate books of the Warships of World War II series, with certain revisions and corrections received by the authors during the past twelve months. Its object is to list those ships extant at the outbreak of the Second World War and then list, in its entirety, the large programme of war construction undertaken. For the sake of completeness the few vessels whose construction was cancelled, or only projected, or whose existence was limited to the " between wars " period, are included as otherwise no recorded details would be available of them.

The following format is standard:—

Displacement: Standard, as defined in the Washington Naval Treaty, is used throughout. Vessels completed prior to this date had their old national displacements re-assessed under Washington rules.

Dimensions: Perpendicular and overall length, beam inside bulges (except where noted) and mean draught at standard displacement.

Machinery: Number of shafts and type of prime mover, designed horse power and speed at standard displacement and mean draught.

Protection: Maximum and minimum thickness of armour on main belt, decks, main turrets and conning tower or director control tower. For deck armour, figures given are the total thickness where there are more than one armoured decks.

Armament: Details of guns, torpedo tubes, mines and aircraft carried. The notations (4×1) (1×2) etc. shown after guns and torpedo tubes indicate four single mountings, one twin mounting etc. Saluting guns (3 pdr.) are omitted as they were removed at the outbreak of war.[1]

Complement: Normal peace time figures are given as full war figures are variable within the same class and not generally available for all types of warships.

Tabular list: Pennant number, present and previous names, builder of hull (superior) and machinery (inferior) if different, launch date and fate including any further change of name or flag.[2]

Notes: Are principally related to any alteration in the above plus brief details of war employment.

[1] *At the end of the First World War flying-off platforms were fitted to the turrets of all capital ships and were either statically fitted before the bridge in cruisers or on revolving structures further aft. Aircraft were launched by either turning the platform or steaming directly into the wind at full speed but as aircraft developed, and their speed increased, they could no longer be launched in this manner. Therefore all flying-off platforms and aircraft were removed until a suitable catapult was evolved. After prolonged experience with the* PEGASUS *and the hopper-barge* SLINGER *the first catapults were fitted in the cruisers of the* **Kent** *class and subsequent new construction and added to capital ships—usually on " X " turret—as they were refitted.*

[2] *The flag superior to pennant numbers underwent some major changes during the war and is detailed in the " Notes ".*

Details of those vessels completed, or under construction, on the outbreak of war are given as for that date and would so include all modifications effected, or proposed, prior to that date. Notes are given where further war modifications are carried out. Details of war construction, on the other hand, are *as designed* and any changes, prior to completion, are similarly dealt with in the notes appended to each class.

Part One, covers capital ships, cruisers and aircraft carriers, giving details as set out in the previous paragraphs.

The Second Part describes the numerous destroyers and submarines which served in the war, together with details of the large war building programmes put in hand. Although 80 of the oldest destroyers have already been listed in WARSHIPS OF WORLD WAR I their complete listing again here was considered justified in view of the many alterations they underwent. The ex-U.S.N. destroyers are included with these older vessels as they belong to the same period. Of considerable interest are those allied and ex-enemy vessels which either served as H.M. Ships or passed under the operational control of the Royal Navy.

Sloops—an all-embracing term including escort vessels, patrol vessels, minesweepers, corvettes and frigates are dealt with in Part Three. Why this diversity of classification was used is not clear as all the vessels listed herein joined together, often taking over each other's functions, and performed the vital task of keeping sea-borne trade moving. This, they could do under the cover afforded by the main fleets and its detached aircraft carrier and cruiser squadrons but they were the initial bulwark against marauding aircraft, submarines and the indiscriminating mine; a combination which accounted for more lost mercantile tonnage than any other agent. In turn they mastered the mine and air and submarine attacks on mercantile trade: equally aided by technical brilliance in the development of new weapons and their own matchless war-acquired efficiency at sea in conjunction with, and supported by, maritime aircraft.

Only thirty-four sloops (six escort, twenty-six minesweeping and two coastal) remained of the large number built during World War I, of these, five had been converted to surveying vessels and all but one reverted to their original roles.

Listed separately are those American vessels transferred to the Royal Navy on "Lend/Lease" and coming within the sloop category. A moot point for inclusion, either here or in Part 2 (Destroyers and Submarines), were the American *destroyer-escorts*. As they were officially designated *frigates*, and were not pressed into service with the main fleets as destroyers, their inclusion, with the sloops, appeared more appropriate.

The auxiliary vessels, both naval built and mercantile conversions, are dealt with in Parts Four, Five and Six. Parts Four and Five embrace all classes except trawlers, drifters and whalecatchers which are dealt with in Part Six. For naval built vessels the same format has been observed as in earlier parts but for the majority of mercantile conversions the following details only have been listed.[1]

(a) pennant number.

(b) name, which in the majority of cases remained unaltered except where it was already borne by an existing warship.

(c) gross tonnage and year built.

(d) date commissioned, or requisitioned, for service in the Royal Navy.

(e) fate at end of naval service.

[1]Where possible, fuller details are given for the more elaborate conversions and vessels lost in naval service.

Inevitably, some mercantile auxiliaries will be listed more than once, when converted for other duties, but this has proved unavoidable as an alternative to elaborate cross-referencing. Finally, notes on armament (unfortunately not as complete as the authors would wish) and service will summarise the duties and activities of the different categories.

Part Seven embraces the coastal craft which, with a very few exceptions, were numbered and not named.

The same format has been observed as in previous parts except that, where known, the *full* displacement and not the *standard*; the *forward* and *after* draughts and not the *mean*; and both the *maximum* and *maximum continuous* horse powers and speeds have been shown wherever possible. The latter difference is important as maximum speed could only be maintained for a short period whereas the maximum continuous speed could be maintained indefinitely.

Part Eight describes the landing ships and craft which in Home Waters, the Mediterranean, and the Pacific, carried the Allied armies and their equipment to their ultimate object—the occupation of enemy home territory.

The co-authors experienced the singular difficulty that, for some type of landing craft, they were unable to ascertain the complete range of numbers involved. The issue was further complicated by the fact that some types of landing craft were modified to perform other functions and were sometimes re-numbered and, on other occasions, retained their original numbers. A typical example were the LCAs, of which over two thousand were built. Those altered to LCA (OC), LCA (HR), and LCA (FT) kept their original numbers (which were by no means consecutive but were selected *ad hoc*), while those converted to LCS (M) (1), (2), and (3), were re-numbered from 1 up, and their original LCA numbers, if allocated, remain a mystery. Thus for strict accuracy, the range of numbers shown against LCAs should exclude the numbers borne by these modified craft but such concise information is, unfortunately, not now available. Similarly, craft received under *Lend/Lease* from the U.S.A. were no by means consecutively numbered (as shown by an examination of LST (2)s and LCI (L)s) and it would, therefore, be incorrect to assume with smaller *Lend/Lease* craft that all the numbers, within a fixed range, were turned over to the Royal Navy.

In continuing the work started by the late Mr. H. M. Le Fleming the co-authors are indebted to Mrs. Le Fleming who kindly made available to them the preparatory notes compiled by her late husband. They would also wish to record their deep regret at the sudden and untimely death of Mr. Le Fleming whose life was bounded by the variety of ships he so ably wrote about.

The co-authors particularly wish to acknowledge the assistance they received from the late Commander A. C. Hardy, B.Sc., A.M.R.I.N.A., Mr. D. Trimingham (Bermuda), Mr. N. McKellar (Australia), Mr. G. Hudson, F.C.A., and Mr. Paul Silverstone (U.S.A.), all of the World Ship Society, and Mr. C. Hope-Johnson of *Shipbuilding & Shipping Record*, for assistance with research; the United States Navy for details of *Lend/Lease* warships and photographs; the very many builders, too numerous to mention, who so kindly co-operated with information and photographs of the vessels they built; Mr. A. P. Young and the staff of the Admiralty Library; Mr. J. F. Golding and the staff of the Imperial War Museum, Mr. G. A. Osbon and Messrs. A. & J. Pavia (Malta), Mr. P. A. Vicary for the fine selection of photographs they made available.

H.T.L.

January 1964 J.C.C.

PART ONE

Capital Ships, Cruisers and Aircraft Carriers

H.M.S. Dorsetshire, 1939.

[*P. A. Vicary*

WARSHIPS OF WORLD WAR 2

ON the outbreak of the Second World War the Royal Navies[1] were composed of a mixture of the old and the new. Practically half the vessels had seen service in, or their design dated from, the First World War whilst the bulk of the remainder had been designed in accordance with restrictive Naval Limitation Treaties. The principal treaties enacted between 1918-1939[2] were:—

(a) *The Washington Naval Treaty* (*1921*) which limited the displacement and armament of capital ships, aircraft carriers and cruisers and, in addition, the first two categories were further bound by age limits and total tonnage allocations.

(b) *The Geneva Naval Conference* (*1927*) which failed to agree on total tonnages for cruisers, destroyers and submarines and led to the maze of intricacies of

(c) *The First London Naval Treaty* (*1930*) which fixed the age limits and total tonnages of cruisers and divided them into two classes: armed with guns either over or under 6.1 in. It dealt similarly with destroyers and submarines but placed no restrictions whatsoever on surface vessels under 600 tons, whilst those between 600-2,000 tons were limited in armament and speed.

The major naval powers—the British Empire and Dominions, the United States of America, Japan, France and Italy—all participated at Washington but France and Italy declined acceptance at Geneva and although they attended, were not signatories, at London (1930). The end of restrictions and disarmament came on December 31st, 1936 when both the Washington and First London Naval Treaties terminated at the insistence of Japan, who henceforth proceeded on unfettered naval construction and drew a convenient veil over her activities. Meanwhile, the United Kingdom embroiled herself in further naval agreements with Germany and Russia, and the United States and France (London, 1936), which further restricted her cruisers to 8,000 tons and 6 in. guns but otherwise achieved nothing. It was in this atmosphere of parsimony and parity that the modest replacement vessels of the *between wars* period were built, woefully deficient in numbers, which shortage not even the vigorous re-armament programmes subsequent to 1936 were able to redress. Not only had the naval treaties placed restrictions on new construction but it also limited the amount of re-construction that was permissible with existing vessels. There was thus little time left, once the treaties were abrogated, to refit old vessels to new standards and the work had to be apportioned with regard to new construction ordered under the re-armament programmes. From 1937 onwards naval and commercial yards worked to capacity in building new, and refitting old, naval vessels.

The full building programmes, from 1918 to the close of the Second World War, are listed below. They can be used in conjunction with the tabular lists, which are chronologically arranged, so that the Estimates under which vessels were completed can be found by inspection.

1921 Estimates
Capital ships: 4 battlecruisers (cancelled)
Cruiser: ADVENTURE

1922 Estimates
Battleships: 2 **Nelson**

[1]An inclusive term for the Royal, Dominion and Colonial Naval Forces.
[2]Only salient details of the relevant treaties can be given.

1924 Estimates
Cruisers: 7 **Kent** (inc. 2 R.A.N.)

1925 Estimates
Cruisers: 4 **London**

1926 Estimates
Cruisers: 2 **Dorsetshire**, 1 **York**

1927 Estimates
Cruisers: 2 **Dorsetshire** (cancelled), 1 **York**

1928 Estimates
Cruisers: 2 **Dorsetshire** (cancelled), 2 **York** (cancelled), 1 **Leander**

1929 Estimates
Cruisers: 1 **Dorsetshire** (cancelled), 1 **York** (cancelled), 1 **Leander**

1930 Estimates
Cruisers: 3 **Leander**

1931 Estimates
Cruisers: 2 **Leander** (inc. 1 R.A.N.), 1 **Arethusa**

1932 Estimates
Cruisers: 2 **Leander** (R.A.N.), 1 **Arethusa**

1933 Estimates
Cruisers: 1 **Leander** (cancelled), 3 **Arethusa** (2 cancelled), 2 **Southampton**

1934 Estimates
Carrier: ARK ROYAL
Cruisers: 1 **Arethusa**, 3 **Southampton**

1935 Estimates
Cruisers: 3 **Southampton**

1936 Estimates
Battleships: 2 **King George V**
Carriers: 2 **Illustrious**
Cruisers: 2 **Southampton**, 5 **Dido**

1937 Estimates
Battleships: 3 **King George V**
Carriers: 2 **Illustrious**
Cruisers: 2 **Dido**, 5 **Fiji**

1938 Estimates
Battleships: 2 **Lion** (cancelled)
Carriers: 1 **Illustrious**, UNICORN
Cruisers: 3 **Dido**, 4 **Fiji**, 3 **Abdiel**

1939 Estimates and War Programme
Battleships: 2 **Lion** (cancelled)
Carriers: 1 **Illustrious**, 5 **Archer** (1 retained U.S.N.)
Cruisers: 6 **Dido**, 2 **Fiji**, 1 **Abdiel**

1940 War Programme
Battleship: VANGUARD
Monitor: ROBERTS

1941 War Programme
Carriers: 8 **Attacker**
Cruisers: 6 **Minotaur** (1 cancelled), 2 **Abdiel**
Monitor: ABERCROMBIE

1942 War Programme
Carriers: 32 **Ruler** (6 retained U.S.N.), 10 **Colossus, 6 Majestic,** 4 **Audacious** (2 cancelled)
Cruisers: 6 **Minotaur** (5 cancelled)

1943 War Programme
Carriers: 3 **Gibraltar** (cancelled), 8 **Hermes** (4 cancelled)

CAPITAL SHIPS

The vessels retained from the First World War were the CENTURION and IRON DUKE (both de-militarised), the **Queen Elizabeth**, **Royal Sovereign** and **Repulse** classes and the HOOD.

The CENTURION was employed as a wireless controlled target ship and was utilised, during the Second World War, as a dummy **King George V** class battleship. She was finally expended as part of the artificial harbour on the Arromanches beaches during the European landings in June, 1944 together with the old cruisers DURBAN and SUMATRA (R.Neth.N.), to which were added the Polish DRAGON after she had been torpedoed whilst covering the operations.

The IRON DUKE had been de-militarised as a Gunnery Training ship[3] and had her boiler power mutilated and speed reduced, her main belt armour removed and two turrets (" B " and " Y ") taken out. Deck and internal armour and the secondary battery were left intact and varying lighter calibre guns were added and removed from time to time for instructional and experimental purposes. Owing to severe bomb damage received early in the Second World War the IRON DUKE was grounded at Scapa Flow but continued to serve as a base ship.

Owing to their high speed priority was given to modernising the **Queen Elizabeth** class. Initially, the entire class had their two funnels trunked into a single uptake, the A.A. armament increased four 4 in. A.A. guns and aircraft and catapult added on " X " turret. The BARHAM was subsequently little further altered except for augmentation of the A.A. armament. The MALAYA was more extensively altered. She was re-engined, hangars added and the catapult made a fixed athwartship type, a pole replaced the tripod mainmast and the A.A. armament was increased. WARSPITE was completely reconstructed and modernised. In addition to alterations effected in the MALAYA the ponderous tripod foremast was replaced by a truncated tower with a light pole mast, the elevation of the main guns was increased, deck and magazine armour thickened, new boilers put in and the bunkerage increased. The battery was reduced by four guns and the T.T. removed but the A.A. armament was considerably enhanced. The QUEEN ELIZABETH and VALIANT followed the pattern set by the RENOWN (see later) and were added refinements on the WARSPITE.

[3]The Japanese battlecruiser HIEI was similarly demilitarised but was rapidly brought back to full combatant strength on the termination of the Washington and First London Naval treaties.

The **Royal Sovereign** class were little altered as being slower and smaller than the **Queen Elizabeth** class they were less adaptable to modern requirements. Such alterations as took place were limited to that undertaken on the BARHAM.

The two vessels of the **Repulse** class received widely differing alteration. The REPULSE had hangars added and the fixed catapult installed, the L.A. battery was reduced, the A.A. armament increased and above water T.T. supplanted submerged ones. Finally, four 4 in. A.A. in twin countersunk turrets were added and led to the adoption of this type of turret in RENOWN, QUEEN ELIZABETH and VALIANT. RENOWN was completely modernised and reconstructed on a scale that even surpassed the WARSPITE. She incorporated all the latter's modifications, had side armour extended and a homogeneous battery of D.P. guns, in ten twin turrets, replaced the former triple and single L.A. and A.A. mountings. To carry the increased weight of gear aloft a light fore tripod mast was re-introduced which was taken a state further in QUEEN ELIZABETH and VALIANT who had light tripod masts fore and aft. Following the loss of the HOOD the RENOWN remained the fastest British capital ship for the rest of the war.

Technically a post-Jutland ship, the HOOD was the fastest unit of the battle fleet and had the lowest priority amongst the vessels earmarked for modernisation. Due to the increased range of modern guns her horizontal protection against plunging fire was considered inadequate and, had time permitted, she would have been altered on similar lines to RENOWN. Her A.A. armament was increased to the standard of the BARHAM and the **Royal Sovereign** class but nothing else was done.

It is, perhaps, significant to note that all the capital ships which had restricted modernisation—the **Royal Sovereign** class excepted—became war losses. The HOOD because of insufficient horizontal armour, the REPULSE exposed to first rate air attack with a second rate A.A. battery and the BARHAM whose internal and magazine protection did not match that of her modernised sisters. The loss of the ROYAL OAK was a notable feat of arms on the part of the enemy but the remainder of the class only owed their immunity to the temerity of their employment. The PRINCE OF WALES, the only modern British capital ship to be lost, was part of an unbalanced force completely devoid of air cover but was nevertheless a signal success for a crack Japanese naval air squadron.

War modifications to capital ships were extensive and their bulk permitted considerable additions to be made. Also, such costly investments as capital ships (like aircraft carriers) received a higher priority than smaller vessels and could evaluate new equipment to a higher degree than small complements which lacked highly technical personnel.

The initial demand was to install warning and gunnery R.D.F. and augment the light A.A. armament with further multiple 2 pdr. mountings and varying numbers of 20 mm. guns. Aircraft and associated equipment was then removed so that further space and weight could be devoted to this purpose. Finally, the 40 mm. gun in multiple mountings tended to supplant the 2 pdr., and in single mountings replaced the 20 mm. In no instance did any capital ship sacrifice main or secondary armaments in order to supplement A.A. fire. Their volume of A.A. progressed steadily with the war as production demands were better met. The VANGUARD, the only war programmed capital ship to be completed, derived complete benefit from early war experience which was reflected in the simplicity of her ordnance. Only three calibres were borne: the main armament of 15 in. guns, a secondary dual purpose battery of 5.25 in. guns and a tertiary light A.A. battery of 40 mm. guns.

As it was unlikely that the **Lion** class would be completed during the duration of the war their construction was abandoned and more immediate requirements undertaken. Generally they would have followed the **King George V** class with three triple 16 in. gun turrets instead of the 14 in. gun arrangement of the latter. The decision to build the VANGUARD was prompted both by the desire to have at least one modern capital ship embracing war experience and the immediate availability of the twin 15 in. gun and mountings removed from the COURAGEOUS and GLORIOUS when converted to aircraft carriers and retained as spares. With the loss of four 15 in. gunned capital ships by the time VANGUARD was put in hand, these guns and mountings became surplus to requirements and as they frequently take longer to manufacture than the ships in which they are installed the construction of the VANGUARD, although not pushed, could have been expedited if required.

BATTLESHIPS

Target Ship

Displacement: 25,000 tons.
Dimensions: 555 (pp) 596 (oa) × 89 × 28 ft.
Machinery: 4-shaft Turbines, S.H.P. 31,000 = 21¾ knots reduced to 16 knots with mutilated boiler power.
Protection: Main belt 4-6 in. (ends), 8-12 in. (amid), deck 1¾-2¾ in.
Armament: Removed.
Complement: 250.

P. No.	Name	Builder	Launched	Fate
I.50	CENTURION	Devonport: Hawthorn Leslie	18.11.11	Expended as breakwater 9/6/44.

Notes:—Converted to Target Ship 1924. Altered as dummy **King George V** class battleship and armed with a few 2 pdr. and 20 mm. A.A. guns 1939-40. Home fleet 1939-41, East Indies 1942-44, U.K. and reduced to C. & M. until expended 1944.

Gunnery Training Ship

Displacement: 21,250 tons.
Dimensions: 580 (pp) 620 (oa) × 90 × 26 ft.
Machinery: 4-shaft Turbines, S.H.P. 31,000 = 21¼ knots reduced to 18 knots with mutilated boiler power.
Protection: Main belt removed but battery 6 in. retained, deck 1½-2½ in. (fwd), 2½-2¾ in. (amid), 1½-4 in. (aft), turrets 3-11 in., C.T. removed.
Armament: 6—13.5 in. (3 × 2), 12—6 in. (12 × 1) Guns.
Complement: 589.

P. No.	Name	Builder	Launched	Fate
18	IRON DUKE	Portsmouth: Cammell Laird	12.10.12	Scrapped Faslane 19/8/46.

Notes:—De-militarised as Gunnery Training ship 1931. Home fleet as Base ship 1939-45.

Queen Elizabeth class

Displacement: BARHAM & MALAYA 31,100 tons, WARSPITE 30,600 tons and QUEEN ELIZABETH & VALIANT 32,700 tons.
Dimensions: 600 (pp) $639\frac{3}{4}$ (oa) × $90\frac{1}{2}$ (104 outside bulges) × $30\frac{3}{4}$ except QUEEN ELIZABETH & VALIANT $32\frac{3}{4}$ ft.
Machinery: 4-shaft geared Turbines S.H.P. 80,000 except BARHAM 4-shaft Turbines S.H.P. 75,000 = 24 knots.
Protection: Main belt 4-6 in. (ends), 8-13 in. (amid), decks $1\frac{1}{4}$-3 in. (ends), $3\frac{1}{4}$-4 in. (amid) except QUEEN ELIZABETH & VALIANT $5\frac{3}{4}$-7 in. (ends), $3\frac{3}{4}$-$5\frac{1}{2}$ in. (amid), turrets 5-13 in., C.T. 11 in.
Armament: 8—15 in. (4 × 2), WARSPITE 8/BARHAM & MALAYA 12—6 in. (8/12 × 1) & 8—4 in. A.A. (4 × 2) and QUEEN ELIZABETH & VALIANT 20—4.5 in. DP (10 × 2), 32 except BARHAM & MALAYA 16—2 pdr. A.A. (2/4 × 8), 16—.5 in. M (4 × 4—WARSPITE, QUEEN ELIZABETH & VALIANT only) Guns; 2—21 in. (2 × 1—fixed) in BARHAM only; 4 except BARHAM 1 aircraft.
Complement: 1,124 (1,184 as Flagship).

04	BARHAM	Clydebank	31.12.14	Lost 25/11/41.
01	MALAYA	Armstrong: Parsons*	18. 3.15	Scrapped Faslane 12/4/48.
00	QUEEN ELIZABETH	Portsmouth: Fairfield*	16.10.13	Scrapped Dalmuir 7/7/48 and Troon (hull only).
02	VALIANT	Fairfield*	4.11.14	Scrapped Cairn Ryan 12/11/48 and Troon 10/3/50 (hull only).
03	WARSPITE	Devonport: Fairfield*	26.11.13	Wrecked 23/4/47 and scrapped *in situ*.

*Re-engined

Notes:—BARHAM, MALAYA and WARSPITE had 16—2 pdr. A.A. (2×8 not in WARSPITE) and several (31 in MALAYA) 20 mm. added. QUEEN ELIZABETH and VALIANT had 52—20 mm. A.A. (26 × 2) added and .5 in MG.'s removed. BARHAM Home fleet 1939-40, Force " H " 1940, Mediterranean fleet 1941. MALAYA Mediterranean fleet and Atlantic escort 1939-40, Force " H " 1941, Home fleet 1941-44, Reserve as accommodation ship 1945. QUEEN ELIZABETH Home fleet 1941, Mediterranean fleet 1941-42, Refit U.S.A. 1942-43, Eastern fleet 1944, East Indies 1945. WARSPITE Mediterranean and Home fleets 1939-42, Eastern fleet 1942-43, Force " H " 1943, Home fleet and Reserve 1944-45. VALIANT Home fleet 1940, Mediterranean fleet 1941-42, Eastern fleet 1942. Force " H " 1943, Home fleet 1943-44, Eastern fleet 1944, East Indies 1945.

Royal Sovereign class

Displacement: 29,150 tons.
Dimensions: 580 (pp) $620\frac{1}{2}$ (oa) × $88\frac{1}{2}$ ($101\frac{1}{2}$/$102\frac{1}{2}$ outside bulges) × $28\frac{1}{2}$ ft.
Machinery: 4-shaft Turbines, S.H.P. 40,000 = $21\frac{1}{2}$ knots.
Protection: Main belt 4-6 in. (ends), 6-13 in. (amid), decks 1-$2\frac{1}{2}$ in. (fwd), $1\frac{3}{4}$-2 in. (amid), 3-$5\frac{1}{2}$ in. (aft), turrets $4\frac{1}{4}$-13 in., C.T. 11-13 in.
Armament: 8—15 in. (4 × 2), 12—6 in. (12 × 1), 8—4 in. A.A. (4 × 2), 16—2 pdr. A.A. (2 × 8) Guns; REVENGE 2/ROYAL OAK 4—21 in. (2/4 × 1—fixed) T.T.; 1 aircraft.
Complement: 1,146.

Left: H.M.S. Barham, 1938. Note twin float plane on "X" gun turret.

[*P. A. Vicary*

Right: H.M.S. Queen Elizabeth at Trincomalee, March 1945. Note shortening effect of camouflage.

[*P. A. Vicary*

07	RAMILLIES	Beardmore	12. 9.16	Completed Cammell Laird; scrapped Cairn Ryan 23/4/48 and Troon 10/49 (hull only).
09	RESOLUTION	Palmers	14. 1.16	Scrapped Faslane 13/5/48.
06	REVENGE (ex-Renown)	Vickers	29. 5.15	Scrapped Inverkeithing 5/9/48.
08	ROYAL OAK	Devonport: Hawthorn Leslie	17.11.14	Lost 14/10/39.
05	ROYAL SOVEREIGN	Portsmouth: Parsons	29. 4.15	Russian ARCHANGELSK (1944-49); scrapped Inverkeithing 18/5/49.

Notes:—All, except ROYAL OAK, had 16/24—2 pdr. A.A. (2/3×8) and several 20 mm. A.A. added. RAMILLIES Home fleet 1939, East Indies and Mediterranean fleet 1940, Atlantic escort 1941, Eastern fleet 1942-43, Home fleet 1944, Reserve as accommodation ship 1945. RESOLUTION Home fleet and Atlantic escort 1939-40, Refit U.S.A. 1941, Eastern fleet 1942-43, Training ship 1944-45. REVENGE Home fleet and Atlantic escort 1939-41, Eastern fleet 1942-43, Training ship 1944-45. ROYAL OAK Home fleet 1939. ROYAL SOVEREIGN Home fleet 1939, Atlantic escort 1940-41, Eastern fleet and refit U.S.A. 1942-43, U.K. and reduced to C. & M. 1944.

BATTLECRUISERS

Repulse class

Displacement: 32,000 tons.
Dimensions: 750 (pp) 794¼ (oa) × 90 (102¾ outside bulges) × 26¾ ft.
Machinery: 4-shaft geared Turbines, S.H.P. 112,000 REPULSE, 120,000 RENOWN = 29 knots.
Protection: Main belt 4-6 in. (fwd), 6-9 in. (amid), 3 in. (aft), deck 2½/3 in. (fwd), 3-4 in. (amid), 3½-4 in. (aft), turrets. 7-11 in., C.T. 10 in.
Armament: 6—15 in. (3 × 2), 20—4.5 in. D.P. (10 × 2—RENOWN), 12—4 in. (4 × 3) & 8—4 in. A.A. (2 × 2 & 4 × 1—REPULSE), REPULSE 16/RENOWN 24—2 pdr. A.A. (2/3 × 8) Guns; 8—21 in. (4 × 2—fixed) T.T. REPULSE only; 4 aircraft.
Complement: 1,181 (1,205 as Flagship).

34	REPULSE (ex-Resistance)	Clydebank	8.1.16	Lost 10/12/41.
72	RENOWN	Fairfield: Cammell Laird*	4.3.16	Scrapped Faslane 1948.

*Re-engined

Notes:—REPULSE only had some 20 mm. A.A. added whilst RENOWN had 4—2 pdr. A.A. (1 × 4) and 62—20 mm. A.A. (18 × 2 & 26 × 1) added and later had 12—4.5 in. D.P. removed. REPULSE Home fleet 1939-41, Eastern fleet 1941. RENOWN South Atlantic 1939, Force " H " 1940-41, Home fleet 1942-44, Eastern fleet 1944, East Indies 1945.

H.M.S. Royal Oak, 1938, flying Admiral's flag. [*P. A. Vicary*

H.M.S. Repulse, May 1937. [*G. A. Osbon*

H.M.S. Renown, 1945, with forward 4.5 in. turrets removed. [*P. A. Vicary*

Displacement: 42,100 tons.
Dimensions: 810 (pp) 860$\frac{1}{2}$ (oa) × 105$\frac{1}{4}$ × 28$\frac{1}{2}$ ft.
Machinery: 4-shaft geared Turbines, S.H.P. 144,000 = 31 knots.
Protection: Main belt 5-6 in. (fwd), 5-12 in. (amid), 6 in. (aft), decks 1$\frac{1}{2}$-2 in. (fwd), 1$\frac{1}{4}$-3 in. (amid), 3-3$\frac{3}{4}$ in. (aft), turrets 11-15 in., C.T. 11-9 in.
Armament: 8—15 in. (4 × 2), 12—5.5 in. (12 × 1), 8—4 in. A.A. (4 × 2), 24—2 pdr. A.A. (3 × 8), 20—.5 in. M (5 × 4) Guns; 4—21 in. (2 × 2—fixed) T.T.
Complement: 1,341.

51	HOOD	Clydebank	22. 8.18	Lost 24/5/41.

Notes:—Original design was for 33,600 tons, 33 knots and 8—15 in. and 16—5.5. in. guns but considerable extra protection was worked in after Jutland, speed reduced and 4—5.5. in. guns suppressed. ANSON (Armstrong), HOWE (Cammell Laird) and RODNEY (Fairfield) were cancelled 1918. HOOD only had some 20 mm. A.A. added and served Home fleet 1939-41.

Displacement: 48,000 tons.
Dimensions: 820 (pp) 856 (oa) × 106 × 32$\frac{1}{2}$ ft.
Machinery: 4-shaft geared Turbines, S.H.P. 160,000 = 32 knots.
Protection: Main belt 12-14 in., deck 4-8 in. (fwd), 5 in. (amid), 3-7 in. (aft), turrets 8-17 in., D.C.T. 6-12 in.
Armament: 9—16 in. (3 × 3), 16—6 in. (8 × 2), 6—4.7 in. A.A. (6 × 1), 32—2 pdr. A.A. (4 × 8) Guns; 2—24.5 in. (2 × 1—fixed) T.T.; 2 aircraft.
Complement: 1,716.

	A	Swan Hunter: Parsons		Cancelled 1921.
	B	Beardmore: Vickers		Cancelled 1921.
	C	Fairfield		Cancelled 1921.
	D	Clydebank		Cancelled 1921.

Notes.—Although never officially named it was understood that they were to be called INVINCIBLE, INFLEXIBLE, INDOMITABLE and INDEFATIGABLE. They were to be followed by four even larger battleships of 48,500 tons armed with 9—18 in. (3 × 3) guns but all construction was halted by the Washington Naval Treaty. The battlecruisers were cancelled and the battleships never more than projected.

CAPITAL SHIPS

Nelson class

Displacement: NELSON 33,950 tons, RODNEY 33,900 tons.
Dimensions: 660 (pp) 710 (oa) × 106 × 28$\frac{1}{2}$ft.
Machinery: 2-shaft geared Turbines, S.H.P. 45,000 = 23 knots.
Protection: Main belt 14 in., deck 3$\frac{3}{4}$-6$\frac{1}{4}$ in., main turrets 9-16 in., D.C.T. 16 in.
Armament: 9—16 in. (3 × 3), 12—6 in. (6 × 2), 6—4.7 in. A.A. (6 × 1), 24—2 pdr. A.A. (2 × 8 & 8 × 1), 12—M Guns; 2—24.5 in. (2 × 1—fixed) T.T.; 1 NELSON, 2 RODNEY aircraft.
Complement: 1,314 (1,361 as Flagship).

Left: H.M.S. HOOD, 1937, flying Admiral's flag.

[*P. A. Vicary*

Right: H.M.S. Nelson at Malta in September, 1943.

[*P. A. Vicary*

28	NELSON	Armstrong	3. 9.25	Scrapped Inverkeithing 15/3/49.
29	RODNEY	Cammell Laird	17.12.25	Scrapped Inverkeithing 26/3/48.

Notes:—Embraced the main features of the cancelled 1921 battlecruisers but with greatly reduced speed to conform with the tonnage limitations of the Washington Naval treaty. 32—2 pdr. A.A. (4 × 8), 16—40 mm. A.A. (4 × 4) and 61/65—20 mm. A.A. were added and single 2 pdr. and MG.'s removed. NELSON Home fleet 1939-42, Force " H " 1943, Home fleet 1943-44, Refit U.S.A. 1944-45, East Indies 1945. RODNEY Home fleet 1939-42, Force " H " 1943, Home fleet 1943-45.

King George V class

Displacement: 35,000 tons.
Dimensions: 700 (pp) 745 (oa) × 103 × $27\frac{3}{4}$ ft.
Machinery: 4-shaft geared Turbines, S.H.P. 110,000 = 29 knots.
Protection: Main belt $4\frac{1}{2}$-$5\frac{1}{2}$ in.–14-15 in., deck 1 in.–5-6 in., main turrets 9-16 in., D.C.T. 16 in.
Armament: 10—14 in. (2 × 4 & 1 × 2), 16—5.25 in. D.P. (8 × 2), 48—2 pdr. A.A. (6 × 8) Guns; 4 aircraft.
Complement: 1,553-1,558.

41	KING GEORGE V	V.A. (Tyne)	21. 2.39	Scrapped Dalmuir 20/1/58 and Troon 5/59 (hull only).
53	PRINCE OF WALES	Cammell Laird	3. 5.39	Lost 10/12/41.
17	DUKE OF YORK (ex-Anson)	Clydebank	28. 2.40	Scrapped Faslane 18/2/58.
79	ANSON (ex-Jellicoe)	Swan Hunter: Wallsend	24. 2.40	Scrapped Faslane 17/12/57.
32	HOWE (ex-Beatty)	Fairfield	9. 4.40	Scrapped Inverkeithing 4/6/58.

Notes:—About 16—20 mm. A.A. (16 × 1) were initially added in all but these were later replaced and supplemented (not in PRINCE OF WALES) by 16 KING GEORGE V; 24 Anson: 40 others 2 pdr. A.A. (2×8 2/6×4), 8—40 mm. A.A. (2×4) and *circa* 16—20 mm. A.A. (8×2). KING GEORGE V Home fleet 1940-43, Force " H " 1943, Home fleet, 1943-44, Pacific fleet 1945. PRINCE OF WALES Home fleet 1940-41, Eastern fleet 1941. DUKE OF YORK Home fleet 1941-45. ANSON Home fleet, 1942-45 Pacific fleet 1945. HOWE Home fleet 1942-43, Force " H " 1943, Home fleet 1943-44, Eastern fleet 1944-45.

Lion class

Displacement: 40,000 tons.
Dimensions: 740 (pp) 785 (oa) × 105 × 30 ft.
Machinery: 4-shaft geared Turbines, S.H.P. 152,000 = 30 knots.
Protection: Main belt 14-15 in., deck 6 in., turrets 16 in., D.C.T. 16 in.
Armament: 9—16 ins. (3 × 3), 16—5.25 in. D.P. (8 × 2), 48—2 pdr. A.A. (6 × 8) Guns.
Complement: 1,500.

H.M.S. RODNEY at Malta in August 1943, showing anti-torpedo boom rigged and 4.7 in. A.A. guns in shields. [*P. A. Vicary*

H.M.S. Duke of York, 1946. [*P. A. Vicary*

27 36	LION TEMERAIRE	V.A. (Tyne) Cammell Laird		Cancelled 1940. Cancelled 1940.
45 49	CONQUEROR THUNDERER	Clydebank Fairfield		Cancelled 1940. Cancelled 1940.

Displacement: 42,500.
Dimensions: 760 (pp) 814¼ (oa) × 107½ × 28 ft.
Machinery: 4-shaft geared Turbines, S.H.P. 130,000 = 29½ knots.
Protection: Main belt 4½-5½-13-14 in., main turrets 4-13 in., deck 5-6 in. D.C.T. 13 in.
Armament: 8—15 in. (4 × 2), 16—5.25 in. D.P. (8 × 2), 71—40 mm. A.A. (10 × 6, 1 × 4 & 7 × 1) Guns. *Complement:* 1,600.

23	VANGUARD	Clydebank	30.11.44	Scrapped Faslane 9/8/60.

MONITORS

Displacement: SOULT 6,400 tons, NEY 6,700 tons.
Dimensions: 340 (pp) 355¾ (oa) × 90¼ (outside bulges) × 10¼ ft.
Machinery: 2-shaft Diesel motors, B.H.P. 1,500 = 6½ knots.
Protection: Main belt 4-6 in., deck 1 in. (fwd), 3-5 in. (amid), 1½ in. (aft), turret 4¼-13 in., C.T. 6 in.
Armament: 2—15 in. (1 × 2), 8—4 in. (8 × 1), 3—3 in. A.A. (3 × 1) Guns. NEY disarmed. *Complement:* 280.

Hulk	MARSHAL NEY (ex-M.13)	Palmers	17. 6.15	VIVID (1920), DRAKE (1934), ALAUNIA II (1947). Scrapped Milford Haven 6/10/57.
I.01	MARSHAL SOULT (ex-M.14)	Palmers	24. 8.15	Scrapped Troon 5/8/46.

Notes:—NEY was a disarmed hulk throughout the war whilst SOULT, after a short period as a training ship, was similarly disarmed and hulked. Flag superior changed to F (1940).

Displacement: 7,200 tons.
Dimensions: 380 (pp) 405 (oa) × 88 (outside bulges) × 11 ft.
Machinery: 2-shaft Reciprocating (V.T.E.), I.H.P. 6,000=12 knots.
Protection: Main belt 4-6 in., deck ¾ in. (fwd), 3-5 in. (amid), 1-1¾ in. (aft), turret 4¼-13 in., upper bridge 1 in. C.T. removed.
Armament: 2—15 in. (1 × 2), 8—4 in. (8 × 1), 2—3 in. AA (2 × 1) Guns.
Complement: 315.

I.02	EREBUS (ex-M.15)	Harland & Wolff (Govan)	19. 6.16	Scrapped Inverkeithing 1946/47.
I.03	TERROR (ex-M.16)	Harland & Wolff (Govan)	18. 5.16	Lost 24/2/41.

Notes:—TERROR was not altered but EREBUS had the 4 in. and 3 in. A.A. removed and 6—4 in A.A. (6 × 1), 8—2 pdr. A.A. (2 × 4) and a few single 20 mm. A.A. added. Flag superior changed to F (1940).

Roberts class

Displacement: ROBERTS 7,970 tons, ABERCROMBIE 7,850 tons.
Dimensions: 373¼ (oa) × 89¾ × 11 ft.
Machinery: 2-shaft geared Turbines, S.H.P. 4,800 = 12 knots.
Protection: Main belt 4-6 in., deck 1-4 in., turret 4¼-13 in., D.C.T. 6 in.
Armament: 2—15 in. (1 × 2), 8—4 in. A.A. (4 × 2), 16—2 pdr. A.A. (1 × 8 & 2 × 4), 16—20 mm. A.A. (4 × 2 & 6 × 1) Guns.
Complement: 350.

F.40	ROBERTS	Clydebank	1. 2.41	For disposal.
F.109	ABERCROMBIE	V.A. (Tyne): Parsons	31. 3.42	Scrapped Barrow 24/12/54.

NOTES:—Were armed with the turrets removed from the SOULT and NEY. 20 mm. were replaced by 6—40 mm. A.A. (6 × 1).

CRUISERS

The vessels retained from the First World War were the ADELAIDE (R.A.N.), and the **Caledon, Ceres, Cardiff, Improved Birmingham, "D"** and **"E"** classes. All, except the **Improved Birmingham** and **"E"** classes, were small vessels which however excellent in their day were not adaptable to modern conditions. The ADELAIDE (sole survivor of the **Birmingham** class) was quite obsolete and only her delayed completion had ensured her retention this long. The various **"C"** and **"D"** classes had been quite outclassed by modern construction and were significantly weak in aerial defence. The **Improved Birmingham** and **"E"** classes were larger and wholly seaworthy vessels and the latter had the dual distinction of being both the fastest and most heavily torpedo armed vessels in the Royal Navy—an agressive combination by any standards. The **Improved Birmingham** class were well armed and armoured and although initially weak in aerial defence their size permitted a sufficient margin for this deficiency to be partially redressed. Although the Naval Limitation treaties had halted capital ship construction it had not directly done so with cruisers. Qualitative, and later total tonnage, limitations only had been placed on them and they could be replaced as soon as over-age. There was no provision to modernise old cruisers which, in the normal course of events, would be scrapped when replaced by modern construction. However, as the major naval powers built up to the limits imposed at Washington the Royal Navy found itself in the unenviable position of having insufficient numbers if it did likewise, owing to the total tonnage limitation with which it was fettered at London (1930). Over-age vessels were therefore retained to make up the number required by the Royal Navy for the protection of its widespread trade and lines of communications.

Two of the **"C"** class, COVENTRY and CURLEW, were re-armed solely as anti-aircraft vessels during the Abyssinian crisis (1936)—a conversion which showed considerable promise and was to be extended to the remainder of the class. But time only allowed the CURACOA and the entire **Capetown** (less the nameship) group to be so re-armed. The **"D"** class had a single 4 in. A.A. gun added on the after shelter deck whilst the **"E"** class except for the addition of aircraft and catapult, remained quite unaltered. EFFINGHAM, of the **Improved Birmingham** class, was completely re-armed and modernised but FROBISHER hurriedly re-shipped her old guns (which had been removed whilst she was employed as a training ship) when war threatened but omitted the beam guns to augment her A.A. armament. HAWKINS only added to her light A.A. armament but nothing was done to again make VINDICTIVE (ex-Cavendish) a combatant unit. She had only recently undergone an extensive conversion to a training ship (vice FROBISHER) and would have absorbed time and labour better devoted elsewhere.

Thus, at the outbreak of the Second World War, only the re-armed A.A. vessels, the **Improved Birmingham** and "E" classes were capable of employment with the main fleets and only EFFINGHAM and the two "E" class carried aircraft. The remainder were mainly suitable for the protection of trade for which their speed, protection and armament were adequate to deal with mercantile raiders although their radius of action was somewhat restricted. With a singular exception (DELHI) war modifications to these old cruisers were not extensive and limited R.D.F. and a few light A.A. guns were added in all. EMERALD sacrificed her quarterdeck 6 in. gun for 4—2 pdr. A.A. (1 × 4) and ENTERPRISE her beam 6 in. guns for 8—2 pdr. A.A. (2 × 4) and both had the two after banks of T.T. removed and the pole mainmast replaced by a tripod. Following action damage the DELHI was completely refitted and re-armed in the U.S.A. with 5—5 in. D.P. (5 × 1), 8—2 pdr. A.A. (2 × 4) and 10—20 mm. A.A. (2 × 2 & 6 × 1) guns and emerged a completely battleworthy unit. As the war progressed these older cruisers were relegated to subsidiary duties as training and base and accommodation ships and only the DELHI and the fleet "E" class (which still retained their aircraft) continued to be actively employed.

The modern cruisers were little altered up to 1939 with the exception of some of the **Kent** class and the LONDON. Cruisers, excluding the minelayers, that preceded the PENELOPE (1933 Estimates) had their single 4 in. A.A. guns replaced by twin mountings (only the **London** class received four additional single guns) and 8/16—2 pdr. A.A. (2 × 4/8) were added in the classes prior to the SOUTHAMPTON (1933 Estimates). This mounting had been experimentally fitted in the ADVENTURE in 1930 but was soon removed, after a successful trial, for general adoption in the fleet.

Four units of the **Kent** class (less the nameship and the R.A.N. vessels) and the LONDON were the only vessels to receive major refits before the outbreak of war. The **Kent** class all had large hangars added aft, the training catapult replaced by a fixed athwartship one and a narrow waterline belt added in addition to the increased A.A. armament mentioned above. The first pair to complete had the freeboard abaft "Y" turret reduced to compensate for the additional weight but this was not done with the last pair. LONDON was completely altered and closely resembled the **Fiji** class but her modifications were otherwise similar to that carried out on the **Kent** class.

The modern cruisers were generally well equipped for the war that followed and showed remarkable powers of resistance due to such invisible assets as strong construction embraced by a seaworthy hull. The need to augment the A.A. armament was more brought about by the continental enemies policy of attrition from the air as they neither possessed the surface fleet (Germany) or the aggressive spirit (Italy) to otherwise perform the task. The Japanese had both these qualities in abundance and a polygot collection of scattered British and Allied ships suffered in consequence.

The war modifications to modern cruisers were extensive and could not possibly be listed in detail within the parameters of this book. The opportunity was taken at every refit or overhaul to add some new item of available equipment and homogeneity within classes soon ceased to exist. The principal modifications effected were:—

(a) installation of warning and gunnery control R.D.F. and the addition of varying numbers of single 20 mm. guns which supplanted the .5 in. MG's.

(b) the removal of aircraft and associated equipment (of diminished importance with long range warning R.D.F.) so that the light A.A. armament could be further supplemented.

(c) the removal of "X" turret in many units for final additions and refinement to the light A.A. armament together with increased gunnery R.D.F. sets. At this stage the 40 mm. gun had completely replaced the 20 mm. and partially replaced the 2 pdr.

Production difficulties hampered heavy augmentation of the A.A. armament whose deficiency was realised at a very early stage. Such difficulties also accounted for two **Dido** class vessels receiving provisional armaments of 8—4.5 in. D.P. until their 5.25 in. guns were available, and one was so lost before this was achieved. Although R.D.F. never equalled the range of aerial reconnaisance it provided sufficient warning so that aircraft, whose installation had been the outcome of considerable effort "between the wars", could be landed and the weight and space be made available for the more pressing need of A.A. defence. Pole masts, which had been such a feature of post-1918 cruiser construction, could no longer support the weight of gear aloft brought about by the advent of R.D.F. and led to the re-introduction of tripods.

Birmingham class

Displacement: 5,100 tons.
Dimensions: 430 (pp) 462¾ (oa) × 49¾ × 15¾ ft.
Machinery: 2-shaft geared Turbines, S.H.P. 25,000 = 25½ knots.
Protection: Main belt 1½ in. (ends), 3 in. (amid), deck 1-2 in., shields 1 in.
Armament: 8—6 in. (8 × 1), 3—4 in. A.A. (3 × 1) Guns.
Complement: 470.

I.47	ADELAIDE (R.A.N.)	Cockatoo	27. 7.18	Scrapped Port Kembla 30/3/49.

Notes:—Sole survivor of a cycle of twenty-one (**Bristol, Weymouth, Chatham, Birmingham** and **Birkenhead** classes) medium sized broadside cruisers. Served Australia 1939-45. Flag superior changed to D (1940).

Caledon class

Displacement: 4,180 tons.
Dimensions: 425 (pp) 450 (oa) × 42¾ × 14¼ ft.
Machinery: 2-shaft geared Turbines, S.H.P. 40,000 = 29 knots.
Protection: Main belt 1¼-2¾ in. (fwd), 3 in. (amid), 2-2½ in. (aft), deck 1 in., shields 1 in., C.T. 6 in. & 4 in. tube.
Armament: 5—6 in. (5 × 1), 2—3 in. A.A. (2 × 1), 2—2pdr. A.A. (2 × 1) Guns; 8—21 in. (4 × 2) T.T.
Complement: 400 (437 as Flagship).

I.53	CALEDON	Cammell Laird	25.11.16	Scrapped Dover 22/1/48.
I.61	CALYPSO	Hawthorn Leslie	24. 1.17	Lost 12/6/40.
I.60	CARADOC	Scotts	23.12.16	Scrapped Briton Ferry 5/4/46.

Notes:—A few single 20 mm. A.A. were added in all, and CALEDON re-armed 8—4 in. A.A. (4 × 2) and 8—2 pdr. A.A. (1 × 8). CALEDON Home fleet 1939, Mediterranean fleet 1940, Red Sea 1940-41, East Indies and Eastern fleet 1942, converted to A.A. vessel 1942-43, Mediterranean 1944-45, Reserve 1945. CALYPSO Home fleet 1939, Mediterranean fleet 1940. CARADOC America and West Indies 1939-42, Eastern fleet 1942-43, South Atlantic 1943-44, Base ship (Colombo) 1944-45, Flag superior changed to D (1940).

Ceres class

Displacement: 4,190 tons.
Dimensions: 425 (pp) 451½ (oa) × 43½ × 14¼ ft.
Machinery: 2-shaft geared Turbines, S.H.P. 40,000 = 29 knots.
Protection: Main belt 1¼-2¼ in. (fwd), 3 in. (amid), 2-2½ in. (aft), deck 1 in., shields 1 in., C.T. 3 in.
Armament: 5—6 in. (5 × 1), 2—3 in. A.A. (2 × 1), 2—2 pdr. A.A. (2 × 1) Guns; 8—21 in. (4 × 2) T.T. except COVENTRY and CURLEW 10—4 in. A.A. (10 × 1), 16—2 pdr. A.A. (2 × 8) Guns and CURACOA 8—4 in. A.A. (4 × 2), 4—2 pdr. A.A. (1 × 4), 8—.5 in. M (2 × 4) Guns.
Complement: 400 (437 as Flagship).

I.58	CARDIFF (ex-Caprice)	Fairfield	12. 4.17	Scrapped Troon 3/46.
I.59	CERES	Clydebank	24. 3.17	Scrapped Blyth 12/7/46.
I.43	COVENTRY (ex-Corsair)	Swan Hunter: Wallsend	6. 7.17	Lost 14/9/42.
I.41	CURACOA	Pembroke: Harland & Wolff	5. 5.17	Lost 2/10/42.
I.42	CURLEW	Armstrong: Vickers	5. 7.17	Lost 26/5/40.

Notes:—COVENTRY and CURLEW were prototype conversions to A.A. vessels later extended to CURACOA and entire **Capetown** class. CERES had 1—2 pdr. A.A. and 4—20 mm. A.A. (4 × 1) added and a few single 20 mm. A.A. were added in others. CARDIFF Home fleet 1939, Training ship 1940-45, Reserve 1945, CERES Home fleet 1939, Mediterranean fleet 1940, East Indies 1940-42, Eastern fleet 1942-43, Reserve as Accommodation ship 1944-45. COVENTRY Home fleet 1939-40, Mediterranean fleet 1940-42. CURACOA Home fleet 1940-42. CURLEW Home fleet 1939-40 Flag superior changed to D (1940).

Capetown class

Displacement: 4,290 tons.
Dimensions: 425 (pp) 451½ (oa) × 43½ × 14¼ ft.
Machinery: 2-shaft geared Turbines, S.H.P. 40,000 = 29 knots.
Protection: Main belt 1¼-2¼ in. (fwd), 3 in. (amid), 2-2½ in. aft, deck 1 in.
Armament: 8—4 in. A.A. (4 × 2), 4—2 pdr. A.A. (1 × 4), 8—.5 in. M (2 × 4) Guns.
Complement: 400 (437 as Flagship).

Left:
H.M.A.S. Adelaide. Fore funnel removed when converted to oil firing 1938/39.

[P. A. Vicary

Right:
H.M.S. Calypso at Malta in 1938.

[A. & J. Pavia

Left:
H.M.S. Cardiff, July 1945. The French destroyer Mistral in the background was commissioned as an H.M. ship.

[*P. A. Vicary*

Right:
H.M.S. Coventry, 1937, re-armed as an A.A. cruiser.

[*P. A. Vicary*

I.87	CAIRO	Cammell Laird	19.11.18	Lost 12/8/42.
I.82	CALCUTTA	Armstrong: Vickers	9. 7.18	Lost 1/6/41.
I.88	CAPETOWN	Cammell Laird	28. 6.19	Completed by Pembroke; scrapped Preston 6/46.
I.67	CARLISLE (ex-Cawnpore)	Fairfield	9. 7.18	Constructive total loss 9/10/45; scrapped Alexandria 1949.
I.89	COLOMBO	Fairfield	18.12.18	Scrapped Newport 5/48.

Notes:—Differed from **Ceres** group by having *trawler* bow fitted. Conversion of CAPETOWN to A.A. vessel did not materialise owing to outbreak of war and she retained original armament 5—6 in. (5 × 1), 2—3 in. A.A. (2 × 1) Guns and 8—21 in. (4 × 2) T.T. A few single 20 mm. A.A. were added in all. CAIRO Home fleet 1939-42, Mediterranean fleet 1942. CALCUTTA Home fleet 1939-40, Mediterranean fleet 1940-41. CAPETOWN Mediterranean fleet 1939-40, East Indies 1941-42, Eastern fleet 1942-43, Reserve as Accommodation ship 1944-45. CARLISLE Home fleet 1939, Red Sea 1940-42, Mediterranean fleet 1942-43, Levant and Base ship (Alexandria) 1943-45. COLOMBO Home fleet 1939, East Indies 1940-41, Eastern fleet 1942, converted to A.A. vessel 1942-43, Mediterranean fleet 1943-45, Reserve 1945. Flag superior changed to D (1940).

Improved Birmingham class

Displacement: 9,770 tons, 9,550 tons, 9,860 tons and 9,800 tons *respectively*.
Dimensions: 565 (pp) 605 (oa) × 58 (65 over bulges) × 17¼ ft.
Machinery: 4-shaft Turbines, S.H.P. 65,000 = 30½ knots.
Protection: Main belt 1½-2½ in. (fwd), 2-3 in. (amid), 2¼-2½ in. (aft), deck 1-1½ in., shields 1-2½ in., C.T. 3 in. (removed in VINDICTIVE and EFFINGHAM).
Armament: 7 except FROBISHER 5—7.5 in. (5/7 × 1), 4 except FROBISHER 5—4 in. A.A. (4/5 × 1), 8—2 pdr. A.A. (2 × 4), 10—20 mm. A.A. (10 × 1) Guns; 6—21 in. (6 × 1—all fixed) T.T. EFFINGHAM 9—6 in. (9 × 1), 8—4 in. A.A. (4 × 2), 8—2 pdr. A.A. (2 × 4), 8—.5 in. M (2 × 4) Guns; 4—21 in. (4 × 1—all fixed) T.T.; 1 aircraft. VINDICTIVE 2—4.7 in. Guns as Training ship.
Complement: 712 (749 as Flagship) except VINDICTIVE 468 + 200 cadets.

I.36	VINDICTIVE (ex-Cavendish)	Harland & Wolff: Parsons	17. 1.18	Scrapped Blyth 14/2/46.
I.98	EFFINGHAM	Portsmouth: Harland & Wolff	8. 6.21	Lost 21/5/40.
I.81	FROBISHER	Devonport: Wallsend	20. 3.20	Scrapped Newport 5/49.
I.86	HAWKINS	Chatham: Parsons	1.10.17	Scrapped Dalmuir 12/47.
	RALEIGH	Beardmore	28. 8.19	Wrecked 8/8/22.

Notes:—VINDICTIVE was completed as an aircraft carrier but was converted back to a cruiser 1923-25, then to a training ship 1936-37 and finally to a repair ship 1940. VINDICTIVE converted to Repair ship 1939-40, South Atlantic 1940-42, Mediterranean fleet 1943-44, Home fleet and Reserve 1945. EFFINGHAM America and West Indies 1939, Atlantic escort and Home fleet 1940. FROBISHER Rearming 1939-42, Eastern fleet 1942-44, Home fleet 1944, Training ship 1945. HAWKINS South Atlantic 1940-41, East Indies 1941-42, Eastern fleet 1942-44, Home fleet 1944, Training ship 1944-45, Reserve 1945. Flag superior changed to D (1940).

"D" class

Displacement: 4,850 tons.
Dimensions: 445 (pp) 472½ (oa) × 46½ × 14½ ft.
Machinery: 2-shaft geared Turbines, S.H.P. 40,000 = 29 knots.
Protection: Main belt 1½-2 in. (ends), 3 in. (amid), deck 1 in., shields 1 in.
Armament: 6—6 in. (6 × 1), 3—4 in. A.A. (3 × 1), 2—2pdr. A.A. (2 × 1) Guns; 12—21 in. (4 × 3) T.T.
Complement: 450 (469 as Flagship).

I.44	DANAE	Armstrong: Wallsend	26. 1.18	Polish CONRAD (1944-46); scrapped Barrow 27/3/48.
I.45	DAUNTLESS	Palmers	10. 4.18	Scrapped Inverkeithing 13/2/46.
I.74	DELHI*	Armstrong: Wallsend	23. 8.19	Scrapped Newport 5/48.
I.46	DRAGON*	Scotts	29.12.17	Polish (name not changed, (1944); expended as breakwater 8/7/44.
I.93	DUNEDIN*	Armstrong: Hawthorn Leslie	19.11.18	Completed Devonport, R.N.Z.N. (1924-37); lost 24/11/41.
I.99	DURBAN*	Scotts	29. 5.19	Expended as breakwater 9/6/44.
I.30	DESPATCH*	Fairfield	21.12.19	Completed Chatham; scrapped Troon 8/46.
I.92	DIOMEDE*	Vickers	29. 4.19	Completed Portsmouth, R.N.Z.N. (1935-37); scrapped Dalmuir 13/5/46.

*trawler bow

Notes:—DAEDALUS (Armstrong), DARING (Beardmore), DESPERATE (Palmer) and DRYAD (Vickers) were cancelled. DIOMEDE had fo'c'sle 6 in. gun in turret. All had a few single 20 mm. A.A. added and DELHI was re-armed with 5—5 in. D.P. (5 × 1), 8—2 pdr. A.A. (2 × 4), 10—20 mm. A.A. (2 × 2 & 6 × 1) guns. DANAE China 1939-41, Eastern fleet 1942-44, Home fleet 1944-45. DAUNTLESS China 1939-41, Eastern fleet 1942-43, Training ship 1943-45. DELHI Home fleet 1939, Mediterranean fleet 1940, South Atlantic 1941-42, Refit U.S.A. 1941-42, Home fleet 1942, Mediterranean fleet 1943-45, Reserve 1945. DRAGON Home fleet 1939, Mediterranean fleet and East Indies 1940, South Atlantic 1940-41, Eastern fleet 1942, Home fleet 1943-44. DUNEDIN Home fleet 1939, America and West Indies 1940, South Atlantic 1941-42. DURBAN China 1939-41, Eastern fleet 1942-43, Home fleet 1944. DESPATCH America and West Indies 1939-42, South Atlantic 1942-43, Home fleet 1944, Reserve as Accommodation ship 1945. DIOMEDE Home fleet 1939, America and West Indies 1940-42, South Atlantic 1942, Home fleet 1942-43, Training ship 1943-45. Flag superior changed to D (1940).

"E" class

Displacement: 7,550 tons and 7,580 tons *respectively*.
Dimensions: 535 (pp) 570 (oa) × 54½ × 16¼ ft.
Machinery: 4-shaft geared Turbines, S.H.P. 80,000 = 33 knots.
Protection: Main belt 1½-2½ in. (fwd), 3 in. (amid), 2 in. (aft), deck 1 in., shields 1 in.
Armament: 7—6 in. (EMERALD 7 × 1, ENTERPRISE 1 × 2 & 5 × 1), 3—4 in. A.A. (3 × 1), 2—2 pdr. A.A. Guns; 16—21 in. (4 × 4) T.T.; 1 aircraft.
Complement: 572.

H.M.S. Diomede, 1938. Note fo'c'sle 6 in. gun in turret and absence of flash screen round forward shelter deck. [*P. A. Vicary*

H.M.S. Dunedin, May 1937. [*G. A. Osbon*

H.M.S. Dauntless, April 1942, with after 4 in. A.A. gun removed and 5-20 mm. A.A. and R.D.F. added. [*I.W.M.*

H.M.S. Delhi, July 1943, with American guns and fire control after re-fit in U.S.A. [*P. A. Vicary*

H.M.S. Emerald at Colombo, January 1944, and still carrying aircraft. [*P. A. Vicary*

H.M.S. Cornwall, June 1938. Hangar added but hull not cut down aft. H.M.S. Berwick was similar. [*P. A. Vicary*

H.M.S. Cumberland, 1938. Hangar added and hull cut down aft. H.M.S. Suffolk was similar. [*P. A. Vicary*

I.66	EMERALD	Armstrong: Wallsend	19. 5.20	Completed Chatham; scrapped Troon 23/7/48.
I.52	ENTERPRISE	Clydebank	23.12.19	Completed Devonport; scrapped Newport 11/4/46.

Notes:—EUPHRATES (Fairfield) was cancelled. ENTERPRISE had both fwd. 6 in. guns in a twin turret and the D.C.T. on the bridge instead of the foremast. Its success led to its adoption in the **Nelson** class battleships as secondary armament. EMERALD had aft 6 in. gun replaced by 4—2 pdr. A.A. (1 × 4) and ENTERPRISE both beam 6 in. guns by 8—2 pdr. A.A. (2 × 4). Both had the two after banks of T.T. removed and several single 20 mm. A.A. added. EMERALD Atlantic escort 1939-40, East Indies 1941-42, Eastern fleet 1942-44, Home fleet 1944, Reserve 1945. ENTERPRISE Atlantic escort 1939-40, Home fleet 1940, South Atlantic 1940-41, East Indies 1941-42, Eastern fleet 1942-43, Home fleet 1943-44, Reserve and trooping 1945. Flag superior changed to D (1940).

Kent class

Displacement: 9,750 tons except SUFFOLK 9,800 tons, KENT and CANBERRA 9,850 tons and AUSTRALIA 9,870 tons.
Dimensions: 590 (pp) 630 (oa) × 68¼ (outside bulges) × 16¼ft.
Machinery: 4-shaft geared Turbines, S.H.P. 80,000 = 31½ knots.
Protection: Main belt 3-5 in., deck 1½ in. 3-4 in., turrets 1½-2 in., D.C.T. 3 in.
Armament: 8—8 in. (4 × 2), 8—4 in. A.A. (4 × 2), 8—2 pdr. A.A. (2 × 4), 8—.5 M (2 × 4) Guns; 8—21 in. (2 × 4 in KENT and R.A.N. vessels only) T.T.; 4 except KENT and R.A.N. vessels 1 aircraft.
Complement: 679 (710 as Flagship).

65	BERWICK	Fairfield	30. 3.26	Scrapped Blyth 12/7/48.
56	CORNWALL	Devonport: Beardmore	11. 3.26	Lost 5/4/42.
57	CUMBERLAND	V.A.(Barrow)	16. 3.26	Converted to trials vessel (1949); scrapped Newport 3/11/59.
54	KENT	Chatham: Hawthorn Leslie	16. 3.26	Scrapped Troon 22/1/48.
55	SUFFOLK	Portsmouth: Parsons	16. 2.26	Scrapped Newport 25/3/48.
I.84	AUSTRALIA (R.A.N.)	Clydebank	17. 3.27	Scrapped Barrow 5/7/55.
I.33	CANBERRA (R.A.N.)	Clydebank	31. 5.27	Lost 9/8/42.

Notes:—Several single 20 mm. A.A. were added and .5 in. MG.'s removed, later supplemented by several 40 mm. A.A. in R.A.N. AUSTRALIA only. BERWICK Home fleet 1939-45. CORNWALL East Indies 1939, South Atlantic 1940-41, East Indies 1941-42, Eastern Fleet 1942. CUMBERLAND South Atlantic 1939-41, Home fleet 1941-44, Eastern fleet 1944-45, East Indies 1945. KENT East Indies 1939-40, Home fleet 1940-44, Reserve 1945. SUFFOLK Home fleet 1939-43, Eastern fleet 1943-45. AUSTRALIA Australia 1939-40, East Indies 1941, Australia 1942-45. CANBERRA Australia 1939-40, South Atlantic and Australia 1940, East Indies 1941, Australia1942. Flag superior changed to D (1940-R.A.N. vessels only).

H.M.A.S. Australia, 1945, Hanger not added. H.M.A.S. Canberra and H.M.S. Kent were similar. [*P. A. Vicary*

A view of H.M.S. London, before reconstruction, showing a Supermarine Walrus Mk. I amphibian on the catapult. [*Aldo Fraccaroli*

London class

Displacement: *First pair* 9,850 tons, *second pair* 9,830 tons.
Dimensions: 595 (pp) 633 (oa) × 66 × 17 ft.
Machinery: 4-shaft geared Turbines, S.H.P. 80,000 = 32¼ knots.
Protection: Main belt 3-5 in. (LONDON only), deck 1½-4 in., turrets 1½-2 in., D.C.T. 3 in.
Armament: 8—8 in. (4 × 2), 8—4 in. A.A. (4 × 2 in LONDON, 8 × 1 others), 8 except LONDON 16—2 pdr. A.A. (2 × 4: 2 × 8), 8—.5 in. M (LONDON only) Guns; 8—21 in. (2 × 4) T.T.; 1 except LONDON 3 aircraft.
Complement: 650.

39	DEVONSHIRE	Devonport: V.A. (Tyne)	22.10.27	Converted to training ship (1947); scrapped Newport 12/12/54.
69	LONDON	Portsmouth: Fairfield	14. 9.27	Scrapped Barrow 3/1/50.
73	SHROPSHIRE	Beardmore	5. 7.28	R.A.N. (1943); scrapped Dalmuir 20/1/55, and Troon 19/9/55 (hull only).
96	SUSSEX	Hawthorn Leslie	22. 2.28	Scrapped Dalmuir 20/1/55.

Notes:—8—2 pdr. A.A. (2 × 4—not in LONDON) and several single 20 mm. A.A. were added in all and .5 in. MG.'s removed. A further 8—2 pdr. A.A. (2 × 4) were added in DEVONSHIRE and SUSSEX when "X" turret was removed, and T.T. were removed in SHROPSHIRE and SUSSEX. Finally, SHROPSHIRE had 8—10 40mm. A.A. (8×1) added and 8—2 pdr. A.A. taken out and LONDON 4—40 mm. A.A. (4×1) added. DEVONSHIRE Home fleet 1939-41, Eastern fleet, 1942-43, Home fleet, 1943-45. LONDON Refit 1939-41, Home fleet 1941-44, Eastern fleet 1944-45. SHROPSHIRE South Atlantic 1939-40, Red Sea and East Indies 1940-41, Home fleet and South Atlantic 1941-42, Australia 1942-45. SUSSEX South Atlantic 1939, East Indies 1940, Home fleet 1940-43, Eastern fleet 1943-45.

Norfolk class

Displacement: 9,975 tons and 9,925 tons *respectively*.
Dimensions: 590 (pp) 630 (oa) × 66 × 17 ft.
Machinery: 4-shaft geared Turbines, S.H.P. 80,000 = 32¼ knots.
Protection: Deck 1½-4 in., turrets 1½-2 in., D.C.T. 3 in.
Armament: 8—8 in. (4 × 2), 8—4 in. A.A. (4 × 2), 16—2 pdr. A.A. (2 × 8) 8—.5 in. M (2 × 4) Guns; 8—21 in. (2 × 4) T.T.; 1 aircraft.
Complement: 650.

40	DORSETSHIRE	Portsmouth: Cammell Laird	29. 1.29	Lost 5/4/42.
78	NORFOLK	Fairfield	12.12.28	Scrapped Newport 3/1/50.
	NORTHUMBER-LAND	Devonport		Cancelled 1/30.
	SURREY	Portsmouth		Cancelled 1/30.

Notes:—Three further projected vessels were cancelled. Several single 20 mm. A.A. were added and .5 in. MG's removed. 16—2 pdr. A.A. (4 × 4) and 4—40 mm. A.A. (4 × 1) added in NORFOLK and "X" turret removed. DORSETSHIRE East Indies 1939, South Atlantic 1940-41, Eastern fleet 1942. NORFOLK Home fleet 1939-45.

York class

Displacement: 8,250 tons and 8,390 tons *respectively.*
Dimensions: 540 (pp) 575 (oa) × 57 YORK, 58 EXETER × 17 ft.
Machinery: 4-shaft geared Turbines, S.H.P. 80,000 = 32 knots.
Protection: Main belt 2-3 in., deck 2 in., turrets 1½-2 in., D.C.T. 3 in.
Armament: 6—8 in. (3 × 2), 4—4 in. A.A. (4 × 1), 2—2 pdr. A.A. (2 × 1) Guns; 6—21 in. (2 × 3) T.T.; 1 YORK, 2 EXETER aircraft.
Complement: 600.

90	YORK	Palmers	17. 7.28	Constructive total loss 26/3/41 and abandoned 22/5/41.
68	EXETER	Devonport: Parsons	18. 7.29	Lost 1/3/42.

Notes:—Three further projected vessels were cancelled. YORK only had a few single 20 mm. A.A. added whilst EXETER had 4—4 in. A.A. (single mtgs. paired), 8—2 pdr. A.A. (2 × 4) and 2—20 mm. A.A. (2 × 1) added. YORK Atlantic escort 1939, Home fleet 1940, Mediterranean fleet 1941. EXETER South Atlantic 1939, Refit and Home fleet 1940-41, Eastern fleet 1942.

Leander class

Displacement: *First group* 7,270 tons, 7,175 tons, 7,215 tons, 7,030 tons and 6,985 tons *respectively. Second group* 6,830 tons, 6,980 tons and 7,105 tons *respectively.*
Dimensions: *First group* 530 (pp) 554½ (oa) × 55¼ × 16 ft. except AJAX 522 (pp) × 55¾ × 15½ ft. *Second group* 530 (pp) 555 (oa) × 56¾ × 15¾ ft.
Machinery: 4-shaft geared Turbines, S.H.P. 72,000 = 32½ knots.
Protection: Main belt 2-4 in., deck 2 in., turrets 1 in., D.C.T. 1 in.
Armament: 8—6 in. (4 × 2), 8—4 in. A.A. (4 × 2), 8—2 pdr. A.A. (2 × 4—not in R.A.N. vessels), 12—.5 in. M (3 × 4) Guns; 8—21 in. (2 × 4) T.T.; 1 aircraft. *Complement:* 550.

75	LEANDER	Devonport: V.A. (Tyne)	24. 9.31	Scrapped Blyth 15/1/50.
20	NEPTUNE	Portsmouth: Parsons	31. 1.33	Lost 19/12/41.
85	ORION	Devonport: V.A. (Tyne)	24.11.32	Scrapped Troon 19/7/49.
70	ACHILLES	Cammell Laird	1. 9.32	R.N.Z.N. (1937-43); R.I.N. DELHI (1948).
22	AJAX	V.A. (Barrow)	1. 3.34	Scrapped Newport 11/49.
I.48	SYDNEY (R.A.N.) (ex-Phaeton)	Swan Hunter: Wallsend	22. 9.34	Lost 19/11/41.
I.29	PERTH (R.A.N.) (ex-Amphion)	Portsmouth: Beardmore	27. 7.34	Lost 1/3/42.
I.63	HOBART (R.A.N.) (ex-Apollo)	Devonport: Beardmore	9.10.34	Scrapped Japan.

Notes:—(*First group*) Several single 20 mm. A.A. were added in all and the .5 in. MG.'s removed. "X" turret was later removed from LEANDER and ACHILLES and replaced by 4—2 pdr. A.A. (1 × 4).

H.M.S. York, 1938, note Supermarine Walrus Mk. I on catapult. [*P. A. Vicary*

H.M.S. Leander, 1937, also carrying Supermarine Walrus Mk. I on catapult. Note foremost twin 4 in. A.A. mounting moved forward. [*G. A. Osbon*

H.M.S. Orion, March 1943, with 7—20 mm. A.A. and R.D.F. added. [*P. A. Vicary*

LEANDER New Zealand 1939-40, Mediterranean fleet and Red Sea 1940, East Indies 1941, New Zealand 1941-43, Refit U.S.A. 1944-45. NEPTUNE South Atlantic 1939, Mediterranean fleet and East Indies 1940, Home and Mediterranean fleets 1941. ORION America and West Indies 1939-40, Mediterranean fleet 1940-45. ACHILLES South Atlantic 1939, New Zealand 1940-43, Home fleet 1943-44, Pacific fleet 1945. AJAX South Atlantic 1939, Mediterranean fleet 1940-42, Force "H" and refit U.S.A. 1943, Mediterranean fleet 1943-45.

(*Second group*) A further projected vessel was cancelled. Only a few single 20 mm. A.A. were added in all. SYDNEY Australia 1939-40, Mediterranean fleet 1940, Australia 1941. PERTH America and West Indies 1939, Australia 1940, Mediterranean fleet 1941, Australia 1941-42. HOBART East Indies 1939-40, Red Sea 1940, Australia 1941-45. Flag superior changed to D (1940).

Arethusa class

Displacement: *First pair* 5,220 tons, *second pair* 5,270 tons.
Dimensions: 480 (pp) 506 (oa) × 51 × 13¾ ft.
Machinery: 4-shaft geared Turbines, S.H.P. 64,000 = 32¼ knots.
Protection: Main belt 2 in., deck 2 in., turrets 1 in., D.C.T. 1 in.
Armament: 6—6 in. (3 × 2), 8—4 in. A.A. (4 × 2), 8—2 pdr. A.A. (2 × 4), 8—.5 in. M (2 × 4) Guns; 6—21 in. (2 × 3) T.T.; 1 aircraft (not in AURORA).
Complement: 450.

26	ARETHUSA	Chatham: Parsons	6. 3.34	Scrapped Troon 9/5/50.
71	GALATEA	Scotts	9. 8.34	Lost 15/12/41.
97	PENELOPE	Harland & Wolff	15.10.35	Lost 18/2/44.
12	AURORA	Portsmouth: Wallsend	20. 8.36	Chinese (Nat.) CHUNG-KING (1948), Chinese (Communist) TCHOUNG KING (1949), lost 3/49 and salved, HSUANG HO (1951), PEI CHING (1951), KUANG CHOU; now harbour hulk.

Notes:—Two further projected vessels were cancelled. Several single 20 mm. A.A. were added in all. ARETHUSA Mediterranean fleet 1939, Home fleet 1940-42, Mediterranean fleet 1942-44, Home fleet 1944, Mediterranean fleet 1945. GALATEA Mediterranean fleet 1939, Home fleet 1940-41, Mediterranean fleet 1941. PENELOPE Mediterranean fleet 1939, Home fleet 1940-41, Mediterranean fleet 1942-44. AURORA Home fleet 1939-41, Mediterranean fleet 1942-45.

Southampton class

(First & Second Groups)

Displacement: *First group* 9,100 tons, *second group* 9,400 tons.
Dimensions: 558 (pp) 591½ (oa) × 61¾ *first group*, 62¼ *second group* × 17 *first group*, 17½ *second group* ft.
Machinery: 4-shaft geared Turbines, S.H.P. 75,000 = 32 knots, *first group*, S.H.P. 82,500 = 32½ knots *second group*.
Protection: Main belt 3-4 in., deck 2 in., turrets 1-2 in., D.C.T. 4 in.
Armament: 12—6 in. (4 × 3), 8—4 in. A.A. (4 × 2), 8—2 pdr. A.A. (2 × 4), 8—.5 in. M (2 × 4) Guns; 6—21 in. (2 × 3) T.T.; 3 aircraft.
Complement: 700.

H.M.S. Penelope, 1936. Running builders trials and not yet commissioned. [*P. A. Vicary*

H.M.S. Southampton dressed overall, May 1937.

[G. A. Osbon

76	NEWCASTLE (ex-Minotaur)	V.A. (Tyne): V.A.(Barrow)	23. 1.36	Scrapped Faslane 19/8/59.
83	SOUTHAMPTON (ex-Polyphemus)	Clydebank	10. 3.36	Lost 11/1/41.
19	BIRMINGHAM	Devonport: Clydebank	1. 9.36	Scrapped Inverkeithing 7/9/60.
21	GLASGOW	Scotts	20. 6.36	Scrapped Blyth 8/7/58.
24	SHEFFIELD	V.A. (Tyne)	23. 7.36	
11	LIVERPOOL	Fairfield	24. 3.37	Scrapped Bo'ness 2/7/58.
15	MANCHESTER	Hawthorn Leslie	12. 4.37	Lost 13/8/42.
62	GLOUCESTER	Devonport: Scotts	19.10.37	Lost 22/5/41.

(Third Group)

Displacement: 10,000 tons.
Dimensions: 579 (pp) 613½ (oa) × 63¼ × 17¼ ft.
Machinery: 4-shaft geared Turbines, S.H.P. 80,000 = 32 knots.
Protection: Main belt 4½ in., deck 2 in., turrets 1-2½ in., D.C.T. 4 in.
Armament: 12—6 in. (4 × 3), 12—4 in. A.A. (6 × 2), 16—2 pdr. A.A. (2 × 8), 8—.5 in. M (2 × 4) Guns; 6—21 in. (2 × 3) T.T.; 3 aircraft.
Complement: 850.

35	BELFAST	Harland & Wolff	17. 3.38	
16	EDINBURGH	Swan Hunter: Wallsend	31. 3.38	Lost 2/5/42.

Notes:—(*First & second groups*) Several single 20 mm. A.A. were added in all and the .5 in. MG.'s removed. Light A.A. received considerable further augmentation, in stages, and entailed removal of "X" turret (not in vessels lost) and addition of 8—2 pdr. A.A. (2 × 4). BIRMINGHAM had 8—40 mm. A.A. (4 × 2) in lieu of multiple 2 pdr. mtgs. and SHEFFIELD had a homogeneous battery of 20—40 mm. A.A. (6 × 2 & 8 × 1). SOUTHAMPTON Home fleet 1939-40, Mediterranean fleet 1941. NEWCASTLE Home fleet 1939-41, South Atlantic 1941-42, Eastern fleet 1942-44, East Indies 1944-45, Home fleet 1945. BIRMINGHAM China 1939, Home fleet 1940, South Atlantic 1941-42, Eastern fleet 1942-44, Mediterranean fleet and refit U.S.A. 1944, Home fleet 1945. GLASGOW Home fleet 1939-40, East Indies 1941-42, Eastern fleet 1942, Home fleet 1942-45. SHEFFIELD Home fleet 1939-40, Force "H" 1940-41, Home fleet 1941-45. LIVERPOOL China 1939-40, Red Sea and Mediterranean fleet 1940, Refit U.S.A. 1941, Home fleet 1942-45. MANCHESTER Home fleet 1939-42, Mediterranean fleet 1942. GLOUCESTER East Indies 1939-40, Mediterranean 1940-41.

(*Third group*) Initially 6—20 mm. A.A. (6 × 1) were added. Later 4—4 in. A.A. (2 × 2) and the .5 in. MG.'s were removed from BELFAST and 20—2 pdr. A.A. (4×4 & 4×1) and 5—40 mm. A.A. (5×1) added, and the hull bulged and beam increased to 69 ft.
BELFAST Home fleet 1938-45. EDINBURGH Home fleet 1939-42.

Dido class

Displacement: *First group* 5,450 tons, *second group* 5,770 tons.
Dimensions: 485 (pp) 512 (oa) × 50½ × 14ft. *first group*, 14¾ *second group.*
Machinery: 4-shaft geared Turbines, S.H.P. 62,000 = 33 knots.
Protection: Main belt 2-3 in., deck ½-1-2 in., turrets 1-2 in., D.C.T. 1 in.

H.M.S. Belfast, October 1948. [P. A. Vicary

Armament: *First group* 10—5.25 in. D.P. (5 × 2), 8—2 pdr. A.A. (2 × 4), 8—.5 in. M (2 × 4) Guns; 6—21 in. (2 × 3) T.T. *Second group* 8—5.25 in. D.P. (4 × 2), 12—2 pdr. A.A. (3 × 4), 12—20 mm. A.A. (6 × 2) Guns; 6—21 in. (2 × 3) T.T.

Complement: *First group* 530 (556 as Flagship), *second group* 535 (551 as Flagship).

37	DIDO	Cammell Laird	18. 7.39	Scrapped Barrow 16/7/58.
42	EURYALUS	Chatham: Hawthorn Leslie	6. 6.39	Scrapped Blyth 18/7/59.
93	NAIAD	Hawthorn Leslie	3. 2.39	Lost 11/3/42.
43	PHOEBE	Fairfield	25. 3.39	Scrapped Blyth 1/4/56.
82	SIRIUS	Portsmouth: Scotts	18. 9.40	Scrapped Blyth 15/10/56.
31	BONAVENTURE	Scotts	19. 4.39	Lost 31/3/41.
74	HERMIONE	Stephen	18. 5.39	Lost 16/6/42.
88	CHARYBDIS	Cammell Laird	17. 9.40	Lost 23/10/43.
33	CLEOPATRA	Hawthorn Leslie	27. 3.40	Scrapped Newport 15/12/58.
98	SCYLLA	Scotts	24. 7.40	Scrapped Barrow 12/4/50.
61	ARGONAUT	Cammell Laird	6. 9.41	Scrapped Newport 19/11/55.
63	BELLONA	Fairfield	29. 9.42	R.N.Z.N. (1948-56); scrapped Briton Ferry 5/2/59.
81	BLACK PRINCE	Harland & Wolff	27. 8.42	R.N.Z.N. (1948); scrapped 2/3/62.
84	DIADEM	Hawthorn Leslie	26. 8.42	R.P.N. BABUR (1956).
89	ROYALIST	Scotts	30. 5.42	R.N.Z.N. (1956).
95	SPARTAN	V.A.(Barrow)	27. 8.42	Lost 29/1/44.

Notes:—(*First group*) About 6—20 mm. A.A. (6× 1) were initially added in all and the .5 in. MG.'s removed. CHARYBDIS and SCYLLA were completed with extemporised armament of 8—4.5 in. D.P. (4 × 2), 8—2 pdr. A.A. (2 × 4) and 8—20 mm. A.A. (8 × 1) owing to non-availability of 5.25 in. turrets. PHOEBE and CLEOPATRA later had " Q " turret removed and replaced by 4—2 pdr. A.A. (1 × 4) and SCYLLA was so re-armed with 40 mm. substituted for 2 pdr. guns. Single 20 mm. were ultimately replaced by either twin 20 mm. or single 40 mm. or combination of both.

(*Second group*) Differed from first group in that they had upright funnels and masts and were completed without " Q " turret in first instance. DIDO Home fleet 1940-41, Mediterranean fleet 1941-44, Home fleet 1944-45. EURYALUS Home fleet 1941, Mediterranean fleet 1941-43, Home fleet 1943-44, East Indies and Pacific fleet 1945. NAIAD Home fleet 1940-41, Mediterranean fleet 1941-42. PHOEBE Home fleet 1940-41, Mediterranean fleet 1941-44. Eastern fleet 1944, East Indies 1945, SIRIUS Home and Mediterranean fleets 1942, Force " H " 1943, Mediterranean fleet 1943-44. BONAVENTURE Home fleet 1940-41, Mediterranean fleet 1941. HERMIONE Home fleet 1941, Force " H " 1941-42, Mediterranean fleet 1942. CHARYBDIS Home fleet and Force " H " 1942, Home fleet 1943. CLEOPATRA Home fleet 1942, Mediterranean fleet 1943-44, Home fleet 1944-45, East Indies 1945. SCYLLA Home fleet 1942, Force " H " 1943, Home fleet 1943-45. ARGONAUT Home fleet 1942, Force " H " and refit U.S.A. 1943, Home fleet 1944, Pacific fleet 1945. BELLONA Home fleet 1943-45. BLACK PRINCE Home fleet 1943-44, Mediterranean fleet 1944, Pacific fleet 1945. DIADEM Home fleet 1943-45. ROYALIST Home fleet 1943-44, Mediterranean fleet 1944-45, East Indies 1945. SPARTAN Home fleet 1943, Mediterranean fleet 1944.

Left:
H.M.S. Euryalus, 1942.

[*P. A. Vicary*

Right:
H.M.S. Diadem, November 1948.

[*P. A. Vicary*

Fiji class

Displacement: 8,000 tons except * 8,800 tons.
Dimensions: 538 (pp) $555\frac{1}{2}$ (oa) × 62 × $16\frac{1}{2}$ ft.
Machinery: 4-shaft geared Turbines, S.H.P. 72,500 = 33 knots.
Protection: Main belt $3\frac{1}{4}$ in., deck 2 in., turrets 2 in., D.C.T. 4 in.
Armament: 12—6 in. (4 × 3), 8—4 in. A.A. (4 × 2), 9—2 pdr. A.A. (2 × 4 & 1 × 1), 8—.5 in. M (2 × 4) except * 9—6 in. (3 × 3), 8—4 in. A.A. (4 × 2), 20—2 pdr. A.A. (5 × 4), 20—20 mm. A.A. (10 × 2) Guns; 6—21 in. (2 × 3) T.T.; 3 aircraft except * nil.
Complement: 730.

58	FIJI	Clydebank	31. 5.39	Lost 22/5/41.
14	KENYA	Stephen	18. 8.39	Scrapped Faslane 29/10/62.
80	MAURITIUS	Swan Hunter: Wallsend	19. 7.39	For disposal.
60	NIGERIA	V.A. (Tyne): Parsons	18. 7.39	R.I.N. MYSORE (1957).
46	TRINIDAD	Devonport: Hawthorn Leslie	21. 3.40	Lost 15/5/42.
30	CEYLON*	Stephen	30. 7.42	Peruvian CORONEL BOLOGNESI (1959).
48	GAMBIA	Swan Hunter: Wallsend	30.11.40	R.N.Z.N. (1943-46).
44	JAMAICA	V.A. (Barrow)	16.11.40	Scrapped Dalmuir 20/12/60 and Troon 1962 (hull only).
66	UGANDA*	V.A. (Tyne): Parsons	7. 8.41	R.C.N. QUEBEC; scrapped Osaka 6/2/61.
52	BERMUDA	Clydebank	11. 9.41	For disposal.
59	NEWFOUND-LAND*	Swan Hunter: Wallsend	19.12.41	Peruvian ALMIRANTE GRAU (1959).

*completed to modified "3-turret" design

Notes:—About 4/8—20 mm. A.A. (4/8 × 1) were initially added and the single 2 pdr. A.A. (not fitted in all) and .5 in. MG.'s were removed, but this was greatly implemented. All, except NIGERIA and GAMBIA and war losses, later had "X" turret removed and 12—2 pdr. A.A. (3 × 4) added and CEYLON, UGANDA and NEWFOUNDLAND were so completed to a modified "3-turret" design. Single 20 mm. A.A. were either increased or replaced by a lesser number of 40 mm. A.A. and KENYA was re-armed with 18—40 mm. A.A. (5 × 2 & 8 × 1) replacing mixed battery of 2 pdr., 40 mm. and 20 mm. A.A. guns. The "3-turret" vessels of the modified design had 8—2 pdr. A.A. (2 × 4) and 4—20 mm. A.A. (2 × 2) less than provided for and only UGANDA offset this by 8—40 mm. A.A. (2 × 4) with a reduced number of 20 mm. A.A. guns. FIJI Home fleet 1940-41, Mediterranean fleet 1941. KENYA Home fleet 1940-43, Eastern fleet 1943-44, East Indies and Home fleet 1945, MAURITIUS Home fleet 1941, East Indies 1941-42, Eastern fleet 1942-43, Mediterranean fleet 1943-44, Home fleet 1944-45. NIGERIA Home fleet 1940-44, Eastern fleet 1944, East Indies 1945. TRINIDAD Home fleet 1941-42. CEYLON Home fleet 1943, Eastern fleet 1944, Pacific fleet and East Indies 1945. GAMBIA Eastern fleet 1942, East Indies and Eastern fleet 1943, Home fleet 1943-44, Eastern fleet 1944, Pacific fleet 1944-45. JAMAICA Home fleet 1942-45. UGANDA Home fleet 1943, Mediterranean fleet 1943-44, Refit U.S.A. 1944, Pacific fleet 1945. BERMUDA Home fleet 1942-45, Pacific fleet 1945. NEWFOUNDLAND Home fleet 1943, Mediterranean fleet 1943-44, Home fleet 1944, Pacific fleet 1945.

H.M.S. Mauritius, at Augusta, 1943, with aircraft, catapult and port crane removed and a total of 24—20 mm. A.A. (24 × 1). [*P .A. Vicary*

Minotaur class

Displacement: 8,800 tons except * 9,550 tons (revised design).
Dimensions: 538 (pp) 555½ (oa) × 63 *first pair*, 64 *others* × 17¼ ft.
Machinery: 4-shaft geared Turbines, S.H.P. 72,500 = 32½ knots except * S.H.P. 80,000 = 31½ knots.
Protection: Main belt 3¼ in., deck 2 in., turrets 2 in., D.C.T. 4 in.
Armament: 9—6 in. (3 × 3), 10—4 in. A.A. (5 × 2), 16—2 pdr. A.A. (4 × 4), 8—40 mm. A.A. (8 × 1) except * 4—6 in. D.P. (2 × 2), 6—3 in. A.A. (3 × 2) Guns; 6—21 in. (2 × 3) T.T. except * nil.
Complement: 730 except * 716.

08	SWIFTSURE	V.A. (Tyne)	4. 2.43	For disposal.
53	MINOTAUR (i)	Harland & Wolff	29. 7.43	R.C.N. ONTARIO (1945); scrapped Japan 1960.
	BELLEROPHON*	Clydebank	25.10.45	TIGER (1945).
50	TIGER	V.A. (Tyne)		BLAKE (1945), BELLEROPHON (1945); cancelled.
34	DEFENCE*	Scotts	2. 9.44	Completed Swan Hunter and engined Wallsend; LION (1957).
25	SUPERB	Swan Hunter: Wallsend	31. 8.43	Scrapped Dalmuir 8/8/60, and Troon 15/5/61 (hull only).
99	BLAKE*	Fairfield	20.12.45	TIGER (1945), BLAKE (1945).
27	HAWKE	Portsmouth		Cancelled.
	CENTURION			Projected.
	EDGAR			Projected.
	MARS			Projected.
	MINOTAUR (ii)			Existence doubtful.
	NEPTUNE			Projected.

Notes:—Closely followed design of modified " **3-turret Fiji** " class. Only three were so completed, six cancelled and the remaining three suspended for nine years before completing to a revised design which substituted rate of fire plus extensive R.D.F. control arrangements for number of guns. SWIFTSURE Home fleet 1944, Pacific fleet 1945. R.C.N. ONTARIO (ex-Minotaur) Pacific fleet 1945.

CRUISER MINELAYERS

Displacement: 6,740 tons.
Dimensions: 500 (pp) 520 (oa) × 59 (outside bulges) × 14½ ft.
Machinery: 4-shaft geared Turbines, S.H.P. 40,000 = 27¾ knots + Diesel-Electric for cruising.
Protection: Main belt 2 in., deck 1 in.
Armament: 4—4.7 in. A.A. (4 × 1), 8—2 pdr. A.A. (1 × 4 & 4 × 1), 10-M Guns; 280 (large), 340 (small) mines.
Complement: 395.

Left:
H.M.S. Superb, July 1947.

[G. A. Osbon

Right:
H.M.S. Adventure, July 1945.

[P. A. Vicary

M.23	ADVENTURE	Devonport: V.A. (Tyne)*	18. 6.24	Scrapped Briton Ferry 10/7/47.

*diesels only

Notes:—An unsuccessful combination being too slow and weakly armed for her size but with a good mine load and novel diesel-electric cruising propulsion. Was converted to a Repairship. Served Home fleet 1939-44, Accommodation ship and converted to Repair ship 1944-45, Home fleet and Reserve 1945.

Abdiel class

Displacement: 2,650 tons.
Dimensions: 400½ (pp) 418 (oa) × 40 × 11¼ ft.
Machinery: 2-shaft geared Turbines, S.H.P. 72,000 = 40 knots.
Armament: 6—4.7 in. (3 × 2), 4—2 pdr. A.A. (1 × 4), 8—.5 in. M (2 × 4) except * 4—4 in. A.A. (2 × 2), 4—40 mm. A.A. (2 × 2), 12—20 mm. A.A. (6 × 2) Guns; 160 mines.
Complement: 242/246.

M.39	ABDIEL	White	23. 4.40	Lost 9/9/43.
M.76	LATONA	Thorneycroft	20. 8.40	Lost 24/10/41.
M.70	MANXMAN	Stephen	5. 9.40	M/S support ship (1963).
M.84	WELSHMAN	Hawthorn Leslie	4. 9.40	Lost 1/2/43.
M.01	APOLLO*	Hawthorn Leslie	5. 4.43	Scrapped Blyth 28/11/62.
M.65	ARIADNE*	Stephen	16. 2.43	

Notes:—A most successful design dependant on high sustained speed for laying operations. *First group* had about 4—20 mm. A.A. (4×1) added and all later had the twin 4.7 in. replaced by twin 4 in. A.A. and 8—20 mm. A.A. (4×2) added. ABDIEL Mediterranean fleet 1941, Eastern fleet 1942, Home fleet 1942-43, Mediterranean fleet 1943. LATONA Mediterranean fleet 1941. MANXMAN Home fleet 1941-42, Eastern fleet 1942-43, Home fleet 1943-45. WELSHMAN Home fleet 1941-42, Mediterranean fleet 1943. ARIADNE Mediterranean fleet 1944, Pacific fleet 1944-45, Home fleet 1945. APOLLO Home fleet 1944-45.

AIRCRAFT CARRIERS

Aircraft carriers extant in 1939, whose construction or design emanated from the First World War, were the PEGASUS (ex-Ark Royal), the **Courageous** class and FURIOUS (all ex-light battlecruisers), the ARGUS, the EAGLE and the HERMES.

The seaplane carrier PEGASUS was the doyen amongst carriers and had been taken over prior to 1914 whilst under construction as a fleet tanker. " Between the wars " she had participated in catapult and Hein mat experiments and then as a minesweeper depot ship before going into Reserve. Long past active employment she again reverted to a catapult ship during the Second World War and filled a useful role.

The FURIOUS, whose original conversion only entailed the removal of the forward turret and its replacement by a flying-off deck with hangars under, later had a landing-on deck with hangars and workshops under added in place of the

Left:
H.M.S. Abdiel off the Sicillian invasion beaches, July 1943. Twin 4 in. A.A. have replaced original 4·7 in. guns.

[*P. A. Vicary*

Right:
H.M.S. Apollo flying her pennants and berth number while entering harbour.

[*P. A. Vicary*

after turret. As the central bridge structure and funnel increased the hazards of alighting aircraft a third conversion saw them removed and a new flight deck, 30 feet above the former one, built in its place. Smoke was discharged through horizontal trunking taken along the hangar sides and as this caused overheating the side was opened up but it was never really a satisfactory means of smoke dispersal. For a short time FURIOUS operated both the original flying-off deck forward and the much larger and higher landing-on deck aft but the use of the former was discontinued and all air operations confined to the new flight deck. The original battlecruiser secondary armament of 5.5 in. guns which had been retained was eventually superseded by 12—4 in. A.A. (6 × 2) and, 24—2 pdr. A.A. (3 × 8) guns and a small " island " superstructure, placed on the starboard side, replaced the retractable charthouse which had been fitted at the fore end of the flight deck.

The ARGUS, adapted from the uncompleted mercantile hull CONTE ROSSO, was also flush decked but from the onset was too slow for fleet work having no margin of speed over the battle fleet. Used as a " Queen Bee " tender to provide realistic air target practice for the fleet she was, however, brought back to active service on the outbreak of war and was subsequently used as a training carrier for deck landings.

The EAGLE was adapted from the partially complete hull of the Chilean battleship ALMIRANTE COCHRANE and a considerable amount of the original light armour was retained. She introduced two novel features—an " island " superstructure[4] and a double-storied hangar. Although the former was adopted for all subsequent carrier construction the inclusion of the latter was restricted to only the larger carriers. The EAGLE'S armament only received minor modification when the single 4 in. A.A. gun between the funnels was replaced by 8—2 pdr. A.A. (1 × 8) and a further multiple mounting was later added before the " island ".

The HERMES was the first vessel in the Royal Navy to be *designed* as an aircraft carrier and was considerably smaller than those vessels which had been converted to this role. Her flight deck extended over the whole hull whose side was considerably flared forward so that flight deck width was not reduced to unworkable dimensions. A standard cruiser two-shaft installation gave her a five knot margin over the battle fleet but restricted hangar space reduced her. air complement from 21 to 12 as naval aircraft continued to develop in size, An " island " superstructure on the starboard side, with an unusual tripod mast installation of square section with only a single trailing leg, gave early indication of many advantages over the " flush-decked " design, which was confirmed by experience with the EAGLE.

The COURAGEOUS and GLORIOUS underwent conversion, on the completion of the EAGLE, on generally similar lines to the FURIOUS (a near sister) but had " island " superstructures and discarded L.A. guns for an entire A.A, armament. They rightly looked to accompanying vessels for cover and support in a surface action and concentrated defensive measures against air attack, to which they were more vulnerable.

These old carriers, the nucleus of a later paramount expression in naval air power, were a very mixed collection. COURAGEOUS, GLORIOUS and FURIOUS were the fastest, had ample flight decks but only light protection. The bulkier EAGLE was more robust but slower whilst ARGUS was quite devoid of protection and had inadequate speed. The HERMES was a good return for

[4]Although not finally completed until after the HERMES the design of the EAGLE was of an earlier date.

her size and sought a possible solution for these costly and (then) vulnerable vessels within moderate dimensions. She was protected on the same scale as the COURAGEOUS but only possessed the bare margin of speed for her role. She was, however, easily the best sea-boat of them all—partly the outcome of being designed for her task.

To these were added the first of the post 1918 carriers—the Royal Australian Navy's ALBATROSS, a seaplane carrier of an already obsolescent type which was later transferred to the Royal Navy in part exchange for three cruisers. During the war she was employed as a mobile base from which her amphibian aircraft could operate an anti-submarine patrol and be serviced.

The final outcome of naval air experience " between the wars " was the ARK ROYAL which embraced all the best features of previous designs and rejected the moderate dimensions of the HERMES as insufficient to accommodate sufficient aircraft. ARK ROYAL had an " island " superstructure, double-storied hangars, an entire A.A. armament, enhanced protection and could stow 72 aircraft against the maximum of 48 borne in the COURAGEOUS. She could keep pace with the fleetest of the old carriers and had two catapults installed at the fore end of the flight deck, which enabled her to launch aircraft even when not under way.

The **Illustrious** class which followed—none were completed before the outbreak of war—introduced a significant innovation with an armoured hangar. The weight of armour, at such a height, entailed some sacrifice and only a single hangar was adopted with aircraft stowage reduced to 36. However, the need for these vessels to carry the maximum numbers of aircraft was foreseen and the last three were altered to incorporate an additional half hangar aft but the thickness of the hangar side armour was considerably reduced to compensate. The armoured hangars served these vessels well and, on more than one occasion, secured their survival. They were otherwise similarly armed to the ARK ROYAL with the light A.A. armament considerably augmented with numerous 20 mm. and 40 mm. guns and with more extensive R.D.F. installation. In keeping with all major vessels completed during the war no two were similarly armed and the installation of their light guns was more prescribed by availability than by designed commitments.

Except for the installation of R.D.F. the older carriers were not greatly affected by war modifications. COURAGEOUS, GLORIOUS, EAGLE and HERMES were relatively early losses whilst PEGASUS, ARGUS and ALBATROSS were, after short spells of active employment, relegated to training and base duties. Only FURIOUS saw the war through in active employment, although she was not latterly risked in the theatres to which the more modern carriers were exposed. The ARK ROYAL was the sole loss amongst the modern carriers when she succumbed to torpedo damage that eventually deprived her of all boiler power so that the inflow of water became unchecked.

All carriers initially suffered from the lack of suitable aircraft, a legacy from the days when the Fleet Air Arm was jointly administered by the Royal Air Force and the Admiralty; under the operational control of the latter but trained and equipped by the former. When, in 1936, the Admiralty finally regained complete control of its Air Arm it was already burdened with heavy programmes of building and reconstruction and had insufficient time to train sufficient air crew, or develop suitable types of maritime aircraft, in the face of equally pressing requirements from its depleted fleet. It was not until American aid was forthcoming, to both train pilots and supply suitable aircraft, that the carriers were able to deploy their full strength. The following details of the numbers and types of aircraft borne by the ILLUSTRIOUS may be taken as typical:—

August, 1940: 5 Fulmars and 8 Swordfish
May, 1942: 6 Martlets and 21 Swordfish
Sept., 1943: 20 Martlets, 10 Seafires and 12 Barracudas
May, 1944: 28 Corsairs and 24 Barracudas
January, 1945: 36 Corsairs and 21 Avengers.

SEAPLANE CARRIERS

Displacement: 6,900 tons.
Dimensions: 352½ (pp) 366 (oa) × 50¾ × 17½ ft.
Machinery: 1-shaft Reciprocating (V.T.E.), I.H.P. 3,000 = 11 knots.
Armament: 4—12 pdr. A.A. (4 × 1) Guns; 10 seaplanes.
Complement: 139.

I.35	PEGASUS (ex-Ark Royal)	Blyth Sbdg.	5. 9.14	Mercantile ANITA I (1947); scrapped Grays 1950.

Notes:—Was converted to a catapult ship 1940 and a few single 20 mm. A.A. were added. Served Home fleet 1939-44, Accommodation ship 1945. Flag superior changed to D (1940).

Displacement: 4,800 tons.
Dimensions: 422 (pp) 443¾ (oa) × 60¾ (over bulges) × 13¾ ft.
Machinery: 2-shaft geared Turbines, S.H.P. 12,000 = 20 knots.
Armament: 4—4.7 in. A.A. (4 × 1), 2—2pdr. A.A. (2 × 1) Guns; 9 seaplanes.
Complement: 450.

I.22	ALBATROSS	Cockatoo	21. 2.28	R.A.N. (1928-38); mercantile HELLENIC PRINCE (1946).

Notes:—Converted to Repair ship 1942 and a few single 20 mm. A.A. were added. Served South Atlantic 1939-42, Eastern fleet 1942-43, Home fleet 1944, Reserve 1945. Flag superior changed to D (1940).

AIRCRAFT CARRIERS

Courageous class

Displacement: 22,500 tons.
Dimensions: 735 (pp) 786¼ (oa) × 90½ (over bulges) × 24 ft.
Machinery: 4-shaft geared Turbines, S.H.P. 90,000 = 30½ knots.
Protection: Main belt 1½-2 in. (fwd), 3 in. (aft), deck 1-1½-3 in.
Armament: 16—4.7 in. A.A. (16 × 1) Guns; 48 aircraft.
Complement: 1,216.

H.M.S. Pegasus, 1937. [*P. A. Vicary*

H.M.A.S. Albatross, flying paying-off pennant while de-ammunitioning. [*R. Perkins*

50	COURAGEOUS	Armstrong: Parsons	5. 2.16	Lost 17/9/39.
77	GLORIOUS	Harland & Wolff	20. 4.16	Lost 8/6/40.

Notes:—Former light battlecruisers (4—15 in., 18—4 in. guns) converted to aircraft carriers 1924-30 on lines generally similar to third reconstruction of FURIOUS but with " island " superstructure. COURAGEOUS Home fleet 1939, GLORIOUS Mediterranean fleet 1939-40, Home fleet 1940.

Displacement: 22,450 tons.
Dimensions: 735 (pp) 786¼ (oa) × 90 (over bulges) × 24 ft.
Machinery: 4-shaft geared Turbines, S.H.P. 90,000 = 30½ knots.
Protection: Main belt 2 in. (fwd), 3 in. (amid), deck 1-1½-3 in.
Armament: 12—4 in. A.A. (6 × 2), 24—2 pdr. A.A. (3 × 8) Guns; 33 aircraft.
Complement: 748 (excluding air crew).

47	FURIOUS	Armstrong: Wallsend	15. 8.16	Scrapped Dalmuir 15/3/48 and Troon (hull only) 22/6/48.

Notes:—Former light battlecruiser (2—18 in., 10—5.5 in. guns) which underwent three major reconstructions finally emerging as a flush-decked aircraft carrier. A small " island " superstructure was later fitted and several single 20 mm. A.A. added. Served Home fleet 1939-44, Reserve 1944-45.

Displacement: 14,000 tons.
Dimensions: 535 (pp) 565 (oa) × 68 (over bulges) × 21 ft.
Machinery: 4-shaft Turbines, S.H.P. 20,000 = 20¼ knots.
Armament: 6—4 in. A.A. (6 × 1) Guns; 20 aircraft.
Complement: 373 (excluding air crew).

1.49	ARGUS (ex-mercantile Conte Rosso)	Beardmore	2.12.17	Scrapped 1946.

Notes:—8—20 mm. A.A. (8 × 1) were added and relegated to training 1942. Served Mediterranean fleet 1939-40, Home fleet 1940-41, Force " H " 1942, Home fleet 1943-44, Reserve as Accommodation ship 1944-45. Flag superior changed to D (1940).

Displacement: 22,600 tons.
Dimensions: 625 (pp) 667 (oa) × 92¾ (105¼ over bulges) × 24 ft.
Machinery: 4-shaft geared Turbines, S.H.P. 50,000 = 24 knots.
Protection: Main belt 4-6-7 in., deck 1-1½-4 in., shields 1 in.
Armament: 9—6 in. (9 × 1), 4—4 in. A.A. (4 × 1), 8—2 pdr. A.A. (1 × 8) Guns; 21 aircraft.
Complement: 748 (excluding air crew).

94	EAGLE (ex-Chilean Almirante Cochrane, ex-Santiago)	Armstrong: Clydebank	8. 6.18	Lost 11/8/42.

Notes:—Former battleship construction suspended 1914, purchased 1917 and modified as result of trials 1920-23. Introduced " island " superstructure and double-storied hangar, 8—2 pdr. A.A. (1 × 8) and 16-20 mm. A.A. (16 × 1) were added. Served China 1939, East Indies 1939-40, Mediterranean fleet 1940-41, South Atlantic 1941-42, Force " H " 1942.

H.M.S. Courageous, the first British aircraft carrier to be sunk during World War II. [*G. A. Osbon*

H.M.S. Glorious, May 1937. [*G. A. Osbon*

H.M.S. Argus, 1939. [*P. A. Vicary*

H.M.S. Hermes, May 1937. She was the first British aircraft carrier to be sunk by Japanese air attack, off Trincomalee, 1942. [*G. A. Osbon*

Displacement: 10,850 tons.
Dimensions: 548 (pp) 598 (oa) × $70\frac{1}{4}$ (over bulges) × $18\frac{3}{4}$ ft.
Machinery: 2-shaft geared Turbines, S.H.P. 40,000 = 25 knots.
Protection: Main belt 2-3 in. (amid), deck 1 in., shields 1 in.
Armament: 6—5.5 in. (6 × 1), 3—4 in. A.A. (3 × 1) Guns; 15 aircraft.
Complement: 664 (excluding air crew).

I.95	HERMES	Armstrong: Parsons	11. 9.19	Lost 9/4/42.

Notes:—First vessel in R.N. *designed* as an aircraft carrier and completed with " island " superstructure. 4—2 pdr. A.A. (1 × 4) and a few single 20 mm. A.A. added. Served Home fleet 1939, East Indies 1939-42, Eastern fleet 1942. Flag superior changed to D (1940).

Displacement: 22,000 tons.
Dimensions: 685 (pp) 800 (oa) × $94\frac{3}{4}$ × $22\frac{3}{4}$ ft.
Machinery: 3-shaft geared Turbines, S.H.P. 102,000 = $30\frac{3}{4}$ knots.
Protection: Main belt $4\frac{1}{2}$ in., deck $2\frac{1}{2}$ in.-3 in.
Armament: 16—4.5 in. A.A. (8 × 2), 48—2 pdr. A.A. (6 × 8), 32—.5 in. M (8 × 4) Guns; 72 aircraft.
Complement: 1,575.

91	ARK ROYAL	Cammell Laird	13. 4.37	Lost 14/11/41.

Notes:—8—20 mm. (8 × 1) added and .5 in. MG.'s removed. Served Home fleet and South Atlantic 1939, Home and Mediterranean fleets 1940, Force " H " 1941.

Illustrious class

Displacement: 23,000 tons except * 26,000.
Dimensions: 673 (pp) $753\frac{1}{2}$ (oa) except * 766 × $95\frac{3}{4}$ × 24 except * 26 ft.
Machinery: 3-shaft geared Turbines, S.H.P. 110,000 = 31 knots except * 4-shaft geared Turbines, S.H.P. 148,000 = 32 knots.
Protection: Main belt $4\frac{1}{2}$ in., hangar side $4\frac{1}{2}$ in. except * $1\frac{1}{2}$in., deck $2\frac{1}{2}$-3 in.
Armament: 16—4.5 in. D.P. (8 × 2), 48—2 pdr. A.A. (6 × 8), 8 except* 38—20 mm. A.A. (8 × 1; 17 × 2 & 4 × 1) Guns; 36 except * 72 aircraft.
Complement: 1,392 except * 1,785.

87	ILLUSTRIOUS	V.A.(Barrow)	5. 4.39	Scrapped Faslane 3/11/56.
38	VICTORIOUS	V.A. (Tyne): Wallsend	14. 9.39	
67	FORMIDABLE	Harland & Wolff	17. 8.39	Scrapped Inverkeithing 11/11/53.
92	INDOMITABLE	V.A.(Barrow)	26. 3.40	Scrapped Faslane 30/9/55.
86	IMPLACABLE*	Fairfield	10.12.42	Scrapped Inverkeithing 3/11/55.
10	INDEFATIG-ABLE*	Clydebank	8.12.44	Scrapped Dalmuir 4/11/56 and Troon (hull only).

Notes:—INDOMITABLE was modified whilst building, with additional half hangar and thinner.

H.M.S. Ark Royal, showing quarter views bow (upper) and stern (lower). Note raised aerial masts flanking the flight deck and distinctive aircraft homing beacon at the masthead.

[*P. A. Vicary*

Left:
H.M.S. Illustrious at Malta, September 1943.

[P. A. Vicary

Right:
H.M.S. Indefatigable, 1947.

[P. A. Vicary

hangar side. Several single and twin 20 mm. A.A. were added in first four. ILLUSTRIOUS Mediterranean 1940-41, Eastern fleet 1942-43, Force " H " 1943, Eastern fleet 1944, Pacific fleet 1945. VICTORIOUS Home fleet 1941-43, South Pacific 1943, Home and Eastern fleets 1944, Pacific fleet 1945. FORMIDABLE East Indies and Mediterranean fleet 1941, Eastern fleet 1942, Force " H " 1943, Home fleet 1944, Pacific fleet 1945. INDOMITABLE Home fleet 1941, Eastern fleet 1942, Home fleet 1942-43, Force " H " 1943, Eastern fleet 1944, Pacific fleet 1945. IMPLACABLE and INDEFATIGABLE Home fleet 1944, Pacific fleet 1945.

Audacious class

Displacement: 36,800 tons.
Dimensions: 720 (pp) 803¾ (oa) × 112¾ × 33¼ ft.
Machinery: 4-shaft geared Turbines, S.H.P. 152,000 = 31½ knots.
Protection: Main belt 8 in. otherwise similar ILLUSTRIOUS with thicker deck.
Armament: 16—4.5 in. D.P. (8 × 2), 58—40 mm. A.A. (8 × 6, 2 × 2 & 6 × 1) Guns; 100 aircraft.
Complement: 2,300.

D.29	AUDACIOUS	Harland & Wolff	19. 3.46	EAGLE (1945).
D.06	AFRICA	Fairfield		Cancelled.
94	EAGLE	V.A. (Tyne)		Cancelled.
91	IRRESISTIBLE	Cammell Laird	3. 5.50	ARK ROYAL (1945).

Gibraltar class

Three larger carriers of 45,000 tons were projected embracing the main features of the **Audacious** class but were not proceeded with on termination of hostilities.

D.68	GIBRALTAR	V.A. (Tyne)		Cancelled 1945.
D.93	MALTA	Clydebank		Cancelled 1945.
D.96	NEW ZEALAND	Cammell Laird		Cancelled 1945.

Displacement: 14,750.
Dimensions: 564 (pp) 640 (oa) × 90 × 19 ft.
Machinery: 2-shaft geared Turbines, S.H.P. 40,000 = 24 knots.
Armament: 8—4.5 in. D.P. (4 × 2), 12—2 pdr. A.A. (3 × 4), 12—20 mm. A.A. (2 × 2 & 8 × 1) Guns; 35 aircraft.
Complement: 1,000

I.72	UNICORN	Harland & Wolff	20.11.41	Scrapped Dalmuir 15/6/59.

Notes:—Aircraft maintenance carrier also used as an operational unit. Served Home and Mediterranean fleets 1943-44, Eastern fleet 1944, Pacific fleet 1945. Flag superior changed to F (1940).

Colossus class

Displacement: 13,190 except * 13,350 tons.
Dimensions: 630 (pp) 695 (oa) × 80¼ × 18¼ ft.
Machinery: 2-shaft geared Turbines, S.H.P. 42,000 = 25 knots.

H.M.S. Unicorn, December 1945.

Armament: 24—2 pdr. A.A. (6 × 4), 19—40 mm. A.A. (19 × 1) except PERSEUS and PIONEER 12—2 pdr. A.A. (3 × 4) 10—20 mm. A.A. (10 × 1) Guns; 48 aircraft (none in PERSEUS and PIONEER).
Complement: 1,076.

15	COLOSSUS	V.A. (Tyne): Parsons	30. 9.43	French ARROMANCHES (1951).
51	PERSEUS* (ex-Edgar)	V.A.(Tyne): V.A.(Barrow)	26. 3.44	Scrapped Port Glasgow 6/5/58.
62	GLORY	Harland & Wolff	27.11.43	Scrapped Inverkeithing 23/8/61.
D.76	PIONEER (ex-Mars. ex-Ethalion)	V.A.(Barrow)	20. 5.44	Scrapped Inverkeithing 9/54.
68	OCEAN	Stephen	8. 7.44	Scrapped Faslane 6/5/52.
64	THESEUS*	Fairfield	6. 7.44	Scrapped Inverkeithing 29/5/62.
16	TRIUMPH*	Hawthorn Leslie	2.10.44	
	VENERABLE	Cammell Laird	30.12.43	R.Neth.N. KAREL DOORMAN (1948).
71	VENGEANCE	Swan Hunter: Wallsend	23. 2.44	R.A.N. (1952-55); Brasilian MINAS GERAIS (1957).
31	WARRIOR* (ex-Brave)	Harland & Wolff	20. 5.44	R.C.N. (1946-48); Argentinian INDEPENDENCIA (1958).

Notes:—Only COLOSSUS, GLORY, VENERABLE and VENGEANCE and the maintenance carriers PERSEUS and PIONEER were operational before the end of the war and all served in the Pacific fleet.

Majestic class

Displacement: 14,000 tons.
Dimensions: 630 (pp) 695 (oa) × $80\frac{1}{4}$ × 23 ft.
Machinery: 2-shaft geared Turbines, S.H.P. 42,000 = $24\frac{1}{2}$ knots.
Armament: 30—40 mm. A.A. (6 × 2 & 18 × 1) Guns; 34 aircraft.
Complement: 1,100.

49	HERCULES	V.A. (Tyne): Parsons	22. 9.45	Completed by Harland & Wolff; R.I.N. VIKRANT (1957).
97	LEVIATHAN	Swan Hunter: Wallsend	7. 6.45	Suspended 5/46; for disposal.
21	MAGNIFICENT	Harland & Wolff	16.11.44	R.C.N. (1946-57).
77	MAJESTIC	V.A.(Barrow)	28. 2.45	R.A.N. MELBOURNE (1955).
95	POWERFUL	Harland & Wolff	27. 2.45	R.C.N. BONAVENTURE (1952).
93	TERRIBLE	Devonport: Parsons	30. 9.44	R.A.N. SYDNEY (1948).

H.M.S. Ocean, September 1954. A Fairey Firefly Mk. 6 can be seen on the afterdeck

[G. A. Osbon

Hermes class

Displacement: 18,300 tons.
Dimensions: 650 (pp) 736½ (oa) × 90 × 20 ft.
Machinery: 4-shaft geared Turbines, S.H.P. 83,000 = 29½ knots.
Protection: Deck 1 in.
Armament: 32—40 mm. A.A. (2 × 6, 8 × 2 & 4 × 1) Guns; 50 aircraft.
Complement: 1,330-1,390.

08	ALBION	Swan Hunter: Wallsend	6. 5.47	
14	ARROGANT	Swan Hunter		Cancelled.
34	BULWARK	Harland & Wolff	22. 6.48	
39	CENTAUR	Harland & Wolff	22. 4.47	
61	ELEPHANT	V.A. (Barrow)	16. 2.53	HERMES (1945).
	HERMES	Cammell Laird		Cancelled.
96	MONMOUTH	Fairfield		Cancelled.
57	POLYPHEMUS	Devonport		Cancelled.

Archer class

Displacement: 8,200 tons except * 9,000 tons.
Dimensions: 468½ (pp) 492¼ (oa) × 66¼ × 23¼ ft.
Machinery: 1-shaft Diesel motors (2 except * 4 per shaft), B.H.P. 8,500 = 16½ knot except * B.H.P. 9,000 = 17 knots.
Armament: 3—4 in. A.A .(3 × 1), 15—20 mm. A.A. (4 × 2 & 7 × 1) Guns; 15 aircraft.
Complement: 555.

D.78	ARCHER* (ex-mercantile Mormacland)	Sun Sbdg.	14.12.39	Returned U.S.N. 18/1/46, mercantile EMPIRE LAGAN (1946), ANNA SALEN (1949), TASMANIA (1955), UNION RELIANCE (1961); scrapped New Orleans 3/62.
D.14	AVENGER (ex- mercantile Rio Hudson)	Sun Sbdg.	27.11.40	Lost 15/11/42.
D.97	BITER (ex-mercantile Rio Parana)	Sun Sbdg.	18.12.40	French DIXMUDE (1945).
	CHARGER (ex-mercantile Rio de la Plata)	Sun Sbdg.	3. 3.42	Retained U.S.N. (CVE. 30) for training R.N. aircrew; mercantile FAIRSEA (1949).
D.37	DASHER (ex-mercantile Rio de Janeiro)	Sun Sbdg.	12. 4.41	Lost 27/3/43.

Notes.—Only had half-hangar under after half of flight deck.

Attacker class

Displacement: 11,420 tons.
Dimensions: 468½ (pp) 492 (oa) × 69½ × 23¼ ft.
Machinery: 1-shaft geared Turbines, S.H.P. 9,350 = 17 knots.
Armament: 2—4 in. A.A. (2 × 1); 8—40 mm. A.A. (4 × 2), 15—20 mm. A.A. (15 × 1) Guns; 18 aircraft.
Complement: 646.

D.02	ATTACKER (ex-U.S.N. Barnes, ex-Steel Artisan)	Western Pipe: G.E.C.	27. 9.41	Returned U.S.N. 5/1/46; mercantile CASTEL FORTE (1948).
D.18	BATTLER (ex-U.S.N. Altamaha, ex-Mormacmail)	Ingalls Sbgd: Westinghouse	4. 4.42	Returned U.S.N. 12/2/46.
D.32	CHASER (ex-U.S.N. Breton, ex-Mormacgulf)	Ingalls Sbdg: Westinghouse	19. 6.42	Returned U.S.N. 12/5/46; mercantile AAGTEKERK (1948).
D.64	FENCER (ex-U.S.N. Croatan)	Western Pipe: G.E.C.	4. 5.42	Returned U.S.N. 11/12/46; mercantile SYDNEY (1948).
D.73	PURSUER (ex-U.S.N. St. George, ex-Mormacland)	Ingalls Sbdg: Westinghouse	18. 7.42	Returned U.S.N. 12/2/46; scrapped 1946.
D.91	STALKER (ex-U.S.N. Hamlin)	Western Pipe: G.E.C.	5. 3.42	Returned U.S.N. 29/12/45; mercantile RIOUW. (1948).
D.12	STRIKER (ex-U.S.N. Prince William)	Western Pipe: G.E.C.	7. 5.42	Returned U.S.N. 12/2/46; scrapped 1946.
D.80	TRAILER (ex-U.S.N. Block Island, ex-Mormacpenn)	Ingalls Sbdg: Westinghouse	22. 5.42	HUNTER (1943), returned U.S.N. 29/12/45; mercantile ALMDIJK. (1948).

Notes:—Had full length hangar under flight deck. Additional 2/6-20 mm. A.A. (2/6 × 1) on hull sponsons.

Ruler class

Displacement: 11,420 tons.
Dimensions: 468½ (pp) 492¼ (oa) × 69½ × 25½ ft.
Machinery: 1-shaft geared Turbine, S.H.P. 9,350 = 17 knots.
Armament: 2—4 in. A.A. (2 × 1), 16—40 mm. A.A. (8 × 2), 20—20 mm. A.A. (20 × 1) Guns; 24 aircraft.
Complement: 646.

D.70	RAVAGER* (ex-Charger)	Seattle-Tacoma	16. 7.42	Returned U.S.N. 27/2/46; mercantile ROBIN TRENT (1948)
D.09	TRUMPETER (ex-Lucifer, ex-U.S.N. Bastian)	Seattle-Tacoma	15.12.42	Returned U.S.N. 6/4/46; mercantile ALBLASSERDIJK. (1948).

D.07	PATROLLER (ex-U.S.N. Keeweenaw)	Seattle-Tacoma	6. 5.43	Returned U.S.N. 13/12/46; mercantile ALMKERK (1948).
D.79	PUNCHER (ex-U.S.N. Willapa)	Seattle-Tacoma	8.11.43	Returned U.S.N. 16/1/46; mercantile MUNCASTER CASTLE (1949); BARDIC (1954); BENNEVIS (1959).
D.82	REAPER (ex-U.S.N. Winjah)	Seattle-Tacoma	22.11.43	Returned U.S.N. 20/5/46; mercantile SOUTH AFRICA STAR (1948).
D.40	SEARCHER	Seattle-Tacoma	20. 6.42	Completed Commercial I.W., returned U.S.N. 29/11/45; mercantile CAPTAIN THEO. (1947).
D.26	SLINGER (ex-U.S.N. Chatham)	Seattle-Tacoma	19. 9.42	Returned U.S.N. 27/2/46; mercantile ROBIN MOWBRAY. (1948).
D.55	SMITER (ex-U.S.N. Vermilion)	Seattle-Tacoma	27. 9.43	Returned U.S.N. 6/4/46; mercantile ARTILLERO (1948).
D.90	SPEAKER* (ex-U.S.N. Delgada)	Seattle-Tacoma	20. 2.43	Returned U.S.N. 17/7/46; mercantile LANCERO (1948).
D.24	TRACKER (ex-U.S.N. Mormacmail)	Seattle-Tacoma	7. 3.42	Returned U.S.N. 29/11/45; mercantile CORRIENTES
D.85	TROUNCER (ex-U.S.N. Perdita)	Seattle-Tacoma	16. 6.43	Returned U.S.N. 3/3/46; mercantile GREY-STOKE CASTLE (1949), GALLIC (1954) BENRINNES (1959).
D.31	ARBITER (ex-U.S.N. St. Simon)	Seattle-Tacoma	9. 9.43	Returned U.S.N. 3/3/46; mercantile CORACERO (1948).
D.01	AMEER (ex-U.S.N. Baffin's Bay)	Seattle-Tacoma	18.10.42	Returned U.S.N. 17/1/46; mercantile ROBIN KIRK (1948).
D.51	ATHELING (ex-U.S.N. Glacier	Seattle-Tacoma	7. 9.42	Returned U.S.N. 13/12/46; mercantile ROMA (1950).
D.38	BEGUM (ex-U.S.N. Balinas)	Seattle-Tacoma	11.11.42	Returned U.S.N. 4/1/46; mercantile RAKI (1948).
B.98	EMPEROR (ex-U.S.N. Pybus)	Seattle-Tacoma	7.10.42	Returned U.S.N. 12/2/46; scrapped 1946.
D.42	EMPRESS (ex-U.S.N. Carnegie)	Seattle-Tacoma	30.12.42	Returned U.S.N. 4/2/46; scrapped 1946.

H.M.S. Battler, August 1943. [P. A. Vicary

H.M.S. Puncher at Malta, carrying Supermarine Seafires. H.M.S. Formidable is visible in the background. [P. A. Vicary

H.M.S. Atheling, 1945. [P. A. Vicary

D.62	KHEDIVE (ex-U.S.N. Cordova)	Seattle-Tacoma	30. 1.43	Returned U.S.N. 26/1/46; mercantile REMPANG (1948).
D.77	NABOB (ex-U.S.N. Edisto)	Seattle-Tacoma	9. 3.43	R.C.N. (1943-44); constructive total loss 22/8/44, returned U.S.N. 16/3/45; mercantile (name not changed, 1951).
D.23	PREMIER (ex-U.S.N. Estero)	Seattle-Tacoma	22. 3.43	Returned U.S.N. 12/4/46; mercantile RHODESIA STAR (1948).
D.19	QUEEN (ex-U.S.N. St. Andrews)	Seattle-Tacoma	2. 8.43	Returned U.S.N. 31/10/46; mercantile ROEBIAH (1948).
D.10	RAJAH (ex-Prince, (ex-U.S.N. McClure)	Seattle-Tacoma	18. 5.43	Returned U.S.N. 13/12/46; mercantile DRENTE (1948).
D.03	RANEE (ex-U.S.N. Niantic)	Seattle-Tacoma	2. 6.43	Returned U.S.N. 21/11/46; mercantile FRIESLAND (1948).
D.72	RULER (ex-U.S.N. St. Joseph)	Seattle-Tacoma	21. 8.43	Returned U.S.N. 29/1/46; scrapped 1946.
D.21	SHAH (ex-U.S.N. Jamaica)	Seattle-Tacoma	21. 4.43	Returned U.S.N. 6/12/45; mercantile SALTA (1948).
D.48	THANE (ex-U.S.N. Sunset)	Seattle-Tacoma	15. 7.43	Constructive total loss 15/1/45; returned U.S.N. 5/12/45; scrapped Faslane.

All engined Allis-Chalmers. * Completed Williamette

Notes:—Had full length hangar under flight deck. Additional 2/6-20mm. (2/6 × 1) on hull sponsons. Original AMEER (ex-Alazon Bay), ATHELING (i) (ex-Anguilla Bay), ATHELING (ii) (ex-Mission Bay), BEGUM (ex-Natoma Bay), KHEDIVE (ex-Hehenta Bay) and EMPEROR (ex-Nassuk Bay) were retained by U.S.N. and replaced by other units.

Escort carriers were mainly based on Greenock and attached to escort groups. Four were with the Mediterranean fleet 1943-44, five were in the Eastern fleet 1944, six were in the Home fleet 1945, twelve—later sixteen—were in the East Indies 1945 and six—later nine—were in the Pacific fleet 1945.

Displacement: 11,800 tons.
Dimensions: 476¼ (pp) 512¾ (oa) × 66½ × 26 ft.
Machinery: 2-shaft Diesel motors, B.H.P. 12,000 = 18 knots.
Armament: 2—4 in. A.A. (1 × 2), 20—20 mm. A. A. (10 × 2) Guns; 15 aircraft. *Complement:* 700.

D.94	ACTIVITY (ex-Telemachus)	Caledon: Kincaid	30. 5.42	Mercantile BRECONSHIRE (1946).

Displacement: 12,450 tons.
Dimensions: 510 (pp) 540 (oa) × 70 × 19 feet.
Machinery: 2-shaft Diesel motors, B.H.P. 11,000 = 17 knots.
Armament: 2—4 in. A.A. (1 × 2), 16—2 pdr. A.A. (4 × 4), 16—20 mm. A.A. (8 × 2) Guns; 15 aircraft. *Complement:* 700.

D.48	CAMPANIA	Harland & Wolff	17. 6.43	Scrapped Blyth 11/11/55.

Displacement: 13,455 tons VINDEX, 14,050 tons NAIRANA.
Dimensions: 499½ (pp) 524 VINDEX, 528½ NAIRANA (oa) × 68½ × 21 ft.
Machinery: 2-shaft Diesel Motors, B.H.P. 11,000 = 17 knots.
Armament: 2—4 in. A.A. (1 × 2), 16—2 pdr. A.A. (4 × 4), 16—20 mm. A.A. (8 × 2) Guns; 15 aircraft.
Complement: 700 VINDEX, 728 NAIRANA.

D.15	VINDEX	Swan Hunter	4. 5.43	Mercantile PORT VINDEX (1947).
D.05	NAIRANA	Clydebank	20. 5.43	R.Neth.N. KAREL DOORMAN (1946), mercantile PORT VICTOR (1948).

Notes:—Above four were adapted from uncompleted mercantile hulls but the construction of further escort carriers was not undertaken by the R.N. as the U.S.N. had them under mass production, a proportion of which were available for the R.N. By avoiding this duplication of effort the R.N. were able to proceed with alternative new construction in other categories.

H.M.A.S. Albatross, July 1945. *[P. A. Vicary*

FLEET DISTRIBUTION

Capital ships, cruisers and aircraft carriers—December, 1939

HOME FLEET

BS.2

Warspite (C-in-C)
Barham
Nelson
Rodney

BCS.

Hood (Flagship)

CS.1

Devonshire
Berwick
Suffolk
Norfolk

CS.2

Edinburgh
Southampton
Glasgow

A.A. Cr.

Curlew

Attached Flotillas

Aurora (Flagship)

LOCAL COMMANDS

Orkney and Shetlands

CS.7

Diomede
Dragon
Caledon
Calypso

CS.11

Colombo
Cardiff
Ceres
Delhi
Dunedin

Portsmouth

Erebus
Adventure
Queen Elizabeth *
Hawkins *
Frobisher *

Nore

Marshal Soult * *
London *
Curacoa *

Humber

Cairo
Calcutta
Coventry

Western Approaches

Royal Sovereign *
Carlisle *
Vindictive *
Centurion *

Rosyth

Belfast *

AMERICA and WEST INDIES

Valiant
Repulse

Furious

Perth
Effingham
Despatch
Caradoc

CS.8

Orion

Halifax Escort Force

BS.3

Resolution
Revenge

York *
Emerald
Enterprise

MEDITERRANEAN FLEET

Malaya

Argus

CS.3

Arethusa
Penelope
Capetown

Attached Flotillas

Galatea (Flagship)

SOUTH ATLANTIC

Renown

Ark Royal
Hermes
Albatross

Cumberland
Shropshire
Sussex
Exeter
Ajax
Achilles
Neptune

EAST INDIES

Eagle

Cornwall
Dorsetshire
Kent
Gloucester
Hobart

Ramillies * * *

Glorious * * *

R.A.N.

Canberra
Australia
Sydney
Adelaide

R.N.Z.N.

Leander

CHINA

CS.5

Liverpool
Birmingham

CS.9

Danae
Dauntless
Durban

Terror

*Refitting * *Training * * *Attached

FLEET DISTRIBUTION

Capital ships, cruisers and aircraft carriers—January 1945

HOME FLEET

BS.2

Rodney (C-in-C)
Anson *
Duke of York *

ACS

Implacable *
Nairana
Campania *
Premier
Trumpeter

CS.1

Norfolk (Flagship)
Berwick
Devonshire

CS.10

Vindex (Flagship)
Mauritius
Bellona
Diadem
Dido

Sussex *
Birmingham *
Belfast *
Glasgow *
Bermuda *
Jamaica *
Apollo
Vindictive

LOCAL COMMANDS

Rosyth

TS

Dauntless
Diomede
Corinthian
Hawkins

Manxman *
Frobisher *
Liverpool *

Portsmouth

Marshal Soult * *
Ceres * *
Ramillies
Conrad *
Scylla (Reserve)

Nore

Argus * *

Attached ANCXF

Warspite
Erebus
Roberts

Adventure

Plymouth

Revenge
Resolution

Western Approaches

Cleopatra *
Cardiff (Training)

TS

Colossus (Flagship)
Patroller
Ranee
Ravager
Reaper
Smiter

Empress * * *
Chaser * * *
Khedive * * *
Puncher * * *
Ruler * * *
Slinger * * *
Speaker * * *

Pretoria Castle (Trials)
Arbiter *
Emperor *
Pursuer *
Queen *
Searcher *

Lent U.S.N.

Atheling
Rajah
Tracker
Trouncer

Ferry Service

Fencer
Striker
Thane
Activity *

Transport

Archer *

RESERVE FLEET

Furious
Biter
Capetown
Despatch
Emerald
Enterprise

Malaya (Reducing)
Nabob ,,
Kent ,,
Albatross ,,

Caledon (to Reduce)
Carlisle ,,
Colombo ,,
Dauntless (to Reduce)
Diomede ,,

MEDITERRANEAN FLEET

CS.15

Ajax
Orion
Aurora
Sirius
Arethusa *

ECS

Royalist (Flagship)
Stalker
Attacker
Hunter

Abercrombie
Carlisle * *

EAST INDIES

BS.3

Queen Elizabeth (Flagship)
Valiant
Renown

ACS

Begum
Shah
Ameer
Battler

CS.5

Newcastle (Flagship)
London
Suffolk
Cumberland
Kenya
Nigeria
Euryalus
Phoebe

PACIFIC FLEET

BS.1

Howe (C-in-C)
King George V (Flagship)

ACS.1

Indomitable (Flagship)
Illustrious
Indefatigable

*Refitting **Base and Accommodation ships ***Working up

BS = Battle Squadron; ACS = Aircraft Carrier Squadron; ECS = Escort Carrier Squadron;
CS = Cruiser Squadron; TS = Training Squadron.
ANCXF = Allied Naval Commander Expeditionary Force.

Victorious
Formidable

CS.4

Swiftsure (Flagship)
Ceylon
Argonaut
Black Prince
Achilles

Gambia *
Newfoundland
Uganda

S.W. PACIFIC

Australia (C-in-C)
Shropshire
Hobart
Adelaide (Reserve)

REFITTING U.S.A.

Nelson
Pursuer
Sheffield
Leander

*Refitting **Base and Accommodation ships ***Working up

BS = Battle Squadron; ACS = Aircraft Carrier Squadron; ECS = Escort Carrier Squadron; CS = Cruiser Squadron; TS = Training Squadron

PART TWO

Destroyers and Submarines

H.M.S. Quail ("**Q**" class) with LA and HA DCTs on bridge. [*I.W.M.*

THE OLD DESTROYERS

RETAINED from the First World War were flotilla leaders of the **Shakespeare** and **Scott** classes and destroyers of the " **R** ", " **S** ", " **V** ", " **W** " and modified " **W** " classes, together with builder's variants of the last three types. They were depleted in numbers, many had been scrapped " between the wars " and they totalled only eighty vessels in all, sub-divided as follows:—

" **R** " *class*:	1	(2 lost and 36 scrapped)
" **S** " *class*:	11	(2 cancelled and 44 scrapped)
" **V** " *class*:	21	(3 lost and 5 scrapped)
(**Thornycroft** *type*):	2	
" **W** " *class*:	17	(1 scrapped)
(**Thornycroft** *type*):	2	
Modified " **W** " *class*:	14	(40 cancelled)
(**Thornycroft** *type*):	2	
Shakespeare *class*:	3	(2 cancelled and 2 scrapped)
Scott *class*:	7	(1 lost and 2 cancelled).

Of these, one **Scott**, three " **V** " and one " **W** " were serving in the Royal Australian Navy and one **Scott** and two " **S** " were de-militarised for the Fleet Target service. It was well realised that most of these old vessels, many of which had seen arduous First World War service, would be unable to stand the strain of modern conflict and plans were formulated for their employment in subsidiary, but equally important, duties to which they lent themselves. Five of the " **S** " class were earmarked for conversion to minelayers and one **Shakespeare**, five " **V** " and four " **W** " were modified for escort work and anticipated the **Hunt** class of escort destroyers. Before even this modest programme could be fully implemented hostilities started and thereafter war expediency dictated further modifications. The remainder, practically without exception, were modified for escort work and underwent (some progressively) three main type of conversions, viz:—

(a) *Escort Destroyers*: This followed the pattern set pre-war and involved considerable structural alteration and complete re-arming with solely A.A. and A/S weapons. It was too extensive to apply to many vessels and only two " **V** ", one **Thornycroft** " **V** " and one " **W** " were taken in hand.

(b) *Short Range Escorts*: This only required minor modification to the armament to improve A.A. and A/S qualities. The after bank of torpedo tubes was replaced by a 3 in. A.A. gun and quarterdeck gun removed to increase depth charge stowage. This conversion was largely undertaken and four so altered were subsequently modified (one **Scott**, two " **W** " and one modified " **W** ") for anti-" E " boat work when a twin 6 pdr. replaced the fo'c'sle gun and an additional 2 pdr. was added on the quarterdeck. The greater majority of the remainder were altered to

(c) *Long Range Escorts*: To increase endurance the forward boiler and its uptake were removed and the space used for additional bunkerage. The fo'c'sle gun was replaced by an ahead throwing weapon (Hedgehog) and the remaining bank of torpedo tubes was removed from most. Those that retained torpedo tubes used them to project 1-ton depth charges.

A small number of vessels (including the five in the R.A.N.) remained materially unaltered mainly because of their early date of loss or because of their employment in areas far removed from home waters. All vessels had from 2 to 6—20 mm. A.A. (supplanting, in some instances, the single 2 pdr. and quadruple .5 in. M.G's already borne) and air and surface warning R.D.F. added as they became available and only the escort destroyers had control R.D.F. added to their H.A. D.C.T's.

Consequent to war losses incurred, and the large number of destroyers damaged at the Dunkirk evacuation, the pressing need for escort vessels resulted in the transfer of fifty over-age destroyers from the United States Navy to the Royal Navy on September 2nd, 1940. Essentially an interim measure to meet current exigencies these vessels filled an essential gap but " over-age " was an apt description—some, indeed, had already been stricken from the U.S.N. list—and no political smoke screen. Their original armament of 4—4 in. (4 × 1), 1—3 in.A.A. and 3—.5 in. A.A. guns and 12—21 in. (4 × 3) T.T. was immediately reduced to improve seaworthiness and augment A/S qualities. Thus, the two forward banks of torpedo tubes were removed and the 3 in. A.A. re-sited on the after shelter deck in place of the aftermost 4 in. gun. This was later considerably reduced, in some, by the removal of the beam 4 in. guns and their substitution by 20 mm. A.A., the two after banks of torpedo tubes were moved forward and the after half of the upper deck was left clear for depth charges and their racks and throwers, a few additional 20 mm. A.A. guns were added aft and an ahead throwing weapon on the fo'c'sle abaft the sole remaining 4 in. gun. Renamed after towns common to both the U.S.A. and British Commonwealth they were not actively employed for long and were replaced as an increased number of new escort vessels became available, but meantimes had filled a critical shortage.

PENNANT NUMBERS

AT the outbreak of war destroyers had flags D, H or F superior to their numeral pennants. The **Tribal** class were originally allotted flag L but this was changed to flag F in December, 1938 and flag L used for escort destroyers building (**Hunt** class) or converting (" **V** " and " **W** " classes). In 1940 flags D and F were changed to I and G and war construction was allotted the latter letter until the " **T** " class, which adopted flag R. A reversion to flag G was made with the **Weapon** and cancelled " **G** " classes and as war losses had left many gaps in the original lists the later **Battle** and " **D** " classes reverted to flag I. Post-war, flag D was allocated to all destroyers and in consequence some re-numbering was required: usually by the addition of 100 or 200 to original numbers.

OLD DESTROYERS

"R" and "S" classes

Displacement: 905 tons except SKATE 900 tons.
Dimensions: 265 (pp) 276 except SKATE 275 (oa) × $26\frac{3}{4}$ × $8\frac{1}{2}$ ft.
Machinery: 2-shaft geared Turbines, S.H.P. 27,000 = 36 knots.
Armament: 1—4 in., 1—3 in. A.A., 8—.5 in. A.A. (2 × 4) or 2 (4 in SKATE and SHIKARI)—20 mm. A.A. (2/4 × 1) guns except* 2—4 in. (2 × 1), 1—2 pdr. A.A. guns. * fitted for minelaying.
Complement: 90.

P. No.	Name	Builder	Launched	Fate
H.39	SKATE	Clydebank	11. 1.17	Scrapped Newport 20/7/47.
H.18	SABRE	Stephen†	23. 9.18	Scrapped Grangemouth 1945/46.
H.54	SALADIN	Stephen	17. 2.19	Scrapped Llanelly 6/47.
H.26	SARDONYX	Stephen	27. 5.19	Scrapped Preston 6/45.
H.21	SCIMITAR	Clydebank	27. 2.18	Scrapped Briton Ferry 30/6/47.
H.51	SCOUT	Clydebank	27. 4.18	Scrapped Briton Ferry 2/3/46.
D.85	SHIKARI	Doxford‡	14. 7.19	Scrapped Newport 4/11/45.
H.50	STRONGHOLD*	Scotts	6. 5.19	Lost 2/3/42.
H.28	STURDY*	Scotts	25. 6.19	Lost 30/10/40.
H.04	TENEDOS	Hawthorn Leslie	21.10.18	Lost 5/4/42.
H.29	THANET	Hawthorn Leslie	5.11.18	Lost 27/1/42.
D.86	THRACIAN*	Hawthorn Leslie§	5. 3.20	Lost 24/12/41, salved as I.J.N. Patrol boat No. 101, and returned R.N. (1945); scrapped 2/46.

‡ completed by Fairfield
† completed by Chatham
§ completed by Sheerness

Notes:—SCOUT, TENEDOS, THANET and THRACIAN were based on Hong Kong and only the latter survived to return to Home waters. THRACIAN was salved by the Japanese and incorporated as their Patrol Boat No. 101 (1942) and then Training Boat No. 1 (1944) and survived the war to be returned to the R.N. All units in Home waters were eventually used for training.

"V", "W" and Modified "W" classes

(Unaltered)

Displacement: "V" class 1,090 tons, "W" class 1,100 tons, Mod. "W" class 1,120 tons.
Dimensions: 300 (pp) 312 (oa) × $29\frac{1}{2}$ × $8\frac{1}{2}$ft.
Machinery: 2-shaft geared Turbines, S.H.P. 27,000 = 34 knots.
Armament: 4—4 in. (4.7 in. in **Mod.** "**W**" class—4 × 1), 1 except **Mod.** "**W**" class 2—2 pdr. A.A. (1/2 × 1) guns; 6—21 in. (2 × 3) T.T.
Complement: 134.

" **V** " class

D.68	VAMPIRE (R.A.N.)	White	21. 5.17	Lost 9/4/42.
D.69	VENDETTA (R.A.N.)	Fairfield	3. 9.17	Scuttled off Sydney Heads 2/7/48.
D.53	VENETIA	Fairfield	29.10.17	Lost 19/10/40.
D.31	VOYAGER (R.A.N.)	Stephen	8. 5.18	Lost 25/9/42.

" **W** " class

H.88 L.91	WAKEFUL	Clydebank	6.10.17	Lost 29/5/40.
D.22	WATERHEN (R.A.N.)	Palmers	26. 3.18	Lost 30/6/41.
D.43	WESSEX	Hawthorn Leslie	12. 3.18	Lost 24/5/40.
D.30	WHIRLWIND	Swan Hunter: Wallsend	15.12.17	Lost 5/7/40.

Mod. " **W** " class

D.88	WREN	Yarrow	11.11.19	Lost 27/7/40.
D.96	WORCESTER	White	24.10.19	YEOMAN (1945); scrapped Grays 2/47.

Notes:—The R.A.N. vessels came to the Mediterranean in 1940 and less WATERHEN (lost) returned to Australian waters in 1942. They had the aft T.T. removed and 1—12 pdr. A.A., 2/4—20 mm. A.A. (2/4 × 1) and 4—.5 in. (1 × 4) guns added. The others all served in Home waters and WORCESTER became an accommodation ship in 1944.

(Escort Destroyers)

Displacement: " **V** " class 1,090 tons, " **W** " class 1,100 tons, **Thornycroft** " **V** " and " **W** " classes, 1,120 tons.
Dimensions: 300 (pp) 312 (oa) × 29½ except **Thornycroft** vessels 30½ × 10¾ ft.
Machinery: 2-shaft geared Turbines, S.H.P. 27,000 = 34 knots except **Thornycroft** vessels S.H.P. 30,000 = 35 knots.
Armament: 4—4 in. A.A. (2 × 2), 2—2 pdr. A.A. (2 × 1—WOOLSTON only), 4—20 mm. A.A. (4 × 1—WOOLSTON only), 8—.5 in. A.A. (2 × 4) guns.
Complement: 125.

" **V** " class

D.49 L.69	VALENTINE	Cammell Laird	24. 3.17	Lost 15/5/40, salved and scrapped 1/53.
L.00	VALOROUS	Denny	8. 5.17	Scrapped Thornaby 1947.
D.28 L.38	VANITY	Beardmore	3. 5.18	Scrapped Grangemouth 1947.
D.52 L.41	VEGA	Doxford	1. 9.17	Scrapped Dunston 26/3/48.
D.93 L.93	VERDUN	Hawthorn Leslie	21. 8.17	Scrapped Granton 4/46.

H.M.S. Scimitar (Admiralty " **S** " class) modified for escort work. [*I.W.M.*

H.M.S. Vega (" **V** " class) converted to an escort destroyer. [*I.W.M.*

H.M.S. Walpole (" **W** " class) with early war alterations only. [*I.W.M.*

D.23 L.29	VIMIERA	Swan Hunter: Wallsend	22. 6.17	Lost 9/1/42.
L.33	VIVIEN	Yarrow	16. 2.18	Scrapped Rosyth and Charlestown 4/48.

Thornycroft " V " class

D.91 L.21	VICEROY	Thornycroft	17.11.17	Scrapped 1946.

" **W** " class

D.45 L.40	WESTMINSTER	Scotts	24. 2.18	Scrapped Rosyth 8/48.
L.23	WHITLEY	Doxford	13. 4.18	Lost 19/5/40.
L.55	WINCHESTER	White	1. 2.18	Scrapped Forth 3/46.
D.56	WOLFHOUND	Fairfield	14. 3.18	Scrapped Granton 1948.
D.21	WRYNECK	Palmers	13. 5.18	Lost 27/4/41.

Thornycroft " **W** " class

D.98 L.02	WOLSEY	Thornycroft	16. 3.18	Scrapped Sunderland 1947.
L.49	WOOLSTON	Thornycroft	27. 1.18	Scrapped Grangemouth 1947.

Notes:—Quadruple .5 in. M.G's replaced by 2—20 mm. A.A. (2 × 1) and a further 2—20 mm. A.A. (2 × 1) added in most (not in WOOLSTON).

(Short Range Escorts)

Displacement: " **V** " class 1,090 tons, " **W** " class 1,100 tons, **Mod.** " **W** " class 1,120 tons, **Thornycroft Mod.** " **W** " class 1,140 tons.
Dimensions: 300 (pp) 312 (oa) × 29½ except **Thornycroft** vessels 30½ × 10¾ ft.
Machinery: 2-shaft geared Turbines, S.H.P. 27,000 = 34 knots except **Thornycroft** vessels S.H.P. 30,000 = 35 knots.
Armament: 3 (2 in VETERAN and WOLVERINE) 4.7 in. (4 in. in VORTIGERN—2/3 × 1), 1—3 in. A.A., 2—2 pdr. A.A. (2 × 1—not in WOLVERINE), 4—20 mm. A.A. (4 × 1—WOLVERINE only) except* 2—4 in. (4.7 in. in WHITSHED—2 × 1), 2—6 pdr. A.A. (1 × 2), 1—3 in. A.A., 3—2 pdr. A.A. (3 × 1), 2—20 mm. A.A. (2 × 1) guns; 3—21 in. (1 × 3) T.T.; 1—A.T.W. (Hedgehog—VETERAN and WOLVERINE only).
Complement: 125.

" **V** " class

D.37	VORTIGERN	White	5.10.17	Lost 15/3/42.

" **W** " class

D.41	WALPOLE*	Doxford	12. 2.18	Scrapped Grays 3/45.
D.42 L.94	WINDSOR*	Scotts	21. 6.18	Scrapped Charlestown 6/49.

Mod. " **W** " class

D.72	VETERAN	Clydebank	26. 8.19	Lost 9/11/42.
D.77	WHITSHED*	Swan Hunter: Wallsend	31. 1.19	Scrapped Gateshead 4/48.
D.62	WILD SWAN	Swan Hunter: Wallsend	17. 5.19	Lost 17/6/42.
D.76	WITHERINGTON	White	16. 1.19	Lost 29/4/47, en-route shipbreakers.
D.66	WIVERN	White	16. 4.19	Scrapped Charlestown 10/48.
D.78	WOLVERINE	White	17. 7.19	Scrapped Troon 9/46.

Thornycroft Mod. " **W** " class

D.67	WISHART	Thornycroft	18. 7.19	Scrapped Forth 1945/46.
D.89	WITCH	Thornycroft	11.11.19	Scrapped Rosyth, 1946.

Notes:—All served in Home waters.

(Long Range Escorts)

Displacement: " **V** " class 1,090 tons, " **W** " class 1,100 tons, **Thornycroft** " **V** " and **Mod.** " **W** " class 1,120 tons.
Dimensions: 300 (pp) 312 (oa) × 29½ except **Thornycroft** vessel 30½ × 10¾ ft.
Machinery: 2-shaft geared Turbines, S.H.P. 18,000 = 24½ knots except **Thornycroft** vessel, S.H.P. 20,000 = 25 knots.
Armament: 2 (3 in VANSITTART)—4 in. (4.7 in. in **Mod.** " **W** " class—2/3 × 1), 1—3 in. A.A. (in VIMY, VANESSA, VISCOUNT, WINCHELSEA and VOLUNTEER only), 2 (3 in WATCHMAN) —2 pdr. A.A. (in VANESSA, VANQUISHER, VANSITTART and WHITEHALL—2/3 × 1) and 2—20 mm. A.A. or 4 (6 in VERITY)—20 mm. A.A. (2/4 × 1) guns; 3—21 in. (1 × 3—VISCOUNT only) T.T.; 1—A.T.W. (Hedgehog—not in VANSITTART).
Complement: 125.

" **V** " class

D.33	VIMY (ex-Vancouver)	Beardmore	28.12.17	Scrapped Rosyth and Charlestown 2/48.
D.29	VANESSA	Beardmore	16. 3.18	Scrapped Charlestown 2/49.
H.33	VANOC	Clydebank	14. 6.17	Lost Penryn 6/46, en-route shipbreakers.
D.54	VANQUISHER	Clydebank	18. 8.17	Scrapped Charlestown 12/48.

D.34	VELOX	Doxford	17.11.17	Scrapped Charlestown 11/47.
D.55	VESPER	Stephen	15.12.17	Scrapped 1946.
D.32	VERSATILE	Hawthorn Leslie	31.10.17	Scrapped Granton 8/49.
D.48	VIDETTE	Stephen	28. 2.18	Scrapped Grangemouth 1947.
D.36	VIVACIOUS	Yarrow	13.11.17	Scrapped Charlestown 10/48.

Thornycroft " **V** " class

D.92	VISCOUNT	Thornycroft	29.12.17	Scrapped Tyne 1947.

" **W** " class

D.27	WALKER	Denny	29.11.17	Scrapped Troon 3/46.
D.25	WARWICK	Hawthorn Leslie	28.12.17	Lost 20/2/44.
D.26	WATCHMAN	Clydebank	2.12.17	Scrapped Inverkeithing 1945.
D.47	WESTCOTT	Denny	14. 2.18	Scrapped Troon 5/46.
D.46	WINCHELSEA	White	15.12.17	Scrapped Rosyth 8/45.
D.35 L.10 I.50	WRESTLER	Swan Hunter: Wallsend	25. 2.18	Constructive total loss 6/6/44 and scrapped Newport 15/8/44.

Mod. " **W** " class

D.64	VANSITTART	Beardmore	17. 4.19	Scrapped Newport 5/5/46.
D.75	VENOMOUS (ex-Venom)	Clydebank	21.12.18	Scrapped Charlestown 8/48.
D.63	VERITY	Clydebank	19. 3.19	Scrapped Newport 14/9/47.
D.71	VOLUNTEER	Denny	17. 4.19	Scrapped Granton 4/48.
D.74	WANDERER	Fairfield	1. 5.19	Scrapped Blyth 1/46.
D.94	WHITEHALL	Swan Hunter: Wallsend	11. 9.19	Scrapped Barrow 27/10/45.

Notes:—All served in Home waters a few being relegated to training 1944-45.

Shakespeare class

Displacement: 1,480 tons.
Dimensions: 318¼ (pp) 329 (oa) × 31¾ × 9 ft.
Machinery: 2-shaft geared Turbines, 43,500 = 36½ knots.
Armament: 2—4.7 in. (2 × 1), 1—3 in. A.A., BROKE 2/KEPPEL 4—20 mm. A.A. (2/4 × 1) guns; 6—21 in. (2 × 3) T.T.; 1—A.T.W. (Hedgehog) except WALLACE 4—4 in. A.A. (2 × 2), 4—2 pdr. A.A. (1 × 4), 2—20 mm. A.A. (2 × 1), 8—.5 in. A.A. (2 × 4) guns.
Complement: 164.

H.M.S. Wolverine (modified " **W** " class), as a short range escort. [I.W.M.

H.M.S. Wanderer (modified " **W** " class), as a long range escort—fuelling at sea. [I.W.M.

Flotilla Leader H.M.S. Keppel, modified for escort work but retaining full torpedo armament. [I.W.M.

D.84	KEPPEL	Thornycroft	23. 4.20	Scrapped Barrow 1945.
D.83	BROKE (ex-Rooke)	Thornycroft	16. 9.20	Lost 9/11/42.
L.64	WALLACE	Thornycroft	26.10.18	Scrapped Dunston 20/3/45.

Notes:—BROKE and KEPPEL were converted to short range escorts and WALLACE to an escort destroyer. All served in Home waters but BROKE was lost in the Mediterranean whilst detached.

Scott class

Displacement: 1,530 tons.
Dimensions: 320 (pp) 332½ (oa) × 31¾ × 9¼ ft.
Machinery: 2-shaft geared Turbines, S.H.P. 40,000 = 36½ knots.
Armament: STUART 5—4.7 in. (5 × 1), 1—3 in. A.A. CAMPBELL 3—4.7 in. (3 × 1), 1—4 in. A.A., 4—20 mm. A.A. (4 × 1). MONTROSE 2—4.7 in. (2 × 1), 2—6 pdr. (1 × 2), 1—4 in. A.A., 2—2 pdr. A.A. (2 × 1), 2—20 mm. A.A. (2 × 1). DOUGLAS and MALCOLM 2—4.7 in. (2 × 1), 1—3 in. A.A., 2—2 pdr. A.A. (2 × 1), 1—1 pdr. (MALCOLM only), 2—20 mm. A.A. (2 × 1), 4—.303 in. (2 × 2—DOUGLAS only) guns; 6 except DOUGLAS and MALCOLM 3—21 in. (1/2 × 3) T.T.; 1—A.T.W. (Hedgehog—DOUGLAS and MALCOLM only). BRUCE dis-armed as target.
Complement: 164/183.

D.81	BRUCE	Cammell Laird	26. 2.18	Lost 22/11/39.
D.60	CAMPBELL	Cammell Laird	21. 9.18	Scrapped Rosyth 6/48.
D.70	MACKAY (ex-Claverhouse)	Cammell Laird	21.12.18	Scrapped Charlestown 6/49.
D.90	DOUGLAS	Cammell Laird	8. 6.18	Scrapped Inverkeithing 20/3/45.
D.19	MALCOLM	Cammell Laird	29. 5.19	Scrapped Barrow 25/7/45.
D.01	MONTROSE	Hawthorn Leslie	10. 6.18	Scrapped Blyth 31/1/46.
D.00	STUART (R.A.N.)	Hawthorn Leslie	22. 8.18	Scrapped Sydney 3/2/47.

Notes:—BRUCE was used as a target, STUART was unaltered and the remainder converted to short range escorts. Except for STUART service was mainly in Home waters.

Town class

(First group)

Displacement: 1,020 tons.
Dimensions: 308 (wl) 315½ (oa) × 30¾ × 7½ ft.
Machinery: 2-shaft geared Turbines, S.H.P. 20,000 = 30 knots.
Armament: 2—2 pdr. A.A. (2 × 1), 5—20 mm. A.A. (5 × 1).
Complement: 146.

1. Flotilla Leader H.M.S. Wallace, converted to an escort destroyer. 2. Flotilla Leader H.M.S. Montrose, modified for escort work with twin 6-pounder in large shield on fo'c'sle. 3. H.M.S. Leeds, (**Town** class—2nd Group), with fo'c'sle and quarter-deck 4 in. guns retained. 4. H.M.S. Ludlow (**Town** class—2nd Group), with beam 4 in. guns retained. [*All photos I.W.M.*

G.68	LEWES (ex-U.S.N. Conway, ex-Craven)	Norfolk	29. 6.18	Scuttled Australia 5/46.

(Second group)

Displacement: 1,020 tons.
Dimensions: 308 (wl) 315½ (oa) × 30¾ × 7½ ft.
Machinery: 3-shaft geared Turbines, S.H.P. 18,500 = 30 knots.
Armament: 2—4 in. (2 × 1), 2—2 pdr. A.A. (2 × 1), 4—20 mm. A.A. (4 × 1) guns.
Complement: 146.

G.27	LEEDS (ex-U.S.N. Conner)	Cramp	21. 8.17	Scrapped Grays 4/3/47.
G.57	LUDLOW (ex-U.S.N. Stockton)	Cramp	17. 7.17	Scrapped 5/7/45.

(Third group)

Displacement: 1,090 tons.
Dimensions: 309 (wl) 314¼ (oa) × 30½ × 8¾ ft.
Machinery: 2-shaft geared Turbines, S.H.P. 25,200 except* 26,000 = 35 knots.
Armament: 3—4 in. (3 × 1), 1—3 in. A.A., 2—.5 in. A.A. (2 × 1), 2—.303 in. A.A. (2 × 1—TWIGGS only) guns; 6—21 in. (2 × 3) T.T. except † 1—4 in., 1—3 in. A.A., WELLS 3/others 4—20 mm. A.A. (3/4 × 1) guns; 3—21 in. (1 × 3) T.T.; 1—A.T.W. (Hedgehog).
Complement: 146.

I.42	CAMPBELTOWN (ex-U.S.N. Buchanan)	Bath I.W.	2. 1.19	Expended 28/3/42.
I.20	CALDWELL (ex-U.S.N. Hale)	Bath I.W.	29. 5.19	R.C.N. (1942-44); scrapped Granton 20/3/45.
I.23	CASTLETON† (ex-U.S.N. Aaron Ward)	Bath I.W.	10. 4.19	Scrapped Bo'ness 4/3/47.
I.35	CHELSEA† (ex-U.S.N. Crowinshield)	Bath I.W.	24. 7.19	R.C.N. (1942-43), Russian DERZKI (1944-49); scrapped Bo'ness 12/7/49.
G.05	LANCASTER (ex-U.S.N. Philip)	Bath I.W.	25. 7.18	Scrapped Blyth 18/2/47.
G.19	LEAMINGTON* (ex-U.S.N. Twiggs)	N.Y. Sbdg.	28. 9.18	R.C.N. (1942-43); Russian ZHGUCHI (1944-50); scrapped Newport 26/7/51.
G.42	LINCOLN*† (ex-U.S.N. Yarnall)	Cramp	19. 6.18	R.N.N. (1941-43); Russian DRUZNI (1944-52); scrapped Rosyth 9/52.

G.76	MANSFIELD† (ex-U.S.N. Evans)	Bath I.W.	30.10.18	R.N.N. (1940-42), R.C.N. (1942-43); scrapped Canada 1944.
G.95	MONTGOMERY† (ex-U.S.N. Wickes)	Bath I.W.	25. 6.18	R.C.N. (1942-43); scrapped Tyne 20/3/45.
G.88	RICHMOND* (ex-U.S.N. Fairfax)	Mare Island	15.12.17	R.C.N. (1942-43), Russian ZHIVUCHI (1944-49); scrapped Bo'ness 12/7/49.
I.52	SALISBURY*† (ex-U.S.N. Claxton)	Mare Island	15. 1.19	R.C.N. (1942-43); scrapped Canada 26/6/44.
I.95	WELLS† (ex-U.S.N. Tillman)	Charleston	7. 7.19	Scrapped Troon 24/7/45.

(Fourth group)

Displacement: 1,060 tons.
Dimensions: 309 (wl) 314¼ (oa) × 30½ × 8½ ft.
Machinery: 2-shaft geared Turbines, S.H.P. 27,000 except* 25,000 = 35 knots.
Armament: 3—4 in. (3 × 1), 1—3 in. A.A., 2 except ST. ALBANS 3—.5 in. A.A. (2/3 × 1), 4—.303 in. A.A. (4 × 1—ST. ALBANS only) guns; 6—21 in. (2 × 3—not in ST. ALBANS) T.T. except† 1—4 in., 1—3 in. A.A., 4—20 mm. A.A. (4 × 1) guns 3—21 in. (1 × 3 T.T.; 1—A.T.W. Hedgehog).
Complement: 146.

I.04	ANNAPOLIS (R.C.N.) (ex-U.S.N. MacKenzie)	Union I.W.	19. 9.18	For disposal 21/6/45.
I.17	BATH* (ex-U.S.N. Hopewell)	Newport News	8. 6.18	R.N.N. (1941); lost 19/8/41.
I.08	BRIGHTON† (ex-U.S.N. Cowell)	Fore River	23.11.18	Russian ZHARKI (1944-49); scrapped Bo'ness 5/4/49.
I.21	CHARLESTOWN* (ex-U.S.N. Abbot)	Newport News	4. 7.18	Scrapped Sunderland 4/3/47.
I.49	COLUMBIA (R.C.N.) (ex-U.S.N. Haraden)	Newport News	4. 7.18	For disposal 7/8/45.
I.40	GEORGETOWN† (ex-U.S.N. Maddox)	Fore River	27.10.18	R.C.N. (1942-43), Russian ZHOSTKI (1944-52); scrapped Inverkeithing 16/9/52.
I.24	HAMILTON† (R.C.N.) (ex-U.S.N. Kalk, ex-Rogers)	Fore River	21.12.18	For disposal 2/8/45.

G.08	NEWARK† (ex-U.S.N. Ringgold)	Union I.W.	14. 4.18	Scrapped Bo'ness 18/2/47.
G.47	NEWMARKET† (ex-U.S.N. Robinson)	Union I.W.	28. 3.18	Scrapped Llanelly 9/45.
G.54	NEWPORT (ex-U.S.N. Sigourney)	Fore River	16.12.17	R.N.N. (1941-42); scrapped Granton 18/2/47.
I.57	NIAGARA (R.C.N.) (ex-U.S.N. Thatcher)	Fore River	31. 8.18	For disposal 13/1/46.
I.07	ROXBURGH† (ex-U.S.N. Foote)	Fore River	14.12.18	Russian DOBLESTNI (1944-49); scrapped Dunston 5/4/49.
I.15	ST. ALBANS* (ex-U.S.N. Thomas)	Newport News	4. 7.18	R.N.N. (1941-44); Russian DOSTOINI (1944-49); scrapped Charlestown 5/4/49.
I.65	St. CLAIR (R.C.N.) (ex-U.S.N. Williams)	Union I.W.	4. 7.18	For disposal 5/3/46.
I.12	St. MARY'S* (ex-U.S.N. Doran, ex-Bagley)	Newport News	19.10.18	Scrapped Rosyth 20/3/45.

(Fifth group)

Displacement: 1,190 tons.

Dimensions: 311 (wl) 314¼ (oa) × 30¾ × 9¼ ft.

Machinery: 2-shaft geared Turbines, S.H.P. 27,000 = 35 knots except BRADFORD, CLARE and STANLEY S.H.P. 13,500 = 25 knots.

Armament: 3—4 in. (3 × 1), 1—3 in. A.A., 2—.5 in. A.A. (2 × 1) except* 1—4 in., 1—3 in. A.A., 4 except ROCKINGHAM 5—20 mm. A.A. (4/5 × 1) guns; 6 except * 3—21 in. (1/2 × 3) T.T.; 1—A.T.W. (Hedgehog in* only).

Complement: 146.

H.46	BELMONT (ex-U.S.N. Satterlee)	Newport News	21.12.18	Lost 31/1/42.
H.64	BEVERLEY* (ex-U.S.N. Branch)	Newport News	19. 4.19	Lost 11/4/43.
H.72	BRADFORD (ex-U.S.N. McLanahan)	Bethlehem (Squantum)	22. 9.18	Scrapped Troon 19/6/46.

H.M.S. Leamington (**Town** class—3rd Group), with only initial alterations affected. [*I.W.M.*

H.M.S. Brighton (**Town** class—4th Group), with topweight considerably reduced for escort work. [*I.W.M.*

H.M.S. Rockingham (**Town** class—5th Group), modified for escort work. Note propeller guard at stern. [*I.W.M.*

H.81	BROADWATER (es-U.S.N. Mason)	Newport News	8. 3.19	Lost 81/10/41.
H.90	BROADWAY* (ex-U.S.N. Hunt)	Newport News	14. 2.20	Scrapped Charlestown 5/48.
H.82	BURNHAM* (ex-U.S.N. Aulick)	Bethlehem	11. 4.19	Scrapped Pembroke 12/48.
H.94	BURWELL* (ex-U.S.N. Laub)	Bethlehem (Squantum)	25. 8.18	Scrapped Milford Haven 4/3/47.
H.96	BUXTON* (ex-U.S.N. Edwards)	Bethlehem (Squantum)	10.10.18	R.C.N. (1943-44); for disposal 21/3/46.
I.05	CAMERON (ex-U.S.N. Welles)	Bethlehem	8. 5.19	Constructive total loss Portsmouth 15/12/40. and scrapped 11/44.
I.28	CHESTERFIELD* (ex-Welborn C. Wood)	Newport News	6. 3.20	Scrapped Tyne 4/3/47.
I.45	CHURCHILL* (ex-U.S.N. Herndon)	Newport News	31. 5.19	Russian DEIATELNYI (1944-45); lost 16/1/45.
I.14	CLARE* (ex-U.S.N. Abel P. Upshur)	Newport News	14. 2.20	Scrapped Troon 3/47.
G.60	RAMSEY (ex-U.S.N. Meade)	Bethlehem (Squantum)	24. 5.19	Scrapped Bo'ness 7/47.
G.71	READING (ex-U.S.N. Bailey)	Bethlehem (Squantum)	5. 2.19	Scrapped Inverkeithing 24/7/45.
G.79	RIPLEY* (ex-U.S.N. Shubrick)	Bethlehem (Squantum)	31.12.18	Scrapped Sunderland 20/3/45.
G.58	ROCKINGHAM* (ex-U.S.N. Swasey)	Bethlehem (Squantum)	7. 5.19	Lost 27/9/44.
I.81	St. CROIX (R.C.N.) (ex-U.S.N. McCook)	Bethlehem	31. 1.19	Lost 20/9/43.
I.93	St. FRANCIS (R.C.N.) (ex-U.S.N. Bancroft)	Bethlehem	21. 3.19	For disposal 2/8/45.
I.80	SHERWOOD (ex-U.S.N. Rodgers, ex-Kalk)	Bethlehem	26. 4.19	Scrapped 1945.
I.73	STANLEY* (ex-U.S.N. McCalla)	Bethlehem	28. 3.19	Lost 19/12/41.

Notes:—All had four funnels except LEEDS and LUDLOW which had only three. BRADFORD, CLARE and STANLEY (and possibly others) had the two forward boilers and funnels removed on conversion to long range escorts. All except LEWES served continuously in Home waters and the North Atlantic. LEWES was in the South Atlantic from 1943-44 and finished up as an air target vessel, based on Sydney, for the Pacific fleet. The class as a whole was responsible for the sinking of eleven U-boats and St. ALBANS had the distinction of sinking, besides U.401, the British minesweeper ALBERIC and the Polish submarine JASTRAB

BRITISH DESTROYER DEVELOPMENT FROM 1918

THE effect of the large destroyer construction programmes embarked on during the First World War resulted in no new vessels being authorised until 1924 when two prototype vessels were put in hand. Wisely, the two foremost destroyer builders were selected—Thornycroft and Yarrow—and were given a free hand within broad Admiralty specifications to evolve a standard type. The Admiralty specified for vessels similar to the most recent design available (Thornycroft's Modified " **W** " class) and the prototypes were generally similar with two knots more speed, all-steel bridges, improved habitability and a wider radius of action. From them stemmed the long line of the "**A**" to " **I** " classes; eight full flotillas of nine vessels, a half flotilla of five vessels plus two additional vessels for the Royal Canadian Navy. Minor improvements in each succeeding class are listed below:—

"**A**" class: (1927) Est.)	Introduced quadruple torpedo tubes and had full shields to their 4.7 in. guns. (The two R.C.N. vessels built to this design had their hulls strengthened for ice navigation).
" **C** " class: (1929 Est.)	A single 3 in. A.A. replaced the two single 2 pdr. A.A. which were moored to the bridge wings and a director control tower the pedestal director.
" **E** " class: (1931 Est.)	Two vessels were designed for rapid conversion to fast minelayers and this was later extended to the entire " **G** ", " **H** " and " **I** " classes. Two quadruple .5 in. M.G. A.A. mountings replaced the single 3 in. A.A.
" **G** " class: (1933 Est.)	One vessel experimentally mounted quintuple torpedo tubes, later adopted in the " **I** ", " **J** ", " **K** " and " **N** " classes.
" **H** " class: (1934 Est.)	Two vessels introduced the angled bridge front which became standard for all subsequent construction and another vessel experimentally carried a twin 4.7 in. mounting later adopted by the **Tribal,** " **J** ", " **K** " and " **N** " classes.

A halt was called to standard construction in view of the large destroyers building abroad and to which it was considered desirable to have British counterparts. This resulted in the **Tribal** class in which the gun armament was doubled, the torpedo armament halved and the A.A. armament (a weak feature of the "**A**" to " **I** " classes) was considerably enhanced.

Whereas the flotilla in the "**A**" to " **I** " classes consisted of eight vessels and an enlarged leader (with two exceptions) this practice was discontinued from the **Tribal** class and one, or more, vessel was merely altered internally to accommodate the additional personnel carried. Further, with the **Tribal** class onwards more extensive A/S qualities replaced the high speed mine sweeps fitted in the "**A**" to " **F** " classes and the minelaying potential of the " **G** " to " **I** " classes.

The **Tribal** class were too expensive to be repeated in large numbers so that a reduced design, which suppressed a twin gun mounting but increased the torpedo armament to full strength with two banks of quintuple tubes, was adopted. The vessels introduced longitudinal framing to British destroyers and accepted the risk incurred by a reduction to two boilers which resulted in a single funnel—a profile new to British destroyers. To this design were built the " **J** " and " **K** " classes but the subsequent " **L** " and " **M** " classes differed slightly in that their guns were fully enclosed in turrets and were dual purpose (low-angle and high-angle) pieces, but size and cost increased alarmingly and the " **N** " class which followed reverted to the earlier, and simpler, design.

The need for fast escort vessels, so that destroyer strength would not be denuded for this essential task, led to the introduction of the *escort destroyer*. They sacrificed torpedo armament and some speed for a purely A.A. and A/S armament and resulted in smaller and cheaper vessels which could be quantity produced. The first group of twenty were ordered before the war but this number was considerably increased in subsequent war programmes.

The outbreak of the Second World War found the Royal Navy short materially in most classes of vessels but especially in the destroyer and escort flotillas. To speed production it was decided to adopt a standard destroyer design which was longitudinally framed with two boilers as in the " **J** " class but armed with single guns as in the "**A**" to " **I** " classes. However, the inadequacy of the A.A. armament was recognised and happily coincided with the belated introduction of the 20 mm. A.A. gun. Provision was made for four mountings in the war standard vessels in the bridge wings to port and starboard and similarly abreast the searchlight platform between the torpedo tubes, whilst the quadruple 2 pdr. A.A. kept its position abaft the funnel. Production difficulties only permitted single 20 mm. being fitted initially and to a large extent they were replaced by twin 20 mm. at a later stage. When the 40 mm. A.A. gun made its even more belated appearance its single mounting partially replaced the twin 20 mm. (which was usually retained in the bridge wings) but its twin mounting completely eclipsed the long standing quadruple 2 pdr. which had given sterling service. The minor differences and improvements in succeeding classes of the war standard vessels (the " **O** " to " **Z** " classes and the four " **C** " groups) are listed below.

" **O** " class: Fitted for minelaying. Owing to shortage of 4.7 in. guns half were armed with old 4 in. guns but had both banks of torpedo tubes whilst the others had a single 4 in. A.A. in lieu of the after bank. Light A.A. comprised 4—2 pdr. (1 × 4) and 4—20 mm. (4 × 1) in all.

" **P** " class: Generally as above but none originally received 4.7 in. guns and half of them had a single 4 in. A.A. in lieu of the after bank of torpedo tubes.

" **Q** " class: Light A.A. increased to 6—20 mm. (6 × 1) by inclusion of two extra guns abreast searchlight.

" **R** " class: Light A.A. further increased to 8—20 mm. (2 × 2 & 4 × 1) by substituting twins for single mountings in bridge wings. Surface warning R.D.F. replaced searchlight between torpedo tubes in some.

" **S** " class: One vessel introduced 4.5 in. D.P. gun. Quadruple 2 pdr. re-sited between torpedo tubes and replaced by 2—40 mm. (2 × 1) or 4—20 mm. (2 × 2) in some and all had 8—20 mm. in addition by general adoption of twin mountings.

" **T** " class: Light A.A. comprised 10—20 mm. (4 × 2 & 2 × 1) later increased to 12 when single mountings in bridge wings were paired, or 2—40 mm. (1 × 2) and 8—20 mm. (4 × 2).

“**U**” class: Introduced lattice masts but light A.A. lacked uniformity and comprised (i) 2—40 mm. (1 × 2) or 4—2 pdr. (1 × 4) and 8—20 mm. (4 × 2) or (ii) 12—20 mm. (6 × 2).

“**V**” class: Light A.A. comprised 2—40 mm. (1 × 2) or 4—2 pdr. (1 × 4) and 8—20 mm. (4 × 2).

“**W**” class: Light A.A. generally 2—40 mm. (1 × 2) and 8—20 mm. (4 × 2) but some units had 4/5—40 mm. (4/5 × 1) with the additional gun in a superfiring position abaft the funnel.

“**Z**” class: Introduced 4.5 in. D.P. gun. Light A.A. generally 2—40 mm. (1 × 2) and 6—20 mm. (2 × 2 & 2 × 1) with only single mountings abaft funnel.

“**C**” groups: Generally 2—40 mm. (1 × 2) and 6/8—20 mm. (2 × 2 & 2 × 1 or 4 × 2)—but very varied as completed.

The construction of escort destroyers was continued together with the war standard fleet destroyers. The *second group* had an additional twin 4 in. A.A. mounting added aft which the *third group* sacrificed for twin torpedo tubes while the enlarged *fourth group* embraced both additional features. With a limited radius of action their employment was circumscribed and they never quite attained their designed speed but were otherwise efficient vessels.

War modifications to the destroyers of the “**A**” to “**I**” classes (including the ex-Brasilian & ex-Turkish vessels) mainly comprised:—

(a) the replacement of the after bank of torpedo tubes by a single 3 in. A.A. gun.

(b) the after funnel was cut down and the mainmast removed to increase the sky arcs of the above.

(c) ‘Y’ gun was removed to increase depth charge stowage and extra throwers were fitted.

(d) the eventual addition of 2/6—20 mm. A.A. guns in the bridge wings, between the funnels (where it supplanted single 2 pdr. and quadruple .5 in. M.G’s originally fitted) and abreast the searchlight.

Vessels more exclusively employed in escort groups had ‘A’ gun replaced by an A.T.W. (Hedgehog) and surface warning R.D.F. took the place of the D.C.T. and R/F on the bridge.

The British **Tribal** class had ‘X’ twin 4.7 in. mounting replaced by a twin 4 in. A.A. and had 2/4—20 mm. A.A. added. The Australian and Canadian (*first group*) **Tribal** class were so completed in the first instance and the latter had up to 12—20 mm. A.A. (6 × 2) added. The Canadian *second group* had a light A.A. armament of 4—40 mm. (1 × 2 & 2 × 1) and 4—20 mm. A.A. (2 × 2) guns and the final pair of the group (completed too late for hostilities) had a main armament of 8—4 in. A.A. (4 × 2).

The **Hunt** groups of escort destroyers had 2/3—20 mm. A.A. added in the bridge wings and on the quarterdeck (in some). Those employed on East Coast convoys had a single 2 pdr. bowchaser added right in the bows, and a few units later had their single 20 mm. A.A. replaced by twin mountings.

The “**J**”, “**K**” and “**N**” classes all had the after bank of torpedo tubes removed and shipped a 4 in. A.A. gun instead and had from 2/4—20 mm. A.A. guns added. They later had the torpedo tubes replaced and the gun taken out. The same held good for the “**L**” and “**M**” classes except that four of the “**L**” class were completed with a main armament of 8—4 in. A.A. (4 × 2) guns and a few units later had their single 20 mm. replaced by twin mountings.

In all the above vessels surface warning R.D.F. was added either on the bridge (generally applicable to destroyers on escort duty) or in place of the searchlight between the torpedo tubes (more generally for destroyers retained for fleet work), air warning R.D.F. was added at the mast head and in the **Tribal**, " **J** ", " **K** " and " **N** " classes the R/F on the bridge was replaced by an H.A. D.C.T. fitted with gunnery R.D.F. A short vertical lattice mast topped by HF/DF aerials was fitted at the fore end of the after shelter deck in most and lattice foremasts replaced tripods (where fitted—but not in the **Hunt** classes) to take the increasing weight of gear aloft.

With the foreseeable end of the European war in sight, the shifting of the major theatre of operations to the Pacific led to the abandonment of the standard war destroyer, which fell short of Pacific requirements, and a new design—the **Battle** class—was evolved. The **Battle** class were considerably larger than the standard destroyer to embrace improved seaworthiness, a greater radius of action and a larger measure of self-support during protracted operations, well away from a main base. As the air war in the Pacific was carried to the enemy mainly by carrier borne aircraft, supporting vessels had to be amply equipped with A.A. guns for their own defence, so that the maximum number of aircraft could be used in offensive strikes. The main gun armament of the **Battle** class was concentrated forward and re-introduced twin turrets (the prototype had been installed in the SAVAGE—" **S** " class) to the British flotilla whilst the after part was devoted to a numerous light A.A. battery and a full torpedo armament. The *first group* had a 4 in. gun abaft the funnel for firing starshell but this was replaced in the *second group* by a 4.5 in. gun.

The primary and dual function of the destroyer was to both protect its own line (whether composed of battleships or aircraft carriers) from torpedo attack and similarly attack the enemy's line. However, the modern, fast battleship with its highly efficient, numerous and R.D.F. controlled secondary battery had practically relegated *surface* torpedo attack to obsolescense but the threat was ever present from *over* and *under* the sea. Therefore, in its defensive role the modern destroyer could dispense with L.A. guns and install a purely A.A. and A/S armament whilst retaining, for the time being, its torpedo tubes. To this new concept was built the **Weapon** class with the novel machinery arrangement of boiler and engine rooms disposed *en echelon*. The original main gun armament of 6—4 in. A.A. (3 × 2) was reduced when a twin mounting was removed and replaced by a new and improved A.T.W.—the Squid. It was tried both forward (in ' **B** ' position) and aft (in ' **X** ' position) and the latter position was ultimately preferred. The cancelled " **G** " class, which would have followed the **Weapon** class, were generally similar but with 4.5 in. D.P. instead of the 4 in. A.A. guns.

The final class of destroyer to be ordered before the end of the war were of an enlarged **Battle** design and the largest vessels of their type ever built for the Royal Navy. Their main guns were in fully automatic turrets with a high rate of fire, and although matchless vessels for their size the latter tended to remove them from the class of the hunter to that of the hunted. Historically, they became the last conventional destroyers to be ordered for the Royal Navy as with the passing of the line of battle the need for the true destroyer lapsed.

DESTROYERS

Prototypes

Displacement: AMAZON 1,352 tons, AMBUSCADE 1,173 tons.
Dimensions: AMAZON 311¾ (pp) 323 (oa) × 31½ × 9¼ ft., AMBUSCADE 307 (pp) 322 (oa) × 31 × 8½ ft.

Machinery: 2-shaft geared Turbines, S.H.P. 39,500 AMAZON, 33,000 AMBUSCADE = 37 knots.
Armament: 4—4.7 in. (4 × 1), 2—2 pdr. A.A. (2 × 1) guns; 6—21 in. (2 × 3) T.T. *Complement:* 138.

D.39	AMAZON	Thornycroft	27. 1.26	Scrapped Troon 25/10/48.
D.38	AMBUSCADE	Yarrow	15. 1.26	Scrapped Troon 23/11/46.

Notes:—The first destroyers to be ordered by the R.N. after the First World War in which the builders were allowed considerable latitude in design within broad Admiralty specifications with the view of evolving a standard type. After service with the Home fleet both spent three years in the Western Approaches and were finally used for training.

Flotilla Leader and "A" class

Displacement: 1,350 tons except R.C.N. vessels 1,337 tons and CODRINGTON 1,540 tons.
Dimensions: 312 (pp) 323 (oa) × 32¼ × 8½ ft. except R.C.N. vessels 309 (pp) 321¼ (oa) × 32¾ × 8½ ft. and CODRINGTON 332 (pp) 343 (oa) × 33¾ × 9 ft.
Machinery: 2-shaft geared Turbines S.H.P. 34,000 except R.C.N. vessels 32,000 and CODRINGTON 40,000 = 35 knots.
Armament: 4 except CODRINGTON 5—4.7 in. (4/5 × 1), 2—2 pdr. A.A. (2 × 1) guns; 8—21 in. (2 × 4) T.T.
Complement: 138 (185 in CODRINGTON).

D.65	CODRINGTON	Swan Hunter: Wallsend	7. 8.29	Lost 27/7/40.
H.09	ACASTA	Clydebank	8. 8.29	Lost 8/6/40.
H.12	ACHATES	Clydebank	4.10.29	Lost 31/12/42.
H.45	ACHERON	Thorny-croft: Parsons	18. 3.30	Lost 17/12/40.
H.14	ACTIVE	Hawthorn Leslie	9. 7.29	Scrapped Troon 20/5/47.
H.36	ANTELOPE	Hawthorn Leslie	27. 7.29	Scrapped Blyth 31/1/46.
H.40	ANTHONY	Scotts	24. 4.29	Scrapped Troon 5/48.
H.41	ARDENT	Scotts	26. 6.29	Lost 8/6/40.
H.42	ARROW	V. A. (Barrow)	22. 8.29	Scrapped Taranto 5/49.
D.79	SAGUENAY (R.C.N.)	Thornycroft	11. 7.30	Constructive total loss 11/42, training, for disposal 30/6/45.
D.59	SKEENA (R.C.N.)	Thornycroft	10.10.30	Lost 25/10/44, salved and scrapped 1946.

Notes:—Introduced quadruple T.T. ACTIVE was mainly based on Gibraltar whilst ANTELOPE, ANTHONY and ARROW, after some service in Home waters, went to Gibraltar and the Mediterranean. Both R.C.N. vessels served in the West Indies to 1940 followed by Escort duty in North Atlantic.

Flotilla Leader and " B " class

Displacement: 1,360 tons except KEITH 1,400 tons.
Dimensions: 312 (pp) 323 (oa) × 32¼ × 8½ ft.
Machinery: 2-shaft geared Turbines, S.H.P. 34,000 = 35 knots.
Armament: 4—4.7 in. (4 × 1), 2—2 pdr. A.A. (2 × 1) guns; 8—21 in. (2 × 4) T.T. *Complement:* 138 (175 in KEITH).

D.06	KEITH	V. A. (Barrow)	10. 7.30	Lost 1/6/40.
H.11	BASILISK	Clydebank	6. 8.30	Lost 1/6/40.
H.30	BEAGLE	Clydebank	26. 9.30	Scrapped Rosyth 6/46.
H.47	BLANCHE	Hawthorn Leslie	29. 5.30	Lost 13/11/39.
H.65	BOADICEA	Hawthorn Leslie	23. 9.30	Lost 13/6/44.
H.77	BOREAS	Palmers	18. 7.30	R.H.N. SALAMIS (1944-51); scrapped Troon 4/52.
H.80	BRAZEN	Palmers	25. 7.30	Lost 20/7/40.
H.84	BRILLIANT	Swan Hunter: Wallsend	9.10.30	Scrapped Troon 4/48.
H.91	BULLDOG	Swan Hunter: Wallsend	6.12.30	Scrapped Rosyth 3/46.

Notes:—KEITH, BASILISK, BLANCHE and BRAZEN all served in Home waters until lost. BEAGLE and BOADICEA were Home fleet and then in the Western Approaches from 1941. BOREAS was in Home waters until 1941, South Atlantic to 1942, then the Mediterranean and was lent to the R.H.N. BRILLIANT served successively in Home waters, South Atlantic, Gibraltar and then Home waters again. BULLDOG was in the Mediterranean and East Indies to 1940 then Home waters, mostly on Western Approaches escort duty.

Flotilla Leaders and " C " and " D " classes

Displacement: 1,375 tons except R.C.N. ASSINIBOINE 1,390 tons and DUNCAN 1,400 tons.
Dimensions: 317¾ (pp) 329 (oa) × 33 × 8½ except R.C.N. ASSINIBOINE and DUNCAN 8¾ ft.
Machinery: 2-shaft geared Turbines, S.H.P. 36,000 = 35½ knots.
Armament: 4—4.7 in. (4 × 1), 2—2 pdr. A.A. (2 × 1), 8—.5 in. A.A. (2 × 4 —" E " class only), guns; 8—21 in. (2 × 4) T.T.
Complement: 145 (175 in R.C.N. ASSINIBOINE and DUNCAN).

D.18	ASSINBOINE (R.C.N.) (ex-Kempenfelt)	White	29.10.31	Lost 10/11/45.
H.00	RESTIGOUCHE (R.C.N.) (ex-Comet)	Portsmouth: Hawthorn Leslie	30. 9.31	For disposal 9/11/45.

H.M.S. Achates ("**A**" class), modified for escort work. SW. RDF. on bridge, AW. RDF at masthead, HF/DF aerial aft and ATW on fo'c'sle. [*I.W.M.*

H.M.C.S. Saguenay (Canadian "**A**" class). [*Thornycroft*

H.M.S. Bulldog (" **B** " class), taking oil hose from H.M.S. Express, 1944. [*I.W.M.*

H.48	FRASER (R.C.N.) (ex-Crescent)	V.A. (Barrow)	29. 9.31	Lost 28/6/40.
H.60	OTTAWA (R.C.N.) (ex-Crusader)	Portsmouth: Hawthorn Leslie	30. 9.31	Lost 14/9/42.
H.83	St. LAURENT (R.C.N.) (ex-Cygnet)	V.A. (Barrow)	29. 9.31	For disposal 9/11/45.
D.99	DUNCAN	Portsmouth: Hawthorn Leslie	7. 7.32	Scrapped Barrow 11/45.
H.53	DAINTY	Fairfield	3. 5.32	Lost 24/2/41.
H.16	DARING	Thornycroft	7. 4.32	Lost 18/2/40.
H.75	DECOY	Thornycroft	7. 6.32	R.C.N. KOOTENAY (1943); scrapped 28/1/46.
H.07	DEFENDER	V.A. (Barrow)	7. 4.32	Lost 11/7/41.
H.38	DELIGHT	Fairfield	2. 6.32	Lost 29/7/40.
H.22	DIAMOND	V.A. (Barrow)	8. 4.32	Lost 27/4/41.
H.49	DIANA	Palmers	16. 6.32	R.C.N. MARGAREE (1940); lost 22/10/40.
H.64	DUCHESS	Palmers	19. 7.32	Lost 12/12/39.

Notes:—The " **C** " class served in Western Approaches and North Atlantic following a short spell in the West Indies. The " **D** " class were all transferred to the Mediterranean from China on the outbreak of War. DUCHESS and DARING soon came to Home waters and the DELIGHT to the Home fleet in 1940. DIANA only returned to Home waters for transfer to the R.C.N. and was lost on her first commission. DUNCAN spent two years at Gibraltar before going to the Western Approaches. The remainder went from the Mediterranean to the South Atlantic and then returned to the Mediterranean. DECOY spent some months with the Eastern fleet prior to transfer to the R.C.N. and was then employed in North Atlantic escort duty.

Flotilla Leaders and " E " and " F " classes

Displacement: " E " class and FEARLESS 1,375 tons, " F " class 1,350 tons and EXMOUTH and FAULKNOR 1,475 tons.
Dimensions: $318\frac{1}{4}$ (pp) 329 (oa) × $33\frac{1}{4}$ × $8\frac{1}{2}$ ft. except EXMOUTH and FAULKNOR 332 (pp) 343 (oa) × $33\frac{3}{4}$ × $8\frac{3}{4}$ ft.
Machinery: 2-shaft geared Turbines, S.H.P. 36,000 = $35\frac{1}{2}$ knots except EXMOUTH and FAULKNOR S.H.P. 38,000 = 36 knots.
Armament: 4 except EXMOUTH and FAULKNOR 5—4.7 in. (4/5 × 1); 8—.5 in A A (2 × 4) guns; 8—21 in (2 × 4) T.T.
Complement: 145 (175 in EXMOUTH and FAULKNOR).

H.02	EXMOUTH	Portsmouth: Fairfield	7. 2.34	Lost 21/1/40.
H.23	ECHO	Denny	16. 2.34	R.H.N. NAVARINON (1944-56); scrapped Dunston 26/4/56.
H.08	ECLIPSE	Denny	12. 4.34	Lost 24/10/43.
H.27	ELECTRA	Hawthorn Leslie	15. 2.34	Lost 27/2/42.

Flotilla Leader H.M.S. Duncan (" **D** " class leader), only had the quarterdeck gun and after bank of tubes removed. *[I.W.M.*

H.M.S. Escapade (" **E** " class). *[R. Perkins*

Flotilla Leader H.M.S. Faulknor (" **F** " class leader), before the war. *[I.W.M.*

H.10	ENCOUNTER	Hawthorn Leslie	29. 3.34	Lost 1/3/42.
H.17	ESCAPADE	Scotts	30. 1.34	Scrapped Grangemouth 2/47.
H.66	ESCORT	Scotts	29. 3.34	Lost 11/7/40.
H.15	ESK	Swan Hunter: Wallsend	19. 3.34	Lost 31/8/40.
H.61	EXPRESS	Swan Hunter: Wallsend	29. 5.34	R.C.N. GATINEAU (1943); scrapped Vancouver 1956.
H.62	FAULKNOR	Yarrow	12. 6.34	Scrapped Milford Haven 22/1/46.
H.78	FAME	V.A. (Tyne): Parsons	28. 6.34	Dominican GENERALISIMO (1948)
H.67	FEARLESS	Cammell Laird	12. 5.34	Lost 23/7/41.
H.79	FIREDRAKE	V.A. (Tyne): Parsons	28. 6.34	Lost 17/12/42.
H.74	FORESTER	White	28. 6.34	Scrapped Rosyth 6/47.
H.68	FORESIGHT	Cammell Laird	29. 6.34	Lost 13/8/42.
H.70	FORTUNE	Clydebank	29. 8.34	R.C.N. SASKATCHEWAN (1943); for disposal 28/1/46.
H.69	FOXHOUND	Clydebank	12.10.34	R.C.N. QU'APPELLE (1944); for disposal 17/12/47.
H.76	FURY	White	10. 9.34	Constructive total loss 21/6/44; scrapped Briton Ferry 9/44.

Notes:—ESK and EXPRESS were adaptable for minelaying and carried their whalers on the fo'c'sle and had tripod mainmasts. ECHO and ECLIPSE served mainly in Home waters until 1943 when they went to the Mediterannean. ELECTRA, ENCOUNTER and EXPRESS went from Home waters to the Eastern fleet in 1942 and the EXPRESS was later transferred to the R.C.N. and served in the Western Approaches. ESCORT went to the Mediterranean in 1940 whilst the three remaining "**E**" class served only in Home waters. FAULKNOR served with the Home fleet to 1943 (with Force "H" 1940-41) and then went to the Mediterranean, to return home again in 1945. The remainder of the "**F**" class except FAME were Home fleet until 1940, then Force "H". FORESIGHT, FORESTER and FURY left Force "H" for the Home fleet in 1942; FORESTER went on to serve in the Western Approaches and the other pair returned to the Mediterranean. FAME went to The Nore in 1942 and finally to the Western Approaches.

Flotilla Leaders and "G" and "H" classes

Displacement: "**G**" class 1,335 tons except GLOWWORM 1,345 tons, "**H**" class 1,340 tons, GRENVILLE 1,485 tons and HARDY 1,505 tons.

Dimensions: 312 (pp) 323 (oa) × 32¼ × 8½ ft. except GRENVILLE 319 (pp) 330 (oa) × 34½ × 8¾ ft. and HARDY 326 (pp) 337 (oa) × 34 × 8¾ ft.

Right: H.M.S. Fame (" **F** " class), still in service with the Dominican Navy.
[*I.W.M.*

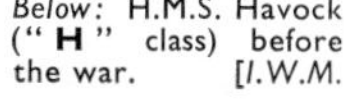

Below: H.M.S. Havock (" **H** " class) before the war. [*I.W.M.*

Right: H.M.S. Hotspur (" **H** " class), during the war and still in service in the Dominican Navy.
[*I.W.M.*

Machinery: 2-shaft geared Turbines, S.H.P. 34,000 = 35½ knots except GRENVILLE and HARDY S.H.P. 38,000 = 36 knots.

Armament: 4 except GRENVILLE and HARDY 5—4.7 in. (4/5 × 1), 8—.5 in. A.A. (2 × 4) guns; 8 except GLOWWORM 10—21 in. (2 × 4/5) T.T.

Complement: 145 (175 in GRENVILLE and HARDY).

H.03	GRENVILLE	Yarrow	15. 8.35	Lost 19/1/40.
H.59	GALLANT	Stephen	26. 9.35	Constructive total loss 5/4/42; expended as blockship at Malta.
H.37	GARLAND	Fairfield	24.10.35	Polish (name not changed, 1939-47); R. Neth.N. MARNIX (1947).
H.63	GIPSY	Fairfield	7.11.35	Lost 21/11/39.
H.92	GLOWWORM	Thornycroft	22. 7.35	Lost 8/4/40.
H.89	GRAFTON	Thornycroft	18. 9.35	Lost 29/5/40.
H.86	GRENADE	Stephen	12.11.35	Lost 29/5/40.
H.05	GREYHOUND	V.A. (Barrow): Parsons	15. 8.35	Lost 22/5/41.
H.31	GRIFFIN	V.A. (Barrow): Parsons	15. 8.35	R.C.N. OTTAWA (ii) (1943); for disposal 28/1/46.
H.87	HARDY	Cammell Laird	7. 4.36	Lost 10/4/40.
H.24	HASTY	Denny	5. 5.36	Lost 15/6/42.
H.43	HAVOCK	Denny	7. 7.36	Lost 6/4/42.
H.93	HEREWARD	V.A. (Tyne): Parsons	10. 3.36	Lost 29/5/41.
H.99	HERO	V.A. (Tyne): Parsons	10. 3.36	R.C.N. CHAUDIERE (1943); for disposal 19/3/46.
H.55	HOSTILE	Scotts	24. 1.36	Lost 23/8/40.
H.01	HOTSPUR	Scotts	23. 3.36	Dominican TRUJILLO (1948).
H.35	HUNTER	Swan Hunter: Wallsend	25. 2.36	Lost 10/4/40.
H.97	HYPERION	Swan Hunter: Wallsend	8. 4.36	Lost 22/12/40.

Notes:—GLOWWORM introduced quintuple T.T. and HERO and HEREWARD angled bridge faces. Both classes were adaptable for rapid conversion to minelayers and had tripod mainmasts and HARDY had a tripod foremast in addition. HEREWARD completed with experimental twin 4.7 in. in "B" position which was removed in 1937. GARLAND joined the Western Approaches from the Mediterranean in 1940, remaining there until 1944 when she served for a time at Freetown before returning to the Mediterranean; finally Home fleet 1945. GALLANT was at the Nore in 1939 before going to the Mediterranean. All the remaining "**G**" class were in the Mediterranean 1939 returning to Home waters in the same year. GRIFFIN went back to the Mediterranean in 1940, to the Eastern fleet 1942 and after transfer to the R.C.N. she served in the North Atlantic. The "**H**" class were in the Mediterranean 1939 and then were divided between the South Atlantic (HARDY, HASTY, HAVOCK,

HERO and HOSTILE) and the West Indies (HEREWARD, HOTSPUR, HUNTER and HYPERION) before joining the Home fleet 1940. The remainder then went back to the Mediterranean only HERO (transferred to the R.C.N.) and HOTSPUR returning to Home waters, where they served in the Western Approaches.

Flotilla Leader and " I " class

Displacement: 1,370 tons except INGLEFIELD 1,530 tons.
Dimensions: 312 (pp) 323 (oa) × 32¼ × 8½ ft. except INGLEFIELD 326 (pp) 337 (oa) × 34 × 9 ft.
Machinery: 2-shaft geared Turbines, S.H.P. 34,000 except INGLEFIELD 38,000 = 36 knots.
Armament: 4 except INGLEFIELD 5—4.7 in. (4/5 × 1), 8—.5 in. A.A. (2 × 4) guns; 10—21 in. (2 × 5) T.T.
Complement: 145 (175 in INGLEFIELD).

D.02	INGLEFIELD	Cammell Laird	15.10.36	Lost 25/2/44.
D.03	ICARUS	Clydebank	26.11.36	Scrapped Troon 29/10/46.
D.61	ILEX	Clydebank	28. 1.37	Scrapped Italy 1948.
D.44	IMOGEN	Hawthorn Leslie	30.10.36	Lost 16/7/40.
D.09	IMPERIAL	Hawthorn Leslie	11.12.36	Lost 29/5/41.
D.11	IMPULSIVE	White	1. 3.37	Scrapped Sunderland 22/1/46.
D.10	INTREPID	White	17.12.36	Lost 27/9/43.
D.87	ISIS	Yarrow	12.11.36	Lost 20/7/44.
D.16	IVANHOE	Yarrow	11. 2.37	Lost 1/9/40.

Notes:—Were adaptable for rapid conversion to minelayers and had tripod mainmasts (tripod foremast in addition in INGLEFIELD), angled bridge faces and quintuple T.T.—all individual features of earlier classes. The " I " class came to the Home fleet from the Mediterranean in 1939. ICARUS and IMPULSIVE remained with Western Approaches and the surviving four returned to the Mediterranean.

Tribal class

Displacement: 1,870 tons except R.A.N. and R.C.N. vessels 1,927 tons.
Dimensions: 355½ (pp) 377½ (oa) × 36½ × 9 ft.
Machinery: 2-shaft geared Turbines, S.H.P. 44,000 = 36 knots.
Armament: R.N. vessels 8—4.7 in. (4 × 2), 4—2 pdr. A.A. (1 × 4), 8—.5 in. A.A. (2 × 4) guns; 4—21 in. (1 × 4) T.T., R.A.N. and R.C.N. vessels 6—4.7 in. (3 × 2), 2—4 in. A.A. (1 × 2), 4—2 pdr. A.A. (1 × 4), 8—.5 in. A.A. (2 × 4) except* 8—4 in. A.A. (4 × 2), 4—40 mm. A.A. (1 × 2 & 2 × 1), 4—20 mm. A.A. (2 × 2) guns 4—21 in. (1 × 4) T.T.
Complement: 190 (219 in AFRIDI, COSSACK, SOMALI and TARTAR) except R.A.N. vessels 250 and R.C.N. vessels 240.

F.07	AFRIDI	V.A. (Tyne): V.A. (Barrow)	8. 6.37	Lost 3/5/40.

F.03	COSSACK	V.A. (Tyne): V.A. (Barrow)	8. 6.37	Lost 27/10/41.
F.20	GURKHA	Fairfield	7. 7.37	Lost 9/4/40.
F.24	MAORI	Fairfield	2. 9.37	Lost 12/2/42.
F.31	MOHAWK	Thornycroft	5.10.37	Lost 16/4/41.
F.36	NUBIAN	Thornycroft	21.12.37	Scrapped Briton Ferry 25/6/49.
F.18	ZULU	Stephen	23. 9.37	Lost 14/9/42.
F.51	ASHANTI	Denny	5.11.37	Scrapped Troon 12/4/49.
F.67	BEDOUIN	Denny	21.12.37	Lost 15/6/42.
F.75	ESKIMO	V.A. (Tyne): Parsons	3. 9.37	Scrapped Troon 27/6/49.
F.59	MASHONA	V.A. (Tyne): Parsons	3. 9.37	Lost 28/5/41.
F.26	MATABELE	Scotts	6.10.37	Lost 17/1/42.
F.21	PUNJABI	Scotts	18.12.37	Lost 1/5/42.
F.82	SIKH	Stephen	17.12.37	Lost 14/9/42.
F.33	SOMALI	Swan Hunter: Wallsend	24. 8.37	Lost 24/9/42.
F.43	TARTAR	Swan Hunter: Wallsend	21.10.37	Scrapped Newport 22/2/48.
I.30	ARUNTA (R.A.N.)	Cockatoo	30.11.40	
I.91	BATAAN (R.A.N.) (ex-Kurnai)	Cockatoo	15. 1.44	For disposal.
I.44	WARRAMUNGA (R.A.N.)	Cockatoo	6. 2.42	
G.07	ATHABASKAN (i) (R.C.N.) (ex-Iroquois)	V.A. (Tyne): Parsons	18.11.41	Lost 29/4/44.
G.63	HAIDA (R.C.N.)	V.A. (Tyne): Parsons	25. 8.42	
G.24	HURON (R.C.N.)	V.A. (Tyne): Parsons	25. 6.42	
G.89	IROQUOIS (R.C.N.) (ex-Athabaskan)	V.A. (Tyne): Parsons	23. 9.41	
R.04	CAYUGA (R.C.N.)*	Halifax	28. 7.45	
R.10	MICMAC (R.C.N.)	Halifax	18. 9.43	
R.96	NOOKTA (R.C.N.)	Halifax	26. 4.44	
R.79	ATHABASKAN (ii) (R.C.N.)*	Halifax	4. 5.46	

Notes:—Four further vessels projected by the R.A.N. were cancelled. The R.N. vessels started the war in two flotillas and served throughout on Fleet duty at Home and in the Mediterranean. The four survivors went to the East Indies in 1945. The R.A.N. vessels served in the S.W. Pacific and the first four R.C.N. vessels in Home waters until 1945 when they returned to Canada. The last four R.C.N. vessels were completed too late for war service.

" J " and " K " classes

Displacement: 1,690 tons except JERVIS and KELLY 1,695 tons.
Dimensions: 339½ (pp) 356½ (oa) × 35¾ × 9 ft.
Machinery: 2-shaft geared Turbines, S.H.P. 40,000 = 36 knots.
Armament: 6—4.7 in. (3 × 2), 4—2 pdr. A.A. (1 × 4), 8—.5 in. A.A. (2 × 4) guns; 10—21 in. (2 × 5) T.T.
Complement: 183 (218 in JERVIS and KELLY).

F.00	JERVIS	Hawthorn Leslie	9. 9.38	Scrapped Troon 3/1/49.
F.22	JACKAL	Clydebank	25.10.38	Lost 12/5/42.
F.34	JAGUAR	Denny	22.11.38	Lost 26/3/42.
F.53	JANUS	Swan Hunter: Wallsend	10.11.38	Lost 23/1/44.
F.61	JAVELIN (ex-Kashmir)	Clydebank	21.12.38	Scrapped Troon 11/49.
F.72	JERSEY	White	26. 9.38	Lost 2/5/41.
	JUBILANT			Cancelled.
F.46	JUNO (ex-Jamaica)	Fairfield	8.12.38	Lost 21/5/41.
F.85	JUPITER	Yarrow	27.10.38	Lost 28/2/42.
F.01	KELLY	Hawthorn Leslie	25.10.38	Lost 23/5/41.
F.28	KANDAHAR	Denny	21. 3.39	Lost 20/12/41.
F.12	KASHMIR (ex-Javelin)	Thornycroft	4. 4.39	Lost 23/5/41.
F.37	KELVIN	Fairfield	19. 1.39	Scrapped Troon 6/49.
F.45	KHARTOUM	Swan Hunter: Wallsend	6. 2.39	Lost 23/6/40.
F.50	KIMBERLEY	Thornycroft	1. 6.39	Scrapped Troon 30/3/49.
F.64	KINGSTON	White	9. 1.39	Constructive total loss 11/4/42; scrapped Malta.
F.91	KIPLING	Yarrow	19. 1.39	Lost 11/5/42.

Notes:—First longitudinally constructed destroyers and a reduction to two boilers only required a single funnel. Tripod foremast and no mainmast. The " **J** " and " **K** " classes all went to the Mediterranean from Home waters in 1940-41 where they suffered heavy losses. Four (JERVIS, JAVELIN, KELVIN and KIPLING) returned to Home waters for a time before going back to the Mediterranean, KIMBERLEY stayed in the Mediterranean and JUPITER went to the Eastern fleet.

" L " and " M " classes

Displacement: 1,920 tons except LAFOREY and MILNE 1,935 tons.
Dimensions: 345½ (pp) 362½ (oa) × 36¾ × 10 ft.
Machinery: 2-shaft geared Turbines, S.H.P. 48,000 = 36 knots.
Armament: 6—4.7 in. D.P. (3 × 2) except * 8—4 in. A.A. (4 × 2). 4—2 pdr. A.A. (1 × 4), 2—20 mm. A.A. (2 × 1), 8—.5 in. A.A. (2 × 4) guns; 8—21 in. T.T. (2 × 4).
Complement: 221 except* 226.

H.M.S. Jupiter (" **J** " class) with H.M.S. Kashmir in the background. 4 in. A.A. has replaced after-bank of tubes but they were later put back. [*I.W.M.*

Flotilla Leader H.M.S. Kelly (" **K** " class leader), was distinguishable from the remainder of the class by the longer after deckhouse. [*I.W.M.*

Flotilla Leader H.M.S. Laforey (" **L** " class leader), with guns in fully enclosed turrets and full torpedo armament. [*I.W.M.*

F.99	LAFOREY	Yarrow	15. 2.41	Lost 30/3/44.
F.87	LANCE*	Yarrow	28.11.40	Constructive total loss 22/10/42; scrapped Grays 6/44.
F.63	GURKHA* (ex-Larne)	Cammell Laird	8. 7.40	Lost 17/1/42.
F.74	LEGION*	Hawthorn Leslie	26.12.39	Constructive total loss 25/3/42.
F.55	LIGHTNING	Hawthorn Leslie	22. 4.40	Lost 12/3/43.
F.40	LIVELY*	Cammell Laird	28. 1.41	Lost 11/5/42.
F.32	LOOKOUT	Scotts	4.11.40	Scrapped Newport 29/2/48.
F.15	LOYAL	Scotts	8.10.41	Constructive total loss 12/10/44; scrapped Milford Haven 5/8/48.
G.14	MILNE	Scotts	30.12.41	Turkish ALP ARSLAM (1958).
G.23	MAHRATTA (ex-Marksman)	Scotts	28. 7.42	Lost 25/2/44.
G.35	MARNE	V.A. (Tyne): Parsons	30.10.40	Turkish MARESAL FEVZI CAKMAK (1958).
G.44	MARTIN	V.A. (Tyne): Parsons	12.12.40	Lost 10/11/42.
G.52	MATCHLESS	Stephen	4. 9.41	Turkish KILICALI PASHA (1958).
G.73	METEOR	Stephen	3.11.41	Turkish PIYALE PASHA (1958).
G.86	MUSKETEER	Fairfield	2.12.41	Scrapped Sunderland 6/12/55.
G.90	MYRMIDON	Fairfield	2. 3.42	Polish ORKAN (1942); lost 8/10/43.

Notes:—The " **L** " class served through most of the war in Force " H" and the Mediterranean. The " **M** " class served in the Home fleet until 1944 and then went to the Mediterranean. Introduced turrets to destroyers, a weighty installation which increased their size.

" N " class

Displacement: 1,690 tons except NAPIER 1,695 tons.
Dimensions: 339½ (pp) 356½ (oa) × 35¾ × 9 ft.
Machinery: 2-shaft geared Turbines, S.H.P. 40,000 = 36 knots.
Armament: 6—4.7 in. (3 × 2), 4—2 pdr. A.A. (1 × 4), 2—20 mm. A.A. (2 × 1), 8—.5 in. A.A. (2 × 4) guns; 10—21 in. (2 × 5) T.T.
Complement: 183 (218 in NAPIER).

G.97	NAPIER	Fairfield	22. 5.40	R.A.N. (1940-45); scrapped Briton Ferry 1/56.
G.65	NERISSA	Clydebank	7. 5.40	Polish PIOURUN (1940-46), NOBLE (ii) (1946); scrapped Dunston 12/55.

1. H.M.S. Lookout (" **L** " class) with 4 in. A.A. gun in place of after bank of tubes. 2. H.M.S. Mahratta (" **M** " class) with twin 20 mm. A.A. guns in wing positions abreast the bridge and the searchlight. 3. Flotilla Leader H.M.S. Napier (" **N** " class) served with the Royal Australian Navy throughout the war. [*All photos I.W.M.*

G.02	NESTOR	Fairfield	9. 7.40	R.A.N. (1941-42); lost 15/6/42.
G.38	NIZAM	Clydebank	4. 7.40	R.A.N. (1941-45); scrapped Grays 16/11/55.
G.84	NOBLE (i)	Denny	17. 4.41	R.Neth.N. VAN GALEN (1942); scrapped Hendrik-Ibo-Ambacht 8/2/57.
G.16	NONPAREIL	Denny	25. 6.41	R.Neth.N. TJERK HIDDES (1942), Indonesian GADJAH MADA (1951).
G.49	NORMAN	Thornycroft	30.10.40	R.A.N. (1941-45); scrapped Newport 4/58.
G.25	NORSEMAN	Thornycroft	4.12.41	NEPAL (1942); scrapped Briton Ferry 1/56.

Notes:—The " **N** " class served in Home waters, the Mediterranean and the Far East except PIORUN (ex-Nerissa) which was mainly employed in Home waters.

" O " and " P " class

Displacement: 1,540 tons except ONSLOW and PAKENHAM 1,550 tons.
Dimensions: 338½ (pp) 345 (oa) × 35 × 9 ft.
Machinery: 2-shaft geared Turbines, S.H.P. 40,000 = 36¾ knots.
Armament: 4—4.7 in. (4 × 1), 4—2 pdr. A.A. (1 × 4), 8—20 mm. A.A. (4 × 2) guns; 8—21 in. (2 × 4) T.T.; * fitted for minelaying.
Complement: 175 (217 in ONSLOW and 228 in PAKENHAM).

G.17	ONSLOW (ex-Pakenham)	Clydebank	31. 3.41	R.P.N. TIPPU SULTAN (1949)
G.39	OBDURATE*	Denny	19. 2.42	Scrapped Rosyth 4/59.
G.48	OBEDIENT*	Denny	30. 4.42	Scrapped Blyth 19/10/62.
G.29	OFFA	Fairfield	11. 3.41	R.P.N. TARIQ (1949); scrapped Sunderland 13/10/59.
G.04	ONSLAUGHT (ex-Pathfinder)	Fairfield	9.10.41	R.P.N. TUGHRIL (1951).
G.80	OPPORTUNE*	Thornycroft	21. 1.42	Scrapped Milford Haven 25/11/55.
G.66	ORIBI (ex-Observer)	Fairfield	14. 1.41	Turkish GAYRET (1946).
G.98	ORWELL*	Thornycroft	2. 4.42	
G.06	PAKENHAM (ex-Onslow)	Hawthorn Leslie	28. 1.41	Lost 16/4/43.
G.69	PALADIN	Clydebank	11. 6.41	Scrapped Dunston 25/10/62.
G.41	PANTHER	Fairfield	28. 5.41	Lost 9/10/43.
G.30	PARTRIDGE	Fairfield	5. 8.41	Lost 18/12/42.
G.10	PATHFINDER (ex-Onslaught)	Hawthorn Leslie	10. 4.41	Constructive total loss 11/2/45; scrapped 1948.

H.M.S. Offa ("**O**") class), one of the four vessels of this class (not used as minelayers) to receive designed gun armament, but had the after set of T.T. replaced by a 3 in. A.A. gun. [*I.W.M.*

H.M.S. Partridge ("**P**" class), showing the utility armament of five old 4 in. A.A. guns, given to this half and the "**O**" classes. HA. DCT only on the bridge. Pathfinder, Penn, Petard and Porcupine had full torpedo armament. [*I.W.M.*

H.M.S. Roebuck (" **R** " class) with twin 20 mm. A.A. guns in bridge wings and four single 20 mm. A.A. guns between the tubes. SW. RDF is also fitted between the tubes. [*I.W.M.*

G.77	PENN	V.A. (Tyne)	12. 2.41	Scrapped Troon 31/1/50.
G.56	PETARD (ex-Persistent)	V.A. (Tyne)	27. 3.41	
G.93	PORCUPINE	V.A. (Tyne)	10. 6.41	Constructive total loss 9/12/42; scrapped 6/5/46.

Notes:—Were designed for rapid conversion to minelayers. None received designed armament. In both classes only single 20 mm. were available and the majority had 4 in. A.A. in lieu of 4.7 in. with an additional mounting in place of the after bank of T.T. The " **O** " class served in the Home fleet throughout the war except for a short period in the Mediterranean by some units. The " **P** " class went to the Mediterranean early in 1942 serving in the Fleet and Force " H ". PORCUPINE was badly damaged 9/12/42 and was thereafter used as a Base ship. PALADIN, PENN, PETARD and PATHFINDER later went to the Far East and the last named sustained damage in this area was and not repaired.

" Q " and " R " classes

Displacement: 1,705 tons except QUILLIAM 1,725 tons and ROTHERHAM 1,750 tons.
Dimensions: $328\frac{3}{4}$ (pp) $358\frac{3}{4}$ (oa) $\times$ $35\frac{3}{4}$ $\times$ $9\frac{1}{2}$ ft.
Machinery: 2-shaft geared Turbines, S.H.P. 40,000 = $36\frac{3}{4}$ knots.
Armament: 4—4.7 in. (4 × 1), 4—2 pdr. A.A. (1 × 4), 8—20 mm. A.A. (4 × 2) guns; 8—21 in. (2 × 4) T.T.
Complement: 175 (225 in QUILLIAM and ROTHERHAM).

G.09	QUILLIAM	Hawthorn Leslie	29.11.41	R.Neth.N. BANKCERT (1945); scrapped Burght 8/2/57.
G.11	QUADRANT	Hawthorn Leslie	28. 2.42	R.A.N. (1945).
G.45	QUAIL	Hawthorn Leslie	1. 6.42	Lost 18/6/44.
G.62	QUALITY	Swan Hunter: Wallsend	6.10.41	R.A.N. (1945); scrapped Japan 1958.
G.70	QUEEN-BOROUGH	Swan Hunter: Wallsend	16. 1.42	R.A.N. (1945).
G.78	QUENTIN	White	5.11.41	Lost 2/12/42.
G.81	QUIBERON	White	31. 1.42	R.A.N. (1942).
G.92	QUICKMATCH	White	11. 4.42	R.A.N. (1942).
H.09	ROTHERHAM	Clydebank	21. 3.42	R.I.N. RAJPUT (1949).
H.11	RACEHORSE	Clydebank	1. 6.42	Scrapped Troon 8/12/49.
H.15	RAIDER	Cammell Laird	1. 4.42	R.I.N. RANA (1949).
H.32	RAPID	Cammell Laird	16. 7.42	
H.41	REDOUBT	Clydebank	2. 5.42	R.I.N. RANJIT (1949).
H.85	RELENTLESS	Clydebank	15. 7.42	
H.92	ROCKET	Scotts	28.10.42	
H.95	ROEBUCK	Scotts	10.12.42	

Notes:—The " **Q** " and " **R** " classes served in groups in the Home and Mediterranean fleets and South Atlantic and in flotillas in the Far East 1944-45.

“S” and “T” classes

Displacement: 1,710 tons except SAUMERAZ and TROUBRIDGE 1,730 tons.
Dimensions: $339\frac{1}{2}$ (pp) $362\frac{3}{4}$ (oa) × $35\frac{3}{4}$ × 10 ft.
Machinery: 2-shaft geared Turbines, S.H.P. 40,000 = $36\frac{3}{4}$ knots.
Armament: 4—4.7 in. (4 × 1) except SAVAGE 4—4.5 in. (1 × 2 & 2 × 1), 2—40 mm. A.A. (1 × 2) and 8—20 mm. (4 × 2) or 12—20 mm. A.A. (6 × 2) guns; 8—21 in. (2 × 4) T.T.
Complement: 180 (225 in SAUMERAZ and TROUBRIDGE).

G.12	SAUMERAZ	Hawthorn Leslie	20.11.42	Scrapped Charlestown 8/9/50.
G.20	SAVAGE	Hawthorn Leslie	24. 9.42	Scrapped Newport 11/4/62.
G.72	SCORPION (ex-Sentinel)	Cammell Laird	26. 8.42	R.Neth.N. KORTENAER (1945).
G.01	SCOURGE	Cammell Laird	8.12.42	R.Neth.N. EVERTSEN (1945).
G.94	SERAPIS	Scotts	25. 3.43	R.Neth.N. PIET HEIN (1945); scrapped Ghent 6/62.
G.03	SHARK	Scotts	1. 6.43	R.N.N. SVENNER (1944); lost 6/6/44.
G.26	SUCCESS	White	3. 4.43	R.N.N. STORD (1943); scrapped Burght 1959.
G.46	SWIFT	White	15. 6.43	Lost 24/6/44.
R.00	TROUBRIDGE	Clydebank	23. 9.42	
R.23	TEAZER	Cammell Laird	7. 1.43	
R.45	TENACIOUS	Cammell Laird	24. 3.43	
R.89	TERMAGANT	Denny	22. 3.43	
R.33	TERPSICHORE	Denny	17. 6.43	
R.11	TUMULT	Clydebank	9.11.42	
R.56	TUSCAN	Swan Hunter: Wallsend	28. 5.42	
R.67	TYRIAN	Swan Hunter: Wallsend	27. 7.42	

Notes:—Light A.A. armament very variable and the twin 40 mm. supplanted the quadruple 2pdr. and single 40 mm. started to replace twin 20 mm. Some units had an additional superfiring 40 mm. gun abaft the funnel. SAVAGE experimentally introduced the 4.5 in. D.P. gun and had her two forward guns in a twin turret which was the prototype later adopted for the **Battle** class. Half of each class were completed with lattice foremasts. The "**S**" class served in the Home fleet and the "**T**" class went to the Mediterranean in 1943, then the East Indies and were with the Pacific fleet by 1945.

“U” and “V” classes

Displacement: 1,710 tons except GRENVILLE and HARDY 1,730 tons.
Dimensions: $339\frac{1}{2}$ (pp) $362\frac{3}{4}$ (oa) × $35\frac{3}{4}$ × 10 ft.
Machinery: 2-shaft geared Turbines, S.H.P. 40,000 = $36\frac{3}{4}$ knots.

1. H.M.S. Savage ("**S**" class). This class introduced the 4.5 in. D.P. gun and this ship had her forward guns in an experimental twin turret later adopted for the **Battle** class. Note the light A.A. of 12—20 mm. in 6 twin mountings in the bridge wings, *en echelon* abaft the funnel and between the tubes. Searchlight has been moved forward and SW. RDF low amidships. 2. H.M.S. Tumult (" **T** " class) with light A.A. armament of 12—20 mm. (6 × 2) guns. 3. H.M.S. Urania (" **U** " class), has SW. RDF on lattice foremast and twin 40 mm. A.A. between tubes. 4. H.M.S. Vigilant (" **V** " class), with HF/DF mast aft.
[*All photos I.W.M.*

Armament: 4—4.7 in. (4 × 1), 2—40 mm. A.A. (1 × 2) and 8—20 mm. A.A. (4 × 2) or 12—20 mm. A.A. (6 × 2) guns; 8—21 in. (2 × 4) T.T.
Complement: 180 (225 in GRENVILLE and HARDY).

R.97	GRENVILLE (ii)	Swan Hunter: Wallsend	12.10.42	
R.83	ULSTER	Swan Hunter: Wallsend	9.11.42	
R.69	ULYSSES	Cammell Laird	22. 4.43	For disposal.
R.53	UNDAUNTED	Cammell Laird	19. 7.43	
R.42	UNDINE	Thornycroft	1. 6.43	
R.05	URANIA	V.A. (Barrow)	19. 5.43	
R.99	URCHIN	V.A. (Barrow)	8. 3.43	
R.22	URSA	Thornycroft	22. 7.43	
R.08	HARDY (ii)	Clydebank	18. 3.43	Lost 30/1/44.
R.17	VALENTINE (ex-Kempenfelt)	Clydebank	2. 9.43	R.C.N. ALONGQUIN (1944).
R.50	VENUS	Fairfield	23. 2.43	
R.28	VERULAM	Fairfield	22. 4.43	
R.93	VIGILANT	Swan Hunter: Wallsend	22.12.42	
R.75	VIRAGO	Swan Hunter: Wallsend	4. 2.43	
R.64	VIXEN	White	14. 9.43	R.C.N. SIOUX (1944).
R.41	VOLAGE	White	15.12.43	

Notes:—Introduced lattice foremasts. The " **U** " class went to the Pacific from the Mediterranean in 1944 and the " **V** " class served in the Home fleet until 1945 when they went to the East Indies, except the R.C.N. vessels which went to Canada.

" W " and " Z " classes

Displacement: 1,710 tons except KEMPENFELT and MYNGS 1,730 tons.
Dimensions: 339½ (pp) 362¾ (oa) × 35¾ × 10 ft.
Machinery: 2-shaft geared Turbines, S.H.P. 40,000 = 36¾ knots.
Armament: 4—4.7 in. (" **W** " class) or 4.5 in. D.P. (" **Z** " class) (4 × 1), 2—40 mm. A.A. (1 × 2) and 8—20 mm. (4 × 2) A.A. or 4—40 mm. A.A. (1 × 2 & 2 × 1) and 4—20 mm. A.A. (2 × 2) or 6—40 mm. A.A. (1 × 2 & 4 × 1) guns; 8—21 in. (2× 4) T.T.
Complement: 186 (222 in KEMPENFELT and MYNGS).

R.03	KEMPENFELT (ex-Valentine)	Clydebank	8. 5.43	Yugoslavian KOTOR (1958).
R.98	WAGER	Clydebank	1.11.43	Yugoslavian PULA (1958).

R.59	WAKEFUL (ex-Zebra)	Fairfield	30. 6.43	
R.78	WESSEX (ex-Zenith)	Fairfield	2. 9.43	S.A.N. JAN VAN RIEBEECK (1950).
R.37	WHELP	Hawthorn Leslie	3. 6.43	S.A.N. SIMON VAN DER STEL (1953).
R.87	WHIRLWIND	Hawthorn Leslie	30. 8.43	
R.72	WIZARD	V.A. (Barrow)	29. 9.43	
R.48	WRANGLER	V.A. (Barrow)	30.12.43	S.A.N. VRYSTAAT (1957).
R.06	MYNGS	V.A. (Tyne): Parsons	31. 5.43	Egyptian EL QUAHER (1955).
R.66	ZAMBESI	Cammell Laird	21.11.43	Scrapped Briton Ferry 12/2/59.
R.39	ZEALOUS	Cammell Laird	28. 2.44	Israeli ELATH (1955).
R.81	ZEBRA (ex-Wakeful)	Denny	8. 3.44	Scrapped Newport 12/2/59.
R.95	ZENITH (ex-Wessex)	Denny	5. 6.44	Egyptian EL FATEH (1955).
R.19	ZEPHYR	V.A. (Tyne): Parsons	15. 7.43	Scrapped Dunston 2/7/58.
R.02	ZEST	Thornycroft	14.10.43	
R.54	ZODIAC	Thornycroft	11. 3.44	Israeli YAFFA (1955).

Notes:—The " **W** " class served in the Home fleet to 1945 and then went to the Pacific whilst the " **Z** " class never left Home waters.

" C " classes

(CA, CH, CO and CR groups)

Displacement: 1,710 tons except CAVENDISH, CHILDERS, COSSACK and CROWN 1,730 tons.
Dimensions: $339\frac{1}{2}$ (pp) $362\frac{3}{4}$ (oa) × $35\frac{3}{4}$ × 10 ft.
Machinery: 2-shaft geared Turbines, S.H.P. 40,000 = $36\frac{3}{4}$ knots.
Armament: 4—4.5 in. D.P. (4 × 1), 4—40 mm. A.A. (1 × 2 & 2 × 1), 4—20 mm. A.A. (2 × 2) guns; 4 except CA group 8—21 in. (1/2 × 4) T.T.
Complement: 186 (222 in CAVENDISH, CHILDERS, COSSACK and CROWN).

R.07	CAESAR (ex-Ranger R.58)	Clydebank	14. 2.44	
R.85	CAMBRIAN (ex-Spitfire)	Scotts	10.12.43	
R.01	CAPRICE (ex-Swallow)	Yarrow	16. 9.43	
R.30	CARRON (ex-Strenuous)	Scotts	28. 3.44	
R.25	CARYSFORT (ex-Pique R.49)	White	25. 7.44	
R.62	CASSANDRA (ex-Tourmaline)	Yarrow	29.11.43	

R.73	CAVALIER (ex-Pellew R.04)	White	7. 4.44	
R.15	CAVENDISH (ex-Sibyl)	Clydebank	12. 4.44	
R.52	CHAPLET	Thornycroft	18. 7.44	For disposal.
R.29	CHARITY	Thornycroft	30.11.44	R.P.N. SHAH JEHAN (1958).
R.61	CHEQUERS (ex-Champion)	Scotts	30.10.44	
R.90	CHEVIOT	Stephen	2. 5.44	Scrapped Inverkeithing, 1962.
R.51	CHEVRON	Stephen	23. 2.44	
R.36	CHIEFTAIN	Scotts	26. 2.45	Scrapped Sunderland 20/3/61.
R.91	CHILDERS	Denny	27. 2.45	For disposal.
R.21	CHIVALROUS	Denny	22. 6.45	R.P.N. TAIMUR (1954).
R.34	COCKADE	Yarrow	7. 3.44	For disposal.
R.26	COMET	Yarrow	22. 6.44	Scrapped Troon 11/62.
R.43	COMUS	Thornycroft	14. 3.45	Scrapped Newport 12/11/58.
R.76	CONSORT	Stephen	19.10.44	Scrapped Swansea 15/3/61.
R.71	CONSTANCE	V.A. (Tyne): Parsons	22. 8.44	Scrapped Inverkeithing 8/3/56.
R.12	CONTEST	White	16.12.44	Scrapped Grays 2/2/60.
R.63	CONCORD (ex-Corso)	Thornycroft	14. 5.45	Scrapped Inverkeithing, 11/62.
R.57	COSSACK	V.A. (Tyne): Parsons	10. 5.44	Scrapped Troon 1/3/61.
R.68	CRISPIN (ex-Craccher)	White	23. 6.45	R.P.N. JAHANGIR (1958).
R.82	CREOLE	White	22.11.45	R.P.N. ALAMGIR (1958).
R.35	CROMWELL (ex-Cretan)	Scotts	6. 8.45	R.N.N. BERGEN (1946).
R.16	CRESCENT (R.C.N.)	Clydebank	20. 7.44	
R.46	CROWN	Scotts	19.12.45	R.N.N. OSLO (1946).
R.27	CROZIERS	Yarrow	19. 9.44	R.N.N. TRONDHEIM (1946); scrapped Belgium 12/61.
R.20	CRUSADER (R.C.N.)	Clydebank	5.10.44	
R.38	CRYSTAL	Yarrow	12. 2.45	R.N.N. STAVANGER (1946).

Notes:—When the " CA " group was ordered in 1942 they were given spare names until they received their "CA" names in 11/42 by which time only two had been laid down. Some "**C**" class were of all-welded construction and the last three groups had remote power control (R.P.C.) fitted to their 4.5 in. guns and sacrificed the forward bank of T.T. to compensate for the additional topweight involved. Only the " CA " group saw war service serving with the Home fleet until 1945 before going to the East Indies.

Battle class
(First and Second groups)

Displacement: *First group* 2,315 tons except R.A.N. vessels, ARMADA, BARFLEUR, SAINTES, ST. JAMES, SOLEBAY and TRAFALGAR 2,325 tons. *Second group* 2,380 tons except AGINCOURT, ALAMEIN, CORUNNA and JUTLAND (ii) 2,400 tons.

Dimensions: 355 (pp) 379 (oa) × 40¼ except R.A.N. vessels 41 × 10½ (*first group*) 10¾ (*second group*) ft.

Machinery: 2-shaft geared Turbines, S.H.P. 50,000 except R.A.N. vessels 54,000 = 35¾ knots.

Armament: *First group* 4—4.5 in. D.P. (2 × 2), 1—4 in. and 12—40 mm. A.A. (4 × 2 & 4 × 1) except* 14—40 mm. A.A. (4 × 2 & 6 × 1) and R.A.N. vessels 12—40 mm. A.A. (3 × 2 & 6 × 1) guns; 8 except R.A.N. vessels 10—21 in. (2 × 4/5) T.T. *Second group* 5—4.5 in. (2 × 2 & 1 × 1), 8—40 mm. A.A. (3 × 2 & 2 × 1) guns; 10—21 in. (2 × 5) T.T.

Complement: *First group* 247 except R.A.N. vessels 290 (308 in ARMADA, BARFLEUR, SAINTES, ST. JAMES, SOLEBAY and TRAFALGAR). *Second group* 232 (268 in AGINCOURT, ALAMEIN, CORUNNA and JUTLAND (ii)).

(First group)

R.14	ARMADA	Hawthorn Leslie	9.12.43	For disposal.
R.80	BARFLEUR	Swan Hunter: Wallsend	1.11.43	For disposal.
R.09	CADIZ*	Fairfield	16. 9.44	R.P.N. KHAIBAR (1957).
R.32	CAMPERDOWN	Fairfield	8. 2.44	For disposal.
R.55	FINISTERRE	Fairfield	22. 6.44	For disposal.
R.47	GABBARD	Swan Hunter: Wallsend	16. 3.45	R.P.N. BADR (1957).
R.24	GRAVELINES*	Cammell Laird	30.11.44	Scrapped Rosyth 4/4/61.
R.74	HOGUE	Cammell Laird	21. 4.44	Sold Singapore 7/3/62.
R.44	LAGOS	Cammell Laird	4. 8.44	For disposal.
R.65	ST. JAMES*	Fairfield	7. 6.45	Scrapped 19/3/61.
R.18	ST. KITTS*	Swan Hunter: Wallsend	4.10.44	Scrapped Sunderland 14/2/62.
R.84	SAINTES*	Hawthorn Leslie	19. 7.44	For disposal.
R.60	SLUYS*	Cammell Laird	28. 2.45	
R.70	SOLEBAY*	Hawthorn Leslie	22. 2.44	For disposal.
R.77	TRAFALGAR	Swan Hunter: Wallsend	12. 1.44	

R.31	VIGO*	Fairfield	27. 9.45	For disposal.
D.59	ANZAC (R.A.N.)	Williamstown	20. 8.48	
D.37	TOBRUK (R.A.N.)	Cockatoo	20.12.47	

(Second group)

I.06	AGINCOURT	Hawthorn Leslie	29. 1.45	
I.22	AISNE	V.A. (Tyne): Parsons	12. 5.45	
I.17	ALAMEIN	Hawthorn Leslie	28. 5.45	For disposal.
I.51	ALBUERA	V.A. (Tyne)	28. 8.45	Cancelled; hull scrapped Inverkeithing 21/11/50.
I.68	BARROSA	Clydebank	17. 1.45	
I.88	BELLE ISLE	Fairfield	7. 2.46	Cancelled; hull scrapped Troon 5/46.
I.97	CORUNNA	Swan Hunter: Wallsend	29. 5.45	
I.09	DUNKIRK	Stephen	27. 8.45	
I.16	JUTLAND (i)	Hawthorn Leslie	2.11.45	Cancelled; hull scrapped Rosyth 10/57.
I.62	MALPLAQUET	Stephen	20. 2.46	JUTLAND (ii) (1947); for disposal.
I.43	MATAPAN	Clydebank	30. 4.45	
I.53	MONS	Hawthorn Leslie		Cancelled.
I.58	NAMUR	Cammell Laird	12. 6.45	Cancelled; hull retained for experimental purposes.
I.82	NAVARINO	Cammell Laird	21. 9.45	Cancelled; hull scrapped Preston 4/46.
I.98	OMDURMAN	Fairfield		Cancelled.
I.02	OUDENARDE	Swan Hunter	11. 9.45	Cancelled; hull scrapped Rosyth 12/57.
I.10	POICTIERS	Hawthorn Leslie	4. 1.46	Cancelled; hull retained for experimental purposes.
I.83	RIVER PLATE	Swan Hunter		Cancelled.
I.42	ST. LUCIA	Stephen		Cancelled.
I.37	SAN DOMINGO	Cammell Laird		Cancelled.
I.31	SOMME	Cammell Laird		Cancelled.
I.72	TALAVERA	Clydebank	27. 8.45	Cancelled; hull scrapped Troon 1/46.
I.59	TRINCOMALEE	Clydebank	8. 1.46	Cancelled; hull scrapped Troon 2/46.
I.07	WATERLOO (ex-Vimiera)	Fairfield		Cancelled.

Two enlarged **Battle** class were projected as follows:—

G.22	VIMIERA	Cammell Laird		Completed as DANAE.
G.83	YPRES	Fairfield		Completed as DELIGHT (ex-Disdain).

Notes:—Designed for Pacific operations with a large radius of action and a heavy A.A. armament for employment in areas where enemy aircraft predominated. TRINCOMALEE had her original pennant number I.86 changed to I.59 when the THRACIAN was recovered from the Japanese, the latter assuming her old pennant number I.86. ARMADA, BARFLEUR, CAMPERDOWN, HOGUE and TRAFALGAR were the only units completed before the end of hostilities and went to the Pacific from the Home fleet in 1945.

Weapon class

Displacement: 1,980 tons.
Dimensions: $341\frac{1}{2}$ (pp) 365 (oa) × 38 × $10\frac{1}{2}$ ft.
Machinery: 2-shaft geared Turbines, S.H.P. 40,000 = 35 knots.
Armament: 6—4 in. A.A. (3 × 2), 6—40 mm. A.A. (3 × 2) guns; 10—21in. (2 × 5) T.T.
Complement: 234 (256 in BATTLEAXE).

G.18	BATTLEAXE	Yarrow	12. 6.45	For disposal.
G.31	BROADSWORD	Yarrow	5. 2.46	
G.82	CARRONADE	Scotts	4.46	Cancelled; hull scrapped Troon 4/46.
G.34	CLAYMORE	Scotts		Cancelled.
G.96	CROSSBOW	Thornycroft	20.12.45	
G.28	CULVERIN	Thornycroft		Cancelled; hull scrapped Grays 1946.
G.74	CUTLASS	Yarrow	20. 3.46	Cancelled; hull scrapped Troon 3/46.
G.23	DAGGER	Yarrow		Cancelled.
G.02	DIRK	Scotts		Cancelled.
G.53	GRENADE	Scotts		Cancelled.
G.99	HALBERD	Scotts		Cancelled.
G.44	HOWITZER	Thornycroft		Cancelled.
G.55	LONGBOW	Thornycroft		Cancelled.
G.78	MUSKET	White		Cancelled.
G.06	PONIARD	Scotts		Cancelled.
	RAPIER			Cancelled.
G.21	RIFLE	Denny		Cancelled.
G.30	SPEAR	Denny		Cancelled.
G.85	SWORD (ex-Celt)	White		Cancelled.
G.64	TOMAHAWK (ex-Centaur)	White	15. 8.46	SCORPION (1946).

Notes:—Introduced *en echelon* arrangement of boiler and engine rooms. Armament reduced by 2—4 in. A.A. (1 × 2) to incorporate A.T.W (two Squids).

1. H.M.S. Zealous (" **Z** " class), with combined HA/LA DCT on bridge and catwalk over tubes. 2, H.M.S. Cambrian (" **CA**" group). The only group of the " **C** " class to mount two sets of torpedo tubes. HF/DF fitted as topmast to lattice foremast. 3. H.M.S. Eglinton (**Hunt** class—type I) with 2 pdr. bowchaser. 4. H.M.S. Chiddingfold (**Hunt** class—type II), had additional twin 4 in. A.A. mounting and multiple 2 pdr. re-sited abaft funnel. [*All photos I.W.M.*

"G" class

Displacement: *ca.* 2,000 tons.
Dimensions: 341½ (pp) 365 (oa) × 39½ × 10½ ft.
Machinery: 2-shaft geared Turbines, S.H.P. 40,000 = 35 knots.
Armament: 4—4.5 in. D.P. (2 × 2), 6—40 mm. A.A. (3 × 2) guns; 10—21 in. (2 × 5) T.T.; 2—A.T.W. (Squid).
Complement:

G.07	GAEL	Yarrow		Cancelled.
G.03	GALLANT	Yarrow		Cancelled.
G.59	GAUNTLET	Thornycroft		Cancelled.
G.19	GUERNSEY	Denny		Cancelled.
G.45	GLOWWORM (ex-Gift G.67)	Thornycroft		Cancelled.
G.76	GRAFTON	White		Cancelled.
G.88	GREYHOUND	White		Cancelled.
G.67	GIFT (ex-Glowworm, ex-Guinivere G.40)	Denny		Cancelled.

Notes:—Similar to **Weapon** class with heavier gun armament.

"D" class

Displacement: 2,610 tons.
Dimensions: 366 (pp) 390 (oa) × 43 × 12¾ ft.
Machinery: 2-shaft geared Turbines, S.H.P. 54,000 = 34¾ knots.
Armament: 6—4.5 in. D.P. (3 × 2), 10—40 mm. A.A. (5 × 2) guns; 10—21 in. (2 × 5) T.T.; 1—A.T.W. (Squid).
Complement: 278 (308 in DARING and DIAMOND).

I.52	DAINTY	White	16. 8.50	
I.05	DANAE (ex-Vimiera G.22)	Cammell Laird		Cancelled.
I.15	DARING	Swan Hunter: Wallsend	10. 8.49	
I.40	DECOY (i)	V.A. (Tyne): Parsons		Cancelled.
I.45	DELIGHT (i)	V.A. (Tyne): Parsons		Cancelled.
I.35	DEMON	Swan Hunter		Cancelled.
I.73	DERVISH	White		Cancelled.
I.19	DESIRE	Hawthorn Leslie		Cancelled.
I.87	DESPERATE	Clydebank		Cancelled.
I.81	DIAMOND	Clydebank	14. 6.50	
I.77	DIANA (i)	Hawthorn Leslie		Cancelled.
I.08	DISDAIN (ex-Ypres G.83)	Fairfield	21.12.50	DELIGHT (ii) (1946).
I.47	DOGSTAR	Stephen	27. 7.50	DEFENDER (1946).

I.56	DRAGON	Yarrow	29. 3.49	DECOY (ii) (1946).
I.26	DRUID	Yarrow	8. 5.52	DIANA (ii) (1946).
I.94	DUCHESS	Thornycroft	9. 4.51	
D.11	VAMPIRE (R.A.N.)	Cockatoo	27.10.56	
D.08	VENDETTA (R.A.N.)	Williamstown	3. 5.54	
D.04	VOYAGER R.A.N.	Cockatoo	1. 3.52	
	WATERHEN (R.A.N.)	Williamstown		Cancelled.

Notes:—An after control position replaced 4—40 mm. A.A. (2 × 2).

ESCORT DESTROYERS

Hunt class

(Type 1)

Displacement: 907 tons.
Dimensions: 264¼ (pp) 280 (oa) × 29 × 7¾ ft.
Machinery: 2-shaft geared Turbines, S.H.P. 19,000 = 26 knots.
Armament: 4—4 in. A.A. (2 × 2), 4 except * 5—2 pdr. A.A. (1 × 4 & 1 × 1), 2—20 mm. A.A. (2 × 1) guns.
Complement: 146.

L.05	ATHERSTONE*	Cammell Laird	12.12.39	Scrapped Port Glasgow 25/11/57.
L.17	BERKELEY*	Cammell Laird	29. 1.40	Lost 19/8/42.
L.35	CATTISTOCK*	Yarrow	22. 2.40	Scrapped Newport 1957.
L.46	CLEVELAND*	Yarrow	24. 4.40	Wrecked 28/6/57 en route shipbreakers.
L.54	COTSWOLD*	Yarrow	18. 7.40	Scrapped Grays 11/9/57.
L.78	COTTESMORE*	Yarrow	5. 9.40	Egyptian IBRAHIM-EL-AWAL (1950), MOHAMED-ALI-EL-KEBIR (1951), Israeli HAIFA (1956).
L.87	EGLINTON*	V.A. (Tyne): Parsons	28.12.39	Scrapped Blyth 28/5/56.
L.61	EXMOOR (i)	V.A. (Tyne): Parsons	25. 1.40	Lost 25/2/41.
L.11	FERNIE*	Clydebank	9. 1.40	Scrapped Port Glasgow 7/11/56.
L.20	GARTH*	Clydebank	14. 2.40	Scrapped Barrow 15/8/58.
L.37	HAMBLEDON*	Swan Hunter: Wallsend	12.12.39	Hulked 1955, scrapped Tyne 4/2/58.

L.48	HOLDERNESS*	Swan Hunter: Wallsend	8. 2.40	Scrapped Preston 20/11/56.
L.60	MENDIP*	Swan Hunter: Wallsend	9. 4.40	Chinese (Nationalist) LIN FU (1948), Egyptian MOHAMED-ALI-EL-KEBIR (1950), IBRAHIM-EL-AWAL (1951).
L.82	MEYNELL*	Swan Hunter: Wallsend	7. 6.40	Ecuadorian VELASCO YBARRA (1954).
L.92	PYTCHLEY*	Scotts	13. 2.40	Scrapped Llanelly 1/12/56.
L.58	QUANTOCK*	Scotts	22. 4.40	Ecuadorian PRESIDENTE ALFARO (1954).
L.66	QUORN*	White	27. 3.40	Lost 3/8/44.
L.25	SOUTHDOWN*	White	5. 7.40	Scrapped Barrow 1/11/56.
L.96	TYNEDALE	Stephen	5. 6.40	Lost 12/12/43.
L.45	WHADDON*	Stephen	16. 7.40	Scrapped Faslane 4/59.

Notes:—Most of Type I served in Home waters—chiefly at The Nore or Rosyth. ATHERSTONE, CLEVELAND, HAMBLEDON, MENDIP, QUANTOCK, TYNEDALE and WHADDON went to the Mediterranean in 1943. Designed armament included 6—4 in. A.A. (3 × 2) and T.T. and ATHERSTONE so completed but 2—4 in. (1 × 2) and the T.T. were suppressed and 2—20 mm. A.A. added.

(Type II)

Displacement: 1,050 tons except * 1,000 tons.
Dimensions: $264\frac{1}{4}$ (pp) $282\frac{1}{2}$ (oa) × $31\frac{1}{2}$ × $7\frac{3}{4}$ ft.
Machinery: 2-shaft geared Turbines, S.H.P. 19,000 = 25 knots.
Armament: 6 except* 4—4 in. A.A. (2/3 × 2), 4 except† 5—2 pdr. A.A. (1 × 4 & 1 × 1), 2/3—20 mm. A.A. (2/3 × 1) guns.
Complement: 168 except* 146.

L.06	AVON VALE†	Clydebank	23.10.40	Scrapped Sunderland 15/5/58.
L.03	BADSWORTH	Cammell Laird	17. 3.41	R.N.N. ARENDAL (1946).
L.14	BEAUFORT	Cammell Laird	9. 6.41	R.N.N. HAUGESUND (1954).
L.26	BEDALE	Hawthorn Leslie	23. 7.41	Polish SLAZAK (1942-45), R.I.N. GODAVARI (1953).
L.34	BICESTER	Hawthorn Leslie	5. 9.41	Scrapped Grays 22/8/56.
L.43	BLACKMORE	Stephen	2.12.41	R.D.N. ESBERN SNARE (1952).
L.30	BLANKNEY	Clydebank	19.12.40	Scrapped Blyth 3/59.
L.24	BLENCATHRA*†	Cammell Laird	6. 8.40	Scrapped Barrow 2/1/57.
L.51	BRAMHAM	Stephen	29. 1.42	R.H.N. THERMISTOCLES (1943).

L.08	BURTON	Swan Hunter: Wallsend	12. 3.41	EXMOOR (ii) (1941); R.D.N. VALDEMAR SEJR (1953).
L.42	BROCKLESBY*	Cammell Laird	30. 9.40	
L.71	CALPE	Swan Hunter: Wallsend	28. 4.41	R.D.N. ROLF KRAKE (1952).
L.31	CHIDDINGFOLD	Scotts	10. 3.41	R.I.N. GANGA (1954).
L.52	COWDRAY	Scotts	22. 7.41	Scrapped Gateshead 3/9/59.
L.62	CROOME	Stephen	30. 1.41	Scrapped Briton Ferry 8/57.
L.63	DULVERTON	Stephen	1. 4.41	Lost 13/11/43.
L.68	ERIDGE	Swan Hunter: Wallsend	20. 8.40	Constructive total loss 29/8/42; scrapped Alexandria 10/46.
L.70	FARNDALE	Swan Hunter: Wallsend	30. 9.40	Scrapped Blyth 4/12/62.
L.77	GROVE	Swan Hunter: Wallsend	29. 5.41	Lost 12/6/42.
L.85	HEYTHROP	Swan Hunter: Wallsend	30.10.40	Lost 20/3/42.
L.84	HURSLEY	Swan Hunter: Wallsend	25. 7.41	R.H.N. KRITI (1943).
L.28	HURWORTH	V.A. (Tyne): Parsons	10. 4.41	Lost 22/10/43.
L.88	LAMERTON	Swan Hunter: Wallsend	14.12.40	R.I.N. GOMATI (1953).
L.95	LAUDERSDALE	Thornycroft	5. 8.41	R.H.N. AIGAION (1946).
L.90	LEDBURY	Thornycroft	27. 9.41	Scrapped Rosyth 4/58.
L.100	LIDDESDALE*†	V.A. (Tyne): Parsons	19. 8.40	Scrapped Gateshead 1948.
L.74	MIDDLETON	V.A. (Tyne): Parsons	12. 5.41	Hulked 1955. scrapped Blyth 4/10/57.
L.72	OAKLEY (i)	V.A. (Tyne): Parsons	30.10.40	Polish KUJAWIAK (1941); lost 16/6/42.
L.108	PUCKERIDGE	White	6. 3.41	Lost 6/9/43.
L.115	SILVERTON	White	4.12.40	Polish KRAKOWIAK (1941-46); scrapped Grays 3/49.
L.10	SOUTHWOLD	White	29. 5.41	Lost 24/3/42.
L.99	TETCOTT	White	12. 8.41	Scrapped Milford Haven 24/9/56.
L.98	TICKHAM	Yarrow	15. 1.42	OAKLEY (ii) (1942); W. German GNEISENAU (1958).

L.122	WHEATLAND	Yarrow	7. 6.41	Hulked 1955, scrapped Bo'ness 9/59.
L.128	WILTON	Yarrow	17.10.41	Scrapped Faslane 12/59.
L.59	ZETLAND	Yarrow	7. 3.42	R.N.N. TROMSO (1954).

Notes:—AVON VALE and COWDRAY served as the R.H.N. AEGEAN and ADMIRAL HASTINGS for a short period in 1944. ERIDGE was heavily damaged in the Mediterranean in 1942 and served as a Base ship at Alexandria from 1944-46.

(Type III)

Displacement: 1,087 tons.
Dimensions: $264\frac{1}{4}$ (pp) $282\frac{1}{2}$ (oa) $\times$ $31\frac{1}{2}$ $\times$ $7\frac{3}{4}$ ft.
Machinery: 2-shaft geared Turbines, S.H.P. 19,000 = 25 knots.
Armament: 4—4 in. A.A. (2 × 2), 4 except* 5—2 pdr. A.A. (1 × 4 & 1 × 1), 2/3—20 mm. A.A. (2/3 × 1) guns; 2—21 in. (1 × 2) T.T.
Complement: 168.

L.07	AIREDALE	Clydebank	12. 8.41	Lost 15/6/42.
L.12	ALBRIGHTON*	Clydebank	11.10.41	W. German RAULE (1958).
L.22	ALDENHAM	Cammell Laird	27. 8.41	Lost 14/12/44.
L.32	BELVOIR	Cammell Laird	18.11.41	Scrapped Bo'ness 10/57.
L.47	BLEAN	Hawthorn Leslie	15. 1.42	Lost 11/12/42.
L.50	BLEASDALE*	V.A. (Tyne): Parsons	23. 7.41	Scrapped Blyth 14/9/56.
L.65	BOLEBROKE	Swan Hunter: Wallsend	5.11.41	R.H.N. PINDOS (1942).
L.67	BORDER	Swan Hunter: Wallsend	3. 2.42	R.H.N. ADRIAS (i) (1942); constructive total loss 22/10/43, scrapped Tyne 11/45.
L.81	CATTERICK	V.A. (Barrow)	22.11.41	R.H.N. HASTINGS (1946).
L.83	DERWENT	V.A. (Barrow)	22. 8.41	Scrapped 1/47.
L.09	EASTON	White	11. 7.42	Scrapped Rosyth 1/53.
L.15	EGGESFORD	White	12. 9.42	W. German BROMMY (1958).
L.36	ESKDALE	Cammell Laird	16. 3.42	R.N.N. (name not changed, 1942); lost 14/4/43.
L.44	GLAISDALE*	Cammell Laird	5. 1.42	R.N.N. NARVIK (1946); scrapped Denmark 12/61.
L.27	GOATHLAND	Fairfield	3. 2.42	Constructive total loss 24/7/44; scrapped Troon 2/46.
L.19	HALDON	Fairfield	27. 4.42	French LA COMBATTANTE (1942); lost 23/2/45.
L.53	HATHERLEIGH	V.A. (Tyne): Parsons	18.12.41	R.H.N. KANARIS (1942).

Left: H.M.S. Derwent (**Hunt** class—type III), closing H.M.S. Illustrious [*I.W.M.*

Below: H.M.S. Brissenden (**Hunt** class—type IV), with fo'c'sle extended well aft. [*I.W.M.*

L.75	HAYDON	V.A. (Tyne): Parsons	2. 4.42	Scrapped Dunston 18/5/58.
L.56	HOLCOMBE	Stephen	14. 4.42	Lost 12/12/43.
L.57	LIMBOURNE	Stephen	12. 5.42	Lost 23/10/43.
L.73	MELBREAK	Swan Hunter: Wallsend	5. 3.42	Scrapped Grays 22/11/56.
L.91	MODBURY	Swan Hunter: Wallsend	13. 4.42	R.H.N. MIAOULIS (1942-60); for disposal.
L.89	PENYLAN	V.A. (Barrow)	17. 3.42	Lost 3/12/42.
L.39	ROCKWOOD	V.A. (Barrow)	13. 6.42	Scrapped Gateshead 8/46.
L.16	STEVENSTONE*	White	23.11.42	Scrapped Dunston 2/9/59.
L.18	TALYBONT	White	3. 2.43	Scrapped Charlestown 10/3/61.
L.69	TANATSIDE	Yarrow	30. 4.42	R.H.N. ADRIAS (ii) (1946).
L.86	WENSLEYDALE	Yarrow	20. 6.42	Scrapped Blyth 15/2/46.

Notes:—Types II and III saw service in Home waters or the Mediterranean, usually on escort duties. Those employed on East Coast convoys had an additional 2 pdr. bowchaser. Four of them operated from Freetown for a year and eight were in the East Indies in 1945.

(Type IV)

Displacement: 1,175 tons.
Dimensions: 276 (pp) 296 (oa) × 33¼ × 8 ft.
Machinery: 2-shaft geared Turbines, S.H.P. 19,000 = 25 knots.
Armament: 6—4 in. A.A. (3 × 2), 4—2 pdr. A.A. (1 × 4), 2—40 mm. A.A. (2 × 1) and 4—20 mm. A.A. (2 × 2) BRECON or 8—20 mm. A.A. (4 × 2) BRISSENDEN guns; 3—21 in. (1 × 3) T.T.
Complement: 170.

L.76	BRECON	Thornycroft	27. 6.42	Scrapped 17/9/62.
L.79	BRISSENDEN	Thornycroft	15. 9.42	For disposal.

Notes:—Were built to the original design proposed by Thornycroft but modified by the Admiralty and resulted in the Type I. For the first time since the prototypes AMAZON and AMBUSCADE the builders were given a free hand and produced vessels superior to the three earlier types. BRECON was in the Home fleet until 1943 and then went to the Mediterranean and finally the East Indies in 1945. BRISSENDEN was in Home waters until 1945 when she went to the Mediterranean.

The following eight vessels were building in the U.K. at the outbreak of war and were acquired by the Royal Navy.

Displacement: 1,340 tons **(ex-Brazilian)**, 1,360 tons **(ex-Turkish).**
Dimensions: 312 (pp) 323 (oa) × 33 × 8½ ft.
Machinery: 2-shaft geared Turbines, S.H.P. 34,000 = 35½ knots.
Armament: 4—4.7 in. (4 × 1), 8—.5 in. A.A. (2 × 4) guns; 8—21 in. (2 × 4) T.T. *Complement:* 145.

Ex-Brazilian

H.19	HANDY (ex-Jurua)	V.A. (Barrow)	29. 9.39	HARVESTER (1940); lost 11/3/43.
H.32	HAVANT (ex-Javary)	White	17. 7.39	Lost 1/6/40.

H.88	HAVELOCK (ex-Jutahy)	White	16.10.39	Scrapped Inverkeithing 31/10/46.
H.57	HEARTY (ex-Juruena)	Thornycroft	1. 8.39	HESPERUS (1940); scrapped Grangemouth 26/11/46.
H.44	HIGHLANDER (ex-Jaguaribe)	Thornycroft	17.10.39	Scrapped Rosyth 27/5/46.
H.06	HURRICANE (ex-Japarua)	V.A. (Barrow)	29. 9.39	Lost 24/12/43.

Ex-Turkish

H.49	INCONSTANT (ex-Muavenet)	V.A. (Barrow)	15.12.40	Turkish MUAVENET (1945).
H.05	ITHURIEL (ex-Gayret)	V.A. (Barrow)	24. 2.41	Damaged beyond repair 28/11/42; scrapped Bo'ness 11/45

Notes:—(Ex-Brazilian) After a short period with the Home fleet all except HAVANT (lost) served in the Western Approaches. (Ex-Turkish) Both initially went to the Eastern fleet and then INCONSTANT went to the Western Approaches and ITHURIEL to the Mediterranean. Two sister vessels, built by Denny, were commissioned as H.M. Ships (DEMIRHISAR—H.80 and SULTANHISAR—H.87) for the passage to Turkey only.

The following Allied vessels served as H.M. Ships from July, 1940.

Ex-FRENCH

Pomone class

Displacement: 610 tons
Dimensions: 249¼ (pp) 264¾ (oa) × 23¾ × 9¼ ft.
Machinery: 2-shaft geared Turbines, S.H.P. 22,000 = 34 knots.
Armament: 2—3.9 in. (2 × 1), 2—37 mm. A.A. (2 × 1), 4—13 mm. A.A. (2 × 2) guns; 2—21.7 in. (1 × 2) T.T. *Complement:* 92.

H.20	BOUCLIER	Ch. Worms	9. 8.37	All retroceded (1945).
H.25	LA CORDELIERE	Normand	9. 9.36	
H.63	LA FLORE	At. & Ch. Bretagne	4. 5.35	
H.47	L'INCOMPRISE	Ch. Worms	14. 4.37	
H.56	LA MELPOMENE	At. & Ch. Bretagne	24. 1.35	

Notes:—BOUCLIER served at Portsmouth until 1940 and was then used for training. LA CORDELIERE, LA FLORE and L'INCOMPRISE were at Portsmouth till 1941 before being used for training. LA MELPOMENE was at The Nore until 1942 and was then used as a target.

Simoun class

Displacement: 1,319 tons.
Dimensions: 325¼ (pp) 347¼ (oa) × 33¼ × 13¾ ft.
Machinery: 2-shaft geared Turbines, S.H.P. 33,000 = 33 knots.
Armament: 4—5.1 in. (4 × 1), 2—37 mm. A.A. (2 × 1) guns; 6—21.7 in. (2 × 3) T.T. *Complement:* 138.

H.03	MISTRAL	F. & Ch. de la Med. (Havre)	6. 6.25	Both retroceded (1945).
H.16	OURAGAN	Ch. Navales Francais	6.12.24	

Notes:—MISTRAL spent most of the war as tender to the gunnery firing ship CARDIFF. OURAGAN served at Portsmouth until 1942 and was then used as a target.

Ex-ROYAL NETHERLANDS NAVY

Displacement: 150 tons.
Dimensions: $162\frac{1}{2} \times 17 \times 4\frac{1}{2}$ ft.
Machinery: 1-shaft Reciprocating (V.T.E.), I.H.P. 2,600 = 25 knots.
Armament: 2—3 in. (2 × 1) guns; 3—17 .7 in. (3 × 1) T.T.
Complement: 44.

H.35	G.13	De Schelde	1913	Scrapped Preston 2/43.
H.66	G.15	Fijenoord	1914	Scrapped Preston 2/43.

Notes:—G.13 was attached to the 2nd Submarine flotilla until paid off in 1942.

Displacement: 264 tons.
Dimensions: $192 \times 19\frac{3}{4} \times 5\frac{1}{2}$ ft.
Machinery: 2-shaft Reciprocating (V.T.E.), I.H.P. 5,500 = 27 knots except BLADE I.H.P. 3,000 = 22 knots.
Armament: 2—3 in. (2 × 1) 2-machine (2 × 1) guns; 4—17.7 in. (1 × 2 & 2 × 1—not in BLADE).
Complement: 48 except BLADE 34.

H.97	BLADE (ex-Z.5)	De Schelde	1915	Scrapped Troon 10/45.
	Z.6	De Schelde	1915	Scrapped Bo'ness 2/43.
H.93	Z.7	De Schelde	1915	Scrapped Llanelly 1947.
H.71	Z.8	De Schelde	1915	Scrapped Newport 8/44.

Notes:—BLADE was tender to 7th Submarine flotilla for most of the war. Z.6 served at Rosyth then Greenock. Z.7 served at Rosyth until paid off 1943. Z.8 was tender to the 1st Submarine flotilla until 1942 then the 7th Submarine flotilla until paid off in 1943.

BRITISH DESTROYER DEPLOYMENT

January, 1940

1st	Flotilla (Harwich):	7 "**G**", 3 Polish.
2nd	Flotilla (S. Atlantic):	5 "**H**".
	(W. Indies):	4 "**H**".
3rd	Flotilla (Home fleet):	7 "**I**".
4th	Flotilla (Home fleet):	8 **Tribal.**
5th	Flotilla (Home fleet):	6 "**K**".
6th	Flotilla (Home fleet):	8 **Tribal.**
7th	Flotilla (Humber):	8 "**J**".
8th	Flotilla (Home fleet):	9 "**F**".

11th	Flotilla (W. Approaches):	10 " **V** & **W** ".
12th	Flotilla (Rosyth):	7 " **E** ".
13th	Flotilla (Gibraltar):	1 "**A**", 6 " **V** & **W** ", 2 old Leaders.
15th	Flotilla (W. Approaches):	7 " **V** & **W** ", 1 old Leader.
16th	Flotilla (Portsmouth):	4 "**A**", 2 " **V** & **W** ", 2 old " **S** ", 1 old Leader.
17th	Flotilla (W. Approaches):	7 " **V** & **W** ", 1 old Leader.
18th	Flotilla (W. Approaches):	4 "**A**", 5 " **V** & **W** ".
19th	Flotilla (Dover):	7 " **B** ".
20th	Flotilla (Portsmouth):	2 " **I** ", 2 " **E** ".
21st	Flotilla (Mediterranean):	7 " **D** ".
Rosyth Escort force:		7 " **V** & **W** ", 1 old Leader.
R.C.N. (W. Indies):		5 " **C** ", 2 "**A**".
China:		1 " **V** & **W** ", 5 old " **S** ".
East Indies:		1 " **D** ", 1 " **B** ", 4 " **V** & **W** " (R.A.N.), 1 old Leader (R.A.N.).
Refitting, etc.:		1 " **G** ", 1 " **B** ", 1 "**A**", 11 " **V** & **W** ", 2 old " **S** ", 1 old " **R** ", 1 old Leader and 1 old Leader for disposal (BRUCE).

January, 1945

1st	Flotilla (Portsmouth):	1 " **G** ", 1 " **B** ", 1 "**A**", 3 " **V** & **W** ".
2nd	Flotilla (Home fleet):	7 " **Z** ".
3rd	Flotilla (Mediterranean):	5 " **M** ", 2 " **L** ", 1 "**A**".
4th	Flotilla (Pacific fleet):	6 " **Q** ".
5th	Flotilla (Mediterranean):	7 **Hunt.**
6th	Flotilla (Home fleet):	7 " **CA** ".
7th	Flotilla (E. Indies):	4 " **N** ".
8th	Flotilla (Plymouth):	2 " **I** ", 1 " **F** ", 2 R.C.N., 2 R.Neth.N., 2 Polish.
10th	Flotilla (E. Indies):	4 **Tribal.**
11th	Flotilla (E. Indies):	8 " **R** ".
12th	Flotilla (Mediterranean):	8 R.H.N.
13th	Flotilla (Gibraltar):	2 " **V** & **W** ", 1 old Leader.
14th	Flotilla (Mediterranean):	2 " **K** ", 2 " **J** ".
15th	Flotilla (Plymouth):	4 **Hunt.**
16th	Flotilla (Harwich):	7 **Hunt,** 1 " **V** & **W** ", 1 old Leader, 1 R.N.N., 2 Polish.
17th	Flotilla (Home fleet):	8 " **O** ".
18th	Flotilla (Mediterranean):	8 **Hunt,**
21st	Flotilla (Sheerness):	16 **Hunt,** 5 " **V** & **W** ".
22nd	Flotilla (Mediterranean):	7 **Hunt,**
23rd	Flotilla (Home fleet):	8 " **S** ".
24th	Flotilla (E. Indies)	4 " **T** ".
25th	Flotilla (Pacific fleet):	8 " **U** ".
26th	Flotilla (E. Indies):	6 " **V** ".
27th	Flotilla (Pacific fleet):	8 " **W** ".
16th	Division (E. Indies):	4 " **P** ".
Divisions (Mediterranean):		7 **Hunt.**
Miscellaneous (Mediterranean):		2 " **I** ", 1 "**A**", 1 **Hunt.**
Submarine escorts (Home fleet):		2 old " **S** ".
Rosyth Escort force:		2 R.N.N., 16 " **V** & **W** ", 5 **Town,** 1 old Leader.

Air targets (Rosyth & Greenock):	I "**A**", I "**V** & **W**", 7 **Town.**
11th Escort group (Derry):	8 R.C.N.
Escort groups (W. Approaches):	3 ex-Brasilian, 2 "**I**", I "**H**", 2 "**F**", I "**E**", 2 "**B**", I R.C.N., 3 "**V** & **W**", I **Town**, 2 old Leaders.
Miscellaneous (Home ports):	2 "**P**", I "**A**", I **Hunt**, 2 "**V** & **W**", 2 **Town**, I old "**S**".
Reserve fleet (Home ports):	I "**A**", 5 "**V** & **W**", 8 **Town**, 2 old Leaders, 3 old "**S**", 2 R.N.N., 2 French.
R.A.N.:	2 **Tribal**, I "**V** & **W**", I old Leader.
R.C.N.:	I **Tribal**, I "**A**", 5 **Town.**

BRITISH SUBMARINE DEVELOPMENT FROM 1918

SUBMARINE development "between the wars" was more on a technical, than material, plane. In 1918 the Royal Navy possessed fleet submarines ("**K**" class), overseas patrol and minelaying submarines ("**L**" class) and coastal submarines ("**H**" class) and these four main types were perpetuated.

The experimental X.1 was born out of the inflated reputation of the German submarine cruisers and was the *only* Royal Naval vessel laid down after the First World War that was scrapped before the opening of the second conflict. The "**O**", "**P**" and "**R**" classes were developments of the "**L**" class but although their increased size permitted a heavier armament, it was only gained at the cost of unhandiness. The **Thames** class, which followed, was the final attempt to produce a fleet submarine. Greater success was achieved as mechanical advancement enabled them to be diesel engined but again their bulk negated their positive qualities. However, as the speed of capital ships was gradually raised to approaching 30 knots all further attempts at fleet submarines were discontinued. The succeeding "**S**" class were most successful and handy craft and, midway in size between the "**H**" and "**L**" classes, they could undertake both their tasks. The **Porpoise** class minelayers were equally successful and at one time were the sole vessels able to maintain communications with Malta in the face of overwhelming enemy opposition. The "**T**" class replaced the ageing "**L**" class (and, eventually, the "**O**", "**P**" and "**R**" classes as well) on overseas work and had the heaviest broadside of any British submarine—ten bow tubes of which four were external. An external stern tube was added later and the two amidships external tubes turned to fire aft and supplement the stern salvo. The "**U**" class were built to replace the "**H**" class for pre-submarine and A/S training and also had a limited patrol capability.

War production was mainly limited to the "**S**", "**T**" and "**U**" classes and their design was kept constantly under review to incorporate war experience. The hull strength of the "**S**" and "**T**" classes was considerably improved by the complete adoption of welding. With the eventual shift of operations to the Pacific (as outlined for destroyers) their radius was extended by converting some ballast tanks to oil fuel bunkers. The war built "**S**" class added a stern torpedo tube but this was discarded when they shipped a 4 in. gun instead of the 3 in. gun previously borne. Warning R.D.F. and a single 20 mm. A.A. were included in most war built "**S**" and "**T**" classes and added in earlier units. The war built "**U**" class discarded the external bow torpedo tubes of the pre-, and immediate post-war vessels and adopted diesel-electric propulsion which greatly facilitated rapid production. The "**V**" class were generally very similar but with slightly greater length brought about by finer ends.

The "**A**" class originated from the need for higher surface speed and greater endurance for Pacific operations. When preparations were well in hand for their production the "**T**" class was discontinued and their assembly started. They were of pre-fabricated and all welded construction but the war ended before any operational experience could be obtained with them.

With two exceptions British submarines did not receive any names until 1926. Soon after the outbreak of the Second World War boats then building lost their names and were numbered from P.31 to P.42. This group was subsequently completed under their original names but all others laid down from 1940 were without names until January and February, 1943, when naming was again resorted to.

The only submarines of First World War design extant in 1939 were the following nine vessels of the "**H**" class and three of the "**L**" class:—H.28, H.31, H.32, H.33, H.34, H.43, H.44, H.49 and H.50: L.23, L.26, and L.27. These served in Home waters, generally on training duties but H.31 was lost on 24/12/41 and H.49 18/10/40. The remainder were scrapped at Troon on the following dates:—H.28 8/44, H.32 11/44, H.33 10/44, H.34 7/45, H.43 11/44, H.44 2/45 and H.50 7/45. The three "**L**" class went to Canada in 1944 for training and were scrapped there; L.23 being lost in tow 5/46 en-route the shipbreakers, and L.26 was expended as an A/S target 25/9/45.

SUBMARINES

Experimental

Displacement: 2,780/3,600 tons. *Dimensions:* 350 (pp) 363½ (oa × 29¾ × 15¾ ft.
Machinery: 2-shaft Diesel/Electric motors, B.H.P. 6,000/2,600 = 19½/9 knots
Armament: 4—5.2 in. (2 × 2), 2—machine guns; 6—21 in. (fixed bow) T.T.
Complement: 110.

	X.1	Chatham	16. 6.23	Scrapped Pembroke 12/12/36.

Notes:—Design was influenced by the German submarine cruisers of the First World War and took nearly four years to build.

"O" class
(First Group)

Displacement: 1,350/1,870 tons except OBERON 1,311/1,831 tons.
Dimensions: 275 (pp) (oa) × 27¾ × 13¼ ft. except OBERON 270 (pp) 296 (oa) × 28 × 13¼ ft.
Machinery: 2-shaft Diesel/Electric motors B.H.P. 3,000/1,350 = 15½/9 knots
Armament: 1—4 in., 2—machine guns; 8—21 in. (6 bow and 2 stern—all fixed) T.T. *Complement:* 54.

N.21	OBERON (ex-O.1)	Chatham	24. 9.26	Scrapped Rosyth 24/8/45.
N.51	OTWAY (ex-OA.2)	V.A. (Barrow)	7. 9.26	R.A.N. (1927-31); scrapped Inverkeithing 24/8/45.
55.P	OXLEY (ex-OA.1)	V.A. (Barrow)	29. 6.26	R.A.N. (1927-31); lost 10/9/39.

Notes:—OBERON and OXLEY served in Home flotillas and the OTWAY in the Mediterranean.

(Second group)

Displacement: 1,475/2,030 tons.
Dimensions: 260 (pp) 283½ (oa) × 29¾ × 13¾ ft.
Machinery: 2-shaft Diesel/Electric motors, B.H.P. 4,400/1,320 = 17½/9 knots.
Armament: 1—4 in., 2—machine guns; 8—21 in. (6 bow and 2 stern—all fixed) T.T. *Complement:* 53.

N.84	ODIN	Chatham	5. 5.28	Lost 14/6/40.
N.35	OLYMPUS	Beardmore	11.12.28	Lost 8/5/42.
N.46	ORPHEUS	Beardmore	26. 2.29	Lost 27/6/40.
N.67	OSIRIS	V.A. (Barrow)	19. 5.28	Scrapped Durban 9/46.
N.58	OSWALD	V.A. (Barrow)	19. 6.28	Lost 1/8/40.
N.92	OTUS	V.A. (Barrow)	31. 8.28	Scuttled off Durban 9/46.

Notes:—ODIN, OLYMPUS, ORPHEUS and OTUS served in the East Indies and then went to the Mediterranean in 1940. The sole survivor, OTUS, returned to Home waters 1942 and then went to the South Atlantic 1943 for A/S training. OSIRIS and OSWALD served in the Mediterranean and only the former boat survived to go to the Eastern theatre as a training vessel.

" P " and " R " classes

Displacement: 1,475/2,040 (" **P** " class), 2,030 (" **R** " class) tons.
Dimensions: 260 (pp) 290 (oa) × 29¾ × 13¾ ft.
Machinery: 2-shaft Diesel/Electric motors, B.H.P. 4,400/1,320 = 17½/9 knots.
Armament: 1—4 in., 2—machine guns; 8—21 in. (6 bow and 2 stern—all fixed) T.T. *Complement:* 53.

N.75	PARTHIAN	Chatham	22. 6.29	Lost 11/8/43.
N.36	PERSEUS	V.A. (Barrow)	22. 5.29	Lost 1/12/41.
N.96	PHOENIX	Cammell Laird	3.10.29	Lost 17/7/40.
	POSEIDON	V.A. (Barrow)	21. 6.29	Lost 9/6/31.
N.29	PROTEUS	V.A. (Barrow)	23. 7.29	Scrapped Troon 26/2/46.
N.42	PANDORA (ex-Python)	V.A. (Barrow)	22. 8.29	Lost 31/3/42, salved 1943 and scrapped 1955.
N.16	RAINBOW	Chatham	14. 5.30	Lost 19/10/40.
N.41	REGENT	V.A. (Barrow)	11. 6.30	Lost 16/4/43.
N.88	REGULUS	V.A. (Barrow)	11. 6.30	Lost 6/12/40.
N.62	ROVER	V.A. (Barrow)	11. 6.30	Scrapped Durban 30/7/46.
	ROYALIST	Beardmore		Cancelled.
	RUPERT	Cammell Laird		Cancelled.

Notes:—All went to the Mediterranean from China in 1940. The only two to survive were used for training from 1943, PROTEUS in Home waters and ROVER in the Far East.

Thames class

Displacement: 1,850/2,723 tons except THAMES 1,805/2,680 tons.
Dimensions: 325 (pp) 345 (oa) × 28¼ except THAMES 28 × 13¾ except THAMES 13½ ft.
Machinery: 2-shaft Diesel/Electric motors, B.H.P. 10,000/2,500 = 22¼ except THAMES 21¾/10 knots
Armament: 1—4 in., 2—machine guns; 8—21 in. (6 bow and 2 stern—all fixed) T.T.
Complement: 61.

N.71	THAMES	V.A. (Barrow)	26. 1.32	Lost 23/7/40.
N.57	SEVERN	V.A. (Barrow)	16. 1.34	Scrapped Bombay 1946.
N.12	CLYDE	V.A. (Barrow)	15. 3.34	Scrapped Durban 30/7/46.

Notes:—Designed with high surface speed for Fleet work. CLYDE and SEVERN, after a short spell based on Freetown, served in Home waters until 1941 when they went to the Mediterranean and finally to the Eastern fleet in 1944.

Porpoise class

Displacement: 1,520/2,157 tons except PORPOISE 1,500/2,053 tons.
Dimensions: 271½ (pp) 289 (oa) × 25½ × 15½ ft. except PORPOISE 267 (pp) 288 (oa) × 29¾ × 13¾ ft.
Machinery: 2-shaft Diesel/Electric motors, B.H.P. 3,300/1,630 = 15/8¾ knots.
Armament: 1—4 in., 2—machine guns; 6—21 in. (all fixed bow) T.T.; 50 mines.
Complement: 59.

N.14	PORPOISE	V.A. (Barrow)	30. 8.32	Lost 19/1/45.
N.56	GRAMPUS	Chatham	25. 2.36	Lost 24/6/40.
N.45	NARWHAL	V.A. (Barrow)	29. 8.35	Lost 7/40.
N.74	RORQUAL	V.A. (Barrow)	21. 7.36	Scrapped Newport 17/3/46.
N.83	CACHALOT	Scotts	2.12.37	Lost 4/8/41.
37.M	SEAL	Chatham	27. 9.38	Captured 5/5/40 and became German UB; scuttled Germany 3/5/45.
P.411	Unnamed	Scotts		Cancelled.
P.412	Unnamed	Scotts		Cancelled.
P.413	Unnamed	Scotts		Cancelled.

Notes:—CACHALOT and NARWHAL were successively Mediterranean, West Indies, Home waters and Mediterranean 1939-41. GRAMPUS went to the Mediterranean from China. PORPOISE returned to Home waters from the Mediterranean in 1939 and went to the Eastern fleet in 1944 after a brief return to the Mediterranean in 1941. RORQUAL went to the Mediterranean from China in 1940 and to the Eastern fleet in 1944. SEAL was en-route China at the outbreak of war and was diverted to the West Indies and then returned to Home waters.

"S" class

(First group)

Displacement: 670/960 tons except *first four* 640/927 tons.
Dimensions: 193 (pp) $208\frac{3}{4}$ (oa) × 24 × $10\frac{1}{2}$ ft. except *first four* 187 (pp) $202\frac{1}{2}$ (oa) × $23\frac{1}{2}$ × $10\frac{1}{4}$ ft.
Machinery: 2-shaft Diesel/Electric motors, B.H.P. 1,550 except SUNFISH 1,900/1,300 = $13\frac{3}{4}$ except SUNFISH 15/10 knots.
Armament: 1—3 in., 1—machine gun; 6—21 in. (all fixed bow) T.T.
Complement: 38.

N.73	STURGEON	Chatham	8. 1.32	R.Neth.N. ZEEHOND (1943-45); scrapped Granton 1947.
N.61	SWORDFISH	Chatham	10.11.31	Lost 16/11/40.
98.S	SEAHORSE	Chatham	15.11.32	Lost 7/1/40.
19.S	STARFISH	Chatham	14. 3.33	Lost 9/1/40.
N.72	SEALION	Cammell Laird	16. 3.34	Expended as A/S target 3/45.
N.54	SHARK	Chatham	31. 5.34	Lost 6/7/40.
N.65	SALMON	Cammell Laird	30. 4.34	Lost 9/7/40.
N.39	SNAPPER	Chatham	25.10.34	Lost 12/2/41.
N.47	SEAWOLF	Scotts	28.11.35	Scrapped Montreal 11/45.
N.69	SPEARFISH	Cammell Laird	21. 4.36	Lost 2/8/40.
N.81	SUNFISH	Chatham	30. 9.36	Russian B.1 (1944); lost 27/7/44.
N.22	STERLET	Chatham	22. 9.37	Lost 18/4/40.

Notes:—SALMON, SEALION, SHARK and SNAPPER returned to Home waters from the Mediterranean in 1939 and joined the remainder of the class. Only four boats survived and were all used for A/S training by 1942-43, SEAWOLF being loaned to Canada for that purpose in 1943 and stationed at Bermuda.

(Second group)

Displacement: 715/990 tons.
Dimensions: $202\frac{1}{2}$ (pp) 217 (oa) × $23\frac{3}{4}$ × $10\frac{1}{2}$ ft.
Machinery: 2-shaft Diesel/Electric motors, B.H.P. 1,900/1,300 = $14\frac{3}{4}$/9 knots.
Armament: 1—3 in., 3—machine guns; 7—21 in. (6 bow and 1 stern (external)—all fixed) T.T. in *earlier boats*. 1—4 in., 1—20 mm. A.A. guns; 6—21 in. (all fixed bow) T.T. in *later boats*.
Complement: 44.

P.211	SAFARI (ex-P.211, ex-P.61)	Cammell Laird	18.11.41	Wrecked 7/1/46 en-route shipbreakers.
P.212	SAHIB (ex-P.212, ex-P.62)	Cammell Laird	19. 1.42	Lost 24/4/43.
P.247	SARACEN (ex-P.213, ex-P.63)	Cammell Laird	16. 2.42	Lost 18/8/43.
P.214	SATYR (ex-P.214, ex-P.64)	Scotts	28. 9.42	French SAPHIR (1952-61); scrapped Charlestown 6/62.

Left: H.M.S. Rorqual (**Porpoise** class), minelaying submarine. [*I.W.M.*

Above: H.M.S. Safari ("**S**" class). [*I.W.M.*

Left: H.M.S. Sportsman ("**S**" class), showing additional stern tube. [*I.W.M.*

P.215	SCEPTRE (ex-P.215, ex-P.65)	Scotts	9. 1.43	Scrapped Gateshead 9/49.
P.216	SEADOG (ex-P.216, ex-P.66)	Cammell Laird	11. 6.42	Scrapped Troon 24/12/47.
P.217	SIBYL (ex-P.217, ex-P.67)	Cammell Laird	29. 4.42	Scrapped Troon 3/48.
P.218	SEA ROVER (ex-P.218, ex-P.68)	Scotts	18. 2.43	Completed by V.A. (Barrow); scrapped Faslane 10/49.
P.219	SERAPH (ex-P.219, ex-P.69)	V.A. (Barrow)	25.10.41	
P.221	SHAKESPEARE (ex-P.221, ex-P.71)	V.A. (Barrow)	8.12.41	Scrapped Briton Ferry 7/46.
P.222	Unnamed (ex-P.72)	V.A. (Barrow)	20. 9.41	Lost 12/12/42.
P.223	SEA NYMPH (ex-P.223)	Cammell Laird	29. 7.42	Scrapped Troon 6/48.
P.224	SICKLE (ex-P.224)	Cammell Laird	27. 8.42	Lost *ca*. 18/6/44.
P.225	SIMOON (ex-P.225)	Cammell Laird	12.10.42	Lost 9/11/43.
P.226	SIRDAR (ex-P.226)	Scotts	26. 3.43	Completed by V.A. (Barrow); hull retained for experimental purposes 1959.
P.227	SPITEFUL (ex-P.227)	Scotts	5. 6.43	French SIRENE (1952-58).
P.228	SPLENDID (ex-P.228)	Chatham	19. 1.42	Lost 21/4/43.
P.229	SPORTSMAN (ex-P.229)	Chatham	17. 4.42	French SIBYLLE (1952); lost 23/9/52.
P.231	STOIC (ex-P.231)	Cammell Laird	9. 4.43	Scrapped Dalmuir 7/50.
P.232	STONEHENGE (ex-P.232)	Cammell Laird	23. 3.43	Lost 22/3/44.
P.233	STORM (ex-P.233)	Cammell Laird	18. 5.43	Scrapped Troon 9/49.
P.234	STRATAGEM (ex-P.234)	Cammell Laird	21. 6.43	Lost 22/11/44.
P.235	STRONGBOW (ex.-P.235)	Scotts	30. 8.43	Scrapped Preston 4/46.
P.236	SPARK (ex-P.236)	Scotts	28.12.43	Scrapped Faslane 28/10/49.
P.237	SCYTHIAN (ex-P.237)	Scotts	14. 4.44	Scrapped Charlestown 8/8/60.
P.238	STUBBORN (ex-P.238)	Cammell Laird	11.11.42	Expended as A/S target 4/46.
P.239	SURF (ex-P.239)	Cammell Laird	10.12.42	Scrapped Faslane 28/10/49.
P.241	SYRTIS	Cammell Laird	4. 2.43	Lost 28/3/44.
P.242	SHALIMAR	Chatham	22. 4.43	Scrapped Troon 7/50.
P.243	SCOTSMAN	Scotts	18. 8.44	For disposal.
P.244	SEA DEVIL	Scotts	30. 1.45	For disposal.
P.245	SPIRIT	Cammell Laird	20. 7.43	Scrapped Grays 7/50.

P.246	STATESMAN	Cammell Laird	14. 9.43	French SULTANE (1952-59).
P.248	STURDY	Cammell Laird	30. 9.43	Scrapped Dunston 9/5/58.
P.249	STYGIAN	Cammell Laird	30.11.43	Scrapped Faslane 28/10/49.
P.251	SUBTLE	Cammell Laird	27. 1.44	Scrapped Charlestown 6/59.
P.252	SUPREME	Cammell Laird	24. 2.44	Scrapped Troon 7/50.
P.253	SEA SCOUT	Cammell Laird	24. 3.44	
P.254	SELENE	Cammell Laird	24. 4.44	Scrapped Gateshead 6/61.
P.255	SENESCHAL	Scotts	23. 4.45	Scrapped Dunston 23/8/60.
P.256	SENTINEL	Scotts	27. 7.45	Scrapped Gillingham 3/62.
P.257	SAGA	Cammell Laird	14. 3.45	Portuguese NAUTILO (1948).
P.258	SCORCHER	Cammell Laird	18.12.44	Hull retained for experimental purposes (1961), scrapped Charlestown 14/9/62.
P.259	SIDON	Cammell Laird	4. 9.44	Lost 16/6/55, salved and expended as A/S target 14/6/57.
P.261	SLEUTH	Cammell Laird	6. 7.44	Scrapped Charlestown 15/9/58.
P.262	SOLENT	Cammell Laird	8. 6.44	Scrapped Troon 8/62.
P.263	SPEARHEAD	Cammell Laird	2.10.44	Portuguese NEPTUNO (1948).
P.264	SPRINGER	Cammell Laird	14. 5.45	Israeli TANIN (1958).
P.265	SPUR	Cammell Laird	17.11.44	Portuguese NARVAL (1948).
P.266	SANGUINE	Cammell Laird	15. 2.45	Israeli RAHAV (1958).
	SEA ROBIN	Cammell Laird		Cancelled.
	SPRIGHTLY	Cammell Laird		Cancelled.
	SURFACE	Cammell Laird		Cancelled.
	SURGE	Cammell Laird		Cancelled.

Notes:—The " **S** " class were offensively employed in the three main theatres of war—Home waters, the Mediterranean and the Far East—and proved a most successful design.

" T " class
(First group)

Displacement: 1,090/1,575 tons except TRITON 1,095/1,579 tons.
Dimensions: 265 (pp) 275 (oa) × $26\frac{1}{2}$ × $14\frac{3}{4}$ ft.

Machinery: 2-shaft Diesel/Electric motors, B.H.P. 2,500/1,450 = 15¼/9 knots.
Armament: 1—4 in., 3—machine guns; 10, except * 11—21 in. (8 bow (2 external) and 2/3 stern (external)—all fixed) T.T.
Complement: 59.

N.15	TRITON	V.A. (Barrow)	5.10.37	Lost 18/12/40.
11.T	THETIS	Cammell Laird	29. 6.38	Lost 1/6/39; salved and renamed THUNDERBOLT (N.25); lost 13/3/43.
N.76	TRIBUNE	Scotts	8.12.38	Scrapped Milford Haven 7/47.
N.52	TRIDENT	Cammell Laird	7.12.38	Scrapped Newport 2/46.
N.18	TRIUMPH	V.A. (Barrow)	16. 2.38	Lost 14/1/42.
N.38	TAKU	Cammell Laird	20. 5.39	Scrapped Llanelly 11/46.
N.17	TARPON	Scotts	17.10.39	Lost 14/4/40.
N.24	THISTLE	V.A. (Barrow)	25.10.39	Lost 10/4/40.
N.63	TIGRIS	Chatham	31.10.39	Lost 10/3/43.
N.53	TRIAD	V.A. (Barrow)	5. 5.39	Lost 20/10/40.
N.68	TRUANT	V.A. (Barrow)	5. 5.39	Wrecked 12/46 en-route shipbreakers.
N.94	TUNA	Scotts	10. 5.40	Scrapped Briton Ferry 6/46.
N.78	TALISMAN	Cammell Laird	29. 1.40	Lost 18/9/42.
N.77	TETRARCH	V.A. (Barrow)	14.11.39	Lost 2/11/41.
N.79	TORBAY	Chatham	9. 4.40	Scrapped Briton Ferry 19/12/45.
N.86	TEMPEST*	Cammell Laird	10. 6.41	Lost 13/2/42.
N.11	THORN*	Cammell Laird	18. 3.41	Lost 6/8/42.
N.37	THRASHER*	Cammell Laird	28.11.40	Scrapped Briton Ferry 3/47.
N.48	TRAVELLER*	Scotts	27. 8.41	Lost 12/12/42.
N.91	TROOPER*	Scotts	5. 3.42	Lost 17/10/43.
N.45	TRUSTY*	V.A. (Barrow)	14. 3.41	Scrapped Milford Haven 7/41.
N.98	TURBULENT*	V.A.(Barrow)	12. 5.41	Lost 14/3/43.

(Second group)

Displacement: 1,090/1,575 tons.
Dimensions: 265 (pp) 275 (oa) × 26½ × 14¾ ft.
Machinery: 2—shaft Diesel/Electric motors, B.H.P. 2,500/1,450 = 15/9 knots.
Armament: 1—4 in., 1—20 mm. A.A., 3—machine guns; 11—21 in. (8 bow (2 external) and 3 stern (all external)—all fixed) T.T.
Complement: 65.

P.311	Unnamed (ex-Tutankhamen, ex-P.91)	V.A. (Barrow)	5. 3.42	Lost 8/1/43.
P.314	TACTICIAN (ex-P.314, ex-P.94)	V.A. (Barrow)	29. 7.42	
P.339	TAURUS (ex-P.313, ex-P.93)	V.A. (Barrow)	27. 6.42	R.Neth.N. DOLFIJN (1948-53); scrapped Dunston 4/60.
P.316	TEMPLAR (ex-P.316, ex-P.96)	V.A. (Barrow)	26.10.42	Scrapped Troon 17/7/59.
P.325	THULE (ex-P.325)	Devonport	22.10.42	Scrapped Inverkeithing 14/9/62.
P.327	TIRELESS (ex-P.327)	Portsmouth	19. 3.43	
P.328	TOKEN (ex-P.328)	Portsmouth	19. 3.43	
P.312	TRESPASSER (ex-P.312, ex-P.92)	V.A. (Barrow)	29. 5.42	Scrapped Gateshead 26/9/61.
P.315	TRUCULENT (ex-P.315, ex-P.95)	V.A. (Barrow)	12. 9.42	Lost 12/1/50, salved 14/3/50 and scrapped Grays 8/5/50.
P.326	TUDOR (ex-P.326)	Devonport	23. 9.42	Scrapped Faslane 7/63.
P.322	TALENT (i) (ex-P.322)	V.A. (Barrow): Clydebank	17. 7.43	R.Neth.N. ZWAARDVISCH (1944).
P.317	TALLY-HO (ex-P.317, ex-P.97)	V.A. (Barrow): Clydebank	23.12.42	For disposal.
P.318	TANTALUS (ex-P.318, ex-P.98)	V.A. (Barrow)	24. 2.43	Scrapped Milford Haven 11/50.
P.319	TANTIVY (ex-P.319, ex-P.99)	V.A. (Barrow): Clydebank	6. 4.43	Expended as target 1951.
P.321	TELEMACHUS (ex-P.321)	V.A. (Barrow)	19. 6.43	Scrapped Charlestown 25/8/61.
P.323	TERRAPIN (ex-P.323)	V.A. (Barrow): Bellis & Morcom	31. 8.43	Constructive total loss 19/5/45; scrapped Troon 4/46.
P.324	THOROUGH (ex-P.324)	V.A. (Barrow)	30.10.43	Scrapped Dunston 29/6/61.
P.332	TIPTOE	V.A. (Barrow): Clydebank	25. 2.44	Scrapped Inverkeithing 14/9/62.
P.352	TOTEM	Devonport	28. 9.43	
P.329	TRADEWIND (ex-P.329)	Chatham	11.12.42	Scrapped Charlestown 14/12/55.
P.331	TRENCHANT	Chatham	24. 3.43	Scrapped Faslane 7/63.
P.333	TRUMP	V.A. (Barrow): Clydebank	25. 3.44	
P.353	TRUNCHEON	Devonport	22. 2.44	

P.342	TABARD	Scotts	21.11.45	
P.334	TACITURN	V.A. (Barrow): Bellis & Morcom	7. 6.44	
P.343	TALENT (ii)	V.A. (Barrow)		Cancelled.
P.335	TAPIR	V.A. (Barrow): Clydebank	21. 8.44	R.Neth.N. ZEEHOND (1948-53).
P.336	TARN	V.A. (Barrow)	29.11.44	R.Neth.N. TIJGERHAAI (1945).
P.337	TASMAN	V.A. (Barrow): Bellis & Morcom	13. 2.45	TALENT (iii) (1945).
P.338	TEREDO	V.A. (Barrow): Clydebank	27. 4.45	
P.341	THEBAN	V.A. (Barrow)		Cancelled.
P.355	THERMOPYLAE	Chatham	27. 6.45	
P.349	THOR	Portsmouth	18. 4.44	Cancelled; scrapped Llanelly 1946.
P.344	THREAT	V.A. (Barrow)		Cancelled.
P.351	TIARA	Portsmouth	18. 4.44	Cancelled; scrapped 1946.
P.354	TURPIN	Chatham	5. 8.44	
	TYPHOON			Projected only.

Notes:—The " **T** " class were employed in the three main war theatres. TARPON and THISTLE were lost in Home waters and the remainder in the Mediterranean.

" U " class

(First group)

Displacement: 540/730 tons.
Dimensions: 180 (pp) 191½ (oa) except * 196¾ (oa) × 16 × 12¾ ft.
Machinery: 2-shaft Diesel-Electric motors, B.H.P. 615/825 = 11¾/9 knots.
Armament: 1—3 in. (not in UNDINE and UNITY), 3—machine guns; 6 except* 4—21 in. (all fixed bow—2 external in 6-tube boats) T.T.
Complement: 27 (*first three*), 31 (*others*).

N.48	UNDINE	V.A. (Barrow)	5.10.37	Lost 7/1/40.
N.66	UNITY	V.A. (Barrow)	16. 2.38	Lost 29/4/40.
N.59	URSULA	V.A. (Barrow)	16. 2.38	Russian B.4 (1944-49); scrapped Grangemouth 5/50.
N.82	UMPIRE* (ex-P.31, ex-Umpire)	Chatham*	30.12.40	Lost 19/7/41.

N.87	UNA* (ex-P.32, ex-Una)	Chatham*	10. 6.41	Scrapped Llanelly 11/4/49.
N.93	UNBEATEN* (ex-P.33, ex-Unbeaten)	V.A. (Barrow)	9. 7.40	Lost 11/11/42.
N.55	UNDAUNTED* (ex-P.34, ex-Undaunted)	V.A. (Barrow)	20. 8.40	Lost 13/5/41.
N.56	UNION* (ex-P.35, ex-Union)	V.A. (Barrow)	1.10.40	Lost 22/7/41.
N.95	UNIQUE (ex-P.36, ex-Unique)	V.A. (Barrow)	6. 6.40	Lost 24/10/42.
N.99	UPHOLDER (ex-P.37, ex-Upholder)	V.A. (Barrow)	8. 7.40	Lost 14/4/42.
N.89	UPRIGHT (ex-P.38, ex-Upright)	V.A. (Barrow)	21. 4.40	Scrapped Troon 3/46.
N.97	URCHIN* (ex-P.39, ex-Urchin)	V.A. (Barrow)	30. 9.40	Polish SOKOL (1940-46); scrapped 1949.
N.17	URGE* (ex-P.40, ex-Urge)	V.A. (Barrow)	19. 8.40	Lost 28/4/42.
N.65	USK* (ex-P.41, ex-Usk)	V.A. (Barrow)	7. 6.40	Lost 3/5/41.
N.19	UTMOST (ex-P.42, ex-Utmost)	V.A. (Barrow)	20. 4.40	Lost 24/11/42.

(Second group)

Displacement: 545/740 tons.
Dimensions: 180 (pp) 196¾ (oa) × 16 × 12¾ ft.
Machinery: 2-shaft Diesel-Electric motors, B.H.P. 615/825 ×= 11¼/9 knots
Armament: 1—3 in., 3—machine guns; 4—21 in. (all fixed bow) T.T.
Complement: 31.

P.31	UPROAR (ex-Ullswater, ex-P.31 (ii))	V.A. (Barrow)	27.11.40	Scrapped Inverkeithing 2/46.
P.32	Unnamed	V.A. (Barrow)	15.12.40	Lost 18/8/41.
P.33	Unnamed	V.A. (Barrow)	28. 1.41	Lost 20/8/41.
P.34	ULTIMATUM (ex-P.34 (ii))	V.A. (Barrow)	11. 2.41	Scrapped Port Glasgow 23/12/49.
P.35	UMBRA (ex-P.35 (ii))	V.A. (Barrow)	15. 3.41	Scrapped Blyth 7/46.
P.36	Unnamed	V.A. (Barrow)	28. 4.41	Lost 31/3/42; salved & scrapped 22/8/58.
P.37	UNBENDING (ex-P.37 (ii))	V.A. (Barrow)	12. 5.41	Scrapped Tyne 5/50.

P.38	Unnamed	V.A. (Barrow)	9. 7.41	Lost 25/2/42.
P.39	Unnamed	V.A. (Barrow)	23. 8.41	Lost 26/3/42.
P.41	UREDD (R.N.N.) (ex-P.41 (ii))	V.A. (Barrow)	24. 8.41	R.N.N. (1941); lost 10/2/43.
P.42	UNBROKEN (ex-P.42 (ii))	V.A. (Barrow)	4.11.41	Russian B.2 (1944-49); scrapped Gateshead 5/50.
P.43	UNISON (ex-P.43)	V.A. (Barrow)	5.11.41	Russian B.3 (1944-49); scrapped Stockton 5/50.
P.44	UNITED (ex-P.44)	V.A. (Barrow)	18.12.41	Scrapped Troon 12/2/46.
P.45	UNRIVALLED (ex-P.45)	V.A. (Barrow)	16. 2.42	Scrapped Briton Ferry 1/46.
P.46	UNRUFFLED (ex-P.46)	V.A. (Barrow)	19.12.41	Scrapped Troon 1/46.
P.47	DOLFIJN (R.Neth.N.) (ex-P.47)	V.A. (Barrow)	27. 7.42	Scrapped Holland 1947.
P.48	Unnamed	V.A. (Barrow)	15. 4.42	Lost 25/12/42.
P.49	UNRULY (ex-P.49)	V.A. (Barrow)	28. 7.42	Scrapped Inverkeithing 2/46.
P.51	UNSEEN (ex-P.51)	V.A. (Barrow)	16. 4.42	Scrapped Hayle 9/49.
P.52	DZIK (Polish) (ex-P.52)	V.A. (Barrow)	11.10.42	Danish SPRINGEREN (ex-U.1—1946-57); scrapped Faslane 4/58.
P.53	ULTOR (ex-P.53)	V.A. (Barrow)	12.10.42	Scrapped Briton Ferry 1/46.
P.54	UNSHAKEN (ex-P.54)	V.A. (Barrow)*	17. 2.42	Scrapped Troon 3/46.
P.55	UNSPARING (ex-P.55)	V.A.(Tyne)*	28. 7.42	Scrapped Inverkeithing 14/2/46.
P.56	USURPER (ex-P.56)	V.A.(Tyne)*	24. 9.42	Lost 3/10/43.
P.57	UNIVERSAL (ex-P.57)	V.A.(Tyne)*	10.11.42	Scrapped Milford Haven 2/46.
P.58	UNTAMED (ex-P.58)	V.A.(Tyne)*	8.12.42	Lost 30/5/43 and salved. VITALITY (1943); scrapped Troon 3/46.
P.59	UNTIRING (ex-P.59)	V.A.(Tyne)*	20. 1.43	R.H.N. AMFITRITI (1945-52); expended as target 25/7/57.
P.61	VARANGIAN (ex-P.61)	V.A.(Tyne)*	4. 4.43	Scrapped Gateshead 6/49.
P.62	UTHER (ex-P.62)	V.A.(Tyne)*	6. 4.43	Scrapped Hayle 4/50.
P.63	UNSWERVING (ex-P.63)	V.A.(Tyne)*	2. 6.43	Scrapped Newport 7/49.
P.64	VANDAL (ex-P.64)	V.A. (Barrow)	23.11.42	Lost 24/2/43.

1. H.M.S. Taku (" **T** " class). [I.W.M.
2. H.M.S. Undine (" **U** " class) with external bow tubes. [I.W.M.
3. H.M.S. Ultor (" **U** " class). [I.W.M.
4. H.M.S. Venturer (" **V** " class). [I.W.M.

P.65	UPSTART (ex-P.65)	V.A. (Barrow)	24.11.42	R.H.N. XIFIAS (1945-52); expended as target 29/7/57.
P.66	VARNE (i) (ex-P.66)	V.A. (Barrow)	22. 1.43	R.N.N. ULA (1943).
P.67	VOX (i) (ex-P.67)	V.A. (Barrow)	23. 1.43	French CURIE (1943-46), P. 67 (1946); scrapped 4/59.

*All engined Davey Paxman & Ricardo.

"V" class

Displacement: 545/740 tons.
Dimensions: 200 (pp) 206 (oa) × 16 × 12¾ ft.
Machinery: 2-shaft Diesel-Electric motors, B.H.P. 800/760 = 13/9 knots.
Armament: 1—3 in., 3—machine guns; 4—21 in. (all fixed bow) T.T.
Complement: 37.

P.93	ULEX	V.A. (Barrow)		Cancelled.
P.11	UNBRIDLED	V.A. (Tyne)		Cancelled.
P.92	UPAS	V.A. (Barrow)		Cancelled.
P.82	UPSHOT	V.A. (Barrow)	24. 2.44	Scrapped Preston 11/49.
P.16	UPWARD	V.A. (Tyne)		Cancelled.
P.83	URTICA	V.A. (Barrow)	23. 3.44	Scrapped Milford Haven 3/50.
P.94	UTOPIA	V.A. (Barrow)		Cancelled.
P.18	VAGABOND	V.A. (Tyne)	19. 9.44	Scrapped Newport 1/50.
P.72	VAMPIRE	V.A. (Barrow)	20. 7.43	Scrapped Gateshead 3/50.
	VANTAGE	V.A. (Tyne)		Cancelled.
P.85	VARIANCE	V.A. (Barrow)	22. 5.44	R.N.N. UTSIRA (1944).
P.81	VARNE (ii)	V.A. (Tyne)	24. 2.44	Scrapped Troon 9/58.
P.25	VEHEMENT	V.A. (Tyne)		Cancelled.
P.71	VELDT	V.A. (Barrow)	19. 7.43	R.H.N. PIPINOS (1943-57); scrapped Dunston 23/2/58.
P.86	VENGEFUL	V.A. (Barrow)	20. 7.44	R.H.N. DELFIN (1944-57); scrapped Gateshead 3/58.
P.27	VENOM	V.A. (Tyne)		Cancelled.
P.68	VENTURER	V.A. (Barrow)	4. 5.43	R.H.N. UTSTEIN (1946).
P.28	VERVE	V.A. (Tyne)		Cancelled.
P.88	VETO	V.A. (Barrow)		Cancelled.
P.74	VIGOROUS	V.A. (Barrow)	15.10.43	Scrapped Thornaby 23/12/49.
P.69	VIKING	V.A. (Barrow)	5. 5.43	R.N.N. UTVAER (1946).
P.84	VINEYARD	V.A. (Barrow)	8. 5.44	French DORIS (1944-47); scrapped 1950.

P.89	VIRILE	V.A. (Barrow)		Cancelled.
P.75	VIRTUE	V.A. (Barrow)	29.11.43	Scrapped Cochin 5/46.
P.95	VIRULENT	V.A. (Tyne)	23. 5.44	R.H.N. ARGONAFTIS (1946-58); scrapped Pasajes 4/61.
P.76	VISIGOTH	V.A. (Barrow)	30.11.43	Scrapped Hayle 4/50.
P.91	VISITANT	V.A. (Barrow)		Cancelled.
P.77	VIVID	V.A. (Tyne)	15. 9.43	Scrapped Faslane 10/50.
P.96	VOLATILE	V.A. (Tyne)	20. 6.44	R.H.N. TRIAINA (1946-58); scrapped Dunston 12/58.
P.78	VORACIOUS	V.A. (Tyne)	11.11.43	Scrapped Cochin 5/46.
P.87	VORTEX	V.A. (Barrow)	19. 8.44	French MORSE (1944-47), R.D.N. SAELEN (1947-58); scrapped Faslane 8/58.
P.29	VOTARY	V.A. (Tyne)	21. 8.44	R.N.N. UTHAUG (1946).
P.73	VOX (ii)	V.A. (Barrow)	28. 9.43	Scrapped Cochin 5/46.
P.79	VULPINE	V.A. (Tyne)	28.12.43	R.D.N. STOREN (1947-58); scrapped Faslane 4/59.

Notes:—(" **U** " and " **V** " classes) All served in Home waters and the Mediterranean only except for five boats which went to the East Indies for A/S training and another four which were lent to the R.C.N. for the same purpose. UNDINE, UNITY, UMPIRE, R.N.N. UREDD and VANDAL were lost in Home waters and the remainder in the Mediterranean. Eight un-named " **V** " class ordered from V.A. (Tyne) were cancelled.

"A" class

Displacement: 1,120/1,620 tons.
Dimensions: 279¾ (pp) 281¾ (oa) × 22¼ × 17 ft.
Machinery: 2-shaft Diesel/Electric motors, B.H.P. 4,300/1,250 = 18/8 knots.
Armament: 1—4 in., 1—20 mm. A.A., 3—machine guns; 10—21 in. (6 bow (2 external) and 4 stern (2 external)—all fixed) T.T.
Complement: 60.

P.451	ABELARD	Portsmouth		Cancelled.
P.452	ACASTA	Portsmouth		Cancelled.
P.414	ACE	Devonport	14. 3.45	Cancelled; scrapped Port Glasgow 6/50.
P.433	ACHATES	Devonport	20. 9.45	Cancelled; expended as target 1950.
P.411	ACHERON	Chatham	25. 3.47	
P.412	ADEPT	Chatham		Cancelled.
P.434	ADMIRABLE	V.A. (Tyne)		Cancelled.
P.457	ADVERSARY	V.A. (Tyne)		Cancelled.
P.427	AENEAS	Cammell Laird	25.10.45	
P.421	AFFRAY	Cammell Laird	12. 4.45	Lost 16/4/51.

P.448	AGATE	Cammell Laird		Cancelled.
P.446	AGGRESSOR	Cammell Laird		Cancelled.
P.443	AGILE	Cammell Laird		Cancelled.
P.454	ALADDIN	Cammell Laird		Cancelled.
P.441	ALARIC	Cammell Laird	18. 2.46	
P.453	ALCESTIS	Cammell Laird		Cancelled.
P.415	ALCIDE	V.A. (Barrow)	12. 4.45	
P.416	ALDERNEY	V.A. (Barrow)	25. 6.45	
P.417	ALLIANCE	V.A. (Barrow)	28. 7.45	
P.418	AMBUSH	V.A. (Barrow)	24. 9.45	
P.422	ANCHORITE (ex-Amphion)	V.A. (Barrow)	22. 1.46	
P.439	AMPHION (ex-Anchorite)	V.A. (Barrow)	31. 8.44	
P.423	ANDREW	V.A. (Barrow)	6. 4.46	
P.424	ANDROMACHE	V.A. (Barrow)		Cancelled.
P.425	ANSWER	V.A. (Barrow)		Cancelled.
P.429	ANTAEUS	V.A. (Barrow)		Cancelled.
P.428	ANTAGONIST	V.A. (Barrow)		Cancelled.
P.431	ANZAC	V.A. (Barrow)		Cancelled.
P.432	APHRODITE	V.A. (Barrow)		Cancelled.
P.435	APPROACH	V.A. (Barrow)		Cancelled.
P.436	ARCADIAN	V.A. (Barrow)		Cancelled.
P.437	ARDENT	V.A. (Barrow)		Cancelled.
P.438	ARGOSY	V.A. (Barrow)		Cancelled.
P.449	ARTEMIS	Scotts	26. 8.46	
P.456	ARTFUL	Scotts	22. 5.47	
P.458	ASGARD	Scotts		Cancelled.
P.444	ASPERITY	V.A. (Tyne)		Cancelled.
P.462	ASSURANCE	Scotts		Cancelled.
P.461	ASTARTE	Scotts		Cancelled.
P.447	ASTUTE	V.A. (Barrow)	30. 1.45	
P.442	ATLANTIS	V.A. (Barrow)		Cancelled.

P.419	AURIGA	V.A. (Barrow)	29. 3.45	
P.426	AUROCHS	V.A. (Barrow)	28. 7.45	
P.445	AUSTERE	V.A. (Tyne)		Cancelled.
P.459	AWAKE	V.A. (Tyne)		Cancelled.
P.455	AZTEC	V.A. (Tyne)		Cancelled.

Notes:—Were designed with an extended radius for Pacific operations but were completed too late for hostilities.

Ex-AMERICAN

The following nine boats were handed over to the Royal Navy under the Lend/Lease Agreement and the survivors returned to the United States Navy at the termination of hostilities.

"R" class

Displacement: 569/680 tons.
Dimensions: 179 (wl) 186 (oa) × 18¼ × 14½ ft.
Machinery: 2-shaft Diesel/Electric motors, B.H.P. 880/934 = 13½/10½ knots.
Armament: 1—3 in. gun; 4—21 in. (all fixed bow) T.T.
Complement: 33.

P. No.	Name	Builder	Launched	Fate
P.511	Unnamed (ex-U.S.N. R.3)	Fore River	18. 1.19	R.N. (1941), U.S.N. (1944); scrapped Troon 2/48.
P.512	Unnamed (ex-U.S.N. R.17)	Union I.W.	24.12.17	R.N. (1942), U.S.N (1944); scrapped 12/45.
P.514	Unnamed (ex-U.S.N. R.19)	Union I.W.	28. 1.18	R.N. (1942); lost 21/6/42.

Notes:—P.511 and P.512 were used for training by 1943, the former in Home waters and the latter at Bermuda on loan to the R.C.N.

"S" class

Displacement: 854/1,062 tons.
Dimensions: 211 (wl) 219¼ (oa) × 20¾ × 16 ft.
Machinery: 2-shaft Diesel/Electric motors, B.H.P. 1,200/1,500 = 14/11 knots.
Armament: 1—4 in. gun; 4—21 in. (all fixed bow) T.T.
Complement: 42.

P.552	Unnamed (ex-U.S.N. S.1)	Fore River	26.10.18	R.N. (1942), U.S.N. (1944); scrapped Durban 6/46.
P.553	Unnamed (ex-U.S.N. S.21)	Bethlehem	18. 8.20	R.N. (1942), U.S.N. (1944); expended as target 20/3/45.
P.554	Unnamed (ex-U.S.N. S.22)	Bethlehem	15. 7.20	R.N. (1942), U.S.N. (1944); scrapped 16/11/45.

P.555	Unnamed (ex-U.S.N. S.24)	Bethlehem	27. 6.22	R.N. (1942), U.S.N. (1944); expended in trials 25/8/47.
P.551	Unnamed (ex-U.S.N. S.25)	Bethlehem	29. 5.22	Polish JASTRZAB (1941); lost 2/5/42.
P.556	Unnamed (ex-U.S.N. S.29)	Bethlehem	9.11.22	R.N. (1942), U.S.N. (1944); beached Portchester 24/1/49.

Notes:—Mostly used for training. P. 553 and P 554 were loaned to the R.C.N. and P.552 served in the Eastern fleet and the South Atlantic.

Ex-TURKISH

The following four boats were building in the U.K. at the outbreak of war and were acquired by the Royal Navy but two were shortly afterwards handed back to Turkey.

Displacement: 683/856 tons.
Dimensions: 193 (pp) 201½ (oa) × 22¼ × 10½ ft.
Machinery: 2-shaft Diesel/Electric motors, B.H.P. 1,550/1,300 = 13¾/10 knots.
Armament: 1—3 in., 1—machine guns; 5—21 in. (4 bow and 1 stern (external)—all fixed) T.T.
Complement:

P. No.	Name	Builder	Launched	Fate
P.611	Unnamed (ex-Turkish Oruc Reis)	V.A. (Barrow)	19. 7.40	Turkish ORUC REIS (1942).
P.612	Unnamed (ex-Turkish Murat Reis)	V.A. (Barrow)	20. 7.40	Turkish MURAT REIS (1942).
P.614	Unnamed (ex-Turkish Burak Reis)	V.A. (Barrow)	19.10.40	Turkish BURAK REIS (1945).
P.615	Unnamed (ex-Turkish Uluc Ali Reis)	V.A. (Barrow)	1.11.40	Lost 15/4/43.

Notes:—P.614 and P.615 were used for training at Freetown 1942 and the former was similarly employed in Home waters in 1943.

Ex-ENEMY

The following ex-enemy boats were captured during the war and incorporated into the Royal Navy.

Type VIIc

Displacement: 769/871 tons.
Dimensions: 213 (pp) 220¼ (oa) × 20¼ × 15¾ ft.
Machinery: 2-shaft Diesel/Electric motors, B.H.P. 2,800/750 = 17/7½ knots.
Armament: 1—3.5 in., 1—37 mm. A.A., 2—20 mm. A.A. (1 × 2) guns; 5—21 in. (4 bow and 1 stern—all fixed) T.T.
Complement: 44.

N.46	GRAPH (ex-German U.570)	Blohm & Voss	1941	Captured 28/8/41; lost 20/3/44.

Notes:—Served in Home waters from time of capture to loss.

Archimede class

Displacement: 880/1,231 tons.
Dimensions: 231¼ (oa) × 22½ × 13 ft.
Machinery: 2-shaft Diesel/Electric motors, B.H.P. 3,000/1,300 = 17/8½ knots.
Armament: 1—3.9 in., 2—13 mm. A.A. (2 × 1) guns; 8—21 in. (4 bow and 4 stern—all fixed) T.T.
Complement: 49.

P.711	X.2 (ex-Italian Galileo Galilei)	Tosi	19. 3.34	Captured 19/6/40; P.711 (1942); scrapped 1946.

Notes:—Was in the East Indies 1941 and the Mediterranean 1944 as a training boat.

Perla class

Displacement: 620/853 tons.
Dimensions: 197 (oa) × 21 × 13 ft.
Machinery: 2-shaft Diesel/Electric motors, B.H.P. 1,350/800 = 14/8½ knots.
Armament: 1—3.9 in., 2—13 mm. A.A. (2 × 1) guns; 6—21 in. (all fixed bow) T.T.
Complement: 41.

P.712	Unnamed (ex-Italian Perla)	Adriatico	1. 5.36	Captured 9/7/42, R.H.N. MATROZOS (1943); scrapped 1954.

Notes:—Served in the Mediterranean until 1945.

Nichelio class

Displacement: 629/864 tons.
Dimensions: 197¼ (oa) × 21¼ × 15½ ft.
Machinery: 2-shaft Diesel/Electric motors, B.H.P. 1,350/800 = 14¾/7 knots.
Armament: 1—3.9 in., 4—13 mm. A.A. (2 × 2) guns; 6—21 in. (4 bow and 2 stern—all fixed) T.T.
Complement: 48.

P.714	Unnamed (ex-Italian Bronzo)	Tosi	28. 9.41	Captured 12/7/43, French NARVAL (1944); scrapped.

The following Allied submarines served under the operational control of the Royal Navy during the war.

Polish: ORZEL (lost 8/6/40) and WILK (N.46).

R.N.N.: B.1.

R.Neth.N.: K.9 (N.39), K.11 (N.53), K.12, K.14 (N.22), K.15 (N.24), O.9 (P.9), O.10 (P.10), O.14 (P.14), O.15, O.19 (N.54—lost 5/45), O.21 (P.21), O.22 (P.22—lost 12/40), O.23 (P.23) and O.24 (P.24).

French: CASABIANCA, CERES (P.32), CREOLE (incomplete), JUNON (P.19), LE GLORIEUX (P.17), MARSOUIN, MINERVE (P.26—lost 19/9/45), NARVAL (i) (lost 16/12/40), ONDINE and ORION (both scrapped 1943), PALLAS (P.41), PERLE (i) (lost 8/7/44), PROTEE (lost 30/12/43), RUBIS (P.15), and SURCOUF (P.17—lost 18/2/42).

R.H.N.: GLAFKOS (lost 4/4/42), KATSONIS (N.16—lost 14/9/43), NEREUS (N.56), PAPANICOLIS and TRITON (lost 16/11/42).

Yugoslavian: NEBOJSCA (ex-L.68—N.61).

Italian: ALAGI (N.58), ATROPO (N.51), BRAGADINO (ex-Marcantonio Bragadino—N.49), BRIN (ex-Benedetto Brin—N.96), CAGNI (ex-Ammaraglio Cagni—N.55), GALATEA (N.71), GIADA (N.88), GOFFREDO MAMELI, H.1 (P.56), JALEA, MENOTTI (ex-Circo Menotti—N.66), PLATINO and ZOEA.

"X" craft

There was no provision pre-war for "midget" submarines in the Royal Navy and their design and production was a purely war-time expedient. Briefly, they were special attack craft designed to penetrate and attack vessels lying in protected harbours. Their armament consisted of two powerful charges, containing two tons of explosives, carried on each side which they deposited under their targets and then secured it to their hulls by lines and magnetic clamps. A feature of the design was a floodable compartment from which a diver could leave, and re-enter, the boat.

Prototypes
Nos. X.3 and X.4 built Varley Marine, 1942. 27/30 tons: 50 × 5½ × 5½ ft.: 1-shaft Diesel/Electric, B.H.P. 42/25 = 6½/4½ knots: complement 3.

Operational (Home waters)
Nos. X.5-10 built V.A. (Barrow) 1942/43, *X.20-25* built V.A. (Barrow) 1944. 27/30 tons: 51¼ × 5¾ × 5¾ ft.: 1-shaft Diesel/Electric, B.H.P. 42/30 = 6½/5½ knots: complement 4.

Training
Nos. XT.1-6 built V.A. (Barrow) 1944. Similar to operational units but less elaborately equipped for training.

Operational (Far East)
Nos. XE.1-12 built Broadbent, Markham (Chesterfield) and Marshall (Gainsborough) 1944/45. 30/34 tons: 53 × 5¾ × 5¾ ft.: 1-shaft Diesel/Electric, B.H.P. 42/30 = 6½/6 knots: complement 4/5.

War losses:—X.5, X.6 and X.7 22/9/43. X.8 17/9/43. X.9 15/10/43. X.10 3/10/43. X.22 7/2/44. XE.11 6/3/45, later salved and scrapped.

Scrapped:— XE.10 cancelled and scrapped incomplete 1945. XE.1-6 in Australia 1945/46. XE 7 and XE.12 1952. XE.8 and XE.9 1953.

BRITISH SUBMARINE DEPLOYMENT

September, 1939.

1st	Flotilla (Mediterranean):	3 " **O** ", 4 " **S** ", 2 **Porpoise**.
2nd	Flotilla (Dundee):	1 " **O** ", 8 " **S** ", 1 " **T** ".
4th	Flotilla (China):	13 " **O**, **P** & **R** ", 1 **Porpoise** and 2 on passage.
5th	Flotilla (Portsmouth):	8 " **H** ", 1 " **L** ", 1 " **O** ", 1 **Thames.**
6th	Flotilla (Blyth):	1 " **H** ", 2 " **L** ", 3 " **U** ".
7th	Flotilla (to form at Freetown)	2 **Thames** on passage.

January, 1942.

1st	Flotilla (Alexandria):	4 " **O** & **P** ", 8 " **T** ".
2nd	Flotilla (Malta):	13 " **U** ", 5 R.H.N., 1 Polish, 1 Yugoslavian.
3rd	Flotilla (Clyde):	3 " **T** ", 2 ex-U.S.N., 2 ex-Turkish.
5th	Flotilla (Portsmouth):	1 " **U** ", 1 " **T** ", 3 " **S** ", 1 **Porpoise,** 1 " **R** ", 1 " **P** ", 1 ex-Turkish, 1 R.N.N., 4 French, GRAPH.
6th	Flotilla (Blyth):	1 " **T** ", 1 " **L** ".
7th	Flotilla (W. Approaches):	2 " **O** ", 2 " **L** ", 7 " **H** ", 3 R.Neth.N., 1 R.N.N., 1 Polish.
8th	Flotilla (Gibraltar):	2 **Thames**, 1 " **O** ", 1 R.Neth.N.
9th	Flotilla (Dundee):	1 " **U** ", 3 R.Neth.N., 2 French.
East Indies:		X.2.
Eastern fleet:		2 " **T** ", 1 " **R** ".
America & West Indies:		1 R.Neth.N., 1 French.
Refitting (U.S.A.):		1 " **P** ".

May, 1944.

1st	Flotilla (Malta):	8 " **U** ", 2 " **S** ", 4 R.H.N., 1 R.Neth.N., 1 Yugoslavian.
3rd	Flotilla (Holy Loch):	5 " **U** ", 7 " **T** ", 9 " **S** ", 3 R.Neth.N., 2 French.
4th	Flotilla (Trincomalee):	10 " **T** ", 1 " **S** ", 1 **Porpoise**, 1 **Thames.**
5th	Flotilla (Portsmouth):	4 " **U** ", 1 " **T** ", 3 " **S** ", 1 **Porpoise**, 1 French, 3 Polish, 1 ex-U.S.N.
6th	Flotilla (Blyth):	4 " **U** ", 2 " **T** ", 1 " **O** ".
7th	Flotilla (Rothesay):	4 " **U** ", 2 " **T** ", 1 " **S** ", 1 " **P** ", 1 " **O** ", 4 R.Neth.N., 1 R.N.N., 1 ex-U.S.N.
8th	Flotilla (Trincomalee):	9 " **S** ".
9th	Flotilla (Dundee):	5 " **U** ", 1 " **T** ", 3 " **S** ", 1 ex-Turkish, 2 R.Neth.N.
10th	Flotilla (Maddalena):	3 " **U** ", 1 " **T** ".

PENNANT NUMBERS (Submarines)

Submarines in service in September, 1939 had numeral pennants and a flag inferior. The flags used were: H or L for the " **H** " and " **L** " classes, P for the " **O** " and " **P** " classes, R for the " **R** " class, F for the **Thames** class, M for the **Porpoise** class, S for the " **S** " class, T for the " **T** " class and C for the " **U** " class.

In 1940 all were given flag N superior to the numeral pennants, the latter remaining unchanged. Flag P superior was later adopted for war construction.

PART THREE

Sloops, Corvettes and Frigates

The former Admiralty yacht H.M.S. Enchantress stripped for war service but still lacking her designed armament. Single 20 mm. A.A. guns were added in the bridge wings, quadruple .5 in. M.G.s at the break of the fo'c'sle and a 3 in. A.A. gun on the quarterdeck. The funnel has been capped and an HF/DF lattice mast added aft. [P. A. Vicary

SLOOPS

FOLLOWING the introduction of steam and iron in the mid-nineteenth century, the sloop tended to diminish in importance and the steam version never quite achieved the same stature as its sailing counterpart. After its brief inclusion with the cruising list during this transitory period it emerged as a smaller vessel (**Fantome** class—1872: 920 tons), mainly for distant or detached service, and its construction lapsed in 1902 with the **Espiegle** class (1,070 tons).

It later reappeared during the First World War when the term sloop was applied to the **Flower** class (four of which survived to take part in the Second World War). Originally classed as *fleet minesweeping vessels* their usefulness outside this role, on escort and patrol duties, was soon apparent and they were loosely referred to as *sloops* from the time of this re-deployment. Of the many escort and patrol vessels built between 1914–18 only those over 1,000 tons (the various groups of the **Flower** class and the " **24** " class) were classed as sloops whilst those under this tonnage were either classed as gunboats (the **Kil** and " **P** " and " **PC** " classes) or descriptively described as paddle (**Ascot** class) or twin-screw (**Hunt** class) minesweepers.

Between the wars only the **Flower** (escort), " **P** " and " **PC** " (patrol) and **Hunt** (minesweeping) classes survived in yearly decreasing numbers until, in 1939, only four **Flower**, two " **PC** " and twenty-six **Hunt** remained together with two of the " **24** " class which had been completed as surveying vessels. From 1927 the **Flower** class, from 1931 the **Hunt** class and from 1933 the " **P** " and " **PC** " class started to be replaced by new construction which embraced, but improved on, their main characteristics. The term sloop was finally dropped in 1937 and the new vessels were classed as either *escort* or *patrol vessels* or *minesweepers*.

Some disappointment was expressed in that the new escort vessels were not built up to naval treaty limits of 2,000 tons, 20 knots and four 6 inch guns and doubts were expressed as to their ability to perform any but " flag showing " functions: criticisms which would have equally applied had they been built up to treaty limits but a point overlooked by their detractors. However, with a limited purse, the Admiralty commenced with a type of vessel that was relatively inexpensive and the combatant equal of the vessels they replaced. On a 1,000 tons they could steam 16 knots and were armed with two 4 inch A.A. guns. They were given a shallow draught as the original intention had been for them to fill the dual function of escort and minesweeping and to operate wire sweeps. As an anti-submarine (A/S) vessel they possessed the necessary qualities to combat contemporary submarines and there is no doubt that the Admiralty gauged the situation better than their critics. Each succeeding class was a little better armed, a little faster and, by 1937, the escort vessel had grown to a vessel of 1,250 tons with a speed of 18 knots and armed with eight 4 inch A.A. guns and equally able to protect trade from the assailant either above or below the waves. It never attempted to counter the marauding capital ship, aircraft carrier or cruiser which were commitments of the main fleets.

For coastal escort work smaller patrol vessels, which replaced the " **P** " and " **PC** " boats, had been evolved purely for A/S duties. Any intention to mass produce them in an emergency unfortunately proved impossible, owing to their turbine machinery for which there were quite insufficient blade-cutting facilities available.

The minesweepers were reduced editions of the first escort vessels and proved so ideal for their size that they were not enlarged upon, contrary to an accepted practice of evolution, and were capable of world-wide employment.

Thus, by 1939, sloops fell into three broad classes as below:—

(a) **Escort**—capable of ocean A/S and A.A. duties.

(b) **Patrol**—capable of coastal A/S duties.

(c) **Minesweeping**—capable of ocean and coastal M/S duties and could be pressed into performing either (a) or (b) above if so required.

ESCORTS—Ocean and Coastal

THE shortage of escorts was well realised before the outbreak of the Second World War and the following measures had been put in hand pre-war to meet it:—

(a) The ordering of twenty fast escort vessels.

(b) The ordering of fifty-six coastal escorts of the whale catcher type.

(c) The conversion of old destroyers for escort work (see Note 1).

(d) Continuing construction of the latest type of ocean escort (the **Black Swan** class).

The final outbreak of hostilities only greatly enlarged this programme. The *fast escort vessels* were, not inappropriately, classed as *escort destroyers* (see Note 1) and the *coastal escorts*, quite inappropriately, as *corvettes* (see Note 2). As a vote for twenty additional destroyers would not have passed Parliament pre-war they were put down in the Naval Estimates as fast escort vessels but by the time the first were completed, in 1940, there was no need to continue the deception. To achieve the requisite quantity production, the corvettes reverted to a plan which had been successfully adopted in the First World War with the **Flower** class sloops, and the affinity between these two, widespread classes was further strengthened by the corvettes also receiving " Flower " names. The scheme was mainly to place their construction in the hands of mercantile shipbuilders and to largely adopt mercantile practice in their design. A design submitted by Smith's Dock, Middlesbrough, adapted from their successful whale catcher SOUTHERN PRIDE, was accepted and the corvette put into quantity production. The design was purposely kept simple and the adoption of reciprocating machinery well suited the engine manufacturers. But the efficiency of coastal patrols, by ships and shore-based maritime aircraft, drove the German submarines further afield and coastal escort work soon became one of mainly providing cover against attacks by aircraft and fast surface vessels (" **E** " boats). The purely A/S corvette was now wholly utilised on ocean escort work, for which it had never been designed, and although an excellent sea-boat it was extremely lively in adverse conditions and too small for this purpose. Its design was modified to accept these new conditions—and it performed yeoman service in this role—but it was clearly recognised that to continue building these vessels for ocean work was akin to the proverbial effort of " putting a quart into a pint pot." Therefore a larger and faster design (the **River** class) was drawn up, which more closely embraced the Naval Staff's conception of an ocean escort vessel, and was put in hand as soon as existing corvette contracts were completed. They retained the well tried commercial machinery of the corvettes but had two sets for their twin screws and following the groundless precedent set by the corvettes were ultimately called *frigates*, although initially referred to as *twin-screw corvettes*.

Note 1: See Part 2 (Destroyers and Submarines) for details of these vessels.

Note 2: As the link between old sailing and modern steam counterparts is one of function and not of size a closer approximation to corvette was the modern light cruiser.

However, as some of the smaller shipbuilders could not accommodate the longer hull of the frigate an enlarged and improved type of corvette (the **Castle** class) were simultaneously embarked on to keep building capacity fully extended.

As the foreseeable future indicated an unrelenting demand for even more escort vessels, prefabricated frigates (the **Loch** class) were planned on mass production methods and, as soon as plans were finalised, no further **River** class were ordered and construction switched to the **Loch** class. As some areas were more exposed to air than submarine attack, a proportion of the **Loch** class were modified primarily as A.A. escorts (the **Bay** class) with limited A/S capabilities—the exact reverse of the **Loch** class—but both were built to the same basic design. Although the **Loch/Bay** class still retained the original corvette reciprocating machinery, it was found possible to engine a few units of them and the **River** class with turbine machinery. Had blade-cutting capacity been equal to the demand the installation of turbines would have been extended.

The war programmed corvettes and frigates provided the bulk of the Royal Navy's expanded escort force, but limited construction of the escort sloop was continued and design stabilised on the **Black Swan** class. Six were building (including two for the Royal Indian Navy) at the outbreak of war and a further seven (again including two for the Royal Indian Navy) were subsequently ordered. An additional twenty-nine (which again included a further pair for the Royal Indian Navy) was the sum total of further war orders. But turbine engined and fitted with all the refinements of warship construction, they could not be built rapidly enough for war purposes and the cessation of hostilities led to the cancellation of the last five.

Although it is a popular misconception that the most efficient escort vessels were destroyers they were, in fact, quite outclassed by sloops in this duty. The destroyer was built to defend its own line from, and similarly attack the enemy's line with, torpedoes. Defensively it required guns and a limited A/S capability, as opportunities for submarine attack on the battle line receded as its speed progressively increased. Offensively it required torpedoes and speed; the latter was expensively obtained as regards space and weight. Its low-angle guns were of no use against aircraft, its torpedoes no use against submarines, its speed was in excess of requirements (it was limited to about 20 knots when using its asdic) and it was not as seaworthy as the sloop. On a smaller displacement, the sloop provided better A.A. and A/S qualities which the destroyer could only match when its gun and torpedo armament had been mutilated out of all recognition, and it still carried a deadweight of high-powered machinery which it would seldom need. On purely economic grounds a greater number of smaller—but equally efficient—sloops could be built, for a given figure, than destroyers and to use the latter for escort work was wasteful in expenditure, although the urgent need to do so was unquestioned. The necessity to press destroyers into escort work, in the absence of a sufficient number of escort vessels, had other far-reaching consequences. The absence of destroyers denuded the main fleets of their A/S screen, without which they were unable to proceed to sea, and on many occasions the battle line was reduced to impotence until sufficient destroyers returned, or could be assembled, to enable it to be employed.

MINESWEEPERS

THE outbreak of war found the minesweeping flotillas of the Royal Navy heavily depleted. Available were the twenty-six **Hunt** class dating from the First World War and the new **Halcyon** class of twenty-one vessels. A total of seven from both classes had been converted to surveying duties but were available for minesweeping in an emergency. This meagre force was supplemented by the escort vessels up to, and including, the **Grimsby** class, which were fitted for minesweeping, and the majority of the destroyers of the "**A**" to "**I**" classes were able to operate high-speed sweeps. But the use of the latter was limited to sweeping ahead of the main fleets, as part of its screen when penetrating waters capable of being mined, and it was not contemplated that they would reinforce the minesweeping flotillas (see Note 3). Twenty minesweepers of the **Bangor** class were under construction, of which half had turbine machinery and the remainder either reciprocating (six vessels) or diesel (four vessels) engines and this diversity of main propulsion anticipated the alternatives which would have to be turned to in an emergency. The **Bangor** class were diminutives of the **Halcyon** class and were equally efficient as wire sweepers against contact mines, but the later war requirement to counter influence (magnetic and acoustic) mines, resulted in their becoming cramped for space and led to a reversion to the larger dimensions of the **Halcyon** class.

The outbreak of war greatly implemented the programme of construction of the **Bangor** class and reciprocating machinery was installed in most. For the reasons stated earlier the **Bangor** class were discontinued and construction started on the larger **Algerine** class and they proved to be most efficient vessels. Again, the greater proportion were reciprocating engined.

Both the **Bangor** and **Algerine** classes were used as escort vessels as the occasion demanded and some, indeed, never streamed a sweep but were permanently employed on this duty. The first twenty-four frigates of the **River** class were, conversely, fitted for minesweeping but were never used in this capacity. The greatest war augmentation of the minesweeping flotillas came from hired trawlers and drifters, plus some of the smaller commercial vessels, but they are outside the scope of this book.

MINELAYERS

ONLY the HASTINGS and the six Royal Navy vessels of the **Grimsby** class were adaptable for minelaying for which purpose they had to land their after gun but they were never so employed.

WAR CONSTRUCTION

REFERENCE to the class lists will show that the burden of war construction was equally shared by the United Kingdom and the Dominions. The constructive effort of Canada is most notable and during the course of the the war the Royal Canadian Navy advanced to the position of the premier Dominion navy, which it has not since relinquished.

Built in Canada were **Flower** class corvettes, **River** class frigates and **Bangor** and **Algerine** class minesweepers. Although scheduled to build **Castle** class corvettes as well, none were, in fact, laid down. Australia built **River** class frigates and a variant of the **Bangor** class minesweeper—the **Bathurst** class. These latter vessels

Note 3: The high-speed mine sweeps were replaced by depth charges with their racks and throwers and there is no record that they were ever called upon to use their minesweeping equipment.

were frequently employed as escort vessels and were thus locally referred to as corvettes. India undertook the construction of a few **Bangor** class minesweepers but the need to ship the machinery from the United Kingdom restricted their building activity. The tiny Crown Colony of Hong Kong also started on four **Bangor** class but the tide of events overtook them and they were lost incomplete to the enemy when Hong Kong was compelled to surrender.

With the exception of some ten Canadian built **Bangor** class minesweepers which were diesel-engined, the remainder of Dominion and Colonial war construction received reciprocating machinery. All turbine-engined vessels were built in the United Kingdom.

The United States made a considerable contribution to the escort and minesweeping forces of the Royal Navy and they are listed separately at the end. But even the United States Navy found itself embarrassed by the shortage of escorts shortly after they entered the war and ten **Flower** class corvettes were turned over to them by the Royal Navy to meet the immediate shortage followed by another eight of the modified **Flower** class. The United States Navy subsequently ordered seven modified **Flower** class corvettes, ten **River** class frigates and nine **Algerine** class minesweepers, but as their vast war construction programme was so soon in full swing they found no need to accept all these vessels and used them to meet their Lend/Lease commitments.

The United States undertook to build for the Royal Navy thirty-two minesweepers, thirty-two diesel-electric and forty-six turbo-electric destroyer escorts, twenty-one frigates modelled on the British **River** class, fifteen coastal escorts and transferred ten of the larger Coastguard cutters. They retained eleven of the minesweepers but made the number up by allocating to the Royal Navy the nine **Algerine** class building in Canada and a further two American built vessels. They only took delivery of two of the frigates building in Canada and made the remainder available to the Royal Navy. All these vessels, less those lost, were returned to the United States Navy at the end of the war except the HOTHAM but only three of the Coastguard cutters were re-incorporated. The HOTHAM was retained by the Royal Navy as a floating generating station at Singapore until 1948 and was ultimately scrapped in the United Kingdom. The United States similarly returned to the Royal Navy the eighteen corvettes loaned to them.

WAR MODIFICATIONS

WAR modifications to sloops were not extensive as their limited size restricted modifications which could be effected. Common additions to all vessels completed pre-war were air and surface warning R.D.F. and from two/four 20 mm. A.A. (2/4 × 1) guns, usually mounted in the wings of the bridge and aft at the break of the fo'c'sle deck.

Neither ABERDEEN or ENCHANTRESS, who both had their two after guns omitted to provide extra accommodation, shipped their designed armament and were the poorer in consequence. The STORK, designed to mount four 4.7 in. (4 × 1) guns like the ENCHANTRESS but completed as an unarmed surveying vessel, was re-armed with six 4 in. A.A. (3 × 2) like her other sister ship, the BITTERN. The four **Halcyon** class minesweepers completed as surveying vessels however were not re-armed to the same standard as the remainder of the class.

Those escort vessels fitted for minesweeping landed this gear and had the space utilised for additional depth charge stowage. The **Kingfisher** class patrol vessels had two 20 mm. A.A. (2 × 1) and four .5 in. A.A. (1 × 4) guns added aft as, up to this stage, they had been quite devoid of anti-aircraft fire! The last seven of the **Black Swan** class, and the modified class that followed, sacrificed the multiple 2 pdr. mounting on the quarterdeck and adopted six light anti-aircraft positions (to port and starboard in the bridge wings, amidships abreast the funnel and on the quarterdeck respectively) in which a variety of weapons were mounted, although intended to ship twin 20 mm. mountings in each of them.

Air warning R.D.F. was fitted at the masthead in all and sea warning R.D.F. on the bridge except in the STORK, and later escort vessels, which had an H.A. D.C.T. on the bridge and the sea warning set was consequently installed aft, on a short lattice mast. The later units of the modified **Black Swan** class introduced lattice foremasts which were able to support the weight of sea warning R.D.F. and it was again moved forward in these vessels.

Many modifications were carried out on the corvettes during the course of the war. Originally designed with a short fo'c'sle and a mast stepped before the bridge they embraced some, or all, of the following alterations:—

(a) Sea warning R.D.F. added abaft bridge.

(b) Fo'c'sle extended well aft.

(c) Mast re-stepped abaft bridge.

(d) Six 20 mm. A.A. (6 × 1) added in bridge wings and along the waist.

(e) An ahead throwing weapon (hedgehog) added forward on the gun platform.

The modified **Flower** class embraced all these additions and had the fo'c'sle gun raised on to a shelter deck and the bridge heightened a further deck. More flare and sheer was built into their hulls to improve sea-worthiness and watertube replaced earlier cylindrical boilers.

The **Castle** class corvettes were generally very similar and had a distinctive funnel cap (also fitted in later **Flower** class vessels) but none carried their designed armament and were four 20 mm. A.A. guns short. The shortage of light anti-aircraft guns was extended to the **River** class which, with a few exceptions, only received four of the designed ten 20 mm. guns. Some variation were made in a few Canadian built vessels of this type which had both the 4 in. guns in a twin A.A. mounting forward and an additional 3 in. A.A. gun added aft. The Australian built **River** class had their single 4 in. guns in A.A. mountings from the onset and altered these to twin mountings for the last three vessels completed. By the time the **Loch/Bay** were built the shortage of light anti-aircraft guns had largely been overcome and they were, practically without exception, armed as designed.

The small **Bangor** class minesweepers had, in effect, to make do with whatever light anti-aircraft guns were available and were usually fitted with either one 2 pdr. or four .5 in. (1 × 4) guns. Later, two 20 mm. A.A. (2 × 1) were added in the bridge wings of most. Both the **Bangor** and **Bathurst** classes were given either a 4 in. or 3 in. A.A. forward: the former was usually fitted if used for escort work and the latter if used for minesweeping but this by no means always applied. Most of the **Algerine** class were initially fitted with four 20 mm. A.A. (4 × 1) guns but these were changed to twin mountings as supplies became available.

PENNANT NUMBERS

AT the outbreak of the Second World War the following flag superiors were worn by the various classes of sloops:—

Escort vessels:	Flag L
Patrol vessels:	Flag L (*see Note 4*)
Minesweepers:	Flag N
Surveying vessels: (ex-sloops)	Flag J

The corvettes under construction were allocated flag M and the patrol vessels were similarly altered. In 1940, with the general re-allocation of flag superiors, the following changes occurred:—

Escort vessels:	to flag U	(*see Note 5*)
Patrol vessels and corvettes:	to flag K	(*see Note 6*)
Minesweepers:	to flag J	(*see Note 7*).

Subsequent war construction conformed with the above and the frigates, as they came into service, also received flag K. Exceptions were the ex-American Coastguard cutters which were given flag Y and the coastal escorts of the **Kil** class which received flag 5.

After the war escort destroyers, escort vessels, corvettes and frigates were all classified as *frigates* and changed to flag F, minesweepers to flag M and surveying vessels to flag A. This involved a certain amount of re-numbering amongst existing vessels but was largely limited to adding, or subtracting, 100, 200, etc. from their original numbers.

ESCORT SLOOPS

Flower class

Displacement: 1,175 tons except FOXGLOVE 1,165 tons.
Dimensions: 255¼ (pp) 267¾ (oa) × 33½ × 11 ft. except FOXGLOVE 250 (pp) 262½ (oa) × 33 × 11 ft.
Machinery: 1-shaft reciprocating (V.T.E.), I.H.P. 2,000 except FOXGLOVE 1,800 = 16 knots.
Armament: 2—4 in. (2 × 1) guns. *Complement:* 100.

P. No.	Name	Builder	Launched	Fate
L.26	FOXGLOVE	Barclay Curle	30. 3.15	Constructive total loss 9/7/40; accommodation ship; scrapped Troon 10/46.
L.19	LUPIN	Simons	31. 5.16	Lost 22/3/46, salved and scrapped Portchester 1947.
L.14	ROSEMARY	Richardson Duck: Blair	22.11.15	Scrapped Milford Haven 17/12/47.

Note 4: They had previously borne flag P.
Note 5: The FLEETWOOD retained flag L.
Note 6: Except PC.74 which was allocated flag Z.
Note 7: The R.A.N. ARARAT received flag K.

Above: H.M.S. Lupin was one of the few surviving **Flower** class sloops of World War I and the only one converted to oil firing. [*P. A. Vicary*

Below: H.M.S. Bridgewater initiated the new sloop programme " between the wars ". [*P. A. Vicary*

Displacement: 1,383 tons.
Dimensions: 255¼ (pp) 277¾ (oa) × 35 × 14½ ft.
Machinery: 1-shaft Reciprocating (V.T.E.), I.H.P. 2,500 = 16½ knots.
Armament: 3—4 in. (3 × 1) guns. *Complement:* 119.

L.09	CORNWALLIS (R.I.N.) (ex-Lynchis)	Hamilton	21. 8.17	Scrapped 1946.

Notes: Mercantile PANSY (name unchanged) was requisitioned by the R.I.N. in 1939 and CORNFLOWER (lost 15/12/41) still existed as a base ship at Hong Kong and LABURNUM (lost 2/42) at Singapore.

"24" class

Displacement: 1,320 tons.
Dimensions: 255 (pp) 276½ (oa) × 35 × 12 ft.
Machinery: 1-shaft Reciprocating (V.T.E.), I.H.P. 2,500 = 17 knots.
Armament: Nil.

T.73	HERALD (ex-Merry Hampton)	Blyth Sbdg.	19.12.18	Lost 2/42; salved and I.J.N. HEIYO (1942); lost 14/11/44.
J.54	MORESBY (R.A.N.) (ex-Silvio)	Barclay Curle	20. 4.18	Scrapped Newcastle (N.S.W.) 3/2/47.

Displacement: 1,210 tons.
Dimensions: 225 (pp) 241½ (oa) × 34 × 12 ft.
Machinery: 2-shaft geared Turbines, S.H.P. 1,900 = 15 knots.
Armament: 2—4 in. (2 × 1) guns. *Complement:* 119.

L.83	LAWRENCE (R.I.N.)	Beardmore	30. 7.19	Scrapped 1947.

Displacement: 1,748 tons.
Dimensions: 240 (pp) 262½ (oa) × 38½ × 14 ft.
Machinery: 2-shaft geared Turbines, S.H.P. 2,000 = 14½ knots.
Armament: 2—4 in. (2 × 1) guns. *Complement:* 119.

L.79	CLIVE (R.I.N.)	Beardmore	10.12.19	Scrapped 1947.

Bridgewater, Hastings, Shoreham and Falmouth classes

Displacement: 1,045 tons except **Falmouth** class 1,060 tons, **Shoreham** class 1,105 tons and HINDUSTAN 1,190 tons.
Dimensions: 250 (pp) 266 (oa) × 34 × 8¼ except **Falmouth** class 8¾ and **Shoreham** class 9 ft. HINDUSTAN 280 (pp) 296½ (oa) × 35 × 8¾ ft.

Machinery: 2-shaft geared Turbines, S.H.P. 2,000 = 16 except HINDUSTAN $16\frac{1}{2}$ knots.

Armament: 2—4 in. A.A. (2 × 1), 4—.5 in. A.A. (1 × 4) guns.

Complement: 100 except HINDUSTAN 119.

L.01	BRIDGEWATER	Hawthorn Leslie	14. 9.28	Scrapped Gelleswick Bay 22/5/47.
L.12	SANDWICH	Hawthorn Leslie	28. 9.28	Mercantile (1946).
L.22	FOLKESTONE	Swan Hunter: Hawthorn Leslie	12. 2.30	Scrapped Gelleswick Bay 22/5/47.
L.27	HASTINGS	Devonport	10. 4.30	Scrapped Troon 2/4/46.
L.28	PENZANCE	Devonport	10. 4.30	Lost 24/8/40.
L.25	SCARBOROUGH	Swan Hunter: Hawthorn Leslie	14. 3.30	Scrapped Thornaby 3/7/49.
L.80	HINDUSTAN (R.I.N.)	Swan Hunter: Hawthorn Leslie	12. 5.30	R.P.N. KARSAZ (1948), hulked 1948; scrapped 1951.
L.43	BIDEFORD	Devonport: White*	1. 4.31	Scrapped Milford Haven 14/7/49.
L.15	FOWEY	Devonport: White*	4.11.30	Mercantile FOWLOCK (1946); scrapped Mombasa 1950.
L.50	ROCHESTER	Chatham: White*	16. 7.31	Scrapped Dunston 6/1/51.
L.32	SHOREHAM	Chatham: White*	22.11.30	Mercantile JORGE FEL JOVEN (1946); scrapped Boom 11/50.
L.84	DUNDEE	Chatham: Hawthorn Leslie	20. 9.32	Lost 15/9/40.
L.34	FALMOUTH	Devonport: Hawthorn Leslie	19. 4.32	R.N.V.R. CALLIOPE (Tyne—1952); for disposal.
L.51	MILFORD	Devonport: Yarrow	11. 6.32	Scrapped Hayle 3/6/49.
L.72	WESTON (ex-Weston-Super-Mare)	Devonport: Yarrow	23. 7.32	Scrapped Gelleswick Bay 22/5/47.

* Part contract with hull builder

Notes.—FOLKESTONE and SCARBOROUGH had been converted to surveying vessels but were re-armed as escort vessels in 1939. Two further vessels of the **Shoreham** class, projected under the 1930 Estimates, were cancelled. Until scrapped ROCHESTER was used as a tender to the Navigation school and was disarmed.

Grimsby class

Displacement: 990 tons except R.A.N. vessels, 1,060 tons and INDUS 1,190 tons.

Dimensions: 250 (pp) 266 (oa) × 36 × 7½ ft. except INDUS 280 (pp) 296½ (oa) × 35½ × 8¾ ft.

Machinery: 2-shaft geared Turbines, S.H.P. 2,000 = 16½ knots.

Armament: First and second groups 2—4.7 in. (2 × 1), 1—3 in. A.A. (not in second group), 4—.5 in. A.A. (1 × 4) guns. Third group 3—4 in. A.A. (3 × 1 first pair, 1 × 2 and 1 × 1 second pair), 4—.5 in. A.A. (second pair only) guns. Fourth group 4—4 in. A.A. (4 × 1 ABERDEEN, 2 × 2 FLEETWOOD), 4—.5 in. A.A. (1 × 4 FLEETWOOD only) guns.

Complement: 100 except INDUS 119.

L.16	GRIMSBY	Devonport: White	19. 7.33	Lost 25/5/41.
L.36	LEITH	Devonport: White	9. 9.33	Mercantile BYRON (1946), FRIENDSHIP (1948), R.D.N. GALATHEA (1949); scrapped 1955.
L.59	LOWESTOFT	Devonport: White	11. 4.34	Mercantile MIRAFLO-RES (1946); scrapped Belgium 5/8/55.
L.65	WELLINGTON	Devonport: White	29. 5.34	Headquarters ship of Honourable Company of Master Mariners (1947).
L.53	DEPTFORD	Chatham: White	5. 2.35	Scrapped Milford Haven 8/3/48.
L.76	LONDONDERRY	Devonport: White	16. 1.35	Scrapped Llanelly 8/6/48.
L.67	INDUS (R.I.N.)	Hawthorn Leslie	24. 8.34	Lost 6/4/42.
L.77	YARRA (R.A.N.)	Cockatoo	28. 3.35	Lost 4/3/42.
L.74	SWAN (R.A.N.)	Cockatoo	28. 3.36	
L.44	PARRAMATTA (R.A.N.)	Cockatoo	18. 6.39	Lost 28/11/41.
L.73	WARREGO (R.A.N.)	Cockatoo	10. 2.40	
L.97	ABERDEEN	Devonport: Thornycroft	22. 1.36	Scrapped Hayle 18/1/49.
L.47	FLEETWOOD	Devonport: Thornycroft	24. 3.36	Scrapped Gateshead 10/10/59.

Notes.—R.A.N. SWAN was converted to a Cadets Training ship and R.A.N. WARREGO to a surveying vessel post war. FLEETWOOD was disarmed and used as an R.D.F. experimental ship, attached to the Signal school, after the end of the war.

Bittern class

Displacement: 1,190 tons.
Dimensions: 266 (pp) 282 (oa) × 37 × 8½ ft.
Machinery: 2-shaft geared Turbines, S.H.P. 3,300 = 18¾ knots.
Armament: 4—4.7 in. (4 × 1) except BITTERN 6—4 in. A.A. (3 × 2), 4—.5 in. A.A. (1 × 4) guns.
Complement: 125.

L.56	ENCHANTRESS (ex-Bittern)	Clydebank	21.12.34	Mercantile LADY ENCHANTRESS (1947); scrapped Dunston 2/52.
L.81	STORK	Denny	21. 4.36	Scrapped Troon 3/6/58.
L.07	BITTERN	White	14. 7.37	Lost 30/4/40.

Notes.—STORK was completed as a surveying vessel but was re-armed as an escort vessel in 1939.

Egret class

Displacement: 1,200 tons.
Dimensions: 276 (pp) 292½ (oa) × 37½ × 8¼ ft.
Machinery: 2-shaft geared Turbines S.H.P. 3,600 = 19¼ knots.
Armament: 8—4 in. A.A. (4 × 2), 4—.5 in. A.A. (1 × 4) guns.
Complement: 188.

L.75	EGRET	White	31. 5.38	Lost 27/8/43.
L.61	AUCKLAND (ex-Heron)	Denny	30. 6.38	Lost 24/6/41.
L.86	PELICAN	Thornycroft	12. 9.38	Scrapped Preston 29/11/58.

Black Swan class

Displacement: 1,250 tons (first six), 1,300 tons (others).
Dimensions: 283 (pp) 299½ (oa) × 37½ × 8½ ft.
Machinery: 2-shaft geared Turbines, S.H.P. 3,600 = 19¼ knots.
Armament: 6—4 in. A.A. (3 × 2), 4—2 pdr. A.A. (1 × 4—not in R.I.N. vessels) and 4—.5 in. A.A. (1 × 4) (first six) or 12—20 mm. A.A. (6 × 2—others) guns.
Complement: 180 except R.I.N. vessels 195.

L.57	BLACK SWAN	Yarrow	7. 7.39	Scrapped Troon 13/9/56.
L.18	FLAMINGO	Yarrow	18. 4.39	W. German GRAF SPEE (1958).
U.03	ERNE	Furness: Richardson Westgarth	5. 8.40	R.N.V.R. WESSEX (Solent—1952).
U.99	IBIS	Furness: Richardson Westgarth	28.11.40	Lost 10/11/42.

H.M.S. Penzance shows the two features common to the earlier sloops—a windlass on the fo'c'sle and a powerful M/S winch aft. [*P. A. Vicary*

H.M.S. Lowestoft, **Grimsby** class, reverted to L.A. guns for the main armament and introduced the forward shelter deck for the H.A. gun. [*P. A. Vicary*

H.M.S. Stork, designed as a sister ship to H.M.S. Enchantress, was completed as a disarmed surveying vessel but when re-armed adopted the armament of her sister ship H.M.S. Bittern. In this illustration, taken at the end of the war, can be seen the lattice foremast, the mainmast struck, " B " mounting replaced by an A.T.W. (Hedgehog) and four single 20 mm. A.A. guns. [*P. A. Vicary*

Above: H.M.S. Bittern as completed. Note light pre-war masting, pole foremast and a tripod mainmast to eliminate shrouds, which would have masked " X " mounting's arcs of fire.

Below: H.M.S. Pelican was developed from H.M.S. Bittern and had a further twin 4 in. A.A. mounting added on the quarterdeck. [*P. A. Vicary*

U.21	JUMNA (R.I.N.)	Denny	16.11.40	
U.95	SUTLEJ (R.I.N.)	Denny	1.10.40	

U.29	WHIMBREL	Yarrow	25. 8.42	Egyptian EL MALEK FAROUQ (1949), TARIK (1954).
U.45	WILD GOOSE	Yarrow	14.10.42	Scrapped Bo'ness 27/2/56.
U.90	WOODCOCK	Fairfield	26.11.42	Scrapped Rosyth 28/11/55.
U.08	WOODPECKER	Denny	29. 6.42	Lost 27/2/44.
U.28	WREN	Denny	11. 8.42	Scrapped Rosyth 2/2/56.
U.52	GODAVARI (R.I.N.)	Thornycroft	21. 1.43	R.P.N. SIND (1948).
U.40	NARBADA (R.I.N.)	Thornycroft	21.11.42	R.P.N. JHELUM (1948); scrapped 15/7/59.

Notes.—R.I.N. SUTLEJ was disarmed and converted to a surveying vessel after the war.

Modified Black Swan class

Displacement: 1,350 tons.
Dimensions: 283 (pp) 299½ (oa) × 38½ × 8¾ ft.
Machinery: 2-shaft geared Turbines, S.H.P. 4,300 = 20 knots.
Armament: 6—4 in. A.A. (3 × 2), 12—20 mm. A.A. (6 × 2) guns.
Complement: 192 except R.I.N. vessels 219.

U.07	ACTAEON	Thornycroft	25. 7.45	W. German HIPPER (1958).
U.60	ALACRITY	Denny	1. 9.44	Scrapped Dalmuir 15/9/56 and Troon (hull only) 3/11/56.
U.16	AMETHYST	Stephen	7. 5.43	Scrapped Plymouth 18/1/57.
U.05	CHANTICLEER	Denny	24. 9.42	Constructive total loss 18/11/43; hulked LUSITANIA (1943); scrapped Lisbon 1946/7.
U.23	CRANE	Denny	9.11.42	For disposal.
U.38	CYGNET	Cammell Laird	28. 7.42	Scrapped Rosyth 16/3/56.
U.58	HART	Stephen	7. 7.43	W. German SCHEER (1958).
U.39	HIND	Denny	30. 9.43	Scrapped Dunston 10/12/58.
U.87	KITE	Cammell Laird	13.10.42	Lost 21/8/44.
U.62	LAPWING	Scotts	16. 7.43	Lost 20/3/44.
U.11	LARK	Scotts	28. 8.43	Constructive total loss 7/2/45; Russian NEPTUN (1945); scrapped 1956.
U.82	MAGPIE	Thornycroft	24. 3.43	Scrapped Blyth 12/7/59.
U.30	MERMAID	Denny	11.11.43	W. German SCHARNHORST (1958).

U.42	MODESTE	Chatham: Yarrow	29. 1.44	Scrapped St. Davids-on-Forth 11/3/61.
U.64	NEREIDE	Chatham: Yarrow	29. 1.44	Scrapped Bo'ness 18/5/58.
U.54	NONSUCH	Chatham		Cancelled 1945.
U.84	NYMPHE	Chatham		Cancelled 1945.
U.33	OPOSSUM	Denny	30.11.44	Scrapped Plymouth 26/4/60.
U.37	PARTRIDGE	Thornycroft		Cancelled 1945.
U.96	PEACOCK	Thornycroft	11.12.43	Scrapped Rosyth 7/5/58.
U.49	PHEASANT	Yarrow	21.12.42	Scrapped Troon 1/61.
U.69	REDPOLE	Yarrow	25. 2.43	Scrapped St. Davids-on-Forth 20/11/60.
U.20	SNIPE	Denny	20.12.45	Scrapped Newport 23/8/60.
U.71	SPARROW	Denny	18. 2.46	Scrapped Rosyth 26/5/58.
U.66	STARLING	Fairfield	14.10.42	For disposal.
U.05	WATERHEN	Denny		Cancelled 2/11/45.
U.31	WRYNECK	Denny		Cancelled 2/11/45.
U.10	CAUVERY (R.I.N.)	Yarrow	15. 6.43	
U.46	KISTNA (R.I.N.)	Yarrow	22. 4.43	

Notes.—REDPOLE and STARLING were disarmed and replaced SCARBOROUGH as tenders to the Navigation school.

MINESWEEPING SLOOPS

Hunt class

Displacement: 710 tons except TEDWORTH 675 tons.
Dimensions: 220 (pp) 231 (oa) × 28½ except TEDWORTH 28 × 7½ ft.
Machinery: 2-shaft Reciprocating (V.T.E.), I.H.P. 2,200 except TEDWORTH 1,800 = 16 knots.
Armament: 1—4 in., 1—3 in. A.A. guns. *Complement:* 73.

N.32	TEDWORTH	Simons	20. 6.17	Scrapped Hayle 11/46.
N.49	ABERDARE	Ailsa	29. 4.18	Sold Belgium for mercantile use 13/3/47.
N.23	ABINGDON	Ailsa: Clark	11. 6.18	Constructive total loss 5/4/42 and scrapped Malta 1950.
N.41	ALBURY	Ailsa	21.11.18	Sold Belgium for mercantile use 13/3/47.
N.06	ALRESFORD	Ailsa: Allen	17. 1.19	Sold Belgium for mercantile use 13/3/47.
N.57	BAGSHOT	Ardrossan: Allen	5.18	MEDWAY II (1945); lost 1/9/51.
N.90	DERBY (ex-Dawlish)	Clyde Sbdg.	8.18	Scrapped Spain 4/7/45.
N.60	DUNDALK	Clyde Sbdg.	30. 1.19	Lost 17/10/40.

Above: H.M.S. Pelican as completed, showing the additional mounting on the quarterdeck which was later replaced by a quadruple 2 pounder.

Below: H.M.S. Sparrow at the end of the war showing the many war modifications adopted from the basic **Black Swan** design. [*P. A. Vicary*

N.52	DUNOON	Clyde Sbdg.	3.19	Lost 30/4/40.
N.39	ELGIN (ex-Troon)	Simons	3. 3.19	Constructive total loss 3/5/54; scrapped Gateshead 20/3/45.
N.89	FAREHAM	Dunlop Bremner	6.18	Hulked (1944); scrapped Hayle 9/48.
N.40	FERMOY	Dundee Sbdg.: Cooper & Greig	5. 2.19	Constructive total loss 30/4/41; scrapped 4/5/41.
N.61	HARROW	Eltringhams: Wallsend	7.18	Scrapped Italy 1950.
N.56	HUNTLEY (ex-Helmsdale)	Eltringhams	1.19	Lost 31/1/41.
N.44	LYDD (ex-Lydney)	Fairfield	4.12.18	Sold Belgium for mercantile use 13/3/47.
N.37	PANGBOURNE (ex-Padstow)	Lobnitz	26. 3.18	
J.03	FITZROY (ex-Pinner, ex-Portreath)	Lobnitz	15. 4.19	Lost 27/5/42.
J.04	FLINDERS (ex-Radley)	Lobnitz	27. 8.19	Scrapped Hayle 1946.
N.45	ROSS (ex-Ramsey)	Lobnitz	12. 6.19	Sold Belgium for commercial use 13/3/47.
N.62	SALTASH	Murdock & Murray: Yarrow	7.18	
N.58	SALTBURN	Murdock & Murray: Yarrow	10.18	Scrapped Bude 1948.
N.18	SELKIRK	Murdock & Murray: Rowan	12.18	Scrapped 1947/8.
N.33	STOKE (ex-Southwold)	Rennoldson: Shields Eng.	8. 7.18	Lost 7/5/41.
N.78	SUTTON (ex-Salcombe)	McMillan: Yarrow	5.18	Scrapped 1947/8.
J.05	KELLETT (ex-Uppinham)	Simons	31. 5.19	Scrapped Wear 1945.
N.55	WIDNES (ex-Withernsea)	Napier & Miller: Rowan	6.18	Lost 20/5/41, salved German U.J. 2109; lost 1943.

Halcyon class

Displacement: 815 tons (first seven), 835 tons (next nine), 875 tons (last five).

Dimensions: 230 (pp) 245 (oa) × 33½ × 6¾ (first seven), 7¼ (next nine), 8 (last five) ft.

Machinery: 2-shaft Reciprocating (V.C. in first five, V.T.E. in next pair), I.H.P. 1,770 (first five) 2,000 (next pair) = 16½/17 knots. Geared Turbines in others, S.H.P. 1,750 = 17 knots.

Above: H.M.S. Dunoon belonged to the coal fired **Hunt** class of minesweeper of World War I
[*P. A. Vicary*

Below: H.M.S. Harrier belonged to the initial group of the **Halcyon** class, was reciprocating engined and had a 4 in. A.A. gun forward and a 4 in. L.A. gun aft.
[*P. A. Vicary*

Armament: 1—4 in., 1—4 in. A.A. (first seven), 2—4 in. A.A. (2 × 1), 4—.5 in. A.A. (1 × 4) in others. *Complement:* 80.

N.42	HALCYON	Clydebank	20.12.33	Scrapped Milford Haven 19/4/50.
N.38	SKIPJACK	Clydebank	18. 1.34	Lost 1/6/40.
N.71	HARRIER	Thornycroft	17. 4.34	Scrapped Gateshead 6/6/50.
N.82	HUSSAR	Thornycroft	27. 8.34	Lost 27/8/44.
N.87	SPEEDWELL	Hamilton: Beardmore	21. 3.35	Mercantile TOPAZ (1946); wrecked 11/5/54 en-route Dutch shipbreakers, and scrapped Dordrecht.
N.73	NIGER	White	29. 1.36	Lost 5/7/42.
N.86	SALAMANDER	White	24. 3.36	Constructive total loss 27/8/44; scrapped Blyth 7/5/47.
N.83	GLEANER	Grays: Cen. Marine	10. 6.37	Scrapped Grays 14/11/50.
N.02	HAZARD	Grays: Cen. Marine	26. 2.37	Scrapped Grays 22/4/49.
N.24	HEBE	Devonport: ?	28.10.36	Lost 22/11/43.
N.68	SHARPSHOOTER	Devonport: ?	10.12.36	SHACKLETON (1953).
N.84	FRANKLIN	Ailsa: Thornycroft	22.12.37	Scrapped Dunston 1955/6.
N.63	GOSSAMER	Hamilton: Stephen	5.10.37	Lost 24/6/42.
N.99	JASON	Ailsa: Thornycroft	6.10.37	Mercantile JASLOCK (1946); scrapped Grays 1950.
N.93	LEDA	Devonport: Richardson Westgarth	8. 6.37	Lost 20/9/42.
N.85	SEAGULL	Devonport: Richardson Westgarth	28.10.37	R.N.V.R. Drillship (Leith—1955); scrapped Plymouth 5/56.
N.11	BRAMBLE	Devonport: Barclay Curle	12. 7.38	Lost 31/12/42.
N.22	BRITOMART	Devonport: Barclay Curle	23. 8.38	Lost 27/8/44.
N.79	SCOTT	Caledon: Parsons	23. 8.38	
N.17	SPEEDY	Hamilton: White	23.11.38	Mercantile SPEEDON (1946); scrapped Aden 1957.
N.69	SPHINX	Hamilton: White	7. 2.39	Lost 3/2/40.

Notes.—GLEANER, FRANKLIN, GOSSAMER, JASON and SCOTT were completed as surveying vessels but were converted back into minesweepers in 1939. At the close of the war FRANKLIN and SCOTT reverted to surveying vessels and SHARPSHOOTER and SEAGULL were similarly adapted.

H.M.S. Sharpshooter as modified for war service with the mainmast struck, SW. RDF added on the bridge, after 4 in. A.A. gun replaced by two single 20 mm. guns and twin M.G.s and a further pair of 20 mm. guns added in the bridge wings. [P. A. Vicary

H.M.S. Leda belonged to the later group of the **Halcyon** class which were turbine engined and had 4 in. A.A. guns forward and aft and a quadruple .5 in. A.A. M.G. mounting amidships. [P. A. Vicary

H.M.S. Seagull was the first all-welded vessel completed for the Royal Navy. [P. A. Vicary

Bangor class

(Diesel-engined)

Displacement: 590 tons.
Dimensions: 153½ (pp) 162 (oa) × 28 × 8¼ ft.
Machinery: 2-shaft Diesel motors, B.H.P. 2,000 = 16 knots.
Armament: 1—3 in. A.A., 4—.5 in. A.A. (1 × 4—British built) or .303 in. A.A. (2 × 2—Canadian built) guns.
Complement: 60.

J.00	BANGOR	Harland & Wolff	23. 5.40	R.N.N. GLOMMA (1946).
J.27	BLACKPOOL	Harland & Wolff	4. 7.40	R.N.N. JANA (1946).
J.65	BRIDLINGTON	Denny: Harland & Wolff	29. 2.40	R.A.F. (name not changed—1946); scrapped Plymouth 6/5/58.
J.50	BRIDPORT	Denny: Harland & Wolff	29. 2.40	R.A.F. CAWLEY (1946); scrapped Plymouth 6/5/58.
J.270	BROCKVILLE	Marine Industries	20. 6.41	R.C.M.P. MACLEOD (1950), re-acquired R.C.N. (1951); scrapped 1961.
J.267	DIGBY	Davie Sbdg.	5. 6.42	R.C.M.P. PERRY (1950); re-acquired R.C.N. (1951).
J.272	ESQUIMALT	Marine Industries	8. 8.41	Lost 16/4/45.
J.264	GRANBY	Davie Sbdg.	9. 6.41	R.C.M.P. COLONEL WHITE (1950), re-acquired R.C.N. (1951) scrapped 1961.
J.266	LACHINE	Davie Sbdg.	14. 6.41	R.C.M.P. STARNES (1950); mercantile JACKS BAY (1952).
J.263	MELVILLE	Davie Sbdg.	7. 6.41	R.C.M.P. CYGNUS (1950); scrapped 1961.
J.265	NORANDA	Davie Sbdg.	13. 6.41	R.C.M.P. IRVINE (1950); scrapped 1961.
J.271	TRANSCONA	Marine Industries	26. 4.41	R.C.M.P. FRENCH (1950); scrapped 1961.
J.269	TROIS RIVIERES	Marine Industries	30. 6.41	R.C.M.P. MACBRIEN (1950); scrapped 1959.
J.268	TRURO	Davie Sbdg.	5. 6.42	R.C.M.P. HERCHMER (1950), mercantile GULF MARINER (1952).

Notes.—The nine surviving R.C.N. vessels were all provisionally turned over to the R.C.M.P. (Marine section) but BROCKVILLE, DIGBY and GRANBY were subsequently re-acquired by the R.C.N. and were initially converted to coastal escort vessels and LACHINE and TRURO were disposed of commercially by the R.C.M.P.

Bangor class

(Reciprocating-engined)

Displacement: 672 tons.
Dimensions: 171½ (pp) 180 (oa) × 28½ × 8¼ ft.
Machinery: 2-shaft Reciprocating (V.T.E.), I.H.P. 2,400 = 16 knots.
Armament: 1—3 in. A.A. (R.N. vessels) or 4 in. (R.C.N. vessels), 1—2 pdr. A.A. or 4—.5 in. A.A. (1 × 4), 4—.303 in. A.A. (2 × 2) guns. R.I.N. vessels, 1—3 in. A.A., 3—20 mm. A.A. (3 × 1) guns.
Complement: 60 (R.N. vessels), 70 (R.C.N. vessels), 87 (R.I.N. vessels).

J.15	BLYTH	Blyth: Whites M.E.	2. 9.40	Mercantile RADBOURNE (1949); conversion never completed and scrapped.
J.116	BUDE	Lobnitz	4. 9.40	Egyptian NASR (1946).
J.200	CLYDEBANK	Lobnitz	20.11.41	R.I.N. ORISSA (1942); scrapped 1949.
J.128	CROMER	Lobnitz	7.10.40	Lost 9/11/42.
J.127	EASTBOURNE	Lobnitz	5.11.40	Scrapped Dunston 10/48.
J.126	FELIXSTOWE	Lobnitz	15. 1.41	Lost 18/12/43.
J.124	FRASERBURGH	Lobnitz	12. 5.41	Scrapped Thornaby 3/1/48.
J.197	LYME REGIS (i)	Lobnitz	31.12.41	R.I.N. RAJPUTANA (1942); scrapped 1961.
J.59	PETERHEAD	Blyth: Whites M.E.	31.10.40	Constructive total loss 8/6/44 but later salved; scrapped 5/48.
J.36	RHYL	Lobnitz	21. 6.40	Scrapped Gateshead 10/48.
J.77	ROMNEY	Lobnitz	3. 8.40	Scrapped Granton 2/50.
J.123	SEAHAM	Lobnitz	16. 6.41	Mercantile (name not changed—1947).
J.47	SIDMOUTH	Robb: Plenty	15. 3.41	Scrapped Charlestown 18/1/50.
J.31	STORNOWAY	Robb: Plenty	10. 6.41	Egyptian MATRUH (1946).
J.228	TILBURY	Lobnitz	18. 2.42	R.I.N. KONKAN (1942).
J.208	LANTAN (ex-Beaulieu)	Hongkong & Whampoa	. 12.41	Mercantile GYOSEI MARU (1943), KAGO. SHIMA MARU (1943)-
J.209	LYEMUN (ex-Looe)	Hongkong & Whampoa	.42	Japanese NANYO (1943); lost 23/12/43.
J.210	TAITAM (ex-Portland)	Taikoo	20. 2.43	Japanese M/S No. 101 (1944); lost 10/3/45.
J.211	WAGLAN (ex-Seaford)	Taikoo	20. 3.43	Japanese M/S No. 102 (1944); R.N. (1947); scrapped Urago 1948.
J.247	BIHAR (R.I.N.)	Garden Reach	7. 7.42	Scrapped 1949.

H.M.S. Bridport was a British built diesel engined minesweeper of the **Bangor** class. [*P. A. Vicary*

H.M.S. Eastbourne was a British built reciprocating engined minesweeper of the **Bangor** class. [*P. A. Vicary*

H.M.S. Seaham stripped of M/S gear and fitted as a fleet tug. [*P. A. Vicary*

J.129	DECCAN (R.I.N.)	Garden Reach	24. 4.44	Scrapped 1949.
J.55	MALWA (R.I.N.)	Garden Reach	21. 6.44	R.P.N. PESHAWAR (1948); sold 22/1/59.
J.245	OUDH (R.I.N.)	Garden Reach	3. 3.42	R.P.N. DACCA (1948); sold 22/1/59.
		(all engined Lobnitz)		
J.08	BAYFIELD	Port Arthur*	26. 5.41	R.C.N. (1941–45); scrapped Gateshead 1/1/48.
J.170	BELLECHASSE (R.C.N.)	Burrard	20.10.41	For disposal 24/10/45.
J.314	BLAIRMORE (R.C.N.)	Port Arthur*	14. 5.42	Turkish BEYCOZ (1958).
J.250	BURLINGTON (R.C.N.)	Dufferin†	23.11.40	For disposal 3/4/46.
J.21	CANSO	North Vancouver*	9. 6.41	R.C.N. (1942–45); scrapped Sunderland 1/1/48.
J.38	CARAQUET	North Vancouver*	2. 6.41	R.C.N. (1942–45); Portuguese ALMIRANTE LACERDA (1946).
J.168	CHEDABUCTO (R.C.N.)	Burrard	14. 4.40	Lost 21/10/43.
J.160	CHIGNECTO (R.C.N.)	North Vancouver*	12.12.40	Scrapped 1957.
J.174	CLAYOQUOT (R.C.N.)	Prince Rupert	3.10.40	Lost 24/12/44.
J.262	COURTENAY (R.C.N.)	Prince Rupert	2. 8.41	For disposal 3/4/46.
J.146	COWICHAN (R.C.N.)	North Vancouver*	9. 8.40	Mercantile (name not changed—1950/1)?
J.253	DRUMMONDVILLE (R.C.N.)	Canadian Vickers	21. 5.41	Mercantile FORT ALBANY (1960).
J.311	FORT WILLIAM (R.C.N.)	Port Arthur*	30.12.41	Turkish BODRUM (1957).
J.259	GANANOQUE (R.C.N.)	Dufferin†	23. 4.41	For disposal 1959.
J.144	GEORGIAN (R.C.N.)	Dufferin†	28. 1.41	For disposal 3/4/46.
J.260	GODERICH (R.C.N.)	Dufferin†	14. 5.41	For disposal 1959.
J.258	GRANDMERE (R.C.N.)	Canadian Vickers	21. 8.41	Mercantile (name not changed—1947), ELDA (1950).
J.52	GUYSBOROUGH	North Vancouver*	21. 7.41	R.C.N. (1942); lost 17/3/45.
J.69	INGONISH	North Vancouver*	30. 7.41	R.C.N. (1943–45); scrapped Dunston 1/1/48.
J.261	KELOWNA (R.C.N.)	Prince Rupert	28. 5.41	Mercantile CONDOR (1950), HUNG HSIN (1950).

J.281	KENORA (R.C.N.)	Port Arthur*	5. 8.42	Turkish BANDIRMA (1957).
J.312	KENTVILLE (R.C.N.)	Port Arthur*	17. 4.42	Turkish BARTIN (1957).
J.100	LOCKEPORT	North Vancouver*	22. 8.41	R.C.N. (1942-45); for disposal.
J.159	MAHONE (R.C.N.)	North Vancouver*	14.11.40	Turkish BEYLERBEYI (1958).
J.148	MALPEQUE (R.C.N.)	North Vancouver*	5. 9.40	For disposal 1959.
J.256	MEDICINE HAT (R.C.N.)	Canadian Vickers	25. 6.41	Turkish BIGA (1957).
J.119	FORT YORK (ex-Mignan)	Dufferin†	24. 8.41	Portuguese COMANDATE ALMEIDA CARVALHO (1950).
J.317	MILLTOWN (R.C.N.)	Port Arthur*	5. 8.42	For disposal 1959.
J.165	MINAS (R.C.N.)	Burrard	23. 1.41	Scrapped Seattle 20/8/59.
J.169	MIRAMICHI (R.C.N.)	Burrard	2. 9.41	Scrapped Vancouver 1949.
J.313	MULGRAVE (R.C.N.)	Port Arthur*	2. 5.42	Constructive total loss 8/10/44; scrapped Llanelly 1947.
J.154	NIPIGON (R.C.N.)	Dufferin†	1.10.40	Turkish BAFRA (1957).
J.161	OUTARDE (R.C.N.)	North Vancouver*	27. 1.41	Mercantile CONTENT (1950), PING HSIN (1950).
J.117	PARRSBOROUGH	Dufferin†	26. 6.41	Scrapped Pembroke Dock 1/48.
J.280	PORT HOPE (R.C.N.)	Dufferin†	14.12.41	For disposal 1959.
J.138	QUALICUM	Dufferin†	3. 9.41	Scrapped Rosyth 6/49.
J.152	QUATSINO (R.C.N.)	Prince Rupert	9. 1.41	Mercantile CONCORD (1950); CHEN HSIN (1950).
J.166	QUINTE (R.C.N.)	Burrard	8. 3.41	Scrapped Sidney (N.S.), 8/47.
J.255	RED DEER (R.C.N.)	Canadian Vickers	5.10.42	For disposal 1959.
J.309	SARNIA (R.C.N.)	Dufferin†	21. 1.42	Turkish BUYUKDERE (1957).
J.212	SHIPPIGAN	Dufferin†	12. 8.41	Scrapped Charlestown 6/49.
J.310	STRATFORD (R.C.N.)	Dufferin†	14. 2.42	For disposal 3/4/46.
J.254	SWIFT CURRENT (R.C.N.)	Canadian Vickers	29. 5.41	Turkish BOZCAADA (1958).
J.220	TADOUSSAC	Dufferin†	2. 8.41	Mercantile (name not changed—1946)?
J.156	THUNDER (R.C.N.)	Dufferin†	19. 3.41	For disposal 3/4/46.
J.149	UNGAVA (R.C.N.)	North Vancouver*	9.10.40	For disposal 3/4/46.

J.257	VEGREVILLE (R.C.N.)	Canadian Vickers	7.10.41	Scrapped Hayle 1947.
J.162	WASAGA (R.C.N.)	Burrard	23. 1.41	For disposal 3/4/46.
J.139	WEDGEPORT	Dufferin†	2. 8.41	Egyptian SOLLUM (1946); lost 7/3/53.
J.318	WESTMOUNT (R.C.N.)	Dufferin†	15. 9.42	Turkish BORNOVA (1958).

* *engined Allis-Chalmers* † *engined Montreal-Loco*

Notes.—Five built in Canada for the R.N. were loaned to the R.C.N. during the war. Eighteen units (BLAIRMORE, DRUMMONDVILLE, FORT WILLIAM, GANANOQUE, GODERICH, KENORA, KENTVILLE, MAHONE, MALPEQUE, MEDICINE HAT, MILLTOWN, MINAS, NIPIGON, PORT HOPE, RED DEER, SARNIA, SWIFT CURRENT and WESTMOUNT) placed on the disposal list post war by the R.C.N. were later re-acquired and converted to coastal escorts.

Bangor class

(Turbine-engined)

Displacement: 656 tons.
Dimensions: 162 (pp) 174 (oa) × 28½ × 8¼ ft.
Machinery: 2-shaft geared Turbines, S.H.P. 2,400 = 16 knots.
Armament: 1—3 in. A.A., 1—2 pdr. A.A. or 4—.5 in. A.A. (1 × 4), 2—20 mm. A.A. guns.
Complement: 60 except R.I.N. vessels 87.

J.131	ARDROSSAN	Blyth: Whites M.E.	22. 7.41	Scrapped Thornaby 29/8/48.
J.07	BEAUMARIS	Ailsa	31.10.40	Scrapped Milford Haven 1/1/48.
J.143	BOOTLE	Ailsa	23.10.41	Scrapped Charlestown 6/49.
J.14	BOSTON	Ailsa	30.12.40	Scrapped Charlestown 6/49.
J.105	BRIXHAM	Blyth: Whites M.E.	21.10.41	Scrapped Dunston 7/7/48.
J.151	CLACTON	Ailsa	19.12.41	Lost 31/12/43.
J.09	CROMARTY	Blyth: Whites M.E.	24. 2.41	Lost 23/10/43.
J.173	DORNOCH	Ailsa	4. 2.42	Scrapped Thornaby 1/1/48.
J.53	DUNBAR	Blyth: Whites M.E.	5. 6.41	Scrapped Southampton 1/1/48.
J.182	GREENOCK	Blyth: Whites M.E.	11. 5.42	R.I.N. BALUCHISTAN (1942), R.P.N. (1948).
J.155	HARTLEPOOL	Blyth: Whites M.E.	14. 7.42	R.I.N. KATHIAWAR (1942), R.P.N. CHITTAGONG (1948); scrapped 1956.
J.190	HARWICH	Hamilton: Parsons	17. 2.42	R.I.N. KHYBER (1942); scrapped 1949.

J.194	HYTHE (ex-Banff)	Ailsa	4. 9.41	Lost 11/10/43.
J.95	ILFRACOMBE	Hamilton: Whites M.E.	29. 1.41	Scrapped Dunston 1/1/48.
J.67	LLANDUDNO	Hamilton: Whites M.E.	8.11.41	Mercantile RORVICK (1947); scrapped 1952.
J.164	MIDDLES-BROUGH	Hamilton: Parsons	2. 5.42	R.I.N. KUMAON (1942); scrapped 1949.
J.199	NEWHAVEN	Hamilton: Parsons	29. 7.42	R.I.N. CARNATIC (1942); scrapped 1949.
J.180	PADSTOW	Hamilton: Parsons	29.10.42	R.I.N. ROHILKAND (1943); scrapped 1961.
J.97	POLRUAN	Ailsa	18. 7.40	Scrapped 6/50.
J.147	POOLE	Stephen	25. 6.41	Scrapped Pembroke Dock 1/48.
J.19	ROTHESAY	Hamilton: White	18. 3.41	Scrapped Milford Haven 19/4/50.
J.76	RYE	Ailsa	19. 8.40	Scrapped Purfleet 9/48.
J.319	LYME REGIS (ii) (ex-Sunderland—J.193)	Stephen	19. 3.42	Scrapped Sunderland 24/8/48.
J.34	TENBY	Hamilton: White	10. 9.41	Scrapped Dunston 1/1/48.
J.121	WHITEHAVEN	Philip: B.T.H.	29. 5.41	Scrapped Briton Ferry 1/1/48.
J.72	WORTHING	Philip: B.T.H.	22. 8.41	Scrapped Dunston 7/7/48.

Bathurst class

Displacement: 650 tons.
Dimensions: 162 (pp) 186 (oa) × 31 × 8¼ ft.
Machinery: 2-shaft Reciprocating (V.T.E.), I.H.P. 1,750 = 15 knots increased to I.H.P. 2,000 = 16 knots in later units.
Armament: 1—4 in. or 3 in. A.A., 1—20 mm. A.A., 4—.303 in. A.A. (2 × 2) guns. *Complement:* 60 except R.I.N. vessels 87.

K.34	ARARAT (R.A.N.)	Evans Deakin	20. 2.43	Scrapped Darwin 6/1/61.
J.240	ARMIDALE (R.A.N.)	Morts Dock	23. 1.42	Lost 1/12/42.
J.184	BALLARAT	Williams-town	10.12.40	Mercantile CARMENCITA (1947).
J.158	BATHURST	Cockatoo	1. 8.40	Scrapped Sydney 31/8/48.
J.323	BENALLA (R.A.N.)	Williams-town	19.12.42	Scrapped Japan 3/58.
J.187	BENDIGO	Cockatoo	1. 3.41	Mercantile CHEUNG HING (1947).
J.285	BOWEN (R.A.N.)	Walkers	11. 7.42	Scrapped Hong Kong 6/56.

H.M. Ships Beaumaris (above) and Poole (below), turbined engined minesweepers of the **Bangor** class.
[*P. A. Vicary*

J.191	BROOME	Evans Deakin	6.10.41	Turkish ALANYA (1946).
J.241	BUNBURY (R.A.N.)	Evans Deakin	16. 5.42	Scrapped Japan 3/62.
J.231	BUNDABERG (R.A.N.)	Evans Deakin	1.12.41	Scrapped Japan 3/62.
J.198	BURNIE	Morts Dock	25.10.40	R.Neth.N. CERAM (1946).
J.183	CAIRNS	Walkers	5. 7.41	R.Neth.N. AMBON (1946), Indonesian BANTENG (1949).
J.244	CASTLEMAINE (R.A.N.) (ex-Castle Harbour)	Williams-town	7. 8.41	Static training ship (Flinders).
J.175	CESSNOCK	Cockatoo	1941	Scrapped Hong Kong 1949
J.242	COLAC (R.A.N.)	Morts Dock	13. 8.41	Training ship (OTC-1962).
J.316	COOTAMUNDRA (R.A.N.)	Poole & Steele	3.12.42	For disposal.
J.351	COWRA (R.A.N.)	Poole & Steele	27. 5.43	Scrapped Japan 1962.
J.232	DELORAINE (R.A.N.)	Morts Dock	26. 7.41	Scrapped Hong Kong 9/56.
J,251	DUBBO (R.A.N.)	Morts Dock	7. 3.42	Scrapped Japan 1958.
J.252	ECCHUCA (R.A.N.)	Williams-town	17. 1.42	R.N.Z.N. (1952).
J.246	FREMANTLE (R.A.N.)	Evans Deakin	18. 8.42	Scrapped Japan 3/62.
J.188	GAWLER	Broken Hill	4.10.41	Turkish AYVALIK (1946).
J.201	GEELONG (R.A.N.)	Williams-town	22. 4.41	Lost 18/10/44.
J.178	GERALDTON	Poole & Steele	16. 8.41	Turkish ANTALYA (1946).
J.324	GLADSTONE (R.A.N.)	Walkers	26.11.42	Mercantile· AKUNA (1956)
J.236	GLENELG (R.A.N.)	Cockatoo	25. 9.42	Scrapped Hong Kong 1957.
J.167	GOULDBURN	Cockatoo	16.11.40	Mercantile BENITA (1947).
J.283	GYMPIE (R.A.N.)	Evans Deakin	30. 1.42	Scrapped Japan 1962.
J.235	HORSHAM (R.A.N.)	Williams-town	23. 5.42	Scrapped Hong Kong 1956.
J.233	INVERELL (R.A.N.)	Morts Dock	2. 5.42	R.N.Z.N. (1952).
J.186	IPSWICH	Evans Deakin	11. 8.41	R.Neth.N. MOROTAI (1946), Indonesian HANG TUAH (1949)
J.362	JUNEE (R.A.N.)	Poole & Steele	16.11.43	Scrapped Sydney 1962
J.192	KALGOORLIE	Broken Hill	7. 8.41	R.Neth.N. TERNATE (1946), Indonesian PATTI UNIS (1949).

J.218	KAPUNDA (R.A.N.)	Poole & Steele	23. 6.42	Scrapped Japan 1962.
J.204	KATOOMBA (R.A.N.)	Poole & Steele	16. 4.41	Scrapped Hong Kong 1957.
J.353	KIAMA (R.A.N.)	Evans Deakin	9. 7.43	R.N.Z.N. (1952).
J.234	LATROBE (R.A.N.)	Morts Dock	19. 6.42	Scrapped Hong Kong 1956.
J.179	LAUNCESTON	Evans Deakin	30. 6.41	Turkish AYANCIK (1946).
J.145	LISMORE	Morts Dock	10. 8.40	R.Neth.N. BATJAN (1946).
J.206	LITHGOW (R.A.N.)	Morts Dock	21.12.40	Scrapped Hong Kong 1956.
J.195	MARYBOROUGH	Walkers	17.10.40	Scrapped Brisbane 1953.
J.207	MILDURA (R.A.N.)	Morts Dock	15. 5.41	Static training ship (Brisbane).
J.361	PARKES (R.A.N.)	Evans Deakin	30.10.43	For disposal.
J.189	PIRIE	Broken Hill	3.12.41	Turkish AMASRA (1946).
J.203	ROCKHAMPTON (R.A.N.)	Walkers	26. 6.41	Scrapped Japan 1962.
J.248	SHEPPARTON (R.A.N.)	Williams-town	15. 8.42	Scrapped Japan 1958.
J.348	STAWELL (R.A.N.)	Williams-town	3. 4.43	R.N.Z.N. (1952).
J.363	STRAHAN (R.A.N.)	Newcastle	12. 7.43	Scrapped Japan 1962.
J.181	TAMWORTH	Walkers	14. 3.42	R.Neth.N. TIDORE (1946).
J.157	TOOWOOMBA	Walkers	26. 3.41	R.Neth.N. BOEROE (1946).
J.205	TOWNSVILLE (R.A.N.)	Evans Deakin	13. 5.41	For disposal.
J.315	WAGGA (R.A.N.)	Morts Dock	5. 7.42	Scrapped 1962.
J.222	WALLAROO (R.A.N.)	Poole & Steele	18. 2.42	Lost 11/6/43.
J.202	WARRNAMBOOL (R.A.N.)	Morts Dock	8. 5.41	Lost 13/9/47.
J.153	WHYALLA (ex-Glenelg)	Broken Hill	12. 5.41	Mercantile RIP (1947).
J.172	WOLLONGONG	Cockatoo	5. 7.41	R.Neth.N. BANDA (1946), Indonesian RADJAWALI (1949).
J.243	BENGAL (R.I.N.)	Cockatoo	28. 5.42	
J.249	BOMBAY (R.I.N.)	Morts Dock	6. 12.41	
J.237	MADRAS (R.I.N.)	Cockatoo	17. 2.42	
J.239	PUNJAB (R.I.N.)	Morts Dock	11.10.41	Scrapped 1949.
J.322	ASSAM (R.I.N.)	Garden Reach		Cancelled 3/45.

H.M.A.S. Mildura, a **Bathurst** class minesweeper, armed with a 4 in. gun. [*I.W.M.*

J.321	GONDWHANA	Garden Reach		Cancelled 3/45.
J.320	SIND (R.I.N).	Garden Reach		Cancelled 3/45.

Notes.—Twenty built in Australia for the R.N. were all loaned to the R.A.N. during the war.

Algerine class

Displacement: 850 tons.
Dimensions: 212½ (pp) 225 (oa) × 35½ × 8½ ft.
Machinery: 2-shaft geared Turbines or Reciprocating (V.T.E.), S.H.P. or I.H.P. 2,000 = 16½ knots.
Armament: 1—4 in., 8—20 mm. A.A. (4 × 2) guns. *Complement:* 85.

Turbine-engined

J.140	ALARM	Harland & Wolff	5. 2.42	Constructive total loss 2/1/43; scrapped 1/44.
J.101	ALBACORE	Harland & Wolff	2. 4.42	For disposal.
J.106	ALERT	Harland & Wolff	14. 4.42	ACUTE (1942); for disposal.
J.213	ALGERINE	Harland & Wolff	22.12.41	Lost 15/11/42.
J.305	BRAVE	Blyth: White	4. 2.43	R.N.V.R. SATELLITE (Tyne—1954); scrapped Dunston 25/11/58.
J.230	CADMUS	Harland & Wolff	27. 5.42	R.B.N. GEORGES LECOINTE (1950); scrapped 1960.
J.387	CHAMELEON	Harland & Wolff	6. 5.44	
J.388	CHEERFUL	Harland & Wolff	22. 5.44	For disposal.
J.214	CIRCE	Harland & Wolff	27. 6.42	R.N.V.R. drillship (Tay—1955).
J.421	CYRUS	Scotts		Cancelled.
J.399	CYBELE	Scotts		Cancelled.
J.216	ESPIEGLE	Harland & Wolff	12. 8.42	
J.308	FANCY	Blyth: White	5. 4.43	R.B.N. DUFOUR (1951), hulked NZADI (1959).
J.224	FANTOME	Harland & Wolff	22. 9.42	Constructive total loss 20/5/43; scrapped Milford Haven 22/5/47.
J.389	HARE	Harland & Wolff	20. 6.44	R.Nig.N. NIGERIA (1959); scrapped Faslane 6/11/62.
J.390	JEWEL	Harland & Wolff	20. 7.44	For disposal.
J.391	LIBERTY	Harland & Wolff	22. 8.44	R.B.N. ADRIEN DE GERLACHE (1949); hulked (1959).

Left: H.M.S. Albacore, British built, turbine-engined **Algerine** class minesweeper cocooned for preservation in Reserve fleet.

Right: H.M.S. Cheerful, British built, turbine-engined **Algerine** class minesweeper showing post-war pennant number.

	MARMION (i)	Harland & Wolff		Cancelled.
	MOON (i)	Harland & Wolff		Cancelled.
J.227	MUTINE	Harland & Wolff	10.10.42	
J.221	ONYX	Harland & Wolff	27.10.42	For disposal.
J.293	PICKLE	Harland & Wolff	3. 8.43	R.Cey.N. PARAKRAMA (1958).
J.294	PINCHER	Harland & Wolff	19. 8.43	Scrapped Dunston 7/3/62.
J.295	PLUCKY	Harland & Wolff	29. 9.43	Scrapped Dunston 15/3/62.
J.217	RATTLER	Harland & Wolff	9.12.42	LOYALTY (1943); lost 22/8/44.
J.223	READY	Harland & Wolff	11. 1.43	R.B.N. JAN VAN HAVERBEKE (1951); scrapped Bruges 7/3/61.
J.298	RECRUIT	Harland & Wolff	26.10.43	
J.299	RIFLEMAN	Harland & Wolff	25.11.43	
J.225	RINALDO	Harland & Wolff	20. 3.43	Scrapped Gateshead 16/8/61.
J.219	ROSARIO	Harland & Wolff	3. 4.43	R.B.N. DE MOOR (1953).
J.226	SPANKER	Harland & Wolff	20. 4.43	R.B.N. DE BROUWER (1953).
J.301	SQUIRREL	Harland & Wolff	20. 4.44	Lost 24/7/45.
J.215	VESTAL	Harland & Wolff	19. 6.43	Lost 26/7/45.

Reciprocating-engined

J.273	BRAMBLE	Lobnitz	26. 1.45	Scrapped 8/61.
J.229	COCKATRICE	Fleming & Ferguson	27.10.42	For disposal.
J.442	DISDAIN	Lobnitz	1. 5.45	NIGER (ii) (1945).
J.453	FIERCE	Lobnitz	11. 9.45	Scrapped Gateshead 2/8/59.
J.464	FIREBALL	Lobnitz		Cancelled.
J.306	FLY	Lobnitz	1. 6.42	R.Per.N. PALANG (1949).
J.465	GABRIEL	Lobnitz		Cancelled.
J.466	HAPPY RETURN	Lobnitz		Cancelled.
J.307	HOUND	Lobnitz	29. 7.42	Scrapped Troon 1/9/62.
J.275	HYDRA	Lobnitz	29. 9.42	Constructive total loss 10/11/44; scrapped Grays 28/10/44.
	LARNE (i)	Simons		Cancelled.

Left: H.M.S. Ready was a British built, turbine-engined minesweeper of the **Algerine** class. Note twin 20 mm. A.A. mountings.

[*P. A. Vicary*

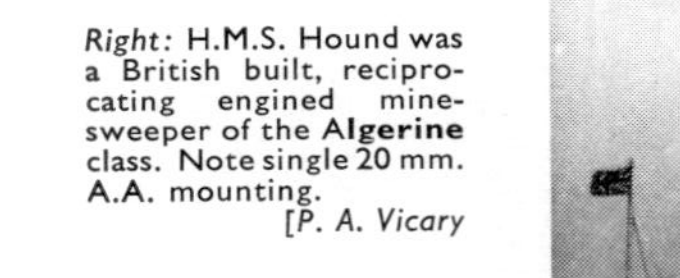

Right: H.M.S. Hound was a British built, reciprocating engined minesweeper of the **Algerine** class. Note single 20 mm. A.A. mounting.

[*P. A. Vicary*

J.274	LARNE (ii)	Lobnitz	2. 9.43	Italian AMMARAGLIO MAGNAHI (1946), ERITREA (1948), ALABARDA (1951).
	LENNOX (i)	Simons		Cancelled.
J.276	LENNOX (ii)	Lobnitz	15.10.43	Scrapped Tyne 1/6/61.
J.277	ORESTES	Lobnitz	25.11.42	Scrapped Troon 4/63.
J.291	PELORUS	Lobnitz	18. 6.43	S.A.N. PIETERMAR-ITZBURG (1947).
J.297	RATTLESNAKE	Lobnitz	23. 2.43	Scrapped Grangemouth 10/59.
J.384	ROWENA	Lobnitz	5. 6.44	Scrapped Gateshead 23/10/58.
J.367	STORMCLOUD	Lobnitz	28.12.43	Scrapped Gateshead 2/8/59.
J.382	SYLVIA	Lobnitz	28. 2.44	Scrapped Gateshead 24/10/58.
J.383	TANGANYIKA	Lobnitz	12. 4.44	For disposal.
J.304	WATERWITCH	Lobnitz	22. 4.43	
J.385	WAVE	Lobnitz	18. 8.44	Scrapped Tyne 4/4/62.
J.386	WELCOME	Lobnitz	14.11.44	Scrapped Gateshead 3/5/62.
J.282	ANTARES (ex-U.S.N.)	Toronto	15. 8.42	Returned U.S.N. 12/46.
J.283	ARCTURUS (ex-U.S.N.)	Redfern	31. 8.42	R.H.N. PYRPOLITIS (1947).
J.284	ARIES (ex-U.S.N.)	Toronto	19. 9.42	R.H.N. ARMATOLOS (1947).
J.349	COURIER (ex-R.C.N. Arnprior)	Redfern	22.12.43	Scrapped Llanelly 25/3/59.
J.344	BORDER CITIES (R.C.N.)	Port Arthur	3. 5.43	Partially scrapped Victoria 6/49; hull for disposal.
J.350	COQUETTE (ex-R.C.N. Bow-manville)	Redfern	24.11.43	Scrapped Rosyth 26/5/58.
J.286	CLINTON (ex-U.S.N.)	Toronto	5.10.42	Returned U.S.N. 1/47.
J.369	FELICITY (ex-R.C.N. Coppercliff)	Redfern	19. 1.44	Mercantile FAIRFREE (1947); scrapped Charlestown 29/8/57.
J.325	PROVIDENCE (ex-R.C.N. Forrest Hill)	Redfern	27.10.43	Scrapped Sunderland 17/5/58.
J.396	FORT FRANCIS (R.C.N.)	Port Arthur	30.10.43	Surveying vessel.
J.398	FRIENDSHIP (ex-U.S.N.)	Toronto	24.10.42	Returned U.S.N. 1/47.
J.287	GOZO (ex-U.S.N.)	Redfern	27. 1.43	R.H.N. POLEMISTIS (1947).
J.379	LYSANDER (ex-R.C.N. Hespeler)	Port Arthur	11.11.43	CORNFLOWER (1950), LYSANDER (1951); scrapped Blyth 23/11/57.

J.376	GOLDEN FLEECE (ex-R.C.N. Humberstone)	Redfern	29. 2.44	Scrapped Llanelly 8/60.
J.378	PROMPT (ex-R.C.N. Huntsville)	Redfern	30. 3.44	Constructive total loss 9/5/45; scrapped Rainham 16/1/47.
J.428	JASEUR	Redfern	19. 4.44	Scrapped Blyth 26/2/56.
J.326	KAPUSKASING (R.C.N.)	Port Arthur	22. 7.43	Canadian coastguard.
J.380	MARINER (ex-R.C.N. Kincardine)	Port Arthur	9. 5.44	Burmese YAN MYO AUNG (1958).
J.433	LAERTES	Redfern	25. 3.44	Scrapped Barrow 21/4/59.
J.354	SERENE (ex-R.C.N. Leaside)	Redfern	18.10.43	Scrapped Llanelly 8/3/59.
J.288	LIGHTFOOT (ex-U.S.N.)	Redfern	14.11.42	R.H.N. NAVAMACHOS (1947).
J.327	REGULUS (ex-R.C.N. Longbranch)	Toronto	18. 9.43	Lost 12/1/45.
J.335	MAENAD	Redfern	8. 6.44	Scrapped Grays 18/12/57.
J.436	MAGICIENNE	Redfern	24. 6.44	Scrapped Newport 20/3/56.
J.437	MAMELUKE	Redfern	19. 7.44	Scrapped Middlesbrough 15/5/50.
J.438	MANDATE	Redfern	9. 8.44	Scrapped Charlestown 12/57.
J.443	MARVEL	Redfern	30. 8.44	Scrapped Charlestown 7/5/58.
J.289	MELITA	Redfern	8.12.42	Scrapped Llanelly 25/2/59.
J.444	MICHAEL	Redfern	20. 9.44	Scrapped Bo'ness 15/11/56.
J.328	MIDDLESEX (R.C.N.)	Port Arthur	27. 5.43	Lost 3/12/46.
J.329	MOON (ii) (ex-R.C.N. Mimico)	Redfern	2. 9.43	Scrapped Gateshead 13/11/57.
J.445	MINSTREL	Redfern	5.10.44	R.Th.N. PHOSAMPTON (1947).
J.454	MYRMIDON	Redfern	21.10.44	Scrapped Briton Ferry 2/12/58.
J.455	MYSTIC	Redfern	11.11.44	Scrapped Llanelly 3/5/58.
J.456	NERISSA	Redfern	25.11.44	Scrapped Llanelly 8/60.
J.397	NEW LISKEARD (R.C.N.)	Port Arthur	14. 1.44	Surveying vessel.
J.457	NICATOR	Toronto		Cancelled.
J.442	NIGER (i)	Toronto		Cancelled.
J.459	NONPAREIL	Toronto		Cancelled.
J.460	NOX	Toronto		Cancelled.

J.290	OCTAVIA	Redfern	31.12.42	Scrapped Gateshead 19/5/50.
J.461	ODIN	Toronto		Cancelled.
J.381	MARMION (ii) (ex-R.C.N. Orangeville)	Port Arthur	15. 6.44	Scrapped Dunston 1959.
J.462	ORCADIA	Port Arthur	8. 8.44	Scrapped Briton Ferry 3/12/58.
J.330	OSHAWA (R.C.N.)	Port Arthur	6.10.43	
J.463	OSSORY	Port Arthur	3.10.44	Scrapped Troon 4/3/59.
J.347	PERSIAN (ex-U.S.N.)	Redfern	22. 2.43	Returned U.S.N. 12/46, mercantile KIKIADES (1947).
J.377	LIONESS (ex-R.C.N. Petrolia)	Redfern	15. 3.44	Scrapped Rosyth 15/11/56.
J.446	PLUTO	Port Arthur	21.10.44	For disposal.
J.447	POLARIS	Port Arthur	3.12.45	Scrapped Briton Ferry 26/9/56.
J.331	PORTAGE (R.C.N.)	Port Arthur	21.11.42	Scrapped Canada 1959.
J.296	POSTILLION (ex-U.S.N.)	Redfern	18. 3.43	R.H.N. MACHITIS (1947).
J.448	PYRRHUS	Port Arthur	19. 5.45	Scrapped Newport 8/9/56.
J.355	ROCKCLIFF (R.C.N.)	Port Arthur	19. 8.43	Scrapped Canada 1960.
J.449	ROMOLA	Port Arthur	19. 5.45	Scrapped Plymouth 19/11/57.
J.439	ROSAMUND	Port Arthur	20.12.44	S.A.N. BLOEM-FONTEIN (1947).
J.332	St. BONIFACE (R.C.N.)	Port Arthur	5.11.42	Mercantile (name not changed 1947), BESS BARRY (1954).
J.333	SEABEAR (ex-R.C.N. St. Thomas)	Redfern	6.11.43	Scrapped Preston 12/12/58.
J.300	SKIPJACK (ex-Scorpion, ex-R.C.N. Solebay)	Redfern	7. 4.43	Scrapped Blyth 1959.
J.334	The SOO (R.C.N.)	Port Arthur	5. 8.42	SAULT Ste. MARIE (1942); scrapped Canada 1959.
J.440	STYX	Port Arthur		Cancelled.
J.302	THISBE	Redfern	12. 4.43	Scrapped Charlestown 12/57.
J.370	FLYING FISH (ex-R.C.N. Tillsonburg)	Redfern	16. 2.44	R.Cey.N. VIJAYA (1949).
J.360	MARY ROSE (ex-R.C.N. Toronto)	Redfern	5. 8.43	Scrapped Gateshead 14/11/57.
J.303	TRUELOVE	Redfern	8. 7.43	Scrapped Blyth 23/11/57.

H.M.S. Romola. Canadian built, reciprocating engined **Algerine** class minesweeper displaying International day signals for a minesweeper and indicating starboard sweep wire out. [*G. A. Osbon*

J.336	WALLACEBURG (R.C.N.)	Port Arthur	17.12.42	R.B.N. GEORGES LECOINTE (1959).
J.356	WELFARE	Redfern	15. 7.43	Scrapped Grays 1957/8.
J.337	WINNIPEG (R.C.N.)	Port Arthur	19. 9.42	R.B.N. DUFOUR (1959).

All engined Montreal Locomotive Works

Notes.—Nine ordered in Canada for the U.S.N. were all loaned to the R.N. under Lend/Lease. The eleven surviving R.C.N. vessels were initially converted to escort vessels after the war. Of these FORT FRANCIS, NEW LISKEARD and OSHAWA were subsequently converted to surveying vessels and the KAPUSKASING lent to the Dept. of Mines and Technical Surveys. British built NIGER was converted to a minesweepers H/Q ship.

PATROL SLOOPS

"PC" class

Displacement: 610 tons PC.74, 661 tons PATHAN.
Dimensions: 233 (pp) 247 (oa) × 26¾ × 8 PC.74, 9 PATHAN ft.
Machinery: 2-shaft geared Turbines, S.H.P. 3,500 = 20 knots.
Armament: 1—4 in., 2—3 in. (2 × 1) guns.
Complement: 56 PC.74, 66 PATHAN.

K.26	PATHAN (R.I.N.) (ex-PC.69)	Workman Clark	11. 3.18	Lost 23/6/40.
Z.74	PC.74	White	4.10.18	Scrapped Pembroke Dock 1947?

Kingfisher class

Displacement: 510 tons (*first three*), 530 tons (*second three*), 580 tons (*last three*)
Dimensions: 234 (pp) 243¼ (oa) × 26½ × 6 (*first three*), 6½ (*second three*) ft., except (*last three*) 224 (pp) 233¼ (oa) × 25½ × 7¼ ft.
Machinery: 2-shaft geared Turbines, S.H.P. 3,600 = 20 knots.
Armament: 1—4 in. gun. *Complement:* 60.

L.70	KINGFISHER	Fairfield	14. 2.35	Scrapped Thornaby 21/4/47.
L.42	MALLARD	Stephen	26. 3.36	Scrapped Gateshead 21/4/47.
L.52	PUFFIN	Stephen	5. 5.36	Constructive total loss 26/3/45; scrapped Grays 16/1/47.
L.30	KITTIWAKE	Thornycroft	30.11.36	Mercantile TUCH SING (1946).
L.06	SHELLDRAKE	Thornycroft	28. 1.37	Mercantile TUCH LOON (1946).
L.62	WIDGEON	Yarrow	2. 2.38	Scrapped Redheugh 25/9/47.
L.89	GUILLEMOT	Denny	6. 7.39	Scrapped Grays 11/50.

Above: P.C. 74 was a " **P** " boat altered to resemble a merchant vessel. The 4 in. gun is visible aft, but both the 3 in. guns are concealed behind lidded ports under the bridge. [*P. A. Vicary*

Below: H.M.S. Kingfisher was the name ship of a class of patrol sloop built to replace the " **P** " and "**PC** " boats. The flag superior was changed to L, then M and finally K. [*P. A. Vicary*

L.21	PINTAIL	Denny	18. 8.39	Lost 10/6/41.
L.39	SHEARWATER	White	18. 4.39	Scrapped Thornaby 21/4/47.

Notes.—SHEARWATER changed pennant numbers from M.39 to K.02 in 1940.

CORVETTES

Flower class

Displacement: 925 tons.
Dimensions: 190 (pp) 205 (oa) × 33 × 11½ ft.
Machinery: 1-shaft Reciprocating (4 cyl. V.T.E.), I.H.P. 2,750 = 16 knots.
Armament: 1—4 in., 1—2 pdr. A.A. or 4—.5 in. A.A. (1 × 4), 4—.303 in. A.A. (2 × 2) guns.
Complement: 85.

K.184	ABELIA	Harland & Wolff	28.11.40	Mercantile KRAFT (1948), ARNE SKONTORP (1954).
K.01	ACANTHUS	Ailsa	26. 5.41	R.N.N. ANDENES (1942), mercantile COLIN FRYE (1956).
K.58	ACONITE	Ailsa	31. 3.41	French ACONIT (1941), mercantile TERJE XI (1948).
K.185	ALISMA	Harland & Wolff	17.12.40	Mercantile LACONIA (1949), CONSTANTINOS S (1950), PARNON (1952); lost 16/7/54.
K.100	ALYSSUM	Brown: Kincaid	3. 3.41	French ALYSSE (1941); lost 8/2/42.
K.17	AMARANTHUS	Fleming & Ferguson	17.10.40	Mercantile (name not changed—1946); scrapped Hong Kong 1953.
K.186	ANCHUSA	Harland & Wolff	15. 1.41	Mercantile SILVERLORD (1949), SIR EDGAR (1954); lost 18/1/60, salved and scrapped Mauritius 4/10/60.
K.48	ANEMONE	Blyth: Clark	22. 4.40	Mercantile PELIKAN (1950).
K.73	ARABIS (i)	Harland & Wolff	14. 2.40	U.S.N. SAUCY (1942), R.N. SNAPDRAGON (ii) (1945), mercantile KATINA (1947), TEWFIK (1950).
K.86	ARBUTUS (i)	Blyth: Clark	5. 6.40	Lost 5/2/42.

K.187	ARMERIA	Harland & Wolff	16. 1.41	Mercantile DEPPIE (1948), CANASTEL (1950), RIO BLANCO (1952), LILLIAN (1955).
K.56	ASPHODEL	Brown: Kincaid	25. 5.40	Lost 9/3/44.
K.188	ASTER	Harland & Wolff	12. 2.41	Scrapped Bo'ness 30/5/46.
K.96	AUBRIETIA	Brown: Kincaid	5. 9.40	Mercantile ARNFINN BERGAN (1948).
K.12	AURICULA	Brown: Kincaid	14.11.40	Lost 6/5/42.
K.25	AZALEA	C. W. & G.: Holmes	8. 7.40	Mercantile NORTE (1946); lost 19/1/55.
K.72	BALSAM (ex-Chelmer)	Brown: Clark	30. 5.42	Scrapped Newport 20/4/47.
K.66	BEGONIA	C. W. & G.: Holmes	18. 9.40	U.S.N. IMPULSE (1942), mercantile BEGONLOCK (1946), FUNDICIONES MOLINAO (1949), ASTILUZU (1951), RIO MERO (1956).
K.114	BELLWORT	Brown: Kincaid	11. 8.41	Irish CLIONA (1946).
K.189	BERGAMOT	Harland & Wolff	15. 2.41	Mercantile SYROS (1947), DELPHINI (1951), DELFINI (1955), EKATERINI (1955).
K.80	BLUBELL	Fleming & Ferguson	24. 4.40	Lost 17/2/45.
K.120	BORAGE	Brown: Kincaid	22.11.41	Irish MACHA (1946).
K.190	VERVAIN (ex-Broom)	Harland & Wolff	12. 3.41	Lost 20/2/45.
K.192	BRYONY	Harland & Wolff	15. 3.41	R.N.N. POLARFRONT II (1947).
K.126	BURDOCK	Crown: N.E. Marine	14.12.40	Scrapped Hayle 8/46.
K.193	BUTTERCUP	Harland & Wolff	10. 4.41	R.N.N. NORDKYN (1942), mercantile THORIS (1957).
K.28	CALENDULA	Harland & Wolff	21. 3.40	U.S.N. READY (1942) mercantile VILLA CISNEROS (1948), VILLA BENS (1949).
K.31	CAMELLIA	Harland & Wolff	4. 5.40	Mercantile HETTY W. VINKE (1948).
K.18	CAMPANULA	Fleming & Ferguson	23. 5.40	Scrapped Dunston 21/8/47.

Left: H.M.S. Kittiwake in 1941 with a quadruple .5 in. A.A. M.G. mounting added aft. [*P. A. Vicary*

Below: H.M.S. Anchusa, a **Flower** class corvette, showing the many modifications effected. Fo'c'sle lengthened, foremast abaft bridge, R.D.F. added on bridge, main mast struck and replaced by W/T spreaders before A.A. position (where it would not mask arc of fire), 20 mm. A.A. guns added in bridge wings and DG coils fitted internally. [*I.W.M.*

K.108	CAMPION	Crown: Clark	26. 4.41	Scrapped Newport 20/4/47.
K.09	CANDYTUFT	Grange-mouth: N.E. Marine	8. 7.40	U.S.N. TENACITY (1942), mercantile MAW HWA (1947), Chinese (Com.)?
K.00	CARNATION	Grange-mouth: N.E. Marine	3. 9.40	R.Neth.N. FRISIO (1943-45), mercantile SOUTHERN LAUREL (1949).
K.75	CELANDINE	Grange-mouth: Ailsa	28.12.40	Scrapped Portaferry 10/48.
K.195	CHRYSANTHE-MUM	Harland & Wolff	11. 4.41	French COMAN-DANTE DROGOU (1942), mercantile TERJE X (1948), Port uguese CARVALHO ARAUJO (1959).
K.88	CLARKIA	Harland & Wolff	7. 3.40	Scrapped Hayle 8/47.
K.36	CLEMATIS	Hill: Richardson Westgarth and Clark	22. 4.40	Scrapped Charlestown 9/49.
K.134	CLOVER	Fleming & Ferguson	30. 1.41	Mercantile CLOVER-LOCK (1947), Chinese (Com.) KAI FENG (19).
K.140	COLTSFOOT	Hall	12. 5.41	Mercantile ALEXANDRA (1947), HERMOPOULIS (1953); lost 20/11/54.
K.94	COLUMBINE	Hill: Richardson Westgarth and Clark	13. 8.40	Mercantile LIEF WELDING (1949).
K.45	CONVOLVULUS	Hill: Richardson Westgarth and Clark	21. 9.40	Scrapped Newport 5/10/47.
K.32	COREOPSIS	Inglis: Kincaid	23. 5.40	R.H.N. KRIEZIS (1943-52); scrapped Sunderland 22/7/52.
K.196	COWSLIP	Harland & Wolff	28. 5.41	Scrapped Troon 4/49.
K.49	CROCUS	Inglis: Kincaid	26. 6.40	Mercantile ANNLOCK (1947); scrapped Ho[illegible] Kong 1951.
K.83	CYCLAMEN	Lewis	20. 6.40	Mercantile SOUTHER[illegible] BRIAR (1948).
K.07	DIANELLA (ex-Daffodil)	Lewis	3. 9.40	Scrapped Portaferry 1948.
K.59	DAHLIA	Lewis	31.10.40	Scrapped Gelleswick Bay 20/10/48.

M.S. Columbine and other **Flower** class corvettes laid-up post war, awaiting sale.

M.S. Gardenia, a **Flower** class corvette, as completed before the flag superior was changed from to K. Note short fo'c'sle, foremast before bridge, only rifle calibre machine guns in A.A.position (later replaced by a 2 pdr.) and external D.G. coils. [*I.W.M.*

M.S. Gloxinia did not follow the ordinary run of modifications to the **Flower** class corvettes. The c'sle was left short and additional berthing was added amidships and a 3 in. A.A. gun replaced the ›dr. A.A. which was re-sited further aft. [*P. A. Vicary*

K.77	DELPHINIUM	Robb: Ailsa	6. 6.40	Scrapped Pembroke Dock 2/49.
K.95	DIANTHUS	Robb: Ailsa	9. 7.40	Mercantile THORSLEP (1950).
K.197	EGLANTINE	Harland & Wolff	11. 6.41	R.N.N. SOROY (1941) mercantile (name not changed—1957).
K.50	ERICA	Harland & Wolff	18. 6.40	Lost 9/2/43.
K.43	FREESIA	Harland & Wolff	3.10.40	Mercantile FREELOCK (1946); lost 1/4/47.
K.199	FRITILLARY	Harland & Wolff	22. 7.41	Mercantile ANDRIA (1947), V.D. CHID-AMBARAM (1949); scrapped India 1955.
K.99	GARDENIA	Simons	10. 4.40	Lost 9/11/42.
K.200	GENISTA	Harland & Wolff	24. 7.41	O.W.S. WEATHER RECORDER (1947); for disposal.
K.90	GENTIAN	Harland & Wolff	6. 8.40	Scrapped Purfleet 21/8/47.
K.16	GERANIUM	Simons	23. 4.40	R.D.N. THETIS (1947)
K.34	GLADIOLUS	Smiths Dock	24. 1.40	Lost 16/10/41.
K.201	GLORIOSA	Harland & Wolff		Cancelled 23/1/41.
K.22	GLOXINIA	Harland & Wolff	2. 7.40	Scrapped Purfleet 15/7/47.
K.72	GODETIA (i)	Smiths Dock	8. 5.40	Lost 6/9/40.
K.226	GODETIA (ii) (ex-Dart)	Crown: Clark	24. 9.41	Scrapped Grays 1947.
K.202	HAREBELL	Harland & Wolff		Cancelled 23/1/41.
K.69	HEATHER	Harland & Wolff	17. 9.40	Scrapped Grays 1947.
K.03	HELIOTROPE	Crown: N.E. Marine	5. 6.40	U.S.N. SURPRISE (1942), mercantile HELIOLOCK (1946), ZIANG TEH (1947), Chinese (Com.) LIN (19)?
K.203	HEMLOCK	Harland & Wolff		Cancelled 23/1/41.
K.24	HIBISCUS	Harland & Wolff	6. 4.40	U.S.N. SPRY (1942), mercantile MADONNA (1947); scrapped Hong Kong 1955.
K.64	HOLLYHOCK	Crown: N.E. Marine	19. 8.40	Lost 9/4/42.
K.27	HONEYSUCKLE	Ferguson	22. 4.40	Scrapped Grays 1950.
K.84	HYACINTH	Harland & Wolff	19. 8.40	R.H.N. APOSTOLIS (1943).

K.39	HYDRANGEA	Ferguson	4. 9.40	Mercantile HYDRALOCK (1948); lost 25/2/57.
K.183	CORIANDER (ex-Iris)	Hall Russell	9. 6.41	French COMANDANTE DETROYAT (1942); scrapped Troon 2/48.
K.204	IVY	Harland & Wolff		Cancelled 23/1/41.
K.23	JASMINE	Ferguson	14. 1.41	Sold 11/9/48.
K.68	JONQUIL	Fleming & Ferguson	9. 7.40	Mercantile LEMNOS (1948), OLYMPIC RIDER (1951); lost 1/12/55.
K.33	KINGCUP	Harland & Wolff	31.10.40	Mercantile RUBIS (1946), SEISLIM (1954) scrapped Holland 1957?
K.82	LARKSPUR	Fleming & Ferguson	5. 9.40	U.S.N. FURY (1942), mercantile LARKSLOCK (1946); scrapped Hong Kong 1953.
K.60	LAVENDER	Hall	27.11.40	Mercantile EUGENE VINKE (1948).
K.205	LING	Harland & Wolff		Cancelled 23/1/41.
K.05	LOBELIA	Hall	15. 2.41	French (name not changed—1941), mercantile THORGEIR (1949).
K.105	LOOSESTRIFE	Hall Russell	25. 8.41	Mercantile KALLSEVNI (1949); scrapped 4/62.
K.93	LOTUS (i)	Hill: Ailsa	17. 1.42	French COMANDANTE D'ESTIENNE D'ORVES (1942); scrapped Troon 5/51.
K.81	MALLOW	Harland & Wolff	22. 5.40	Yugoslavian NADA (1944), PARTIZANKA (1948), Egyptian EL SUDAN (1948).
K.54	MARGUERITE	Hall Russell	8. 7.40	O.W.S. WEATHER OBSERVER (1947); scrapped Ghent 8/9/61.
K.87	MARIGOLD	Hall Russell	4. 9.40	Lost 9/12/42.
K.206	MARJORAM	Harland & Wolff		Cancelled.
K.144	MEADOWSWEET	Hill: Richardson Westgarth and Clark	28. 3.42	Mercantile GERRIT W. VINKE (1951).
K.38	MIGNONETTE	Hall Russell: N.E. Marine	28. 1.41	Mercantile ALEXANDROUPLIS (1948); lost 30/11/48.

K.11	MIMOSA	Hill: Richardson Westgarth and Clark	18. 1.42	French (name not changed—1942); lost 9/6/42.
K.207	MONKSHOOD	Fleming & Ferguson	17. 4.41	Mercantile W.R. STRANG (1948).
K.208	MONTBRETIA	Fleming & Ferguson	27. 5.41	R.N.N. (name not changed—1941); lost 18/11/42.
K.65	MYOSOTIS	Lewis	28. 1.41	Mercantile GRUN-NINGUR (1948), THORON (1949).
K.74	NARCISSUS	Lewis	29. 3.41	Mercantile ESTE (1946).
K.212	NETTLE	Hall	23. 9.41	HYDERBAD (1941); scrapped Portaferry 10/48.
K.19	NIGELLA	Philip: Clark	21. 9.40	Mercantile NIGELOCK (1947); lost 10/3/55.
K.76	ORCHIS	Harland & Wolff	15.10.40	Constructive total loss 21/8/44.
K.123	OXLIP	Inglis: Kincaid	28. 8.41	Irish MAEV (1946).
K.15	HEARTSEASE (ex-Pansy)	Harland & Wolff	20. 4.40	U.S.N. COURAGE (1942), mercantile ROSKVA (1951), DOUGLAS (1956), SEA-BIRD (1958); lost 12/58.
K.111	PENNYWORT	Inglis: Kincaid	18.10.41	Scrapped Troon 2/49.
K.40	PEONY	Harland & Wolff	4. 6.40	R.H.N. SAKHTOURIS (1943); scrapped Dunston 21/4/52.
K.61	PENTSTEMON	Philip: Clark	18. 1.41	Mercantile GALAXIDI (1947), ROSA VLASSI (1951).
K.55	PERIWINKLE	Harland & Wolff	24. 2.40	U.S.N. RESTLESS (1942), mercantile PERILOCK (1947); scrapped Hong Kong 1953.
K.79	PETUNIA	Robb: Kincaid	19. 9.40	Chinese (Nat.) FU PO (1946); lost 19/3/47.
K.130	LOTUS (ii) (ex-Phlox)	Robb: Ailsa and N.E. Marine	16. 1.42	Mercantile SOUTHERN LOTUS (1948).
K.63	PICOTEE	Harland & Wolff	19. 7.40	Lost 12/8/41.
K.71	PIMPERNEL	Harland & Wolff	16.11.40	Scrapped Portaferry 10/48.
K.137	PINK	Robb: Ailsa and N.E. Marine	16. 2.42	Constructive total loss 27/6/44; scrapped Llanelly.
K.47	POLYANTHUS	Robb: Kincaid	30.11.40	Lost 21/9/43.

K.213	POPPY	Hall	20.11.41	Mercantile RAMI (1946); hulked 1955.
K.214	POTENTILLA	Simons	18.12.41	R.N.N. (name not changed—1942-44); scrapped Gateshead 1946.
K.91	PRIMROSE	Simons	8. 5.40	Mercantile NORFINN (1949).
K.14	PRIMULA	Simons	22. 6.40	Mercantile MARY-LOCK (1947); scrapped Hong Kong 1953.
K.117	RANUNCULUS	Simons	25. 6.41	French RENONCULE (1941), mercantile SOUTHERN LILY (1947).
K.78	RHODODEN-DRON	Harland & Wolff	2. 9.40	Mercantile MAJ VINKE (1950).
K.51	ROCKROSE	Hill: Richardson Westgarth and Clark	26. 7.41	S.A.N. PROTEA (1947).
K.102	ROSE	Simons	22. 9.41	R.N.N. (name not changed—1941); lost 26/10/44.
K.97	SALVIA	Simons	6. 8.40	Lost 24/12/41.
K.128	SAMPHIRE	Smiths Dock	14. 4.41	Lost 30/1/43.
K.04	SAXIFRAGE	Hill: Richardson Westgarth and Clark	24.10.41	R.N.N. POLARFRONT 1 (1947).
K.10	SNAPDRAGON (i)	Simons	3. 9.40	Lost 19/12/42.
K.67	SNOWDROP	Smiths Dock	12. 5.41	Scrapped Tyne 9/49.
K.08	SPIRAE	Inglis: Kincaid	31.10.40	Mercantile THESSA-LONIKA (1948).
K.20	STARWORT	Inglis: Kincaid	12. 2.41	Mercantile SOUTHERN BROOM (1948).
K.142	STONECROP	Smiths Dock	12. 5.41	Mercantile SILVER KING (1949), MARTHA VINKE (1950).
K.57	SUNDEW	Lewis	28. 5.41	French ROSELYS (1941); scrapped Troon 5/48.
K.41	SUNFLOWER	Smiths Dock	19. 8.40	Scrapped Hayle 8/47.
K.209	SWEETBRIAR	Smiths Dock	26. 6.41	Mercantile STAR IX (1949).
K.216	TAMARISK (ex-Ettrick)	Fleming & Ferguson	28. 7.41	R.H.N. TOMPAZIS (1943); scrapped U.K. 20/3/52.

K.210	THYME	Smiths Dock	25. 7.41	O.W.S. WEATHER REPORTER (1946), WEATHER EXPLORER (1947), mercantile EPOS (1958).
K.29	TULIP	Smiths Dock	4. 9.40	Mercantile OLYMPIC CONQUERER (1950), OTORI MARU No. 8 (1956), THORLYN (1957).
K.85	VERBENA	Smiths Dock	1.10.40	Mercantile conversion failed to materialise and scrapped Blyth 1/10/51.
K.37	VERONICA	Smiths Dock	17.10.40	U.S.N. TEMPTRESS (1942), mercantile VEROLOCK (1947); lost 1/47, salved and scrapped Blyth 1951.
K.132	VETCH	Smiths Dock	27. 5.41	Mercantile PATRAI (1948), OLYMPIC HUNTER (1951), OTORI MARU No. 18 (1956).
K.35	VIOLET	Simons	30.12.40	Mercantile LA AGUERA (1947), LA GUERA (1949).
K.44	WALLFLOWER	Smiths Dock	14.11.40	Mercantile ASBJORN LARSEN (1949).
K.53	WOODRUFF	Simons	28. 2.41	Mercantile SOUTHERN LUPIN (1948); scrapped Odense 11/59.
K.211	SNOWFLAKE (ex-Zenobia)	Smiths Dock	22. 8.41	O.W.S. WEATHER WATCHER (1947); scrapped Dublin 5/5/62.
K.98	ZINNIA	Smiths Dock	28.11.40	Lost 23/8/41.
	LA BASTIAISE (French)	Smiths Dock	8. 4.40	Lost 22/6/40.
K.122	FLEUR DE LYS (ex-French La Dieppoise)	Smiths Dock	21. 6.40	Lost 14/10/41.
K.46	LA MALOUINE (ex-French)	Smiths Dock	21. 3.40	Scrapped Gelleswick Bay 22/5/47.
K.107	NASTURTIUM (ex-French La Paimpolaise)	Smiths Dock	4. 7.40	Mercantile CANIA (1948).
K.129	AGASSIZ (R.C.N.)	Burrard	15. 8.40	Sold 16/11/45.
K.103	ALBERNI (R.C.N.)	Canadian Yarrow	22. 8.40	Lost 21/8/44.
K.127	ALGOMA (R.C.N.)	Port Arthur	17.12.40	Venezuelan CONSTITUCION (1946).
K.148	AMHERST (R.C.N.)	St. John	4.12.40	Venezuelan FEDERACION (1946); scrapped 1956.

K.145	ARROWHEAD	Marine Industries	8. 8.40	R.C.N. (1941-45), mercantile SOUTHERN LARKSPUR (1948); scrapped Odense 11/59.
K.113	ARVIDA (R.C.N.)	Morton: J. Inglis	21. 9.40	Mercantile LA CEIBA (1950).
K.147	BADDECK (R.C.N.)	Davie Sbdg.	20.11.40	Mercantile EFTHALIA (1947), YUSUF Z. ALIREZA (1948), Saudi-Arabian (1955).
K.175	WETASKIWIN (R.C.N.) (ex-R.C.N. Banff)	Burrard	18. 7.40	Venezuelan VICTORIA (1946).
K.138	BARRIE (R.C.N.)	Collingwood: Dom. Eng. Wks.	23.11.40	Mercantile GASESTADO (1947); Argentinian CAPITAN CANEPA (1956/7).
K.165	BATTLEFORD (R.C.N.)	Collingwood	15. 4.41	Venezuelan LIBERTAD (1946); lost 12/4/49.
K.182	BITTERSWEET	Marine Industries	12. 9.40	R.C.N. (1941-45), scrapped Rosyth 15/7/47.
K.149	BRANDON (R.C.N.)	Davie Sbdg.	29. 4.41	Sold 5/10/45.
K.218	BRANTFORD (R.C.N.)	Midland	6. 9.41	Mercantile OLYMPIC ARROW (1950), OTORI MARU No. 11 (1956).
K.179	BUCTOUCHE (R.C.N.)	Davie Sbdg.	20.11.40	Sold 23/10/45.
K.231	CALGARY (R.C.N.)	Marine Industries	23. 8.41	Sold 30/8/46.
K.154	CAMROSE (R.C.N.)	Marine Industries	16.11.40	Scrapped Canada 6/47.
K.116	CHAMBLY (R.C.N.)	Canadian Vickers	29. 7.40	Mercantile SONIA VINKE (1952).
K.244	CHARLOTTETOWN (R.C.N.)	Kingston	10. 9.41	Lost 11/9/42.
K.156	CHICOUTIMI (R.C.N.)	Canadian Vickers	16.10.40	Scrapped Canada 6/46.
K.131	CHILLIWACK (R.C.N.)	Burrard	14. 9.40	Sold 5/10/45.
K.124	COBALT (R.C.N.)	Port Arthur: Dom. Eng. Wks.	17. 8.40	Mercantile JOHANNA W. VINKE (1953); scrapped S. Africa 15/12/61.
K.180	COLLINGWOOD (R.C.N.)	Collingwood	27. 7.40	Scrapped Canada 7/50.
K.157	DAUPHIN (R.C.N.)	Canadian Vickers	24.10.40	Mercantile CORTES (1949), SAN ANTONIO (1955).
K.104	DAWSON (R.C.N.)	Victoria	8. 2.41	Lost 22/3/46.

K.167	DRUMHELLER (R.C.N.)	Collingwood	5. 7.41	Sold 30/8/46.
K.229	DUNDAS (R.C.N.)	Victoria	25. 7.41	Sold 23/10/45.
K.177	DUNVEGAN (R.C.N.)	Marine Industries	11. 2.40	Venezuelan INDEPENDENCIA (1946); scrapped 1953.
K.106	EDMUNDSTON (R.C.N.)	Canadian Yarrow	22. 2.40	Mercantile AMAPALA (1948).
K.150	EYEBRIGHT	Canadian Vickers	22. 7.40	R.C.N. (1941-45), mercantile ALBERT W. VINKE (1950).
K.194	FENNEL	Marine Industries	20. 8.40	R.C.N. (1941-45), mercantile MILLIAM KIHL (1948).
K.273	LA MALBAIE (R.C.N.) (ex-R.C.N. Fort William—K.236)	Kingston	25.10.41	Sold 17/10/45.
K.245	FREDERICTON (R.C.N.)	Marine Industries	2. 9.41	Sold 14/7/45.
K.163	GALT (R.C.N.)	Collingwood	28.12.40	Sold 5/10/45.
K.237	HALIFAX (R.C.N.)	Collingwood	4.10.41	Mercantile (name not changed—1945).
K.159	HEPATICA	Davie Sbdg.	6. 7.40	R.C.N. (1941-45), scrapped Llanelly 1/1/48.
K.176	KAMLOOPS (R.C.N.)	Victoria	7. 8.40	Sold 19/10/45.
K.171	KAMSACK (R.C.N.)	Port Arthur	5. 5.41	Venezuelan CARABOBO (1945); lost 12/45
K.125	KENOGAMI (R.C.N.)	Port Arthur	5. 9.40	Scrapped Canada 1/50.
K.240	VANCOUVER (R.C.N.) (ex-R.C.N. Kitchener)	Canadian Yarrow	26. 8.41	Sold 5/10/45.
K.160	LETHBRIDGE (R.C.N.)	Canadian Vickers	21.11.40	Mercantile NICOLAAS VINKE (1952).
K.115	LEVIS (R.C.N.)	G. T. Davie	4. 9.40	Lost 20/9/41.
K.143	LOUISBURG (i) (R.C.N.)	Morton	27. 5.41	Lost 6/2/43.
K.151	LUNENBURG (R.C.N.)	G. T. Davie	10. 7.41	Scrapped Canada 6/46.
K.112	MATAPEDIA (R.C.N.)	Morton	14. 9.40	Scrapped Canada 12/50.
K.191	MAYFLOWER	Canadian Vickers	3. 7.40	R.C.N. (1941-45), scrapped Inverkeithing 20/9/49.
K.220	MIDLAND (R.C.N.)	Midland	25. 6.41	Sold 19/11/45.
K.139	MONCTON (R.C.N.)	St. John	11. 8.41	Mercantile WILLEM VINKE (1955).
K.164	MOOSE-JAW (R.C.N.)	Collingwood	9. 4.41	Scrapped Canada 9/49.

K.170	MORDEN (R.C.N.)	Port Arthur	5. 5.41	Scrapped Canada 11/56.
K.101	NANAIMO (R.C.N.)	Canadian Yarrow	28.10.40	Mercantile RENE W. VINKE (1953).
K.118	NAPANEE (R.C.N.)	Kingston	31. 8.40	Scrapped Canada 6/46.
K.228	NEW WESTMINSTER (R.C.N.)	Victoria: Dom. Eng. Wks.	14. 5.41	Mercantile ELISA (1950), PORTOVIEJO (1952), AZUA (1954).
K.178	OAKVILLE (R.C.N.)	Port Arthur	21. 6.41	Venezuelan PATRIA (1946).
K.119	ORILLIA (R.C.N.)	Collingwood	15. 9.40	Scrapped Canada 1/51.
K.146	PICTOU (R.C.N.)	Davie Sbdg.	5.10.40	Mercantile OLYMPIC CHASER (1950), OTORI MARU No. 7 (1956).
K.233	PORT ARTHUR (R.C.N.)	Port Arthur	18. 9.41	Sold 23/10/45.
K.161	PRESCOTT (R.C.N.)	Kingston	7. 1.41	Sold 19/9/45.
K.242	VILLE DE QUEBEC (R.C.N.) (ex-R.C.N. Quebec)	Morton	12.11.41	Mercantile DISPINA (1946), DOROTHEA PAXOS (1947), TANYA (1948), MEDEX (1949).
K.133	QUESNELL (R.C.N.)	Victoria	12.11.40	R.C.N. (1941); sold 5/10/45.
K.234	REGINA (R.C.N)	Marine Industries	14.10.41	Lost 8/8/44.
K.121	RIMOUSKI (R.C.N.)	Davie Sbdg.	3.10.40	Scrapped Canada 12/50.
K.169	ROSTHERN (R.C.N.)	Port Arthur	30.11.40	Scrapped Canada 6/46.
K.181	SACKVILLE (R.C.N)	St. John	15. 5.41	
K.158	SASKATOON (R.C.N.)	Canadian Vickers	7.11.40	Mercantile TRALOSMONTES (1948), OLYMPIC FIGHTER (1950), OTORI MARU No. 6 (1956).
K.136	SHAWINIGAN (R.C.N.)	G. T. Davie	16. 5.41	Lost 24/11/44.
K.110	SHEDIAC (R.C.N.)	Davie Sbdg.	29. 4.41	Mercantile JOOSKE W. VINKE (1954).
K.152	SHERBROOKE (R.C.N.)	Marine Industries	25.10.40	Scrapped Canada 5/47.
K.166	SNOWBERRY	Davie Sbdg.	8. 8.40	R.C.N. (1941-45), scrapped Middlesbrough 1947.
K.153	SOREL (R.C.N.)	Marine Industries	16.11.40	Sold 16/11/45.
K.198	SPIKENARD	Davie Sdbg.	10. 8.40	R.C.N. (1940); lost 11/2/42.
K.162	SUDBURY (R.C.N.)	Kingston	31. 5.41	Mercantile (name not changed—1949).

K.141	SUMMERSIDE (R.C.N.)	Morton	7. 5.41	Scrapped Canada 6/46.
K.168	THE PAS (R.C.N.)	Colling-wood	16. 8.41	Sold 16/9/45.
K.223	TIMMINS (R.C.N.)	Canadian Yarrow : J. Inglis	26. 6.41	Mercantile GUAYA-QUIL (ex-Trujillo—1948); lost 3/8/60.
K.174	TRAIL (R.C.N.)	Burrard	16.10.40	Scrapped Canada 8/50.
K.172	TRILLIUM	Canadian Vickers	26. 6.40	R.C.N. (1941-45), mercantile OLYMPIC RUNNER (1950), OTORI MARU No. 10 (1956).
K.225	KITCHENER (R.C.N.) (ex-R.C.N. Vancouver)	G. T. Davie	18.11.41	Scrapped Canada 9/49.
K.173	WEYBURN (R.C.N.)	Port Arthur	26. 7.41	Lost 22/2/43.
K.155	WINDFLOWER	Davie Sbdg.	4. 7.40	R.C.N. (1940); lost 7/12/41.
K.238	WOODSTOCK (R.C.N.)	Colling-wood	10.12.41	Mercantile OLYMPIC WINNER (1951), OTORI MARU No. 20 (1956), AKITSU MARU (1957).

Notes.—Three of the four ordered in the U.K. for the French Navy were taken over by the R.N. after June 1940. The fourth unit was lost whilst running trials under the French flag. ROCKROSE was sold to the S.A.N. after the war and converted to a surveying vessel. Only QUESNELL of the ten units built in Canada for the R.N. was taken over: the remainder were all lent to the R.C.N. during the war. Post war, SACKVILLE was converted to a coastal minelayer by the R.C.N.

Modified Flower class

Displacement: 980 tons.
Dimensions: 193 (pp) 208¼ (oa) × 33¼ × 11 ft.
Machinery: 1-shaft Reciprocating (4-cyl. V.T.E.), I.H.P. 2,880 = 16 knots.
Armament: 1—4 in., 1—2 pdr. A.A., 6—20 mm. A.A. (6 × 1) guns; 1—A.T.W. (Hedgehog). *Complement:* 109.

K.385	ARABIS (ii)	Brown: Kincaid	28.10.43	R.N.Z.N. (1944-48); scrapped Grays 8/51.
K.403	ARBUTUS (ii)	Brown: Kincaid	26. 1.44	R.N.Z.N. (1944-48); scrapped Dunston 6/51.
	BALM	Hall		Cancelled 12/11/42.
K.274	BETONY	Hall	22. 4.43	R.I.N. SIND (1945), R.Th.N. PRASE (1947); lost 13/1/51.
K.275	BUDLEIA	Hall	19. 6.43	R.C.N. GIFFARD (1944); scrapped Canada 10/52.

Left: H.M.S. Peony was also modified as H.M.S. Gloxinia. She had an entire A.A. armament comprising a 3 in. gun forward, quadruple .5 in. M.G.s and two 20 mm. amidships and a 2 pdr. and single 20 mm. further aft.
[*P. A. Vicary*

Right: H.M.S. Arbutus belonged to the **Modified Flower** class and incorporated all the alterations effected in the earlier corvettes. Note the A.T.W. (Hedgehog) abaft the 4 in. gun and to starboard.
[*P. A. Vicary*

K.306	BUGLOSS	Crown: Clark and N.E. Marine	21. 6.43	R.I.N. ASSAM (1945-47); scrapped.
K.307	BULRUSH	Crown: Clark	11.10.43	R.C.N. MIMICO (K.485—1944); mercantile OLYMPIC VICTOR (1950), OTORI MARU No. 12 (1956).
K.348	BURNET	Ferguson	31. 5.43	R.I.N. GONDWANA (1945), R.Th.N. BANGPAKONG (1947).
K.382	CANDYTUFT (ii)	Inglis: Kincaid	30. 8.43	R.C.N. LONG-BRANCH (K.487—1944), mercantile REXTON KENT II (1947), REXTON KENT (1948).
K.360	CEANOTHUS	Ferguson	27.10.43	R.C.N. FORREST HILL (K.486—1944); for disposal.
K.395	CHARLOCK	Ferguson	16.11.43	R.I.N. MAHRATTA (1946-47), scrapped.
K.358	ASBESTOS (R.C.N.)	Morton	22.11.43	Scrapped New Orleans 3/49.
K.15	ATHOLL (R.C.N.)	Morton	5. 5.43	Scrapped Canada 10/52.
K.540	BEAUHARNOIS (R.C.N.)	Morton	11. 5.44	Israeli WEDGEWOOD (1950); scrapped 1956.
K.332	BELLEVILLE (R.C.N.)	Kingston	17. 6.44	Dominican JUAN BAUTISTA CAMBIASO (1947).
	BRAMPTON (R.C.N.)	Morton		Cancelled 12/43.
K.333	COBOURG (R.C.N.)	Midland: Enterprise Engr.	14. 7.43	Mercantile CAMEO (1945), DUNDAS KENT (1948), PUERTO DEL SOL (1951).
K.277	COMFREY	Collingwood	28. 7.42	U.S.N. ACTION (1943), mercantile ARNE PRESTHUS (1952).
K.278	CORNEL	Collingwood	4. 9.42	U.S.N. ALACRITY (1943), mercantile RIO MARINA (1948), PORTO FERRAIO (1951).
K.279	DITTANY (ex-U.S.N. Beacon)	Collingwood	31.10.42	Mercantile OLYMPIC CRUISER (1950); OTORI MARU No. 2 (1956).

K.686	FERGUS (R.C.N.) (ex-R.C.N. Fort Francis)	Colling-wood	30. 8.44	Mercantile CAMCO II (1945), HARCOURT KENT (1948); lost 22/11/49.
K.284	FLAX	Kingston	15. 6.42	U.S.N. BRISK (1943), mercantile FLAX (1947), ARIANA (1951), ARVIDA BAY (1955).
K.335	FRONTENAC (R.C.N.)	Kingston	2. 6.43	For disposal.
K.687	GUELPH (R.C.N.)	Colling-wood	20.12.43	Mercantile (name not changed—1946) JOSEPHINE LANASA (1955), BURFIN (1956).
K.415	HAWKESBURY (R.C.N.)	Morton: C.P.R.	16.11.43	Mercantile CAM-PUCHEA (1950); scrapped Hong Kong 1956.
K.285	HONESTY (ex-U.S.N. Caprice)	Kingston	28. 9.42	Returned U.S.N. 5/1/46.
K.336	INGERSOLL (R.C.N.)	Morton		Cancelled 12/43.
K.440	LACHUTE (R.C.N.)	Morton	9. 6.44	Dominican CRISTO-BAL COLON (1947).
K.282	LINARIA (ex-U.S.N. Clash)	Midland	18.11.42	Mercantile PORTO OFFURO (1948)?
K.338	LINDSAY (R.C.N.)	Midland	4. 6.43	Mercantile NORTH SHAW (1946).
K.439	LISTOWEL (R.C.N.)	Kingston		Cancelled 12/43.
K.401	LOUISBURG (ii)	Morton	13. 7.43	Dominican JUAN ALEJANDRO ACOSTA (1947).
K.287	MANDRAKE	Morton	22. 8.42	U.S.N. HASTE (1943), mercantile PORTO AZZURO (1949).
	MEAFORD (R.C.N.)	Midland		Cancelled 12/43.
K.288	MILFOIL	Morton	5. 8.42	U.S.N. INTENSITY (1943), mercantile OLYMPIC PRO-MOTER (1950), OTORI MARU No. 5 (1956).
K.289	MUSK	Morton	15. 7.42	U.S.N. MIGHT (1943), mercantile OLYMPIC EXPLORER (1950), OTORI MARU No. 3 (1956), KYO MARU No. 12 (1957).

K.290	NEPETA	Morton	29.11.42	U.S.N. PERT (1943), mercantile OLYMPIC LEADER (1950), OTORI MARU No. 1 (1956), KYO MARU No. 15 (1957).
K.520	NORSYD (R.C.N.)	Morton	31. 7.43	Mercantile BALBOA (1948), Israeli HAGANAH (1950); scrapped 1956.
K.339	NORTH BAY (R.C.N.)	Colling-wood Enterprise Engr.	27. 4.43	Mercantile KENT COUNTY II (1946), GALLOWAY KENT (1950), BEDFORD II (1951).
K.340	OWEN SOUND (R.C.N.)	Colling-wood	15. 6.43	Mercantile CADIO (1946).
K.341	PARRY SOUND (R.C.N.)	Midland	13.11.43	Mercantile OLYMPIC CHAMPION (1950), OTORI MARU No. 15 (1956).
K.342	PETER-BOROUGH (R.C.N.)	Kingston	15. 1.44	Dominican GERARD JANSEN (1947).
K.688	MERRITTONIA (R.C.N.) (ex-R.C.N. Pointe Claire)	Morton	24. 6.44	Lost 30/11/45.
K.291	PRIVET	Morton	4.12.42	U.S.N. PRUDENT (1943), Italian ELBANO (1949), STAFFETTA (1951).
K.452	RENFREW (R.C.N.)	Kingston		Cancelled 12/43.
K.357	RIVIERE DU LOUP (R.C.N.)	Morton	2. 7.43	Dominican JUAN BAUTISTA MAGGI-OLO (1947).
K.286	ROSEBAY (ex-U.S.N. Spendor)	Kingston	11. 2.43	Mercantile BENMARK (1947), FRIDA (1950).
K.343	St. LAMBERT (R.C.N.)	Morton: C.P.R.	6.11.43	Mercantile CHRYSI HONDROULIS (1946), LOULA (1955).
	SIMCOE (R.C.N.)	Morton		Cancelled 12/43.
K.280	SMILAX (ex-U.S.N. Tact)	Colling-wood	24.12.42	Argentinian REPUB-LICA (1946).
K.345	SMITHS FALLS (R.C.N.)	Kingston	19. 8.44	Mercantile OLYMPIC LIGHTNING (1950), OTORI MARU No. 16 (1956).
K.281	STATICE (ex-U.S.N. Vim)	Colling-wood	10. 4.43	Returned U.S.N. 21/6/46.
K.457	STELLARTON (R.C.N.)	Morton	27. 4.44	Chilean CASMA (1946).
K.455	STRATHROY (R.C.N.)	Midland	30. 8.44	Chilean CHIPANA (1946).

K.394	THORLOCK (R.C.N.)	Midland	15. 5.44	Chilean PAPUDO (1946).
K.368	TRENTONIAN (R.C.N.)	Kingston	1. 9.43	Lost 22/2/45.
K.369	WEST YORK (R.C.N.)	Midland	25. 1.44	Mercantile GAUTEMALA (1946), MOULAY BOUCHAIB (1946), ESPRESSO (1953), FEDERAL EXPRESS (1960); lost 5/5/60.
K.346	WHITBY (R.C.N.)	Midland	18. 9.43	For disposal 30/8/46.
K.283	WILLOWHERB (ex-U.S.N. Vitality)	Midland	24. 3.43	Returned U.S.N. 11/6/46; scrapped Hamburg 1961.

Notes.—The U.S.N. acquired eight units building in Canada for the R.N. and conversely turned over to the R.N. eight units which they had ordered.

Castle class

Displacement: 1,010 tons.
Dimensions: 225 (pp) 252 (oa) × $36\frac{3}{4}$ × 10 ft.
Machinery: 1-shaft Reciprocating (4-cyl. V.T.E.), I.H.P. 2,880 = $16\frac{1}{2}$ knots.
Armament: 1—4 in., 10—20 mm. A.A. (2 × 2 & 6 × 1) guns; 1—ATW (Squid). *Complement:* 120.

K.689	ALLINGTON CASTLE (ex-Amaryllis)	Fleming & Ferguson	29. 2.44	Scrapped Sunderland 20/12/58.
K.405	ALNWICK CASTLE	Brown: Kincaid	23. 5.44	Scrapped Gateshead 12/58.
	ALTON CASTLE	Fleming & Ferguson		Cancelled.
K.386	AMBERLEY CASTLE	Austin: Clark	27.11.43	O.W.S. WEATHER ADVISER (1960).
	APPLEBY CASTLE	Austin		Cancelled.
K.412	BAMBOROUGH CASTLE	Lewis	11. 1.44	Scrapped Llanelly 22/5/59.
K.694	BARNARD CASTLE	Brown: Kincaid	5.10.44	Completed as mercantile EMPIRE SHELTER (1945); scrapped Belgium 29/7/55.
	BERE CASTLE	Brown		Cancelled.
K.387	BERKLEY CASTLE	Barclay Curle	19. 8.43	Scrapped Grays 26/9/55.
K.690	CAISTOR CASTLE	Lewis	22. 5.44	Scrapped Troon 3/56.
	CALDECOT CASTLE	Brown		Cancelled.
	CALSHOT CASTLE	Inglis		Cancelled.

K.379	CARISBROOKE CASTLE	Caledon: Clark	31. 7.43	Scrapped Faslane 14/6/58.
K.696	DENBIGH CASTLE	Lewis	5. 8.44	Lost 13/2/45.
	DOVER CASTLE	Inglis		Cancelled.
	DUDLEY CASTLE	Inglis		Cancelled.
K.388	DUMBARTON CASTLE	Caledon: Hargreaves	28. 9.43	Scrapped 16/11/60.
K.413	FARNHAM CASTLE	Crown: Clark	25. 4.44	Scrapped Gateshead 31/10/60.
K.383	FLINT CASTLE	Robb: Plenty	1. 9.43	Scrapped Faslane 10/7/58.
K.529	GOREY CASTLE	Crown: Clark	30.10.44	HEDINGHAM CASTLE (ii) (1945); scrapped 1957.
K.378	GUILDFORD CASTLE	Robb: Walker	13.11.43	R.C.N. HESPELER (K. 489—1944), mercantile CHILCOTIN (1947), STELLA MARIS (1958).
K.355	HADLEIGH CASTLE	Smiths Dock	21. 6.43	For disposal.
K.396	HEDINGHAM CASTLE (i)	Robb: Plenty	26. 1.44	R.C.N. ORANGEVILLE (K. 491—1944) mercantile TA TUNG (1947), HSI LING (1947), SHIH LIN (1947), Chinese (Nat.) TE AN (1951).
K.521	HEVER CASTLE	Blyth: White	24. 2.44	R.C.N. COPPERCLIFF (K.495—1944), mercantile TA LUNG (1947), WAN LEE (1947), Chinese (Com.)
K.416	HURST CASTLE	Caledon: Thornycroft	23. 2.44	Lost 1/9/44.
K.420	KENILWORTH CASTLE	Smiths Dock	17. 8.43	Scrapped Llanelly 20/6/59.
K.389	KNARES-BOROUGH CASTLE	Blyth: White	28. 9.43	Scrapped Port Glasgow 16/3/56.
K.691	LANCASTER CASTLE	Fleming & Ferguson	14. 4.44	Scrapped Gateshead 6/9/60.
K.397	LAUNCESTON CASTLE	Blyth: White	27.11.43	Scrapped St. Davids-on-Forth 3/8/59.
K.384	LEEDS CASTLE	Pickersgill: Clark	12.10.43	Scrapped Grays 5/6/58.
K.443	MAIDEN CASTLE	Fleming & Ferguson	8. 6.44	Completed as mercantile EMPIRE LIFEGUARD (1944); scrapped Belgium 22/7/55.
	MONMOUTH CASTLE (ex-Peel Castle)	Lewis		Cancelled.

K.693	MORPETH CASTLE	Pickersgill: Clark	26.11.43	Scrapped Llanelly 9/8/60.
K.447	NORHAM CASTLE (ex-Totnes Castle)	Inglis: Harland & Wolff and Fawcett, Preston	12. 4.44	R.C.N. HUMBERSTONE (K.497—1944), mercantile TA WEI (1947), CHANG CHENG (1947), KING KANG (1949), TAI SHAN (1950), FLYING DRAGON (1951), SAN BLAS (1951), SOUTH OCEAN (1954); scrapped Hong Kong 9/59.
	NORWICH CASTLE	Brown		Cancelled.
K.446	NUNNERY CASTLE	Pickersgill: Clark	26. 1.44	R.C.N. BOWMANVILLE (K.493—1944), mercantile TA SHUN (1947), YUAN PEI (1947), Chinese (Com.) KUANO CHOU (1951).
K.530	OAKHAM CASTLE	Inglis: Harland & Wolff and Robey	20. 7.44	O.W.S. WEATHER REPORTER (1958).
	OSWESTRY CASTLE	Crown		Cancelled.
K.692	OXFORD CASTLE	Harland & Wolff	11.12.43	Scrapped Briton Ferry 6/9/60.
K.450	PEMBROKE CASTLE	Ferguson	12. 2.44	R.C.N. TILLSONBURG (K.496—1944), mercantile TA TING (1947), CHIU CHIN (1947), Chinese (Nat.) KAO AN (1952).
	PENDENNIS CASTLE	Crown		Cancelled.
K.449	PEVENSEY CASTLE	Harland & Wolff	11. 1.44	O.W.S WEATHER MONITOR (1960).
K.362	PORTCHESTER CASTLE	Swan Hunter	21. 6.43	Scrapped Clyde 14/5/58.
K.695	RAYLEIGH CASTLE	Ferguson	19. 6.44	Completed as mercantile EMPIRE REST (1944); scrapped.
	RHUDDLAN CASTLE	Crown		Cancelled.
K.398	RISING CASTLE	Harland & Wolff	8. 2.44	R.C.N. ARNPRIOR (K.494—1944), Uruguayan MONTEVIDEO (1948).
K.372	RUSHEN CASTLE	Swan Hunter	16. 7.43	O.W.S. WEATHER SURVEYOR (1960).

K.373	SANDGATE CASTLE	Smiths Dock	28.12.43	R.C.N. St. THOMAS (K.488—1944), mercantile CAMOSUN (1946), CHILCOTIN (1958), YUKON STAR (1958).
K.536	SCARBOROUGH CASTLE	Fleming & Ferguson	8. 9.44	Completed as mercantile EMPIRE PEACE-MAKER (1945); scrapped Belgium 6/55
K.453	SHERBORNE CASTLE	Harland & Wolff	24. 2.44	R.C.N. PETROLIA (K.498—1944); for disposal, 23/5/46.
K.374	SHREWSBURY CASTLE	Swan Hunter	16. 8.43	R.N.N. TUNSBERG CASTLE (1944); los 12/12/44.
K.393	TAMWORTH CASTLE	Smiths Dock	26. 1.44	R.C.N. KINCARDINE (K.490—1944), mercantile SAADA (1947)
	THORNBURY CASTLE	Ferguson		Cancelled.
K.399	TINTAGEL CASTLE	Ailsa	13.12.43	Scrapped 1958.
	TONBRIDGE CASTLE	Austin		Cancelled—would have become R.C.N.
K.460	WALMER CASTLE	Smiths Dock	10. 3.44	R.C.N. LEASIDE (K.492—1944), mercantile COQUITLAM (1947), GLACIER QUEEN (1958).
	WARKWORTH CASTLE	Fleming & Ferguson		Cancelled.
K.461	WOLVESEY CASTLE	Ailsa	24. 2.44	R.C.N. HUNTSVILLE (K.499—1944), mercantile WELLINGTON KENT (1947), BELLE ISLE II (1951), los 19/8/60.
K.537	YORK CASTLE	Ferguson	20. 9.44	Completed as mercantile EMPIRE COMFORT (1945); scrappe Belgium 6/55.
	AYDON CASTLE	Kingston		Cancelled.
	BARNWELL CASTLE	Kingston		Cancelled.
	BEESTON CASTLE	Kingston		Cancelled.
	BODIAM CASTLE	Collingwood		Cancelled.
	BOLTON CASTLE	Collingwood		Cancelled.
	BOWES CASTLE	Kingston		Cancelled.
	BRAMBER CASTLE	Collingwood		Cancelled.

H.M.S. Tintagel Castle belonged to the **Castle** class of corvette. Noteworthy features are the capped funnel, lattice foremast with HF/DF aerial on the topmast and an A.T.W. (Squid) on the forward shelter deck. [*P. A. Vicary*

	BRIDGNORTH CASTLE	Colling-wood		Cancelled.
	BROUGH CASTLE	Colling-wood		Cancelled.
	CANTERBURY CASTLE	Midland		Cancelled.
	CAREW CASTLE	Midland		Cancelled.
	CHEPSTOW CASTLE	Colling-wood		Cancelled.
	CHESTER CASTLE	Colling-wood		Cancelled. Cancelled.
	CHRISTCHURCH CASTLE	Midland		Cancelled.
	CLARE CASTLE	Colling-wood		Cancelled.
	CLAVERING CASTLE	Colling-wood		Cancelled.
	CLITHEROE CASTLE	Colling-wood		Cancelled.
	CLUN CASTLE	Midland		Cancelled.
	COLCHESTER CASTLE	Midland		Cancelled.
K.527	CORFE CASTLE	?		Cancelled.
K.528	CORNET CASTLE	Colling-wood		Cancelled.
	COWES CASTLE	Colling-wood		Cancelled.
	COWLING CASTLE	Midland		Cancelled.
	CRICCIETH CASTLE	Morton		Cancelled.
	CROMER CASTLE	Midland		Cancelled.
	DEVIZES CASTLE	Kingston		Cancelled.
	DHYFE CASTLE	Colling-wood		Cancelled.
	DUNSTER CASTLE	Midland		Cancelled.
	EGREMONT CASTLE	Kingston		Cancelled.
	FOTHERINGAY CASTLE	Morton		Cancelled.
	HELMSLEY CASTLE	Morton		Cancelled.
	MALLING CASTLE	Morton		Cancelled.
	MALMESBURY CASTLE	Morton		Cancelled.
	RABY CASTLE	Morton		Cancelled.
	TREMATON CASTLE	Morton		Cancelled.
	TUTBURY CASTLE	Morton		Cancelled.
	WIGMORE CASTLE	Midland		Cancelled.

Notes.—Five were completed as mercantile rescue ships during the war.

FRIGATES

River class

Displacement: 1,370 tons.
Dimensions: 283 (pp) 301¼ (oa) × 36½ × 9 ft.
Machinery: 2-shaft Reciprocating (4 cyl. V.T.E.) I.H.P. 5,500, except † geared Turbines, S.H.P. 6,500 = 20 knots.
Armament: 2—4 in., 10—20 mm. A.A. (10 × 1) except * 2—4 in. A.A. (1 × 2), 1—3 in. A.A., 6—20 mm. A.A. (2 × 2 & 2 × 1) and ‡ 4—4 in. A.A. (2 × 2), 2—40 mm. A.A. (2 × 1), 4—20 mm. A.A. (2 × 2) guns; 1—A.T.W. (Hedgehog). *Complement:* 140 except ‡ 177.

K.262	AIRE	Fleming & Ferguson	22. 4.43	TAMAR (1946), AIRE (1946); lost 23/12/46.
K.404	ANNAN	Hall Russell: Thornycroft	29.12.43	R.C.N. (1944-45), R.D.N. NIELS EBBESEN (1945).
K.97	AVON	Hill: Bellis & Morcom	19. 6.43	Portuguese NUNO TRISTAO (1949).
K.526	AWE	Fleming & Ferguson	28.12.43	Portuguese DIOGO GOMES (1949).
K.255	BALLINDERRY	Blyth: Hawthorn Leslie and Fletcher	7.12.42	Scrapped Barrow 7/7/61.
K.256	BANN	Hill: Bellis & Morcom	29.12.42	R.I.N. TIR (1947).
K.263	BRAID	Simons	30.11.43	French L'AVENTURE (1943).
K.264	CAM†	Brown: Parsons	31. 7.43	Scrapped Tyne 22/6/45.
K.221	CHELMER†	Brown: Parsons	27. 3.43	Scrapped Charlestown 8/57.
K.21	DART	Blyth: Hawthorn Leslie	10.10.42	Scrapped Newport 1957.
K.257	DERG	Robb: Plenty	7. 1.43	R.N.V.R. CAMBRIA (S. Wales—1947); scrapped 1960.
K.265	DEVERON	Smiths Dock	12.10.42	R.I.N. DHANUSH (1945), R.P.N. ZULFIQUAR (1948).
K.411	DUDDON	Blyth: Clark	10.11.43	RIBBLE (K.525—1944), R.C.N. (1944-46), scrapped Blyth 9/7/57.
K.254	ETTRICK†	Crown: Parsons	5. 2.43	R.C.N. (1944-45); scrapped Grays 6/56.
K.92	EXE	Fleming & Ferguson	19. 3.42	Scrapped Preston 20/9/56.
K.266	FAL	Smiths Dock	9.11.42	Burmese MAYU (1947).
K.267	FROME	Blyth: Hawthorn Leslie	1. 6.43	French L'ESCARMOUCHE (1943).

K.417	HALLADALE†	Inglis: Parsons	28. 1.44	Mercantile (name not changed—1949), NORDEN (1962), TURIST EXPRESSEN (1962).
K.252	HELFORD	Hall Russell: Yarrow	6. 2.43	Scrapped Troon 29/6/56.
K.253	HELMSDALE†	Inglis: Parsons	5. 6.43	Scrapped Faslane 7/11/57.
K.227	ITCHEN	Fleming & Ferguson	29. 7.42	Lost 22/9/43.
K.235	JED	Hill: Bellis & Morcom	30. 7.42	Scrapped Milford Haven 25/7/57.
K.241	KALE	Inglis: Hawthorn Leslie	24. 6.42	Scrapped Newport 1957.
K.259	LAGAN	Smiths Dock	28. 7.42	Constructive total loss 20/9/43; scrapped Troon 21/5/46.
K.268	LAMBOURNE	Fleming & Ferguson	14.10.43	DOVEY (K.523—1944); scrapped Preston 2/11/55.
K.365	LOCHY	Hall Russell	30.10.43	Scrapped Troon 29/6/56.
K.269	MEON	Inglis: Fleming & Ferguson	4. 8.43	R.C.N. (1944-45).
K.441	MONNOW	Hill: Bellis & Morcom	4.12.43	R.C.N. (1944-45), R.D.N. HOLGER DANSKE (1945); for disposal.
K.261	MOURNE	Smiths Dock	24. 9.42	Lost 15/6/44.
K.260	MOYOLA	Smiths Dock	27. 8.42	French TONKINOIS (1943), LA CONFIANCE (19).
K.392	NADDER	Smiths Dock	15. 9.43	R.C.N. (1944-45), R.I.N. SHAMSHER (1945), R.P.N. (name not changed—1948).
K.270	NENE	Smiths Dock	9.12.42	R.C.N. (1944-45); scrapped Briton Ferry 21/7/55.
K.219	NESS	Robb: Plenty	30. 7.42	Scrapped Newport 1956.
K.215	NITH	Robb: Yarrow	25. 9.42	Egyptian DOMIAT (1948); lost 31/10/56.
K.356	ODZANI	Smiths Dock	19. 5.43	Scrapped Newport 1957.
K.271	PLYM	Smiths Dock	4. 2.43	R.N.V.R. drillship (1948); expended 3/10/52.

K.251	RIBBLE	Simons	23. 4.43	R.Neth.N. JOHAN MAURITS VAN NASSAU (1943); R.C.N. (1944-45); scrapped 1959.
K.224	ROTHER	Smiths Dock	20.11.41	Scrapped Troon 22/4/55.
K.246	SPEY	Smiths Dock	18.12.41	Egyptian RASHEED (1948).
K.258	STRULE (ex-Glenarm)	Robb: Smiths Dock	8. 3.43	French CROIX DE LORRAINE (1943).
K.217	SWALE	Smiths Dock	16. 1.42	Scrapped Faslane 26/2/55.
K.367	TAFF	Hill: Bellis & Morcom	11. 9.43	Scrapped Newport 1957.
K.272	TAVY	Hill: Bellis & Morcom	3. 4.43	Scrapped Newport 18/7/55.
K.232	TAY	Smiths Dock	18. 3.42	Scrapped Rosyth 28/9/56.
K.293	TEES	Hall Russell	20. 5.43	Scrapped Newport 16/7/55.
K.458	TEME	Smiths Dock	11.11.43	R.C.N. (1944-45), constructive total loss 29/3/45; scrapped Llanelly 8/12/45.
K.239	TEST	Hall Russell	30. 5.42	R.I.N. NEZA (1945-46); scrapped Faslane 25/2/55.
K.222	TEVIOT	Hall Russell	12.10.42	Scrapped Briton Ferry 9/3/55.
K.292	TORRIDGE	Blyth: Clark	16. 8.43	French LA SURPRISE (1943).
K.294	TOWY	Smiths Dock	4. 3.43	Scrapped Port Glasgow 6/56.
K.243	TRENT	Hill: Bellis & Morcom	10.10.43	R.I.N. KUKRI (1946), R.P.N. INVESTI-GATOR (1948).
K.250	TWEED†	Inglis: Parsons	24.11.42	Lost 7/1/44.
K.295	USK	Smiths Dock	3. 4.43	Egyptian ABIKIR (1948), scuttled 10/56 and salved and scrapped 1957.
K.248	WAVENEY	Smiths Dock	30. 4.42	Scrapped Troon 9/11/57.
K.230	WEAR	Smiths Dock	1. 6.42	Scrapped Sunderland 29/10/57.
K.270	WINDRUSH	Robb: Plenty	18. 6.43	French LE DECOUVERTE (1943); for disposal.
K.371	WYE	Robb: Lobnitz	16. 8.43	Scrapped Faslane 1954.

J.467	BALMAIN (R.A.N.)	Sydney		Cancelled 1944.
K.375	BARCOO (R.A.N.)	Cockatoo	26. 8.43	
K.406	BARWON (R.A.N.)	Cockatoo	3. 8.44	Scrapped Japan 8/62.
K.09	BOGAM (R.A.N.)	Newcastle		Cancelled 1944.
K.376	BURDEKIN (R.A.N.)	Walkers	30. 6.43	Scrapped Japan 1/62.
K.24	CAMPASPE (R.A.N.)	Sydney		Cancelled 1944.
K.698	CONDAMINE (R.A.N.)‡	Newcastle	4.11.44	Scrapped Japan 1/62.
K.532	MACQUARIE (R.A.N.) (ex-Culgoa)	Morts Dock	3. 3.45	Scrapped Japan 8/62.
K.377	DIAMANTINA (R.A.N.)	Walkers	6. 4.44	
K.354	GASCOYNE (R.A.N.)	Morts Dock	20. 2.43	
K.363	HAWKESBURY (R.A.N.)	Morts Dock	24. 7.43	Scrapped Japan 1962.
K.364	LACHLAN (R.A.N.)	Morts Dock	25. 3.44	R.N.Z.N. (1950).
K.408	CULGOA(R.A.N.)‡ (ex-Macquarrie)	Williams-town	22. 9.44	
K.442	MURCHISON (R.A.N.)‡	Evans Deakin	31.10.44	Scrapped Japan 1962.
K.534	MURRUM-BIDGEE (R.A.N.)	Melbourne		Cancelled 1944.
K.55	NAOMI (R.A.N.)	Sydney		Cancelled 1944.
K.468	NEPEAN (R.A.N.)			Cancelled 1944.
K.535	SHOALHAVEN (R.A.N.)‡	Walkers	14.12.44	Scrapped Japan 8/62.
K.533	WARBURTON (R.A.N.)	Evans Deakin		Cancelled 1944.
K.66	WILLIAMSTOWN (R.A.N.)			Cancelled.
K.86	WIMMERA (R.A.N.)	Sydney		Cancelled 1944.
	WOLLONDILLY (R.A.N.)	Sydney		Cancelled 1944.
K.269	ADUR	Canadian Vickers	22. 8.42	R.C.N. NADUR (1942), U.S.N. ASHEVILLE (1942), Argentinian HERCULES (1947).
	ALEXANDRIA (R.C.N.)	Montreal		Cancelled 12/43.
K.677	ROYAL MOUNT (R.C.N.) (ex-R.C.N. Alvington)	Canadian Vickers	15. 4.44	Scrapped Canada 18/11/47.
K.297	ANNAN	Canadian Vickers	12. 9.42	U.S.N. NATCHEZ (1942), Dominican JUAN PABLO DUARTE (1946).
K.661	ANTIGONISH (R.C.N.)*	Canadian Yarrow	10. 2.44	

K.289	BARLE (ex-U.S.N.)	Canadian Vickers	26. 9.42	Returned U.S.N 27/2/46.
K.407	BEACON HILL (R.C.N.)	Canadian Yarrow	6.11.43	
K.662	PRESTONIAN (R.C.N.) (ex-Beauharnois)	Davie Sbdg.	22. 6.44	R.N.N. TROLL (1956).
K.663	CAP DE LA MADELEINE (R.C.N.)	Morton	13. 5.44	
K.350	CAPE BRETON (R.C.N.)	Morton	24.11.42	Expended as breakwater 1948.
K.409	CAPILANO (R.C.N.)	Canadian Yarrow	8. 4.44	Mercantile IRVING FRANCES M (1948); lost 1953.
K.664	CARLPLACE (R.C.N.)	Davie Sbdg.	6. 7.44	Dominican PRESIDENTE TRUJILLO (1946).
K.244	CHARLOTTETOWN (R.C.N.)	G. T. Davie	16. 9.43	Expended as breakwater 1948.
K.317	CHEBOGUE (R.C.N.)	Canadian Yarrow	16. 8.43	Constructive total loss 4/10/44; scrapped 1948.
K.410	COATICOOK (R.C.N.)	Davie Sbdg.	25.11.43	Scuttled 14/12/61.
K.299	CUCKMERE (ex-U.S.N.)	Canadian Vickers	24.10.42	Returned U.S.N. 6/11/46.
K.665	EASTVIEW (R.C.N.)	Canadian Vickers	17.11.43	Expended as breakwater 1948.
K.300	EVENLODE (ex-U.S.N. Danville)	Canadian Vickers	8.11.42	Returned U.S.N. 8/3/46.
K.301	FINDHORN (ex-U.S.N.)	Canadian Vickers	5.12.42	Returned U.S.N. 20/3/46.
	FOSTER (R.C.N.)	Lauzon		Cancelled 12/43.
K.538	TORONTO (R.C.N.) (ex-Giffard —K.402)	Davie Sbdg.	18. 9.43	R.N.N. GARM (1956).
K.671	LAUZON (R.C.N.) (ex- Glace Bay)	G. T. Davie	10. 6.44	
K.518	GROU (R.C.N.)	Canadian Vickers	7. 8.43	Scrapped Victoria 1948.
K.666	HALLOWELL (R.C.N.)	Canadian Vickers	28. 3.44	Israeli MISNAK (1950).
	HARDROCK (R.C.N.)	Montreal		Cancelled 12/43.
	HENRYVILLE (R.C.N.)	Lauzon		Cancelled 12/43.
K.667	INCH ARRAN	Davie Sbdg.	6. 6.44	
K.302	INVER (ex-U.S.N.)	Canadian Vickers	12.12.42	Returned U.S.N. 4/3/46.
K.418	JOLIETTE (R.C.N.)	Morton	12.11.43	Chilean IQUIQUE (1946).
K.318	JONQUIERE (R.C.N.)	G. T. Davie	28.10.43	

K.419	KONKANEE (R.C.N.)*	Canadian Yarrow	27.11.43	Mercantile BENGAL (1950).
K.668	LA HULLOISE (R.C.N.)*	Canadian Vickers	29.10.43	
K.519	LA SALLE (R.C.N.)	Davie Sbdg.	12.11.43	Expended as breakwater 1948.
K.670	FORT ERIE (R.C.N.) (ex-La Tuque)	G. T. Davie	27. 5.44	
K.669	LANARK (R.C.N.)	Canadian Vickers	10.12.43	
K.414	GLACE BAY (R.C.N.) (ex-Lauzon)	G. T. Davie	26. 4.44	Chilean ESMERALDA (1946), BAQUEDANO (1952).
	LE HAVRE (R.C.N.)	Victoria		Cancelled 12/43.
K.400	LEVIS (R.C.N.)	G. T. Davie	26.11.43	Expended as breakwater 1948.
	LINGABAR (R.C.N.)	Lauzon		Cancelled 12/43.
K.672	LONGUEUIL (R.C.N.)	Canadian Vickers	30.10.43	Scrapped Canada 1949.
K.303	LOSSIE (ex-U.S.N.)	Canadian Vickers	30. 4.43	Mercantile TETI (1947), ADRIATIKI (1955).
K.673	MAGOG (R.C.N.)	Canadian Vickers	22. 9.43	Constructive total loss 14/10/44; scrapped Sorel 1945/46.
K.444	MATANE (R.C.N.) (ex-Stormont)	Canadian Vickers	29. 5.43	Expended as breakwater 1948.
K.394	SEA CLIFF (R.C.N.) (ex-Megantic)	Davie Sbdg.	3. 7.44	Chilean CAVADONGA (1946).
K.319	MONTREAL (R.C.N.) (ex- Stormont)	Canadian Vickers	12. 6.43	Scrapped Canada 1948.
K.320	NEW GLASGOW (R.C.N.)	Canadian Yarrow	5. 5.43	
K.321	NEW WATERFORD (R.C.N.)	Canadian Yarrow	3. 7.43	
K.448	ORKNEY (R.C.N.)	Canadian Yarrow	18. 9.43	Mercantile VIOLETTA (1947), Israeli MIVTAKH (1950), R.Cey. N. MAHASENA (1959).
	NORTHUMBERLAND (R.C.N.)	Victoria		Cancelled 12/43.
K.322	OUTREMONT (R.C.N.)	Morton	3. 7.43	
K.304	PARRET (ex-U.S.N.)	Canadian Vickers	30. 4.43	Returned U.S.N. 5/2/46.

	PESAQUID (R.C.N.)	Victoria		Cancelled 12/43.
	PLESSIVILLE (R.C.N.)	Lauzon		Cancelled 12/43.
K.326	PORT COLBORNE (R.C.N.)	Canadian Yarrow	21. 4.43	Scrapped Canada 1948.
K.675	POUNDMAKER (R.C.N.)	Canadian Vickers	21. 4.44	Peruvian TENIENTE FERRE (1947), FERRE (1953).
K.324	PRINCE RUPERT (R.C.N.)	Canadian Yarrow	3. 2.43	Expended as breakwater 1947.
	RANNEY FALLS (R.C.N.)	Lauzon		Cancelled 12/43.
K.685	BUCKINGHAM (R.C.N.) (ex-Royal Mount)	Davie Sbdg.	28. 4.44	
K.676	PENETANG (R.C.N.) (ex-Rouyn)	Davie Sbdg.	6. 7.44	R.N.N. DRAUG (1956)
K.678	RUNNYMEDE (R.C.N.)	Canadian Vickers	27.11.43	For disposal (partially dismantled).
	St. AGATHE (R.C.N.)	Quebec		Cancelled 12/43.
K.325	St. CATHERINES (R.C.N.)	Canadian Yarrow: Dom. Eng.	6.12.42	O.W.S. (name not changed—1950).
	St. EDOUARD (R.C.N.)	Lauzon		Cancelled 12/43.
K.337	KIRKLAND LAKE (R.C.N.) (ex-St. Jerome)	Morton	27. 4.44	Scrapped Canada 1947/8.
K.456	St. JOHN (R.C.N.)	Canadian Vickers	25. 8.43	Scrapped Canada 1948.
K.680	St. PIERRE (R.C.N.)	Davie Sbdg.	1.12.43	Peruvian TENIENTE PALACIOS (1947), PALACIOS (1953).
	St. ROMAULD (R.C.N.)	Lauzon		Cancelled 12/43.
K.454	St. STEPHEN (R.C.N.)	Canadian Yarrow	6. 2.44	O.W.S. (name not changed—1947).
K.366	Ste. THERESE (R.C.N.)	Davie Sbdg.	16.10.43	
K.305	SHIEL (ex-U.S.N.)	Canadian Vickers	26. 5.43	Returned U.S.N. 4/3/46.
	SHIPTON (R.C.N.)	Quebec		Cancelled 12/43.
K.323	SPRINGHILL (R.C.N.)	Canadian Yarrow	7. 9.43	Scrapped Canada 1948.
K.681	STETTLER (R.C.N.)	Canadian Vickers	10. 9.43	
K.531	STONETOWN (R.C.N.)	Canadian Vickers	28. 3.44	O.W.S. (name not changed—1950).
K.327	STORMONT (R.C.N.)	Canadian Vickers	14. 7.43	Mercantile CHRISTINA (1951).

K.682	STRATHADAM (R.C.N.)	Canadian Yarrow	20. 3.44	Israeli MISGAV (1951), R.Cey.N. GAJABAHU (1959).
K.328	SWANSEA (R.C.N.)*	Canadian Yarrow	19.12.42	
K.459	THETFORD MINES (R.C.N.)	Morton	30.10.43	Mercantile 1946/7.
	TISDALE (R.C.N.)	Montreal		Cancelled 1/44.
K.683	SUSSEXVALE (R.C.N.)(ex-R.C.N. Valdorian)	Davie Sbdg.	12. 7.44	
K.329	VALLEYFIELD (R.C.N.)	Morton	.43	Lost 7/5/44.
K.388	DUNVER(R.C.N.) ex-Verdun (of Canada, ex-R.C.N. Verdun)	Morton	10.11.42	Expended as breakwater 1948.
K.684	VICTORIAVILLE (R.C.N.)	G. T. Davie	23. 6.44	
K.330	WASKESIU (R.C.N.)	Canadian Yarrow	6.12.42	Mercantile HOOGHLY (1950).
K.331	WENTWORTH (R.C.N.)	Canadian Yarrow	6. 3.43	Scrapped Canada 1948.
	WESTBURY (R.C.N.)	Montreal		Cancelled 12/43.
	WULASTOCK (R.C.N.)	Victoria		Cancelled 12/43.

Notes.—EXE, MEON and WAVENEY were converted to LSH (S) after the war. R.I.N. TIR was converted to a training and INVESTIGATOR to a surveying, vessels after the partition of the former R.I.N. R.P.N. ZULFIQUAR and SHAMSHER were similarly converted. LACHLAN was completed as a surveying vessel by the R.A.N. and later lent to the R.N.Z.N. The U.S.N. only accepted two of the ten units ordered in Canada and turned the remainder over to the R.N. under Lend/Lease. R.C.N. St. CATHERINES, St. STEPHEN and STONETOWN were converted to O.W.S. post war.

Loch/Bay class

Displacement: **Loch** class 1,435 tons, **Bay** class, 1,580 tons, DERBY HAVEN and WOODBRIDGE HAVEN 1,652 tons.
Dimensions: 286 (pp) $307\frac{1}{4}$ (oa) $\times$ $38\frac{1}{2}$ $\times$ $8\frac{3}{4}$ (**Loch**) $9\frac{1}{2}$ (**Bay**), $9\frac{3}{4}$ (DERBY HAVEN and WOODBRIDGE HAVEN) ft.
Machinery: 2-shaft Reciprocating (4 cyl. V.T.E.), I.H.P. 5,500 except * geared Turbines, S.H.P. 6,500 = 20 knots.
Armament: **Loch** 1—4 in., 4—2 pdr. A.A. (1 × 4), 6—20 mm. A.A. (2 × 2 & 2 × 1) guns; 2—A.T.W. (Squid). **Bay** 4—4 in. A.A. (2 × 2), 4—40 mm. A.A. (2 × 2), 4—20 mm. A.A. (2 × 2) guns; 1—A.T.W. (Hedgehog), DERBY HAVEN and WOODBRIDGE HAVEN, 2—4 in. A.A. (1 × 2), 6—20 mm. A.A. (6 × 1) guns.
Complement: **Loch** 114, **Bay** 157, DERBY HAVEN and WOODBRIDGE HAVEN 120.

K.424	LOCH ACHANALT (ex-Naver)	Robb: Hall Russell	23. 3.44	R.N.Z.N. PUKAKI (1948).
K.426	LOCH ACHRAY	Smiths Dock	7. 7.44	R.N.Z.N. KANIERE (1948).
K.600	St. BRIDES BAY (ex-Loch Achilty)	Harland & Wolff	16. 1.45	Scrapped Faslane 3/9/62.
K.601	LOCH AFRIC	Ailsa		Cancelled.

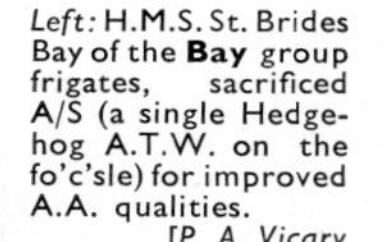

Left: H.M.S. St. Brides Bay of the **Bay** group frigates, sacrificed A/S (a single Hedgehog A.T.W. on the fo'c'sle) for improved A.A. qualities.
[*P. A. Vicary*

Right: H.M.S. Loch Arkaig was one of the few frigates of the **Loch** group to be turbine engined. The A/S armament (two Squid A.T.W.) was considerably superior to that fitted in corvettes.
[*P. A. Vicary*

K.428	LOCH ALVIE	Barclay Curle	14. 4.44	
K.602	TRANSVAAL (S.A.N.) (ex-Loch Ard)	Harland & Wolff	2. 8.44	
K.603	LOCH ARKAIG*	Caledon: B.T.H.	7. 6.45	Scrapped Gateshead 1/60.
K.604	START BAY (ex-Loch Arklet)	Harland & Wolff	15. 2.45	For disposal.
K.605	TREMADOC BAY (ex-Loch Arnish)	Harland & Wolff	29. 3.45	Scrapped Genoa 18/9/59.
K.438	DERBY HAVEN (ex-Loch Assynt)	Swan Hunter	14.12.44	R.Per.N. BABR (1949).
	LOCH AWE	Harland & Wolff		Cancelled.
	LOCH BADCALL	Pickersgill		Cancelled.
K.432	GOOD HOPE (S.A.N.) (ex-Loch Boisdale)	Blyth: White	5. 7.44	
K.435	ENARD BAY (ex-Loch Bracadale)	Smiths Dock	31.10.44	Scrapped Faslane 15/11/57.
K.606	BIGBURY BAY (ex-Loch Carloway)	Hall Russell	16.11.44	Portuguese PACHECO PEREIRA (1959).
	LOCH CAROY	Pickersgill		Cancelled.
K.436	SURPRISE (ex-Gerrans Bay, ex-Loch Carron)	Smiths Dock	14. 3.45	
K.607	LOCH CLUNE	Ailsa		Cancelled.
K.608	PADSTOW BAY (ex-Loch Coulside)	Robb: Barclay Curle	24. 8.45	Scrapped Spezia 11/8/59.
K.609	LOCH CRAGGIE	Harland & Wolff	23. 5.44	Completed Clydebank; for disposal.
K.430	NATAL (S.A.N.) (ex-Loch Cree)	Swan Hunter	19. 6.44	
	LOCH CRERAN	Smiths Dock		Cancelled.
	LOCH DOINE	Smiths Dock		Cancelled.
K.425	LOCH DUNVEGAN	Hill: Fletcher	25. 3.44	Scrapped Briton Ferry 25/8/60.
	LOCH EARN	Hill		Cancelled.
K.422	LOCH ECK	Smiths Dock	25. 4.44	R.N.Z.N. HAWEA (1948).
K.611	DAMPIER (ex-Herne Bay, ex-Loch Eil)	Smiths Dock	15. 5.45	Completed Chatham.
	LOCH ENOCH	Harland & Wolff		Cancelled.
K.612	LOCH ERICHT	Ailsa		Cancelled.

.613	LOCH ERISORT	Barclay Curle		Cancelled.
	LOCH EYE	Harland & Wolff		Cancelled.
	LOCH EYNORT	Harland & Wolff		Cancelled.
.390	LOCH FADA	Clydebank	14.12.43	
.614	HOLLESLEY BAY (ex-Loch Fannich)	Smiths Dock		Cancelled.
.423	LARGO BAY (ex-Loch Fionn)	Pickersgill: Clark	3.10.44	Scrapped Inverkeithing 11/7/58.
.615	WIDEMOUTH BAY (ex-Loch Frisa)	Harland & Wolff	19.10.44	Scrapped Blyth 11/57.
.429	LOCH FYNE	Burntisland: Rowan	24. 5.44	
.616	WIGTOWN BAY (ex-Loch Garasdale)	Harland & Wolff	26. 4.45	Scrapped Faslane 4/59.
.617	LOCH GARVE	Hall Russell		Cancelled.
.618	LOCH GLASHAN	Smiths Dock		Cancelled.
.427	DALRYMPLE (ex-Luce Bay, ex-Loch Glass)	Pickersgill: Clark	12. 4.45	Completed Devonport.
.619	LOCH GLENDHU	Burntisland: Rowan	18.10.44	Scrapped Dunston 14/11/57.
	LOCH GOIL	Harland & Wolff		Cancelled.
.620	LOCH GORM	Harland & Wolff	8. 6.44	For disposal.
.621	LOCH GRIAM	Swan Hunter		Cancelled.
.622	BURGHEAD BAY (ex-Loch Harport)	Hill: Robey	3. 3.45	Portuguese ALVARES CABRAL (1959).
.623	LOCH HARRAY	Smiths Dock		Cancelled.
.624	MORECAMBE BAY (ex-Loch Heilen)	Pickersgill: Clark	1.11.44	Portuguese DON FRANCESCO DE ALMEIDA (1961).
	LOCH HOURN	Harland & Wolff		Cancelled.
	LOCH INCHARD	Harland & Wolff		Cancelled.
.433	LOCH INSH	Robb: Whites M.E.	10. 5.44	
625	LOCH KATRINE	Robb: Plenty	21. 8.44	R.N.Z.N. ROTOITI (1948).
626	LOCH KEN	Smiths Dock		Cancelled.

K.627	MOUNTS BAY (ex-Loch Kilbernie)	Pickersgill: Clark	8. 6.45	Portuguese VASCO DA GAMA (1961).
K.391	LOCH KILLIN	Burntisland: Rowan	29.11.43	Scrapped Newport 24/8/60.
K.628	LOCH KILLISPORT	Harland & Wolff	6. 7.44	
K.629	LOCH KIRBISTER	Swan Hunter		Cancelled.
	LOCH KIRKAIG	Harland & Wolff		Cancelled.
	LOCH KISHORN	Robb		Cancelled.
	LOCH KNOCKIE	Pickersgill		Cancelled.
	LOCH LANO	Harland & Wolff		Cancelled.
K.630	CARDIGAN BAY (ex-Loch Laxford)	Robb: Whites M.E.	28.12.44	
K.631	LOCH LINFERN	Smiths Dock		Cancelled.
K.632	LOCH LINNHE	Pickersgill		Cancelled.
K.437	LOCH LOMOND	Caledon: Duncan Stewart	19. 6.44	
K.633	WHITESAND BAY (ex-Loch Lubnaig)	Harland & Wolff	16.12.44	Scrapped Charlestown 13/2/56.
	LOCH LURGAN	Harland & Wolff		Cancelled.
K.634	St. AUSTELL BAY (ex-Loch Lyddoch)	Harland & Wolff	18.11.44	Scrapped Rosyth 4/7/59.
K.635	LOCH LYON	Swan Hunter		Cancelled.
	LOCH MABERRY	Hall Russell		Cancelled.
K.636	CARNARVON BAY (ex-Loch Maddy)	Robb: Whites M.E.	15. 3.45	Scrapped Spezia 28/8/59.
K.637	LOCH MINNICK	Smiths Dock		Cancelled.
K.638	COOK (ex-Pegwell Bay, ex-Loch Mochrom)	Pickersgill: Clark	1. 9.45	Completed Devonport.
K.639	LOCH MORE	Caledon: Aitchison Blair	3.10.44	
K.517	LOCH MORLICH	Swan Hunter	25. 1.44	R.N.Z.N. TUTIRA (1948); sold 15/12/6
K.640	OWEN (ex-Thurso Bay, ex-Loch Muick)	Hall Russell	19.10.45	Completed Chatham.
K.641	LOCH NELL	Robb		Cancelled.
K.642	LOCH ODAIRN	Robb		Cancelled.

Left: H.M.S. Widemouth Bay, a frigate of the **Bay** group.
[*P. A. Vicary*

Right: Loch Killisport. A postwar view with flag superior changed from K to F and single 40 mm. A.A. exchanged for twin 20 mm. guns aft but otherwise unaltered. [*A. & J. Pavia*

K.643	LOCH OSSIAN	Smiths Dock		Cancelled.
K.434	LOCH QUOICH	Blyth: White	2. 9.44	Scrapped Dunston 13/11/57.
K.644	CAWSAND BAY (ex-Loch Roan)	Blyth: White	26. 2.45	Scrapped Genoa 5/9/59.
	LOCH RONALD	Harland & Wolff		Cancelled.
K.645	LOCH RUTHVEN	Hill: Belliss & Morcom	3. 6.44	
K.646	LOCH RYAN	Pickersgill		Cancelled.
K.647	ALERT (ex-Dundrum Bay, ex-Loch Scamadale)	Blyth: White	10. 7.45	
K.648	LOCH SCAVAIG	Hill: Belliss & Morcom	9. 9.44	Scrapped Genoa 5/9/59.
K.649	LOCH SCRIVAIN	Pickersgill		Cancelled.
K.650	PORLOCK BAY (ex-Loch Seaforth, ex-Loch Muick)	Hill: Robey	14. 6.45	
	LOCH SHEALLAG	Harland & Wolff		Cancelled.
	LOCH SHIEL	Harland & Wolff		Cancelled.
K.421	LOCH SHIN	Swan Hunter	23. 2.44	R.N.Z.N. TAUPO (1948); sold 15/12/6
	LOCH SKAIG	Smiths Dock		Cancelled.
	LOCH SKERROW	Hill		Cancelled.
	LOCH STEMSTER	Harland & Wolff		Cancelled.
	LOCH STENNESS	Smiths Dock		Cancelled.
	LOCH STRIVEN	Harland & Wolff		Cancelled.
	LOCH SUNART	Harland & Wolff		Cancelled.
K.651	VERYAN BAY (ex-Loch Swannay)	Hill: Clark	11.11.44	Scrapped Charlestown 1/7/59.
	LOCH SWIN	Harland & Wolff		Cancelled.
K.652	LOCH TANA	Blyth		Cancelled.
K.431	LOCH TARBERT	Ailsa	19.10.44	Scrapped Genoa 18/9/59.
K.653	LOCH TILT	Pickersgill		Cancelled.
K.654	WOODBRIDGE HAVEN (ex-Loch Torridon)	Swan Hunter	13. 1.45	
K.655	LOCH TRALAIG*	Caledon: B.T.H.	12. 2.45	For disposal.
	LOCH TUMMELL	Harland & Wolff		Cancelled.

H.M.S. St. Austell Bay as completed with four 4 in. A.A. (2 × 2), four 40 mm. A.A. (2 × 2) aft and four 20 mm. A.A. (4 × 1) in upper and lower bridge wings. [*P. A. Vicary*

H.M.S. Veryan Bay, 20 mm. guns forward were replaced by single 40 mm. guns in upper bridge wings only. [*G. A. Osbon*

H.M.S. Frolic was one of the diesel-electric minesweepers loaned to the Royal Navy under *Lend/Lease*. [*P. A. Vicary*

K.656	LOCH URIGILL	Blyth		Cancelled.
	LOCH VANAVIE	Harland & Wolff		Cancelled.
K.657	LOCH VENNACHER	Blyth		Cancelled.
K.658	LOCH VEYATIE	Ailsa	8.10.45	
K.659	LOCH WATTEN	Blyth		Cancelled.

Notes.—ALERT and SURPRISE were completed as Despatch vessels, DERBY HAVEN and WOODBRIDGE HAVEN as Depot ships for Coastal Forces, COOK, DALRYMPLE, DAMPIER and OWEN as surveying vessels and S.A.N. GOOD HOPE was converted to a Despatch vessel and training ship and NATAL to a surveying vessel after the war.

ESCORT SLOOPS

(Ex-American Coastguard cutters)

Banff class

Displacement: 1,546 tons.
Dimensions: (pp) 256 (oa) × 42 × 16 ft.
Machinery: 2-shaft Turbines/Electric motors, S.H.P. 3,200 = 16 knots.
Armament: 1—5 in., 2 except TOTLAND and WALNEY 3—3 in. A.A. (2/3 × 1—not in GORLESTON), 4 except GORLESTON 2—20 mm. A.A. (2/4 × 1), 10—.5 in. A.A. (2 × 4 & 2 × 1—GORLESTON only), 4—.303 in. A.A. (2 × 2—in most) guns.
Complement: 200.

Y.43	BANFF (ex-U.S.C.G. Saranac)	G.E.C.	12. 4.30	U.S.C.G. TAMPA (1946).
Y.87	CULVER (ex-U.S.C.G. Mendota)	Bethlehem	1928	Lost 31/1/42.
Y.59	FISHGUARD (ex-U.S.C.G. Tahoe)	Bethlehem	28. 9.27	Returned U.S.C.G. 2/46.
Y.92	GORLESTON (ex-U.S.C.G. Itasca)	G.E.C.	16.11.29	U.S.C.G. ITASCA (1946).
Y.00	HARTLAND (ex-U.S.C.G. Pontchartrain)	Bethlehem	1928	Lost 8/11/42, salved and scuttled 26/10/49.
Y.56	LANDGUARD (ex-U.S.C.G. Shoshone)	G.E.C.	11. 9.30	Scrapped Colombo 1949/50.
Y.60	LULWORTH (ex-U.S.C.G. Chelan)	Bethlehem	1928	Returned U.S.C.G. 1/46.
Y.21	SENNEN (ex-U.S.C.G. Champlain)	Bethlehem	1928	U.S.C.G. CHAMPLAIN (1946).

Y.88	TOTLAND (ex-U.S.C.G. Cayuga)	Bethlehem	7.10.31	U.S.C.G. MOCOMA (1946).
Y.04	WALNEY (ex-U.S.C.G. Sebago)	G.E.C.	1930	Lost 8/11/42.

MINESWEEPING SLOOPS (Ex-American)

Catherine class

Displacement: 890 tons.
Dimensions: 215 (pp) $220\frac{1}{2}$ (oa) × 32 × $9\frac{1}{2}$ ft.
Machinery: 2-shaft Diesel/Electric motors, B.H.P. 3,500 = 18 knots.
Armament: 1—3 in. A.A., 6—20 mm. A.A. (6 × 1) guns.
Complement: 80.

	AKBAR (ex-BAM.1)	General Engineering (Alameda)	12.12.42	Retained as U.S.N. CHAMPION (AM.314).
	ALICE (ex-BAM.2)	,,	5. 1.43	Retained as U.S.N. CHIEF (AM.315).
	AMELIA (ex-BAM.3)	,,	9. 1.43	Retained as U.S.N. COMPETENT (AM.316).
	AMITY (ex-BAM.4)	,,	18.2.43	Retained as U.S.N. DEFENSE (AM.317).
	AUGUSTA (ex-BAM.5)	,,	19.4.43	Retained as U.S.N. DEVASTATOR (AM.318).
	BLAZE (ex-BAM.6)	,,	7. 5.43	Retained as U.S.N. GLADIATOR (AM.319).
	BRUTUS (ex-BAM.7)	,,	21.5.43	Retained as U.S.N. IMPECCABLE (AM.320).
	BUFFALO (ex-BAM.8)	,,	22.6.43	Retained as U.S.N. ARDENT (AM.340).
.12	CATHERINE (ex-BAM.9)	Assoc. Sbdg. (Seattle)	7. 9.42	Turkish ERDEMLI (1947).
.16	CATO (ex-BAM.10)	,,	7. 9.42	Lost 6/7/44.
.23	PIQUE (ex-Celerity, ex-BAM.11)	,,	20. 6.43	Turkish EREGLI (1947).
.28	CHAMOIS (ex-BAM.12)	,,	26.10.42	Constructive total loss 21/7/44; mercantile MORNING STAR (1948); abandoned incomplete and scrapped.
340	CHANCE (ex-BAM.13)	,,	26.10.42	Turkish EDREMIT (1947).
341	COMBATANT (ex-BAM.14)	,,	27.11.42	Returned U.S.N. 15/12/46.

J.345	CYNTHIA (ex-BAM.15)	Assoc. Sbdg. (Seattle)	27.11.42	Returned U.S.N. 31/12/46.
J.402	ELFREDA (ex-BAM.16, ex-U.S.N. Overseer)	,,	25. 1.43	Turkish CESMI (1947).
J.342	GAZELLE (es-BAM.17)	Savannah Machinery	10. 1.43	Returned U.S.N. 11/12/46.
J.346	GORGON (ex-BAM.18)	,,	24. 1.43	Returned U.S.N. 11/12/46.
J.352	GRECIAN (ex-BAM.19)	,,	10. 3.43	Turkish EDINCIK (1947).
J.400	MAGIC (ex-BAM.20)	,,	24. 5.43	Lost 6/7/44.
J.401	PYLADES (ex-BAM.21)	,,	27. 6.43	Lost 8/7/44.
	ERRANT (ex-BAM.22)	Assoc. Sbdg. (Seattle)	25. 2.43	Retained as U.S.N. SPEAR (AM.322).
	ESPOIR (ex-BAM.23)	,,	25. 2.43	Retained as U.S.N. TRIUMPH (AM.323).
	EXPLOIT (ex-BAM.24)	,,	5. 4.43	Retained as U.S.N. VIGILANCE (AM.324).
J.403	FAIRY (ex-BAM.25)	,,	5. 4.43	Returned U.S.N. 11/12/46.
J.404	FLORIZIEL (ex-BAM.26)	,,	20. 5.43	Mercantile AIDA (1947).
J.405	FOAM (ex-BAM.27)	,,	20. 5.43	Returned U.S.N. 11/12/46.
J.406	FROLIC (ex-BAM.28)	,,	22. 7.43	Turkish CANDARLI (1947).
J.407	JASPER (ex-BAM.29)	,,	20. 6.43	Returned U.S.N. 12/46, mercantile PANDELIS (?).
	SEPOY (ex-BAM.30)	Gulf Sbdg. Chickasaw	17. 1.43	Retained as U.S.N. DEXTROUS (AM.341).
J.375	STEADFAST (ex-BAM.31)	,,	17. 1.43	Returned U.S.N. 24/12/46.
J.374	TATTOO (ex-BAM.32)	,,	27. 1.43	Turkish CARSAMBA (1947).
J.338	STRENUOUS (ex-U.S.N. Vital)	,,	7. 9.42	Mercantile EVENING STAR (1948), PRIDE OF THE WEST (1949) abandoned and scrapped Germany 7/56.
J.339	TOURMALINE (ex-U.S.N. Usage)	,,	4.10.42	Turkish CARDAK (1947).

FRIGATES (Ex-American Destroyer Escorts)

Captain class

(Diesel-electric)

Displacement: 1,085 tons.
Dimensions: (pp) 289½ (oa) × 35 × 9ft

Machinery: 2-shaft Diesel-Electric motors, B.H.P. 6,000 = 20 knots.
Armament: 3—3 in. A.A. (3 × 1), 2—40 mm. A.A. (1 × 2), 10—20 mm. A.A. (10 × 1) guns. *Complement:* 200.

K.310	BAYNTUN (ex-DE.1)	Boston	27. 6.42	Returned U.S.N. 22/8/45.
K.311	BAZELY (ex-DE.2)	,,	27. 6.42	Returned U.S.N. 20/8/45.
K.312	BERRY (ex-DE.3)	,,	23.11.42	Returned U.S.N. 15/2/46.
K.313	BLACKWOOD (ex-DE.4)	,,	23.11.42	Lost 15/6/44.
K.347	BURGES (ex-DE.12)	,,	26. 1.43	Returned U.S.N. 27/2/46.
K.316	DRURY (ex-Cockburn, ex-DE.46)	Philadelphia	24. 7.43	Returned U.S.N. 20/8/45.
K.470	CAPEL (ex-DE.266)	Boston	22. 4.43	Lost 26/12/44.
K.471	COOKE (ex-D.E.267)	,,	22. 4.43	Returned U.S.N. 5/3/46.
K.472	DACRES (ex-D.E.268)	,,	14. 5.43	Returned U.S.N. 26/1/46.
K.473	DOMETT (ex-DE.269)	,,	3. 9.43	Returned U.S.N. 5/3/46.
K.474	FOLEY (ex-DE.270)	,,	19. 5.43	Returned U.S.N. 22/8/45.
K.475	GARLIES (ex-DE.271)	,,	19. 5.43	Returned U.S.N. 20/8/45.
K.476	GOULD (ex-DE.272)	,,	4. 6.43	Lost 1/3/44.
K.477	GRINDALL (ex-DE.273)	,,	4. 6.43	Returned U.S.N. 20/8/45.
K.478	GARDINER (ex-DE.274)	,,	8. 7.43	Returned U.S.N. 12/2/46.
K.479	GOODALL (ex-DE.275)	,,	8. 7.43	Lost 29/4/45.
K.480	GOODSON (ex-DE.276)	,,	8. 7.43	Constructive total loss 25/6/44; returned U.S.N. 21/10/45.
K.481	GORE (ex-DE.277)	,,	8. 7.43	Returned U.S.N. 2/5/46.
K.482	KEATS (ex-DE.278)	,,	17. 7.43	Returned U.S.N. 27/2/46.
K.483	KEMPTHORNE (ex-DE.279)	,,	17. 7.43	Returned U.S.N. 20/8/45.
K.484	KINGSMILL (ex-DE.280)	,,	13. 8.43	Returned U.S.N. 22/8/45.
K.514	LAWFORD (ex-DE.516)	,,	. 8.43	Lost 8/6/44.
K.515	LOUIS (ex-DE.517)	,,	9.11.43	Returned U.S.N. 20/3/46.
K.516	LAWSON (ex-DE.518)	,,	13. 8.43	Returned U.S.N. 20/3/46.
K.564	PASLEY (ex-Lindsay, ex-DE.519)	,,	30. 8.43	Returned U.S.N. 20/8/45.

Right: H.M.S. Duckworth was one of the turbo-electric frigates loaned to the Royal Navy under *Lend/Lease*. They generally mounted three 3 in. and ten 20 mm. A.A. guns and the latter were mounted four before the bridge and six abaft the funnel. [*P. A. Vicary*

H.M.S. Hargood was a turbo-electric frigate of the **Captain** class loaned to the Royal Navy under *Lend/Lease*. A 2 pdr. bowchaser has been added. [*P. A. Vicary*

H.M.S. Sarawak, a **Colony** class frigate loaned to the Royal Navy under *Lend-Lease*, closely followed the design of the River class. [*P. A. Vicary*

K.565	LORING (ex-DE.520)	Boston	30. 8.43	Returned U.S.N. 7/1/47.
K.566	HOSTE (ex-Mitchell, ex-DE.521)	,,	24. 9.43	Returned U.S.N. 22/8/45.
K.567	MOORSOM (ex-DE.522)	,,	11.12.43	Returned U.S.N. 25/10/45.
K.568	MANNERS (ex-DE.523)	,,	17.12.43	Constructive total loss 26/1/45; returned U.S.N. 8/11/45.
K.569	MOUNSEY (ex-DE.524)	,,	24. 9.43	Returned U.S.N. 25/2/46.
K.570	INGLIS (ex-DE.525)	,,	2.11.43	Returned U.S.N. 20/3/46.
K.571	INMAN (ex-DE.526)	,,	2.11.43	Returned U.S.N. 1/3/46.

Captain class

(Turbo-electric)

Displacement: 1,300 tons.
Dimensions: 300 (pp) 306 (oa) × 36¾ × 9 ft.
Machinery: 2-shaft geared Turbines-Electric motors, S.H.P. 12,000 = 26 knots.
Armament: 3—3 in. A.A. (3 × 1), 1—2 pdr. A.A. in *, 2—40 mm. A.A. (1×2 and 8—20 mm. A.A. (8 × 1) or 10—20 mm. A.A. (10 × 1) Guns.
Complement: 200.

K.314	BENTINCK (ex-DE.52)	Bethlehem (Hingham)	22. 8.42	Returned U.S.N. 5/1/46.
K.315	BYARD (ex-DE.55)	,,	6. 3.43	ReturnedU.S.N.12/12/45.
K.349	CALDER (ex-DE.58)	,,	27. 3.43	Returned U.S.N. 19/10/45.
K.351	DUCKWORTH (ex-DE.61)	,,	1. 5.43	Returned U.S.N. 17/12/45.
K.352	DUFF (ex-DE.64)	,,	22. 5.43	Constructive total loss 30/11/44; returned U.S.N. 22/8/45.
K.353	ESSINGTON (ex-DE.67)	,,	19. 6.43	Returned U.S.N. 19/10/45.
K.462	AFFLECK (ex-DE.71)	,,	30. 6.43	Constructive total loss 26/12/44; mercantile hulk NOSTRA SENORA DE LALUZ (1954).
K.463	AYLMER (ex-DE.72)	,,	10. 7.43	Returned U.S.N. 5/11/45.
K.464	BALFOUR (ex-DE.73)	.	10. 7.43	Returned U.S.N. 25/10/45.
K.465	BENTLEY (ex-DE.74)	,,	17. 7.43	Returned U.S.N 5/11/45.
K.466	BICKERTON (ex-DE.75)	,,	24. 7.43	Lost 22/8/44.
K.467	BLIGH (ex-DE.76)	,,	31. 7.43	Returned U.S.N. 12/11/45.
K.468	BRAITHWAITE (ex-DE.77)	,,	31. 7.43	Returned U.S.N. 13/11/45.

K.460	BULLEN (ex-DE.78)	Bethlehem (Hingham)	7. 8.43	Lost 6/12/44.
K.508	BYRON (ex-DE.79)	,,	14. 8.43	Returned U.S.N. 24/11/45.
K.509	CONN (ex-DE.80)	,,	21. 8.43	Returned U.S.N. 26/11/45.
K.510	COTTON (ex-DE.81)	,,	21. 8.43	Returned U.S.N. 5/11/45.
K.511	CRANSTOUN (ex-DE.82)	,,	28. 8.43	Returned U.S.N. 3/12/45.
K.512	CUBITT (ex-DE.83)	,,	11. 9.43	Returned U.S.N. 4/3/46.
K.513	CURZON (ex-DE.84)	,,	18. 9.43	Returned U.S.N. 27/3/46.
K.550	DAKINS (ex-DE.85)	,,	18. 9.43	Constructive total loss 25/12/44; scrapped Holland 9/1/47.
K.551	DEANE (ex-DE.86)	,,	29. 9.43	Returned U.S.N. 4/3/46.
K.552	EKINS* (ex-DE.87)	,,	2.10.43	Constructive total loss 16/4/45; scrapped Holland 1947.
K.553	FITZROY (ex-DE.88)	,,	1. 9.43	Returned U.S.N. 5/1/46.
K.554	REDMILL (ex-DE.89)	,,	2.10.43	Constructive total loss 27/4/45; returned U.S.N. 20/1/47.
K.555	RETALICK (ex-DE.90)	,,	9.10.43	Returned U.S.N. 25/10/45.
K.556	HALSTED (ex-Reynolds, ex-DE.91)	,,	14.10.43	Constructive total loss 10/6/44 and canibalised for spares; scrapped Holland 28/3/47.
K.557	RIOU (ex-DE.92)	,,	23.10.43	Returned U.S.N. 25/2/46.
K.558	RUTHERFORD (ex-DE.93)	,,	23.10.43	Returned U.S.N. 25/10/45.
K.559	COSBY (ex-Reeves, ex-DE.94)	,,	30.10.43	Returned U.S.N. 4/3/46.
K.560	ROWLEY (ex-DE.95)	,,	30.10.43	Returned U.S.N. 12/11/45.
K.561	RUPERT (ex-DE.96)	,,	31.10.43	Returned U.S.N. 20/3/46.
K.562	STOCKHAM (ex-DE.97)	,,	31.10.43	Returned U.S.N. 15/2/46.
K.563	SEYMOUR (ex-DE.98)	,,	1.11.43	Returned U.S.N. 5/1/46.
K.572	SPRAGGE* (ex-DE.563)	,,	16.10.43	Returned U.S.N. 28/2/46.
K.573	STAYNER* (ex-DE.564)	,,	6.11.43	Returned U.S.N. 24/11/45.
K.574	THORNBROUGH (ex-DE.565)	,,	13.11.43	Returned U.S.N. 29/1/47.
K.575	TROLLOPE (ex-DE.566)	,,	20.11.43	Constructive total loss 6/7/44; scrapped Troon 5/51.

K.576	TYLER (ex-DE.567)	Bethlehem (Hingham)	20.11.43	Returned U.S.N. 12/11/45.
K.577	TORRINGTON (ex-DE.568)	,,	27.11.43	Returned U.S.N. 11/6/46.
K.578	NARBROUGH (ex-DE.569)	,,	27.11.43	Returned U.S.N. 4/2/46.
K.579	WALDEGRAVE (ex-DE.570)	,,	4.12.43	Returned U.S.N. 3/12/35.
K.580	WHITTAKER (ex-DE.571)	,,	12.12.43	Constructive total loss 1/11/44; scrapped 1947.
K.581	HOLMES* (ex-DE.572)	,,	19.12.43	Returned U.S.N. 3/12/45.
K.582	HARGOOD* (ex-DE.573)	,,	19.12.43	Returned U.S.N. 4/3/46.
K.583	HOTHAM (ex-DE.574)	,,	22.12.43	Returned U.S.N. 13/3/56; scrapped U.K.

FRIGATES (Ex-American)

Colony class

Displacement: 1,318 tons.
Dimensions: 285½ (pp) 304 (oa) × 37½ × 12 ft.
Machinery: 2-shaft Reciprocating (V.T.E.), I.H.P. 5,500 = 18 knots.
Armament: 3—3 in. A.A. (3 × 1), 4—40 mm. A.A. (2 × 2), 4—20 mm. A.A. (4 × 1) guns. *Complement:* 120.

K.500	ANGUILLA (ex-Hallowel, ex-PF.72)	Walsh Kaiser	14. 7.43	Returned U.S.N. 5/46.
K.501	ANTIGUA (ex-Hammond, ex-PF.73)	,,	26. 7.43	Returned U.S.N. 5/46.
K.502	ASCENSION (ex-Hargood, ex-PF.74)	,,	6. 8.43	Returned U.S.N. 31/5/46.
K.503	BAHAMAS (ex-Hotham, ex-PF.75)	,,	17. 8.43	Returned U.S.N. 11/6/46.
K.504	BARBADOS (ex-Halsted, ex-PF.76)	,,	27. 8.43	Returned U.S.N. 13/4/46.
K.505	CAICOS (ex-Hannam, ex-PF.77)	,,	6. 9.43	Argentinian SANTISIMA TRINIDAD (1947), TRINIDAD (1947).
K.506	CAYMAN (ex-Harland, ex-PF.78)	,,	22. 8.43	Returned U.S.N. 22/4/46.
K.507	DOMINICA (ex-Harnam, ex-PF.79)	,,	14. 9.43	Returned U.S.N. 23/4/46.

K.584	LABUAN (ex-Gold Coast, ex-Harvey, ex-PF.80)	Walsh Kaiser	21. 9.43	Returned U.S.N. 2/5/46.
K.585	TOBAGO (ex-Hong Kong, ex-Holmes, ex-PF.81)	,,	17. 8.43	Returned U.S.N. 13/5/46; Egyptian (1950) but conversion from mercantile abandoned 1956 and scrapped.
K.586	MONTSERRAT (ex-Hornby, ex-PF.82)	,,	28. 8.43	Returned U.S.N. 11/6/46.
K.587	NYASALAND (ex-Hoste, ex-PF.83)	,,		Returned U.S.N. 13/4/46.
K.588	PAPUA (ex-Howett, ex-PF.84)	,,	10.10.43	Returned U.S.N. 13/5/46; Egyptian (1950) but conversion from mercantile abandoned 1956 and scrapped.
K.589	PITCAIRN (ex-Pilford, ex-PF.85)	,,	15.10.43	Returned U.S.N. 11/6/46.
K.590	St. HELENA (ex-Pasley, ex-PF.86)	,,	20.10.43	Returned U.S.N. 23/4/46.
K.591	SARAWAK (ex-Patton, ex-PF.87)	,,	25.10.43	Returned U.S.N. 31/5/46.
K.592	SEYCHELLES (ex-Pearl, ex-PF.88)	,,	30.10.43	Returned U.S.N. 11/6/46.
K.593	PERIM (ex-Sierra Leone, ex-Phillimore, ex-PF.89)	,,	5.11.43	Returned U.S.N. 22/5/46.
K.594	SOMALILAND (ex-Popham, ex-PF.90)	,,	11.11.43	Returned U.S.N. 31/5/46.
K.595	TORTOLA (ex-Peyton, ex-PF.91)	,,	16.11.43	Returned U.S.N. 22/5/46.
K.596	ZANZIBAR (ex-Prowse, ex-PF.92)	,,	21.11.43	Returned U.S.N. 31/5/46

PATROL SLOOPS (Ex-American Coastal Escorts)

Kil class

Displacement: 795 tons.
Dimensions: 176½ (pp) 184¼ (oa) × 33 × 9½ ft.
Machinery: 2-shaft Diesel motors, B.H.P. 1,500/1,800 = 18 knots.

Armament: 1—3 in. A.A., 3—40 mm. A.A. (3 × 1), 4—20 mm. A.A. (4 × 1) guns *Complement:* 100.

5.01	KILBIRNIE (ex-BEC.1, ex-U.S.N. PCE.827)	Pullman Standard Car (Chicago)	2. 5.43	Mercantile HAUGE-SUND (1947).
5.02	KILBRIDE (ex-BEC.2, ex-U.S.N. PCE.828)	,,	15. 5.43	Returned U.S.N. 12/46.
5.03	KILCHATTAN (ex-BEC.3, ex-U.S.N. PCE.829)	,,	27. 5.43	Mercantile STAVANGER (1947).
5.04	KILCHRENAN (ex-BEC.4, ex-U.S.N. PCE.830)	,,	13. 6.43	Returned U.S.N. 12/46.
5.05	KILDARY (ex-BEC.5, ex-U.S.N. PCE.831)	,,	26. 6.43	Mercantile RIO VOUGA (1947).
5.06	KILDWICK (ex-BEC.6, ex-U.S.N. PCE.832)	,,	10. 7.43	Returned U.S.N. 12/46.
5.07	KILHAM (ex-BEC.7, ex-U.S.N. PCE.833)	,,	2. 8.43	Returned U.S.N.
5.08	KILKENZIE (ex-BEC.8, ex-U.S.N. PCE.834)	,,	19. 8.43	Mercantile (name not changed—1947). NADDODD (1948), GOVERNOR WRIGHT (1952),
5.09	KILHAMPTON (ex-BEC.9, ex-U.S.N. PCE.835)	,,	3. 9.43	Mercantile GEORGIOS F (1947).
5.10	KILMACOLM (ex-BEC.10, ex-U.S.N. PCE.836)	,,	17. 9.43	Mercantile RIO AGUEDA (1947).
5.11	KILMARNOCK (ex-BEC.11, ex-U.S.N. PCE.837)	,,	1.10.43	Mercantile ARION (1947); lost 5/1/51.
5.12	KILMARTIN (ex-BEC.12, ex-U.S.N. PCE.838)	,,	13.10.43	Mercantile MARI-GOULA (1947).
5.13	KILMELFORD (ex-BEC.13, ex-U.S.N. PCE.839)	,,	23.10.43	Returned U.S.N. 12/46.
5.14	KILMINGTON (ex-BEC.14, ex-U.S.N. PCE.840)	,,	2.11.43	Mercantile ATHINAI (1947); TRIAS (1950), AGIOB GERASSIMOS (1954).
5.15	KILMORE (ex-BEC.15, ex-U.S.N. PCE.841)	,,	9.11.43	Mercantile DESPINA (1947).

SLOOP DEPLOYMENT

Escort Vessels — December 1939

Western Approaches (Belfast):	1st A/S Striking Force (4 Kingsfisher, JASON and SCOTT (M/S) and 3 sloops).
Home Fleet:	2nd A/S Striking Force (4 Kingfisher, PC.74 and GLEANER (M/S)).
Dover:	1 Kingfisher (damaged).
Rosyth Escort Force:	9 sloops.
North Atlantic (Gibraltar):	GOSSAMER (M/S).
South Atlantic:	7 sloops.
America and West Indies:	2 sloops.
East Indies and Persian Gulf:	6 sloops (including 2 R.I.N.).
Australia:	MORESBY (R.A.N.).
China:	6 sloops.

Escort Vessels — January 1944

With the Battle of the Atlantic in full swing most escorts were based at either end of the convoy routes between America and the United Kingdom. The western section was under Canadian command and operated out of Halifax and Newfoundland ports. Canadian escort groups were also based on Londonderry and were designated C.1, C.2, etc., whilst the British groups were named B.1, B.2, etc.

Harwich:	1st Corvette Flotilla (7 Kingfisher).
Western Approaches (Derry):	6th, 24th and 39th Escort Groups and Escort Groups B.1, B.4, B.7, C.1, C.2, C.3, C.4 and C.5 (3 sloops, 14 frigates and 62 corvettes).
(Belfast):	3rd and 4th Escort Groups (12 frigates) and 37 frigates not allocated to groups.
(Liverpool):	2nd Escort Group and Escort Groups B.2, B.5 and B.6 (10 frigates and 16 corvettes).
(Greenock):	7th, 23rd and 40th Escort Groups and Escort Group B.3 (2 sloops, 10 frigates and 15 corvettes) and 4 sloops, 11 frigates and 10 corvettes not allocated to groups.
Royal Canadian Navy	
(Atlantic coast):	10 frigates, 54 corvettes and 35 minesweepers.
(Pacific coast):	6 corvettes and 3 minesweepers.
Mediterranean (Gibraltar):	38th and 41st Escort Groups (5 sloops, 2 frigates and 7 corvettes). 51st A/S Group (7 Kils).
(Algiers):	37th, 46th, 47th, 48th, 49th and 50th Escort Groups (3 sloops, 7 frigates and 19 corvettes).
(Malta):	36th Escort Group (1 sloop and 3 corvettes).
(Levant):	5 sloops.
Eastern Fleet	
(Kilindine Escort Force):	2 sloops, 5 cutters, 1 frigate and 13 corvettes.
(Ceylon Escort Force):	4 sloops, 4 corvettes and 14 minesweepers.
Royal Indian Navy:	5 sloops.
Australia:	Minesweepers were used as escorts as requisite

West Africa	6 sloops, 2 cutters, 2 frigates and 11 corvettes.
(Freetown Escort Force):	50th A/S Group (8 Kils).
South Atlantic:	9 frigates and 3 corvettes.

Minesweepers — June 1940

1st Flotilla (Scapa Flow):	7 Halcyon (HEBE at Dover wearing flag of F.O.C.).
2nd Flotilla	
(part—East Indies):	3 Hunt.
(part—China):	2 Hunt.
3rd Flotilla (Mediterranean):	5 Hunt.
4th Flotilla (Grimsby):	2 Halcyon (both at Dover) and 5 Hunt (two at Dover).
5th Flotilla (Dover):	2 Halcyon and 6 Hunt.
6th Flotilla (Dover):	6 Halcyon.

Minesweepers — May 1944

1st Flotilla (Harwich):	9 Halcyon.
2nd Flotilla (Mediterranean):	5 Hunt.
4th Flotilla (Portland):	9 Hunt.
6th Flotilla (Harwich):	8 Algerine.
7th Flotilla (Harwich):	8 Algerine.
9th Flotilla (Portsmouth):	8 Bangor.
12th Flotilla (Mediterranean):	8 Algerine.
13th Flotilla (Mediterranean):	6 Bangor.
14th Flotilla (Plymouth):	8 Bangor.
15th Flotilla (Humber):	8 Bangor.
16th Flotilla (Plymouth):	9 Bangor.
17th Flotilla (Mediterranean):	2 Halcyon (A/S).
18th Flotilla (Portsmouth):	8 Algerine.
19th Flotilla (Mediterranean):	8 Algerine.
24th Flotilla (S.W. Pacific):	38 Bathurst (R.A.N.).
26th Flotilla (S.W. Pacific):	
27th Flotilla (S.W. Pacific):	
31st Flotilla (Plymouth):	10 Bangor (R.C.N.).
32nd Flotilla (Plymouth):	4 Bangor (R.C.N.).
37th Flotilla (Eastern Fleet):	4 Bathurst and 9 Bangor (all R.I.N.) (A/S or M/S).
40th Flotilla (Granton):	9 Catherine.
41st Flotilla (Granton):	12 Catherine.
42nd Flotilla (for Granton):	4 Catherine (still in U.S.A.).
R.C.N. Atlantic:	27 Bangor.
R.C.N. Pacific:	7 Bangor.
Eastern Fleet:	13 Bathurst (R.A.N.) (A/S or M/S).

H.M.S. Coquette. Canadian built reciprocating-engined **Algerine** class minesweeper, displaying pennant number M. 350 in International Code flags. Flotilla number on funnel.

[*G. A. Osbon*

PART FOUR

Auxiliary Fighting Vessels

H.M.S. Largs, originally an Ocean Boarding Vessel, was later converted to a Headquarters Ship.

[I.W.M.

ESCORT CARRIERS

Although escort carriers were dealt with in Part 1 they were, with the sole exception of the ARCHER, adapted from uncompleted mercantile hulls and were thus able to have much of standard warship construction incorporated into their design. The ARCHER, a sister ship to the prototype escort carrier LONG ISLAND, was converted before the entry of the United States into the war and peace-time conditions enabled it to be completely carried through.

The two following vessels were converted during the war from completed mercantile vessels and, under the stimulus of wartime conditions, neither could be expected to come up to the standard of the American built escort carriers, whose task was much simplified by having an incomplete and bare standard hull to work on plus the experience gained with the LONG ISLAND.

The German prize EMPIRE AUDACITY (ex-Hannover) provided the Royal Navy with its first escort carrier. The conversion was simple and rapid and was little more than the addition of a flight deck over the existing hull. Six aircraft were carried which were permanently parked on the flight deck as neither hangar or lift was provided. With her name shorted to AUDACITY she rendered brief but valuable service. The PRETORIA CASTLE had originally been requisitioned as an armed merchant cruiser but was converted into an escort carrier in 1943 and was used for deck landing and other training duties.

Displacement: 17,392 tons gross.
Dimensions: 560 (pp) $594\frac{1}{2}$ (oa) × $76\frac{1}{2}$ × $29\frac{1}{4}$ ft.
Machinery: 2-shaft Diesel motors, B.H.P. 11,350 = 17 knots.
Armament: 4—4 in. A.A. (2 × 2), 16—2 pdr. A.A. (4 × 4), 20—20 mm. A.A. (10 × 2) Guns; 15 aircraft.

P. No.	Name	Builder	Launched	Fate
F.61	PRETORIA CASTLE	Harland & Wolff	12.10.38	Mercantile WARWICK CASTLE (1947); scrapped Spain 9/62

Notes:—Converted from an A.M.C. to an escort carrier 1943 and used for training.

Displacement: 5,537 tons gross.
Dimensions: $434\frac{3}{4}$ (pp) 475 (oa) × 56 × $27\frac{1}{4}$d. ft. (F.D. 460 × 60 ft.).
Machinery: 2-shaft Diesel motors, B.H.P. 4,750 = 15 knots.
Armament: 1—4 in., 6—20 mm. A.A. (6 × 1); 6 aircraft.

P. No.	Name	Builder	Launched	Fate
D.10	AUDACITY (ex-mercantile Empire Audacity, ex-Hannover)	Bremer Vulkan	29. 3.39	Lost 21/12/41.

Notes:—Former German prize which became first escort carrier in the Royal Navy.

MERCHANT AIRCRAFT CARRIERS

In spite of the fact that they flew the red ensign the inclusion of merchant aircraft carriers is justified by the originality of their concept and the technical interest of their design. Only their air crew (and the necessary maintenance

Above: This view of H.M.S. Pretoria Castle clearly shows her light A.A. armament of two quadruple 2 pdr. and 5 twin 20 mm. mountings along the starboard side; this arrangement was duplicated along the port side. [*P. A. Vicary*

Below: H.M.S. Archer (ex-Mormacland), first escort carrier received from the U.S.A. [*U.S. Navy Official*

staff) were naval personnel and they were otherwise commanded and manned by merchant service officers and crew.

They could only be adapted from bulk carriers, which could dispense with the hatches and derricks essential to the general trader, and fell into two classes—grain carriers and oil tankers. They superseded the earlier catapult (CAM) ships and provided air cover in that vital area of the North Atlantic which was outside the range of shore-based maritime aircraft from both sides. They successfully combined the dual functions of merchant ship and aircraft carriers without detriment to the efficiency of either and their development was only arrested by the numbers of escort carriers which were later made available.

The minimum requirements originally given by the Admiralty were for vessels of a speed of 14/15 knots and dimensions capable of providing a flight deck of 490 × 62 feet, but these were reduced to 11 knots and 390 × 62 feet respectively so that they could be incorporated in a war standard cargo hull. Six grain ships and four oil tankers were built as merchant aircraft carriers and nine existing tankers from the Anglo-Saxon Petroleum Company's fleet were altered to this role. Two of the latter were under the Dutch flag and continued in their hands after conversion and had the distinction of being the first aircraft carrying vessels to operate under the flag of the Netherlands. The essential difference between the two types were that the grain carriers had an hangar and lift for their aircraft whereas the oil tankers had a longer flight deck of which the after 100 feet was used as a permanent deck park.

Empire MacAlpine class

Displacement: *First* and *second pair* 7,950 tons gross, *third pair* 8,250 tons gross.

Dimensions: *First pair* 412½ (pp) 433¾ (oa) × 56¾ × 24½ ft. (F.D. 413¾ × 62 ft). *Second pair* 425 (pp) 445¾ (oa) × 56 × 24¾ ft. (F.D. 423 × 62 ft.). *Third pair* 425 (pp) 444½ (oa) × 57¾ × 24½ ft. (F.D. 424¼ × 62 ft.).

Machinery: 1-shaft Diesel motor, B.H.P. 3,300 = 12½ knots.

Armament: 1—4 in., 2—40 mm. A.A. (2 × 1), 4—20 mm. A.A. (4 × 1) guns; 4 aircraft.

Complement: 107.

EMPIRE MACALPINE	Burntisland	23.12.42	DERRYNAN (1951), HUNTSBROOK (1959). SUVA BREEZE (1960).
EMPIRE MACKENDRICK	Burntisland	29. 9.43	GRANPOND (1950), CONDOR (1955), SALTERSGATE (1957), VASSIL LEVSKY (1959).
EMPIRE MACANDREW	Denny	3. 5.43	DERRYHEEN (1947), CAPE GRAFTON (1951).
EMPIRE MACDERMOTT	Denny	24. 1.44	LA CUMBRE (1948), PARNON (1959).
EMPIRE MACRAE	Lithgows	21. 6.43	ALPHA ZAMBESI (1947), TOBON (1954).

H.M.S. Audacity was the first escort carrier in the Royal Navy and was converted from a German prize. [*I.W.M.*

The war-built M.V. Empire Mackendrick served in the dual role of aircraft and grain carrier. [*Courtesy Burntisland Sbdg. Co*

M.V. Empire Macandrew was another combined aircraft and grain carrier. [*I.W.M*

EMPIRE MACCALLUM	Lithgows	12.10.43	DORIS CLUNIES (1947), SUNROVER (1951), EUDOXIA (1957), PHORKYSS (1959); scrapped Osaka 11/60.

Notes:—Grain carriers.

Displacement: 8,908 tons gross.
Dimensions: 460 (pp) 482$\frac{3}{4}$ (oa) × 59 × 27$\frac{1}{2}$ ft. (F.D. 460 × 62 ft.).
Machinery: 1-shaft Diesel motor, B.H.P. 3,300 = 11 knots.
Armament: 1—4 in., 8—20 mm. A.A. (8 × 1) guns; 4 aircraft.
Complement: 110.

EMPIRE MACKAY	Harland & Wolff (Govan)	17. 6.43	BRITISH SWORDFISH (1946); scrapped Rotterdam 21/5/59.

Displacement: 9,133 tons gross.
Dimensions: 463 (pp) 481$\frac{1}{2}$ (oa) × 61$\frac{3}{4}$ × 27$\frac{3}{4}$ ft (F.D. 461 × 62 ft.).
Machinery: 1-shaft Diesel motor, B.H.P. 3,300 = 11 knots.
Armament: 1—4 in., 8—20 mm. A.A. (8 × 1) guns; 4 aircraft.
Complement: 110.

EMPIRE MACCOLL	Cammell Laird	24. 7.43	BRITISH PILOT (1946); scrapped Faslane 8/62.

Displacement: 8,856 tons gross.
Dimensions: 460 (pp) 483 (oa) × 59 × 27$\frac{1}{2}$ ft. (F.D. 461$\frac{1}{2}$ × 62 ft.).
Machinery: 1-shaft Diesel motor, B.H.P. 3,300 = 11 knots.
Armament: 1—4 in., 8—20 mm. A.A. (8 × 1) guns; 4 aircraft.
Complement: 110.

EMPIRE MACMAHON	Swan Hunter: Hawthorn Leslie	2.7.43	NANINIA (1946); scrapped Hong Kong 17/3/60.

Displacement: 9,249 tons gross.
Dimensions: 463 (pp) 485$\frac{3}{4}$ (oa) × 61$\frac{3}{4}$ × 27$\frac{1}{2}$ ft. (F.D. 461 × 62 ft.).
Machinery: 1-shaft Diesel motor, B.H.P. 3,300 = 11 knots.
Armament: 1—4 in., 8—20 mm. A.A. (8 × 1) guns; 4 aircraft.
Complement: 110.

EMPIRE MACCABE	Swan Hunter: Hawthorn Leslie	18.5.43	BRITISH ESCORT (1946), EASTHILL ESCORT (1959); scrapped Hong Kong 1962.

Notes:—Above four were oil tankers.

Rapana class

Displacement: 16,600 tons (8,000 tons gross).
Dimensions: 463 except * 465 (pp) 481 except * $482\frac{3}{4}$ (oa) × 59 × $27\frac{1}{2}$ ft. (F.D. $461\frac{3}{4}$ × 62 ft.).
Machinery: 1-shaft Diesel motor, B.H.P. 4,000 except * 3,500 = 13 knots.
Armament: 1—4 in., 8—20 mm. A.A. (8 × 1) guns; 4 aircraft.
Complement: 100.

ACAVUS* (8010 t.g.)	Workman Clark: Hawthorn Leslie	24.11.34	IACRA (1952); scrapped Italy 4/63.
ADULA* (8040 t.g.)	Blythswood: Kincaid	28. 1.37	Scrapped Briton Ferry 15/5/53.
ALEXIA (8016 t.g.)	Bremer Vulkan	20.12.34	IANTHINA (1951); scrapped Blyth 17/8/54.
AMASTRA* (8031 t.g.)	Lithgow: Kincaid	18.12.34	IDAS (1951); scrapped Spezia 27/6/55.
ANCYLUS* (8017 t.g.)	Swan Hunter: Hawthorn Leslie	9.10.34	IMBRICARIA (1952); scrapped Spezia 4/12/54.
GADILA (7999 t.g.)	Howaldts-werke	1.12.34	Scrapped Hong Kong 6/6/58.
MACOMA (8011 t.g.)	Netherlands Dock & Sbdg.	31.12.35	Scrapped Hong Kong 14/12/59.
MIRALDA (8003 t.g.)	Netherlands Dock & Sbdg.	7.36	MARISA (1950); scrapped Hong Kong 21/7/60.
RAPANA (8017 t.g.)	Wilton Fijenoord	4.35	ROTULA (1950); scrapped Osaka 1958.

Notes:—Converted from oil tankers 1942-43. GADILA and MACOMA were operated under the Netherlands mercantile flag.

AIRCRAFT TRANSPORTS

The continued and increasing strength of naval aviation, culminating in the main striking force of the fleet being transferred from capital ships to aircraft carriers required additional vessels in the support category. A single aircraft maintenance vessel—the UNICORN—had been laid down pre-war but was completed as a light fleet carrier and the early years of the war saw fleet carriers used as aircraft transports during the Norwegian campaign and in the Mediterranean. Two mercantile hulls, incomplete at the outbreak of war, were subsequently acquired and completed as aircraft transports to serve the widespread and growing carrier squadrons, a smaller class was built to transport aircraft within more restricted limits and many escort carriers were also engaged in ferrying aircraft.

Displacement: 7,473 tons gross.
Dimensions: 457 (pp) $487\frac{3}{4}$ (oa) × 63 × $28\frac{1}{2}$ ft.
Machinery: 2-shaft Reciprocating (V.T.E.), I.H.P. 8,300 = 17 knots.

Left: The merchant aircraft carrier M.V. Empire Maccallum. [*Courtesy Lithgows Ltd.*

Right: The war-built M.V. Empire Maccoll was a combined tanker and aircraft carrier. [*I.W.M.*

Armament: 1—4 in., 1—4 in. A.A., 2—2 pdr. A.A. (2 × 1), 12—20 mm. A.A. (12 × 1) guns; 40 aircraft.

D.25	ATHENE (ex-Clan Brodie)	Greenock D.Y.: Kincaid	10.40	Completed Clydebank; mercantile CLAN BRODIE (1946); scrapped Hong Kong 6/63.
D.71	ENGADINE (ex-Clan Buchanan)	Denny: Kincaid	26. 5.41	Mercantile CLAN BUCHANAN (1946); scrapped Spain 11/62

Notes:—Another sister ship was requisitioned as the depot ship BONAVENTURE.

Displacement: 990 tons.
Dimensions: 160 (pp) 172 (oa) × 30 × 10 ft.
Machinery: 2-shaft Diesel motors, B.H.P. 960 = 10½ knots.
Armament: 1—12 pdr. A.A., 2—20 mm. A.A. (2 × 1) guns.

F.113	BLACKBURN	Blyth Sbdg.: Whites M.E.	4. 2.46	R.N.V.R. (Clyde—1950).
F.106	RIPON	Pollock: Crossley	15. 3.45	Sold 25/2/59.
F.122	ROC	Blyth Sbdg.: Whites M.E.	28. 3.45	Mercantile (1959)
F.114	SEA FOX	Pollock: Crossley	16. 5.46	For disposal.
	SEA GLADIATOR	Pollock: Crossley	24. 9.49	Completed as mercantile GOLDLYNX (1948), SPRINGWOOD (1951), LEAFOAM (1953).
	SEA HURRICANE	Pollock: Crossley	18.12.48	Completed as mercantile GOLDHIND (1949); PURPLE EMPEROR, (1951). TOWAI (1955).
F.116	WALRUS	Blyth Sbdg.: Whites M.E.	28. 5.45	SKUA (1953); mercantile SERGEN (1962).

Notes:—SEA GLADIATOR and SEA HURRICANE were lengthened and completed as single screw mercantile vessels.

In addition, the following three vessels were requisitioned: the FOSSBECK and CRESCENCE as transports for crashed aircraft and the MANELA as a depot ship for floatplanes.

Displacement: 4,876 tons gross.
Dimensions: 336 (pp) 345 (oa) × 60¼ × 22¾ ft.
Machinery: 1-shaft Reciprocating, N.H.P. 522 = 10½ knots.

Y.O1	FOSSBECK (ex-Foss Beck, ex-Beldagny, ex-Port Alfred)	Smiths Dock	11. 4.30	Boom carrier (1942).

Above: M.V. Rapana was a tanker of the Anglo-Saxon Petroleum Co., converted to a merchant aircraft carrier. [*I.W.M.*

Below: H.M.S. Ripon was one of the small aircraft transports specially built for the Royal Navy. [*Courtesy Jas. Pollock Sons & Co.*

The aircraft transporter H.M.S. Athene was adapted from an uncompleted Clan Line cargo vessel building at the outbreak of war. [*U.S. Navy Official*

Displacement: 255 tons gross.
Dimensions: $114\frac{1}{2}$ (pp) $120\frac{1}{4}$ (oa) × $25\frac{1}{2}$ × 9 ft.
Machinery: 1-shaft Diesel motor, B.H.P. 345 = $9\frac{1}{2}$ knots.

D.75	CRESCENCE (ex-William Beatty)	Goole Sbdg: Deutz	5.9.36	Returned 1945.

Notes:—Stationed at Hatson 1941–43 and Scapa 1943–45

Displacement: 8,030 tons gross.
Dimensions: 450 (pp) (oa) $58\frac{1}{4}$ × $32\frac{3}{4}$ ft.
Machinery: 2-shaft geared Turbines, N.H.P. 926 = 14 knots.

F.58	MANELA	Barclay Curle	9.10.20	R.A.F. (1941).

Notes:—Transferred to R.A.F. as accommodation ship for Coastal Command.

ARMED MERCHANT CRUISERS

Fifty-six passenger liners, all twin screw vessels with a service speed of at least 15 knots, were requisitioned as armed merchant cruisers between 1939-40. During 1941 they were supplemented, in the East Indies, by the special service vessels BOTLEA (F.113), CAPE SABLE (F.112), CITY OF DURBAN (F.114) and KING GRUFFYD (F.116); the latter with a concealed armament of seven 4-inch guns and four 21-inch T.T. But in the same year they were found too vulnerable for ocean escort work—fifteen had already been lost—and they began to be withdrawn, although some were kept in commission until much later in the South Atlantic and East Indies. By January, 1943 only seventeen were left in commission (six in the South Atlantic, eight in the East Indies and two in Australian and one in New Zealand waters) and this had been reduced to eight by January, 1944 (four in the East Indies and four in West Africa). By May, 1944 only the damaged ASTURIAS remained: laid up at Freetown.

Of the remaining forty: one was converted to an escort carrier, one to an auxiliary anti-aircraft ship, two to Depot ships, four to Repair ships, eight to Infantry Landing ships, two to Headquarter ships and twenty-two to troopships in which capacities they served with signal success. The Depot and Repair ships were later purchased outright and retained in the post-war fleet.

They were generally armed with six/eight 6-in., two 3-in. A.A. and several light A.A. and machine guns and fitted with rudimentary fire control equipment and surface warning R.D.F. as it became available. A few had an aircraft and catapult added and the CORFU, with nine 6-in. (9 × 1), four 4-in. A.A. (2 × 2), two 2-pounder A.A. (2 × 1) and nineteen 20 mm. A.A. (19 × 1) guns, an aircraft and catapult, air and surface warning R.D.F. and an H.A. D.C.T. fitted with gunnery control R.D.F., was one of the best equipped.

Displacement: 13,950 tons gross.
Dimensions: $520\frac{1}{4}$ (pp) 540 (oa) × $65\frac{1}{4}$ × $31\frac{1}{2}$ ft.
Machinery: 2-shaft geared Turbines, S.H.P. 8,500 = 15 knots.
Armament: 8—6 in. (8 × 1), 2—3 in. A.A. (2 × 1) guns.

F.	ANDANIA	Hawthorn Leslie	1.11.21	Lost 16/6/40.

Displacement: 20,277 tons gross.
Dimensions: $600\frac{3}{4}$ (pp) 624 (oa) × $73\frac{3}{4}$ × $32\frac{3}{4}$ ft.
Machinery: 2-shaft geared Turbines, S.H.P. 12,500 = $17\frac{1}{2}$ knots.
Armament: 8—6 in. (8 × 1), 2—3 in. A.A. (2 × 1) guns.

F.	CARINTHIA	V.A. (Barrow)	24. 2.25	Lost 7/6/40.

Displacement: 15,241 tons gross.
Dimensions: $523\frac{1}{2}$ (pp) 545 (oa) × $70\frac{1}{4}$ × $42\frac{1}{4}$d. ft.
Machinery: 2-shaft Reciprocating (VQE), I.H.P. 13,000 = 17 knots.
Armament: 7—6 in. (7 × 1), 2—3 in. A.A. (2 × 1) guns.

F.49	COMORIN	Barclay Curle	31.10.24	Lost 6/4/41.

Displacement: 15,007 tons gross.
Dimensions: 530 (pp) 560 (oa) × $71\frac{1}{2}$ × 35 ft.
Machinery: 2-shaft Diesel motors, B.H.P. 13,500 = 17 knots.
Armament: 8—6 in. (8 × 1), 2—3 in. A.A. (2 × 1) guns.

F.	DUNVEGAN CASTLE	Harland & Wolff	26. 3.36	Lost 28/8/40.

Displacement: 16,402 tons gross.
Dimensions: $548\frac{1}{4}$ (pp) 563 (oa) × $70\frac{1}{2}$ × 28 ft.
Machinery: 2-shaft geared Turbines, N.H.P. 2,532 = 17 knots.
Armament: 8—6 in. (8 × 1), 2—3 in. A.A. (2 × 1) guns.

F.	FORFAR (ex-Montrose)	Fairfield	14.12.20	Lost 2/12/40.

Displacement: 11,200 tons gross.
Dimensions: $490\frac{3}{4}$ (pp) 517 (oa) × $62\frac{1}{4}$ × 35d. ft.
Machinery: 2-shaft geared Turbines, S.H.P. 8,000 = $15\frac{1}{2}$ knots.
Armament: 6—6 in. (6 × 1), 2—3 in. A.A. (2 × 1) guns.

F.45	HECTOR (11,198 t.g.)	Scotts	18. 6.24	Constructive total loss 5/4/42; salved & scrapped 1946.
F.	PATROCLUS (11,314 t.g.)	Scotts	17. 3.23	Lost 4/11/40.

Displacement: 14,164 tons gross.
Dimensions: $530\frac{1}{2}$ (pp) $548\frac{1}{2}$ (oa) × $68\frac{1}{4}$ × $33\frac{1}{4}$ ft.
Machinery: 2-shaft geared Turbines, S.H.P. 9,000 = 15 knots.
Armament: 8—6 in. (8 × 1), 2—3 in. A.A. (2 × 1) guns.

F.40	JERVIS BAY	V.A. Barrow	17. 1.22	Lost 5/11/40.

Displacement: 18,724 tons gross.
Dimensions: 578¼ (pp) 600 (oa) × 75½ × 40½d. ft.
Machinery: 3-shaft Reciprocating (VTE—wing shafts) & exhaust Turbine (centre shaft), S.H.P. 15,000 = 16½ knots.
Armament: 7—5.5 in. (7 × 1), 3—4 in. A.A. (3 × 1) guns.

F.	LAURENTIC	Harland & Wolff	16. 6.27	Lost 3/11/40.

Displacement: 16,600 tons gross.
Dimensions: 547¾ (pp) 570 (oa) × 71¼ × 28¼ ft.
Machinery: 2-shaft Reciprocating (VQE), I.H.P. 15,000 = 17 knots.
Armament: 8—6 in. (8 × 1), 2—3 in. A.A. (2 × 1) guns.

F.	RAJPUTANA (16,644 t.g.)	Harland & Wolff (Greenock) Harland & Wolff (Belfast)	6. 8.25	Lost 13/4/41.
F.	RAWALPINDI (16,697 t.g.)	Harland & Wolff (Greenock)	26. 3.25	Lost 23/11/39.

Displacement: 10,549 tons gross.
Dimensions: 483½ (pp) 502 (oa) × 60¼ × 29¾ ft.
Machinery: 2-shaft Diesel motors, B.H.P. 7,700 = 15½ knots.
Armament: 6—6 in. (6 × 1), 2—3 in. A.A. (2 × 1) guns.

F.	SALOPIAN (ex-Shropshire)	Fairfield	10. 6.26	Lost 13/5/41.

Displacement: 17,000 tons gross.
Dimensions: 552½ (pp) 578½ (oa) × 70¼ × 29 ft.
Machinery: 2-shaft geared Turbines, S.H.P. 13,500 = 15½ knots.
Armament: 8—6 in. (8 × 1), 2—3 in. A.A. (2 × 1) guns.

F.	SCOTSTOUN (ex-Caledonia, 17,046 t.g.)	Stephen	21. 4.25	Lost 13/6/40.
F.	TRANSYLVANIA (16,923 t.g.)	Fairfield	11. 3.25	Lost 10/8/40.

Displacement: 13,245 tons gross.
Dimensions: 510½ (pp) 526 (oa) × 64¼ × 39¼d. ft.
Machinery: 2-shaft Reciprocating (VQE), I.H.P. 7,500 = 14½ knots.
Armament: 8—6 in. (8 × 1), 2—3 in. A.A. (2 × 1) guns.

F.47	VOLTAIRE	Workman Clark	14. 8.23	Lost 4/4/41.

Above: H.M.S. Rajputana was one of four sister ships requisitioned from the P. & O. Steam Navigation Co. The second funnel has been removed; searchlights added in the bridge wings and at the after end of the boat deck: and a rangefinder fitted over the bridge. [*Courtesy P. & O. S.N. Co.*

Below: H.M.S. Rawalpindi was the first armed merchant cruiser to be lost. She was sunk, in gallant action, by the German battlecruisers Scharnhorst and Gniesenau. [*Courtesy P. & O. S.N. Co.*

P. No.	Name Armament	Gross tonnage Built	Commiss- ioned	Fate
F.17	ALAUNIA 8—6 in. (8 × 1) 2—3 in. A.A. (2 × 1)	14030/25	27. 9.39	Repair ship (1944).
F.88	ALCANTARA 8—6 in. (8 × 1) 2—3 in. A.A. (2 × 1)	22209/26	20.12.39	Troopship (1943).
F.21	ANTENOR 6—6 in. (6 × 1) 2—3 in. A.A. (2 × 1)	11174/25	7.11.39	Troopship (1942).
F.12	ARAWA (ex-Esperance Bay) 7—6 in. (7 × 1) 2—3 in. A.A. (2 × 1)	14462/22	17.10.39	Troopship (1941).
F.68	ASCANIA 8—6 in. (8 × 1) 2—3 in. A.A. (2 × 1)	14013/25	16.10.39	Troopship (1942), LSI(L) (1943).
F.71	ASTURIAS 8—6 in. (8 × 1) 2—3 in. A.A. (2 × 1)	22048/25	10.39	Laid up damaged 4/44.
F.28	AURANIA 8—6 in. (8 × 1) 2—3 in. A.A. (2 × 1)	13984/24	15.10.39	Repair ship ARTIFEX (1942).
F.53	AUSONIA 8—6 in. (8 × 1) 2—3 in. A.A. (2 × 1)	13912/21	7.11.39	Repair ship (1942).
F.82	BULOLO 7—6 in. (7 × 1) 2—3 in. A.A. (2 × 1)	6267/38	4. 1.40	Headquarter ship (1942).
F.55	CALIFORNIA 8—6 in. (8 × 1) 2—3 in. A.A.	16792/23	10.39	Troopship (1942); lost 11/7/43.
F.97	CANTON 9—6 in. (9 × 1) 4—4 in. A.A. (2 × 2)	15784/38	11.39	Troopship (1944).
F.25	CARNARVON CASTLE 8—6 in. (8 × 1) 2—3 in. A.A. (2 × 1)	20122/26	9.10.39	Troopship (1944).

The armed merchant cruiser H.M.S. Aurania belonged to a class of six Cunard liners all of which were requisitioned by the Royal Navy. [*I.W.M.*

H.M.S. California (ex. Anchor line) served as an armed merchant cruiser. [*I.W.M.*

H.M.S. Canton was one of the many P. & O. liners which served as an armed merchant cruiser and she was fitted with an aircraft and catapult. [*I.W.M.*

F.99	CARTHAGE 8—6 in. (8 × 1) 2—3 in. A.A. (2 × 1)	14182/31	1.40	Troopship (1943).
F.05	CATHAY 8—6 in. (8 × 1) 2—3 in. A.A. (2 × 1)	15225/25	11.10.39	Troopship (1942).
F.18	CHESHIRE 6—6 in. (6 × 1) 2—3 in. A.A. (2 × 1)	10552/27	30.10.39	Troopship (1943).
F.57	CHITRAL 7—6 in. (7 × 1) 3—4 in. A.A. (3 × 1)	15346/25	10.39	Troopship (1944).
F.54	CILICIA 8—6 in. (8 × 1) 2—3 in. A.A. (2 × 1)	11136/38	15.10.39	Troopship (1944).
F.91	CIRCASSIA 8—6 in. (8 × 1) 2—3 in. A.A. (2 × 1)	11136/37	1.40	Troopship (1942), LSI(L) (1943).
F.86	CORFU 9—6 in. (9 × 1) 4—4 in. A.A. (2 × 2) 2—2 pdr. A.A. (2 × 1) 19—20 mm. A.A. (19 × 1) 1 aircraft	14170/31	11.39	Troopship (1944).
F.	DERBYSHIRE 6—6 in. (6 × 1) 2—3 in. A.A. (2 × 1)	11660/35	11.39	Troopship (1942), LSI(L) (1943).
F.34	DUNOTTAR CASTLE 7—6 in. (7 × 1) 2—3 in. A.A. (2 × 1)	15007/36	14.10.39	Troopship (1942).
F.67	ESPERANCE BAY 7—6 in. (7 × 1) 2—3 in. A.A. (2 × 1)	14204/22	28.11.39	Troopship (1941).
F.23	KANIMBLA (R.A.N.) 6—6 in. (6 × 1) 2—3 in. A.A. (2 × 1)	10985/36	11.39	Headquarter ship (1943).
F.42	LACONIA 8—6 in. (8 × 1) 2—3 in. A.A. (2 × 1)	19695/22	1.40	Troopship (1941); lost 12/9/42.

With her original foremast and most of her boats removed and her top mast struck the Union Castle liner Carnarvon Castle presents a bare profile as an armed merchant cruiser. [*Courtesy Union Castle Line*

With two of her four masts struck the former Bibby liner H.M.S. Cheshire presents an unfamiliar picture as an armed merchant cruiser. [*I.W.M.*

H.M.S. Cilicia and her sister ship, the Circassia, were both requisitioned as armed merchant cruisers. [*I.W.M.*

F.16	LETITIA 8—6 in. (8 × 1) 2—3 in. A.A. (2 × 1)	13475/25	10.39	Troopship (1941).
F.26	MALOJA 8—6 in. (8 × 1) 2—3 in. A.A. (2 × 1)	20914/23	10.39	Troopship (1941).
F.48	MANOORA (R.A.N.) 8—6 in. (8 × 1) 2—3 in. A.A. (2 × 1)	10856/35	12.12.39	LSI(L) (1942).
F.59	MONOWAI (R.N.Z.N.) (ex-Razmak) 8—6 in. (8 × 1) 2—3 in. A.A. (2 × 1)	10852/24	30. 8.40	LSI(L) (1944).
F.85	MONTCLARE (ex-Metapedia) 7—5.5 in. (7 × 1) 3—4 in. A.A. (3 × 1)	16314/22	10.39	Depot ship (1943).
F.75	MOOLTAN 8—6 in. (8 × 1) 2—3 in. A.A. (2 × 1)	20952/23	10.39	Troopship (1941).
F.11	MORETON BAY 7—6 in. (7 × 1) 2—3 in. A.A. (2 × 1)	14193/21	10.39	Troopship (1941).
F.61	PRETORIA CASTLE 8—6 in. (8 × 1) 2—12 pdr. A.A. (2 × 1)	17392/38	11.39	Escort carrier (1943).
F.89	PRINCE DAVID (R.C.N.) 4—6 in. (4 × 1) 2—3 in. A.A. (2 × 1)	6892/30	12.40	LSI(M) (1943); CHARLTON MONARCH (1948).
F.70	PRINCE HENRY (R.C.N.) (ex-North Star, ex-Prince Henry) 4—6 in. (4 × 1) 2—3 in. A.A. (2 × 1)	6893/30	12.40	LSI(M) (1943); EMPIRE PARKESTON (1946).
F.56	PRINCE ROBERT (R.C.N) 4—6 in. (4 × 1) 2—3 in. A.A. (2 × 1)	6892/30	12.40	Aux. A.A. vessel (1943); CHARLTON SOVEREIGN (1948).

F.73	QUEEN OF BERMUDA 7—6 in. (7 × 1) 2—3 in. A.A. (2 × 1) 1 aircraft	22575/33	28.10.39	Troopship (1943).
F.15	RANCHI 8—6 in. (8 × 1) 2—3 in. A.A. (2 × 1)	16738/25	23.10.39	Troopship (1943).
F.93	RANPURA 8—6 in. (8 × 1) 2—3 in. A.A. (2 × 1)	16583/25	12.39	Repair ship (1944).
F.95	WESTRALIA (R.A.N.) 8—6 in. (8 × 1) 2—3 in. A.A. (2 × 1)	8108/29	17. 1.40	LSI(L) (1943).
F.37	WOLFE (ex-Montcalm) 7—6 in. (7 × 1) 2—12 pdr. A.A. (2 × 1)	16418/21	10. 1.40	Depot ship (1941).
F.29	WORCESTER-SHIRE 6—6 in. (6 × 1) 2—3 in. A.A. (2 × 1) 2—2 pdr. A.A. (2 × 1) 4—20 mm. A.A. (4 × 1)	11402/31	11.39	Troopship (1943).

In addition, the following vessel was also requisitioned but her conversion to an armed merchant cruiser was not completed, viz:—

F.	RIMUTAKA	16575/23		Returned 1939.

Notes:—These vessels are listed in two groups. The first group comprises those vessels lost as A.M.C's for which constructional details are given while the second group, arranged alphabetically, shows the various duties to which the remainder, with a solitary exception, were converted. Details of those converted for alternative naval duties will be found in this, and later parts, of this series.

DEPLOYMENT

March 1940

Orkney & Shetlands

California
Carinthia
Cilicia
Corfu
Derbyshire
Forfar

Mediterranean

Antenor
Voltaire

Halifax Escort Force

Ascania
Alaunia

South Atlantic
(Escort duty)

Bulolo (in U.K.)
Carnarvon Castle
Cheshire
Dunottar Castle
Dunvegan Castle
Esperance Bay (in U.K.)

Left: The ocean boarding vessel H.M.S. Cavina was returned to Elders & Fyffes in 1943 owing to the shortage of refrigerated cargo vessels. [*I.W.M.*

Right: H.M.S. Corinthian as a training ship with the forward 6 in. gun removed and replaced by a deckhouse and the light A.A. armament considerably enhanced. [*I.W.M.*

Orkney & Shetlands
Contd.

Letitia
Maloja
Patroclus
Salopian
Scotstoun
Transylvania
Wolfe
Worcestershire

(Refitting)

Andania
Asturias
Aurania
Canton
Chitral
Laurentic
Montclare

Halifax Escort Force
Contd.

Ausonia
Laconia

R.C.N.
(Fitting out)

Prince David
Prince Henry
Prince Robert

East Indies

Carthage
Cathay
Ranchi

China

Arawa
Kanimbla
Moreton Bay

South Atlantic
Contd.

Jervis Bay
Mooltan
Pretoria Castle
Ranpura

(Patrol Duty)

Alcantara
Comorin
Queen of Bermuda

R.A.N.

Manoora
Westralia

R.N.Z.N.

Hector
Monowai (fitting out)

The functions of ocean boarding vessels and armed boarding vessels were very similar. The former operated on the high seas and the latter usually in coastal waters, intercepting neutral and suspected enemy merchant vessels. Their work was sometimes referred to as *contraband control* and sometimes as *examination service*. There were also very many small craft (examination vessels) engaged on this latter duty working in the entrance to harbours.

The arduous work of the ocean and armed boarding vessels incurred heavy losses but with the overrunning of the European continent by Germany, in 1940, their work dwindled to almost nothing and they were then adapted for other duties.

OCEAN BOARDING VESSELS

These vessels were usually armed with two 6 in. guns and lighter A.A. guns and were of medium size with a better than average turn of speed. With the diminished need for them after 1940, four were fitted with a fighter aircraft and catapult and were used for the protection of convoys. So fitted, they were able to engage enemy reconnaisance aircraft which shadowed and reported on convoys and then homed marauding U-boats into attack.

P. No.	Name	Gross tonnage Built	Requisi-tioned	Fate
F.105	ARIGUANI	6746/26	1940	Fighter/Catapult ship (1941); returned 1943.
	CAMITO	6833/15	1940	Lost 6/5/41.
	CAVINA	6907/24	1940	Returned 1943.
F.103	CORINTHIAN	3151/38	1940	Training ship (1943); returned 1945.
	CRISPIN	5051/35	1940	Lost 3/2/41.
F.22	HILARY	7403/31	1940	Headquarter ship (1943); returned 1946.
	LADY SOMERS	8194/29	1940	Lost 15/7/41.
F.43	LARGS (ex-Charles Plumier) 2—6 in. (2 × 1) 1—3 in. A.A. 6—20 mm. A.A. (6 × 1)	4504/38	1940	Headquarter ship (1943); returned 1945.

Originally an ocean boarding vessel the Booth Liner H.M.S. Hilary later served as a headquarters ship. [*I.W.M.*

F.104	MANISTEE 2—6 in. (2 × 1)	5368/20	1940	Lost 24/2/41.
F.107	MAPLIN (ex-Erin) 2—6 in. (2 × 1)	5824/32	1940	Fighter-Catapult ship (1941); returned 1946.
F.87	MARON 2—6 in. (2 × 1) 1—3 in. A.A.	6487/30	1940	Returned 1945.
	MALVERNIAN 2—6 in. (2 × 1) 1—3 in. (A.A.)	3133/37	1940	Lost 19/7/41.
	MARSDALE 2—6 in. (2 × 1)	4890/40	1940	Returned 1945.
	PATIA 2—6 in. (2 × 1)	5355/22	1940	Fighter/Catapult ship (1941); lost 27/4/41.
F.106	REGISTAN 2—6 in. (2 × 1)	5886/30	1940	Fighter/Catapult ship (1943); returned 1946.
	TORTUGUERO 2—6 in. (2 × 1)	5285/21	1941	Returned 1942.

ARMED BOARDING VESSELS

These vessels were smaller and lighter armed, generally with only one/two 4 in. guns, and suffered disastrously in coastal waters. The few that survived were adapted for other duties or returned to mercantile service.

	CHAKDINA	3033/14	1940	Lost 5/12/41.
	CHAKLA	3081/14	1939	Lost 29/4/41.
	CHANTALA	3129/20	1939	Lost 7/12/41.
	DISCOVERY	1062/29	1940	Returned 1945.
	FAROE ISLE 4—5.5 in. (4 × 1)	.../...	19...	
	FIONA	2190/27	1939	Lost 18/4/41.
	FRATTON	757/25	1940	B.B.V. (1943); lost 18/8/44.
	GOODWIN	1570/17	1940	Aux. A.A. vessel (1941).
	KING ORRY	1877/13	1939	Lost 30/5/40.
	LAIRDS ISLE (ex-Riviera)	1784/11	1939	Training ship (1940), Headquarter ship (1944); returned 1945.
	MONA'S ISLE (ex-Onward)	1644/05	1939	Aux. A.A. vessel (1941); accommodation ship (1943); returned 1945.
	ST. TUDNO	2326/26	1939	Depot ship (1940); returned 1947.
	VANDYCK	13241/21	1940	Lost 10/6/40.

Notes:—For further vessels used as A.B.V.s see under yachts and trawlers.

SPECIAL SERVICE VESSELS

This category covered a variety of little-publicised roles including decoy (" Q ") ships. There was little opportunity to emulate the decoy vessels of the First World War as merchant vessels were so rapidly, and effectively, armed that submarines became unwilling to engage in surface gun action and went in with the torpedo.

Four special service vessels were employed as A.M.C.'s in the Pacific, possibly with the hope of falling in with an auxiliary raider, but their lack of success in this field led to their early re-deployment.

(a) *Decoy ships*

X.72	ANTOINE (ex-Orchy)	1,090/30	6.10.39	To M.O.W.T. 18/6/41.
X.96	BRUTUS (ex-City of Durban)	5,945/21	17. 9.39	A.M.C. CITY OF DURBAN (F.114-1941); to M.O.W.T. 4/42.
X.85	CHATSGROVE (ex-R.N. PC.74)	610/18		Patrol sloop PC.74 (1941).
X.44	CYPRUS (ex-Cape Sable)	4,398/36	19. 9.39	A.M.C. CAPE SABLE (F.112–1941); to M.O.W.T. 6/42.
X.39	EDGEHILL (ex-Willamette Valley)	4,702/28	17. 9.39	Lost 29/6/40.
D.57	FIDELITY (ex-Le Rone)	2,456/20	24. 9.40	Lost 30/12/42.
X.15	LAMBRIDGE (ex-Botlea)	5,119/17	16. 9.39	A.M.C. BOTLEA (F.113–1941); to M.O.W.T. 12/41.
X.63	LOOE (ex-Beauly)	1,030/24	6.10.39	To M.O.W.T. 20/6/41.
X.28	MAUNDER (ex-King Gruffyd)	5,072/19	14. 9.39	A.M.C. KING GRUFFYD (F.116–1941); to M.O.W.T. 12/41.
X.02	PRUNELLA (ex-Cape Howe)	4,443/30	15. 9.39	Lost 21/6/40.

Notes:—Were armed according to size, with four/nine 4 in. guns, two/four 21 in. T.T. and depth charges. KING GRUFFYD was armed with seven 4 in. (7 × 1) guns and four 21 in. (4 × 1) T.T.; FIDELITY with three 4 in. (3 × 1), two 75 mm. (2 × 1), one 37 mm. A.A., three 25 mm. A.A., and one 20 mm. A.A. guns; and CITY OF DURBAN with eight (later nine) 4 in. (8/9 × 1), one 12 pdr. A.A., and two 2 pdr. A.A. guns. Their identity was concealed behind R.F.A. names and pennant numbers and, with the exception of FIDELITY, their employment was terminated in 1941. FIDELITY, however continued in this service and was rearmed with four 4 in. (4 × 1) guns, four 21 in. T.T., two aircraft, and one MTB (No. 105).

(b) *Dummy warships*

	MAMARI	7924/11	1939	Dummy aircraft carrier HERMES; lost 4/6/41.
	PAKEHA	7909/10	1939	Dummy battleship REVENGE; returned 1941.
	WAIMANA	7852/11	1939	Dummy battleship RESOLUTION; returned 1942.

CONVOY ESCORTS

These two ships, the only vessels so classified, spent the war in the Mediterranean and were too lightly armed (and too small) to be rated as armed merchant cruisers but were considerably larger than most auxiliary patrol vessels.

4.209	ANTWERP	2957/20	1940	F.D.S. (1944); returned 1945.

4.214	MALINES	2980/21	1940	Returned 1945.

BARRAGE BALLOON VESSELS

These vessels comprised two groups: the sea-going group which proceeded with the coastal convoys and was mainly drawn from small mercantile vessels and tugs, and those vessels which generally flew their balloons in harbour and composed of trawlers and drifters. The former group, listed below, began forming in July, 1940 and was based on Sheerness until 1943 when it was disbanded.

	ASTRAL (ex-Pilote 14)	451/30	Wreck locating vessel (1943).
	BOREALIS (ex-Pilote 15)	451/30	Lost 10/8/40.
	BUNGAY (ex-Maidstone)	688/26	Returned 1943.
	DEAL	691/28	Returned 1943.
	ELAN II*		Target service (1941).
B.16	FRATTON	757/25	Examination service (1943); lost 18/8/44.
	HASLEMERE	756/25	Laid up 1943; returned 1945.
	MAMMOUTH*	954/18	Rescue tug (1943).
	PINGOUIN*	700/17	Target service (1943).
	PINTADE*	700/17	Target service (1943).
	RAMIER*	685/17	Salvage vessel (1943).
	RENE LE BESNERAIS*	246/31	
	ROEBUCK	769/25	ROEBUCK II (1942).
	SAMBUR	769/25	TOREADOR (1942).

*Tug

Notes:—For further vessels of this type see under trawlers and drifters (Part 6).

AUXILIARY ANTI-AIRCRAFT VESSELS

(Seagoing)

These vessels were amongst the most battleworthy conversions undertaken and for the aerial defence of convoys were practically the equal of a modern cruiser. They had their twin mounted 4 in. A.A. guns placed on the centre line, extensive air and sea warning R.D.F. and H.A. D.C.T.'s fitted with gunnery R.D.F. With convoys or invasion fleets their moderate speed was no great disadvantage and allowed them a sufficient reserve for emergencies but such elaborate conversions were necessarily limited in numbers.

Displacement: 5,150 tons gross.
Dimensions: $420\frac{1}{4}$ (pp) 434 (oa) × 54 × $25\frac{3}{4}$ ft.
Machinery: 2-shaft Diesel motors, B.H.P. 2,500 = 12 knots.
Armament: 8—4 in. A.A. (4 × 2), 8—2 pdr. A.A. (2 × 4), 6-20 mm. A.A. (6 × 1), 8—.5 in. A.A. (2 × 4) guns; 1 aircraft (SPRINGBANK only).

P. No.	Name	Builder	Launched	Fate
F.84	ALYNBANK (5151 t.g.)	Harland & Wolff (Govan)	13. 1.25	Expended as blockship 9/6/44; salved and scrapped Troon 12/45.

The Blue Funnel (Alfred Holt & Co.) liner H.M.S. Maron as an ocean boarding vessel. [I.W.M.

The Southern Railway steamer H.M.S. Fratton, served first as an armed boarding vessel, then as a barrage balloon vessel and was finally lost in the examination service. [P. A. Vicary

H.M.S. Fidelity was a special service vessel with a concealed armament which eventually included two aircraft and an M.T.B. [I.W.M.

F.	SPRINGBANK (5155 t.g.)	Harland & Wolff (Govan)	13. 4.26	Lost 27/9/41.

Displacement: 5,582 tons gross.
Dimensions: 426¾ (pp) (oa) × 57¼ × 26¼ ft.
Machinery: 2-shaft Diesel motors, B.H.P. 2,900 = 12 knots.
Armament: 8—4 in. A.A. (4 × 2), 8—2 pdr. A.A. (2 × 4), 4—20 mm. A.A. (4 × 1) guns.

F.	FOYLEBANK	Harland & Wolff	12. 6.30	Lost 4/7/40.

Displacement: 1,895 tons gross.
Dimensions: 295½ (pp) 306½ (oa) × 45 × 17½ ft.
Machinery: 1-shaft Diesel motors, B.H.P. 2,640 = 16¼ knots.
Armament: 6—4 in. A.A. (3 × 2), 8—2 pdr. A.A. (2 × 4), 8—20 mm. A.A. (8 × 1), 8—.5 in. (2 × 4) guns.

F.98	PALOMARES (1,896 t.g.)	Doxford	20.10.37	Fighter direction ship (1943); returned 4/46.
4.261	POZARICA (1,893 t.g.)	Doxford	6. 9.37	Lost 13/2/43; salved and scrapped Italy 5/51.

Displacement: 6,982 tons gross.
Dimensions: 366½ (pp) 385 (oa) × 57 × 16½ ft.
Machinery: 2-shaft geared Turbines, S.H.P. 19,500 = 22¼ knots.
Armament: 10—4 in. A.A. (5 × 2), 8—2 pdr. A.A. (2 × 4), 6—20 mm. A.A. (6 × 1) guns. *Complement:* 241.

F.56	PRINCE ROBERT (R.C.N.)	Cammell Laird	4. 3.30	Mercantile CHARLTON SOVEREIGN (1948).

Displacement: 2,376 tons gross.
Dimensions: 314½ (pp) 329 (oa) × 46 × 13½ ft.
Machinery: 2-shaft geared Turbines, S.H.P. 8,000 = 21 knots.
Armament: 6—4 in. A.A. (3 × 2), 8—2 pdr. A.A. (4 × 4), 4—20 mm. A.A. (4 × 1) guns.

D.69	TYNWALD	V.A. (Barrow)	16.12.36	Lost 12/11/42.

Displacement: 3,791 tons gross.
Dimensions: 346 (pp) 359 (oa) × 46¼ × 15¼ ft.
Machinery: 2-shaft Diesel motors, B.H.P. 4,155 = 18 knots.

bove: The French tug Mammouth was originally employed as a barrage balloon vessel and later as a escue tug. [*I.W.M.*

elow: The auxiliary A.A. vessel H.M.S. Springbank had the refinements of a regular warship. Note win A.A. guns on the centre line, tripod masts with AW. RDF and an HA. DCT on the re-modelled ridge. [*I.W.M.*

The MacAndrew's fruit carrier H.M.S. Pozarica extensively altered as an auxiliary A.A. vessel. [*I.W.M*

With her two former fore funnels trunked into a single uptake and the superstructure accommodatio removed the Canadian National Railways liner H.M.S. Prince Robert was difficult to distinguish from regular naval vessel and was manned by the R.C.N. [*I.W.M*

H.M.S. Tynwald was the only auxiliary A.A. vessel to have HA. DCT's fore and aft and served with tl Irish Sea escort force. [*I.W.M*

Armament: 6—4 in. A.A. (3 × 2), 8—2 pdr. A.A. (2 × 4), 10—20 mm. A.A. (10 × 1) guns.

F.118	ULSTER QUEEN	Harland & Wolff	28. 3.29	Fighter Direction ship (1943); returned 4/46.

Notes:—PALOMARES and ULSTER QUEEN later had 3—6 in. A.A. (3 × 1) in place of the twin 4 in. A.A. mountings.

AUXILIARY ANTI-AIRCRAFT VESSELS

(Coastal)

Although the aerial defence of coastal convoys would have been best met by shore based fighter aircraft many circumstances, and conflicting priorities, prevented this policy from being fully implemented. Therefore, provision had to be made for suitable vessels to be converted to purely coastal anti-aircraft vessels in addition to the A/S cover given by coastal escorts, mostly of limited A.A. firepower. Coastal convoys frequently found themselves harrowed in estuarial waters (such as the Thames estuary) where, once committed to the navigational deep-water channels, they were unable to take any form of avoiding action and thus simplified the task of attacking aircraft. Fortunately, the steadily mounting minesweeper construction programme enabled practically all the requisitioned paddle minesweepers to be released for this purpose, and together with other paddle vessels not taken up for minesweeping and some miscellaneous small vessels they were converted, or adapted, as coastal auxiliary A.A. vessels. The paddle vessels enjoyed the additional advantage that their shallow draught did not wholly restrict them to the deep water channels and they virtually provided A.A. cover from harbour entrance to harbour entrance. Their armament was of a makeshift nature and consisted of numerous close range weapons as their light construction did not permit heavier pieces being mounted. Generally, it consisted of single 2 pdr. A.A. guns fitted forward and aft, a few 20 mm. A.A. guns before and abaft the paddle boxes, which usually had quadruple .5 in. M.G.'s. on top of them, quadruple Boulton & Paul aircraft turrets on the bridge and superstructure, several single or twin vintage M.G.'s disposed overall and one or more 4-barrelled rocket projectors of capricious nature. The latter were ultimately replaced by 20 mm. guns as they became more readily available. At close range they were able to confront attacking aircraft with a considerable, but ill-directed, volume of A.A. fire (there were no H.A. control arrangements) and their true measure of success was more in the number of air attacks they broke up than in the actual number of aircraft brought down.

Displacement: 544 tons gross.
Dimensions: 215 (pp) 222½ (oa) × 27½ × 16½d. ft.
Machinery: Paddle Diesel/Electric, S.H.P. 1,300 = 17 knots.
Armament: 2—2 pdr. A.A. (2 × 1), 5—20 mm. A.A. (5 × 1), 8—.303 in. A.A. (2 × 4 B & P), 6—M (1 × 2 & 4 × 1 LG) guns.

4.200	ARISTOCRAT (ex-Talisman)	Inglis: English Elec.	10. 4.35	Ferry service (1945); returned 1946.

Left: The diesel-engined H.M.S. Ulster Queen, here shown as an auxiliary A.A. vessel, was later converted to a fighter direction ship. [*I.W.M.*

Right: The auxiliary A.A. vessel H.M.S. Aristocrat had diesel-electric propulsion to her paddles. [*I.W.M.*

Displacement: 473 tons gross.
Dimensions: 236 (pp) (oa) × 27 × 9½ ft.
Machinery: Paddle Reciprocating (DC), N.H.P. 300 = 20 knots.
Armament: 2—2 pdr. A.A. (2 × 1), 8—.5 in. A.A. (2 × 4 VG), 8—.303 in. A.A. (2 × 4 B & P), 7—M guns.

4.241	BALMORAL	McKnight: Hutson	15. 5.00	Accommodation ship (1944); returned 1945, scrapped 1946.

Displacement: 350 tons gross.
Dimensions: 200 (pp) (oa) × 24 × 8 ft.
Machinery: Paddle Reciprocating (DC), N.H.P. 94 = 12½ knots.
Armament: 2—2 pdr. A.A. (2 × 1), 8—.303 in. (2 × 4 B & P), 5—M guns.

4.270	BOURNEMOUTH QUEEN (ex-R.N. Bourne, ex-Bournemouth Queen)	Ailsa Sbdg.: Hutson	18. 5.08	Accommodation ship (1944); returned 1945.

Displacement: 886 tons gross.
Dimensions: 193½ (pp) 234¾ (oa) × 30½ × 13½ ft.
Machinery: 2-shaft Reciprocating (VTE), I.H.P. 1,865 = 15¼ knots.
Armament: 1—12 pdr., A.A., 2—2 pdr. A.A. (2 × 1), 6—20 mm. A.A. (6 × 1), 8—.5 in. A.A. (2 × 4 VG), 8—.303 in. M (4—L.G. and 4 HG) guns.

F.33	CONQUEROR (ex-Emerald, ex-Marynthia)	Thornycroft	16. 1.11	Ex-armed yacht; returned 1945.

Displacement: 3,044 tons gross.
Dimensions: 332 (pp) (oa) × 53 × 20½d. ft.
Machinery: 2-shaft Reciprocating (VTE), I.H.P. 2,087 = 10¼ knots.
Armament: 2—3 in. A.A., 2—2 pdr. A.A. (2 × 1) guns.

	CORONATION	Vickers	8. 8.02	Ex-dredger; INZ WENDA (1947)

Displacement: 1,110 tons gross.
Dimensions: 299¾ (pp) 309¼ (oa) × 34½ × 11½ ft.
Machinery: Paddle Reciprocating (DTE), I.H.P. 3,148 = 18¾ knots.
Armament: 3—2 pdr. A.A. (3 × 1) guns.

	CRESTED EAGLE	White	26. 3.35	Lost 29/5/40.

Displacement: 534 tons gross.
Dimensions: 217¼ (pp) (oa) × 25 × 8½ ft.
Machinery: Paddle Reciprocating (DC), I.H.P. 1,422 = 14½ knots.

Left: H.M.S. Emperor of India served with the Royal Navy in both World Wars and was named Mahratta for the earlier war. [*I.W.M.*

Right: The auxiliary A.A. vessel H.M.S. Goatfell. Her armament included four single 2 pdr. disposed fore and aft and over the paddle boxes, six single 20 mm. and two quadruple Boulton & Paul MG turrets amidships. [*I.W.M.*

Armament: 2—2 pdr. A.A. (2 × 1), 8—.5 in. A.A. (2 × 4 VG), 8—.303 in. A.A. (2 × 4 B & P) guns; 4—RP (1 × 4).

4.237	EMPEROR OF INDIA (ex-R.N. Mahratta, ex-Emperor of India, ex-Princess Royal)	Thornycroft	1906	Ex-P.M.S., harbour service (1943); returned 1946.

Displacement: 509 tons gross.
Dimensions: 220 (pp) (oa) × 27 × 9 ft.
Machinery: Paddle Reciprocating (DC), N.H.P. 165 = 17 knots.
Armament: 3—2 pdr. A.A. (3 × 1), 4—20 mm. A.A. (4 × 1), 8—.303 in. (2 × 4 B & P), 4—M (4 × 1 LG) guns.

4.392	GLEN AVON	Ailsa Sbdg.:	30. 5.12	Lost 2/9/44.

Displacement: 524 tons gross.
Dimensions: 224¼ (pp) (oa) × 28 × 9 ft.
Machinery: Paddle Reciprocating (DC), N.H.P. 165 = 17 knots.
Armament: 3—2 pdr. A.A. (3 × 1), 4—20 mm. A.A. (4 × 1), 8—.303 in. (2 × 4 B & P), 4—M (2 × 2 LG) guns.

4.377	GLEN USK	Ailsa Sbdg.:	27. 5.14	Ex-P.M.S.; returned 1945.

Displacement: 553 tons gross.
Dimensions: 235 (pp) 242 (oa) × 28½ × 9 ft.
Machinery: Paddle Reciprocating (DC), I.H.P. 1,800 = 17½ knots.
Armament: 4—2 pdr. A.A. (4 × 1), 5—20 mm. A.A. (5 × 1), 8—.303 in. (2 × 4 B & P), 3—M (2 × 1 HG, 1 × 1 LG) guns.

4.368	GLEN MORE (ex-Glen Gower)	Ailsa Sbdg.: Thomson	14. 2.22	Ex-P.M.S.; returned 1945.

Displacement: 624 tons gross.
Dimensions: 223 (pp) 229½ (oa) × 30 × 6½ ft.
Machinery: Paddle Reciprocating (DTE), I.H.P. 1750 = 16½ knots.
Armament: 4—2 pdr. A.A. (4 × 1), 6—20 mm. A.A. (6 × 1), 16—.303 in. A.A. (4× 4 B & P) guns.

4.36	GOATFELL (ex-Caledonia)	Denny	1. 2.34	Ex-P.M.S.; returned 1945.

Displacement: 793 tons gross.
Dimensions: 275 (pp) (oa) × 32 × 10¾ ft.
Machinery: Paddle Reciprocating (DTE), I.H.P. 2,700 = 18 knots.

Armament: 4—2 pdr. A.A. (4 × 1), 2—20 mm. A.A. (2 × 1), 8—.303 in. A.A. (2 × 4 B & P), 2—M (1 × 2 LG) guns, 8—RP (2 × 4).

4.236	GOLDEN EAGLE	Clydebank	1909	Returned 1945.

Displacement: 642 tons gross.
Dimensions: 223 (pp) 230½ (oa) × 30 × 9¾ ft.
Machinery: Paddle Reciprocating (DTE), I.H.P. 2,000 = 17 knots.

	HELVELLYN (ex-Juno)	Fairfield	25. 5.37	Ex-P.M.S.; constructive total loss 20/3/41.

Displacement: 635 tons gross.
Dimensions: 249¾ (pp) 257½ (oa) × 30 × 9½ ft.
Machinery: Paddle Reciprocating (DTE), N.H.P. 338 = 18¼ knots.
Armament: 2—2 pdr. A.A. (2 × 1), 4—20 mm. A.A. (4 × 1), 8—.5 in. (2 × 4 VG), 16—.303 in. A.A. (4 × 4 B & P), 8—M (8 × 1 HG) guns.

4.29	JEANNIE DEANS	Fairfield	7. 4.31	Ex-P.M.S.; returned 1944.

Displacement: 971 tons gross.
Dimensions: 223¼ (pp) (oa) × 36 × 13¼ ft.
Machinery: 1-shaft Reciprocating (VTE), N.H.P. 106 = 11 knots.

	KAMPAR	Hong Kong & Whampoa	1915	Lost 13/12/41.

Displacement: 617 tons gross.
Dimensions: 249 (pp) (oa) × 30 × 10d. ft.
Machinery: Paddle Reciprocating (DTE), I.H.P. 2500 = 16 knots.
Armament: 1—12 pdr. A.A., 2—2 pdr. AA., (2 × 1), 4—20 mm. A.A. (4 × 1), 8—.303 in. A.A. (2 × 4 B & P) guns, 8—RP (2 × 4).

4.373	LAGUNA BELLE (ex-Southend Belle)	Denny	11. 3.96	Ex-P.M.S.; accommodation ship (1943); returned 1944.

Displacement: 410 tons gross.
Dimensions: 220½ (pp) (oa) × 26 × 9¼ ft.
Machinery: Paddle Reciprocating (DC), N.H.P. 248 = 16 knots.
Armament: 2—2 pdr. A.A. (2 × 1), 5—20 mm. A.A. (5 × 1), 6—M (2 × 2 LG and 2 × 1 HG) guns.

4.402	LORNA DOONE	Napier, Shanks, & Ball: Rowan	27. 5.91	Ex-P.M.S., accommodation ship (1944); returned 1946.

Although converted to an auxiliary A.A. vessel H.M.S. Jeannie Deans still has her minesweeper pennant number painted up. [*I.W.M.*

The auxiliary A.A. vessel H.M.S. Laguna Belle was later relegated to harbour duties as an accommodation ship. [*I.W.M.*

The turbine-engined H.M.S. Queen Eagle was requisitioned at the outbreak of war while still under construction and completed as an auxiliary A.A. vessel. [*I.W.M.*

Displacement: 438 tons gross.
Dimensions: 225 (pp) 233 (oa) × 26 × 9½ ft.
Machinery: Paddle Reciprocating (DC), I.H.P. 2,600 = 20 knots.
Armament: 3—2 pdr. A.A. (3 × 1), 8—.303 in. (2 × 4 B & P) guns.

4.385	PLINLIMMON (ex-Cambria, ex-R.N. Cambridge, ex-Cambria)	McIntyre: Hutson	10. 4.95	Ex-P.M.S.; accommodation ship (1944); constructive total loss 8/46, scrapped Grays 11/46.

Displacement: 388 tons gross.
Dimensions: 195 (pp) (oa) × 24¼ × 8 ft.
Machinery: Paddle Reciprocating (DC), N.H.P. 94 = 12½ knots.
Armament: 1—12 pdr. A.A., 2—2 pdr. A.A. (2 × 1), 3—20 mm. A.A. (3 × 1), 8—M (4 × 2 LG) guns.

4.403	PRINCESS ELIZABETH	Day Summers	2. 6.27	Ex-P.M.S.; returned 1944.

Displacement: 1,781 tons gross.
Dimensions: 269½ (pp) 282 (oa) × 37½ × 12 ft.
Machinery: 2-shaft geared Turbines, N.H.P. 650 = 21 knots.
Armament: 4—2 pdr. A.A. (4 × 1), 16—.303 in. A.A. (4 × 4 B & P), 2—M (2 × 1 LG) guns, 4—RP (1 × 4).

4.247	QUEEN EAGLE (ex-Empress Queen)	Ailsa Sbdg.: Harland & Wolff	3.40	Returned 1945.

Notes:—Later re-armed 4—2 pdr. AA (4 x 1), 5—20 mm. AA (5 x 1), 4—.303 in. AA (1 x 4 B & P) guns.

Displacement: 411 tons gross.
Dimensions: 210 (pp) (oa) × 25½ × 8½ ft.
Machinery: Paddle Reciprocating (DC), N.H.P. 178 = 15 knots.
Armament: 2—2 pdr. A.A. (2 × 1), 4—20 mm. A.A. (4 × 1), 11—M (4 × 2 and 3 × 1 LG) guns.

4.399	QUEEN EMPRESS	Murdoch & Murray: Rankin & Blackmore	20. 4.12	Ex-P.M.S.; returned 1944; scrapped 1946.

Displacement: 391 tons gross.
Dimensions: 215 (pp) (oa) × 24 × 8½ ft.
Machinery: Paddle Reciprocating (DC), N.H.P. 205 = 18 knots.
Armament: 3—2 pdr. A.A. (3 × 1), 3—20 mm. A.A. (3 × 1), 16—.303 in (4 × 4 B & P), 2—M (2 × 1 HG) guns.

4.328	RAVENSWOOD	McKnight: Barclay Curle	27. 4.91	Ex-P.M.S.; returned 1945.

Notes:—Was re-engined in 1909 when original simple machinery (by Hutson & Corbett) was replaced by compound set.

Displacement: 1,538 tons gross.
Dimensions: 289¾ (pp) (oa) × 33 × 7 ft.
Machinery: Paddle Reciprocating (DTE), I.H.P. 2,875 = 18 knots.
Armament: 6—2 pdr. A.A. (6 × 1), 6—20 mm. A.A. (6 × 1), 12—.303 in. A.A. (3 × 4 B & P), 1—M (LG) guns, 8—RP (2 × 4).

4.239	ROYAL EAGLE	Cammell Laird	24. 2.32	Returned 5/45.

Displacement: 603 tons gross.
Dimensions: 220 (pp) 223 (oa) × 29 × 7¼ ft.
Machinery: Paddle Reciprocating (DTE), I.H.P. 1000 = 14 knots.
Armament: 3—2 pdr. A.A. (3 × 1), 6—20 mm. A.A. (6 × 1), 8—.303 in. A.A. (2 × 4 B & P), 16—M (8 × 2 LG) guns.

4.39	RYDE	Denny	23. 4.37	Ex-P.M.S.; returned 2/45.

Displacement: 684 tons gross.
Dimensions: 216 (pp) 223 (oa) × 29 × 10 ft.
Machinery: Paddle Reciprocating (DTE), I.P.H. 1000 = 14 knots.
Armament: 1—12 pdr. A.A., 2—2 pdr. A.A. (2 × 1), 4—20 mm. A.A. (4 × 1). 8—.303 in. (2 × 4 B & P) guns, 4—RP (1 × 4).

4.15	SANDOWN	Denny	1. 5.34	Ex-P.M.S.; returned 1944.

Notes:—Later re-armed with 3—2 pdr. A.A. (3 x 1), 5/6 20 mm. A.A. (5/6 x 1) guns.

Displacement: 642 tons gross.
Dimensions: 223 (pp) 230½ (oa) × 30 × 9¾ ft.
Machinery: Paddle Reciprocating (DTE), I.H.P. 2000 = 17 knots.
Armament: 4—2 pdr. A.A. (4 × 1), 6—20 mm. A.A. (6 × 1), 16—.303 in. (4 × 4 B & P) guns.

4.22	SCAWFELL (ex-Jupiter)	Fairfield	9. 4.37	Ex-P.M.S.; returned 1945.

Displacement: 459 tons gross.
Dimensions: 230 (pp) (oa) × 26½ × 9½ ft.
Machinery: Paddle Reciprocating (DC), N.H.P. 304 = 20 knots.
Armament: 1—12 pdr. A.A., 2 pdr. A.A. (2 × 1) guns.

4.301	SKIDDAW (ex-Britannia, ex-R.N. Britain, ex-Britannia)	McKnight: Hutson	14. 5.96	Ex-P.M.S.; returned 1945.

Left: H.M.S. Queen Empress was one of the many paddle steamers originally taken up as a minesweeper and later converted to an auxiliary A.A. vessel. [*I.W.M.*

Right: H.M.S. Royal Eagle was another one of the General Steam Navigation Co. paddle steamers adapted for A.A. duties. [*I.W.M.*

Displacement: 517 tons gross.
Dimensions: 240 (pp) (oa) × 28 × $9\frac{1}{4}$ ft.
Machinery: Paddle Reciprocating (DTE), I.H.P. 1250 = 17 knots.
Armaments: 1—12 pdr. A.A., 2—2 pdr. A.A. (2 × 1), 4—20 mm. A.A. (4 × 1), 8—.303 in. A.A. (2 × 4 B & P), 1-M (LG) guns, 4-RP (1 × 4).

4.380	THAMES QUEEN (ex-Queen of Southend, ex-Yarmouth Belle)	Denny	7. 4.98	Ex-P.M.S.; returned 2/47.

Displacement: 438 tons gross.
Dimensions: 225 (pp) (oa) × 26 × $9\frac{1}{2}$ ft.
Machinery: Paddle Reciprocating (DC), N.H.P. 277 = 17 knots.
Armament: 1—12 pdr. A.A., 2—2 pdr. A.A. (2 × 1), 8—.303 in. (2 × 4 B & P) guns.

4.390	WESTWARD HO! (ex-Westward Queen, ex-R.N. Westhope, ex-Westward Queen)	McKnight: Hutson	17. 4.94	Ex-P.M.S.; accommodation ship (1944); returned 3/46 & scrapped Newport 1/8/46.

Displacement: 825 tons gross.
Dimensions: 244 (pp) 250 (oa) × 30 × 7 ft.
Machinery: Paddle Reciprocating (DC), N.H.P. 196 = 16 knots.
Armament: 3—2 pdr. A.A. (3 × 1), 4—20 mm. A.A. (4 × 1), 2—M (2 × 1 HG) guns.

4.404	WHIPPINGHAM	Fairfield	1. 5.30	Ex-P.M.S.; returned 4/45.

ANTI-AIRCRAFT GUARDSHIPS

Displacement: 2,450 tons.
Dimensions: 328 (pp) (oa) × $39\frac{1}{4}$ × 13 ft.
Machinery: 2-shaft geared Turbines, S.H.P. 10,000 = 20 knots.
Armament: 1—2 pdr. A.A., 2—40 mm. A.A. (2 × 1) guns.

P. No.	Name	Builder	Launched	Fate
	L'IMPASSIBLE	Lorient	17. 6.39	Scrapped 1952.

Notes:—Uncompleted French target ship, without machinery, converted to harbour A.A. ship 1942 and stationed at Plymouth.

Right: H.M.S. Skiddaw served with the Royal Navy in both World Wars; she was named Britain in World War I. Although her minesweeping gear has been removed she still wears herminesweeper pennant number. [*I.W.M.*

Right: H.M.S. Thames Queen is typical of the older paddle steamers with the funnel before the bridge. [*I.W.M.*

P. No.	Name	Gross tonnage Built	Requisi-tioned	Fate
4.68	GOODWIN	1570/17	1941	Ex-A.B.V. A/P (1942).
4.47	MONA'S ISLE	1644/05	1941	Ex-A.B.V. ; returned 1945.

Notes:—GOODWIN was armed with 1—12 pdr. A.A. and 5—20 mm. (5×1) guns and MONA'S ISLE with 1—12 pdr. A.A., 2—2pdr. A.A. (2×1) and 2—20 mm. A.A. (2×1) guns.

AUXILIARY PATROL VESSELS

Auxiliary patrol vessels were mainly requisitioned for coastal escort work and were usually armed with a single 12-pdr. or 4 in. gun, a few light A.A. pieces, depth charges and asdic (in some).

They were largely acquired by the Dominion navies for service in home waters. Far fewer were taken up by the Royal Navy and the majority were locally acquired and employed in the Far East, while a proportion were solely engaged as examination vessels.

They ranged from sea-going tugs to small, coastal passenger vessels and their principal characteristic was their diversity of type. A few of the newer, and faster, vessels—such as the R.I.N. SONAVATI—were fully operational vessels quite the combatant equal of comparative naval vessels but the need for them steadily declined as the Allied navies enlarged their command of the seas and the war construction of escort vessels and maritime aircraft gained impetus.

Trawlers, drifters and whalers requisitioned as auxiliary patrol vessels are dealt with separately in part 6.

P. No.	Name	Gross tonnage Built	Requisi-tioned	Fate
	ARCADIA (R.C.N.)	846/13	1939	Returned 1946.
FY.079	BADORA (R.I.N.)	274/14	1939	Returned 1944.
	BAN HONG LIONG	1671/08	1940	Returned 1942.
FY.065	BHADRAVATI (R.I.N.)	1449/32	1939	Returned 1945.
FY.88	BINGERA (R.A.N.)	922/35	1939	Returned 1946.
	BIRCHGROVE PARK (R.A.N.)	640/30	1940	Returned 1946.
	B. O. DAVIES	173/32	1941	Examination service; returned 1946.
	BOMBO (R.A.N.)	540/30	1940	Store carrier (1944); returned 1946.
FY.85	BONTHORPE (R.A.N.)	273/27	1939	Returned 1946.
.405	BRENDA		1939	Examination service; returned 1945.
	BURRABRA (R.A.N.)	458/08	1942	Training ship (1942); returned 1944.
	CHANDBALI (R.I.N.)	362/19	1939	Returned 1943.
	CHANDAVATI (R.I.N.)	556/33	1939	Returned 1940.
	CORONIA	227/34	1939	Returned 1945.
	DHAMRA (R.I.N.)	490/10	1940	Returned 1940.

4.406	EXPLORER		1939	Examination service; returned 1945.
	FRENCH (R.C.N.)	226/38	1939	Returned 1946.
4.407	FREYA	280/04	1940	Examination service; returned 1946.
	FUH WO	955/22	1940	Lost 2/42.
	GANGA (R.I.N.) 1—3 pdr.	89/31	1939	Harbour service; returned 1946.
	GEORGES LEVEDIER	279/30	1940	Examination service; returned 1946.
	GIANG BEE	1646/08	1940	Lost 3/3/42.
	GOODWIN	1570/17	1942	Ex-A.A. guardship, ex-A.B.V., rescue ship (1943); returned 1945.
	GUTHIE (R.I.N.)		1940	Returned 1941.
	HAIDERI (R.I.N.)	1510/20	1939	Lost 2/4/43 & salved; returned 1946.
	HASHEMI (R.I.N.) (ex-Padma, ex-Wearmouth, ex-R.N. Kildorough)	634/18	1939	Returned 1944; lost 24/11/48, salved and scrapped.
FY.87	HEROS (R.A.N.)* (ex-R.N. St. Erth) 1—4 in.	382/18	1940	Returned 1946.
4.215	HIRAVATI (R.I.N.)	580/30	1940	Returned 1946.
	INDIRA (ex-Embleton, ex-R.N. Kildysart)	637/18	1940	Lost 15/12/41
4.186	IRRAWADI (R.I.N.)	1243/13	1939	Returned 1945.
	JAMNAGAR (R.I.N.)	576/24	1941	Returned 1943, EMPIRE BULBUL (1943).
FY.035	KEDAH	2499/27	1939	Accommodation ship (1943); returned 1946.
F.166	KELANTAN	1106/21	1940	Repair ship (1943); returned 1947.
	KELENA	300/	1941	Lost 2/42, salved & Japanese SUKEI No. 22 (1943).
	KERNOT (ex-Pilote 16)	423/30	1940	Returned 1945.
	KEVERNE*	120/08	1939	Examination service; returned 1946.
	KING BAY (R.A.N.)	237/38	1940	Examination service; returned 1945.
	KUALA	954/11	1940	Lost 14/2/42.
	KUDAT	1725/14	1940	Base ship (1941); lost 30/12/41.
FY.086	KUTUBTARI (R.I.N.)	237/15	1939	Returned 1946.
FY.90	KYBRA (R.A.N.)	858/26	1940	Returned 1946.
	LADY CRADDOCK (R.I.N.)		1939	Lost 16/10/42.
	LARUT	894/27	1940	Lost 22/1/42.
	LAURIER (R.C.N.)	201/36	1939	Returned 1946.
FY.090	LAXMI (R.I.N.)	310/18	1939	Returned 1946.

	LILAVATI (R.I.N.) 1—12 pdr.	293/11	1939	M/S (1943); returned 1945.
	LIPIS	845/27	1939	Lost 13/2/42.
	LI WO 1—4 in.	707/38	1940	Lost 14/2/42.
	LOCH ALINE	230/04	1940	Examination service; returned 1946.
	MATA HARI	1020/15	1940	Lost 28/2/42.
	MINNA	290/39	1940	Examination service; returned 1945.
,123	NETRAVATI (R.I.N.) 1—4 in.	1540/09	1939	Returned 1945.
.409	NORNA	457/09	1939	Examination service; returned 1945.
	NULCHIRA (R.I.N.)	272/08	1939	Returned 1944.
	OOSTCAPPELLE (R.I.N.) 1—12 pdr. 2—M (1 × 2 LG)	751/21	1939	M/S (1942); returned 1944.
	PADMAVATI (R.I.N.)	252/04	1939	Returned 1945.
	PANSY (R.I.N.) (ex-R.N.)		1939	Returned 1946.
.179	PARVATI (R.I.N.)	1548/27	1939	Lost 30/4/41.
	PATHFINDER (R.I.N.)	495/38	1939	Returned 1940.
	PRABNAVATI (R.I.N.)	556/33	1939	Lost 8/12/41,
	PRINCESS MARIE JOSE	1820/22	1940	Returned 1945.
	PYGMALION*	569/06	1939	Examination service; returned 1944.
.111	RAMDAS (R.I.N.) 1—4 in.	406/36	1939	Training ship (1944); returned 1946.
.198	RATNAGIRI (R.I.N.) 1—4 in.	590/35	1939	Returned 1946.
	RAUB	1161/26	1939	Lost 22/1/42.
	RONA	180/38	1940	Examination service; returned 1945.
Y.075	RUKMAVATI (R.I.N.)	266/04	1939	Returned 1946.
Y.86	ST. GILES (R.A.N.)* (ex-Khalifa, ex-R.N. St. Giles).	380/19	1939	Returned 1942; re-acquired 1945 as Rescue tug.
	ST. SILIO	314/36	1939	Examination service; returned 1946.
	SANDIP (R.I.N.)	285/15	1939	Returned 1944.
	SANDOWAY (R.I.N.) 1—12 pdr	291/15	1939	M/S (1942); returned 1944.
Y.073	SATYAVATI (R.I.N.) 1—12 pdr.	295/11	1939	M/S (1943); returned 1945.
	SELAMA (R.I.N.)	291/14	1939	Returned 1944.
	SHUH KWANG	788/24	1939	Lost 12/2/42.
	SIANG WO	2595/26	1940	Lost 13/2/42.
	SITAKHOOND (R.I.N.)	280/10	1939	Returned 1943.
206	SONAVATI (R.I.N.) 2—4 in. (2 × 1)	1638/36	1940	Returned 1945.
	SOPHIE MARIE (R.I.N.)	1138/23	1939	Lost 19/3/42.
33	TANJORE (R.I.N.)		1942	Returned 1943.
	TIEN KWANG	787/25	1939	Lost 2/42.

	TUNG WO	1337/14	1940	Examination service; lost 13/12/41.
	VICTORIA MARIE (R.I.N.)	1432/27	1939	Returned 1945.
FY.06	VIGILANT (R.A.N.) 1—3 pdr.	106/38	1939	SLEUTH (1944), HAWK (1945); returned 1946.
T.373	VITI (R.A.N.—Fijian)	676/40	1940	Returned 1946.
	VIVA (R.I.N.)		1940	Returned 1943.
	VYNER BROOKE	1670/28	1940	Lost 14/2/42.
	WOODBRIDGE	102/26	1941	Examination service; returned 1946.
FY.92	WYRALLAH (R.A.N.) 1—4 in.	1049/34	1940	WILCANIA (1942); returned 1947.
FY.91	YANDRA (R.A.N.) 1—4 in., 1—2 pdr. A.A.	990/28	1940	Returned 1946.
T.303	ZULFAQUAR (R.I.N.)		1939	Returned 1946.

*Tug

AUXILIARY MINESWEEPERS

Only a small regular force of minesweepers had been maintained up to th outbreak of war and the re-inforcement of the minesweeping flotillas was princi pally derived from the following sources:—

(a) the fishing fleets
(b) war construction
(c) paddle vessels
(d) auxiliary vessels

The main augmentation was from the trawlers and drifters, listed in Part 6 and from the naval war building programmes, listed in Parts 3 (minesweepin sloops) and 8 (motor minesweepers). The shallow draught paddle vessels wer available only in the United Kingdom, and only in limited numbers, and auxiliar minesweepers were requisitioned under similar circumstances as those applicabl to auxiliary patrol vessels. The Royal Navy took up a greater proportion c auxiliary minesweepers than auxiliary patrol vessels and they were locall acquired and employed over a wider area and included many allied vessels whic had escaped to British ports from the Continent.

It is interesting to note that the seven small tugs SALVO, SCYTHE, SERV TOR, SHAKO, SLOGAN, SOLITAIRE and SOUVENIR were all requisitione in November, 1939 and fitted out on the Thames for *electric minesweeping* an were one of the first group of vessels formed to combat the magnetic mine Also, that a former **Hunt** class minesweeper, the WEXFORD, sold out comme cially in 1921 was requisitioned to take up her former role as the R.A.N DOOMBA in 1939.

Usually employed in coastal and estuarial waters the work of auxiliary mine sweepers was arduous, but unspectacular, and what armament they receive was extremely varied: none usually carried a gun heavier than a 12 pdr. and th smaller vessels had no more than machine guns.

P. No.	Name	Gross tonnage Built	Requisi-tioned	Fate
	AIK LAM	155/41	1941	Returned 1946.

	ALARM* (ex-R.N. St. Ewe)	432/19	1941	ALARM II (1942); returned 1946.
	ALCIS*		1942	Returned 1945.
	AL HATHERA*	279/27	1941	Returned 1944.
	ALLENWOOD (R.A.N.)	398/20	1941	Returned 1945.
	ANDROMEDA*	658/10	1941	Lost 18/4/42.
	ANSAY*		1942	Returned 1945.
	AZANIA	375/26	1941	Returned 1945.
	BANKA	623/14	1940	Lost 10/12/41.
FY.81	BERMAGUI (R.A.N.)	402/12	1939	Returned 1945.
	BREEZE (R.N.Z.N.)	625/33	1942	Returned 1946.
	CHANGTEH*	244/14	1941	Lost 14/2/42.
FY.353	CHINTHE	688/32	1941	Returned 1942.
	CIRCE 1—4 in.	778/12	1940	MEDEA (1942); returned 1945.
	CONQUERANTE*		1940	Returned 1945.
	CONTROL*		1941	Returned 1946.
.25	COOLEBAR (R.A.N.)	479/11	1939	Returned 1945.
	COOMBAR (R.A.N.)	581/12	1940	Returned 1946.
4.109	DIPAVATI (R.I.N.)	840/36	1939	Returned 1946.
.01	DOOMBA (R.A.N.) (ex-R.N. Wexford) 1—4 in.	750/19	1939	Returned 1946.
	DRANQUET*		1940	Returned 1945.
T. 370	GALE (R.N.Z.N.)	625/35	1940	Returned 1945.
	GEMAS	207/25	1941	Lost 2/3/42.
FY.98	GUNBAR (R.A.N.)	481/11	1940	Returned 1946.
T.398	HAWERA (R.N.Z.N.)	188/12	1941	Returned 1/46.
	HUATONG	280/27	1941	Lost 13/2/42.
	JARAK	208/27	1941	Lost 17/2/42.
	JERAM	210/27	1941	Lost 15/2/42, salved & Japanese SUKEI No. 21 (1943).
	JERANTUT	217/27	1941	Lost 8/3/42.
	KAI	1746/21	1941	Returned 1946.
	KAIWAKA (R.N.Z.N.)	169/37	1941	Returned 1946.
.158	KALAVATI (R.I.N.)	1408/28	1939	Returned 1945.
T.400	KAPUNI (R.N.Z.N.)	190/09	1941	Returned 1946.
	KIANGA (R.A.N.)	338/22	1941	Returned 1946.
	KLIAS	207/27	1941	Lost 15/2/42.
	KOOPA (R.A.N.)	416/11	1940	Returned 1945.
	MALACCA	211/27	1941	Lost 18/2/42.
	MARRAWAH (R.A.N.)	472/10	1941	U.S.N. (1943).
	MEDUSA	793/13	1940	Returned 1943.
	MINNIE MOLLER*	377/09	1940	Lost 31/12/41.
	MIRIMAR (R.A.N.)	.../...	1940	Returned 1945.
	MURITAI (R.N.Z.N.)	462/23	1940	Controlled minelayer (1945).
	NAMBUCCA (R.A.N.)	489/36	1939	U.S.N. (1943).
	NARANI (R.A.N.)	381/14	1940	Returned 1946.
Y.092	NAUTILUS (R.I.N.) 1—12 pdr. A.A.	290/13	1942	RDF Calibrating ship (1943); returned 1946.
	OCEAN EAGLE* (R.C.N.) (ex-R.N. St. Arvans)	420/18	1939	Returned 1944.

J.130	ORARA (R.A.N.) 1—4 in.	1297/07	1939	Returned 1945.
	PANGKOR	1250/29	1939	Accommodation ship (1943); returned 1946.
	PATERSON (R.A.N.)	446/20	1940	Returned 1946.
	PURIRI (R.N.Z.N.)	927/40	1940	Lost 14/5/41.
	RAHMAN	209/26	1940	Lost 1/3/42.
	RATA (R.N.Z.N.)	974/29	1940	Returned 1944.
	REO II* (R.C.N.)	129/31	1941	Returned 1946.
	ROSS NORMAN (R.C.N.)	297/37	1940	DG vessel (1941); returned 1946.
	ST. ANGELO*	../..	1939	Lost 30/5/42.
4.149	ST. ANTHONY (R.I.N.)	452/36	1939	Returned 1945.
	ST. AUBIN*	468/18	1941	Returned 1945.
	ST. SAMPSON*	451/19	1939	Lost 7/3/42.
FY.1672	SALVO* (ex-Astrid)		11/39	Returned 11/45.
	SCOTT HARLEY	620/13	1940	Lost 3/3/42.
	SCYTHE* (ex-Baltic)		11/39	Returned 7/47.
FY. 1673	SERVITOR* (ex-Captain A. Letzer)		11/39	Returned 1945.
FY. 1657	SHAKO* (ex-Hercules)		11/39	Returned 11/45.
	SIN AIK LEE	198/28	1941	Lost 2/42.
	SLOGAN* (ex-Samson)		11/39	Returned 1945.
FY. 1674	SOLITAIRE* (ex-The Schelde)		11/39	Lost 20/6/44.
	SOUTH SEA (R.N.Z.N.) (ex-Ferriby)	322/13	1940	Lost 19/12/42.
	SOUVENIR* (ex-Wrestler)		11/39	Returned 1945.
	SPRAY* (R.C.N.)	118/07	1941	Returned 1945.
	STANDARD COASTER (R.C.N.)	150/27		
J.141	TAMBAR (R.A.N.) 1—12 pdr. A.A.	456/12	1939	BDV (Z.83—1943); returned 1945.
	TAPAH	208/26	1940	Lost 2/42.
FY.99	TERKA (R.A.N.) 1—2 pdr. A.A.	420/25	1941	Water carrier (1944); lost 26/3/45.
	THASOS*	130/97	1940	Returned 1945.
	TITAN	574/28	1940	Returned 1946.
FY.00	TOLGA (R.A.N.)	418/25	1940	Water carrier (1944); scuttled 4/46.
FY.01	TOORIE (R.A.N.)	414/25	1940	Returned 1943.
	TRANG	205/12	1940	Lost 14/2/42.
FY.80	UKI (R.A.N.) 1—12 pdr.	545/23	1939	U.S.N. (1943).
	WARRAWEE (R.A.N.)	423/09	1941	Returned 1946.
	WEST COCKER	.../...	1940	Lost 9/4/42.
	WO KWANG*	350/27	1940	Lost 2/42.

*Tug

PADDLE MINESWEEPERS

The following vessels were all requisitioned in 1939, except the WHIPPINGHAM in 1941, and were originally formed into six minesweeping flotillas (the 7th–12th

Early in 1940 there were five flotillas in service, as follows:—

7th Minesweeper flotilla (Rosyth): 7 vessels.
8th Minesweeper flotilla (North Shields): 5 vessels.
10th Minesweeper flotilla (Dover): 8 vessels.
11th Minesweeper flotilla (Greenock): 5 vessels.
12th Minesweeper flotilla (Harwich): 5 vessels.

By January, 1943, this had been reduced to one flotilla (the 7th) of three vessels based at Granton and a further two were employed on training duties. The remainder had been converted to auxiliary A.A. vessels (" Eagle " ships) or were being used as accommodation ships.

Many of the older vessels had been requisitioned during the First World War, which accounts for the previous naval names shown against them, whilst two—QUEEN OF KENT and QUEEN OF THANET—were former Admiralty paddle minesweepers sold out commercially after the First World War and not unnaturally requisitioned for service again in 1939. Paddle minesweepers were initially armed with a 12 pdr. A.A. gun forward and several light A.A. pieces and, even before the majority were subsequently converted to auxiliary A.A. vessels, were possessed of a good A.A. armament of light guns for their own defence.

P. No.	Name	Gross tonnage Built	Fate
J.109	AMBASSADOR (ex-Embassy, ex-Duchess of Norfolk)	381/11	Training ship (1944); returned 1945.
J.117	BRIGHTON BELLE (ex-Lady Evelyn)	320/00	Lost 28/5/40.
J.28	BRIGHTON QUEEN (ex-Lady Moyra, ex-Gwalia)	519/05	Lost 1/6/40.
J.92	CITY OF ROCHESTER	235/04	Lost 19/5/41.
J.113	DEVONIA	520/05	Lost 31/5/40.
J.115	DUCHESS OF FIFE	336/03	Returned 1/45.
J.107	DUCHESS OF ROTHESAY	338/94	Accommodation ship (1942); returned 1946.
J.106	EMPEROR OF INDIA (ex-Princess Royal)	534/06	Aux. A.A. vessel (1940).
J.101	ESSEX QUEEN (ex-Walton Belle)	592/97	Hospital ship (1940); returned 3/43, PRIDE OF DEVON (1946).
J.104	GLEN AVON	509/12	Lost 2/9/44.
.26	GLEN USK	524/14	Aux. A.A. vessel (1942).
J.16	GLEN GOWER	553/22	GLEN MORE (1941), Aux. A.A. vessel (1942).
.125	GOATFELL (ex-Caledonia)	624/34	Aux. A.A. vessel (1942).
.100	GRACIE FIELDS	393/36	Lost 29/5/40.
.120	HELVELLYN (ex-Juno)	642/37	Aux. A.A. vessel (1941).
.108	JEANNIE DEANS	635/31	Aux. A.A. vessel (1941).
	KYLEMORE (ex-Vulcan, ex-Britannia, ex-Kylemore)	318/97	Netlayer (1940).

J.112	LAGUNA BELLE (ex-Southend Belle)	617/96	Aux. A.A. vessel (1942).
J.135	LORNA DOONE	427/91	Aux. A.A. vessel (1942).
J.114	MARMION 1—12 pdr. A.A. 8—.5 in. A.A. (2 × 4) 4—.303 in. A.A. (1 × 4 B & P) 2—.303 in. A.A. (1 × 2 LG)	409/06	Constructive total loss 9/4/41; scrapped 1941.
J.48	MEDWAY QUEEN	318/24	Training ship (1942); returned 5/47.
J.102	MERCURY	621/34	Lost 25/12/40.
J.110	ORIOLE (ex-Eagle III)	441/10	Accommodation ship (1944); returned 1945.
J.66	PLINLIMMON (ex-Cambria, ex-R.N. Cambridge, ex-Cambria)	438/95	Aux. A.A. vessel (1942).
J.111	PRINCESS ELIZABETH	388/27	Aux. A.A. vessel (1942).
J.128	QUEEN EMPRESS	411/12	Aux. A.A. vessel (1942).
J.74	QUEEN OF KENT (ex-R.N. Atherstone)	798/16	Returned 1946, LORNA DOONE (1949); scrapped 1952.
J.30	QUEEN OF THANET (ex-R.N. Melton)	792/16	Returned 1946, SOLENT QUEEN (1949); scrapped 1951.
J.	RAVENSWOOD	391/91	Aux. A.A. vessel (1942).
J.132	RYDE	603/37	Aux. A.A. vessel (1942).
J.20	SANDOWN	684/34	Aux. A.A. vessel (1942).
J.103	SCAWFELL (ex-Jupiter)	642/37	Aux. A.A. vessel (1941).
J.80	SKIDDAW (ex-Britannia, ex-R.N. Britain, ex-Britannia)	459/96	Aux. A.A. vessel (1942).
J.118	SNAEFELL (ex-Waverley, ex-Barry)	477/07	Lost 5/7/41.
J.113	SOUTHSEA	825/30	Constructive total loss 16/2/41.
J.12	THAMES QUEEN (ex-Queen of Southend ex-Yarmouth Belle)	517/98	Aux. A.A. vessel (1942).
J.51	WAVERLEY	537/99	Lost 29/5/40.
J.43	WESTWARD HO! (ex-Westward Queen, ex-R.N. Westhope, ex-Westward Queen)	438/94	Aux. A.A. vessel (1942).
J.136	WHIPPINGHAM	825/30	Aux. A.A. vessel (1942).

MINE DESTRUCTOR VESSELS

These mercantile conversions were amongst the earliest attempts at combatin the magnetic mine and were all converted early in 1940. They carried a 300-tc electro-magnet in the bows (which necessitated a vessel of larger than norm minesweeper dimensions) with which to create a magnetic field to actuate magnet mines. The magnetic field they created was too close to the ship and led structural damage, and even loss, in 'sweeping operations and they were only a limited success. Fortunately, the LL sweep was perfected and proved extremely effective against influence mines, with the added advantage that it could be fitted in small vessels down to wooden M.F.V's. with a small permanent ship's magnetism while larger, steel-built minesweepers attained immunity by fitting DG gear. Between them DG gear, which gave individual immunity, and the LL sweep completely mastered the magnetic mine.

P. No.	Name	Gross tonnage Built	Requisi-tioned	Fate
F.123	ANDELLE	1832/22	1940	M/S maintenance ship (1944); scrapped 4/45.
FY.758	BORDE 2—12 pdr. A.A. (2 × 1) 2—2 pdr. A.A. (2 × 1) 2—MG (2 × 1)	2014/21	1940	M/S maintenance ship (1942); scrapped 7/45.
F.130	BURLINGTON	2068/40	1940	SOOTHSAYER (1941), FAIRFAX (1941), M/S maintenance ship (1944); scrapped 1945.
F.119	BUSHWOOD	2314/30	1940	D.G.V. (1942); returned 11/46.
FY. 1951	CORBRAE 8—20 mm. A.A. (8 × 1)	1788/12	1940	M/S maintenance ship (1944); returned 11/46.
	CORBURN	1786/36	1940	Lost 21/5/40.
	CORFIELD	1791/37	1940	Lost 8/9/41.
	QUEENWORTH	2047/24	1940	Lost 9/5/41.
	SPRINGDALE	1597/37	1940	D.P.V. (1943); returned 1946.
4.94	SPRINGTIDE	1597/37	1940	D.P.V. (1943); returned 1946.

MINELAYERS

Practically every vessel, either naval or mercantile, can be adapted for the laying of mines and this initially resulted in an aversion to building specific naval minelayers in the parsimonious years " between the wars ". It was recognised that for laying in enemy waters speed was of greater importance than mine load whilst the exact reverse was more applicable in waters removed from enemy control. As a result of First World War experience the following naval minelayers were ordered up to 1939, viz.:

(*a*) the cruiser-minelayer ADVENTURE in 1922.
(*b*) the submarine minelayers of the **Porpoise** class (7 vessels) from 1930.
(*c*) the destroyer minelayers of the " **E** " (2 vessels), " **G** " (8 vessels), " **H** " (8 vessels) and " **I** " (8 vessels) classes from 1931.
(*d*) the fast cruiser-minelayers of the **Abdiel** class (4 vessels) from 1938.

The outbreak of war resulted in the construction of two further fast, cruiser-minelayers and the destroyers of the " **O** " and " **P** " classes (16 vessels) were built for rapid conversion to minelayers, like their pre-war prototypes. In addition to these vessels many merchant ships were acquired but, for minelaying deep in enemy waters no vessel—surface or submerged—surpassed the minelaying aircraft of the Royal Air Force. Out of the grand total of nearly 300,000 mines laid by British forces during the war, about 20 per cent of them were laid from the air, generally in areas otherwise inaccessible to naval vessels.

AUXILIARY MINELAYERS

While it was left to the naval built minelayers to undertake lays in enemy waters the following mercantile conversions of large mine capacity and radius of action were taken over for the laying of mine barrages in areas relatively safe from enemy interference. AGAMEMNON, MENETHEUS, PORT NAPIER, PORT QUEBEC and SOUTHERN PRINCE, supplemented at times by one or more of the cruiser-minelayers, formed the 1st Minelaying squadron from 1940–43, based on port "ZA" (Scotland). The TEVIOTBANK served in Home waters until 1941, in the Eastern fleet until 1944 and then in the Mediterranean. The R.A.N. BUNGAREE served in Australian waters and the locally acquired KUNG WO in the Far East. They were only defensively armed with one or two 4 in. guns plus lighter A.A. pieces and operated under the cover of the main fleets.

P. No.	Name	Gross tonnage Built	Requisi-tioned	Fate
M.10	AGAMEMNON 400 mines	7593/29	1940	Amenities ship (1944); returned 1946.
M.29	BUNGAREE (R.A.N.) 423 mines	3155/37	9. 6.41	Returned 1946.
M.19	HAMPTON (ex-Hampton Ferry) 270 mines	2839/34	1940	Returned 1941.
	KUNG WO	4636/21	1941	Lost 14/2/42.
M.93	MENESTHEUS 410 mines	7493/29	1940	Amenities ship (1944); returned 1946.
	PORT NAPIER 550 mines	9600/40	1940	Lost 27/11/40.
M.59	PORT QUEBEC 550 mines	8490/39	1940	Repair ship DEER SOUND (1945).
M.03	PRINCESS VICTORIA 244 mines	2197/39	1939	Lost 19/5/40.
M.83	SHEPPERTON (ex-Shepperton Ferry) 270 mines	2839/35	1940	Constructive total loss 5/5/41; returned 1945
M.47	SOUTHERN PRINCE 560 mines	11447/29	1940	Accommodation ship (1945); returned 1946.

The mine destructor H.M.S. Corbrae is typical of the coastal colliers acquired for this type of conversion. The fore well deck has been plated in flush with the fo'c'sle and the additional superstructure built on the former hatches abaft the original bridge to provide the extra accommodation and space required as a minesweeping maintenance vessel. [*I.W.M.*

The auxiliary minelayer H.M.S. Agamemnon was a former Blue Funnel Liner (A. Holt & Co.) [*I.W.M.*

The Prince Line's Southern Prince was the largest of the auxiliary minelayers and later served as an accommodation ship for repair staffs which could not be housed aboard their parent ships. [*I.W.M.*

M.04	TEVIOTBANK 280 mines	5087/38	1939	Returned 1944.

Notes:—Armaments were as follows AGAMEMNON 3—4 in. A.A. (3×1), 2—2 pdr. A.A. (2×1), 4—20 mm. A.A. (4×1), 4—.5 in. A.A. (2×2) guns; R.A.N. BUNGAREE 2—4 in. (2×1), 1—12 pdr. A.A., 8—20 mm. A.A. (8×1) guns; MENESTHEUS 2—4 in. (2×1), 2—2 pdr. A.A. (2×1), 12—20 mm. A.A. (12×1) guns; PORT NAPIER 2—4 in. A.A. (2×1), 2—2 pdr. A.A. (2×1), 4—20 mm. A.A. (4×1), 4—.5 in. A.A. (2×2) guns; PORT QUEBEC 2—4 in. A.A. (2×1), 2—2pdr. A.A. (2×1), 13—20 mm. A.A. (13×1) guns; SHEPPERTON 1—4 in., 2—20 mm. A.A. (2×1), guns; SOUTHERN PRINCE 2—4 in. A.A. (2×1), 2—2 pdr. A.A. (2×1), 7—20 mm. A.A. (7×1), 4—.5 in. A.A. (2×2) guns; TEVIOTBANK 1—4 in., 1—12 pdr. A.A., 4—20 mm. A.A. (2×2), 4—.5 in. A.A. (2×2) guns.

COASTAL AND CONTROLLED MINELAYERS

For the protection of naval and commercial harbours, and where local conditions suited, controlled minefields were laid which could be activated—or made safe—from ashore or from a controlled minelayer. The fields were laid from small, coastal and controlled minelayers and were then tended from the latter. A nucleus had been created pre-war with the coastal minelayer PLOVER and the controlled minelayers of the **Linnet** class, which could proceed abroad, and were supplemented by a war programme of a further eight controlled minelayers plus conversions from merchant ships (as controlled minelayer base ships), trawlers and tugs.

Mining instruction, both before and during the war, was carried out from small monitors retained from the First World War and converted to coastal minelayers.

COASTAL MINELAYERS

Displacement: 535 tons.
Dimensions: 170 (pp) 177 (oa) × 31 × 6¾ ft.
Machinery: 2-shaft Reciprocating (VTE), I.H.P. 400 = 10 knots.
Armament: 52 mines.
Complement: 52.

P. No.	Name	Builder	Launched	Fate
F.06	MEDUSA (ex-M. 29)	Harland & Wolff	22. 5.15	Depot ship TALBOT (1941), MEDWAY II (1943); MEDUSA (1944); scrapped 9/9/46.
F.04	MELPOMENE (ex-M. 31)	Harland & Wolff	25. 6.15	MENELAUS (1940); scrapped Llanelly 1/48.
F.00	MINERVA (ex-M. 33)	Workman Clark	22. 5.15	Hulk C.23 (1946).

Notes:—Former small monitors converted to coastal minelayers in 1921. MEDUSA was C & M at Malta until 1941 when she became a submarine depot ship. MELPOMENE and MINERVA were employed in training throughout the war based at Plymouth and Portsmouth respectively: the former had a single 21 in. torpedo tube added on the foc's'le.

Displacement: 805 tons.
Dimensions: 180 (pp) 195¼ (oa) × 33¾ × 8¼ ft.
Machinery: 2-shaft Reciprocating (VTE), I.H.P. 1,400 = 14¾ knots.
Armament: 1—12 pdr. A.A., 1—20 mm. A.A. guns; mines.
Complement: 69.

M.26	PLOVER	Denny	8. 6.37	

Notes:—Served at Dover until 1940, The Nore to 1943 and then Portsmouth to the end of the war.

The coastal minelayer H.M.S. Plover performed sterling war service and laid over 15,000 mines. [*I.W.M.*

CONTROLLED MINELAYERS

Displacement: 498 tons.
Dimensions: 145 (pp) 163¾ (oa) × 27¼ × 8 ft.
Machinery: 2-shaft Reciprocating (VTE), I.H.P. 400 = 10½ knots.
Armament: 1—20 mm. A.A., 2—.303 in. A.A. (2 × 1) guns; 12 mines.
Complement: 24.

M.69	LINNET	Ardrossan: Ferguson	3. 5.38	
M.62	REDSTART	Robb: Whites M.E.	14. 4.38	Lost 19/12/41.
M.77	RINGDOVE	Robb: Whites M.E.	15. 6.38	Mercantile (1951).

Notes:—LINNET was based at Rosyth for the whole war except for a few months during 1943 when at Gibraltar. REDSTART was lost at Hong Kong and RINGDOVE served at Scapa and Rosyth 1939-45.

Displacement: 346 tons.
Dimensions: 110¼ (pp) 122½ (oa) × 26½ × 8 ft.
Machinery: 2-shaft Diesel motors, B.H.P. 360 = 10 knots.
Armament: 1—20 mm. A.A., 2—.303 in. A.A. (2 × 1) guns; 10 mines.

M.19	M.1	Philip	6. 7.39	MINER I (1943).
M.34	M.2	Philip	18. 8.39	MINER II (1943), GOSSAMER (1949).
M.53	M.3	Philip	16.11.39	MINER III (1943).
M.68	M.4	Philip	6. 8.40	MINER IV (1943); for disposal.
M.74	M.5	Philip	2.11.40	MINER V (1943). BRITANNIC (1960); for disposal.
M.94	M.6	Philip	7. 2.42	MINER VI (1943).
	M.7 (i)	Singapore		Lost incomplete 2/42
M.88	M.7 (ii)	Philip	29. 1.44	MINER VII (1943). STEADY (1959).
M.98	M.8	Philip	24. 4.43	MINER VIII (1943).

Notes:—All served in Home waters except MINER VI which went to the Mediterranean in 1943.

P. No.	Name	Gross tonnage Built	Requisi-tioned	Fate
T.372	MATAI (R.N.Z.N.)	1050/30	1940	Troopship (1944); returned 1944.
M.	MURITAI (R.N.Z.N.)	462/23	1940	Ex-M/S; conversion not completed; returned 1946.
M.	RHU	254/40	1941	Lost 15/2/42, believed I.J.N. A/S vessel No. 21.

Notes:—RHU was fitting out at Singapore in 1/42 and it is believed she became the Japanese A/S vessel No. 21 and, as such, was still in service in 1944.

For trawlers converted to controlled minelayers see Part 6. These included BLACKBIRD, DABCHICK, STONECHAT and WHITETHROAT (Isles

The controlled minelayer H.M.S. Ringdove.

[I.W.M.

class), CORNCRAKE and REDSHANK (**Fish** class), and ALSEY, JAY, LOCH NEVIS, SNAKEFLY and SPINDRIFT (ex-mercantile).

CONTROLLED MINELAYER BASE SHIPS

M.72	ALCA	3712/27	1940	Returned 1946.
M.44	ATREUS	6546/11	1940	Ex-mine carrier (Y6.4); returned 1944.
M.49	HELVIG	2250/37	1940	Seaward defence ship (1944).
M.17	MANCHESTER CITY	7278/37	1939	Returned 1946.

Notes:—ALCA based at Freetown until 1942 and the rest of her service in Home waters. ATREUS served throughout in the East Indies except for a short spell during 1943 when on loan to the R.A.N. HELVIG served continuously in Home waters except for a short period in the Mediterranean during 1943. MANCHESTER CITY was in Home waters until 1941, then East Indies.

OBSERVATION MINELAYERS

	CHAFFINCH (ex-Nacqueville)		1940	Returned 1945.
	GOLDFINCH (i) (ex-Antwerp 33)		1940	GREENFINCH (ii) (1943); returned 1945.
	GREENFINCH (ex-Lama)		1940	Returned 1943.
	HAWFINCH (ex-Honfleurais)		1940	Returned 1945.

Notes:—All ex-tugs. CHAFFINCH based at Plymouth, HAWFINCH at Harwich; others Portsmouth.

The following coastal minelayers of the Royal Netherlands Navy served in, or with, the Royal Navy from June, 1940, viz:—
MEDUSA, DOUWE AUKES (converted to convoy leader 1941), VAN MEERLANT (M.36), NAUTILUS (M.12), JAN VAN BRAKEL (M.80) and WILLEM VAN DER ZAAN (M.08).

RIVER GUNBOATS

The large, and old, gunboats of the **Insect** class were due for early replacement—two had already been scrapped—when the outbreak halted this programme. Three (GNAT, CRICKET and LADYBIRD) were transferred to the Mediterranean in 1940 where they rendered sterling service with the Inshore Squadron. The remainder of the gunboats stayed in Chinese waters where they suffered disasterously when the Japanese entered the war in 1941. Three were trapped in the upper reaches of the rivers and were turned over to the Chinese, one was lost at Shanhai, four at Hong Kong and the three newest vessels (SCORPION, DRAGONFLY and GRASSHOPPER) at Singapore. Six managed to extricate themselves for further service while two new vessels, completing in the United Kingdom, were retained in Home waters, one being lost at Dunkerque.

The captured Persian gunboats were manned by the Royal Indian Navy and were not flat-bottomed, river craft like the British vessels, but were incapable of facing the open sea and used for harbour defence and training duties.

Insect class

Displacement: 625 tons.
Dimensions: 230 (pp) 237½ (oa) × 36 × 4 ft.
Machinery: 2-shaft Reciprocating (VTE), I.H.P. 2,000 = 14 knots.
Armament: 2—6 in. (2 × 1), 1—3 in. A.A., 10-M (10 × 1) guns.
Complement: 55.

P. No.	Name	Builder	Launched	Fate
T.57	APHIS	Ailsa Sbdg.	15. 9.15	Scrapped Singapore 1947.
	BEE	Ailsa Sbdg.	8.12.15	Scrapped Shanghai 22/3/39.
T.71	CICALA	Barclay Curle	10.12.15	Lost 21/12/41.
T.72	COCKCHAFER	Barclay Curle	17.12.15	Scrapped Singapore 1947.
T.75	CRICKET	Barclay Curle	17.12.15	Constructive total loss 30/6/41; scrapped Alexandria 1944.
	GLOWWORM	Barclay Curle	5. 2.16	Scrapped 9/28
T.60	GNAT	Lobnitz	.15	Constructive total loss 21/10/41; scrapped 1945.
T.58	LADYBIRD	Lobnitz	.15	Lost 12/5/41.
T.69	MANTIS	Sunderland Sbdg.: N.E. Marine	14. 9.15	Scrapped 1946.
T.70	MOTH	Sunderland Sbdg.: N.E. Marine	.15	Lost 21/12/41, salved & Japanese SUMA (1942); lost 19/3/45.
T.59	SCARAB	Wood Skinner: N.E. Marine	7.10.15	Scrapped Singapore 5/48.
T.62	TARANTULA	Wood Skinner: N.E. Marine	8.12.15	Expended as target 1/5/46.

Notes:—BEE AND GLOWWORM were scrapped before the start of World War 2. APHIS was at China until 1940 then went to the Mediterranean and finally the Pacific in 1945. COCKCHAFER was converting to a minesweeper at Hong Kong during 1940 but this was not completed. She served East Indies from 1940, Mediterranean from 1943 and finished in the Pacific. CRICKET, also earmarked for conversion to a minesweeper, went to the Mediterranean in 1941 and was mined soon afterwards and remained inoperative thereafter. GNAT arrived in the Mediterranean in 1940 and was torpedoed the following year but she was beached and used as an A.A. platform. LADYBIRD also came to the Mediterranean in 1940 and was bombed and sunk in Tobruk harbour in 1941 but as her upperworks remained above water they were fitted with light A.A. guns and manned by the Army. MANTIS was awaiting disposal at Shanghai in 1940 and was still there when the Japanese attacked while MOTH, lost at Hong Kong, was salved by the Japanese and was again lost as their SUMA. SCARAB and TARANTULA went to the East Indies in 1941. The latter remained in this theatre throughout the war but SCARAB went to the Mediterranean in 1943 before finally returning to the Pacific.

The River gunboat H.M.S. Aphis. [I.W.M.

Displacement: 262 tons.
Dimensions: 160 (pp) 168 (oa) × 27 × 4 ft.
Machinery: 2-shaft geared Turbines, S.H.P. 1,370 = 14 knots.
Armament: 2—3 in. A.A. (2 × 1), 8-M (8 × 1) guns. *Complement:* 55.

T.43	SEAMEW	Yarrow	16. 1.28	Scrapped Basra 1947.
T.64	TERN	Yarrow	29. 8.27	Lost 19/12/41.

Displacement: 310 tons.
Dimensions: 177 (pp) 184¾ (oa) × 29 × 3¼ ft.
Machinery: 2-shaft geared Turbines, S.H.P. 2,250 = 16 knots.
Armament: 2—3 in. A.A. (2 × 1), 8-M (8 × 1) guns. *Complement:* 55.

T.08	GANNET	Yarrow	10.11.27	Chinese YING SHAN (1942).
T.21	PETEREL	Yarrow	18. 7.27	Lost 8/12/41.

Displacement: 354 tons.
Dimensions: 146 (pp) 150 (oa) × 28¾ × 4¾ ft.
Machinery: 2-shaft geared Turbines S.H.P. 2,250 = 15 knots.
Armament: 1—3.7 in. howitzer, 2—6 pdr. (2 × 1), 10-M (10 × 1) guns.
Complement: 55.

T.74	FALCON	Yarrow	18. 5.31	Chinese LUNG HUAN (1942), YING TEH (1948), NAN CHIANG (1950).

Displacement: 185 tons.
Dimensions: 160 (pp) (oa) × 30¾ × 1¾ ft.
Machinery: 2-shaft Reciprocating (VTE), I.H.P. 600 = 11¼ knots.
Armament: 1—3.7 in. howitzer, 1—6 pdr., 8-M (8 × 1) guns.
Complement: 35.

T.41	SANDPIPER	Thornycroft	9. 6.33	Chinese YING HAO (1942).

Displacement: 226 tons.
Dimensions: 150 (pp) (oa) × 26¾ × 3 ft.
Machinery: 2-shaft Reciprocating (VTE), I.H.P. 800 = 12¾ knots.
Armament: 1—3.7 in. howitzer, 1—6 pdr., 8—M (8 × 1) guns.
Complement: 35.

T.65	ROBIN	Yarrow	7. 3.34	Boom Defence Depot ship (1941); lost 25/12/41.

Displacement: 670 tons.
Dimensions: (pp) 208¾ (oa) × 34½ × 5 ft.
Machinery: 2-shaft geared Turbines, S.H.P. 4,500 = 17 knots.
Armament: 2—4 in. (2 × 1), 1—3.7 in. howitzer, 2—3 pdr. (2 × 1), 8-M (8 × 1) guns. *Complement:* 93.

T.67	SCORPION	White	20.12.37	Lost 13/2/42.

Note:—SCORPION was to have been converted to an A/S vessel.

Displacement: 585 tons.
Dimensions: (pp) 197 (oa) × 33 × 5 ft.
Machinery: 2-shaft geared Turbines, S.H.P. 3,800 = 17 knots.
Armament: 2—4 in. (2 × 1), 1—3.7 in. howitzer, 8-M (8 × 1) guns.
Complement: 74.

T.61	BEE	White		Cancelled 1940.
T.11	DRAGONFLY	Thornycroft	8.12.38	Lost 14/2/42.
T.85	GRASSHOPPER	Thornycroft	19. 1.39	Lost 14/2/42.
T.28	LOCUST	Yarrow	28. 9.39	H.Q.S. (1944), R.N.V.R. (Severn—1951). Drillship
T.94	MOSQUITO	Yarrow	14.11.39	Lost 1/6/40.

Displacement: 331 tons.
Dimensions: 170 (pp) (oa) × 22 × 6 ft.
Machinery: 2-shaft Diesel motors, B.H.P. 900 = 15½ knots.
Armament: 1—12 pdr. A.A., 1—20 mm. A.A. guns.

T.301	HIRA (R.I.N.) (ex-Persian Chahbaaz)	Cant. Nav. Ruiniti	3. 8.31	Captured 1941; retroceded 1946.
T.299	LAL (R.I.N.) (ex-Persian Simorgh)	Cant. Partenopei	3. 8.31	Captured 1941; retroceded 1946.
T.300	MOTI (R.I.N.) (ex-Persian Karkas)	Cant. Partenopei	3. 8.31	Captured 1941; scrapped Bombay 1946.
T.302	NILAM (R.I.N.) (ex-Persian Charogh)	Cant. Partenopei	26. 7.31	Captured 1941; retroceded 1946.

Notes:—These vessels were based on Bombay and employed in harbour A/S patrol and training

SURVEYING AND CABLE VESSELS

The small surveying fleet was greatly depleted at the outbreak of the Second World War when all former escort and minesweeping sloops resumed their former roles (see Part 3) or, in the case of the older vessels, were required for harbour duties. Work was stopped on the incomplete RESEARCH and only the CHALLENGER was left to undertake survey work, to be joined later by the former yachts WHITE BEAR and GULNARE; the latter perpetuating a traditional surveying name. Survey work did not exactly come to a standstill as all operational vessels actively contributed but became limited to the areas of conflict.

Cable laying, and its maintenance, was more a commercial than a naval enterprise but the need, during war, to preserve communications was of utmost importance. The mercantile cable vessels were not requisitioned by the Royal Navy but, from time to time, came under its specific control for certain operations. Many participated in the Normandy landings, during 1944, and laid the undersea pipe-line between the British south coast and the French beach-heads. Naval cable ships were otherwise employed in laying and maintaining asdic loops at the main ports.

SURVEYING VESSELS

Displacement: 1,280 tons.
Dimensions: (pp) 241¼ (oa) × 34¼ × 11¾ ft.
Machinery: 1-shaft Reciprocating (VTE), I.H.P. 1,100 = 13 knots.
Armament: Not armed. *Complement:* 139.

J.91	ENDEAVOUR	Fairfield	30. 3.12	Mercantile (1945).

Notes:—Boom defence depot at Singapore until 1942 then went to Colombo and the Eastern Mediterranean.

Displacement: 1,572 tons.
Dimensions: 226 (pp) 247 (oa) × 37½ × 13½ ft.
Machinery: 2-shaft Reciprocating (VTE), I.H.P. 2,275 = 12½ knots.
Armament: 1—4.7 in., 2—20 mm. A.A. (2 × 1), 2—.303 in. A.A. (2 × 1) guns.
Complement: 109.

J 81	INVESTIGATOR (R.I.N.) (ex-mercantile Patrick Stewart)	Simons	13. 3.25	Sold 1951.

Notes:—Was converted to an A/S sloop 1941 and then used as a training ship from 1943 serving in East Indies throughout the war.

Displacement: 1,140 tons.
Dimensions: 200 (pp) 220 (oa) × 36 × 12½ ft.
Machinery: 1-shaft Reciprocating (VTE), I.H.P. 1,200 = 12½ knots.
Armament: Not armed. *Complement:* 84.

J.98	CHALLENGER	Chatham	1. 6.31	Scrapped Dover 1/54.

Notes:—Served in Home waters until 1942, then in the Eastern fleet and East Indies.

Displacement: 757 tons.
Dimensions: (pp) 142½ (oa) × 34 × 13¼ ft.
Machinery: 1-shaft Diesel motor, B.H.P. 160 = 6½ knots.
Armament: Not armed.

.96	RESEARCH	Philip	4. 4.39	Scrapped incomplete Plymouth 10/52.

Notes:—Composite built brigantine rigged vessel constructed entirely of non-magnetic material.

For sloops converted to surveying vessels see Part 3. These included HERALD and R.A.N. MORESBY (" **24** " class), FITZROY, FLINDERS and KELLETT (**Hunt** class minesweepers), GLEANER, FRANKLIN, GOSSAMER, JASON and SCOTT (**Halcyon** class), FOLKESTONE and SCARBOROUGH (**Hastings** class) and STORK (**Bittern** class).

Displacement: 1,715 tons gross.
Dimensions: 285 (pp) 310 (oa) × 37¾ × 16½ ft.

Machinery: 1-shaft Reciprocating (4 cyl. VTE), N.H.P. 345 = 13½ knots.
Armament: 4—20 mm. A.A. (4 × 1) guns.

J.30	WHITE BEAR (ex-Iolanda)	Ramage & Ferguson	1908	Ex-A/P yacht; sold 1947.

Notes:—Equipment included complete chart reproduction facilities. A small yacht, the GULNARE (J.134), was also taken over for surveying duties.

CABLE VESSELS

Displacement: 895 tons.
Dimensions: 170 (pp) 182 (oa) × 30 × 11¾ ft.
Machinery: 1-shaft Reciprocating (VTE), I.H.P. 700 = 10 knots.
Armament: 2—20 mm. A.A. (2 × 1), 2-M (2 × 1 LG) guns.

Z.85	KILMUN	Smiths Dock	11.10.19	Sold 1947.

Notes:—Sole naval survivor of a class of 86 patrol gunboats built during World War I of which a large number were subsequently sold out commercially. The mercantile MEAD (ex-Kilmead) was requisitioned by the S.A.N. in 1940, the mercantile INDIRA (ex-Kildysart) and the yacht FOINAVON (ex-Kilmartin), by the R.N. in 1940 and the mercantile HASHEMI (ex-Kildorough) by the R.I.N in 1939.

Displacement: 910 tons.
Dimensions: 180 (pp) 205 (oa) × 35¼ × 9¾ ft.
Machinery: 2-shaft Reciprocating (VTE), I.H.P. 1,100 = 13 knots.
Armament: 1—12 pdr. A.A., 2—20 mm. A.A. (2 × 1) guns.

Z.76	LASSO	Thornycroft	17. 3.38	Scrapped Burght 18/5/59.

Displacement: 1,950 tons.
Dimensions: 228¾ (pp) 252 (oa) × 36¼ × 16¼ ft.
Machinery: 2-shaft Reciprocating (VTE), I.H.P. 1,300 = 13 knots.
Armament: 1—12 pdr. A.A., 2—20 mm. A.A. (2 × 1) guns.

Z.176	BULLFINCH	Swan Hunter	19. 8.40	
Z.260	BULLFROG	Swan Hunter	26. 1.44	Mercantile RETRIEVER (1947), CABLE RESTORER (1961)
Z.236	BULLHEAD	Swan Hunter	3.10.44	Mercantile ELECTRA (1947), CABLE GUARDIAN (1959).
	BULLSEYE	Swan Hunter	1945	Completed as mercantile ALERT (1945).
Z.259	ST. MARGARETS	Swan Hunter	13.10.43	

The following mercantile cable vessels were in service during the war, under Admiralty control, and many were requisitioned for the laying of the under-water fuel pipe line (*PLUTO*) to the continent in 1944.
ACCRUITY (Cable carrier), ALERT, ALGERIAN, AQUILLA, ARIEL, BANKVILLE, BANGALOW (Repair ship—R.A.N.), BRITANNIC, BULAN, CABLE ENTERPRISE, CABLE RECORDER (ex-Iris), CAMBRIA, CASTLE ROCK, CECILE MAPLESON (S.A.N.), CYRUS FIELD (R.C.N.), DUNAVON, ELDORADO, EMILE BAUDOT (French), GLENMORISTON, GOLI

Above: The R.I.N. surveying ship H.M.I.S. Investigator was used as an escort vessel and later as a boys' training ship.

Below: H.M.S. Bullhead was one of the war-built naval cable layers. [*I.W.M.*

Above: The G.P.O. cable ship S.S. Alert served under naval control and was armed with a single 12 pdr. A.A. aft, two single 20 mm. A.A. abaft the bridge and three twin Lewis guns. [*I.W.M.*

Below: The armed yacht H.M.S. Coila was used for A/S work. [*I.W.M.*

Left: Originally employed on A/S duties the armed yacht Conqueror was later converted to an auxiliary A.A. vessel. [*I.W.M.*

Right: The armed yachts Cutty Sark (illustrated) and the R.C.N. Renard, were modelled on contemporary destroyer lines and were initially employed as A/S vessels. [*I.W.M.*

BELL, GOLD DRIFT, HOLDFAST (ex-London), INNISFALL (Repai ship—R.A.N.), IRVIN, JOHN W. MACKAY (R.C.N.), LADY DENISON PENDER, LADY LAURIER, LATIMER, LAWSON, LORD KELVIN (R.C.N.), MARIE LOUISE MACKAY (Cable carrier), MAY, MEAD (ex Kilmead—S.A.N.), MIRROR, MONARCH, NORSEMAN, OCEANIC ORANGE, PACIFIC, PERSEPHONE (Lighter), RAMSGATE, RECORDER RETRIEVER, RUNIC, ST. ORAN, SANCROFT, SANKATY (R.C.N. SAXON QUEEN, SOUTHERN BREEZE, SPRAYVILLE, STRAIDE, STORI NORDISKE and VIKING.

ARMED YACHTS

(Over 100 tons T.M.)

A great number of yachts, down to quite small craft, were requisitioned for wa service and the larger vessels are listed here in four main groups:—

(a) A/S yachts. (c) Yachts on miscellaneous services.
(b) M/S yachts. (d) Yachts used as accommodation ship

Many of the smaller yachts, not included in the following lists, were used as ai sea rescue vessels or as harbour defence patrol craft and are only omitte because space does not permit listing the large numbers involved.

A/S YACHTS

Nine anti-submarine groups (the 81st to 89th) were fitted out in the first thre months of the war, each to have comprised from four to six vessels. Many o these entered service armed with only depth charges—one/two 3/12 pdr. bein added later.

All the yachts requisitioned by the Royal Canadian Navy, except the AMBLE and SANS PEUR (ex-Trenora), were purchased in the United States in 194

P. No.	Name	Thames measurement/ Built	Fate
FY.001	AARLA	471/03	Returned 1945.
FY.002	ALASTOR	340/26	A/P (4.282—1941).
FY.045	ALETES		Returned 1946.
FY.003	ALICE	527/30	Accommodation ship (1943).
	ALTAIR	161/31	Training ship (1941), A/S (1943).
FY.004	ANNA MARIE	344/30	TORRENT (1940); lost 6/4/41.
FY.046	BLACK BEAR (ex-Xarifa)	756/30	Attached F.A.A. (Trinidad—1941).
	CAMPEADOR V	120/38	Lost 22/6/40.
FY.005	COILA 1—4 in., 1—M.G.	355/22	Returned 1946.
FY.006	CONQUEROR (ex-Emerald, ex-Marynthia)	900/11	Aux. A.A. vessel (1941).
FY.047	CORSAIR	2181/30	Attached F.A.A. (Bermuda—1941); returned 1945.
FY.007	CUTTY SARK 1—4in. 1—2 pdr. A.A. 2—·5 in. A.A. (1 × 2) 2—·5 M.G. (1 × 2)	828/20	Submarine tender (4.19—1940); returned 1945.

Y.048	DOROTHY DUKE	307/18	Returned 1/46.
Y.009	EVADNE	581/31	Returned 1/45.
Y.010	GLEN STRATHALLAN	356/28	Returned 1945.
Y.011	HINIESTA	330/02	Calibrating vessel (4.60—1942); returned 1946.
Y.012	IOLAIRE	999/02	Accommodation ship (1941); PERSEPHONE (1945); returned 1946.
Y.008	KALAN		
Y.049	KENORA II	536/30	
Y.014	LADY BLANCHE	405/07	Accommodation ship (1942); returned 11/45.
Y.015	LADY SHAHRAZAD	439/04	Returned 1946.
Y.016	LADY VAGRANT	484/03	Returned 1940.
Y.017	MAID MARION	506/38	Submarine tender (1944); returned 1945.
Y.1001	MARAVEL (ex-Chelsea)	295/26	Returned 1/46.
Y.019	MIGRANTE	909/29	Sold 1946.
Y.018	MOLLUSC (ex-Medusa)	627/06	Lost 17/3/41.
Y.020	ORACLE (ex-Osprey)	745/29	Lost 29/1/44.
Y.1002	OWERA	429/07	Returned 1945.
Y.021	PRINCESS	751/24	Lost 11/1/40.
Y.022	RADIANT	550/27	Training ship (1941), A/S (1942); returned 1945.
Y.023	RHODORA	709/29	Lost 7/9/40.
Y.024	RION	324/28	NOIR (1944); returned 1945.
Y.025	ST. MODWEN		Returned 1945.
.60	SEABELLE (ex-Seabelle II)	1057/28	Returned 1946.
Y.026	SHEMARA	834/38	Returned 3/46.
Y.027	SONA	555/22	Accommodation ship (1940); lost 1/42.
Y.036	STAR OF INDIA	735/88	Accommodation ship (1944); returned 1946.
Y.1003	SUMAR	447/26	Examination service (1944); sold 1946.
	SURPRISE	1322/96	Lost 28/2/42.
Y.1612	TROUBADOUR	1245/24	Accommodation ship (1942); sold 1947.
Y.044	TUSCARORA	591/97	Returned 1946.
Y.028	VALENA	882/08	Returned 1945.
Y.029	VENETIA	568/05	Returned 1946.
Y.031	VIRGINIA	712/30	Returned 1946.
Y.030	VIVA II	502/29	Lost 8/5/41.
Y.032	WARRIOR II	1266/04	Lost 11/7/40.
	WILNA	457/05	Lost 24/3/41.
Y.033	ZAZA	455/05	Accommodation ship (1941); sold 1948.

	AMBLER (R.C.N.)	273/22	5.41	Training ship (1944); returned 1/46.

BEAVER (R.C.N.) (ex-Aztec)	890/02	4.41	Returned 8/45.
CARIBOU (R.C.N.) (ex-Elfreda)	301/28	10.40	Training ship (1944); returne 9/45.
COUGAR (R.C.N.) (ex-Breezing Thru)	226/16	9.40	Returned 9/45.
ELK (R.C.N.) (ex-Arcadia)	576/26	9.40	Training ship (1944); returne 9/45.
GRIZZLY (R.C.N.) (ex-Machigonne)	216/09	7.41	Returned 12/44.
HUSKY (R.C.N.) (ex-Wild Duck)	360/30	7.40	Examination service (1943); returned 8/45.
LYNX (R.C.N.) (ex-Ramona)	445/22	8.40	Hulked (1943); returned 5/4
MOOSE (R.C.N.) (ex-Cleopatra)	263/30	9.40	Examination service (1943); returned 8/45.
OTTER (R.C.N.) (ex-Conseco)	416/21	10.40	Lost 5/3/41.
RACCOON (R.C.N.) (ex-Halonia)	358/31	12.40	Lost 1/9/42.
REINDEER (R.C.N.) (ex-Mascotte)	337/26	7.40	Training ship (1944); return 10/45.
RENARD (R.C.N.) (ex-Winchester)	466/16	5.40	Training ship (1944); return 11/45.
SANS PEUR(R.C.N.) (ex-Trenora)	821/33	4.40	Training ship (1944); return 6/47.
VISON (R.C.N.) (ex-Avalon)	422/31	10.40	Training ship (1944); return 11/45.
WOLF (R.C.N.) (ex-Blue Water)	300/15	10.40	Returned 12/45.

M/S YACHTS

These were not formed into groups, like the A/S yachts but were employ as Senior Officers' ships at minesweeping bases or as danlayers.

	ARONIA	193/33	Returned 1942.
FY.050	BOY PAT		Returned 1946.
	CALAMARA (ex-Cala Mara)	313/98	Returned 1945.
4.40	GREY MIST	197/20	Examination service (194 sold 1947.
4.49	GUELDER ROSE		Examination service (194 returned 1945.
	GULZAR	201/34	Lost 29/7/40.
4.53	HINBA	154/03	Examination service (194 sold 1948.
FY.061	LEXA	133/36	Returned 1946.
4.66	OMBRA	275/02	Returned 1947.
FY.053	SARGASSO	223/26	Lost 6/6/43 & salved.
FY.054	SIR SIDNEY		Echo yacht (1941).

H.M.C.S. Husky was a R.C.N. armed yacht which later served in the examination service. [I.W.M.

Above: H.M.C.S. Reindeer was another of the R.C.N. armed yachts. [*I.W.M*

Below: H.M.S. Duena was one of the smaller yachts used for harbour defence. [*I.W.M*

4.90	SYLVANA	487/07	Sold 1946.
FY.057	TARANSAY	175/30	Examination service (1942); sold 1948
FY.1602	THALIA	161/04	Lost 11/10/42.
FY.1565	YARTA	357/98	A/S (1942); returned 1947.

Yachts on miscellaneous services

P. No.	Name	Thames measurement/ Built	Fate
FY.89	ADELE (R.A.N.)	327/06	Examination service; returned 1946.
	ADVENTURESS	322/98	Examination service; returned 1945.
	AISHA	177/34	H.D.P.C.; lost 11/10/40.
	ALISDAIR	120/37	H.D.P.C.; calibrating ship (1943); returned 1945.
	AMALFI	124/25	H.D.P.C.; returned 1943.
4.62	ANGLIA	326/13	A.B.V.; sold 1946.
	AMAZONE	229/36	A/P.
4.286	ANNE	121/25	H.D.P.C.; Examination service (1941); submarine tender (1942); returned 1946.
	ARLETTE II	163/36	Examination service; returned 1946.
4.224	ATMAH	1746/98	Attached F.A.A., accommodation ship (1944); sold 1946.
	ATTENDANT	357/13	Lost 11/43.
4.92	AZUR	136/29	H.D.P.C.; returned 1945.
4.84	BREDA (ex-Sapphire)	1421/12	A/P, submarine tender (1940); lost 18/2/44.
4.73	CACOUNA	202/32	Examination service, escort yacht (1943); returned 1946.
	CALANTHE	429/98	Examination service; lost 24/4/41.
4.155	CALETA	138/30	H.D.P.C. returned 1945.
	CARIAD	153/03	B.B.V. (not commissioned).
4.295	CETO	130/35	Calibrating vessel; returned 1945.
4.37	CHARLES MCIVER	428/36	A.B.V.; returned 12/45.
	CHRYSTOBEL II	111/28	H.D.P.C.; returned 1945.
FY.008	CYNARA	702/13	
4.340	DORADE II	211/06	H.D.P.C.; returned 1945.
	DUENA 1—3 pdr. 3—MG (1 × 2 & 1 × 1)	140/37	H.D.P.C. returned 1945.
4.285	FREELANCE	106/08	A/P.; returned 1944.
	GAEL	115/04	H.D.P.C.; lost 24/11/40.
	GELERT	122/81	H.D.P.C.; returned 1945.
	GIROFLEE	118/35	Examination service; returned 1945.
	GOLDEN HIND	144/31	B.B.V. (not commissioned).

	GRIVE	687/05	Attached F.A.A.; lost 1/6/40.
4.191	HELIOPOLIS	766/03	Attached F.A.A.; returned 1946.
4.74	IONA	279/20	Examination service, calibrating ship (1943); sold 1947.
4.304	ISLE OF MAY	138/96	Examination service, calibrating ship (1942); sold 1947.
	JANETHA IV	164/30	H.D.P.C.; returned 1946.
4.242	KIHNA	574/30	A/P. submarine tender (1941); returned 1945.
	KILORAN	277/30	Contraband control, accommodation ship (1941); returned 1945.
	KIRIN	202/13	B.B.V. (not commissioned).
	LAURABADA(R.A.N.)	150	Returned 1945.
4.65	LORNA	484/04	A.B.V.; returned 1943.
	MAIMIE	112/14	B.B.V. (not commissioned).
4.67	MALAHNE	458/37	Attached F.A.A.; returned 1946.
4.296	MARION	715/96	H.D.P.C.; returned 1945.
	MARTINETTA	115/29	H.D.P.C.; returned 1947.
	MELISANDE	367/83	Depot ship for A/P; returned 1946.
	MINONA	249/06	Examination service, depot ship (1941); returned 1947.
	PANOPE	122/28	B.B.V. (not commissioned).
4.12	PHILANTE 1—4 in. 2—20 mm. A.A. (2 × 1) 4—.5 in. A.A. (2 × 2)	1629/37	Attached F.A.A., escort yacht (1940), training ship (1943); sold 1947.
	QUEEN OF THE MAY	270/95	Calibrating vessel.
	ROSABELLE	614/01	A.B.V.; lost 11/12/41.
	ROSAURA	1538/05	A.B.V.; lost 18/3/41.
4.56	ST. CATHERINE	379/28	Examination service; returned 1945.
4.26	SAGITTA	756/08	Contraband control; returned 1947.
	SAPPHO	327/35	Contraband control; lost 30/9/40.
4.72	SAYONARA	762/11	A.B.V.; returned 1947.
	SOUTHERN CROSS (R.A.N.); 1—4 in.	357/33	Examination service; returned 1946.
	SUNBEAM II	659/29	H.D.P.C., accommodation ship (1944); returned 11/45.
	SURF	560/02	Contraband control; lost 6/4/41.
	TENGGAROH		A/P; believed became Japanese.
	THENDARA	147/37	B.B.V. (not commissioned).
4.83	TIERCEL	489/13	A.B.V. accommodation ship (1941); returned 1946.
	TITAN	103/35	H.D.P.C.; returned 1945.
	TROPHY		B.B.V. (not commissioned).
4.197	TYRANT	149/30	A/P, training ship (1943); returned 1946.

Above: H.M.S. Philante was one of the largest of the armed yachts and was finally used for training. [*I.W.M.*

Below: M.Y. Sister Anne was used as an accommodation ship and was armed with two 20 mm. A.A. guns. [*I.W.M.*

	VADURA	109/26	H.D.P.C.
4.02	WHITE BEAR (ex-Iolanda)	1822/08	A/P, submarine tender (1940), surveying vessel (1944); sold 1947.
	ZITA	283/94	A/P, accommodation ship (1941), mooring hulk (1945); 1946.

Yachts used as accommodation ships

BOADICEA	447/82	CARMELA	148/03
CARMENITA		FLORINDA	135/73
FOINAVON (ex-R.N. Kilmarten)	670/19	GYPSY (lost 11/5/41).	261/
MAHELA	137/98	MAJESTA	170/99
MURAENA	330/07	SISTER ANNE (F.47)	250/29
VALHALLA		VIGILANT	145/04

Notes:—These yachts were not generally commissioned.

PENNANT NUMBERS

It proved impossible to retain a uniform system of flag superiors for the mercantile auxiliary vessels owing to their constantly changing employment. Unlike the regular naval vessels therefore, their flag superior was not a reliable indication of the type or employment of auxiliary vessels as shown below:—

Escort carriers, large aircraft transports and transports for crashed aircraft	Flag D
Small aircraft transports	Flag F
Armed merchant cruisers, ocean and armed boarding vessels	Flag I changed to Flag F (1940).
Special service vessels	Flag F or D
Convoy escorts	Flag 4
Auxiliary anti-aircraft ships	Flag F, D or 4
Auxiliary patrol vessels	Flag 4 or T or FY pennant
Auxiliary minesweepers	Flag J, T or 4 or FY pennant
Paddle minesweepers	Flag N changed to Flag J (1940)
Mine destructors	FY pennant
Auxiliary minelayers	Flag M
Coastal and controlled minelayers	Flag I changed to Flag F or M (1940)
River gunboats	Flag T
Surveying vessels	Flag N changed to Flag J (1940)
Cable vessels	Flag Z
Armed yachts	Flag 4 or FY pennant

PART FIVE

Auxiliary Support Vessels

The destroyer depot ship H.M.S. Tyne had her twin 4·5 in. A.A. guns all on the centre line and had tripod masts fore and aft. [A. & J. Pavia

DEPOT AND REPAIR SHIPS

DEPOT and repair ships performed similar functions but not to the extent that they were interchangeable. The latter were used by the fleet generally for repair work they were not able to undertake themselves, while the former catered for flotilla vessels and, in addition to repair facilities, provided those base and personnel services which the smaller vessels lacked. The increasingly technical nature of the equipment borne in H.M. Ships resulted in a greater demand for depot and repair ships in the Second than the First World War.

To supplement the sole repair ship, five intermediate liners (four were ex-armed merchant cruisers) were purchased by the Royal Navy after the outbreak of war and converted to this role. It was found that in accommodating the large repair staff required, encroachment was made on repair shop space and resulted in separate *accommodation ships* for them to live in. This tended to restrict the use of repair ships in forward areas and a compromise was effected in the repair ships received under *Lend/Lease* from the United States Navy. In them repair facilities and consequently repair staff, were reduced, to produce self-contained units with greater flexibility of employment.

Although a number of mercantile vessels were purchased for large and permanent conversions to depot ships, such extensive alterations were necessarily limited. This led to the equipping of war standard mercantile hulls as *maintenance ships*, whose description is self-explanatory, rather than the Royal Navy placing orders for special depot ships in yards familiar with naval work at the expense of combatant units.

The world-wide nature of the Second World War frequently led to the creation of bases in isolated areas where there was limited, or no shore, facilities. Base offices and staffs had therefore to be accommodated in suitable vessels and resulted in *base ships*, from where command was exercised, and further *accommodation ships*. Thus, the simple categories of *depot ships* and *repair ships*, which sufficed pre-war, were enlarged as a result of war-time improvisation. Only the *maintenance ships* were retained post-war and although they kept this classification assumed near-depot ship status as a result of addition and refinement.

The ultimate provision was for two *amenities ships* for Pacific operations. They were amply provided with recreational facilities such as cinemas, " wet " canteens, etc. where the personnel of the fleet, in the total absence of shore facilities, could relax between operations and were manned by mercantile crews of the Royal Fleet Auxiliary service.

DEPOT AND REPAIR SHIPS

The following depot ships, dating from the First World War, were still serving on the 3rd September, 1939, and, with the exception of the ALECTO and the R.A.N. PLATYPUS, were all ex-mercantile conversions.

Displacement: 6,600 tons.
Dimensions: 338 (pp) 387¾ (oa) × 47½ × 20¾ ft.
Machinery: 1-shaft reciprocating (VTE), I.H.P. 6,350 = 14½ knots.
Armament: 2—3 in. guns.
Complement: 238.

P.No.	Name	Builder Hull: Engine	Launched	Remarks
F.08	COCHRANE (ex-Ambrose)	Raylton Dixon: N.E. Marine	31. 3.03	Paid off 30/11/47.

Notes:—Removed from the effective list in 1938 but used as a harbour depot ship for submarines.

Displacement: 11,300 tons.
Dimensions: 460 (pp) 477 (oa) × 55 × 21¼ ft.
Machinery: 1-shaft reciprocating (VTE), I.H.P. 3,500 = 13 knots.
Armament: 2—4 in. (2 × 1) guns.
Complement: 266.

P.No.	Name	Builder Hull: Engine	Launched	Remarks
F.31	CYCLOPS (ex-Indrabarah)	Laing	27.10.05	Scrapped Newport 7/47.

Notes:—Submarine depot ship in Mediterranean 1939 returning to Home waters in that year where she was employed for the remainder of the war.

Displacement: 5,805 tons.
Dimensions: 350 (pp) 367½ (oa) × 45¼ × 18¾ ft.
Machinery: 1-shaft reciprocating (VTE), I.H.P. 2,750 = 12¾ knots.
Armament: Nil.
Complement: 262.

P.No.	Name	Builder Hull: Engine	Launched	Remarks
F.27	LUCIA (ex-Spreewald)	Furness: Richardson Westgarth	21.11.07	Mercantile SINAI (1948); scrapped Spezia 2/51.

Notes:—Submarine depot ship in the East Indies 1939, base ship for Red Sea force 1940, Eastern fleet as submarine depot ship 1942-45.

Displacement: 935 tons.
Dimensions: 190 (pp) 212 (oa) × 32½ × 11 ft.
Machinery: 1-shaft reciprocating (VTE), I.H.P. 1,400 = 11 knots.
Armament: Nil.
Complement: 76.

P.No.	Name	Builder Hull: Engine	Launched	Remarks
J.10	ALECTO	Laird	29. 8.11	Scrapped Faslane 1948.

Notes:—Submarine depot ship at Portsmouth 1939-40, then for boom defence vessels.

Displacement: 5,250 tons.
Dimensions: 335 (pp) 350 (oa) × 46¼ × 18½ ft.
Machinery: 1-shaft reciprocating (VTE) I.H.P. 3,200 = 14½ knots.
Armament: Nil.
Complement: 249.

P.No.	Name	Builder Hull: Engine	Launched	Remarks
F.32	TITANIA	Clyde Sbdg.	4. 3.15	Scrapped Faslane 9/49.

Notes:—Submarine depot ship in Home waters throughout the war.

H.M.S. Cochrane, wearing an Admiral's flag, served as a harbour depot ship. [I.W.M.

Displacement: 8,100 tons.
Dimensions: 390 (pp) 402 (oa) × 52 × 19¾ ft.
Machinery: 1-shaft reciprocating (VTE), I.H.P. 2,500 = 11 knots.
Armament: 4—4 in. (4 × 1), 1—3 in. A.A. guns.
Complement: 224.

F.10	GREENWICH	Dobson: Swan Hunter	5. 7.15	Completed Swan Hunter; mercantile HEMBURY (1947), NAVEM HEMBURY (1955).

Notes:—Destroyer depot ship at Scapa Flow 1939-41, then served Canada, Iceland 1942 and finished the war with Home fleet.

Displacement: 11,500 tons.
Dimensions: 470 (pp) 485 (oa) × 58 × 20 ft.
Machinery: 1-shaft reciprocating (VTE), I.H.P. 3,300 = 10½ knots.
Armament: 4—4 in. (4 × 1), 1—3 in. A.A. guns.
Complement: 357.

F.92	SANDHURST (ex-Manipur)	Harland & Wolff	14.12.05	Scrapped Dalmuir 4/46.

Notes:—Served Dover 1939-40, depot ship for escort vessels 1941 first at Londonderry and then Greenock.

Displacement: 3,455 tons.
Dimensions: 310 (pp) 325 (oa) × 44 × 15¾ ft.
Machinery: 2-shaft reciprocating (VTE), I.H.P. 3,500 = 15½ knots.
Armament: Nil.
Complement: 357.

	PLATYPUS (R.A.N.) (ex-Penguin, ex-Platypus)	Clydebank	28.10.16	For disposal 12/57.

Notes:—Served in Australian waters throughout the war and was base ship at Darwin from 1941.

As experience in the First World War had clearly shown the need for depot and repair ships—the former for flotilla craft and the latter for the fleet generally—the following vessels were specially built for the purpose.

Displacement: 14,650 tons.
Dimensions: 545 (pp) 580 (oa) × 85 × 21 ft.
Machinery: 2-shaft Diesel motors, B.H.P. 8,000 = 15 knots.
Armament: 2—4 in. (2 × 1), 4—4 in. A.A. (4 × 1) guns.
Complement: 400.

25	MEDWAY	V.A. (Barrow)	19. 7.28	Lost 30/6/42.

Notes:—Submarine depot ship China 1939, Mediterranean 1940. The name MEDWAY II was borne by the minelayer MEDUSA 1943-44 and the minesweeper BAGSHOT from 1945.

Above: H.M.S. Medway was the first large submarine depot ship built for the Royal Navy and was diesel engined. [*I.W.M.*

Below: H.M.S. Woolwich at Capetown in 1942. A 12 pdr. A.A. gun has been added on the foc'sle and a zareba placed around the 4 in. A. A. guns amidships.

Displacement: 12,300 tons.
Dimensions: 500 (pp) 530 (oa) × 83 × 17¼ ft.
Machinery: 2-shaft geared Turbines, S.H.P. 7,500 = 15 knots.
Armament: 4—4 in. A.A. (4 × 1) guns.
Complement: 581.

F.79	RESOURCE	V.A. (Barrow)	27.11.28	Scrapped Inverkeithing 2/54.

Notes:—Fleet repair ship, Mediterranean 1939-44 except for short spell at Freetown 1940, Eastern fleet 1944-45.

Displacement: 8,750 tons.
Dimensions: 575 (pp) 610¼ (oa) × 64 × 14¾ ft.
Machinery: 2-shaft geared Turbines, S.H.P. 6,500 = 15 knots.
Armament: 4—4 in. A.A. (4 × 1) guns.
Complement: 666.

F.80	WOOLWICH	Fairfield	20. 9.34	Scrapped Dalmuir 18/10/62.

Notes:—Destroyer depot ship that served successively in Home waters, the Mediterranean and the East Indies.

Displacement: 8,900 tons.
Dimensions: 497 (pp) 531 (oa) × 73 × 16½ ft.
Machinery: 2-shaft geared Turbines, S.H.P. 7,000 = 17 knots.
Armament: 8—4.5 in. A.A. (4 × 2), 8—2 pdr. A.A. (2 × 4) guns.
Complement: 1,167.

F.07	FORTH	Clydebank	11. 8.38	
F.44	MAIDSTONE	Clydebank	21.10.37	

Notes:—Submarine depot ships. FORTH served with the 2nd Submarine flotilla 1939-41 and then with the 3rd Submarine flotilla until the end of the war. MAIDSTONE served in the Mediterranean, South Atlantic and Rosyth 1939-40 and then successively in the Mediterranean, Eastern fleet and the Pacific fleet.

Displacement: 10,850 tons.
Dimensions: 585 (pp) 623 (oa) × 66 × 16½ ft.
Machinery: 2-shaft geared Turbines, S.H.P. 7,500 = 17 knots.
Armament: 8—4.5 in. A.A. (4 × 2), 8—2 pdr. A.A. (2 × 4) guns.
Complement: 818.

F.20	HECLA	Clydebank	14. 3.40	Lost 12/11/42.
F.24	TYNE	Scotts	28. 2.40	

Notes:—Destroyer depot ships. HECLA was based at Greenock, then Iceland and finally in the Mediterranean. TYNE served with the Home fleet until 1944 when she was transferred to the Pacific fleet.

Displacement: 12,500 tons.
Dimensions: 620 (pp) 658 (oa) × 70½ × 16½ ft.
Machinery: 2-shaft geared Turbines, S.H.P. 8,000 = 17 knots.
Armament: 8—4.5 in. A.A. (4 × 2), 16—2 pdr. A.A. (4 × 4) 8—20 mm. A.A. (8 × 1) 8—·5 in. A.A. (2 × 4) guns.
Complement: 1,273.

F.64	ADAMANT	Harland & Wolff	30.11.40	

Notes:—Submarine depot ship. Eastern fleet until 1944 and then went to the Pacific fleet.

Above: H.M.S. Forth could be distinguished from the Maidstone by the additional HA.DCT aft. Note the conspicuous well separating the bridge from the amidships superstructure. [*I.W.M.*

Below: The submarine depot ship H.M.S. Maidstone had her twin 4.5 in. A.A. guns, in open shields, disposed lozenge-fashion and multiple 2pdr. mountings were placed at the fore end of the amidships superstructure. Two 20mm. A.A. guns have been added in the bridge wings and 2—2pdr. A.A. (2×1) and 3—20 mm. A.A. guns at the aft end of the amidships superstructure. [*I.W.M.*

Above: H.M.S. Adamant, depot ship for submarines, generally followed the lines but was an enlargement of the Tyne. Additional multiple 2 pdr. A.A. mountings were added abreast the after funnel and multiple .5 in. M.G.s were added in the bridge wings plus several single 20 mm. A.A. guns overall [*I.W.M*

Below: H.M.S. Derby Haven was a modified **Loch/Bay** frigate completed as a depot ship for coasta forces and was only lightly armed with a twin 4 in. A.A. mounting forward and three single 20 mm A.A. guns aft. [*I.W.M*

The outbreak of the Second World War resulted in an immediate demand for additional depot and repair ships. This was met in three ways, viz.:—

(a) by converting selected warships,

(b) by requisitioning and converting mercantile tonnage,

(c) by a programme of war construction.

The latter were built to the restricted number of standard mercantile war designs as regards their hull and main machinery and were then equipped for their particular role. Like the American built escort carriers these adaptations, from a bare hull, were considerably superior to conversions from completed merchant ships.

(a) **Warship conversions**

F.01	MARSHAL SOULT (ex-M.14)	Ex-monitor converted to a depot ship for patrol vessels and stationed at Portsmouth from 1940.
D.36	VINDICTIVE (ex-Cavendish)	Ex-training cruiser converted to a repair ship and served with the Home fleet, at Freetown and in the Mediterranean. Returned to the Home fleet in 1945 and converted to a destroyer depot ship.
M.23	ADVENTURE	Ex-minelaying cruiser converted to a repair ship in 1944 for the European invasion.
D.22	ALBATROSS	Ex-seaplane carrier converted to a repair ship in 1941.
J.61	ENDEAVOUR	Ex-surveying vessel converted to a boom defence depot ship at Singapore 1941 and then served in the Mediterranean from 1942 onwards.
K.438 K.654	DERBY HAVEN (ex-Loch Assynt) WOODBRIDGE HAVEN (ex-Loch Torridon)	Ex-frigates completed as depot ships for coastal forces.
F.06	TALBOT (ex-Medusa, ex-M.29)	Ex-coastal minelayer which served as a submarine depot ship at Malta from 1941 and was re-named MEDWAY II in 1943.
D.11 D.00	COURBET PARIS	Ex-French battleships which served as depots ships for auxiliary patrol vessels.
U.63 U.93	BELFORT COUCY	Ex-French patrol vessels which served as depot ships for coastal forces and auxiliary patrol vessels respectively.
	DILIGENTE	Ex-French patrol vessel which served as a depot ship for auxiliary patrol vessels.

(b) Mercantile conversions

Displacement: 19,000 tons except WAYLAND 18,750 tons.
Dimensions: 519¾ (pp) 538 (oa) × 65¼ × 27¼ except WAYLAND 27 ft.
Machinery: 2-shaft geared Turbines, S.H.P. 8,500 = 15 knots.
Armament: 20—20 mm. A.A. (20 × 1) except WAYLAND 4—4 in. A.A. (4 × 1), 8—2 pdr. A.A. (2 × 4), 8—20 mm. A.A. (8 × 1) guns.
Complement: 592 except WAYLAND 596.

P.No.	Name	Builder Hull: Engine	Launched	Fate
F.15	ALAUNIA	Clydebank	7. 2.25	Ex-A.M.C.; scrapped Blyth 10/9/57.
F.28	ARTIFEX (ex-Aurania)	Swan Hunter: Wallsend	6. 2.24	Ex-A.M.C.; scrapped Italy 1/61.
F.53	AUSONIA	Armstrong Whitworth	22. 3.21	Ex-A.M.C.
F.137	WAYLAND (ex-Antonia)	V.A. (Barrow)	11. 3.21	Requisitioned 1940; scrapped Cairn Ryan 6/45 and Troon 2/49 (hull only).

Notes:—Purchased outright 1942-44 and converted to repair ships. All served in the East Indies, WAYLAND from 1943 and the remainder from 1944-45.

Displacement: 16,600 tons.
Dimensions: 503 (pp) 528½ (oa) × 63¼ × 25¼ ft.
Machinery: 2-shaft geared Turbines S.H.P. 6,800 = 14½ knots.
Armament: 4—4 in. A.A (4 × 1), 8—2 pdr. A.A. (2 × 4), PHILOCTETES 4, BLENHEIM 8—20 mm. A.A. (4 × 1/2) guns.
Complement: 674.

P.No.	Name	Builder Hull: Engine	Launched	Fate
4.221	BLENHEIM (ex-Achilles)	Scotts	23.12.19	Purchased 1940; scrapped Barrow 16/3/48.
F.134	PHILOCTETES	Scotts	25. 5.22	Purchased 1940; scrapped Newport 1/3/48.

Notes:—Depot ships for destroyers. BLENHEIM Home fleet 1942, Iceland 1943 and Mediterranean 1944-45. PHILOCTETES Freetown 1942-45.

Displacement: 10,423 tons.
Dimensions: 457 (pp) 487 (oa) × 62¾ × 28½ ft.
Machinery: 2-shaft Reciprocating (VTE), and exhaust turbine, I.H.P. 8,300 = 16 knots.
Armament: 2—4 in. A.A. (1 × 2), 12—20 mm. A.A. (4 × 2 & 4 × 1) guns.

P.No.	Name	Builder Hull: Engine	Launched	Fate
F.139	BONAVENTURE (ex-Clan Davidson ex-Clan Campbell)	Greenock: Kincaid	27.10.42	Completed Scotts; purchased 1942; mercantile CLAN DAVIDSON (1948).

Notes:—Depot ship for " **X** " craft. Home waters until 1945 then to the Pacific.

Left: H.M.S. Artifex was a former A.M.C. purchased outright from the Cunard Line and converted to a repair ship. She was defensively armed with 20—20 mm. A.A. (20×1) guns. [*I.W.M.*

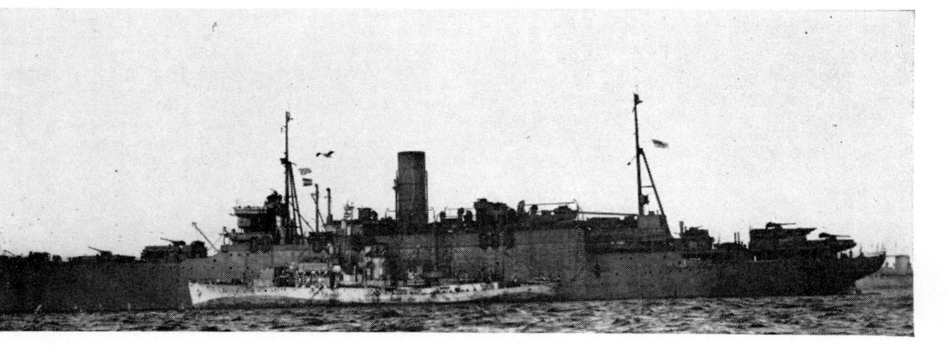

Right: H.M.S. Wayland was the first of the purchased Cunard liners to be converted to a repair ship and differed from the other three by having tripod masts and a heavier A.A. armament, which included 4—4 in. (4×1), 8—2 pdr. (2×4) and 8—20 mm. (8×1) guns. [*I.W.M.*

H.M.S. Blenheim (above) and a sister ship H.M.S. Philoctetes (left), were purchased from the Blue Funnel Line and converted to destroyer depot ships. They both mounted 4—4 in. A.A. guns fore and aft, had multiple 2 pdr. A.A. mountings on either side abaft the funnel and had single or twin 20 mm. A.A. mountings on the fo'c'sle and poop.
[*I.W.M. and P. A. Vicary*

H M.S. Bonaventure belonged to the same sister ship group as the aircraft transports Athene and Engadine and was converted, while building, to a depot ship for 'X' craft. Heavy lift derricks were fitted to each mast for hoisting out the midget submarines stowed on deck. [I.W.M.

Displacement: 21,550 tons.
Dimensions: 546 (pp) 570 (oa) × 70 × 27¾ ft.
Machinery: 2-shaft geared Turbines S.H.P. 13,500 = 16 knots.
Armament: 4—4 in. A.A. (2 × 2), 32—2 pdr. A.A. (4 × 8), 19—20 mm. A.A. (19 × 1) guns. *Complement:* 1,302.

F.85	MONTCLARE	Clydebank	18.12.21	Ex-A.M.C.; scrapped Inverkeithing 3/2/58.
F.37	WOLFE (ex-Montcalm)	Clydebank	3. 7.20	Ex-A.M.C.; scrapped Faslane 11/52.

Notes:—Purchased outright 1942 and converted to depot ships for submarines. MONTCLARE Pacific fleet 1944-45. WOLFE served with 3rd Submarine flotilla until 1944 when she went to the Eastern fleet.

Displacement: 18,250 tons.
Dimensions: 548¼ (pp) 570 (oa) × 71¼ × 28¼ ft.
Machinery: 2-shaft Reciprocating (VQE), I.H.P. 15,000 = 17 knots.
Armament: 20—20 mm. A.A. (20 × 1) guns. *Complement:* 600.

F.39	RANPURA	Hawthorn Leslie	13. 9.24	Ex-A.M.C.; scrapped Italy 4/61.

Notes:—Purchased outright 1942 and converted to repair ship and served with the Pacific fleet.

Displacement: 16,479 tons *gross*.
Dimensions: 575¼ (pp) 600¾ (oa) × 67¾ × 41¼ d.ft.
Machinery: 3-shaft Reciprocating (4 cyl. VTE—wing shafts) and exhaust Turbine (centre shaft), I.H.P. 12,200 = 16 knots.
Armament: Nil.

F.87	WESTERNLAND (ex-Regina)	Harland & Wolff (Glasgow): Harland & Wolff (Belfast)	1918	Purchased 1942; scrapped Blyth 7/47.

Notes:—Purchased 1943 and converted to repair ship.

P.No.	Name	Gross tonnage Built	Requisitioned	Fate
F.74	ABERDONIAN	1648/9	1940	D.S. for C.F.; returned 27/3/45.
F.123	ANDELLE	1832/22	1944	Ex-M.D., M.S. for M/S; scrapped 4/45.
F.169	AMBITIOUS (ex-Algoma)	1849/13	1940	D.S. for M/S; returned 6/45.
	BORDE 2—12 pdr. A.A. (2 × 1) 2—2 pdr. A.A. (2 × 1) 2—M (2 × 1-HG)	2014/21	1942	Ex-M.D., M.S. for M/S; scrapped 7/45.
	CELEBRITY		1940	D.S. for M.D. (1941), for M/S (1942); paid off 7/45.

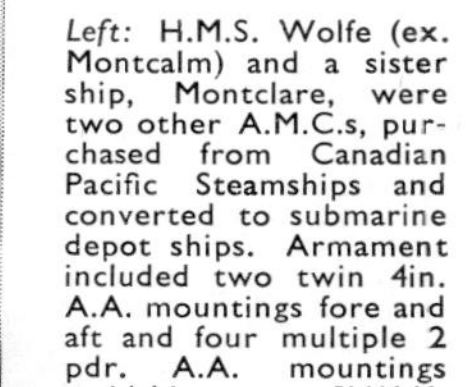

Left: H.M.S. Wolfe (ex. Montcalm) and a sister ship, Montclare, were two other A.M.C.s, purchased from Canadian Pacific Steamships and converted to submarine depot ships. Armament included two twin 4in. A.A. mountings fore and aft and four multiple 2 pdr. A.A. mountings amidships. [*I.W.M.*

Right: H.M.S. Ranpura also commenced service as an A.M.C. and was purchased from the P. & O. for conversion to a repair ship. [*A. & J. Pavia*

F.99	DEER SOUND (ex-Port Quebec-M.59)	5936/39	1944	Ex-Aux. M/L, R.S. for aircraft components, returned 12/47.
F.166	KELANTAN	1106/21	1943	R.S. for M/S; for disposal 2/47.
	PLYMOUTH TRADER	122/16	1941	Cable D.S.
	St. COLUMBA	827/12	1940	D.S. for boom defence; returned 1946.
4.43	St. TUDNO 1—12 pdr. A.A. 2—20 mm. A.A. (2 × 1)	2326/26	1939	Ex-A.B.V., D.S. for M/S; returned 1947.
F.138	VIENNA	4227/29	1941	D.S. for C.F.; returned 1945.
	WHANG PU	3024/20	1942	D.S. for submarines, R.A.N. (1944) as R.S.; returned 1946.
F.30	WUCHANG	3204/14	1941	D.S. for submarines, returned 4/46.

Notes:—ABERDONIAN served Fort William 1941 and Dartmouth 1942-45. AMBITIOUS was stationed at Scapa Flow. DEER SOUND was with the Pacific fleet. PLYMOUTH TRADER served Plymouth 1941-45. St. COLUMBA was stationed at Greenock throughout the war, St. TUDNO served similarly at The Nore. VIENNA served Mediterranean 1942-45. WUCHANG was locally employed with the Eastern fleet.

(c) War construction

Displacement: 10,000 tons.
Dimensions: 431 (pp) 447 (oa) × 56 × 26¾ ft.
Machinery: 1-shaft Reciprocating (VTE), I.H.P. 2,500 = 11 knots.
Armament: 12—20 mm. A.A. (12 × 1) guns.

P.No.	Name	Builder Hull: Engine	Launched	Remarks
F.187	BEAULY FIRTH	Redhead	24. 8.44	M.S. for hull repair; mercantile STANFIRTH (1948).
F.188	CUILLIN SOUND	Gray	2.11.44	M.S. for aircraft components; mercantile JAMES CLUNIES (1948).
F.185	DULLISK COVE	Short Bros.	4. 9.44	M.S. for hull repair; mercantile KAFALONIA (1948).
F.189	HOLM SOUND (ex-Empire Labuan)	Gray	5. 9.44	M.S. for aircraft components; mercantile AVISBAY (1948).
F.62	MORAY FIRTH	Redhead	10. 7.44	M.S. for aircraft components; mercantile LINORIA (1948).
F.186	MULLION COVE	Bartram	10. 7.44	M.S. for hull repair; mercantile MARGARET CLUNIES (1948)

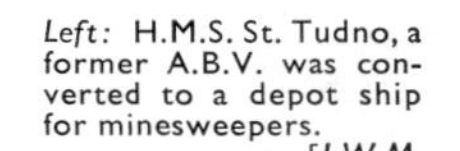

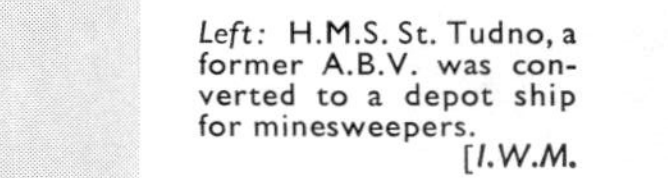

Left: H.M.S. St. Tudno, a former A.B.V. was converted to a depot ship for minesweepers.
[*I.W.M.*

Right: A maintenance ship for hull repairs H.M.S. Mullion Cove was adapted from a British war standard cargo hull.
[*I.W.M.*

F.190	SOLWAY FIRTH	Short Bros.	31.10.44	M.S. for hull repair; mercantile KONGSBORG (1948).

Notes:—CUILLIN SOUND and SOLWAY FIRTH (Home waters), the remainder to the Pacific.

Displacement: 8,580 tons.
Dimensions: 425 (pp) 441 (oa) × 57 × 20 ft.
Machinery: 1-shaft Reciprocating (VTE), I.H.P. 2,500 = 11 knots.
Armament: 16—20 mm. A.A. (16 × 1) guns.

F.02	BEACHY HEAD	Burrard	27. 9.44	M. & R.S. R. Neth. N. VULKAAN (1946-49), R.C.N. CAPE SCOTT (1954).
F.18	BERRY HEAD	Burrard	21.10.44	M. & R.S.
F.36	BUCHAN NESS	West Coast Sbdr.	10. 2.45	D.S. for landing craft; scrapped 9/59.
F.49	CAPE WRATH	West Coast Sbdr.	24. 8.45	M. & R. S.; mercantile MARINE FORTUNE (1951).
F.19	DODMAN POINT	Burrard	14. 4.45	D.S. for landing craft.
F.58	DUNCANSBY HEAD	Burrard	17.11.44	M. & R.S.
F.46	DUNGENESS	West Coast Sbdr.	15. 3.45	D.S. for landing craft; mercantile LEVUKA (1947).
F.29	FIFE NESS	Burrard	30. 4.45	D.S. for landing craft, R.A.F. ADASTRAL (1947).
F.88	FLAMBROUGH HEAD	Burrard	7.10.44	M. & R.S., R.C.N. CAPE BRETON (1954).
F.04	GIRDLE NESS	Burrard	29. 3.45	D.S. for landing craft.
F.25	HARTLAND POINT	Burrard	4.11.44	M. & R.S.
F.26	MULL OF GALLOWAY (ex-Kinnaird Head)	North Vancouver	26.10.44	M. & R.S.
F.86	MULL OF KINTYRE	North Vancouver	5. 4.45	M. & R.S.
F.96	MULL OF OA (ex-Trevose Head)	North Vancouver	11. 8.45	Completed as mercantile TURAN (1946).
F.67	ORFORD NESS	West Coast Sbdr.	12. 4.45	Completed as mercantile RABAUL (1946).
F.05	PORTLAND BILL	Burrard	18. 5.45	M. & R.S.; mercantile ZINNIA (1951).
F.34	RAME HEAD	North Vancouver	22.11.44	M. & R.S.
F.73	RATTRAY HEAD	North Vancouver	8. 6.45	Completed as mercantile IRAN (1946).
F.54	SELSEY BILL	Burrard	11. 7.45	Completed mercantile WAITEMATA (1946).
F.42	SPURN POINT	Burrard	8. 6.45	D.S for landing craft; mercantile LAKEMBA (1947).

H.M.S. Berry Head (above left) and H.M.S. Flambrough Head (below) were Canadian war standard cargo hulls completed as maintenance and repair ships and were armed with 16—20 m.m. A.A. (16 × 1) guns. Note vertically stowed position of derricks and landing craft carried on deck, [*Both I.W.M.*

F.84	TARBAT NESS	West Coast Sbdr.	29. 5.45	Completed as mercantile LAUTOKA (1946).

Notes:—FIFE NESS, GIRDLE NESS, DODMAN POINT, DUNGENESS and SPURN POINT remained in Home waters whilst the others served either in the East Indies or in the Pacific.

Displacement: 14,250 tons.
Dimensions: 416 (pp) 441½ (oa) × 57 × 27½ ft.
Machinery: 1-shaft Reciprocating (VTE), I.H.P. 2,500 = 11 knots.
Armament: 1—5 in., 10—40 mm. A.A. (5 × 2), 2—20 mm. A.A. (2 × 1) guns.
Complement: 489.

F.173	ASSISTANCE (ex-U.S.N. AR.17)	Bethlehem (Fairfield)	20. 6.44	Returned U.S.N. 15/8/46.
F.174	DILIGENCE (ex-U.S.N. AR.18)	Bethlehem (Fairfield)	8. 7.44	Returned U.S.N. 29/1/46.
F.175	HECLA (ii) (ex-U.S.N. AR.19)	Bethlehem (Fairfield)	31. 7.44	Retained as U.S.N. XANTHUS.
F.176	DUTIFUL (ex-Reliance, ex-U.S.N. AR.20)	Bethlehem (Fairfield)	13. 9.44	Retained as U.S.N. LAERTES
F.177	FAITHFUL (ex-U.S.N. AR.21)	Bethlehem (Fairfield)	10.10.44	Retained as U.S.N. DIONYSUS.

Notes:—Ex-U.S.N. repair ships made available under *Lend/Lease*.

BASE AND ACCOMMODATION SHIPS

BASE and accommodation ships were brought about by the shortage, or absence, of these facilities ashore and they were adapted from a variety of vessels from large liners to small yachts. Some, like those intended to accompany the repair ships, were wholly sea-worthy; others were only saved from the shipbreakers by the outbreak of war. As the war progressed many of the older, requisitioned vessels were conveniently relegated to this service.

P.No.	Name	Gross tonnage Built	Requisitioned	Fate
	ALICE	527/30	1943	Ex-armed yacht; returned 1946.
	AL RAWDAH (ex-Ville de Beyrouth, ex-Chenals)	3549/11	1943	Accomodation ship; returned 1945.
	ANKING	3472/25	1941	Base ship; lost 3/3/42
F.41	AORANGI	17490/24	1944	Accommodation ship returned 1946.
4.224	ATMAH	1746/98	1944	Ex-armed yacht; Sold 1946.
F.111	BALDUR (ex-St. Clair)	1637/37	1940	Base ship; convoy rescue ship (1943).
	BALMORAL	473/00	1944	Ex-aux. A.A. vessel returned 1945, scrapped 1946.
	BOURNEMOUTH BELLE	353/08	1944	Ex-aux. A.A. vessel returned 1945.

	DUCHESS OF ROTHESAY	338/94	1942	Ex-P.M.S.; returned 1946.
2	DUNLUCE CASTLE	8114/04	1939	Base ship; scrapped Inverkeithing 7/45.
	DURHAM CASTLE	8217/04	1939	Base ship; lost 26/1/40.
	EASTERN ISLES (ex-Western Isles, ex-Tynewald)	937/91	1940	Accommodation ship; returned 1945.
F.83	EDINBURGH CASTLE	13329/10	1939	Base ship; scuttled Freetown 5/11/45.
	EMPEROR OF INDIA	534/06	1943	Ex-aux. A.A. vessel; returned 1946.
	IOLAIRE	999/02	1941	Ex-armed yacht. PERSOPHONE (1945); returned 1946
	KEDAH	2499/27	1943	Ex-A.P.V.; returned 1946.
	KILLARNEY (ex-Classic, ex-Magic)	2081/93	19—	Accommodation ship; returned 1945.
	KILORAN	277/30	1941	Ex-armed yacht; returned 1945.
	KUDAT	1725/14	1941	Ex-A.P.V., base ship lost 30/12/41.
	LADY BLANCHE	405/07	1942	Ex-armed yacht; returned 11/45.
4.373	LAGUNA BELLE	617/96	1943	Ex-aux. A.A. vessel; returned 1943.
4.402	LORNA DOONE	410/91	1944	Ex-aux. A.A. vessel; returned 1946.
	MONA'S ISLE (ex-Onward)	1644/05	1943	Ex-aux. A.A. vessel; returned 1943.
	ORIOLE	441/10	1944	Ex-P.M.S.; returned 1945.
	PANGKOR	1250/29	1943	Ex-A.M.S.; returned 1946.
.385	PLINLIMMON	438/95	1944	Ex-aux. A.A. vessel; constructive total loss 8/46, scrapped Grays 11/46.
	St. MAGNUS	1312/24	1939	Accommodation ship for examination service; returned 1941.
	St. SUNNIVA	1368/32	1939	Accommodation ship for examination service; convoy rescue ship (1942), lost 22/1/43.
	SONA	555/22	1940	Ex-armed yacht; lost 4/1/42.
	SOUTHERN PRINCE	11447/29	1945	Ex-aux. M/L; returned 1946.
	STAR OF INDIA	735/88	1944	Ex-armed yacht; returned 1946.

H.M.S. Assistance was a *Lend/Lease* repair ship adapted from a **Liberty** type mercantile hull. [I.W.M.

The old Union-Castle liner Edinburgh Castle was salved from the shipbreakers to serve as an accommo dation ship. [I.W.M

An early war photograph of the netlayer H.M.S. Guardian—note external DG coil around the hul [I.W.M

	SUNBEAM II	659/29	1944	Ex-armed yacht; returned 11/45.
4.83	TIERCEL	489/13	1941	Ex-armed yacht; returned 1946.
	TROUBADOR	1245/24	1942	Ex-armed yacht; sold 1947.
	WESTWARD HO!	438/94	1944	Ex-aux. A.A. vessel; returned 3/46, scrapped Newport 1/8/46.
	ZAZA	455/05	1941	Ex-armed yacht; sold 1948.
	ZITA	283/94	1941	Ex-armed yacht, mooring vessel (1945); sold 1946.

AMENITIES SHIPS

THESE vessels were specially converted for Pacific operations conducted from forward bases quite devoid of normal shore facilitities and far removed from main bases. They provided recreational facilities far in excess of that normally borne shipboard, even by depot ships, and were for use by the fleet generally and not only by flotilla craft.

	AGAMEMNON	7829/29	1944	Ex. Aux. M/L; returned 1946.
	MENESTHEUS	7493/29	1944	Ex. Aux. M/L; returned 1946.

Notes:—These vessels were operated under the blue ensign of the R.F.A.

HARBOUR DEFENCE

ALL naval and commercial harbours, where geographical conditions permitted, were protected by strong booms once hostilities commenced. Initially, until the necessary craft and material had been assembled, a small number of blockships were used but such measures were necessarily limited.

The Royal Navy finished the First World War with a wealth of experience in this type of work but with only a handful of mooring vessels, once requisitioned craft had been returned to commercial ownership. The residue of vessels also included sixty dumb barrage vessels, specially built for the Dover barrage, but no such ambitious scheme as this was attempted in the Second World War.

In the years " between the wars " the Royal Navy prepared a sound nucleus for the boom defence organisation. As boom vessels of all categories were relatively cheap they were included, in small numbers, in the annual estimates where their low cost did not attract the attention focussed on the larger warships.

For laying, tending and operating booms both *mooring* and *gate vessels* were required; the former to lay the buoys from which the boom was suspended and secured and the latter to work that part of the boom made as a gate to allow vessels to enter or leave the protected area. Many of the dumb barrage vessels were adapted for the latter purpose which created the illusion that non-propelled craft were suitable for gate operations and resulted in a further class of dumb gate vessels later on. But the inability of both types to make ocean voyages resulted in some commercial trawlers being purchased and converted to *boom defence vessels*, to perform both mooring and gate duties, whilst a naval-designed vessel capable of world-wide employment was put in hand and evaluated. This resulted in the ubiquitous "**Bar**" class which served everywhere and could perform any of the duties connected with boom defence. As buoy-laying was not solely confined to boom defence, a further class of mooring vessels were built during the war but the difference between them and the boom defence vessels was more one of definition and employment than of construction. Generally, the boom defence vessels wore the white ensign and the mooring vessels the blue ensign of the Royal Fleet Auxiliaries.

In addition to the seven trawlers purchased before the outbreak of war some one hundred and thirty were hired, or purchased, during the war and will be dealt with in Part 6.

NETLAYERS AND BOOM CARRIERS

THE need to rapidly render safe an exposed anchorage, or an undefended harbour, resulted in the construction of two netlayers designed to carry, lay and retrieve a net defence system (see *Note 1*). They proved most useful vessels whose utility was further enhanced by being fitted to work with the fleet target and photographic service.

The outbreak of war resulted in six, small merchant vessels being requisitioned as *auxiliary netlayers* and eight larger ones as *boom carriers*. The latter carried a most complete outfit of booms, buoys, etc. which the small boom craft laid, operated and maintained.

Displacement: 2,860 tons.
Dimensions: 310 (pp) 338 (oa) × 53 × 11¼ ft.
Machinery: 2-shaft geared Turbines, S.H.P. 6,500 = 18 knots
Armament: 2—4 in. A.A. (2 × 1) guns.
Complement: 181.

P.No.	Name	Builder Hull: Engine	Launched	Fate
T.89	GUARDIAN	Chatham: Wallsend	1. 9.32	Scrapped Troon 12/62.

Displacement: 2,900 tons.
Dimensions: 310 (pp) 338 (oa) × 50 × 11½ ft.
Machinery: 2-shaft geared Turbines, S.H.P. 9,000 = 20 knots.
Armament: 1—4 in. A.A., 4—.5 in. A.A. (1 × 4) guns.
Complement: 190.

P.No.	Name	Builder Hull: Engine	Launched	Fate
T.98	PROTECTOR	Yarrow	20. 8.36	

Notes:—GUARDIAN had the two single 4 in. A.A. replaced by a twin mounting aft only and quadruple .5 in. A.A. added forward. PROTECTOR had the single 4 in. A.A. mounting replaced by twin one. The quadruple .5 in. A.A. was subsequently removed from both and up to ten 20 mm. A.A (4 × 2 & 2 × 1) added. GUARDIAN was in Home waters up to 1941 and then went to the East Indies PROTECTOR was in the South Atlantic 1939, Home waters 1940, Mediterranean 1940-41 and spent the rest of the war at Bombay, under repair.

Note 1: Generally, a light net defence system were referred to as "nets" and a heavy net system of a more permanent nature, as "booms".

AUXILIARY NETLAYERS

P.No.	Name	Gross tonnage/ year built	Requi- sitioned	Fate
T.143	ATALANTA	486/06	1940	Returned 4/45.
T.197	BRITTANY	1445/33	1940	Returned 1945.
	KYLEMORE	319/97	1940	Ex-P.M.S.; lost 21/8/40
T.198	MINSTER	707/24	1940	Lost 8/6/44.
T.245	RINGWOOD	682/24	1940	Returned 1945.
	TONBRIDGE	683/24	1940	Lost 22/8/41.

Notes:—All served in Home waters except BRITTANY in Eastern fleet 1942 and Mediterranean 1943-44.

BOOM CARRIERS

P.No.	Name	Gross tonnage/ year built	Requi- sitioned	Fate
	ASTRONOMER	8401/17	1940	Lost 2/6/40.
Z.168	DEVON CITY	4928/33	1940	Returned 2/46.
Z.167	ETHIOPIAN	5424/36	1940	Returned 1/46.
Z.208	FERNMOOR	4972/36	1940	Returned 1946.
	FOSSBECK	4918/30	1942	Ex-aircraft transport; returned 1/46.
Z.199	KIRRIEMOOR	4990/35	1940	Returned 1946.
Z.243	LAOMEDON	6490/12	1940	Returned 1945.
Z.197	LEONIAN	5420/36	1940	Returned 1946.
	2—12 pdr. A.A. (2 × 1) 6—20 mm. A.A. (6 × 1)			

MOORING AND GATE VESSELS

THESE two types utilised craft available after the First World War. Whereas the mooring vessels had to be self-propelled the gate vessels could perform their duties moored and needed power only for the boom winch. The availability of the dumb barrage vessels, suitable for conversion to gate vessels, rather forced this decision on them and was only briefly perpetuated.

As both types were only capable of restricted employment they were dropped in favour of an all-purpose *boom defence vessel* capable of proceeding overseas. A further class of mooring vessels were built during the war but of a size that permitted a wide range of employment plus a useful heavy lift capability.

GATE VESSELS

Displacement: 270 tons.
Dimensions: 96 except * 99 (oa) × 25 × 8½ ft.
Machinery: Dumb.
Armament: 1—3 in. A.A. gun.

P.No.	Name	Builder	Launched	Fate
	BV.1	Workman Clark	12.11.17	

	BV.2	Workman Clark	12.11.17	
Z.24	SANDGATE (ex-BV.4)	Workman Clark	28.11.17	Lost 13/2/47.
Z.06	PARKGATE (ex-BV.5)	Workman Clark	12.11.17	BV.5 (1940); scrapped 1945.
Z.07	POLEGATE (ex-BV.7)	Workman Clark	12.11.17	BV.7 (1940); scrapped 1945.
Z.25	SOUTHGATE (ex-BV.8)	Workman Clark	12.11.17	Scrapped 1945.
	BV.10	Workman Clark	28.11.17	Sold 1945.
Z.88	WESTGATE (ex-BV.17)	Robertson	14. 3.18	Scrapped 1946.
	BV.18*	Robertson	12. 4.18	
Z.11	REIGATE (ex-BD.30)	Warren	21. 9.18	Sold 1958.
	BV.41	Robertson	6. 9.18	
	BV.42	Robertson	22.10.18	Lost 22/12/43.
Z.12	ROGATE (ex-BD.46)	Camper & Nicholson	1.10.18	Scrapped 1946.

Notes:—Survivors of a class of sixty dumb barrage vessels built during the war for the Dover barrage and laid up from 1919-33. BV. 1, 2, 5, & 10 were gate vessels at Sheerness 1940/45 and all except BV. 5 were converted to moored A.A. vessels in 1944. BV. 18 was gate vessel at Sheerness 1940/41 and then joined BV. 41 & 42 at Inchkeith.

Displacement: 290 tons except * 345 tons.
Dimensions: 98½ (oa) × 26 except * 25 × 8 except * 9 ft.
Machinery: Dumb.
Armament: 1—3 in. A.A. gun.

Z.68	ALDGATE	Hong Kong & Whampoa	5. 4.34	Lost 19/12/41.
Z.66	BISHOPSGATE	Robb	15.11.32	Scrapped Charlestown 1959.
Z.17	DOWGATE	Hong Kong & Whampoa	24. 9.35	Lost /2/42.
Z.45	LUDGATE	Hong Kong & Whampoa	30. 9.35	Lost /2/42.
Z.71	MOORGATE*	Bow McLachlan	28. 7.31	Sold 1958.
Z.56	WATERGATE	Hong Kong & Whampoa	5. 4.34	Lost 19/12/41.

Notes:—Two gate vessels captured by the Japanese were used at Changi until 5/43 and were probably DOWGATE and LUDGATE.

The following were requisitioned as gate vessels:—

CLAYMORE (R.N.Z.N.); Z.270 GUNBAR (R.A.N.); Z.221 KARA KARA (R.A.N.); Z.96 KINCHELA (R.A.N.); KOOMPARTOO (R.A.N.); KURAMIA (R.A.N.); Z.253 LANAKIA (R.A.N.); WHAKARIRE (R.N.Z.N.).

MOORING VESSELS

P. No.	Name	Displacement/ built	Requi- sitioned	Fate
	MESSENGER	100/16	1916	Sold 1950.
	ANCHORITE (ex-Progress)	750/16	1916	HERMIT (1944); scrapped Rosyth 2/48.
	BUFFALO	750/16	1916	Lost 4/4/41.
	STEADY	750/16	1916	Lost 17/7/40.
	VOLENS (ex-Volunteer)	750/16	1916	Sold 1947.

Displacement: 767 tons.
Dimensions: 138 (pp) 148 (oa) × 29 × 10½ ft.
Machinery: 1-shaft Reciprocating, (VTE), I.H.P. 600 = 9 knots.
Armament: 1—12 pdr. A.A. gun.

P.No.	Name	Builder Hull: Engine	Launched	Fate
	MOOR	Bow McLachlan	1919	Lost 8/4/42.
	MOORDALE	Bow McLachlan	15. 8.19	Sold 1961.
	MOORFOWL	Bow McLachlan	1919	
	MOORHILL	Bow McLachlan	1919	For disposal.
	MOORLAKE	Bow McLachlan	24.12.19	Sold 1946.
	MOORSTONE	Bow McLachlan	24.12.19	Sold 1949.

Displacement: 720 tons.
Dimensions: 135 (pp) 145 (oa) × 31 × 10 ft.
Machinery: 1-shaft Reciprocating (VTE), I.H.P. 500 = 10 knots.
Armament: 2—20 mm. A.A. (2 × 1) guns.

P.No.	Name	Builder	Launched	Fate
	MOORLAND	Simons	22.11.38	

Displacement: 1,000 tons.
Dimensions: 149 (pp) 159 (oa) × 34 × 11 ft.
Machinery: 1-shaft Reciprocating (VTE), I.H.P. 500 = 9 knots.
Armament: 1—12 pdr. A.A., 2—20 mm. A.A. (2 × 1) guns.

P.No.	Name	Builder	Launched	Fate
	MOORBERRY	Taikoo		Lost incomplete /12/41.
	MOORBURN	Goole Sbdg.	16. 4.42	For disposal.
4.396	MOORCOCK	Goole Sbdg.	27. 6.42	For disposal.
	MOORESS	Goole Sbdg.	16. 9.43	For disposal.
	MOORFIELD		1941	For disposal.
	MOORFIRE	Devonport	1941	Scrapped 4/63.
4.395	MOORFLY	Goole Sbdg.	14. 7.42	

	Name	Builder	Launched	Fate
	MOORGRASS	Goole Sbdg.	25. 7.42	For disposal.
	MOORGRIEVE	Goole Sbdg.	4. 9.44	
	MOORHEN	Goole Sbdg.	30. 9.43	
	MOOR MYRTLE	Goole Sbdg.	15. 3.45	For disposal.
	MOORPOUT	Chatham	1944	
	MOORSIDE	Goole Sbdg.	25. 8.45	Scrapped 4/63.
	MOORSMAN	Chatham	1944	
	MOORWIND	Singapore Hbr. Board		Lost incomplete ../2/42.

BOOM DEFENCE VESSELS

BOOM defence vessels were the final outcome of experience with boom operating craft. They were built sufficiently large to proceed overseas and yet kept small enough to retain the degree of manoeuvrability that their work demanded. They were coal-fired and reciprocating-engined: machinery with which trawler reserve personnel, who would man them in an emergency, were well acquainted.

The prototype vessel DUNNET was followed by the **Bar** and **Net**, classes but war construction again reverted to the former.

Prototype

Displacement: 385 tons.
Dimensions: 125 (pp) 134½ (oa) × 26½ × 9 ft.
Machinery: 1-shaft Reciprocating (VTE), I.H.P. 350 = 10 knots.
Armament: 1—3 in. A.A. gun. *Complement:* 15.

P.No.	Name	Builder	Launched	Fate
Z.14	DUNNET	Lytham Sbdg. & Eng.	5. 8.36	Sold 3/46.

Bar class

Displacement: 730 tons.
Dimensions: 150 (pp) 173¾ (oa) × 32¼ × 9½ ft.
Machinery: 1-shaft Reciprocating (VTE), I.H.P. 850 = 11¾ knots.
Armament: 1—3 in. A.A. gun. *Complement:* 32.

P.No.	Name	Builder	Launched	Fate
Z.01	BARBAIN	Blyth: N.E. Marine	8. 1.40	
Z.18	BARBARIAN	Blyth: N.E. Marine	21.10.37	Turkish AG.1 (1946).
Z.276	BARBASTEL	Philip: Holmes	26. 7.45	For disposal.
Z.286	BARBECUE	Ardrossan: Lobnitz	19.12.44	
Z.257	BARBERRY	Ferguson	11. 2.43	For disposal.

Left:
M.V.Mooress,
mooring vessel.

The mooring vessel H.M.S. Moorsman had two sheaves set into the bows, two overhanging sheaves on the horns with a round-down fairlead between them and a short, heavy lift derrick rigged from a tripod mast. Two single 20 mm. A.A. guns were positioned over the bridge and a 12 pdr. A.A. gun aft. [*I.W.M.*

Z.	BARBETTE (i)	Blyth: N.E. Marine	15.12.37	Turkish (1941). AG.2 (1946).
Z.242	BARBETTE (ii)	Simons	18. 6.43	For disposal.
Z. 43	BARBICAN	Blyth: N.E. Marine	14. 3.38	
Z.169	BARBOUR	Blyth: Swan Hunter	9. 4.41	Scrapped Bo'ness 5/42.
Z.170	BARBOURNE	Simons	4. 5.42	For disposal.
Z.173	BARBRAKE	Simons	29. 6.42	S.A.N. FLEUR (1951).
Z.222	BARBRIDGE	Lobnitz	8. 8.41	For disposal.
Z. 03	BARBROOK	Blyth: Whites M.E.	28. 5.38	For disposal.
Z.287	BARCAROLE	Ardrossan: Lobnitz	14. 3.45	
Z. 09	BARCASTLE	Blyth: Whites M.E.	23. 7.38	For disposal.
Z. 70	BARCLIFF (ex-Barwick)	Lobnitz	10. 5.40	For disposal.
Z.174	BARCLOSE	Blyth: Swan Hunter	9. 7.41	Scrapped Dalmuir 8/8/62.
Z.177	BARCOCK	Blyth: Swan Hunter	3. 9.41	R.B.N. (1946–49); for disposal.
Z. 16	BARCOMBE	Goole: Amos & Smith	28. 7.38	Stranded 13/1/58; for disposal.
Z.214	BARCONIA	Hill		Cancelled.
Z. 52	BARCOTE	Blyth: N.E. Marine	8. 2.40	For disposal.
Z. 22	BARCROFT	Goole: Amos & Smith	24. 9.38	For disposal.
Z.185	BARCROSS	Blyth: Swan Hunter	12.10.41	S.A.N. SOMERSET (1951).
Z.195	BARDELL	Blyth: Swan Hunter	12. 1.42	For disposal.
Z.171	BARDOLF	Blyth: Swan Hunter	14. 4.42	For disposal.
Z. 31	BARFAIR	Lewis	31. 5.38	Turkish AG.3 (1946).
Z. 42	BARFIELD	Lewis	28. 7.38	
Z.184	BARFLAKE	Philip: Plenty	18. 4.42	Lost 22/11/43.
Z.182	BARFOAM	Simons	8. 9.41	
Z.194	BARFOIL	Philip: Plenty	18. 7.42	
Z.202	BARFOOT	Lewis	25. 9.42	
Z.209	BARFORD	Simons	21.10.41	For disposal.
Z.200	BARFOSS	Simons	17. 2.42	
Z.190	BARFOUNT	Simons	5. 1.42	For disposal.
Z.205	BARGLOW	Lewis	10.11.42	
Z.225	BARHILL	Ferguson	26.11.42	
Z.211	BARHOLM	Ardrossan: Whites M.E.	31.12.42	
Z. 17	BARILLA	Lewis	7. 1.43	Scrapped 7/58.
Z.271	BARITONE	Philip: Holmes	3. 3.45	For disposal.

bove: The boom defence vessel H.M.S. Barlow, note rounded and unobstructed stern for working edge anchors and boom wires. [*I.W.M.*

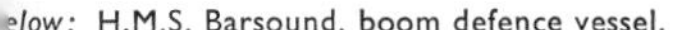

elow: H.M.S. Barsound, boom defence vessel.

Z.181	BARKING	Lobnitz	25. 9.41	
Z.277	BARKIS	Ferguson	29. 3.45	For disposal.
Z. 39	BARLAKE	Blyth: N.E. Marine	16. 9.40	For disposal.
Z. 48	BARLANE	Lobnitz	27. 6.38	Sold 1958.
Z.256	BARLEYCORN	Lewis	6. 3.43	
Z. 57	BARLIGHT	Lobnitz	10. 9.38	Lost 19/12/41, salved and I.J.N. No. 101 (1942); lost 15/6/44; salved and Chinese.
Z. 60	BARLOW	Simons	26. 8.38	For disposal.
Z. 67	BARMILL	Blyth: N.E. Marine	16.10.40	For disposal.
Z.232	BARMOND	Simons	24.12.42	
Z. 77	BARMOUTH	Simons	11.10.38	
Z.237	BARNABY	Simons	8. 3.43	
Z.241	BARNARD	Lewis	17. 8.42	
Z. 92	BARNDALE	Lobnitz	30.11.39	
Z.245	BARNEATH	Lewis	27. 8.42	For disposal.
Z. 84	BARNEHURST	Blyth: N.E. Marine	21.10.39	R.Neth.N. (194?–55).
Z.250	BARNESS			Cancelled 2/41.
Z. 37	BARNSTONE	Blyth: N.E. Marine	25.11.39	
Z. 46	BARNWELL	Lobnitz	13. 2.40	For disposal.
Z.262	BARON	Philip: Plenty	11. 4.44	Mercantile (name unchanged 1946–58), R.Cey.N. (1959).
Z. 87	BARONIA	Hill: Plenty	28. 4.41	Sold 1959.
Z. 94	BAROVA	Hill: Plenty	5. 7.41	
Z. 54	BARRAGE	Hall Russell	2.12.37	
Z. 65	BARRANCA	Hall Russell	18. 1.38	For disposal.
Z. 40	BARRHEAD	Simons	17.10.40	
Z. 83	BARRICADE (ex-Ebgate)	Hill: Plenty	7. 2.38	Scrapped Bo'ness 5/52.
Z. 98	BARRIER (ex-Bargate)	Hill: Plenty	17. 5.38	For disposal.
Z. 59	BARRINGTON	Simons	15.11.40	
Z. 73	BARRYMORE	Simons	13. 2.41	For disposal.
Z. 75	BARSING	Simons	31. 3.41	For disposal.
Z. 89	BARSOUND	Simons	25. 5.41	For disposal.
Z.224	BARSPEAR	Ferguson	25. 3.43	
Z. 32	BARSTOKE	Simons	9. 7.41	Mercantile (name unchanged 1946–60), sold 8/60.
Z. 95	BARTHORPE	Lobnitz	22. 3.40	For disposal.
Z.261	BARTIZAN	Ardrossan: Lobnitz	20. 5.43	
Z. 58	BARWIND	Ferguson	22. 9.42	
Z. 80	KANGAROO (R.A.N.)	Cockatoo	4. 5.40	
Z.216	KARANGI (R.A.N.)	Cockatoo	16. 8.41	

Z. 69	KOALA (R.A.N.)	Cockatoo	4.11.39	

Net class

Displacement: 530 tons.
Dimensions: 135 (pp) 159¾ (oa) × 30½ × 9 ft.
Machinery: 1-shaft Reciprocating (VTE), I.H.P. 850 = 11½ knots.
Armament: 1—3 in. A.A. gun.
Complement: 32.

Z.05	BAYONET (ex-Barnehurst)	Blyth: N.E. Marine	8.11.38	Lost 21/12/39.
Z.90	BOWNET	Blyth: N.E. Marine	19. 1.39	Sold 1958.
Z.33	BURGONET	Blyth: N.E. Marine	14. 3.39	Sold 1958.
Z.82	DRAGONET	Blyth: N.E. Marine	2. 6.39	Mercantile FOUNDATION VENTURE (1961).
Z.19	FALCONET (ex-Barnham)	Blyth: N.E. Marine	5.12.38	Sold 1958.
Z.27	MAGNET (ex-Barnsley)	Smiths Dock	22.11.38	Sold 1958.
Z.41	MARTINET (ex-Barnstone)	Smiths Dock	8.12.38	Sold 1958.
Z.50	PLANET (ex-Barnwell)	Lobnitz	26.12.38	Sold 1958.
Z.63	PLANTAGANET (ex-Barwood)	Lobnitz	23. 2.39	Mercantile AMALTHÉE (1959).
Z.10	SIGNET	Blyth: Whites M.E.	3. 5.39	Sold 1958.
Z.47	SONNET	Blyth: Whites M.E.	12. 7.39	Scrapped Holland 22/4/59.
Z.15	KOOKABURRA (R.A.N.)	Cockatoo	29.10.38	

Com Class

Z.273	COMPACT	Curtis		Cancelled 1945.
Z.272	COMPANION	Doig		Cancelled 2/45.
Z.274	COMPATRIOT	Doig		Cancelled 2/45.
Z.280	COMPEER	Doig		Cancelled 10/44.
Z.281	COMPETENT	Doig		Cancelled 10/44.
Z.275	COMPETITOR	Curtis		Cancelled 1945.
Z.278	COMPLETE	Wivenhoe		Cancelled 1945.
Z.279	COMPLEX	Wivenhoe		Cancelled 10/44.
Z.282	COMPLIMENT	Curtis		Cancelled 10/44.
Z.283	COMPOSURE	Curtis		Cancelled 10/44.

Notes:—Composite construction.

Displacement: 1,058 tons.
Dimensions: 172 (pp) 194½ (oa) × 34½ × 11 ft.
Machinery: 1-shaft Diesel-Electric motors, B.H.P. 1,200 = 14 knots.
Armament: 1—3 in. A.A., 2—20 mm., A.A. (2 × 1) guns.
Complement: 44.

Z.266	PRECEPT (ex-U.S.N. AN.73 ex-YN. 79)	Barbour Boat Works	11. 4.44	Returned U.S.N. 4/1/46.
Z.285	PRECISE (ex-U.S.N. Boxelder AN.74 ex-YN. 80)	,,	20. 7.44	Returned U.S.N. 14/12/45.
Z.263	PREFECT (ex-U.S.N. AN.75 ex-YN. 88)	American Car & Fdry.: Busch Sulzer	8. 3.44	Returned U.S.N. 28/12/45.
Z.284	PRETEXT (ex-Protect, ex-U.S.N. Satinwood AN.76, ex-YN. 89)	,,	23. 5.44	Mercantile JOHN BISCOE (1947), ENDEAVOUR (1956).
Z.265	PREVENTER (ex-U.S.N. Seagrape AN.77 ex-YN. 90)	,,	9. 8.44	Returned U.S.N. 10/1/46.

Notes:—Wooden hull. Ex-U.S.N. netlayers made available under *Lend/Lease*. Twenty vessels of this type (YN.77-96) were to have been transferred but the remaining fifteen were retained by U.S.N

In 1933 a naval "**Castle**" class and two purchased trawlers were converted to boom defence vessels and were supplemented by a further four trawlers purchased in 1939. They were considerably augmented from the large number of trawlers requisitioned after the outbreak—listed in Part 6 (Trawlers, whalers and drifters) —plus the following mercantile conversion:—

P.No.	Name	Gross tonnage/ Built	Requi-sitioned	Fate
Z.83	TAMBAR (R.A.N.)	456/12	1943	Ex-A.M.S.; returned 1945.

TUGS AND SALVAGE VESSELS

THE naval built tugs broadly fell into two types divided, not by size, but by employment. The *harbour tugs* were only equipped for restricted duties in ports and rivers while the *fleet tugs* were fitted for ocean service and were principally used for target towing pre-war.

War brought alternative employment for the fleet tugs in towing back to port, vessels damaged by enemy action which would have otherwise foundered and they were supplemented by the already existing commercial deep-sea towing organisations, brought under naval control and their vessels requisitioned.

The vital need to conserve all possible mercantile tonnage resulted in a war programme of sea-going rescue tugs built by the leading commercial tug builders, to whom their design was largely entrusted. They were classed as *rescue tugs* as their principal employment now lay in the towing of damaged merchantmen and to continue to call them fleet tugs seemed hardly appropriate.

Concurrently, a much smaller war programme of harbour tugs was undertaken but only on a replacement scale.

The salvage vessels were complementary to the rescue tugs. While the latter aided damaged, but floating, vessels to safety, the former were called in once they were sunk: providing it was in a depth of water not outside the normal limits of salvage. As neither the commercial nor naval salvage organisations amounted to a great deal before the outbreak of hostilities, they both had to be built up from scratch for war purposes and a programme of *ocean* and *coastal salvage vessels* was put in hand—the ocean vessels of a size sufficient to proceed independently abroad.

As a general rule the fleet and rescue tugs and the ocean salvage vessels wore the white ensign and the harbour tugs and coastal salvage vessels the blue ensign of the R.F.A.

TUGS

(a) **Paddle tugs for dockyard service**

Displacement: 690 tons except *first five* 700 tons.
Dimensions: 144 (pp) 150¾ (oa) × 27¼ × 11 ft.
Machinery: Paddle Reciprocating (DC), I.H.P. 1,250 = 12 knots.

P.No.	Name	Builder	Launched	Fate
W.24	ADVICE	London & Glasgow	2.10.99	Scrapped Cork 10/50.
W.19	CRACKER	London & Glasgow	7.12.99	Scrapped Grays 7/56.
W.71	ENERGETIC	Clydebank	22. 3.02	Scrapped Lower Rainham 6/53.
W.32	INDUSTRIOUS	Barclay Curle	19. 6.02	Scrapped Holland 12/59.
W.61	VOLATILE (ex-Volcano)	Barclay Curle	21. 9.99	Scrapped Grays 4/57.
W.54	ANCIENT (ex-Veteran)	Thornycroft	30. 8.15	Scrapped Italy 1954.
W.38	CAMEL	Bow McLachlan	19.10.14	Scrapped 1962.
W.15	FIRM	Chatham	23. 8.10	Scrapped Belgium 9/60.
W.26	GRAPPLER	Chatham	4. 9.08	Scrapped Dover 5/57.
W.86	HELLESPONT	Earle's Sbdg.	10. 5.10	Lost /4/42.
W.80	RAMBLER	Clydebank	21.12.08	Scrapped 1955.
W.28	ROBUST	Bow McLachlan	24. 9.07	Scrapped 1955.
W.48	SANDBOY (ex-Strenuous)	Thornycroft	7.12.12	Expended 6/47.
W.53	SPRITE	Thornycroft	23. 8.15	Scrapped Holland 3/60.
W.12	SWARTHY (ex-Sturdy)	Thornycroft	12.11.12	Scrapped Passage West 3/61.

Displacement: 1,023 tons.
Dimensions: 170 (pp) 178 (oa) × 36 × 12 ft.
Machinery: Paddle Reciprocating (DC), I.H.P. 2,000 = 13 knots.

W.42	PERT	Thornycroft	5. 4.16	Scrapped 1962.

(b) Screw tugs for dockyard service

Displacement: 615 tons.
Dimensions: 145 (pp) 153 (oa) × 29 × 12 ft.
Machinery: 2-shaft Reciprocating (VTE), I.H.P. 1,400 = 11 knots.

W.77	ALLIANCE	Chatham	23. 8.10	Lost 19/12/41.
W.41	ATLAS	Chatham	2. 9.09	Sold 1958.
W.03	PILOT	Chatham	2. 9.09	Scrapped Holland 3/60.
W.21	RECOVERY (ex-Rollicker, ex-Rover)	Chatham	12.10.08	Scrapped Passage West 9/57.

Displacement: 1,400 tons.
Dimensions: 175 (pp) 182 (oa) × 34 × 14 ft.
Machinery: 2-shaft Reciprocating (VTE), I.H.P. 2,400 = 14 knots.

W.85	RESOLVE	Ayrshire Co.	30. 7.18	Sold 1950.
W.92	RESPOND	Ayrshire Co.	21.11.18	Scrapped Italy 1956.
W.84	RETORT	Day, Summers	1918	Sold 1958.
W.00	ROLLICKER	Ferguson	16. 1.19	Scrapped Dunston 5/52.
W.91	ROYSTERER	Thornycroft	4. 2.19	Sold 1950.

Notes:—Foc's'le not fitted on RESOLVE and RETORT.

Displacement: 425 tons.
Dimensions: 109 (pp) 116$\frac{3}{4}$ (oa) × 28$\frac{1}{2}$ × 9 ft.
Machinery: 1-shaft Reciprocating (VTE), I.H.P. 1,100 = 11 knots.

W.08	PERSEVERANCE (ex-mercantile Imara)	Fleming & Ferguson	5. 2.31	

Notes:—Purchased 1932.

Displacement: 395 tons.
Dimensions: 105 (pp) 116$\frac{3}{4}$ (oa) × 26$\frac{1}{2}$ × 13d. ft.
Machinery: 2-shaft Reciprocating (VTE), I.H.P. 1,000 = 12 knots.

W.51	ALLIGATOR	Dunston (Hessle)	16.10.40	Lost 3/45.
W.88	CROCODILE	Dunston (Hessle)	2.12.40	Wrecked /5/46; salved & scrapped 1/47

Paddle tugs used in dockyard service—

Top: Cracker

Centre: Firm

Below: The screw tug Perseverance

Displacement: 365 tons.
Dimensions: 90 (pp) 97 (oa) × 28 × 14d. ft.
Machinery: 1-shaft Reciprocating (VTE), I.H.P. 800 = 10 knots.

W.100	DRIVER	Hall	9.10.42	
W.101	ENERGY	Hall	26.10.42	
W. 31	FLAMER	Hall	23. 5.40	
W. 79	HANDMAID (ex-Fresco)	Hall	20. 6.40	
W. 60	IMPETUS	Hall	25. 1.40	

Displacement: 300 tons.
Dimensions: 120 (pp) 128 (oa) × 24½ × 6 ft.
Machinery: 1-shaft Reciprocating (VTE), I.H.P. 450 = 9½ knots.

W. 76	GRINDER	Hong Kong	5. 5.43	Captured incomplete and became I.J.N. NAGASHIMA (1942)
W.102	LANTAKA	Singapore		Lost incomplete 3/42.
	SKILFUL	Taikoo		Lost incomplete 12/41.
W.22	WAVE	Taikoo	. .39	WAVELET (1945).

Notes:—WAVE was a combined tug/water tank.

Displacement: 300 tons.
Dimensions: 95 (pp) 102¼ (oa) × 24 × 10 ft.
Machinery: 1-shaft Diesel-Electric motors, S.H.P. 1,000 = 12 knots.
Armament: 2-MG. (2 × 1).

	BUSY (ex-U.S.N. BYT.1)	Gulfport	3.11.41	Returned U.S.N. 1/47.
	CONFIDENT (ex-U.S.N. BYT.2)	,,	. .42	Returned U.S.N. 1946.
	HELPFUL (ex-U.S.N. BYT. 3)	,,	. .42	Retained as U.S.N. EDENSHAW (YT. 459).
	INTENT (ex-U.S.N. BYT. 4)	,,	. .42	Retained as U.S.N. DEKANISORA (YT. 252).
	RESOLUTE (ex-U.S.N. BYT. 5)	,,	. .42	Retained as U.S.N. EVEA (YT. 458).

Notes:—U.S.N. harbour tugs made available under *Lend/Lease* and employed as rescue tugs in t[he] West Indies and later in the Eastern fleet and the Mediterranean.

(c) **Fleet tugs**

Saint class

Displacement: 860 tons.
Dimensions: 135½ (pp) 143 (oa) × 29 × 12 ft.

Machinery: 1-shaft Reciprocating (VTE), I.H.P. 1,250 = 12 knots.
Armament: 1—12 pdr. A.A. gun.
Complement: 30.

W.02	St. ABBS	Ferguson	17.12.18	Lost 1/6/40.
W.46	St. BLAZEY	Cran & Somerville	16. 1.19	Expended 1947.
W.56	St. BREOCK (ex-St. James)	Hong Kong & Whampoa	. .19	Lost 14/2/42.
W.06	St. CLEARS	Livingstone & Cooper	. .19	Sold 1950.
W.	St. CYRUS	Crichton	. .19	Lost 22/1/41.
W.55	St. DAY	Taikoo: Cockburns	. .19	Mercantile URSUS (1955).
W.66	St. DOGMAEL	Taikoo	. .19	Sold 1950.
W.74	St. FAGAN	Lytham Sbdg.	. .19	Lost 1/6/40.
W.25	St. ISSEY	Napier & Miller	. .18	Lost 28/12/42.
W.90	St. JUST	Napier & Miller	. .19	Lost 14/2/42.
W.27	St. MARTIN	Livingstone	. .19	Sold 1947.
W.81	St. MELLONS	Harland & Wolff (Govan)	. .18	Sold 1948.
W.63	St. MONANCE	Hong Kong & Whampoa	. .19	Sold 1948.
W.34	St. OMAR	Ferguson	15. 9.19	Sold 1948.
W.04	TOIA (R.N.Z.N.) (ex-St. Boniface, ex-St. Fergus)	Fleming & Ferguson	16. 6.19	Sold 1955.

Notes:—The above vessels were survivors of a class af 48 built during the First World War of which the Brazilian ANNIBAL MENDOZA (ex-Times, ex-St. Keyne) and D.N.O.G. (ex-Parana, ex-St. Teath), the Iraqui ALARM (ex-St. Ewe) and the Spanish CICLOPE (ex-St. Clement) were sold abroad and many others were sold out commercially.

At the outbreak of war the St. DOMINIC, CAROLINE MOLLER (ex-St. Mabyn), ABEILLE 22 (ex-St. Minver) and St. OLAVES were called back to naval service as tugs, the St. AUBIN, R.C.N. OCEAN EAGLE (ex-St. Arvans), ALARM (ex-St. Ewe) and St. SAMPSON were requisitioned as A.M.S's. and R.A.N. HEROS (ex-St. Erth) and R.A.N. St. GILES (ex-Khalifa, ex-St. Giles) as A.P.V's.

Brigand class

Displacement: 840 tons.
Dimensions: 165 (pp) 174 (oa) × 32 × $10\frac{3}{4}$ ft.
Machinery: 2-shaft Reciprocating (VTE), I.H.P. 3,000 = $15\frac{1}{2}$ knots.
Armament: 1—3 in. A.A., 1—20 mm. A.A., 2—M (2 × 1—LG) guns.
Complement: 43.

W.69	BANDIT	Fleming & Ferguson	15. 2.38	BRITON (1947); mercantile (1960).
W.83	BRIGAND	,,	8. 7.37	Scrapped Italy 23/9/60.

W.49	BUCCANEER	,,	7. 9.37	Lost 25/8/46.
W.01	FREEBOOTER	,,	29.11.40	Sold 1961.
W.98	MARAUDER	,,	9.11.38	Mercantile EMERSON K (1958).

Nimble class

Displacement: 890 tons.
Dimensions: 165 (pp) 175 (oa) × 35¾ × 11 ft.
Machinery: 2-shaft Reciprocating (VTE), I.H.P. 3,500 = 16 knots.
Armament: 1—3 in. A.A., 2—20 mm. A.A. (2 × 1) guns.
Complement: 42.

W.171	CAPABLE	Hall Russell	22.11.45	
W.172	CAREFUL	Hall	23.10.45	
W.173	EXPERT	Fleming & Ferguson	14. 2.45	
W.123	NIMBLE	Fleming & Ferguson	4.12.41	

Bustler class

Displacement: 1,120 tons.
Dimensions: 190 (pp) 205 (oa) × 38½ × 12½ ft.
Machinery: 2-shaft Diesel motors, B.H.P. 4,000 = 16 knots.
Armament: 1—3 in. A.A., 1—2 pdr. A.A., 2—20 mm. A.A. (2 × 1), 4—M (2 × 2 LG) guns.
Complement: 42.

W. 72	BUSTLER	Robb: Atlas & British Aux.	4.12.41	Mercantile (name unchanged 1947–58).
W.105	GROWLER	,,	10. 9.42	Mercantile CAROLINE MOLLER (1952), CASTLE PEAK (1954), WELSHMAN (1962).
W.106	HESPERIA (ex-Hesper)	,,	10.11.42	Lost 9/2/45.
W.125	MEDIATOR	,,	21. 6.44	
W.164	REWARD	,,	13.10.44	Mercantile (1962).
W. 23	SAMSONIA (ex-Samson)	,,	1. 4.42	Mercantile FOUNDATION JOSEPHINE (1948–1952).
W.169	TURMOIL	,,	14. 7.44	Mercantile (name unchanged 1948).
W.170	WARDEN	,,	28. 6.45	Mercantile TWYFORD (1946–51).

Notes:— First fleet tugs with diesel engines.

Above: The fleet tug St. Clears was one of a large class built during World War I.

Below: H.M.S. Growler, a large diesel-engined tug of the **Bustler** class, and armed with a 12 pdr. A.A. abaft the mainmast and two single 20 mm. A.A. guns in the bridge wings. [*I.W.M.*

H.M.S. Samsonia, one of the **Bustler** class built by Henry Robb, Leith, was armed with a 12 pdr. A.A. on the foc's'le, a 2 pdr. abaft the mainmast and 2 single 20 mm. A.A. guns in the bridge wings. [*I.W.M.*

H.M.S. Allegiance, a reciprocating engined tug of the **Assurance** class built by Cochrane & Sons, Selby. They were smaller than the **Bustler** class and owing to the short foc's'le, the 12 pdr. was moved abaft the funnel, note tripod foremast and heavy belting. [*I.W.M.*

Assurance class

Displacement: 700 tons.
Dimensions: 142½ (pp) 156¾ (oa) × 33¼ × 10½ ft.
Machinery: 1-shaft Reciprocating (VTE), I.H.P. 1,350 = 13 knots.
Armament: 1—3 in. A.A., 2—20 mm. A.A. (2 × 1), 2—M (2 × 1) guns.
Complement: 31.

W.107	ADEPT	Cochrane: Holmes	25. 8.41	Lost 17/3/42.
W.108	ADHERENT	,,	24. 9.41	Lost 14/1/44.
W. 50	ALLEGIANCE	,,	22. 2.43	Mercantile ALLEGIANCE II (1949), KOWLOON DOCKS (1955).
W.141	ANTIC (ex-Ant)	,,	24. 3.43	R.Neth.N. (1943–45).
W.142	ASSIDIOUS	,,	4. 6.43	Mercantile IRVING TAMARACK (1958).
W. 59	ASSURANCE	,,	23. 5.40	Lost 18/10/41.
W.109	CHARON	,,	21.11.41	ALLIGATOR (1947); scrapped 1/59.
W.111	DEXTEROUS	,,	3. 4.42	Mercantile (name unchanged—1945), ZURMAND (1957).
W.143	EARNER (ex-Earnest)	,,	3. 7.43	
W. 11	FRISKY	,,	27. 5.41	Mercantile HASAN (1948), VERNICOS MARINA (1950).
W.112	GRIPER	,,	16. 5.42	Mercantile (name unchanged—1946), SURABAJA (1962).
W.110	HENGIST (ex-Decision)	,,	20.12.41	Sold 1956.
W. 97	HORSA (ex-Rescue)	,,	29. 7.42	Lost 16/3/43.
W. 30	JAUNTY	,,	11. 6.41	
W. 96	PROSPEROUS	,,	29. 6.42	
W. 73	PRUDENT	,,	6. 8.40	CAUTIOUS (1947).
W. 39	RESTIVE	,,	4. 9.40	
W.131	SAUCY (ii)	,,	26.10.42	
W.144	SESAME	,,	1.10.43	Lost 11/6/44.
W. 87	STORMKING (ex-Stormcock)	,,	24.11.42	TRYPHON (1947); mercantile MELANIE FAIR (1958).
W. 18	TENACITY (ex-Diligent)	,,	22. 6.40	ADHERENT (1947), mercantile HERMES (1960).

Envoy class

Displacement: 868 tons.
Dimensions: 160 (pp) 174½ (oa) × 36 × 11¼ ft.

Above: H.M.S. Prosperous, also of the **Assurance** class—details the same as Allegiance see p. 374.
[*I.W.M.*

Below: H.M.S. Enchanter, also by Cochrane, was slightly larger than **Assurance** class and had not the same piled-up appearance. Note greater clearance between bridge and funnel, and life boats carried abaft bridge as compared with **Assurance** class.
[*I.W.M.*

Machinery: 1-shaft Rcciprocating (VTE), I.H.P. 1,700 = 13 knots.
Armament: 1—3 in. A.A., 2—20 mm. A.A. (2 × 1), 4—M (2 × 2) guns.
Complement: 33.

W.178	ENCHANTER	Cochrane: Holmes	2.11.44	Mercantile ENGLISHMAN (1947), CINTRA (1962).
W.179	ENCORE	,,	2.12.44	
W.177	ENFORCER	,,	22. 7.44	Scrapped St. Davids Hbr. 1963.
W.175	ENIGMA	,,	22. 6.44	Lost 21/12/46.
W.166	ENTICER	,,	11. 3.44	
W.165	ENVOY	,,	11. 2.44	

Displacement: 783 tons.
Dimensions: 135 (pp) 143 (oa) × 33¼ × 13½ ft.
Machinery: 2-shaft Diesel-Electric motors, B.H.P. 1,875 = 14 knots.
Armament: 1—3 in. A.A., 2—20 mm. A.A. (2 × 1) guns. *Complement:* 34.

P.No.	Name	Builder Hull: Engine	Completed	Fate
W.117	ORIANA (ex-U.S.N. BAT.1)	Gulfport: Allis Chalmers	22.12.42	Mercantile OCEAN PRIDE (1946), PAN AMERICA (1947), ZEELAND (1956).
	MARICOPA (ex-U.S.N. BAT.2)	,,	30. 9.42	Retained as U.S.N. ATA.146(ex-ATR.90); mercantile SEA RANGER (1946); CAPTAIN ROY (19).
W.119	FAVOURITE (ex-U.S.N. BAT.3)	Levingston: General Motors	15. 6.42	Mercantile SUSAN A. MORAN (1946), EUGENE F. MORAN (1946) MONSANTO (1947).
W. 14	INTEGRITY (ex-U.S.N. BAT.4)	,,	23.10.42	Returned U.S.N. 19/2/46.
W. 17	LARIAT (ex-U.S.N. BAT.5)	,,	10. 8.42	Mercantile MING 308 (1946).
W. 20	MASTERFUL (ex-U.S.N. BAT.6)	,,	28. 8.42	Mercantile EUGENIA M. MORAN (1948), COMANCHE (1960).
W.113	AIMWELL (ex-U.S.N. BAT.7)	Defoe: General Motors	6. 6.42	Sold 14/3/48.
W.114	BOLD (ex-U.S.N. BAT.8)	,,	29. 6.42	Sold 2/10/48.

Above: H.M.S. Encore—read as for Enchanter. [*I.W.M.*

Below: H.M.S. Eminent belonged to a large group of steel-built tugs received from the United States Navy under *Lend/Lease*. They were diesel-engined and of welded construction with the belting formed of half-round rod. No boats were carried only Carley floats and inflatable rafts; they carried a U.S. pattern 3 in. A.A. gun on the foc's'le. [*I.W.M.*

W.115	DESTINY (ex-U.S.N. BAT.9)	Defoe: General Motors	30. 7.42	Mercantile FROSTY MOLLER (1948), CHRISTINE MOLLER (1950), OCEANUS (1951), GELE ZEE (1953).
W.116	EMINENT (ex-U.S.N. BAT.10)	,,	14. 9.42	Mercantile MING 305 (1946)?
W.149	RESERVE (ex-U.S.N. BAT.11)	Levingston: General Motors	12.10.42	R.A.N. (1944); for disposal.
W.103	SPRIGHTLY (ex-U.S.N. BAT.12)	,,	23.11.42	R.A.N. (1944).
W.104	TANCRED (ex-U.S.N. BAT.13)	Gulfport: General Motors	18. 2.43	R.A.N. (1944); mercantile (name unchanged—1947).
W.120	WEAZEL (ex-U.S.N. BAT.14)	,,	10. 4.43	Mercantile MING 106 (1946).
W.133	ADVANTAGE (ex-U.S.N. ATR.41)	Levingston: General Motors	19. 4.43	Mercantile MING 309 (1946).
W.134	ASPIRANT (ex-U.S.N. ATR.42)	,,	3. 5.43	Mercantile VIVI (1948).
W.135	MINDFUL (ex-U.S.N. ATR.48)	,,	31. 8.43	Mercantile GAY MORAN (1947), SEA LION (1949), HARRY J. MOSSER (1955), MARGARET WALSH (1957).
W.136	VAGRANT (ex-U.S.N. ATR.49)	,,	2.10.43	Mercantile MARION MORAN (1947).
W.118	PATROCLUS (ex-U.S.N. ATR.91)	,,	22.10.43	Mercantile KEVIN MORAN (1947), MOHAWK (1960).
W.150	ATHLETE (ex-U.S.N. ATR.92)	,,	13.11.43	Lost 17/7/45.
W.151	FLARE (ex-U.S.N. ATR.93)	,,	7.12.43	Mercantile MING 301 (1946).
W.152	FLAUNT (ex-U.S.N. ATR.94)	,,	21.12.43	Mercantile MING 102 (1946), MING 302 (1951).
W.153	CHEERLY (ex-U.S.N. ATR.95)	,,	18. 1.44	Returned U.S.N. 19/2/46.
W.154	EMPHATIC (ex-U.S.N. ATR.96)	,,	27. 1.44	Philipino IFIGUA (1947).

Notes:—U.S.N. rescue tugs made available under *Lend/Lease*.

H.M.S. Advantage, of the same description as Eminent. [I.W.M.

Displacement: 1,360 tons.
Dimensions: 147 (pp) 165 (oa) × 33½ × 15 ft.
Machinery: 1-shaft Reciprocating (VTE), I.H.P. 1,875 = 12 knots.
Armament: 1—3 in. A.A., 2—20 mm. A.A. (2 × 1) guns.
Complement: 32.

P.No.	Name	Builder	Launched	Fate
W.137	DIRECTOR (ex-U.S.N. BATR.17)	Camden	28.12.43	Returned U.S.N. 23/4/46.
W.138	EMULOUS (ex-U.S.N. BATR.18)	,,	2. 2.44	Returned U.S.N. 30/4/46.
W.139	FREEDOM (ex-U.S.N. BATR.19)	,,	20. 3.44	Returned U.S.N. 23/4/46.
W.140	JUSTICE (ex-U.S.N. BATR.20)	,,	24. 4.44	Mercantile ST. CHRISTOPHER (1948).

Notes:—Wooden hull. U.S.N. rescue tugs made available under *Lend/Lease*.

(d) **Requisitioned tugs**

Dockyard and Harbour Tugs

P.No.	Name	Gross tonnage/ built	Requi- sitioned	Fate
	ABEILLE 5	211/10	1940	Returned M.O.W.T. 1946.
	ABEILLE 20	179/24	1940	Returned 1945.
	ABEILLE 21	260/25	1940	Returned 1944/45.
	CALSHOT	679/30	1940	Ferry service; returned 1946.
	CERVIA	157/25	1941	Returned 1945.
	FABIA	151/19	1941	Returned 1945.
W.129	FALCON	124/92	1941	Returned 1945.
	GONDIA*	200/27	1940	Returned 1945.
	GUARDSMAN	102/05	1939	Lost 15/11/40.
	JAVA	155/18	1940	Returned 1945.
	KESTREL II	161/18	1940	Boom defence tender returned 1945.
	NAPIA	155/14	1939	Lost 20/12/39.
	NESS POINT	85/37	1941	MARTELLO (1945—nominal base ship); returned 1946.
	RENE LE BESNERAIS	246/31	1943	Ex-B.B.V.; returned 1945.
	RISBAN	159/24	1941	Returned M.O.W.T. 1945.
	SUN II	197/09	1939	Returned 1945.
	SUN III	197/09	1939	Returned 1945.
	SUN V	200/15	1939	Returned 1945.
	SUN VII	202/17	1939	Lost 6/3/41.
	SUN VIII	196/19	1939	Returned 1945.
	SUN IX	196/20	1939	Lost 21/12/40.
	SUN XII	183/25	1939	Returned 1945.

H.M.S. Director was one of four wooden-hulled, reciprocating-engined tugs also received under *Lend/Lease* from the United States Navy. [*I.W.M.*

Above: The French commercial tug Abeille No. 21 served with the Royal Navy. [*I.W.M.*

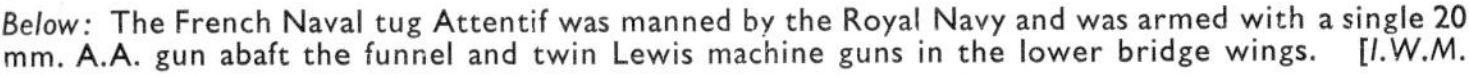

Below: The French Naval tug Attentif was manned by the Royal Navy and was armed with a single 20 mm. A.A. gun abaft the funnel and twin Lewis machine guns in the lower bridge wings. [*I.W.M.*

	TWENTE	239/37	1940	Lost 12/6/40.
	VICTOR	153/98	1940	Returned 1941/42.
	WILLIAM RYAN	102/28	1940	Returned 1945.

* Paddle.

Rescue tugs

W. 94	ABEILLE 4	327/39	1940	Returned 1945.
	ABEILLE 22 (ex-R.N. St. Minver)	433/19	1940	Returned 1945, scrapped 1951.
	AL HATHERA (ex-Kifaru)	279/27	1939	Kenya and Zanzibar R.N.V.R.: returned E.A.R. & H. 1945.
	AMSTERDAM	368/37	1940	Returned 1945.
W. 68	ATTENTIF 1—20 mm. A.A. 2—MG	*672/39	1940	Returned 1945.
W.174	BARWICK	418/19	1942	BEHEST (1944), SANSONE (1947), OPUS (1953).
W.148	CAPTIVE (ex-Max Barendt)	766/23	1942	Salved 1942; sold 1946.
W. 09	CAROLINE MOLLER (ex-R.N. St. Mabyn)	444/19	1940	Lost 7/10/42.
W. 35	CHAMPION 1—20 mm. A.A. 4—MG (4 × 1)	*672/39	1940	Returned 1945.
W. 99	CHERBOURGEOIS 3	281/13	1940	Returned M.O.W.T. 1945.
W.107	CHERBOURGEOIS 4	293/30	1940	Returned M.O.W.T. 1946.
	CORINGA	294/14	1939	Lost 23/6/40.
	DANUBE III (1—12 pdr.)	234/24	1939	Examination service; lost 13/10/40.
W. 36	DANUBE V	241/35	1939	Examination service, rescue tug; returned 1946.
	DANUBE VI	241/35	1939	Examination service; returned 1945.
	DIVERSION (ex-Norman)	222/29	1941	Returned 1943.
	ELAN II		1943	Ex-B.B.V.; target service.
	ENGLISHMAN	487/37	1939	Returned 1943?
	FAIRPLAY II	282/21	1939	Lost 2/3/40.
W.126	FORCEFUL	288/25	1941	Returned 1944.
W.121	GOLIATH	354/21	1940	Returned 1945.
	HENDON	241/24	1939	Returned 1941?
W. 02	HUDSON	294/39	1940	Returned 1946.
	INDIRA	637/18	1940	Lost 15/12/41.
	JAMES E. HUGHES	293/14	1943	Returned M.O.W.T. 1946.

Above: The French Naval tug Champion, requisitioned by the Royal Navy and armed with a single 20 mm. A.A. gun abaft the funnel and four Hotchkiss M.G.s forward. [*I.W.M.*

Below: The requisitioned tug Seaman had a single 20 mm. A.A. gun abaft the funnel and a twin .5 in. A.A. mounting on the foc's'le. [*I.W.M.*

The Sea Giant was one of the two American mercantile tugs acquired for naval service and was armed with twin ·5 in. A.A. mounting aft and two

W. 47	KENIA	200/27	1939	Returned 1945.
	KROOMAN	230/38	1940	Returned 1941?
	LADY BRASSEY	362/13	1939	Returned 1946.
W. 56	MAMMOUTH	*954/18	1943	Ex-B.B.V.; returned 1946.
	MASTODONTE	*954/19	1940	Returned 1946.
	MURIA	192/14	1939	Lost 8/11/40.
	NGUVU	179/25	1939	Kenya and Zanzibar R.N.V.R.; returned E.A.R. & H. 1945.
	PINGOUIN	*700/17	1943	Ex-B.B.V., target service; returned 1945.
	PINTADE	*700/17	1943	Ex-B.B.V.; target service; returned 1945.
	RAMIER	*685/17	1943	Ex-B.B.V.; target service; returned 1945.
W. 62	REVUE	245/39	1940	Returned M.O.W.T. 1946.
W.162	ROODE ZEE‡	468/38	1940	Lost 24/4/44.
	St. DOMINIC (ex-R.N.)	451/19	1940	Lost 8/12/41.
	St. GILES (R.A.N.) (ex-R.N.)	380/19	1945	Ex-A.P.V.; returned 1946.
	St. OLAVES (ex-R.N.)	468/19	1939	Lost 21/9/42.
W. 74	SABINE	488/17	1940	Scrapped Gateshead 1950.
	SALVAGE KING	1164/25	1940	Lost 12/9/40.
W. 43	SALVONIA	571/39	1939	Returned 1946.
	SAUCY (i)	579/18	1939	Lost 4/9/40.
W.193	SEA GIANT (ex-U.S.N. Contocook) 2—.5 in. A.A. (1 × 2) 2—MG	508/20	1940	Returned 1946.
W. 44	SEAMAN 1—20 mm. A.A. 2—.5 in. A.A. (1 × 2)	369/24	1939	Returned 1944.
W.156	SCHELDE	359/26	1940	Returned 1945.
W. 07	STALWART† (ex-Theodor Woker)	621/39	1939	Returned S.A.R. & H. 1946.
W. 89	SUPERMAN 1—20 mm. A.A. 2—.5 in. A.A. (1 × 2) 4—LG (2 × 2)	359/33	1939	Returned 1945.
	THAMES‡	624/38	1940	Returned 1945.
W.128	WAREE (R.A.N.)	233/39	1942	Returned 1946.
	WATERMEYER† (ex-T. H. Watermeyer)	621/39	1939	Returned S.A.R. & H. 1946?
W.127	WATO (R.A.N.)	292/04	1941	Returned 1946.

The requisitioned tug Superman had a single 20 mm. A.A. gun abaft the funnel and a twin .5 in. A.A. mounting on the foc's'le. [I.W.M.

W.163	ZWARTE ZEE‡	793/33	1940	Returned 1945.

* displacement. † twin screw. ‡ diesel.

Notes:—Included with the above were Belgian (GOLIATH), French (ABEILLE 4, 5, 20, 21 and 22, CHERBOURGEOIS 3 and 4, ELAN II and RENE LE BESNERAIS) and Netherlands (AMSTERDAM, HUDSON, ROODE ZEE, SCHELDE, THAMES and ZWARTE ZEE) mercantile and French naval (ATTENTIF, CHAMPION, MAMMOUTH, MASTODONTE, PINGOUIN, PINTARD and RAMIER) tugs which wore either the white ensign or their national flags. The SABINE and SEA GIANT were purchased in the U.S.A., the BARWICK was made available under *Lend/Lease* and the CAPTIVE was an ex-German tug scuttled at Alexandria and salved by the Royal Navy in 1942. Some were employed on examination service and other duties and the DIVERSION, HENDON, LADY BRASSEY, SEAMAN and SUPERMAN were initially operated under the red ensign. In May, 1943, there were forty-three rescue tugs disposed in British ports, one at Iceland, one at the Azores, one at St. Johns (Newfoundland), two at Bermuda, two at Freetown, twenty-three in the Mediterranean, one at Durban, one at Kilindini, one at Aden, one at Bombay, two at Ceylon and three at Australia.

OCEAN SALVAGE VESSELS

King Salvor class

Displacement: 1,440 tons except * 1,550 tons.
Dimensions: $200\frac{1}{4}$ (pp) 217 except * $217\frac{3}{4}$ (oa) × $37\frac{3}{4}$ × 13 except * $13\frac{1}{2}$ ft.
Machinery: 2-shaft Reciprocating (VTE), I.H.P. 1,500 = 12 knots.
Armament: 4—20 mm. A.A. (4 × 1) guns.
Complement: 72 except * 84.

P.No.	Name	Builder Hull: Engine	Launched	Fate
W.191	KING SALVOR	Simons	18. 5.42	KINGFISHER (1954), Argentine TEHUELCHE (1960).
	OCEAN SALVOR	Simons	31. 8.43	Mercantile BRITISH RECOVERY (1960).
W. 05	PRINCE SALVOR	Goole Sbdg: Whites M.E.	8. 3.43	Mercantile (1948).
W. 34	SALVAGE DUKE	Simons	1.11.43	Turkish IMROZ (1948); lost 14/1/59.
	SALVALOUR	Goole Sbdg: Amos & Smith	2.11.44	
	SALVENTURE	Simons	24.11.42	R.H.N. SOTIR (1948).
	RECLAIM* (ex-Salverdant)	Simons: Aitchison Blair	12. 3.48	
W.176	SALVESTOR	Simons	28. 8.42	
W.190	SALVICTOR	Simons	11. 3.44	
	SALVIGIL	Simons	30. 4.45	Mercantile (1960).
	SALVIKING	Simons	22.12.42	Lost 14/2/44.
	SALVIOLA	Simons	9. 7.45	Turkish IMROZ II (1959).
	SEA SALVOR	Goole Sbdg: Whites M.E.	22. 4.43	

Notes:—SALVERDANT was completed as a deep diving and submarine rescue vessel and re-named RECLAIM.

Displacement: 1,250 tons.
Dimensions: 185 (pp) 195 (oa) × 34½ × 13 ft.
Machinery: 2-shaft Reciprocating (VTE), I.H.P. 1,200 = 12 knots.
Armament: 4—20 mm. A.A. (4 × 1) guns.
Complement: 62.

	SALVEDA	Cammell Laird	9. 2.43	Mercantile (name unchanged 1947–57); for disposal.

Displacement: 1,360 tons.
Dimensions: 200 (pp) 213¾ (oa) × 39 × 12 ft.
Machinery: 2-shaft Diesel-Electric motors, B.H.P. 2,780 = 16½ knots.
Armament: 2—40 mm. A.A. (2 × 1), 4—20 mm. A.A. (4 × 1) guns.
Complement: 45.

	CALEDONIAN SALVOR (ex-U.S.N. BARS.1)	Basalt Rock	22. 8.42	R.A.N. (1943); mercantile SUDBURY II (1947).
	CAMBRIAN SALVOR (ex-U.S.N. BARS.2)	,,	7. 9.42	R.A.N. (1943); mercantile (1947): CARIBSCHE ZEE (1962)
	ATLANTIC SALVOR (ex-U.S.N. BARS.3)	,,	24.10.42	Retained as U.S.N. CLAMP (ARS.33).
	PACIFIC SALVOR (ex-U.S.N. BARS.4)	,,	24.10.42	Retained as U.S.N. GEAR (ARS.34).

Notes:—U.S.N. salvage vessels made available under *Lend/Lease.*

COASTAL SALVAGE VESSELS

Displacement: 800 tons.
Dimensions: 170 (pp) 183¼ (oa) × 37 × 14¾ ft.
Machinery: 2-shaft Diesel-Electric motors, B.H.P. 1,200 = 12 knots.
Armament: 1—3 in. A.A., 2—20 mm. A.A. (2 × 1) guns.
Complement: 35.

P.No.	Name	Builder	Launched	Fate
	AMERICAN SALVOR (ex-U.S.N. BARS.5)	Barbour Boat Wks.	1943	Returned U.S.N. 1946.
	BOSTON SALVOR (ex-U.S.N. BARS.6)	Barbour Boat Wks.	1943	Constructive total loss 1944, scrapped Antwerp 3/45.
	PLYMOUTH SALVOR (ex-U.S.N. BARS.7)	American Car & Fdry.	21. 4.43	Retained as U.S.N. WEIGHT (ARS.35).
	YORK SALVOR U.S.N. BARS.8)	American Car & Fdry.	6. 5.43	Retained as U.S.N. SWIVEL (ARS.36).

Above: Laid down as a salvage vessel, H.M.S. Reclaim was completed as a submarine rescue and diving vessel.

Below: The ocean salvage vessel M.M.S. Salvigil was specially fitted for the salvage of sunken vessels and was only lightly armed with 4-20 mm. A.A. (4×1) guns. [*I.W.M.*

Above: The mercantile Sudbury II was the former ocean salvage vessel Caledonian Salvor, loaned to the Royal Navy under *Lend/Lease* and now employed as a tug on the Canadian Pacific Coast.
[*Shipbuilding & Shipping Record*

Below: The Caledonian Salvor, a steel-hulled salvage vessel which the Royal Navy transferred to the Royal Australian Navy.
[*U.S. Navy Official*

The coastal salvage vessel H.M.S. Swin was of a similar type to the mooring vessels. Only 2—20 mm. A.A. (2×1) guns were carried as a defensive armament. [I.W.M.

LINCOLN SALVOR (ex-U.S.N. BARS.9)	Bellingham I.W.	1943	Returned U.S.N. 9/46.
SOUTHAMPTON SALVOR (ex-U.S.N. BARS.10)	Bellingham I.W.	1943	Returned U.S.N. 10/46.
QUEBEC SALVOR (ex-U.S.N. BARS.11)	Bellingham I.W.	10. 5.43	Retained as U.S.N. VALVE (ARS.28).
QUEEN SALVOR (ex-U.S.N. BARS.12)	Bellingham I.W.	30. 6.43	Retained as U.S.N. VENT (ARS.29).

Notes:—Wooden hull, U.S.N. salvage vessels made available under *Lend/Lease.*

Displacement: 950 tons.
Dimensions: 150 (pp) 179¼ (oa) × 35½ × 11 ft.
Machinery: 1-shaft Reciprocating (VTE), I.H.P. 600 = 9 knots.
Armament: 2—20 mm. AA. (2 × 1) guns.
Complement: 34.

	DISPENSER	Smiths Dock	22. 4.43	Mercantile (1955).
	HELP	Smiths Dock	5. 5.43	Mercantile, name unchanged (1950).
	KINBRACE	Hall	17. 1.45	
	KINGARTH (ex-Sledway)	Hall	22. 5.44	R.H.N. (1946–49).
	KINGUSSIE (ex-Solway)	Robb		Cancelled 10/44.
	KINLOSS	Hall	14. 4.45	
	LIFELINE	Smiths Dock	17. 8.43	Mercantile (1947–60); for disposal.
	RESTFUL	Hall		Cancelled 10/44.
	SUCCOUR	Smiths Dock	18. 8.43	
	SWIN (ex-Shipway)	Hall	25. 3.44	
W.06	UPLIFTER	Smiths Dock	29.11.43	

WRECK LOCATION AND DISPERSAL VESSELS

IN 1942 it was decided to make a start in clearing the numerous wrecks sunk in fairways and harbours as a result of enemy action; mainly on the south and east coasts of England. These wrecks had first to be located and then dispersed by explosive charges and the following vessels were therefore fitted out.

Above: The coastal salvage vessel H.M.S. Uplifter belonged to a group that was kept busily employed in keeping esturial waters clear of wrecks that impeded navigation. Note the tall mainmast and radar on port sampson post. [*A. & J. Pavia*

Below: The convoy rescue ship Empire Rest was the former corvette H.M.S. Rayleigh Castle, she was mercantile manned and operated. Ships of this class carried additional boats with which to pick up survivors, special quarters where they could be accommodated and invariably carried a naval medical team. They were not subject to special immunity and were accordingly armed and the Empire Rest had a 12 pdr. A.A. gun aft and 5-20 mm. A.A. (5 × 1) guns. [*I.W.M.*

(a) **Wreck location vessels**

P.No.	Name	Tonnage/ year built	Requi- sitioned	Fate
4.147	ASTRAL (ex-Pilote 14)	451/30	1943	Ex-B.B.V.; returned 1945.

(b) **Wreck dispersal vessels**

P.No.	Name	Tonnage/ year built	Requi- sitioned	Fate
4.48	ARY (ex-Ary Scheffer)	642/04	1943	Returned to M.O.W.T. 4/46.
FY.523	COLCHESTER	1280/18	1942	Returned 2/46.
4.82	RAMPANT (ex-Empire Sentinel, ex-Phaedra)	619/98	1943	W.D. (name unchanged —1946); returned to M.O.W.T. 12/46.

Notes:—In addition to the above vessels two further W.L.V. (an ex-trawler and an ex-drifter) and eleven W.D.V. (all ex-trawlers) are listed in Part 6 together with a wreck dispersal store carrier (ex-trawler).

CONVOY RESCUE SHIPS

THESE vessels, like the merchant aircraft carriers, were mercantile manned and operated (see *Note 2*). They were selected from amongst the smaller merchant vessels with an above average turn of speed and were fitted to pick up and accommodate survivors from vessels sunk in convoy. They were mainly employed in North Russian and North Atlantic convoys where survival, in sub-arctic conditions, was limited to only a few minutes so that their task had to be performed with celerity and precision. They are included with this series because they assisted, even if only passively, in preserving sea communications and their presence in convoys was as re-assuring as that of the armed escorts.

The importance of convoy rescue ships is best illustrated by the vessels listed below which were all converted from regular and auxiliary warships released from naval service. Additionally, but not listed here, were those vessels which were not ex-naval.

P.No.	Name	Tonnage/ year built	Requi- sitioned	Fate
	EMPIRE COMFORT (ex-R.N. York Castle)	1333/44	1944	To M.O.W.T. 1946 as troopships.
	EMPIRE LIFE-GUARD (ex-R.N. Maiden Castle)	1333/44	1944	
	EMPIRE PEACE-MAKER (ex-R.N. Scarsbrough Castle	1333/44	1944	
	EMPIRE REST (ex-R.N. Rayleigh Castle)	1334/44	1944	
	EMPIRE SHELTER (ex-R.N. Barnard Castle)	1336/45	1945	

	GOODWIN	1570/17	1943	Ex-A/P.V., ex-A.A. guardship, ex-A.B.V. returned 1945.
	St. CLAIR (ex-R.N. Baldur) ex-St. Clair)	1637/37	1943	Ex-Base ship; returned 8/45.
	St. SUNNIVA	1368/31	1942	Ex-Accommodation ship; lost 22/1/43.

Note 2: They were all placed under the management of the General Steam Navigation Co. Ltd. London

MISCELLANEOUS VESSELS

Displacement: 4,700 tons.
Dimensions: 380 (pp) 439¼ (oa) × 50¼ × 21¼ ft.
Machinery: 2-shaft Reciprocating (VTE—4 cyl.), I.H.P. 11,800 = 20 knots.
Armament: 2—pdr. (2 × 1) guns.
Complement: 363.

	VICTORIA & ALBERT	Pembroke: Humphrys and Tennant	9. 5.99	Scrapped Faslane 1954.

Notes:—Served as accommodation ship at Portsmouth right through war.

Displacement: 528 tons.
Dimensions: 200½ (pp) (oa) × 24 × 6 ft.
Machinery: Paddle Reciprocating (CD), I.H.P. 1,000 = 15 knots.

X.77	HARLEQUIN (ex-Strathmore)	Russell: Rankin & Blackmore	11. 3.97	Lost 1943 and wreck sold 3/43.

Notes:—Purchased 1908 and used as a ferry. Sister KYLEMORE served as aux. netlayer (ex-PMS).

Displacement: 651 tons.
Dimensions: 185 (pp) (oa) × 26 × 10 ft.
Machinery: 2-shaft Reciprocating (VTE), I.H.P. 1,300 = 15 knots.

X.76	NIMBLE (ex-Roslin Castle)	Hawthorn	14. 3.06	Sold 11/10/48.

Notes:—Purchased 1908 and used as a ferry between Chatham and Sheerness.

Displacement: 298 tons NIGHTINGALE, 302 tons VERNON.
Dimensions: 98 (pp) 106¼ VERNON, 110 NIGHTINGALE (oa) × 24½ × 7½ ft.
Machinery: 2-shaft Reciprocating (VTE), I.H.P. 400 = 10 knots.
Complement: 15.

T.82	NIGHTINGALE	Portsmouth	30. 9.31	Scrapped Southampton 2/58.

T.83	VERNON (ex-Skylark)	Portsmouth	15.11.32	VESUVIUS (1941); scrapped Southampton 2/58.

Notes:—Mining tenders attached to Torpedo school (Portsmouth).

Displacement: 222 tons ELFIN, 225 tons REDWING.
Dimensions: 100 (pp) 108½ ELFIN, 112 REDWING (oa) × 25 × 6½ ft.
Machinery: 2-shaft Reciprocating (VTE), I.H.P. 250 = 9½ knots.
Complement: 12.

T.25	ELFIN	White	20.11.33	NETTLE (1941—T.94); sold 1957.
T.36	REDWING	White	19.10.33	Sold 1957.

Notes:—ELFIN was tender to the 3rd, 5th and 7th Submarine flotillas respectively and REDWING tender to the Submarine depot at Portland.

Displacement: 132 tons.
Dimensions: 83½ (pp) 91 (oa) × 19 × 6½ ft.
Machinery: 2-shaft Reciprocating (VTE), I.H.P. 350 = 9¼ knots.
Complement: 12.

T.92	DWARF	Philip	1936	

Notes:—Tender to the 5th Submarine flotilla until 1941, then the 3rd Submarine flotilla.

Displacement: 1,090 tons.
Dimensions: 206 (pp) (oa) × 37½ × 20½d. ft.
Machinery: 2-shaft Reciprocating (V.T.E.), I.H.P. 1,220 = 13 knots.

X.97	MAGICIAN	Ailsa Sbdg.	27.9.39	MAGICIAN II (1946); scrapped Faslane 1952.

Notes:—Built to replace HARLEQUIN and NIMBLE, but turned over to the Army on completion for use as a hospital ship; returned to the Royal Navy 1945.

P.No.	Name	Gross tonnage Built	Requisitioned	Fate
Y1.3	BRECONSHIRE	9776/39	1939	Fleet supply ship; lost 27/3/42.
	BRUCE (ex-Manxmaid)	1505/10	1941	RDF.TS CAESAREA (1941); to M.O.W.T. 1945; scrapped Barrow 11/50.
4.293	CADUCEUS (ex-Manxman)	2030/04	1941	RDF.TS; to M.O.W.T. 1945; scrapped Preston 9/8/49.
4.250	GLENEARN	9784/38	1939	Fleet supply ship; LSI (L) (1941).
4.196	GLENGYLE	9919/39	1939	Fleet supply ship; LSI (L) (1941).
4.256	GLENROY	9809/38	1939	Fleet supply ship; LSI (L) (1941).

	HELVIG	2250/37	1944	Ex-aux M/L; Seaward defence ship; returned 3/46.
	MASHOBRA	8324/20	1940	MNBDO ship; lost 25/5/40.
	SIR FRANCIS DRAKE	478/08	1941	Exam Service; returned 6/6/46.
	SIR JOHN HAWKINS	930/29	1941	Exam Service, ferry service (1942); returned 26/10/45.
	SIR RICHARD GRENVILLE	896/31	1941	Exam Service, ferry service (1942); returned 19/1/46.
D.65	SIR WALTER RALEIGH	478/08	1941	Exam Service, tender (1942); returned 12/8/46.

Notes:—The BRECONSHIRE and the three " Glens " belonged to a sister ship group which included the escort carrier ACTIVITY (ex-Telemachus). BRECONSHIRE was employed in the Mediterranean, CADUCEUS in Home waters and the MASHOBRA as a mobile naval base defence organisation unit.

PENNANT NUMBERS

THE flag superiors for the vessels listed in this part were far more uniform than in Part 4. At the outbreak of war the following were in use:—

Depot ships:	Flag I or N
Repair ships:	No flag superior
Netlayers and tenders:	Flag T
Boom defence vessels:	Flag P

These were altered, in 1940, with the general re-allocation of flag superiors, by which time several additional ones had been introduced to cover the large variety of auxiliary vessels requisitioned for naval service, as below:—

Depot ships:	Flag F or J (see *Note 1*)
Repair and Maintenance ships:	Flag F
Base and Accommodation ships:	Flag F or 4 (see *Note 2*)
Netlayers and tenders:	Unchanged
Gate, mooring and boom defence vessels:	Flag Z
Tugs and salvage vessels:	Flag W
Auxiliary vessels:	Flag 4
Miscellaneous vessels:	Flag X
Store carriers:	Flag Y

Note 1: RESOURCE had no flag superior while BLENHEIM used flag 4. Depot ships converted from former warships kept their original flag superior.
Note 2: DUNLUCE CASTLE had no flag superior.

One of the large handsome **Bustler** class tugs, H.M.S. Reward, armed with a 12 pdr. A.A. on the foc's'le, a 2 pdr. A.A. abaft the mainmast and two single 20 mm. A.A. guns in the bridge wings. [*I.W.M.*

PART SIX

Trawlers, Whalers and Drifters

H.M.S. St. Geraint. 1—12 pdr. A.A., 1—20mm. A.A., 2—MG (2 × 1).
[*I.W.M.*

NAVAL TRAWLERS AND DRIFTERS

NAVAL trawler construction during World War I assumed very modest proportions up to the close of 1916. Until then it had been limited to some vessels building for the Russian Navy and acquired by the Royal Navy following the outbreak of war (the **Axe** class) and the equally small **Military** class and "**Z**" class whalers. Wholsale requisitioning had otherwise met naval commitments but, by the latter part of 1916, the Admiralty had taken up so many trawlers and drifters that it was not possible to requisition any more if the supply of fish for the population was not to be imperilled. The Admiralty, therefore, ordered two hundred and fifty trawlers and one hundred and fifty steam drifters for their own account supplemented, at a later stage, by equally large orders for trawlers in the U.K., Canada and India.

The trawlers embraced three main classes based on their builders' mercantile prototypes and comprised Cochrane's **Mersey** class, Smith's Dock's **Castle** class and Hall, Russell's **Strath** class. In total, over one hundred and twenty **Merseys,** nearly three hundred **Castles** and one hundred and sixty **Straths** were ordered and were given names taken from the muster rolls of the VICTORY and ROYAL SOVEREIGN at the time of Trafalgar. A small number of mercantile trawlers, under construction at this time, were requisitioned and allotted to one of the three main classes according to dimensions and were known as *non-standard* **Merseys,** etc. and, included in the overall totals above, amounted to at least five **Merseys,** seventeen **Castles** and twenty **Straths.** The termination of hostilities resulted in eighty-two of these vessels being cancelled whilst a further one hundred and thirty-three were completed as mercantile trawlers. These large groups were nearly all sold out commercially between the wars, until, in 1939 only fourteen **Merseys,** three **Castles** and a solitary **Strath** remained in service, plus four of the **Axe** class. Their ranks were considerably augmented by requisitioning in 1939 when some thirty **Merseys,** a hundred and twenty-five **Castles** and seventy-five **Straths,** plus two **Axe** and two **Military** classes, again reverted to H.M. Ships.

In 1935 the naval prototype BASSET was launched which had a larger foc's'le, the bridge placed more amidships and slightly more speed than her purely functional mercantile counterparts. The success of the BASSET is best illustrated by the fact that the two hundred and fifty naval trawlers that followed her in the succeeding ten years deviated little from her basic design.

In the same year, as a result of the Abyssinian crisis, twenty modern trawlers were purchased and were equally appointed for A/S (with **Gem** names) and M/S (with **Tree** names) work. A further twenty were acquired between 1936–39 for A/S, M/S, boom defence and depot ship duties together with six whalers, all building in 1939, which were completed as A/S vessels. These vessels, together with twenty-five survivors from World War I and some half-dozen **Bassets,** were the total trawler strength available to the Royal Navy at the outbreak of war in 1939, plus forty **Bassets (Tree** and **Dance** classes) under construction. But the organisation of the trawler reserve was equal to the emergency and hundreds of trawlers and drifters were rapidly mobilised and placed in the service of the Royal Navy. Heavy demands were made on trawlers for A/S and M/S work in the opening stages of the war and they proceeded far afield, even to providing the A/S screen for early war ocean convoys. Their weatherly qualities, always of the highest order, often resulted in their being the only form of escort operative in heavy weather and they could keep the seas when even destroyers were compelled to seek shelter.

War construction was mainly confined to the **Basset** type (**Shakespearian** and **Isles** classes) with the addition of three very similar vessels for the Royal New Zealand Navy. Contracts were also placed in Burma and India for **Bassets,** in Canada for **Isles** and in New Zealand for **Castles.** The vessels building in Burma were lost incomplete as a result of the Japanese invasion while the necessity for the Indian built vessels to have their machinery shipped out from the U.K. resulted in half of them being subsequently cancelled. Orders for commercial type trawlers were also placed in Portugal and Brazil but the latter were turned over to the Brazilian navy on their entry into the war. A limited number of commercial type trawlers were also built in the U.K. based on designs by Hall Russell, Cochrane and Cook, Welton & Gemmell; the latter replacing Smith's Dock, now wholly occupied with the production of corvettes and frigates, from the original trio of World War I.

The naval trawlers were usually armed with a 4-inch gun when intended for A/S work and a 12-pounder when intended for M/S work and this generally applied to the requisitioned vessels as well, after an initial period when they had to make use of scratch armaments of vintage 3-pounder and 6-pounder guns until the supply position had improved. Similarly, the original anti-aircraft machine guns fitted in both naval and requisitioned vessels were subsequently replaced by 20 mm. guns in practically all. In the naval built trawlers the mast stepped before the bridge was invariably re-stepped abaft it, A.W. R.D.F. was added at the mast head and all-steel bridgework replaced the former mattress protected wood or canvas structures. Reciprocating machinery with which reserve engine room personnel were familiar was adhered to throughout, except in the Portugese built trawlers which were diesel engined, and from the prototype BASSET coal-firing was adopted for cylindrical boilers.

Building was so regulated that relatively few trawlers were cancelled at the termination of hostilities, when requisitioned vessels were rapidly returned to trade and large numbers of naval built trawlers accompanied them into commercial ownership.

During the war years the Royal Navy transferred many of its trawlers to allied navies. Eight trawlers were transferred to France in 1939 followed, at wide intervals, by two to the Royal Netherlands Navy. In 1942 twenty trawlers and two whalers were loaned to the United States Navy for a short period, to meet a critical shortage of escort vessels, and eight whalers to the Russian Navy; one of which was unfortunately lost en-route. Six naval and three requisitioned trawlers were loaned to Portugal in 1943, of which four naval trawlers were retained post-war and a further pair were later acquired. With the steady completion of the large **Isles** class four were respectively transferred to the Royal New Zealand Navy and the Royal Norwegian Navy, which enabled the latter to release six/seven of their older requisitioned vessels to the Royal Hellenic Navy. A requisitioned trawler was also lent to Poland in 1944.

An unintended transfer was the trawler LARWOOD, lost during the Norwegian campaign, which was salved by the German Navy and became their VPG.III. The loss was made good by a similar vessel captured by the Royal Norwegian Navy and incorporated as their HONINGSVAAG but was British manned and, in 1942, a German trawler captured by the Royal Navy was placed in service as the MARIA.

The largest single transfer after the cessation of hostilities was made to Italy in 1946 when sixteen naval built trawlers were turned over for minesweeping but the greatest demand by far for these vessels was from the commercial, and not the naval, market to make good the heavy losses sustained during the war.

NAVAL TRAWLERS AND DRIFTERS

Axe class

Displacement: 390 tons.
Dimensions: 130 (pp) 139 (oa) × 23½ × 12 ft.
Machinery: 1-shaft Reciprocating (VTE), I.H.P. 525 = 10½ knots.
Armament: 1—3 in. gun.
Complement: 18.

P. No.	Name	Builder Hull: Engine	Launched	Fate
T.20	DEE (ex-Battleaxe, ex-Russian T.16)	Smiths Dock	19. 6.16	Mercantile SAFIR (1946).
T.63	GARRY (ex-Goldaxe, ex-Russian T.13)	Smiths Dock	1. 6.16	Mercantile (name unchanged—1946).
T.78	KENNET (ex-Iceaxe, ex-Russian T.17)	Smiths Dock	17. 7.16	Sold 5/46.
T.81	LIFFEY (ex-Stoneaxe, ex-Russian T.14)	Smiths Dock	1. 6.16	Sold 1947.

Notes:—Former Russian vessels building in the U.K. and acquired by the R.N. during World War I.

Strath class

Displacement: 311 tons.
Dimensions: 115 (pp) 123 (oa) × 22 × 10 ft.
Machinery: 1-shaft Reciprocating (VTE), I.H.P. 430 = 10½ knots.
Armament: 1—3 in. gun ; 24 mines.
Complement: 18.

P. No.	Name	Builder	Launched	Fate
FY. 1594	STRATHCOE (ex-Vernon, ex-Strathcoe)	Hall Russell	12. 16	Mercantile (name unchanged—1946) lost 4/2/59.

Notes:—Two of this class, GEORGE IRELAND and HENRY JENNINGS, were unsuccessfully fitted with a form of jet propulsion in 4/18.

Castle class

Displacement: 360 tons.
Dimensions: 125 (pp) 134 (oa) × 23½ × 12 ft.
Machinery: 1-shaft Reciprocating (VTE), I.H.P. 480 = 10½ knots.
Armament: 1—3 in. gun.
Complement: 18.

Z.30	CORONET (ex-Robert Cloughton)	Bow Mac-Lachlan	18.12.17	Scrapped Northam 1953.
T.00	WAKAKURA (R.N.Z.N.) (ex-TR.1)	Port Arthur	1917	Sold 1947.
T.33	MADRAS (R.I.N.)	Burn: Hawthorn Leslie	1917	Laid up 1942.

Mersey class

Displacement: 438 tons.
Dimensions: 138½ (pp) 148 (oa) × 23½ × 13 ft.
Machinery: 1-shaft Reciprocating (VTE), I.H.P. 600 = 11 knots.
Armament: 2—3 in. (2 × 1) guns.
Complement: 20.

Z.100	BARNET (ex-mercantile Earl Haig ex-R.N. John Mann)	Cochrane	1919	Turkish KILYAS (1945).
T.04	BLACKWATER (ex-William Inwood)	Cochrane	10.18	Mercantile SPLEIS (1946); lost 12/2/56
T.29	BOYNE (ex-William Jones)	Cochrane: Holmes	9.18	Mercantile NYPUBERG (1946); scrapped 4/57.
T.03	CHERWELL (ex-James Jones)	Cochrane	1918	Sold 1946.
T.17	COLNE (ex-Isaac Chant)	Lobnitz	1918	Sold 1947.
T.35	DOON (ex-Fraser Eaves)	Cochrane	2.10.17	Sold 1947.
T.49	EDEN (ex-S.A.N. Immortelle, ex-Eden, ex-Thomas Jones)	Cochrane	7.18	Hulked 1942; sold 1945.
T.47	EXCELLENT (ex-Nith, ex-Andrew Jewer)	Cochrane: Holmes	1918	Mercantile MALVERN (1946); scrapped 1954.
T.05	FASTNET (ex-mercantile Frobisher, ex-R.N. Benjamin Hawkins)	Goole Sbdg.	1919	R.Neth.N. (name unchanged—1942); lost 4/42.
T.48	FOYLE (ex-S.A.N. Sonneblom, ex-Foyle, ex-John Edmund)	Goole Sbdg.	1918	W.D. (name unchanged—1946).

T.16	JAMES LUDFORD	Cochrane	6.18.	Lost 14/12/39.
T.79	MOY (ex-Alexander Hills)	Cochrane	22. 5.17	Mercantile CORAL ISLAND (1946); FORBES (1954).
T.80	OUSE (ex-Andrew King)	Cochrane	19. 4.17	Lost 20/2/41.
FY. 1592	STOUR (ex-Pembroke, ex-Stour, ex-Daniel Fearall)	Cochrane	2.11.17	Sold 1945.

Notes:—BARNET and FASTNET were re-acquired in 1933 and together with CORONET were converted to B.D.V's.

Armentiers class

Displacement: 440 tons.
Dimensions: 130 (pp) 139 (oa) × 25 × 13 ft.
Machinery: 1-shaft Reciprocating (VTE), I.H.P. 480 = 10½ knots.
Armament: 1—3 in. gun.
Complement: 18.

J.29	ARMENTIERS (R.C.N.)	Canadian Vickers	1918	Mercantile ARCTIC ROVER (1946).
J.46	FESTUBERT (R.C.N.)	Polson I.W.	2. 8.17	Mercantile INVERLEIGH (1946).
J.70	YPRES (R.C.N.)	Polson I.W.	6. 6.17	Lost 12/5/40.

Notes:—Out of the twelve original units of this class THIEPVAL was lost in 1930, MESSINES, ST. JULIEN and VIMY were sold out commercially, and ARLEUX, ARRAS, GIVENCHY, LOOS and St. ELOI were re-acquired.

ADMIRALTY DRIFTERS

SOME two hundred and eighty drifters were ordered during the First World War about a third of which were of wooden construction and a further hundred, also of wood, were ordered in Canada and numbered CD.1–100. Of these, at least six were cancelled, one hundred and three were completed as commercial drifters and the bulk of the remainder were sold out between the wars. By 1939 only twenty-four remained in service, but some sixty were re-acquired by the Royal Navy out of a total of about five hundred drifters requisitioned for the Second World War.

Displacement: 199 tons except wooden vessels 175 tons.
Dimensions: 86 (pp) 93 (oa) × 18½ × 9 ft.
Machinery: 1-shaft Reciprocating (VTE), I.H.P. 270 = 9 knots.
Armament: 1—6 pdr. gun.

P. No.	Name	Builder	Completed	Fate
	BRINE	Ouse Sbdg.	17. 7.18	BD tender; sold 1950.
	CASCADE	Ouse Sbdg.	21. 6.18	Harbour service; sold 1945.
FY. 3 Z.08	CLOUD	Duthie Torry	17. 5.18	TRV (1941); sold 1946.

Above: Drifter H.M.S. Shower.

Left: Trawler H.M.S. Berberis. 1—12 pdr. A.A.

H.M.S. Basset. 1—12 pdr., 2—.5 in. (1 × 2), 3—LG. (3 × 1), with twin MG. mounting added aft. [*I.W.M.*

FY. 4 Z.23	COLDSNAP	Duthie Torry	21. 3.18	Sold 1945.
FY. 5 Z.28	CRESCENT MOON	Duthie Torry	30. 6.18	M/S; sold 1946.
FY.10 Z.35	EBBTIDE* (ex-CD.1)	Canada	18	Harbour service; sold 1946
FY.12 Z.49	EDDY	Hall	27. 8.18	M/S; lost 26/5/42.
FY.16 Z.36	FUMAROLE*	Colby	11. 1.19	Sold 1947.
	RALEIGH (ex-Glitter)	Hall	18	Harbour service; scrapped 4/60.
FY.21 Z.38	HALO	Hall	4. 5.18	Sold 1948.
FY.23 Z.72	HARMATTAN	Hall	17. 4.18	Sold 1948.
FY.24 Z.53	HORIZON	Hall	30. 3.18	TRV (1941); sold 1946.
FY.28 Z.86	INDIAN SUMMER	Lewis	8. 2.18	TRV (1941); sold 1941.
FY.30 Z.97	LANDFALL	Lewis	7.18	M/S; sold 1946.
FY.31 Z.93	LEEWARD	Lewis	2.18	Sold 1947.
FY.32 Z.62	LUNAR BOW	Lewis	19. 7.18	Sold 1945.
FY.40 Z.55	MIST	Lewis	12.18	For disposal 1943.
FY.45 Z.79	NOONTIDE*	Colby	9.18	Target service (1941); scrapped Rosyth 25/3/60
	ONYX* (ex-CD.82)	Canada	18	Harbour service; sold 1946.
FY.50 Z.61	SEABREEZE	Hall	24.12.18	Sold 1945.
FY.51 Z.64	SHEEN	Brooke Marine	31. 8.18	TRV (1941); scrapped 1955.
FY.52 Z.81	SHOWER	Brooke Marine	30. 9.18	Sold 1945.
FY.54	SUNSET	Webster & Bickerton	22. 6.18	M/S; scrapped Malta 7/43.
FY.60 Z.91	WHIRLPOOL	Hall	30. 3.20	Target service (1941); scrapped Faslane 28/3/56

*wooden hull

Notes:—The flag superior was changed from the FY pendant to flag Z in 1940 which necessitated complete re-numbering to prevent duplication with boom defence vessels, which also wore flag Z.

PURCHASED TRAWLERS AND WHALERS

P. No.	Name	Gross tonnage/ Year built	Purchased	Fate
T.87	AGATE (ex-Mavis Rose)	627/34	1935	A/S; lost 6/8/41.

T.84	ALDER (ex-Lord Davidson)	500/29	1939	M/S; lost 22/10/41.
T.88	AMBER (ex-Cape Barfleur)	700/34	1939	A/S; mercantile ETONIAN (1946), ARCTIC CRUSADER (1950), ETONIAN (1952), GLENELLA (1955).
T.12	AMETHYST (ex-Phyllis Rosalie)	627/34	1935	A/S; lost 24/11/40.
T.44	BEECH (ex-Lord Dawson)	540/29	1939	M/S; lost 22/6/41.
T.46	BERBERIS (ex-Lord Hewart)	540/28	1939	M/S; mercantile BERGEN (1947).
T.34	BERYL (ex-Lady Adelaide)	615/35	1939	A/S; mercantile RED KNIGHT (1946).
T.01	CEDAR (ex-Arab)	649/33	1935	M/S; sold 7/46.
T.07	CORAL (ex-Cape Duner)	700/35	1939	A/S; lost 4/42 and scrapped *en situ* 1943.
T.15	CORNELIAN (ex-Cape Warwick)	568/33	1935	A/S; mercantile LINCOLN CITY (1947).
T.09	CYPRESS (ex-Cape Finisterre)	548/30	1935	M/S; mercantile VARDBERG (1946).
T.118	GUAVA (ex-British Columbia)	134/35	1939	A/S; mercantile BRITISH COLUMBIA (1946).
T.32	HAWTHORN (ex-Cape Guardafui)	593/30	1935	M/S; mercantile HAVBORGIN (1947).
T.19	HOLLY (ex-Kingston Coral)	590/30	1935	M/S; mercantile DRAGABERG (1947).
T.53	HORNBEAM (ex-Lord Trent)	530/29	1939	M/S D/L; mercantile RANKIN (1946).
T.56	JADE (ex-Lady Lillian)	615/33	1939	A/S; lost 10/4/42 and scrapped *en situ* 1943.
T.14	JASPER (ex-Balthasar)	581/32	1935	A/S; lost 1/12/42.
Z.21	JENNET (ex-Bunsen)	358/26	1939	B.D.V.; mercantile WESTHERON (1946).
T.96	LARCH (ex-St. Alexandra)	550/28	1939	M/S; mercantile WESTHILL (1946); scrapped U.K. 1952.
T.29	LAUREL (ex-Kingston Cyanite)	590/30	1935	M/S D/L, WDV (4.417—1944); mercantile STRATHYRE (1948).
T.26	LILAC (ex-Beachflower)	593/30	1935	M/S; mercantile ROBERT HEWITT (1946).
T.31	MAGNOLIA (ex-Lord Brentford)	557/30	1935	M/S; mercantile ORANJEZICHT (1948).
T.38	MAPLE (ex-St. Gerontius)	550/29	1939	M/S; mercantile SUMATRA (1946).

T.90	MOONSTONE (ex-Lady Madeleine)	615/34	1939	A/S; mercantile RED LANCER (1947).
T.91	MYRTLE (ex-St. Irene)	550/28	1939	M/S; lost 14/6/40.
T.54	OAK (ex-St. Romanus)	545/28	1939	M/S; sold 3/46.
T.22	PEARL (ex-Dervish)	649/34	1935	A/S; mercantile WESTELLA (1946).
Z.04	PUNNET (ex-Cape Matapan)	321/25	1939	B.D.V., Turkish ERDEK (1941); sold 1/46.
Z.44	QUANNET (ex-Dairycoates)	350/26	1939	B.D.V.; sold 1/46.
T.86	REDWOOD (ex-St. Rose)	545/28	1939	M/S; sold 1946.
Z.99	RENNET (ex-Deepdale Wyke)	335/28	1939	B.D.V.; Turkish (1940) mercantile RED ARCHER (1946); scrapped 1958.
T.24	RUBY (ex-Cape Bathurst)	568/33	1935	A/S; mercantile CARELLA (1947).
T.27	SAPPHIRE (ex-Mildenhall)	608/35	1935	A/S; mercantile DUNSBY (1946), FINDUS I (1953), SKAIDI (1954).
T.37	SYCAMORE (ex-Lord Beaver-brook)	573/30	1935	M/S; mercantile DRATTUR (1947).
T.55	SYRINGA (ex-Cape Kanin)	574/30	1935	M/S; mercantile DAVARR ISLAND (1947), CAPE KANIN (1948); scrapped 1954.
T.97	TAMARISK (ex-St. Gatien)	540/29	1939	M/S; lost 12/8/40.
T.40	TOPAZE (ex-Melbourne)	608/35	1935	A/S; lost 20/4/41.
T.42	TOURMALINE (ex-Berkshire)	641/35	1935	A/S; lost 5/2/41.
T.45	TURQUOISE (ex-Warwickshire)	641/35	1935	A/S; mercantile St. OSWALD (1946), WOOLTON (1950), WYRE WOOLTON (1954).
T.51	VULCAN (ex-Mascot, ex-Aston Villa)	623/33	1936	D.S. for C.F.; mercantile FOTHERBY (1947). MIRIAM (1950), POLLUX (1953).

T.66	WILLOW (ex-Cape Spartivento)	574/30	1935	M/S; mercantile TRONDUR-I-GOTTU (1946).

Lake class

Displacement: 560 tons.
Dimensions: 138½ (pp) 147½ (oa) × 26½ × 14¾ ft.
Machinery: 1-shaft Reciprocating (VTE), I.H.P. 1,400 = 13¾ knots.
Armament: 1—12 pdr. A.A., 1—20 mm. A.A., 2—5 in. A.A., (1 × 2) guns.

P. No.	Name	Builder	Launched	Fate
FY.205	BUTTERMERE (ex-Kos XXV)	Smiths Dock	30. 6.39	Mercantile TIERN (1948).
FY.204	ELLESMERE (ex-Kos XXIV)	Smiths Dock	17. 6.39	Lost 24/2/45.
FY.239	GRASSMERE (ex-Kos XXVIII)	Smiths Dock	31. 8.39	WASTWATER (1940): sold 5/46.
FY.206	THIRLMERE (ex-Kos XXVI)	Smiths Dock	5. 7.39	Mercantile KOS XXVI (1946).
FY.252	ULLSWATER (ex-Kos XXIX)	Smiths Dock	31. 8.39	Lost 9/11/42.
FY.207	WINDERMERE (ex-Kos XXVII)	Smiths Dock	21. 7.39	Mercantile KOS XXVII (1946).

NAVAL TRAWLERS

Basset Class

Displacement: 460 tons except MASTIFF 520 tons and R.I.N. vessels 545 tons.
Dimensions: 150 (pp) 163½ except BASSET 160½ (oa) × 27½ × 10½ except R.I.N. vessels, 13½ ft.
Machinery: 1-shaft Reciprocating (VTE), I.H.P. 850 = 12 knots except MASTIFF I.H.P. 950 = 13 knots
Armament: 1—4 in. & 2—M (2 × 1—LG) except R.I.N. vessels 1—12 pdr. A.A., 1—20 mm. A.A., 4—M (2 × 2—LG) guns.
Complement: 33 except R.I.N. vessels 48.

P. No.	Name	Builder Hull: Engine	Launched	Fate
T.68	BASSET	Robb	28. 9.35	Mercantile RADFORD (1948); scrapped
T.10	MASTIFF	Robb	17. 2.38	Lost 20/11/39.
R.C.N. vessels				
J.64	COMOX	Burrard*	9. 8.38	Mercantile SUNG MING (1950).
J.88	FUNDY	Collingwood*	18. 6.38	For disposal 29/7/45
J.94	GASPE	Morton*	12. 8.38	Mercantile SUNG LI (1950).
J.35	NOOKTA	Canadian* Yarrow	26. 9.38	NANOOSE (1944); Mercantile SUNG LING (1950).

* Engined Marine Industries

R.I.N. vessels

T.254	AGRA	Hooghlie*	18. 3.42	Sold 1946.
T.264	AHMEDABAD	Burn*	44	Sold 1947.
T.317	ALLAHABAD	Hooghlie		Cancelled 3/45.
T.320	AMBALA	Alcock Ashdown		Cancelled 3/45.
T.261	AMRITSAR	Garden Reach†	19.12.42	Sold 1947.
T.331	BANNU	Shalimar		Cancelled 3/45.
T.319	BAREILLY	Shalimar		Cancelled 3/45.
T.270	BARISAL (ex-Sholapore)	Burn		Cancelled 3/45.
T.249	BARODA	Shalimar	22.10.41	R.P.N. BAHAWALPUR (1947); sold 22/1/59.
T.318	BENARES	Hooghlie		Cancelled 1/45.
T.256	BERAR	Hooghlie*	31. 7.42	Sold 1946.
T.339	CALCUTTA	Hooghlie‡	8. 3.43	Sold 1947.
T.346	CAWNPORE	Burn		Cancelled 1/45.
T.265	CHITTAGONG	Burn		Cancelled 3/45.
T.315	COCHIN (ex-Multan)	Burn*	29.12.43	
T.251	CUTTACK	Burn*	44	Sold 1946.
T.252	DACCA	Burn		Cancelled 3/45.
T.326	DINAPORE	Calcutta		Cancelled 1/45.
T.325	GAYA	Calcutta		Cancelled 1/45.
T.323	JUBBALPORE (ex-Quetta)	Scindia		Cancelled 1/45.
T.262	KARACHI	Alcock Ashdown	1942	
T.330	KIAMARI	Scindia		Cancelled 1/45.
T.266	KOLABA (ex-Cochin)	Alcock Ashdown		
T.253	LAHORE	Shalimar	20.12.41	Sold 1946.
T.267	LUCKNOW	Alcock Ashdown	3. 4.42	
T.268	MADURA	Garden Reach †	21.12.42	Sold 1946.
T.327	MONGHYR	Alcock Ashdown		Cancelled 1/45.
T.322	MULTAN (ex-Cochin, ex-Kolaba)	Scindia		
T.269	NAGPUR	Burn		Cancelled 3/45.
T.258	NASIK	Shalimar	24. 5.44	Sold 1/50.
T.324	PACHMARI	Calcutta		Cancelled 1/45.
T.255	PATNA	Hooghlie‡	1. 9.42	Sold 1946.
T.263	PESHAWAR	Alcock Ashdown	1942	
T.260	POONA	Garden Reach	3. 4.42	Sold 1946.
T.328	PURI	Alcock Ashdown		Cancelled 1/45.
T.332	QUETTA (ex-Jubbalpore)	Alcock Ashdown		Cancelled 3/45.

T. 12	RAMPUR (ex-Barisal)	Burn*	19. 7.41	R.P.N. LAHORE (1947); sold 22/1/59.
T.250	SHILLONG	Burn*	42	Sold 1946.
T.259	SHOLAPORE	Burn		Cancelled 1/45.
T.321	SIALKOT	Alcock Ashdown		Cancelled 3/45.
T.329	SYLHET (ex-Sholapore)	Scindia		Cancelled 1/45.
T.312	TRAVANCORE	Garden Reach	8. 7.41	Sold 1/47.
T.314	TRICHINO-POLY	Burn		Cancelled 1/45.
T.313	VIZAGAPATAM	Burn		Cancelled 1/45.

Engined Lobnitz* Engined Whites M.E.† Engined Holmes‡

	BAY INNAUNG	Irrawadi Flotilla		Lost incomplete 3/42.
	COCHRANE	Irrawadi Flotilla		Lost incomplete 3/42.
	ELARA	Irrawadi Flotilla		Lost incomplete 3/42.
	GEMUNU	Irrawadi Flotilla		Lost incomplete 3/42.

Notes:—ELARA and GEMUNU were ordered for the Ceylon government.

Tree class

Displacement: 530 tons.
Dimensions: 150 (pp) 164 (oa) × 27½ × 10½ ft.
Machinery: 1-shaft Reciprocating (VTE), I.H.P. 850 = 11½ knots.
Armament: 1—12 pdr. A.A., 2—.5 in. A.A. (1 × 2), 4—M (2 × 2—LG) guns.
Complement: 35.

T. 02	ACACIA	Ardrossan: Plenty	7. 3.40	Mercantile (name unchanged—1947), BRAND V (1949); lost 15/6/53.
T.	ALMOND	Ardrossan: Plenty	22. 5.40	Lost 2/2/41.
T. 39	ASH	Cochrane: Amos & Smith	13.12.39	Lost 5/6/41.
T. 77	BAY	Cochrane: Amos & Smith	12.12.39	Mercantile (name unchanged—1947), TRISTANIA (1952).
T. 93	BIRCH	C.W. & G.: Holmes	13.11.39	Mercantile (name unchanged—1952).
T.100	BLACKTHORN	C.W. & G.: Holmes	29.11.39	Mercantile MAY-THORN (1949), KLAN (1955).
T.	CHESTNUT	Goole Sbdg: Amos & Smith	24. 2.40	Lost 30/11/40.

H.M.I.S. Travancore 1—12 pdr., 3—20 mm., mast re-sited abaft bridge and MGs. replaced by 20 mm.

H.M.S. Bay. 1—12 pdr., 2—.5 in. (1 × 2), 2—LG. (2 × 1) as completed. [I.W.M.

H.M.S. Coverley. 1—4 in., 3—20 mm., funnel raised and cowl added; steel bridge; mainmast struck and MG.s replaced by 20 mm. [I.W.M.

T.124	DEODAR	Goole Sbdg.: Amos & Smith	26. 3.40	Mercantile MOLLEX VI (1947), WERNER FELTER (1955).
T.105	ELM	Inglis: Aitchison Blair	12.12.39	Mercantile HELM (1946), MAGUL (1950).
T.129	FIR	Inglis: Aitchison Blair	27. 1.40	Sold 1946.
T.108	HAZEL	Robb: Whites M.E.	27.12.39	Sold 3/46.
T.116	HICKORY	Robb: Whites M.E.	24. 2.40	Lost 22/10/40.
T.123	JUNIPER	Ferguson	15.12.39	Lost 8/6/40.
T.112	MANGROVE	Ferguson	15. 2.40	Portugese P.2 (1943), FAIAL (1946).
T.126	OLIVE	Hall Russell Russell	26. 2.40	Mercantile SAMBA (1949); lost 28/12/56.
T.101	PINE	Hall Russell	25. 3.40	Lost 31/1/44.
T.119	ROWAN	Smiths Dock	12. 8.39	Mercantile MAIKEN (1947).
T.103	WALNUT	Smiths Dock	12. 8.39	Sold 1948.
T.127	WHITETHORN	Smiths Dock	10.11.39	Sold 3/46.
T.113	WISTARIA	Smiths Dock	10.11.39	Sold 3/46.

Dance class

Displacement: 530 tons.
Dimensions: 150 (pp) 160½ (oa) × 27½ × 10½ ft.
Machinery: 1-shaft Reciprocating (VTE), I.H.P 850 = 11½ knots.
Armament: 1—4 in., 3—20 mm. A.A. (3 × 1) guns.
Complement: 35.

T.104	COTILLION	Ardrossan: Plenty	21.12.40	Sold 28/3/47.
T.106	COVERLEY	Ardrossan: Plenty	27. 5.41	Mercantile JANNIKKE (1947), OFOTFJORD (1949).
T.107	FANDANGO	Cochrane: Amos & Smith	26. 3.40	Mercantile (name unchanged—1946).
T.109	FOXTROT	Cochrane: Amos & Smith	23. 4.40	W.D. (name unchanged —1946); scrapped Barrow 30/9/51.
T.115	GAVOTTE	C.W. & G.: Holmes	7. 5.40	Italian RD.312 (1946).
T.120	HORNPIPE	C.W. & G.: Holmes	21. 5.40	Italian RD.316 (1946).

T. 30	MAZURKA	Ferguson	28.11.40	Sold 3/46.
T.131	MINUET	Ferguson	1. 3.41	Italian RD.307 (1946).
T.117	MORRIS DANCE	Goole Sbdg.: Amos & Smith	6. 8.40	Sold 1947.
T. 39	PIROUETTE	Goole Sbdg.: Amos & Smith	22. 6.40	Mercantile TRIDENTE (1946).
T.139	POLKA	Hall Russell	29. 1.41	Sold 4/46.
T.133	QUADRILLE	Hall Russell	15. 3.41	Mercantile ELSA (1946), MURTEN (1950).
T.122	RUMBA	Inglis: Aitchison Blair	31. 7.40	Mercantile (name unchanged—1946), BUK HAE HO (1953).
T.125	SARABANDE	Inglis: Aitchison Blair	29. 8.40	Mercantile VOLEN (1946), BETTY (1953).
T.128	SALTARELO	Robb: Whites M.E.	6. 8.40	Portugese SALVADOR CORREIA (1947).
T.132	SWORD DANCE	Robb: Whites M.E.	3. 9.40	Lost 5/7/42.
T.146	TANGO	Smiths Dock	29.11.40	Sold 7/46.
T.142	TARANTELLA	Smiths Dock	27. 1.41	TWO STEP (1943); Italian RD.308 (1946).
T.151	VALSE	Smiths Dock	12. 3.41	W.D. (name unchanged —1946); scrapped Port Glasgow 9/51.
T.130	VELETA	Smiths Dock	28. 3.41	Sold 3/46.

Shakespearian class

Displacement: 545 tons.
Dimensions: 150 (pp) 164 (oa) × 27¾ × 11 ft.
Machinery: 1-shaft Reciprocating (VTE), I.H.P. 950 = 12 knots.
Armament: 1—12 pdr. A.A., 3—20 mm. A.A. (3 × 1) guns.
Complement: 35.

T.134	CELIA	Cochrane: Amos & Smith	15. 9.40	Mercantile (name unchanged—1946).
T.140	CORIOLANUS	Cochrane: Amos & Smith	2.10.40	Lost 5/5/45.
T.157	FLUELLEN	Cochrane: Amos & Smith	1.11.40	Scottish Home Dept. (name unchanged—1947).

T.167	HAMLET	C.W. & G.: Holmes	24. 7.40	Mercantile EIFONN (1947), FORT LAMALGUE (1950), UNION (1954).
T.153	HORATIO	C.W. & G.: Holmes	8. 8.40	Lost 7/1/43.
T.136	JULIET	C.W. & G.; Holmes	2.10.40	Mercantile PETERJON (1947), PLASSY (1951).
T.137	LAERTES	C.W. & G.: Holmes	16.10.40	Lost 25/7/42.
T.138	MACBETH	Goole Sbdg.: Amos & Smith	3.10.40	Mercantile (name unchanged—1947); lost 10/10/50.
T. 05	OPHELIA	Goole Sbdg.: Amos & Smith	3. 9.40	Mercantile TOTTAN (1946).
T. 76	OTHELLO	Hall Russell	7.10.41	Italian RD.310 (1946).
T. 10	ROMEO	Inglis: Aitchison Blair	20. 3.41	Sold Belgium 1946.
T.135	ROSALIND	Inglis: Aitchison Blair	3. 5.41	R.N.V.R. (Kenya & Zanzibar—1947), R.E.A.N. (19); for disposal.

Isles class

Displacement: 545 tons.
Dimensions: 150 (pp) 164 (oa) × 27½ × 10½ ft.
Machinery: 1-shaft Reciprocating (VTE), I.H.P. 850 = 12 knots
Armament: 1—12 pdr. A.A. (not in danlayers), 3—20 mm. A.A. (3 × 1) guns
Complement: 40.

T.377	AILSA CRAIG	C.W. & G.: Holmes	16.10.43	Mercantile VESLEMOY (1946), TORAN (1952); lost 19/2/55.
T.341	ANNET	C.W. & G.: Holmes	25. 3.43	WDV (DV.2—1946), FPV ULVA (1958).
T. 06	ARRAN	C.W. & G.: Holmes	16.11.40	Mercantile ASSAN REIS (1946); PROFESSOR HENKING (1952).
T. 50	BALTA	C.W. & G.: Holmes	2.12.40	Mercantile CHING HAI (1946)
T.273	BARDSEY	Fleming & Ferguson	17. 7.43	WDV (DV.3—1946), TCV (1950).
T.379	BENBECULA	C.W. & G.: Holmes	28.10.43	H.M.C. & E. VIGILANT (1946); for disposal.
T.294	BERN	C.W. & G.: Holmes	2. 5.42	WDV (DV.4—1946), TCV (1956); for disposal.

T.404	BIGGAL	Ferguson	4.12.44	Mercantile FRANKFURT-MAIN (1946); scrapped Hamburg 2/61
T.214	BRESSAY	C.W. & G.: Amos & Smith	20. 1.42	Sold 3/46.
T. 99	BRORA	C.W. & G.: Holmes	18.12.40	Lost 6/9/41.
T.246	GWEAL (ex-Broreray)	C.W. & G.: Holmes	17. 6.42	Mercantile VELOX (1948).
T.236	BRURAY	C.W. & G.: Holmes	1. 6.42	Portugese P.1 (1943), SAN MIGUEL (1946); scrapped Lisbon 1957.
T.350	BRYHER	C.W. & G.: Holmes	8. 4.43	Sold 1947.
T.158	BURRA	Goole Sbdg.: Amos & Smith	29. 3.41	Italian RD.301 (1946).
T.168	BUTE	Goole Sbdg.: Amos & Smith	12. 5.41	Sold 3/46.
T.359	CALDY	Lewis	31. 8.43	WDV (DV.5—1946), TCV (1951).
T.383	CALVAY	C.W. & G.: Holmes	29.11.43	Mercantile WM. FEN-TON (1948).
T.161	CANNA	Cochrane Holmes	18.11.40	Lost 5/12/42.
T.145	CAVA	Fleming & Ferguson	3. 3.41	Mercantile LUCIA VENTURI (1947).
T.207	COLL	Ardrossan: Plenty	7. 4.42	WDV (DV.6—1946), TCV (1950).
T.384	COLSAY	C.W. & G.: Holmes	15.12.43	Lost 2/11/44.
T.147	COPINSAY	Cochrane: Amos & Smith	2.12.40	W.D. (name unchanged —1946), mercantile ION (1956).
T.380	CROWLIN	C.W. & G Holmes	15.11.43	Mercantile (name unchanged—1946), THERMO (1955).
T.154	CUMBRAE	Cochrane Amos & Smith	20.12.40	Italian RD.302 (1946).
T.208	DAMSAY	Brown Aitchison Blair	27. 6.42	WD store carrier (DVC.2—1946); scrapped Troon 28/8/59.
T.201	EDAY	Cochrane	26. 6.41	R.N.N. TROMOY (ii) (1944), mercantile FJELLBERG (1948), SEMPACH (1952); lost 27/4/53.

Top to bottom: H.M.S. Tango. 1—4 in., 4—LG. (1 × 2 and 2 × 1) as completed. H.M.S. Biggal. 1—12 pdr. A.A., 3—20 mm. A.A. (3 × 1). H.M.S. Calvay as danlayer. Note RDF on bridge, 3—20 mm. A.A. (3 × 1). [*All I.W.M.*

T.215	EGILSAY	C.W. & G.; Holmes	7. 2.42	Italian RD.306 (1946).
T.216	ENSAY	C.W. & G.; Holmes	5. 3.42	Italian RD.314 (1946).
T.217	ERISKAY	Fleming & Ferguson	28. 8.42	Portugese P.8 (1943–44); lost 12/11/45.
T.162	FARA	Cochrane: Amos & Smith	27. 1.41	Sold 12/7/46.
T.353	FARNE	C.W. & G.: Holmes	22. 4.43	Mercantile (name unchanged—1946); lost 27/12/48.
T.202	FETLAR	Cochrane	10. 7.41	WDV (DV.8—1946); scrapped Belgium 22/6/60.
T.238	FIARAY	Goole Sbdg.: Amos & Smith	13. 6.42	Mercantile ATLAS (1946), ARIS (1955).
T.212	FILLA	Crown: Holmes	2. 4.42	Italian RD.305 (1946).
T.354	FLATHOLM	C.W. & G.: Holmes	8. 5.43	WDV (DV.9—1946); scrapped Belgium 8/60.
T.171	FLOTTA	Cochrane: Amos & Smith	13. 2.41	Lost 6/11/41.
T.203	FOULA	Cochrane	28. 7.41	Italian RD.313 (1946).
T.342	FOULNESS	Lewis	23. 3.42	TCV (1957).
T.385	FUDAY	C.W. & G.: Holmes	1. 1.44	Mercantile SIMON DE DANSER (1946)
T.290	GAIRSAY	Ardrossan: Plenty	28. 5.42	Lost 3/8/44.
T.376	GANILLY	C.W. & G.: Holmes	22. 5.43	Lost 5/7/44.
T.386	HARRIS (ex-Gilsay)	C.W. & G.: Holmes	29. 1.44	Mercantile LYNGAS (1947), FORT MALBOUSQUET (1950), SHEILA MARGARET (1952).
T.355	GILLSTONE	Cochrane: Amos & Smith	19. 7.43	Mercantile ARGO (1947).
T.387	GORREGAN	Ardrossan: Whites M.E.	30.12.43	Scrapped Charlestown 10/57.
T.291	GRAEMSAY	Ardrossan: Plenty	3. 8.42	WDV (DV.10—1946). TCV (1956).
T.360	GRAIN	Cochrane: Amos & Smith	17. 8.43	Italian RD.309.
T.344	GRASSHOLM	Lewis	20. 4.43	Mercantile (name unchanged—1946).
T.239	GRUINARD	Crown: Holmes	20.11.42	Portugese P.7 (1943-44), mercantile PRESIDENT F. D. ROOSEVELT (1946), ODIN (1950).

T.297	EARRAID (ex-Gruna)	Crown: Whites M.E.	18.12.41	WDV (DV.7—1946); sold 3/51.
T.365	GULLAND	C.W. & G.: Holmes	5. 8.43	Sold 3/46.
T.389	HANNARAY	C.W. & G.: Holmes	12. 2.44	Mercantile WODAN (1947).
T.390	HASCOSAY	C.W. & G.: Holmes	28. 3.44	Mercantile YPAPANDI (1947); lost 13/1/52.
T.271	HAYLING	C.W. & G.: Holmes	17. 8.42	Portuguese P.3 (1943), TERCEIRA (1946).
T.391	HELLISAY	Cochrane: Amos & Smith	27. 3.44	Mercantile ELPIS (1947). ELPIS II (1954).
T.392	HERMETRAY	Cochrane: Amos & Smith	11. 4.44	Mercantile COIMBRA (1947), FURKA (1952).
T.173	HILDASAY	C.W. & G.: Amos & Smith	29. 4.41	Lost 21/6/45.
T. 16	HOXA	C.W. & G.: Amos & Smith	15. 1.41	Mercantile SUNG HWEI (1946).
T.114	HOY	C.W. & G.: Amos & Smith	1. 2.41	Mercantile DUNAY (1946).
T.298	HUNDA	Ferguson	4. 2.42	Sold 5/46.
J.422	IMERSAY	Cochrane: Amos & Smith	21. 8.44	D/L; sold 1/59.
T. 18	INCHCOLM	C.W. & G.: Holmes	3. 3.41	W.D. (name unchanged —1946), CELESTE AIDA (1952).
T.155	INCHKEITH	Lewis	10. 7.41	R.N.Z.N. (1942).
T.166	INCHMARNOCK	Lewis	25. 8.41	R.N.N. KARMOY (1944), mercantile TILTHORN (1947), NADOR (1952), SERVANNAISE (1955).
T.172	ISLAY	Smiths Dock	10. 4.41	Mercantile ISLY (1946) ST. ANNE (1949); lost 14/3/50.
T.169	JURA	Ardrossan: Plenty	22.11.41	Lost 7/1/43.
T.200	KERRERA	Fleming & Ferguson	24. 9.41	R.N.N. OKSOY (1944) mercantile JASON (1946); lost 1/3/50.
T.174	KILLEGRAY	C.W. & G.: Holmes	25. 5.41	R.N.Z.N. (1942).
T.165	KINTYRE	Ardrossan: Plenty	21.10.41	Sold 1946.
T.382	KITTERN	C.W. & G.: Holmes	21. 8.43	Sold 4/46.

T.361	LINDISFARNE	C.W. & G.: Holmes	17. 6.43	WDV (DV.11—1946); scrapped Dover 26/4/58.
J.423	LINGAY	Cochrane: Amos & Smith	6. 9.44	D/L; mercantile TULIP-DALE (1947);
T.366	LONGA	Cochrane: Holmes	15.10.43	FPV (name unchanged —1946).
T.272	LUNDY	C.W. & G.: Holmes	29. 8.42	WDV (DV.12—1946), TCV (1956).
T.374	MEWSTONE	C.W. & G.: Holmes	16. 9.43	Sold 1946.
T.362	MINALTO	C.W. & G.: Holmes	3. 7.43	Sold 1947.
T.388	MINCARLO	Ardrossan: Whites M.E.	28. 3.44	R.N.N. TROMOY (iii) (1944), mercantile KRISTIANBORG (1948) SVERRE HUND (1950).
T.295	MOUSA	Goole Sbdg.: Amos & Smith	1. 6.42	Italian RD.311 (1946).
T.110	MULL	C.W. & G.: Holmes	27. 3.41	W.D. (name unchanged —1946).
T.247	NEAVE	C.W. & G.: Holmes	16. 7.42	WDV (DV.14—1946); sold 7/51.
T.204	ORFASY	Hall	17. 3.42	Lost 22/10/43.
T.375	ORONSAY	Cochrane: Amos & Smith	30.10.43	Sold 1946.
J.450	ORSAY	Cochrane: Amos & Smith	1. 1.45	D/L; sold 1957.
T.296	OXNA	Inglis: Aitchison Blair	26. 1.43	W.D. (name unchanged —1947).
T.144	PLADDA	C.W. & G.: Holmes	16. 4.41	Mercantile (name unchanged—1946).
T.292	SHEPPEY (ii) (ex-Raasay)	C.W. & G.: Holmes	1. 4.42	W.D. (name unchanged —1947); scrapped Plymouth 24/3/59.
T.149	RONALDSAY	Cochrane: Amos & Smith	14. 2.41	Mercantile DAH LAI (1946).
J.429	RONAY	Cochrane: Amos & Smith	15. 2.45	D/L; for disposal.
T.363	ROSEVEAN	C.W. & G.: Holmes	17. 7.43	Sold 3/46.
T.210	ROUSAY	Goole Sbdg.: Amos & Smith	20.12.41	Mercantile TOVA (1947), EINAR HUND (1954).

T.211	RUSKHOLM	Goole Sbdg.: Amos & Smith	4. 2.42	Portugese BALDAQUE DA SILVA (1947).
T.164	RYSA	Cochrane: Amos & Smith	15. 3.41	Lost 8/12/43.
T.352	ST. AGNES	Lewis	19. 5.43	Mercantile CAPTAIN ARSENE BLONDE (1947), THOR (1950).
T.209	ST. KILDA	Hall	29. 5.42	Mercantile CLAES COMPAEN (1948), PROFESSOR HENSEN (1952).
T.160	SANDA	Goole Sbdg.: Amos & Smith.	12. 7.41	R.N.Z.N. (1942); for disposal.
J.424	SANDRAY	C.W. & G.: Holmes	5.10.44	D/L.: sold 1961.
T.237	SCALPAY	C.W. & G.: Amos & Smith	2. 6.42	WDV (DV.15—1946); mercantile (name unchanged—1947).
J.425	SCARAVAY	C.W. & G.: Holmes	22.10.44	D/L.; sold 11/46.
T.175	SCARBA	C.W. & G.: Holmes	26. 6.41	R.N.Z.N. (1942); for disposal.
T.176	SHAPINSAY	Cochrane: Amos & Smith	29. 3.41	Mercantile EL HASCIMY (1946), EL FAYEZ (1955).
M.15	BLACKBIRD (ex-Sheppey (i))	C.W. & G.: Holmes	20. 2.43	Controlled M/L; mercantile GOODMAR (1949), IASON (1953); lost 13/3/53.
T.170	SHIANT	Goole Sbdg.: Amos & Smith	9. 8.41	R.N.N. JELOY (1944-46), mercantile ARTEMIS (1946); lost 31/7/60.
J.426	SHILLAY	C.W. & G.: Holmes	18.11.44	D/L; scrapped Italy 11/58.
T.376	SKOKHOLM	C.W. & G.: Holmes	29. 9.43	Mercantile SKOGHOLM (1946), HOCHMEISTER (1960).
T.381	SKOMER	Lewis	17. 6.43	WDV (DV.16—1946), TCV (1956).
T.163	SKYE	Robb: Whites M.E.	17. 3.42	Scrapped Bo'ness 29/5/58.
T.177	SLUNA	Cochrane: Amos & Smith	14. 4.41	Mercantile SHUN WA (1946), HAI MA (1948); lost 13/10/50, salved & scrapped.
T.159	STAFFA	Robb: Whites M.E.	15. 6.42	Italian RD.304 (1946).

T.356	STEEPHOLM	Lewis	15. 7.43	WDV (DV.17—1946); scrapped Antwerp 18/6/60.
T.150	STROMA	Hall Russell	19.11.41	Italian RD.315 (1946).
T.178	STRONSAY	Inglis: Aitchison Blair	4. 3.42	Lost 5/2/43.
J.427	SURSAY	C.W. & G.: Holmes	16.12.44	D/L; for disposal.
T.179	SWITHA	Inglis: Aitchison Blair	3. 4.42	WDV (DV.18—1946), T.C.V. (1950).
J.452	TAHAY	C.W. & G.: Holmes	31.12.44	D/L; for disposal.
M.22	DABCHICK (ex-Thorney)	C.W. & G.: Holmes	9. 3.43	Controlled M/L, R.Mal.N. PENYU (1954); for disposal.
T.180	TIREE	Goole Sbdg.: Amos & Smith	6. 9.41	WDV (DV.19–1946); scrapped Antwerp 3/9/60.
J.451	TOCOGAY	C.W. & G. Holmes	7. 2.45	D/L; scrapped Italy 11/58.
J.431	TRODDAY	C.W. & G. Holmes	3. 3.45	D/L; scrapped Spezia 7/60.
T.181	TRONDRA	Lewis	4.10.41	WDV (DV.20–1946); scrapped Charlestown 11/57.
T.248	ULVA	C.W. & G.: Holmes	30. 7.42	Mercantile SALVO (1946), PLICO (1948), SURINAME (1950), ANNE T. WILLIAMS (1951).
T.213	UNST	Ferguson	28. 5.42	Italian RD.303 (1946).
J.432	VACEASAY	C.W. & G.: Holmes	17. 3.45	D/L; for disposal.
.434	VALLAY	C.W. & G.: Holmes	10. 4.45	D/L; sold 1/59.
T.378	VATERSAY	Cochrane: Amos & Smith	13.11.43	Mercantile VOURI (1946), NAM VIET (1954).
T.345	WALLASEA	Robb: Whites M.E.	22. 4.43	Lost 6/1/44.
T.182	WESTRAY	Lewis	4.11.41	Mercantile (name unchanged—1946).
T.293	WHALSAY	C.W. & G.: Holmes	4. 4.42	Portugese P.3 (1943), SANTA MARIA (1946).
.441	WIAY	C.W. & G.: Holmes	26. 4.44	D/L; sold 10/61.
M.25	STONECHAT (ex-......)	C.W. & G.: Holmes	28. 8.44	Controlled M/L, R.C.N. (1944); sold 1946.
M.03	WHITETHROAT (ex-......)	C.W. & G. Holmes	6. 9.44	Controlled M/L, R.C.N. (1944).

T.274	ANTICOSTI	Collingwood	1. 4.42	Mercantile GULOY (1946), BARBRO (1948), GUISEPPINA (1957).
T.275	BAFFIN*	Collingwood	13. 4.42	Mercantile (name unchanged—1947), NIEDERMEHNEN (1952).
T.276	CAILIFF	Collingwood	30. 4.42	Mercantile BORGENES (1947).
T.277	MISCOU* (ex-Bowell, ex-Campenia)	Collingwood	1. 6.42	Mercantile CLEVELAND (1946), SIGURD HUND (1950).
T.278	CAMPOBELLO	Collingwood	19. 6.42	Lost 16/3/43.
T.286	DOCHET	G.T. Davie	26. 6.42	West German EIDER (1946).
T.287	FLINT	G.T. Davie	14. 7.42	West German TRAVE (1947).
T.288	GATESHEAD	G.T. Davie	1. 8.42	Scrapped Rotterdam 9/59.
T.289	HERSCHELL	G.T. Davie: Canadian Bridge	9.11.42	Mercantile EIRIKUR HIN REIDI (1946), RADNI (1947).
T.284	IRONBOUND*	Kingston	14. 1.42	Mercantile TUROY (1946), CHRISTINA (1949), KORSO (1954).
T.285	LISCOMB*	Kingston	23. 3.42	Mercantile AALESUND (1946).
T.279	MAGDALEN*	Midland	7. 3.42	Mercantile MAROY (1946), CINZIA (1951).
T.280	MANITOULIN*	Midland	23. 4.42	Mercantile RAN. (1946), RAN.B (1951), BLUE PETER II (1951).
T.281	PORCHER (ex-Procher)	Midland	26. 5.42	W.D. (name unchanged —1947), mercantile TULIPGLEN (1951).
T.282	PROSPECT	Midland: Con. Mining & Smelting	16. 6.42	W.D. (name unchanged —1946); sold Greece 12/59.
T.283	TEXADA	Midland	27. 7.42	Sold Belgium 3/46.

*All R.C.N. (1942-45).

Admiralty type

Displacement: 600 tons.
Dimensions: 150 (pp) 156 (oa) × 30 × 13 ft.
Machinery: 1-shaft Reciprocating (VTE), I.H.P. 1,000 = 14 knots.
Armament: 1—4 in., 1—20 mm. A.A. guns. *Complement:* 35.

T.102	KIWI (R.N.Z.N.)	Robb: Plenty	7. 7.41	
T.233	MOA (R.N.Z.N.)	Robb: Plenty	15. 5.41	Lost 7/4/43.
T.234	TUI (R.N.Z.N.)	Robb: Plenty	26. 8.41	

Portuguese type

Displacement: *First group:* 525 tons. *Second group:* 550 tons.
Dimensions: 129 (pp) 139 (oa) × 27¾ × 11 ft. 133 (pp) 148 (oa) × 27¾ × 11 ft.
Machinery: *Both groups:* 1-shaft Diesel motors, B.H.P. 550 = 11 knots.
Armament: 1—12 pdr. A.A. gun.
Complement: 30.

First Group (*wooden hull*)

T.190	PRONG (ex-Port Stanley)	A. Monica: British Auxiliaries	1. 7.41	Mercantile SJOSTKERK (1946); scrapped 1954.
T.191	PROOF (ex-Port Royal)	,,	1. 8.41	Sold 1946.
T.192	PROPERTY (ex-Portrush)	,,	1. 9.41	Mercantile PORTRUSH (1946), PROPERTY (1947), VAAGNESS (1955).
T.194	PROPHET (ex-Portobello)	,,	1. 7.41	Sold 1946.
T.195	PROTEST (ex-Port Patrick)	M.M.B. Monica	1. 8.41	Mercantile (1946).
T.196	PROWESS (ex-Provost, ex-Portreath)	M.M.B. Monica	1. 9.41	Sold 1946.

Second Group (*steel hull*)

T.186	PROBE (ex-Portaferry)	Alfeite: Ruston & Hornsby	. .42	Mercantile POLO NORTE (1946).
T.185	PROCTOR (ex-Portisham, ex-Portadown)	,,	23.10.42	Mercantile ARRABIDA (1946).
T.187	PRODIGAL (ex-Porthleven)	Uniao Fabril	26. 4.41	Sold 1946.
T.188	PRODUCT (ex-Port Jackson)	,,	12. 4.41	M/S Repair ship (1943), R.H.N. HERMES (1946).
T.189	PROFESSOR (ex-Portmadoc)	,,	28. 5.41	Mercantile ALGENIB (1946).
T.193	PROMISE (ex-Port Natal)	,,	20. 9.41	Mercantile ALDEBARAN (1946).

Notes:—Two other steel trawlers were ordered in 1942 from the Alfeite Yard but since no material had been received by 12/42 they were cancelled, while two others, ordered from Uniao Fabril, were completed as the mercantile IHLA GRACIOSA and HAIL DO FAIAL.

Brazilian type

Displacement: 680 tons.
Dimensions: 160 (pp) 176½ (oa) × 28 × 14 ft.
Machinery: 1-shaft Reciprocating (VTE), I.H.P. 1,000 = 12½ knots.
Armament: 1—12 pdr. A.A., 4—20 mm. A.A. (4 × 1) guns.
Complement: 40.

Top to bottom: H.M.S. Blackbird as controlled minelayer. 1—20 mm. A.A. H.M.S. Texada, Canadian built. 1—12 pdr. A.A., 3—20 mm. A.A. (3 × 1). H.M.S. Butser. 1—12 pdr. A.A., 3—20 mm. A.A (3 × 1). H.M.S. Sir Tristram. 1—12 pdr. A.A., 1—20 mm. A.A., 2—MG. (2 × 1). [*All I.W.M.*

T.152	PAMPANO	Nac. Nav. Costeira	11. 6.42	Brazilian MATIAS DE ALBUQUERQUE (1942).
T.156	PAPATERA	,,	7.42	Brazilian FELIPE CAMARAO (1942).
T.148	PARATI	,,	11. 6.42	Brazilian FERNANDES VIEIRA (1942).
T.141	PARGO	,,	26. 8.42	Brazilian HENRIQUE DIAS (1942).
T.183	PARU	,,	2.45	Brazilian BARRETO MENEZES (1942).
T.184	PELEGRIME	,,	42	Brazilian VIDAL DE NEGREIROS (1942).

Notes:—All transferred to Brazilian Navy in 1942.

Castle class

Displacement: 625 tons.
Dimensions: 125 (pp) 134 (oa) × 23½ × 12 ft.
Machinery: 1-shaft Reciprocating (VTE), I.H.P. = 10 knots.
Armament: 1—12 pdr. A.A., 4—M (2 × 2—LG) guns. *Complement:* 32.

T.396	AROHA (R.N.Z.N.)	Stevenson & Cook‡ Price		Mercantile MATONG (1947).
T.397	AWATERE (R.N.Z.N.)	Patent Slip		Mercantile (name unchanged—1946).
T.340	HAUTAPU (R.N.Z.N.)	Stevenson & Cook	43	Sold 1947.
T.399	HINAU* (R.N.Z.N.)	Senior Fdry.		Sold 1955.
T.338	MAIMAI (R.N.Z.N.)	Stevenson & Cook‡		Mercantile (name unchanged—1946).
T.401	MANUKA* (R.N.Z.N.)	Senior Fdry.	42	Sold 1946.
T.351	PAHAU (R.N.Z.N.)	Stevenson & Cook: N.Z.Rly.		Mercantile (name unchanged—1947).
T.402	RIMU* (R.N.Z.N.)	Seager	42	Sold 1955.
T.348	TAWHAI* (R.N.Z.N.)	Seager	22. 7.43	Sold 1947.
T.364	WAIRUA (R.N.Z.N.)	Mason		
T.403	WAIHO	Stevenson & Cook‡ Price		R.N.Z.N. (1944) mercantile MOONA (1947).
	WAIITI	Stevenson & Cook		Cancelled 1945.
	WAIKAKA	Stevenson & Cook		Cancelled 1945.
	WAIKANAE	Stevenson & Cook		Cancelled 1945.
T.343	WAIKATO (R.N.Z.N.)	Mason: N.Z. Rly.	16.10.43	Mercantile TAIAROA (1946).

T.349	WAIMA (R.N.Z.N.)	Stevenson & Cook‡		Mercantile MALDONNA (1946).
T.357	WAIPU (R.N.Z.N.)	Stevenson & Cook‡		Mercantile MULLOKA (1955).

* Composite construction

‡ All engined A. G. Price

Hills class

Displacement: 750 tons.
Dimensions: $166\frac{1}{4}$ (pp) $181\frac{1}{4}$ (oa) × 28 × 12 ft.
Machinery: 1-shaft Reciprocating (VTE), I.H.P. 970 = 11 knots.
Armament: 1—12 pdr. A.A., 3—20 mm. A.A. (3 × 1) guns.
Complement: 35.

T.218	BIRDLIP	C.W. & G.: Holmes	9. 7.41	Lost 13/6/44.
T.219	BUTSER	,,	29. 7.41	Mercantile BALTHAZAR (1946), ROYAL MARINE (1952).
T.223	BREDON	,,	20.11.41	Lost 8/2/43.
T.220	DUNCTON	,,	6. 9.41	Mercantile COLWYN BAY (1945).
T.224	DUNKERY	,,	4.12.41	Sold 1947.
T.225	INKPEN	,,	22.12.41	Mercantile STELLA CAPELLA (1946).
T.221	PORTSDOWN	,,	24. 9.41	Mercantile SOLLUM (1946), HARGOOD (1949), RED SABRE (1955).
T.222	YESTOR	,,	21.10.41	Mercantile CAPE CLEVELAND (1946), STELLA CARINA (1947), CAPE FINISTERRE (1949), DRAGOON (1952).

Notes:—Design based on builders mercantile BARNETT (482/37).

Fish class

Displacement: 670 tons.
Dimensions: 146 (pp) 162 (oa) × $25\frac{1}{4}$ × $12\frac{1}{2}$ ft.
Machinery: 1-shaft Reciprocating (VTE), I.H.P. 700 = 11 knots.
Armament: 1—4 in., 3—20 mm. A.A. (3 × 1) guns. *Complement:* 35.

T.231	BONITO	Cochrane: Holmes	8.10.41	Mercantile BLAEFELL (1946); BENJAMIN GELCER (1956)
T.306	BREAM	Cochrane: Amos & Smith	10.12.42	Sold 1946.
T.243	GRAYLING	,,	4. 3.42	Mercantile BARRY CASTLE (1946); lost 1/11/55.

T.368	GRILSE	,,	6. 4.43	Mercantile CARDIFF CASTLE (1946); scrapped Sunderland 10/6/60.
T.307	HERRING	,,	24.12.42	Lost 22/4/43.
M.55	CORNCRAKE (ex-Mackerel)	,,	3.42	Controlled M/L; lost 25/1/43.
T.311	MULLET	,,	14. 8.42	Sold 1946.
T.347	POLLACK	,,	22. 4.43	Mercantile SWANSEA CASTLE (1946), JULIA BRIERLEY (1952).
M.31	REDSHANK (ex-Turbot)	,,	28. 8.42	Controlled M/L; scrapped Sunderland 9/5/57.
T.232	WHITING	Cochrane: Holmes	22.10.41	Mercantile BURFELL (1946); scrapped Sunderland 10/6/60.

Notes:—Design based on builder's mercantile GULFOSS (358/29).

Round Table class

Displacement: 440 tons.
Dimensions: 126 (pp) 137¾ (oa) × 23¾ × 11½ ft.
Machinery: 1-shaft Reciprocating (VTE), I.H.P. 600 = 12 knots.
Armament: 1—12 pdr. A.A., 1—20 mm. A.A., 2—M (2 × 1—LG) guns.
Complement: 35.

T.230	SIR AGRAVAINE	Lewis	5. 3.42	Mercantile (name unchanged—1946), UTHEIM (1954).
T.226	SIR GALAHAD	Hall Russell: Hall	18.12.41	D/L (1944), mercantile STAR OF FREEDOM (1946), ROBERT LIMBRICK (1956). lost 5/2/57.
T.227	SIR GARETH	Hall Russell	19. 1.42	Mercantile STAR OF THE EAST (1946).
T.240	SIR GERAINT	Lewis	15. 4.42	Mercantile STAR OF THE SOUTH (1946).
T.241	SIR KAY	Hall Russell	26.10.42	Mercantile STAR OF THE NORTH (1946), ROBERT CROHN (1956).
T.242	SIR LAMORACK	Hall Russell	23.11.42	Mercantile BRACON-BANK(1946), BRACON (1954).
T.228	SIR LANCELOT	Lewis	4.12.41	D/L (1944), FRS (name unchanged—1946).
T.229	SIR TRISTRAM	Lewis	17. 1.42	Sold 1947.

Notes:—Design based on Hall Russell's mercantile STAR OF ORKNEY (273/36).

Top to Bottom: H.M.S. Coldstreamer. 1—4 in., 4—20 mm. A.A. (4 × 1). H.M.S. Grenadier. 1—4 in., 4—20 mm. A.A. (4 × 1). Belgian A/P Trawler Adriatic. 1—1 pdr., 3—MG. (3 × 1). [*I.W.M.*

Military class

Displacement: 750 tons.
Dimensions: 175 (pp) 193 (oa) × 30 × 13 ft.
Machinery: 1-shaft Reciprocating (VTE), I.H.P. 1,000 = 11 knots.
Armament: 1—4 in., 4—20 mm. A.A. (4 × 1) guns.
Complement: 40.

T.304	BOMBARDIER	C.W. & G.: Holmes	23. 1.43	Mercantile NORMAN (1946); lost 4/10/52.
T.337	COLDSTREAMER	,,	10.12.42	Mercantile ESQUIMAUX (1946).
T.305	FUSILIER	,,	23.12.42	Mercantile SERRON (1946).
T.334	GRENADIER	,,	26. 9.42	Mercantile ISERNIA (1946).
T.393	GUARDSMAN	,,	7. 6.44	Mercantile THURINGIA (1946).
T.394	HOME GUARD	,,	8. 7.44	Mercantile LOYAL (1946).
T.335	LANCER	,,	26.10.42	Mercantile STELLA ORION (1946); lost 7/11/55.
T.395	ROYAL MARINE	,,	22. 7.44	Mercantile SISAPON (1946).
T.336	SAPPER	,,	11.11.42	Mercantile CAPE GLOUCESTER (1946).

Notes:—Design based on builder's mercantile type.

REQUISITIONED TRAWLERS, WHALERS AND DRIFTERS

P. No.	Name	Gross tonnage/ Year built	Requisi- tioned	Fate
FY.284	ABERDOUR (D)	93/08	1940	BBV; returned 1946.
	ABIDING STAR (D)	117/17	1940	MRV, D/G; returned 1946.
FY.734	ABRONIA	242/06	11.39	M/S; scrapped 1947.
	ACCORD (AD)	100/18	8.39	Harbour service; sold 1946.
FY.902	ACHIEVABLE (D)	96/27	11.39	MRV; returned 1/46.
FY.914	ACHROITE	314/34	8.39	M/S; returned 1945.
	ACORN (AD)	96/19	1940	Harbour service; returned 1946.
	ACQUIRE (D)	94/07	1940	BBV; returned 1945.
	ACQUISITION (D)	83/13	3.40	S/M tender, MWU; returned 1944.
	ACRASIA (D) (ex-Moed en Werk)	108/31	1940	D/L, A/P; returned 1946.
FY.1618	ADAM* (ex-R.N. Thomas Maloney)	324/19	2.40	M/S; returned 1945.
	ADELE (D)	100/15	1941	Harbour service; returned 1946.

(AD) = Admiralty Drifter. (D) = Drifter. (W) = Whaler. * ex-"Mersey" class. † ex-"Castle" class. ‡ ex-"Strath" class.

FY.533	ADMIRAL SIR JOHN LAWFORD	338/30	8.39	M/S, WDV (4.415); returned 1/46.
	ADMIRE (D)	93/08	1941	Harbour service; returned 1945.
4.375	ADONIS	500/15	9.39	A/P; lost 15/4/43.
	ADORATION (D)	93/12	1940	Exam.; returned 1945.
4.410	ADRIATIC (Belgian)	147/36	10.40	A/P; returned 6/45.
FY.1500	ADVISABLE (D)	115/30	11.39	M/S; returned 1945.
T.01	AFRICANA (S.A.N.)	313/30	9.39	M/S; returned 4/47.
	AFTERGLOW (AD) (ex-Port Richard, ex-R.N. Afterglow)	112/19	1941	M/S; returned 1945.
	AGNES GARDNER (AD) (ex-R.N. Radiation)	96/20	1941	Harbour service; returned 1945.
4.274	AGNES NUTTEN	183/15	6.40	A/P; returned 1/46.
4.279	AGNES WETHERLY (ex-Agnes H. Wetherly)	229/17	6.40	A/P; returned 12/45.
FY.727	AGNES WICKFIELD	219/09	11.39	M/S; returned 12/45.
FY.1841	AIGLON (French)	305/07	7.40	M/S; returned 7/46.
FY.610	AKITA	314/39	8.39	M/S; returned 10/45.
FY.513	AKRANES	358/29	8.39	M/S; lost 4/7/41.
FY.715	ALAFOSS	357/29	8.39	M/S; sold 1946.
	ALBERIC	286/10	1940	M/S; lost 3/5/41.
T.41	ALBERT HULETT (S.A.N.) (W)	250/29	2.41	M/S, LANGLAAGTE (1942); returned 4/46.
FY.1525	ALCMARIA	148/16	11.39	M/S; R.N.N. (name unchanged—1940).
FY.960	ALCOR (D)	../..	11.39	M/S; returned 9/45.
	ALEX HASTIE	206/14	10.39	A/P; returned 12/39.
	ALEX WATTS	86/13	1940	TRV; returned 1945.
	ALEXANDRE GABRIELLE (Belgian) (D)	../..	7.40	BBV;
FY.515	ALEXANDER SCOTT† (ex-R.N.)	274/17	9.39	M/S, D/L; returned 1945.
FY.560	ALEXANDRITE	313/33	9.39	M/S; returned 11/45.
FY.97	ALFIE CAM (R.A.N.)	282/20	6.40	M/S; returned 1944.
4.52	ALFREDIAN	293/13	11.39	A/P; returned 9/46.
	ALGOA BAY† (S.A.N.) (ex-R.N. TR.)	270/19	10.39	M/S; returned 12/40.
Z.152	ALIDA	270/15	1940	BDV; returned 1945.
	ALL HALLOWS (ex-Jamaica)	205/14	1944	Esso: returned 1945.
	ALLERSIE (D)	../..	1940	BBV; returned 1944.
	ALLOCHY (AD)	96/18	1941	Hospital drifter; returned 1945.
FY.1747	ALMA (Dutch)	206/15	1943	M/S R. Neth. N. (name unchanged—1940); returned 1945.
FY.645	ALMANDINE	295/32	8.39	M/S; sold 12/45.
FY.101	ALOUETTE (ex-Esquimaux)	520/39	9.39	A/S; lost 19/9/42.
M.51	ALSEY	416/32	1940	M/L; returned 1945.
	ALTRUIST (D) (ex-Speedwell)	96/07	1940	Harbour service; returned 1944.
4.118	ALVIS† (ex-R.N. Peter Hall)	280/18	5.40	A/P, M/S; returned 3/45.
FY.1502	AMALIA (D)	139/17	11.39	M/S; returned 3/45.
	AMARANTHE	.../..	1942	Mine-watcher; returned 1945.
4.434	AMBITION (ex-Thrush)	166/02	1944	Esso; returned 1945.
FY.346	AMBROSE PARE (French)	326/06	7.40	A/S; returned 3/46.
	AMIABLE (D)	92/10	1940	MWU; returned 1945.
4.119	AMPULLA	248/13	1940	A/P, M/S; sold 1946.
4.120	AMROTH CASTLE	255/13	1940	A/P, M/S; returned 1945.
	A.N.2 (W)	221/26	10.40	A/P; lost 8/11/40.
	ANCRE ESPERANCE (D) (Belgian)	110/35	1940	A/P;
	ANDANES	320/16	10.40	BDV; returned 1946.
FY.559	ANDRADITE	313/34	8.39	M/S; returned 1/46.
FY.1798	ANDRE ET LOUISE (French)	284/07	7.40	M/S; returned 4/45.
	ANDRÉ-MARCEL (D) (French)	125/36	8.40	A/P, KBV; returned 1945.
	ANDRE MONIQUE (Belgian)	152/37	7.40	A/P; returned 1945.
	ANDRONIE-CAMIEL (Belgian)	139/36	7.40	A/P, ferry service; returned 1945.
FY.1921	ANDYK (Dutch) (ex-Amsterdam)	241/13	1941	M/S; returned 1/46.

FY.1708	ANGELE MARIE (French)	238/29	7.40	M/S; returned 1/46.
FY.201	ANGLE	531/36	9.39	A/S; returned 10/45.
	ANIMATE (D)	88/17	1941	Harbour service; returned 1946.
	ANIMATION (D)	99/25	1940	BBV, TRV; returned 1945.
FY.1945	ANN MELVILLE	201/09	2.40	M/S, Esso; returned 10/44.
	ANNABELLE‡ (ex-R.N. George Borthwick)	202/17	11.39	A/P, BBV; returned 12/44.
	ANNE MARIE (Belgian)	252/16	1940	A/P; returned 1945.
	ANNIE (Belgian) (D)	../..	7.40	A/P; returned 1945.
	ANSON	211/05	10.39	A/P;
FY.1746	ANTIOCHE II (French)† (ex-R.N. James Cepell)	300/18	7.40	M/S; returned 1945.
	APPLETREE (D)	84/07	1940	A/C Observation; lost 15/10/40.
4.00	AQUAMARINE	357/27	8.39	ABV, A/S; returned 9/44.
FY.202	ARAB	531/36	9.39	A/S; returned 11/45.
4.442	ARABESQUE‡ (ex-Yesso, ex-R.N. Henry Flight)	209/18	11.39	A/P, BBV, Esso; returned 11/44.
Y7.2	ARACARI	245/08	1.43	Esso; lost 3/10/43.
	ARAGONITE	315/34	8.39	M/S; lost 22/11/39.
FY.1598	ARCADY (D)	96/..	11.39	M/S; returned 6/45.
FY.111	ARCANES	.../..	9.39	M/S;
	ARCHIMEDES (D)	83/11	4.40	BBV; returned 12/44.
FY.162	ARCTIC EXPLORER	501/37	8.39	A/S U.S.N. (name unchanged—1942); sold 1945.
FY.1614	ARCTIC HUNTER	356/29	8.39	M/S; returned 5/45.
FY.164	ARCTIC PIONEER	501/37	9.39	A/S; lost 27/5/42.
FY.186	ARCTIC RANGER	493/37	8.39	A/S; sold 1946.
	ARCTIC TRAPPER	352/28	6.40	A/P; lost 3/2/41.
FY.1867	ARGO (French) (D)	.../38	7.40	M/S; returned 2/46.
	ARGYLLSHIRE	540/38	9.39	A/S; lost 1/6/40.
T.18	ARISTEA (S.A.N.)	261/35	12.39	M/S; returned 12/44.
FY.653	ARKWRIGHT	370/30	8.39	M/S; sold 12/45.
FY.620	ARLEY	304/14	8.39	M/S; lost 3/2/45.
	ARLEUX (R.C.N.)	357/18	1939	M/S, BGV; returned 1946.
FY.1809	ARMANA	375/30	6.40	A/P, M/S, D/L; returned 11/45.
FY.1939	ARNOLD BENNETT	374/30	6.40	M/S; returned 7/45.
	ARRAS (R.C.N.)	357/18	1939	M/S; returned 1945.
Z.246	ARREST (ex-Buzzard)	181/98	6.40	BDV; returned 7/45.
FY.140	ARSENAL	398/33	8.39	A/S; lost 16/11/40.
FY.1855	ARTEGAL‡ (ex-Henriette, ex-R.N. Robert Harding)	204/18	11.39	M/S; returned 3/45.
FY.566	ARTHUR CAVANAGH† (ex-R.N.)	277/18	8.39	M/S; sold 1/46.
T.10	ARUM (S.A.N.)	194/26	1.40	M/S; returned 10/44.
	ASAMA	303/29	8.39	M/S; lost 21/3/41.
FY.949	ASCONA	138/30	11.39	M/S; returned 11/45.
FY.370	ASIE (French)	551/14	9.40	A/S; returned 4/46.
FY.261	ASTON VILLA	546/37	9.39	A/S; lost 3/5/40.
Z.130	ASTROS† (ex-R.N. William Spencer)	275/17	12.39	BDV; returned 1946.
	ATHELSTON	202/11	11.39	A/P; returned 1/40.
FY.757	ATHENIAN	218/19	11.39	M/S, Esso (Y7.1); returned 9/46.
FY.789	ATMOSPHERE (W) (ex-Gos 2)	247/28	12.40	M/S; returned 12/45.
	AURORA II (D)	74/06	1941	M/S; lost 24/5/41.
FY.931	AURILIA (D)	87/14	11.39	M/S; returned 1945.
	AVAILABLE (D)	102/12	11.39	A/P; returned 1/46.
FY.1895	AVALANCHE (ex-Balmoral)	222/16	11.39	M/S, BBV; returned 1945.
	AVALON (ex-Nordhav I)	644/15	1940	A/P; returned 1945.
FY.1886	AVANTURINE	296/30	10.39	M/S; lost 1/12/43.
FY.1730	AVOLA	255/13	8.39	M/S; returned 4/46.
4.177	AVON	250/07	5.40	A/P; returned 12/41.
	AVONA	.../..	8.39	M/S;
	AVONDEE‡ (ex-R.N. Thomas Evinson)	202/18	3.44	Esso; returned 10/44.
4.432	AVONGLEN	275/17	1940	Exam. hospital trawler; returned 8/46.
FY.1529	AVONSTREAM	251/15	9.39	M/S; returned 7/45.
Z.119	AVONWATER	260/30	9.39	BDV; returned 1945.

Left: Belgian A/P Drifter Ancre Esperence. 1—1 pdr., 1—MG. [*I.W.M.*

Right: Belgian A/P Trawler Andre Monique. 1—1 pdr., 3—MG. (3 × 1—HG). [*I.W.M.*

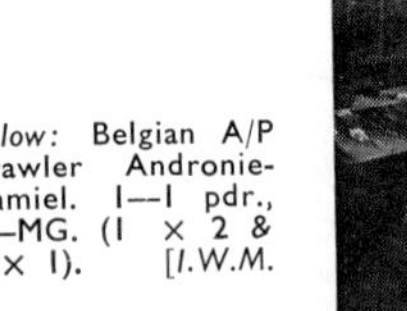

Below: Belgian A/P Trawler Andronie-Camiel. 1—1 pdr., 4—MG. (1 × 2 & 2 × 1). [*I.W.M.*

FY.225	AYRSHIRE	540/38	9.39	A/S; returned 10/45.
T.20	BABIANA (S.A.N.)	262/35	9.39	M/S; returned 12/44.
FY.824	BADINAGE (ex-Sabreur)	188/16	1940	M/S; returned 1945.
	BAHRAM (D)	72/24	1940	HDPC; lost 3/4/41.
FY.788	BANDOLERO	440/35	8.39	A/S; lost 30/12/40.
	BANNERET (D) (ex-Verbena)	.../..	1941	Harbour service; returned 1944.
FY.1600	BANSHEE (D)	.../29	11.39	M/S; returned 1/46.
	BARBADOS	211/05	10.39	A/P; returned 1945.
Z.155	BARBARA ROBB	263/30	9.39	BDV; returned 12/44.
	BARBARA ROBERTSON* (ex-R.N. ?)	325/19	1939	A/P; lost 23/12/39.
	BARBE AUGUSTE (French) (D)	.../..	1940	M/L tender; returned 1945.
4.443	BARNESNESS	173/07	2.40	BBV, Esso; returned 12/44.
Z.106	BASUTO	402/32	1.40	BDV; returned 1/46.
Z.247	BEAULNE VERNEUIL† (French) (ex-R.N. John Brice)	268/18	7.40	BGV; returned 3/46.
	BEATHWOOD	209/12	11.39	A/P, returned 1/40; lost 11/9/40.
FY.993	BEAUMARIS CASTLE† (ex-R.N. James Burgess)	275/17	2.40	M/S; returned 11/45.
	BEAVER (D) (ex-Energy)	.../..	1941	M/S; lost 5/4/42.
	BEDLINGTON (W) (ex-Terje 3)	335/36	4.40	A/S; to M.O.W.T. 9/45.
FY.141	BEDFORDSHIRE	443/35	8.39	A/S; U.S.N. (name unchanged—1942); lost 11/5/42.
	BELLDOCK	236/17	11.39	A/P; returned 1940.
	BELLE O'MORAY (D)	83/11	3.40	Harbour service; returned 2/46.
	BELTON‡(ex-R.N. Thomas Foley)	202/18	1940	Exam.; returned 1945.
	BELVOIR CASTLE (D)	.../..	1940	BBV; returned 1944.
FY.1511	BEN AND LUCY (D)	83/10	10.39	M/S; returned 1945.
	BEN ARDNA‡ (ex-R.N. John Bradford)	226/17	8.39	Exam.; lost 12/5/42.
FY.1681	BEN BHEULAH† (ex-R.N. Thomas Dowding)	275/17	8.39	M/S; returned 10/45.
FY.997	BEN BHRACKIE	235/16	3.40	M/S; returned 12/45.
FY.336	BEN BREAC	235/16	6.40	M/S; returned 12/45.
FY.690	BEN DEARG† (ex-R.N. Thomas Alexander)	280/20	8.39	M/S; returned 6/46.
FY.999	BEN EARN	235/16	2.40	M/S; returned 2/46.
	BEN GAIRN	234/16	6.40	M/S; lost 4/5/41.
FY.808	BEN GLAS	234/17	11.39	A/P, M/S, Esso; returned 10/44.
FY.1680	BEN GULVAIN	197/14	8.39	M/S; returned 8/46.
FY.765	BEN HEILEM	224/19	11.39	M/S; returned 4/46.
FY.1766	BEN IDRIS	232/31	8.39	Exam., M/S; returned 9/45.
FY.1818	BEN MEIDIE	234/17	1.40	M/S; returned 3/46.
Z.120	BEN ROSSAL	260/29	9.39	BDV; returned 3/46.
FY.1557	BEN ROY	260/29	2.40	M/S; returned 2/45.
Z.212	BEN TARBERT	197/12	6.40	BDV, store carrier; returned 2/45.
FY.807	BEN TORC	199/15	11.39	M/S; returned 9/46.
FY.1569	BEN URIE	234/16	2.40	M/S; returned 12/45.
FY.749	BENACHIE (AD) (ex-R.N. White Horses)	96/19	10.39	M/S, S/M tender; returned 1946.
	BENGAL	211/05	11.39	A/P; returned 1/40.
FY.165	BENGALI	455/37	8.39	A/S; lost 5/12/42.
4.444	BENJAMIN COLEMAN‡ (ex-R.N.)	202/18	11.39	A/P, Esso; returned 9/45.
T.54	BENONI (S.A.N.) (W) (ex-Pol V)	221/25	5.42	M/S; returned 4/46.
FY.710	BENVOLIO	352/30	9.39	M/S; lost 23/2/40.
FY.774	BERENGA	227/17	11.39	BBV; returned 9/45.
FY.183	BERKSHIRE	466/36	10.39	A/S; returned 11/45.
Z.175	BERNADETTE (French)	302/14	7.40	BDV; returned 12/45.
FY.200	BERNARD SHAW	335/29	9.39	M/S; returned 9/45.
	BERU	195/11	10.39	A/P; returned 12/39.
FY.847	BERVIE BRAES‡ (ex-R.N. George Burton)	203/17	11.39	A/P, M/S, Esso; returned 10/44.
	BERYL II (D)	88/09	1941	Harbour service; returned 1944.

FY.71	BERYL II (R.A.N.) (ex-Beryl)	248/14	9.39	M/S, BGV (Z.101); returned 1945.
	BETSY SLATER (D)	84/11	1940	BBV; returned 1945.
4.365	BETTY BODIE (D)	96/18	8.39	Exam.; returned 6/46.
	BETTY INGLIS (D)	104/95	12.39	M/S, Harbour service; returned 3/46.
T.49	BEVER (S.A.N.) (W) (ex-Hektor X)	252/30	10.41	M/S; lost 30/11/44.
FY.836	BILLOW (W) (ex-Gos 3)	247/28	1941	M/S; returned 1945.
FY.503	BILSDEAN	242/17	2.40	M/S; returned 11/45.
FY.1712	BJERK (R.N.N.) (W)	182/12	9.40	M/S; returned 10/45.
T.32	BLAAWBERG (S.A.N.) (W)	307/35	12.40	A/S; returned 5/46.
FY.116	BLACKBURN ROVERS	422/34	8.39	A/S; lost 2/6/40.
FY.117	BLACKFLY (ex-Barnett)	482/37	8.39	A/S; sold 1945.
	BLANCHE MADELEINE (Belgian)	.../..	8.40	Harbour service; returned 1945.
	BLANCHE MARGUERITE (Belgian) (D)	.../..	8.40	A/P; returned 1944.
	BLIA (D)	.../36	1941	/ ; lost 11/11/41.
FY.505	BLIGHTY* (ex-R.N. John Cottrell)	325/19	1940	M/S; Polish PODOLE (1944).
	BLIZZARD (W) (ex-Gos 4)	217/28	5.41	M/S; returned 7/45.
T.17	BLOMVLEI (S.A.N.)	252/35	3.40	A/S; returned 3/45.
FY.1757	BLUE HAZE (AD) (ex-R.N.)	97/19	5.40	TRV; returned 2/46.
	BLUE TIT (Belgian) (D) (ex-Anna Leopold)	.../..	1940	Observation M/L;
T.21	BLUFF (S.A.N.)	262/35	9.39	M/S; returned 12/44.
FY.315	BOARHOUND (W) (ex-Terje II)	335/36	8.40	A/S; returned 1945.
	BODO (R.N.N.) (W) (ex-Gos 8)	351/36	1940	M/S; lost 4/1/43.
T.46	BOKSBURG (S.A.N.) (W) (ex-Uni 3)	240/26	10.40	M/S; returned 7/46.
	BOMBAY	229/07	10.39	A/P, returned 1/40; lost 6/8/42.
	BOREALIS (W) (ex-Gos 6)	264/35	5.41	M/S; returned 10/45.
	BORDER KING (D)	92/14	8.39	Harbour service; returned 10/45.
	BORTIND (R.N.N.) (W)	328/12	1940	M/S; returned 1946.
FY.707	BOTANIC	348/28	8.39	M/S; lost 18/2/42.
	BOUNTEOUS (D)	.../..	1942	Exam.; returned 1946.
	BOUNTEOUS SEA (D)	.../..	1941	Harbour service; returned 1946.
FY.1693	BOUVET 1 (W)	245/30	3.40	M/S; returned 1945.
FY.1695	BOUVET 2 (W)	245/30	3.40	M/S; returned 4/46.
FY.1698	BOUVET 3 (W)	245/30	3.40	M/S; returned 4/46.
FY.1701	BOUVET 4 (W)	245/30	3.40	M/S; returned 6/46.
	BOW WAVE (AD) (ex-R.N.)	97/19	11.40	TRV; returned 1945.
	BOY ALAN (D)	109/14	11.39	M/S; lost 10/2/41.
	BOY ALEX (D)	.../..	11.39	M/S; returned 1945.
	BOY ANDREW (AD) (ex-R.N. Sunburst)	97/18	1940	A/P; lost 9/11/41.
	BOY DAVIE (D)	.../..	1941	D/G; returned 1944.
FY.1961	BOY JOHN (D)	87/14	12.39	M/S; returned 7/45.
FY.731	BOY PHILIP	128/30	10.39	M/S; W.D. 8/43.
	BOY RAY (D)	.../..	6.40	Water carrier; returned 1946.
	BOY ROY (D)	95/11	11.39	Flare drifter; lost 28/5/40.
FY.1865	BOY SCOUT (D)	.../..	11.39	BBV; returned 12/44.
FY.586	BRABANT† (ex-R.N. Emmanuel Camelaire)	280/18	8.39	M/S; returned 12/45.
FY.1988	BRACKENDALE	88/16	8.39	D/G; returned 1946.
FY.1812	BRACONDENE	235/16	8.40	M/S; returned 8/46.
	BRACONHEATH	201/06	2.40	D/L; returned 1945.
	BRACONHILL‡ (ex-R.N. William Bentley)	203/19	11.39	Exam.; returned 7/45
	BRACONLYNN	206/13	11.39	A/P; returned 1/40.

FY.686	BRACONMOOR‡ (ex-R.N. Samuel Baker)	194/17	8.39	M/S; returned 8/46.
	BRACONBURN‡ (ex-R.N. Richard Driscoll)	203/18	1944	To be blockship; lost 30/7/44.
FY.189	BRADMAN	452/37	8.39	A/S; lost 25/4/40.
	BRAE FLETT (D)	.../02	1941	Harbour service; lost 22/9/43.
	BRAES O'BUCKIE (D)	84/10	1942	Water carrier; returned 1946.
FY.1641	BRAEMAR (D)		12.39	A/P; returned 1945.
T.23	BRAKVLEI (S.A.N.) (W) (ex-Hektor 4)	234/29	7.40	M/S; returned 6/46.
T.42	BRAKPAN (S.A.N.) (W) (ex-Terje, ex-Terje 6)	335/36	4.43	M/S; returned 11/46.
FY.291	BRANCH (D)	93/08	1939	A/S; returned 1945.
	BRAS D'OR† (R.C.N.) (ex-R.N. TR.18)	221/01	9.39	M/S ; lost 19/10/40.
FY.507	BRECON CASTLE	274/16	8.39	M/S; returned 12/45.
4.272	BREEZE (ex-Gustave Denis)	184/34	7.41	A/P; sold 3/46.
FY.266	BRETWALDA	.../..	1940	A/S; sold 1947.
FY.1825	BREVIK (R.N.N.) (W) (ex-Kos XII)	258/32	1.42	M/S; returned 1946.
FY.254	BRIMNES	413/33	9.39	A/S; sold 1945.
FY.506	BRITISH	406/30	8.39	M/S; returned 12/45.
	BRITISH CROWN (D)	85/13	1941	MRV; returned 1945.
FY.271	BRITISH GUIANA	146/36	11.39	A/S; returned 3/46.
FY.272	BRITISH HONDURAS	147/37	12.39	A/S; returned 1/46.
FY.1973	BROADLAND (D)	76/13	1939	A/P; lost 6/6/45.
FY.621	BROCK	304/14	8.39	M/S; sold 1945.
FY.118	BRONTES	428/34	8.39	A/S; sold 1945.
	BRUINSVISCH (Dutch) (D)	164/29	7.40	M/S, Esso; returned 1946.
	BRUNSWICK BAY	.../..	12.39	M/S; returned 1940.
FY.1514	B.T.B. (D)	89/11	11.39	M/S; returned 1/46.
FY.815	BUCEPHALUS (ex-Venture)	193/05	1944	Esso; returned 1945.
	BUCENTAUR	184/07	11.39	A/P; returned 1/40.
FY.335	BUCHANS II‡ (ex-R.N. Pat Caherty)	203/18	7.40	A/P; returned 8/46.
Z.121	BUCKINGHAM	253/30	8.39	M/S, BDV; returned 12/45.
	BUCKLER (D)	88/11	1942	Harbour service; returned 1945.
FY.605	BURKE	363/30	9.39	M/S, WDV; returned 1/46.
	BURNBANKS	193/05	2.40	D/L; sold 1946.
FY.1607	BURNHAVEN (AD) (ex-R.N. Gust)	96/18	8.39	Harbour service; returned 1945.
FY.1889	BUSEN 3 (W)	210/24	12.40	M/S; ICICLE (1941), returned 1/46.
FY.1854	BUSEN 7 (W)	254/26	1940	M/S; SILHOUETTE (1941), R.N.N. (name unchanged—1941), R.H.N. ACHELOOS (1943), returned 2/47.
FY.1842	BUSEN 11 (W)	279/31	1940	M/S; SNOWDRIFT (1941), R.N.N. (name unchanged —1941), R.H.N. THASOS (1943), lost 24/10/45.
	BUSH	222/08	1940	A/P; returned 1944.
FY.1870	BYNG (AD) (ex-R.N. Elephanta)	107/20	10.39	BDV, BBV; returned 1946.
Z.121	CADELLA	314/13	10.39	BDV; returned 1946.
FY.1651	CADORNA	255/17	5.40	M/S; returned 5/45.
	CAERPHILLY CASTLE† (ex-Ebor Elect, ex-R.N. William Coburn)	275/19	8.39	M/S, sold 1/40; lost 27/1/41.
	CALDY	222/08	12.39	M/S; renamed.
Z.131	CALIBAN† (ex-R.N.)	277/19	12.39	BDV; sold 12/46.
	CALLIOPSIS (AD)	97/18	1944	Harbour service; returned 1945.

M/S Drifter H.M.S. Arcady. 1—20 mm. A.A. [I.W.M.

M/S Trawler H.M.S. Arctic Hunter. 1—12 pdr. A.A., 2—5 in. A.A., (1 × 2) 2—MG. (2 × 1). [I.W.M.

A/S Trawler H.M.S. Cape Portland. 1—4 in., 2—.5 in. A.A. (1 × 2), 2—MG. [I.W.M.

	CALM (W) (ex-Gos 7)	264/35	1940	M/S; returned 1945
FY.775	CALVERTON	214/13	11.39	M/S; lost 29/11/40.
	CALVI	363/30	9.39	M/S; lost 29/5/40.
FY.1850	CALVINIA	191/01	1.40	M/S; returned 12/45.
	CAMBRIAN	338/24	9.39	BDV; lost 30/5/40.
FY.142	CAMBRIDGESHIRE	443/35	8.39	A/S; sold 1945.
4.153	CAMPINA	290/13	1939	A/P; lost 22/7/40.
FY.166	CANADIAN PRINCE	455/37	9.39	A/S; French LA BONOISE (1939), scrapped 1945.
FY.350	CAP D'ANTIFER (French)	.../..	1940	M/S; lost 13/2/44.
FY.1797	CAP FERRAT (French) (D)	.../..	1940	M/S; returned 1945.
FY.190	CAPE ARGONA	494/36	8.39	A/S; sold 1945.
4.122	CAPE BARRACOUTA	390/30	8.39	A/P, M/S; returned 1/46.
FY.119	CAPE CHELYUSKIN	494/36	8.39	A/S; lost 29/4/40.
FY.143	CAPE COMORIN	504/36	8.39	A/S; sold 1945.
	CAPE FINISTERRE	591/39	1940	A/S; lost 2/8/40.
4.172	CAPE MARIATO	497/36	6.40	A/S; returned 12/45.
FY.651	CAPE MELVILLE	342/29	8.39	M/S; returned 8/45.
FY.670	CAPE NYEMETSKI	422/36	8.39	M/S; returned 9/45.
FY.256	CAPE PALLISER	497/36	9.39	A/S; returned 9/45.
FY.270	CAPE PASSARO	510/39	9.39	A/S; lost 21/5/40.
FY.246	CAPE PORTLAND	497/36	9.39	A/S, ABV; Portuguese P.5 (1943–44), returned 1945.
FY.263	CAPE SIRETOKO	590/39	9.39	A/S; lost 29/4/40.
	CAPE SPARTEL	346/29	8.39	M/S; lost 2/2/42.
4.190	CAPE TRAFALGAR* (ex-R.N. Edward Williams)	326/17	5.40	A/P, BDV; sold 1/47.
FY.167	CAPE WARWICK (ex-Compton)	516/37	8.39	A/S; U.S.N. (name unchanged—1942), sold 2/46.
	CAPORAL PEUGEOT (French) (D)	102/23	1940	A/P; returned 1945.
	CAPRICE (ex-Holly)	.../..	1940	Exam., CAPRICORN (1943); returned 7/46.
	CAPRICORNUS	219/17	11.39	A/P, M/S; lost 7/12/40.
4.174	CAPSTONE† (ex-R.N. James Robertson)	275/17	6.40	A/P, M/S (FY.1555); returned 10/45.
4.17	CARBINEER II	297/15	5.40	A/P, BDV; returned 7/46.
FY.512	CARDIFF CASTLE	276/19	8.39	M/S; returned 1/46.
FY.295	CARENCY	233/16	1940	A/S, Exam.; sold 2/47.
FY.583	CARISBROOKE	230/28	8.39	M/S; sold 1946.
FY.1729	CAROLINE (Dutch)	253/30	1940	M/S; lost 28/4/41.
	CARRY ON (AD) (ex-R.N.?)	93/19	12.39	BBV; lost 17/12/40.
	CASSIOPEIA (AD) (ex-Windrise)	97/18	2.40	Hospital drifter; returned 1945.
FY.355	CASTELNAU (French)* (ex-R.N. John Jacobs)	337/18	8.40	A/S; returned 2/46.
	CASTLE BAY (AD) (ex-R.N. Daylight)	108/18	11.39	M/S; returned 7/46.
	CASTLE STUART (D)	80/10	1941	Harbour service; returned 1945.
	CASTLETON	211/04	11.39	A/P, returned 1/40; lost 28/6/40.
FY.500	CASWELL	276/17	2.40	M/S; returned 7/46.
	CATHERINE	78/14	1939	A/P; lost 8/6/42.
4.163	CAULONIA	296/12	1939	A/P, M/S; lost 31/3/43.
FY.791	CAYRIAN	216/11	11.39	M/S; returned 12/45.
FY.191	CAYTON WYKE	373/32	8.39	A/S; lost 8/7/40.
T.31	CEDARBERG (S.A.N.) (W)	307/35	3.41	A/S; returned 5/46.
FY.996	CEDRIC	230/06	11.39	A/P, M/S, BBV; returned 1945.
	CELTIA	239/07	11.39	A/P; returned 1/40.
FY.524	CERISIO	338/15	9.39	M/S; sold 1945.
Y7.16	CEVIC	250/08	1943	Fuel carrier, water carrier returned 8/44.
FY.1853	CEYLONITE† (ex-R.N. Thomas Buckley)	249/18	4.40	M/S; returned 1946.
4.124	CHALCEDONY	357/28	8.39	A/P, M/S; sold 1945.
	CHARDE (AD)	99/19	11.39	M/S; lost 21/6/40.
	(ex-R.N. Hurricane)	200/19	11.39	

	CHANDOS‡ (ex-R.N. Thomas Goodchild)	200/19	11.39	A/P; returned 1/40.
	CHARLES BOYES† (ex-R.N.)	275/18	9.39	M/S; lost 25/5/40.
	CHARLES DENISE (Belgian)	114/35	1940	BBV; returned 1945.
FY.597	CHARLES DORAN† (ex-R.N.)	273/17	1940	M/S; returned 11/45.
4.267	CHARLES HENRI (D) (Belgian)	110/35	7.40	A/P; returned 9/45.
FY.1804	CHARLES VAILLANT (French)	224/16	7.40	M/S; returned 3/46.
FY.1793	CHASSE MARIE (French)	.../..	7.40	M/S; returned 1945.
FY.1857	CHASSIRON	258/13	9.39	M/S; returned 8/45.
4.125	CHILTERN* (ex-R.N. John Cormack)	324/17	6.40	A/P; returned 1945.
4.428	CHOICE (ex-Stalka)	197/99	1944	Esso; lost 25/8/44.
Z.153	CHORLEY	284/14	1.40	BDV; lost 25/4/42.
	CHRISTANIA T. PURDY‡ (ex-R.N. John Mason)	213/17	1939	A/P, BBV; returned 1945.
	CHRISTINE ROSE (D) (French)	.../..	1940	Exam.; lost 10/9/41.
	CHRYSEA	210/12	4.40	BBV; returned 1/45.
FY.1827	CHRYSOLITE	251/16	8.40	M/S; returned 1/46.
FY.1872	CITRON (D)	78/11	1.40	BBV; returned 8/44.
	CITY OF ABERDEEN	194/98	12.39	A/P; returned 1/40.
FY.1716	CLAESJE (Dutch)	229/33	1940	M/S; returned 1945.
FY.1960	CLAN MACKAY (D)	.../..	1939	D/L; returned 1945.
	CLARA SUTTON (D)	102/17	1940	Tender; returned 1945.
FY.1828	CLARIBELLE‡ (ex-R.N. William Barrow)	204/18	1941	M/S; returned 1945.
	CLARICE (ex-Daffodil)	.../..	1940	Harbour service; returned 1945.
Z.132	CLARINET	.../..	1.40	BDV; returned 1946.
	CLAVIS (D)	.../..	1940	BBV; returned 1945.
	CLEON (Dutch) (D)	.../..	1941	BBV; returned 1945.
FY.678	CLEVELLA	387/30	9.39	M/S; returned 5/46.
FY.898	CLIFTON	194/15	11.39	M/S; returned 3/46.
FY.534	CLOTILDE	289/13	2.40	M/S; returned 12/45.
4.446	CLOUGHSTONE	233/07	12.40	BBV; returned 4/45.
	CLOUGHTON WYKE* (ex-R.N. John Johnson)	324/18	6.40	A/P, M/S; lost 2/2/42.
FY.987	CLOVERDALE	100/07	11.39	M/S, A/P; returned 12/45.
FY.508	CLYNE CASTLE	307/29	8.39	M/S, WDV; returned 11/45.
FY.1596	CLYTHNESS† (ex-R.N. Daniel Dick)	276/20	8.39	M/S; returned 7/45.
	COBBERS (ex-R.N. William Knight)	275/19	1939	A/P; lost 3/3/41.
	COCKADE (ex-Anson)	211/05	11.39	A/P, Water carrier, STOCKADE (1944); returned 1945.
	COCKER (W) (ex-Kos XIX)	303/36	1941	A/S; lost 3/6/42.
Z.151	COLLENA	293/15	1.40	BDV; sold 1946.
FY.1879	COMELY BANK (D)	87/14	12.39	BBV; returned 1945.
	COMET	301/24	1939	M/S; lost 30/9/40.
	COMFORT (D)	.../..	1939	D/L; lost 29/5/40.
FY.633	COMITATUS	290/19	1939	M/S; returned 1945.
FY.113	COMMANDER EVANS	344/24	6.40	A/P, M/S, D/L; returned 8/45.
FY.111	COMMANDER HOLBROOK	227/15	6.40	A/P; returned 11/45.
FY.516	COMMANDER NASMITH	227/15	6.40	A/P, M/S; returned 5/45.
FY.636	COMMILES† (ex-R.N. Matthew Flynn)	264/18	8.39	M/S; returned 10/45.
FY.634	COMMODATOR† (ex-R.N. Richard Bacon)	281/18	8.39	M/S; returned 10/45.
FY.635	COMPUTATOR† (ex-R.N. Eglias Akerman)	286/19	1939	M/S; lost 21/1/45.
	COMRADES (D)	114/28	9.39	A/P, target service; returned 4/46.
FY.637	CONCERTATOR† (ex-R.N. John Thorling)	275/17	8.39	M/S; returned 1/46.
FY.1550	CONCORDIA (D)	91/13	12.39	M/S; returned 5/46.

	CONFIANCE (Belgian) (D)	.../..	7.40	Harbour service; ret. 1945.
	CONFIDE (D)	95/07	1940	Harbour service; ret. 1945.
FY.1919	CONGRE (French)† (ex-R.N. John Geoghan)	299/18	7.40	M/S; returned 1/46.
FY.833	CONISTON	217/04	11.39	A/P, M/S;
	CONQUISTADOR	224/15	11.39	A/P, M/S; lost 25/11/40.
Z.107	CONSBRO	350/30	1.40	BDV; returned 9/45.
FY.1539	CONSOLATION (AD) (ex-R.N. Sleet)	97/18	11.39	M/S; returned 9/45.
FY.1933	CONSTANT FRIEND (D)	.../..	1940	M/S; returned 1945.
	CONSTANT HOPE (D)	.../..	1940	BBV; returned 1945.
FY.543	CONTENDER	236/30	2.40	M/S; returned 10/45.
FY.290	CONTRIVE (D)	95/11	5.40	MWU; returned 2/46.
4.447	CONTROLLER	201/13	1.40	A/P, BBV, Esso; returned 9/44.
	CONVALLARIA (AD) (ex-R.N. Watershed)	96/19	4.40	A/P; returned 3/46.
	CONWAY	228/04	11.39	A/P; returned 1940.
FY.509	CONWAY CASTLE	274/16	8.39	M/S; returned 10/45.
FY.337	COPIOUS (AD) (ex-R.N. Current)	96/19	1.40	A/S; returned 8/45.
	CORAL BANK (D)	85/14	1940	M/S; returned 1/46.
FY.293	CORCYRA	225/14	11.40	A/P, water carrier; sold 8/46.
FY.713	CORDELA	355/30	8.39	M/S; sold 1946.
FY.709	CORENA	352/24	8.39	M/S; sold 4/46.
	COR JESU (D)	97/31	1940	BBV; lost 8/6/41.
	CORN RIG (D)	97/11	1941	Harbour service; returned 1945.
	CORNUCOPIA (AD)	96/18	1940	Harbour service; returned 1944.
Z.204	CORONATIA	185/02	1939	BGV; returned 1944.
	CORTINA	213/13	11.39	A/P, M/S; lost 7/12/40.
	CORUSCATION (D)	.../..	1940	A/P; returned 1945.
	CORYPHENE	.../..	1944	Esso; returned 1945.
FY.550	COTSMUIR† (ex-R.N. Thomas Groble)	275/17	2.40	M/S; returned 11.45.
Z.109	COUNT	410/29	1940	BDV; returned 1945.
FY.1823	COURSER	227/05	9.40	M/S, CAVALCADE (1945); returned 12/46.
4.266	COURONNE (French)	227/35	7.40	A/P, water carrier; returned 1947.
FY.592	COURTIER	225/29	8.39	M/S; returned 7/45.
FY.267	COVENTRY CITY	546/37	9.39	A/S U.S.N. (name unchanged—1942); returned 8/45.
FY.1948	CRAFTSMAN (ex-Coriolanus)	226/17	8.40	M/S, D/L; returned 10/44.
FY.1957	CRAIG ALVAH	80/09	12.39	Harbour service; returned 12/45.
FY.1770	CRAIGCOILLEACH	233/17	8.40	M/S; returned 7/45.
Z.157	CRAIG ISLAND	243/13	11.39	BDV; returned 11/44.
FY.1669	CRAIGMILLAR	210/05	1.40	M/S; returned 11/45.
FY.287	CRAIG ROY (AD)	96/18	12.39	A/S; returned 10/45.
	CRAMOND ISLAND	180/10	11.39	BDV; lost 2/4/41.
FY.539	CRANEFLY* (ex-Cotswold, ex-R.N. George Andrew)	312/17	8.39	M/S; returned 1945.
FY.279	CRANNOCK (D)	84/11	11.39	A/S; returned 1/46.
T.19	CRASSULA (S.A.N.)	261/35	10.39	M/S; returned 12/46.
	CREAGH MHOR (D)	.../..	1940	BBV; returned 1945.
	CRESTFLOWER	367/30	8.39	M/S; lost 19/7/40.
4.435	CREVETTE‡ (ex-R.N. Thomas Henrix)	203/18	11.39	A/P, Esso; returned 10/44.
Z.150	CUIRASS	321/15	9.39	BDV; sold 1945.
	CUMULUS (D)	.../..	1940	Harbour service; returned 1945.
FY.674	CURTANA	354/29	8.39	M/S; returned 10/45.
Y7.8	CYELSE	237/12	8.40	Water carrier; returned 3/46.
	DAGNY (Icelandic)	136/04	1942	BDV; returned 1944.

	DAISY (D)	50/02	1940	Harbour service; lost 25/4/42.
	DAISY (D)	.../..	1940	Harbour service; returned 1945.
	DAISY II (ex-Daisy)	248/12	9.39	Harbour service; returned 11/45.
	DAISY II (D)	100/08	1940	Harbour service; returned 1945.
FY.1964	DAISY BANK (D)	84/11	5.40	Harbour service; returned 7/44.
4.156	DALE CASTLE	246/09	5.40	A/P, target service; returned 3/46.
FY.844	DALMATIA	357/28	9.39	M/S, D/L; sold 4/46.
FY.521	DAMITO† (ex-R.N. Oliver Peckin)	275/17	8.39	M/S, Store carrier (Y7.9) returned 1/46.
	DANDOLO	207/10	1944	Esso; returned 1945.
FY.554	DANE	346/11	1.40	M/S; returned 1/46.
FY.123	DANEMAN	516/37	8.39	A/S; lost 8/5/43.
FY.531	DANIEL CLOWDEN† (ex-R.N.)	280/19	8.39	M/S; returned 10/45.
	DARCY COOPER (D)	126/28	1940	Exam.; lost 9/4/41.
FY.1985	DARNAWAY (D)	94/18	12.39	Harbour service; returned 9/45.
FY.542	DARNETT NESS† (ex-R.N. Thomas Boudige)	277/20	8.39	M/S; returned 9/45.
	DAROGAH	221/14	12.39	M/S; lost 27/1/41.
FY.676	DARTHEMA	373/29	1939	M/S; returned 1945.
FY.1859	DARWEN	227/16	11.39	A/P, M/S; returned 2/46.
T.13	DAVID HAIGH† (S.A.N.) (ex-R.N. T.R.?)	276/18	9.39	BDV; returned 6/46.
FY.720	DAVID OGILVIE† (ex-R.N.)	276/17	9.39	M/S; returned 7/46.
FY.147	DAVY	450/36	8.39	A/S; sold 1945.
	DAYBREAK (W) (ex-Kos VII)	248/29	1941	M/S; returned 1945.
	DAYLIGHT (AD) (ex-R.N.)	94/18	1940	Harbour service; returned 1944.
	DAYLIGHT (W) (ex-Globe I)	206/25	1941	M/S; returned 1945.
	DAYSPRING (AD)	108/18	1940	A/P; returned 1944.
	DEBRA HUYSENNE (Belgian)	.../..	7.40	BBV; returned 1945.
	DE DRIE GEZUSTERS (Dutch) (D)	105/12	7.40	A/P; returned 1945.
	DEFENSOR (AD)	97/20	1940	Harbour service; returned 1/46.
	DE HOOP (Belgian)	.../..	7.40	A/P; returned 1945.
	DE HOOP (Dutch)	140/12	1940	BBV; returned 1945.
4.129	DE LA POLE† (ex-R.N. Joshua Arabin)	290/19	5.40	A/P, M/S (FY.558); returned 12/45.
4.273	DELILA‡ (ex-R.N. John Hunter)	202/19	6.40	A/P; returned 1/46.
4.244	DELPHIN II (Polish)	253/38	1940	Exam.; returned 1/46.
FY.846	DELPHINUS	257/06	11.39	M/S; sold 1945.
	DEO VOLANTE (D)	.../..	1940	A/P; returned 1945.
FY.171	DERBY COUNTY	339/38	8.39	A/S; sold 1945.
	DE ROSA (Belgian)	.../..	1940	A/P; returned 1945.
	DERVISH	346/11	6.40	M/S; lost 9/9/40.
	DESIREE	212/12	11.39	M/S; lost 16/1/41.
FY.1719	DESTINN	226/14	1.40	A/P; returned 8/45.
	DEVON COUNTY (D)	86/10	11.39	M/S; lost 1/7/41.
	DEVOTION (D)	88/10	1941	Water carrier; returned 1945.
FY.1721	DEW (W) (ex-Kos VIII)	248/29	1941	M/S, firefloat; returned 5/46.
	DEWEY EVE (D)	109/16	1.40	M/S; lost 9/6/40.
4.131	DHOON	323/15	5.40	A/P, M/S, DHOON GLEN (1943); returned 11/45.
	DIANA LUCIE (Belgian)	.../..	1940	A/P, MWU; returned 1945
Z.188	DIGIT (ex-Heron)	223/02	1940	BDV; sold 1946.
	DILIGENT (D)	80/02	1940	BBV; returned 194..
	DILIMER	139/16	1940	A/P; returned 1945.
FY.1745	DIRKJE (Dutch)	234/34	1940	M/S; returned 1945.

	DISA (S.A.N.)	197/24	9.39	M/S; returned 5/40.
Z.133	DOCTOR LEE	307/14	12.39	BDV; returned 11/44.
FY.1761	DOLFIJN (Dutch)	168/20	1940	M/S, GOEREE (1943); returned 1945.
	DOLORES (ex-Rainbow)	176/06	1.40	D/L; sold 1946.
FY.1764	DOMINO (W) (ex-Sabra)	245/30	3.40	M/S; sold 7/45.
4.132	DONNA NOOK	307/16	6.40	A/P, M/S (FY.1559); lost 25/9/43.
4.235	DOONIE BRAES‡ (ex-R.N. George Coulston)	213/18	5.40	A/P; returned 1/45.
	DOORIE BRAE (AD) (ex-R.N. Rift)	94/20	11.39	A/P; returned 1945.
FY.705	DORIENTA (D)	101/14	9.39	M/S; returned 5/46.
Z.148	DORILEEN‡ (ex-R.N. William Barlow)	226/17	1.40	BDV; sold 5/46.
FY.623	DORINDA	270/17	8.39	M/S; returned 11/45.
4.222	DOROTHY GRAY	199/08	7.40	A/P; returned 12/44.
FY.558	DOROTHY LAMBERT	299/23	2.40	M/S; returned 2/46.
	DOURSWOLD (Dutch)	.../..	1940	BBV; returned 1945.
	DRAINIE (AD) (ex-R.N. Mackerel Sky)	92/18	1940	Water carrier; sold 1947.
FY.195	DRANGEY	434/35	8.39	A/S; sold 1946.
	DREEL CASTLE	97/08	11.39	M/S; returned 1940.
	DROBAK (R.N.N.) (W) (ex-Kos IV)	248/29	1940	M/S; returned 1946.
	DROMIO	380/29	8.39	M/S; lost 22/12/39.
	DRUMMER (ex-R.N.)	297/15	8.39	M/S; lost 4/8/40.
FY.851	DRUMMER BOY	209/16	11.39	M/S; returned 8/45.
FY.341	DUCHESSE DE BRABANT (Belgian)	338/24	7.40	A/S; returned 1945.
FY.826	DULCIBELLE‡ (ex-R.N. Barnard Boyle)	203/18	11.39	A/P; returned 11/44.
	DUNGENESS	263/14	5.40	A/P; lost 15/11/40.
FY.570	DUNRAVEN CASTLE	276/17	3.40	M/S; returned 9/45.
FY.1916	DUSK (ex-Estrella do Mar)	327/14	1941	M/S; sold 1946.
FY.93	DURRAWEEN† (R.A.N.) (ex-R.N. T.R.?)	271/19	1939	M/S; returned 1946.
	DUTHIES	89/14	8.39	/ ; lost 25/10/40.
FY.1820	D. W. FITZGERALD	235/16	8.40	M/S; returned 1/45.
FY.1892	EADWINE (D)	96/14	10.40	A/P; returned 3/46.
FY.990	EAGER (D)	102/12	11.39	M/S; returned 10/44.
FY.852	EARL ESSEX	225/14	11.39	M/S; returned 2/46.
FY.1633	EARL KITCHENER	348/15	8.39	M/S; returned 4/46.
	EAST COAST	192/07	1944	Esso; returned 1945.
FY.1771	EASTCOATES† (ex-R.N. John Graham)	277/19	8.39	M/S; returned 1945.
	EASTER ROSE (D)	87/14	1940	BBV, S/M tender; returned 1945.
4.157	EBOR ABBEY	220/11	1.40	A/P; returned 2/46.
	EBOR JEWEL	.../..	1940	BBV; returned 1945.
FY.1601	EBOR WYKE	348/29	8.39	M/S; lost 2/5/45.
	ECCLESHILL	226/11	2.40	BBV; returned 1/45.
	EDITH M. PURDY‡ (ex-R.N. John Francis)	205/18	2.40	BBV; returned 5/45.
FY.1832	EDOUARD VAN VLAAN- DEREN (Belgian)	324/25	7.40	A/P; lost 22/2/41.
FY.691	EDWARDIAN	348/31	9.39	M/S; sold 1/46.
FY.624	EDWARD WALMSLEY† (ex-R.N. David Dillon)	276/19	8.39	M/S; returned 7/46. A/P; returned 5/45.
4.134	EDWINA	267/15	5.40	M/S; returned 1/45.
FY.251	EGELAND (W)	153/12	1941	D/L; lost 29/11/41.
FY.576	EGERIA (D) (ex-Bellona)	184/07	11.39	
	EILEEN DUNCAN	223/10	1.40	M/S; lost 30/9/41.
FY.1992	EILEEN EMMA (D)	102/14	11.39	A/P; returned 4/46.
FY.656	ELBURY (ex-Pict)	394/25	9.39	M/S; returned 7/45.
FY.571	ELDORADO	180/02	2.40	M/S; returned 12/45.
4.159	ELECTRA II (Belgian)	269/04	5.40	A/P; returned 2/46.

FY.573	ELENA (ex-Viola)	228/05	11.39	M/S; returned 1/45.
	ELISABETH GUILBERT (Belgian) (D)	67/29	1940	A/P; returned 1945.
FY.767	ELIZABETH ANGELA	253/28	1939	M/S; lost 13/8/40.
	ELIZABETH THERESE	156/34	6.40	M/S; lost 4/7/45.
4.24	ELK	181/02	10.39	A/P, M/S; lost 27/11/40.
FY.1581	ELOQUENT (D)	71/11	12.39	M/S; returned 1946.
FY.255	ELSE RYKENS	266/35	12.39	A/S; returned 11/45.
FY.1646	ELSIE CAM (ex-Sophie Busse)	250/22	5.40	M/S; returned 1/46.
FY.1914	ELSIE & NELLIE (D)	101/16	1.40	BBV; returned 2/45.
	ELYSIAN DAWN (D)	.../..	1940	Harbour service; returned 1945.
	EMBRACE (D)	94/07	1940	HDPC; lost 2/8/40.
FY.853	EMILION	201/14	11.39	M/S; lost 24/10/41.
FY.873	EMPYRIAN	215/14	11.39	M/S, store carrier, (Y7.10); returned 1/45.
FY.1743	EN AVANT (Dutch)	264/11	1940	M/S; returned 1945.
	ENZIE (D)	93/08	1940	Harbour service; returned 1945.
FY.310	EPHRETAH (AD) (ex-R.N. Quicksand)	96/18	1940	A/S; returned 1945.
FY.682	EPINE	358/29	9.39	M/S; returned 1/46.
FY.668	EQUERRY	369/29	8.39	M/S; returned 4/45.
4.427	ERIDANUS (ex-Pelican)	205/05	4.44	Esso; returned 11/44.
	ERILLUS	201/14	11.39	A/P; returned 1/40.
FY.569	ERIMO	265/30	9.39	M/S; returned 1945.
	ERIN	394/33	1940	A/S; lost 18/1/42.
FY.578	ERITH	.../..	1940	M/S; returned 1945.
Z.112	ERNA	330/15	5.40	BDV; returned 1945.
FY.518	EROICAN	225/14	4.40	M/S, Esso (4.144); returned 2/45.
	ESCALLONIA (D)	.../..	1940	A/P; returned 1944.
	ETHEL TAYLOR† (ex-R.N. James Hunniford)	276/27	1939	A/P; lost 22/11/40.
	ETOILE POLAIRE (French) (D)	.../..	1940	D/L; returned 1945.
Z.187	ETRURIA	376/30	5.40	BDV; returned 2/46.
FY.854	ETRUSCAN	202/13	11.39	A/P, M/S. Esso; returned 11/44.
FY.1636	EUCLASE	295/31	2.40	M/S; returned 4/46.
FY.1543	EUNICE & NELLIE (AD)	96/18	12.39	M/S, TRV; returned 114/4.
	EVELINA‡ (ex-R.N. John Howard)	202/19	11.39	A/P; lost 16/12/40.
FY.756	EVELINE (Dutch)	206/12	7.40	M/S; lost 27/1/42.
4.136	EVELYN ROSE* (ex-R.N. William Jackson)	327/18	5.40	A/P, M/S; returned 1945.
FY.1516	EVENING PRIMROSE (D)	88/11	1939	M/S; returned 1945.
FY.1645	EVERTON	240/15	12.39	D/L, A/P; returned 3/46.
	EVESHAM	239/15	12.39	A/P; lost 27/5/41, salved & scrapped 4/46.
FY.1733	EWALD (Dutch)	209/13	6.40	M/S; returned 1945.
FY.1873	EX FORTIS (D)	90/14	12.39	BBV; returned 9/45.
FY.961	EXCHEQUER (D)	86/14	5.40	Exam.; returned 4/46.
FY.878	EXYHANE	226/14	11.39	M/S; returned 12/45.
	FAIR BREEZE (D)	92/25	9.39	A/P; lost 1/6/40.
	FAIRHAVEN (AD) (ex-R.N. Sleet)	96/19	1940	BBV; lost 5/9/44.
4.23	FAIRWAY* (ex-R.N. Richard Jewell)	326/18	5.40	A/P, M/S (FY.1551); returned 3/46.
	FAIR WEATHER (AD) (ex-R.N.)	93/18	1.40	A/P; returned 12/45.
FY.941	FAIRY KNOWE (D)	86/13	11.39	M/S, target service; returned 12/45.
	FAITHFUL STAR (D)	103/27	9.39	A/P; returned 3/46.
	FALK (W)	307/37	3.41	A/S; returned 10/46.
	FARADAY	322/16	1940	A/P;
FY.358	FARSUND (R.N.N.) (W) (ex-Kos VI)	248/29	7.40	A/S; returned 1945.
	FAVOUR (D)	93/08	1940	A/P; returned 1945.
FY.302	FAWN (D)	.../..	1.40	A/S; returned 1945.

FY.891	FEACO (D)	123/24	10.39	M/S; returned 11/45.
	FEAR NOT (D)	101/08	1940	A/P, Store carrier, Exam. returned 1945.
FY.928	FEASIBLE (D)	103/12	11.39	M/S; returned 8/45.
	FEE DES EAUX (French) (D)	.../..	9.40	A/P; returned 1944.
	FELLOWSHIP (D)	99/14	11.39	M/S; returned 1946.
	FEMERN (Dutch) (W)	257/32	1941	M/S; returned 1946.
	FENELLA (D) (ex-Unity)	.../..	4.40	Exam.; returned 1945.
FY.868	FENTONIAN	221/12	11.39	M/S, Esso (Y7.11); returned 2/45.
	FERTILE VALE (AD)	91/17	12.39	Exam.; lost 17/7/41.
FY.587	FEZENTA	228/14	11.39	M/S; returned 11/45.
FY.551	FIDGET (D) (ex-Formidable)	88/17	11.39	MRV, A/P, ASR; sold 1/46
	FIELDGATE (ex-Collingwood)	180/02	1941	BGV; returned 1945.
	FIFESHIRE	540/38	9.39	A/S; lost 20/2/40.
FY.679	FILEY BAY	370/31	8.39	M/S; returned 3/45.
FY.1683	FINESSE (ex-Trevo Terceiro)	296/12	1941	M/S; sold 1946.
FY.253	FINTRAY	195/06	2.40	M/S; returned 1/45.
FY.673	FIREFLY (ex-St. Just)	394/30	9.39	M/S; returned 10/45.
FY.1725	FIRMAMENT (W) (ex-Kos IX)	248/30	5.41	M/S; lost 30/5/44.
FY.1505	FISHER BOY (D)	91/14	11.39	MRV; sold 7/46.
	FISHER GIRL (D)	85/13	1940	MWU; lost 25/11/41.
FY.282	FISHER LAD (D)	.../..	12.39	A/S; returned 11/45.
	FISHER QUEEN (D)	88/16	10.40	HDPC; returned 9/46.
FY.600	FLANDERS† (ex-R.N. Charles Antram)	289/20	8.39	M/S; returned 12/45.
FY.1715	FLANDRE	226/15	6.40	A/P, M/S; returned 12/45.
	FLASH (W) (ex-Globe II)	206/25	4.41	M/S; returned 11/45.
	FLEMING	356/29	8.39	M/S; lost 24/7/40.
FY.719	FLICKER (W) (ex-Kos X)	260/32	5.41	M/S; returned 12/45.
	FLIXTON‡ (ex-R.N. William Harvey)	201/19	8.39	Exam.; returned 7/46.
Z.117	FLORENCE BRIERLEY* (ex-R.N. John Dunn)	330/18	1.40	BDV; sold 8/46.
T.34	FLORIDA (S.A.N.) (W) (ex-Gun 9)	256/30	12.40	M/S; returned 3/46.
FY.988	FLORIO	314/16	8.39	M/S; returned 4/45.
	FLOW (AD) (ex-R.N.)	95/20	9.39	Exam.; returned 3/46.
	FLUSH (AD) (ex-R.N.)	97/19	1940	BBV; returned 1945.
	FLYING ADMIRAL† (ex-R.N. John Bullock)	275/17	1940	A/P;
FY.880	FLYING WING	226/15	11.39	A/S, M/S; sold 1946.
4.204	FOAMCREST† (ex-Heron, ex-R.N. T.R. 47)	275/19	6.40	A/P; sold 3/46.
	FONTENOY† (ex-R.N. Siam Duffy)	276/18	8.39	M/S; lost 19/11/40.
	FORCE	327/17	2.40	M/S; lost 27/6/41.
	FORECAST (D)	96/25	11.39	A/P; lost 10/4/44.
	FORERUNNER (D)	92/11	11.39	M/S; lost 14/10/41.
	FORESIGHT (D)	87/11	1941	Harbour service; returned 1946.
4.243	FORFEIT (ex-Cornelian)	262/17	1.40	A/P; returned 6/46.
	FORSETTI	.../..	1940	BBV; returned 1945.
FY.762	FORT ROBERT‡ (ex-R.N. James Bentole)	203/18	11.39	M/S; returned 8/45.
4.275	FORT ROSE‡ (ex-R.N. Matthew Crooke)	212/17	5.40	A/P; returned 1945.
FY.711	FORT ROYAL	351/31	8.39	M/S; lost 9/2/40.
Z.156	FORT RYAN	255/32	9.39	BDV, BGV; returned 12/44.
	FORTUNA	259/06	6.40	A/P; lost 3/4/41.
Z.144	FOSS	275/16	1.40	BDV; returned 7/46.

Above: M/S Trawler H.M.S. Delphinus. 1—12 pdr. A.A., 2—.5 in. A.A. (1 × 2), 2—MG. (2 × 1). [*I.W.M.*

Left: Drifter H.M.S. Fisher Boy. 2—MG. (2 × 1—HG.). [*I.W.M.*

Below: M/S Trawler H.M.S. Fyldea. 1—12 pdr. A.A., 2—MG. (2 × 1). [*I.W.M.*

4.70	FRANC TIREUR	314/16	5.40	A/P, M/S (FY.1560); lost 25/9/43.
	FRAGRANT (D)	94/08	1941	Harbour service; returned 1945.
	FRANCOLIN	322/16	6.40	A/P; lost 12/11/41.
FY.1778	FRERES COQUELIN (French) (D)	.../..	7.40	M/S; returned 2/46.
FY.904	FRIARAGE	210/30	9.39	M/S, Exam., A/P; returned 12/45.
FY.1663	FRIESLAND (Dutch)	180/24	1940	M/S; returned 1945.
FY.962	FRONS OLIVAE (D)	93/16	11.39	MRV; returned 1945.
FY.680	FULL MOON (W) (ex-Kos XI)	258/32	5.41	M/S; returned 5/46.
	FURZE	99/11	1941	Water carrier; returned 1945.
	FUTURIST (R.N.Z.N.)	234/20	1940	M/S; returned 1944.
FY.666	FYLDEA	377/30	9.39	M/S; returned 12/45.
	GABRIELLE DENISE (Belgian)	.../..	7.40	M/S, Target service; returned 1945.
	GABRIELLE-MARIA (Belgian) (D)	102/31	1940	M/S; returned 1946.
FY.517	GADFLY† (ex-Tenedos, ex-R.N. Dominick Addison)	290/19	8.39	M/S; returned 9/45.
	GADRA	219/09	11.39	A/P, returned 1/40; lost 6/1/41.
	GALLINULE	238/07	11.39	A/P; returned 1/40.
4.71	GALVANI	353/29	6.40	A/P; returned 8/45.
FY.865	GAROLA	249/12	11.39	M/S, store carrier (Y7.4); returned 5/46.
FY.1679	GASTON RIVIERE (French)	.../..	1940	M/S; returned 1946.
	GAUL	550/36	9.39	A/S; lost 3/5/40.
4.14	GAVA† (ex-R.N. ?)	256/20	11.39	A/P, target service; returned 6/46.
	GELLYBURN (D)	86/08	9.39	Water carrier; returned 4/45.
	GEMMA	.../..	1941	M/S; sold 1949.
FY.724	GENERAL BIRDWOOD*	324/19	8.39	M/S, Esso; sold 5/46.
FY.599	GENERAL BOTHA	245/16	7.40	M/S; returned 11/45.
	GENERAL FOCH (French)	248/16	1940	A/P; returned 1946.
	GENERAL LEMAN (Belgian)	.../..	1940	BBV; returned 1945.
	GENEVA (D)	/..	1940	BBV; returned 1944.
FY.748	GENIUS (AD) (ex-R.N. Waft)	96/19	10.39	M/S; returned 11/45
FY.1950	GEORDIE (D)	.../..	12.39	M/S, harbour service; returned 5/46.
FY.1910	GEORGE & ALBERT (D)	.../..	12.39	M/S; returned 1/46.
FY.1926	GEORGE ADGELL† (ex-R.N.)	290/20	6.40	A/P, M/S; returned 1/46.
Z.178	GEORGE BLIGH* (ex-R.N.)	324/17	9.39	BDV; returned 12/45.
FY.627	GEORGE COUSINS† (ex-R.N.)	276/19	8.39	M/S; returned 7/45.
Z.249	GEORGE D. IRVIN	194/11	5.40	BDV, M/S; returned 7/45.
FY.685	GEORGE ROBB	217/30	8.39	M/S; sold 1/46.
4.135	GEORGE R. PURDY‡ (ex-R.N. Israel Aldcroft)	212/17	8.39	Exam.; returned 10/44.
FY.804	GEORGETTE‡ (ex-R.N. James Hartwell)	203/18	11.39	M/S; returned 5/46.
FY.1779	GERBERDINA JOHANNA (Dutch)	255/12	1940	M/S; returned 1945.
T.47	GERMISTON (S.A.N.) (W) (ex-Uni IV)	197/23	8.41	M/S: returned 5/46.
	GERVAIS RENTOUL (D)	100/17	11.39	Flare drifter, A/P; returned 5/46.
	G. G. BAIRD (AD)	97/18	1941	Harbour service; returned 1946.
	GILBERT EUGENE (French)	.../..	1940	A/P, Mine tender; returned 1945.
4.408	GILLIAN‡ (ex-R.N. John Elliot)	206/19	8.39	Exam.; returned 8/45.
FY.963	GILT EDGE (D)	88/16	11.39	M/S, D/L; returned 8/45.

	GIPPSLAND (R.A.N.)	133/08	1942	A/P; returned 1944.
Z.179	GIRAFE (French)	.../..	1940	BDV; returned 1945.
Z.186	GIRARD* (ex-R.N. Edward Druce)	326/18	6.40	BDV; sold 1/47.
	GIRL CHRISTIAN (D)	.../..	1940	A/P; returned 1945.
FY.1975	GIRL ELLEN (D)	93/14	12.39	A/P; returned 3/46.
	GIRL ENA (D)	89/07	1941	Harbour service; returned 1945.
FY.1655	GIRL ETHEL (D)	88/14	5.40	MWU; returned 4/45.
FY.1991	GIRL GLADYS (D)	110/17	11.39	Flare drifter, A/P, Exam.; returned 2/46.
	GIRL LIZZIE (AD) (ex-R.N. Hailstorm)	98/18	5.40	Harbour service; returned 6/46.
Z.304	GIRL MARGARET (D)	99/14	11.39	M/S, BDV; returned 3/46.
	GIRL MINNA (D)	.../..	1940	Target service; returned 1945.
FY.1940	GIRL NANCY (D)	.../..	1940	M/S, A/P; returned 1/46.
	GIRL PAMELA (D)	93/12	11.39	Flare drifter; lost 29/5/40.
	GIRL PAT (D)	.../..	1940	M/S, A/P; returned 1945.
	GIRL VIOLET (D)	.../..	3.40	Exam.; returned 11/45.
FY.1999	GIRL WINIFRED (D)	90/12	12.39	A/P; returned 12/45.
	GIVENCHY (R.C.N.)	357/18	1940	M/S; returned 1945.
4.257	GLACIER (ex-Magnolia)	260/09	5.40	A/P; returned 6/44.
	GLADYS* (ex-R.N. John Arthur)	286/17	11.39	BDV; returned 4/46.
FY.881	GLATIAN	220/13	11.39	A/P; returned 1945.
	GLEAM (D)	57/22	1941	Harbour service; lost 15/6/44.
	GLEAM ON (AD) (ex-R.N. Flurry)	100/19	12.39	M/S, Exam.; returned 12/45.
	GLEN ALBYN (D)	82/09	12.39	A/P; lost 23/11/39.
FY.556	GLEN HEATHER (D)	95/13	11.39	M/S; returned 11/45.
4.77	GLEN KIDSTON	360/30	8.39	M/S; returned 7/45.
FY.1556	GLOAMIN (AD)	94/19	12.39	M/S; returned 3/45.
	GLORIA	187/07	2.40	BBV; returned 9/44.
FY.964	GLOW (AD)	96/18	12.39	M/S; returned 11/45.
	GO AHEAD (D)	100/19	1939	M/S; lost 18/11/40.
	GOLDEN CHANCE (D)	.../..	1941	FAA safety vessel; returned 1/46.
	GOLDEN DAWN (D)	85/14	2.40	Harbour service; lost 4/4/40.
FY.1534	GOLDEN EFFORT (D)	86/14	12.39	M/S; lost 23/9/43.
	GOLDEN EMBLEM (AD)	95/18	1.40	A/P; returned 12/45.
FY.1994	GOLDEN GIFT (D)	89/10	11.39	Flare drifter, A/P; lost 6/4/43.
FY.708	GOLDEN HARVEST (D)	89/14	9.39	M/S; returned 6/46.
	GOLDEN LINE (AD) (ex-R.N. Minstrel)	99/19	1941	Harbour service; returned 1946.
	GOLDEN MILLER (D)	83/10	11.39	A/P; returned 9/45.
FY.1510	GOLDEN NEWS	95/14	11.39	M/S; returned 3/46.
FY.1968	GOLDEN SUNBEAM (D)	84/20	11.39	Flare drifter, A/P; lost 19/8/43.
	GOLDEN THYME (D)	.../..	1939	A/P; returned 1945.
FY.745	GOLDEN VIEW (AD) (ex-R.N. Node)	96/18	10.39	M/S; returned 3/46.
	GOLDEN WEST (D)	.../..	1941	Harbour service; lost 15/1/45.
	GOLDEN WEST (D)	88/14	10.40	D/G; lost 15/1/45.
	GOODWILL	.../..	1.40	A/P; returned 1946.
FY.75	GOOLGWAI† (R.A.N.) (ex-R.N. TR. ?)	271/19	10.39	M/S; returned 1946.
FY.94	GOONAMBEE (R.A.N.)	222/19	8.40	M/S; returned 1944.
FY.74	GOORANGAI (R.A.N.)	223/19	10.39	M/S; lost 20/11/40.
Y7.20	GOOSANDER	238/08	11.39	Water carrier, Esso; returned 2/46.
FY.316	GORSE (D)	99/11	12.39	A/S; returned 11/45.
FY.649	GOTH	394/25	8.39	M/S; sold 11/45.
T.03	GOULDING (S.A.N.) (W) (ex-R. L. Goulding)	224/21	1940	M/S; returned 1946.
FY.1962	GOWAN (D)	84/07	12.39	Exam.; returned 4/45.
FY.1544	GOWAN CRAIG (D)	82/15	12.39	M/S; returned 6/46.

	GOWAN HILL (AD) (ex-R.N. Puff)	96/20	8.39	Harbour service; lost 7/5/41.
Z.239	GRAAF VAN VLANDEREN (Belgian)	375/25	9.40	BDV; returned 4/45.
FY.546	GRAMPIAN	409/30	8.39	M/S; returned 3/46.
	GRATEFUL	213/03	1939	A/P, MRV; returned 2/46.
4.146	GREAT ADMIRAL	284/08	5.40	A/P; returned 6/45.
FY.156	GREENFLY (ex-Quantock)	441/36	9.39	A/S; sold 1945.
FY.632	GREEN HOWARD	349/27	8.39	M/S; returned 3/46.
FY.591	GREEN PASTURES (AD)	97/19	12.39	M/S; returned 11/45.
FY.1875	GREGORY	355/30	8.39	M/S; returned 7/45.
T.50	GRIBB (S.A.N.) (W) (ex-Hektor 9)	280/30	6.41	M/S; returned 4/46.
FY.125	GRIMSBY TOWN	422/34	8.39	A/S; returned 11/45.
FY.1956	GRIMSTAD (R.N.N.) (W) (ex-Kos XV)	258/32	7.40	M/S; returned 1/46.
T.04	GRIMWOOD (S.A.N.) (ex-S. H. Grimwood)	219/24	5.40	M/S; returned 5/46.
	GROENLAND (French)	1220/30	1940	To M.W.T. 1941.
FY.671	GROSMONT CASTLE† (ex-R.N. John Pollard)	276/17	2.40	M/S; returned 2/46.
FY.965	GUIDE ON (D)	91/11	11.39	M/S; returned 2/46.
FY.354	GUIDING LIGHT (D)	99/..	12.39	A/S; returned 6/45.
FY.718	GULA	81/36	1940	D/L, harbour service; returned 1945.
FY.710	GULFOSS	358/29	8.39	M/S; lost 9/3/41.
FY.568	GUNNER	350/27	9.39	M/S, D/L; returned 2/46.
	GVAS II (R.N.N.)	251/26	6.40	M/S; returned 6/46.
FY.544	GWENLLIAN	220/11	11.39	M/S; returned 1/46.
Z.135	GWMAHO† (ex-R.N. Thomas Crofton)	276/17	11.39	BDV; returned 1/46.
FY.306	HAARLEM	431/38	6.40	A/S; returned 5/46.
FY.1825	HAILSTORM (W) (ex-Kos XIII)	258/32	5.41	M/S, D/L; returned 9/45.
FY.149	HAMMOND	452/36	8.39	A/S; lost 25/4/40.
FY.173	HAMPSHIRE	425/34	9.39	A/S; French LA TOULONNAISE (1939).
FY.741	HARLECH CASTLE	275/16	2.40	M/S; returned 7/45.
	HARMONY (D) (ex-Unison)	79/10	1940	M/S; lost 15/11/41.
FY.538	HARRY MELLING† (ex-R.N. John Evans)	275/19	8.39	M/S; returned 7/45.
FY.1847	HARSTAD (R.N.N.) (W) (ex-Kos XVII)	258/32	7.40	M/S; lost 27/2/43.
	HARVEST GLEANER (AD) (ex-R.N. Blizzard)	96/18	11.39	M/S; lost 28/10/40.
	HARVEST HOPE (D)	91/11	6.40	A/P; returned 1945.
	HARVEST MOON (D)	72/04	12.39	Expended as blockship 9/9/40.
FY.1528	HARVEST REAPER (D)	98/25	12.39	M/S, harbour service; returned 11/46.
FY.662	HATANO	297/25	9.39	M/S; returned 5/46.
FY.1749	HATSUSE	295/27	8.39	M/S; returned 8/45.
FY.1752	HAUG I (R.N.N.) (W)	212/24	12.40	M/S; returned 6/46.
	HAUKEN (R.N.N.) (W)	251/26	5.40	M/S; returned 3/46.
FY.1759	HAV (W)	249/30	3.40	M/S; returned 1945.
FY.139	HAYBOURNE WYKE* (ex-R.N. Robert Barton)	324/17	5.40	A/P, M/S; lost 2/1/45.
	HEATHER SPRIG (D)	83/13	4.40	BBV, harbour service; returned 8/46.
	HEATHERY BRAE (D)	90/10	10.40	BBV; returned 1944.
.24	HEKTOR (S.A.N.) (W) (ex-Hektor 5)	233/29	7.40	M/S; returned 6/46.
	HEKTOR 7 (W)	233/29	1940	M/S; returned 1945.
.09	HEKTOR FRANS (Belgian)	102/18	10.40	A/P; returned 10/45.
	HELEN SLATER (AD)	.../..	1941	Harbour service; returned 1945.
	HELEN WEST (AD) (ex-R.N. Bluster)	96/25	1939	A/P; returned 1945.
Y.312	HELIER II (W)	341/36	3.40	A/S; returned 10/45.
.86	HELVETIA	260/17	6.40	A/P, M/S; returned 9/46.

Top to bottom: D/L Drifter H.M.S. Gilt Edge. 1—20 mm. A.A., 2—MG. (2 × 1). A/S Trawler H.M.S Kingston Amber. 1—4 in., 2—.5 in. A.A. (1 × 2), 2—MG. (2 × 1). A/S Trawler H.M.S. Kingsto Olivine. 1—4 in., 3—20 mm. A.A. (3 × 1). M/S Trawler H.M.S. Liberia. 1—12 pdr. A.A., 2—.5 in A.A (1 × 2), 2—MG. (2 × 1). [*All I.W.M*

	HENRIETTE‡ (ex-R.N. Robert Harding)	204/19	6.40	A/P, M/S; lost 26/12/41.
FY.1731	HERCULES (Dutch)	255/05	1940	M/S; returned 1/46.
	HERDIS (Dutch)	.../..	6.40	BBV; returned 1945.
FY.1866	HEROINE (ex-Hero)	217/07	6.40	M/S, Esso; returned 11/44.
	HERON	233/02	11.39	A/P, returned 1/40; lost 12/7/42.
FY.176	HERTFORDSHIRE	458/38	1939	A/S, U.S.N. (name unchanged—1942); returned 1945.
	HIGH TIDE (AD) (ex-R.N.)	97/19	8.40	Exam.; lost 30/3/45.
FY.1949	HILDA COOPER	127/28	9.39	Exam.; returned 10/44.
FY.541	HILDINA† (ex-R.N. William Leek)	276/18	8.39	M/S; returned 4/46.
J.112	HINNOY (R.N.N.) (W) (ex-Globe VII)	249/35	4.41	M/S; returned 1/46.
4.325	H. J. BULL (W)	569/35	1940	A/P, R.N.N. NAMSOS (1942); returned 1946.
FY.1982	HOLLYDALE (AD) (ex-R.N. Fireball)	93/19	5.40	Exam.; returned 1945.
	HOLYROOD	210/14	12.39	A/P; returned 1/40.
	HONEYDEW (D)	99/11	1941	Harbour service; ret. 1946
	HONINGSVAAG (R.N.N.) (ex-Malangen)	487/40	4.40	A/P; returned 1945.
FY.661	HONJO	308/28	1939	M/S; lost 18/1/42.
4.322	HORTEN (R.N.N.) (W) (ex-Kos II)	248/29	7.40	A/S, ASR; returned 1945.
FY.1795	HORTENSIA	244/07	7.40	M/S; returned 11/45.
FY.950	HOSANNA	132/30	11.39	M/S; returned 11/44.
FY.557	HOVERFLY (ex-Euryalus)	242/17	1939	M/S; returned 1/45.
FY.197	HUDDERSFIELD TOWN	399/33	1939	A/S; sold 1945.
FY.102	HUGH WALPOLE	498/37	8.39	A/S; sold 4/46.
	HUMPHREY (R.N.Z.N.)‡ (ex-R.N. Robert Faircloth)	207/17	10.39	M/S; returned 8/44.
J.393	HVAL V (R.N.N.) (W)	248/29	7.40	M/S; returned 3/46.
	HYPERION (D)	.../..	1940	A/P; returned 1944.
4.448	IBIS II (Belgian) (ex-Ibis)	160/37	1940	Harbour service, Esso; returned 1945.
FY.612	IJUIN	282/20	8.39	M/S; returned 1/46.
	IMBAT (D)	92/18	1940	Harbour service; lost 4/2/41.
Z.136	IMELDA	251/14	12.39	BDV; returned 1/46.
T.53	IMHOFF (S.A.N.) (W)	224/27	7.41	M/S; returned 5/46.
T.45	IMMORTELLE (S.A.N.) (W) (ex-Terje IX)	335/36	11.41	M/S; returned 12/46.
	IMPALA (W) (ex-A.N.4)	223/24	11.40	A/P; returned 4/46.
FY.813	IMPERIA	213/12	11.39	BGV; returned 11/45
FY.126	IMPERIALIST	520/39	8.39	A/S; returned 10/45.
FY.735	INCHGOWER‡ (ex-R.N. John Jackson)	202/18	11.39	M/S; returned 2/46.
FY.208	INDIAN STAR	463/36	10.39	A/S; returned 10/45.
FY.938	INDUSTRY (D)	100/08	11.39	M/S, Harbour service; returned 12/45.
FY.977	INTERNOS (D)	93/08	11.39	M/S, TRV; returned 3/46.
	INVERNESS (D)	.../..	11.39	A/P; returned 1/40.
FY.288	INVERCAIRN (D)	94/16	12.39	A/S; returned 11/45.
FY.1938	INVERCAULD	262/17	7.40	M/S; returned 11/45.
	INVERCLYDE	215/14	8.39	M/S; lost 16/10/42.
FY.729	INVERFORTH	248/14	11.39	M/S; returned 7/45.
FY.1748	INVERTAY	230/16	8.40	M/S; returned 7/46.
FY.976	INVERUGIE (D)	93/08	12.39	M/S, BBV; returned 8/45.
	IRANIAN	202/13	11.39	A/P; returned 1/40.
	IRMA ALICE (Belgian) (D)	.../ .	1940	A/P; returned 1945.
	IRONAXE (ex-R.N., ex-Russian T.22)	296/16	1940	Salvage vessel; returned 1945.
FY.663	IRVANA† (ex-R.N. Arthur Lessimore)	276/17	2.40	M/S; lost 16/1/42.
FY.896	ISABEL (Dutch)	166/06	1940	M/S; returned 1945.

FY.150	ISTRIA	409/35	9.39	A/S; sold 1946.
4.138	JACINTA	290/15	5.40	A/P, M/S, WDV; sold 5/46.
FY.923	JACKETA (D)	.../26	11.39	M/S; returned 3/46.
FY.958	JACK EVE (AD)	96/19	11.39	M/S; returned 11/45.
	JACK GEORGE (D)	98/13	1942	Water carrier; returned 1945.
FY.1783	JACQUELINE CLASINE (Dutch)	206/06	1940	M/S, Esso; returned 2/46.
	JACQUELINE FLORIMONDE (Belgian) (D)	.../..	1940	Harbour service; returned 1945.
	JACQUES MORGAND (French)	155/36	6.40	A/P; returned 1945.
Z.110	JAMES BARRIE	338/28	1.40	BDV; returned 11/45.
	JAMES COSGROVE† (R.N.Z.N.) (ex-R.N.)	277/18	10.39	M/S, BGV; returned 1946.
FY.667	JAMES LAY† (ex-R.N.)	278/18	9.39	M/S; returned 10/44.
M.06	JAY (ex-Nautilus)	352/26	1940	M/L, SANDMARTIN (1944); sold 1947.
Z.231	JAN DE WAELE (Belgian)	324/25	9.40	BDV; returned 12/45.
FY.169	JARDINE	452/36	8.39	A/S; lost 30/4/40.
	JEAN BOUZARD (French)	.../..	1940	KBV; returned 1945.
FY.1677	JEAN EDMUNDS	216/16	1.40	M/S; returned 9/45.
	JEAN FREDERIC* (Dutch) (ex-R.N. James Hulbert)	329/19	11.40	M/S; lost 1/5/41.
	JEANNE D'ARC (Belgian) (D)	.../..	7.40	A/P, BBV; returned 1945.
	JEANNE ET GENEVIEVE (D)	.../..	1940	KBV; returned 1945.
	JEANNIE HOWIE (D)	99/12	5.40	BDV; returned 1945.
FY.935	JEANNIE LEASK (D)	95/09	11.39	M/S; returned 1944.
	JEANNIE MACKAY (D)	.../..	1940	A/P; returned 1/46.
FY.1635	JEANNIE MACKINTOSH	88/15	1940	M/S, A/P; returned 2/46.
FY.701	JELOY (R.N.N.) (W) (ex-Pol II)	240/26	4.41	M/S, LEVANTER (1942); returned 8/46.
FY.1634	JENNIFER (ex-Braemar)	212/27	4.40	M/S, A/P; returned 1942.
FY.980	JENNY IRVIN (AD) (ex-R.N. Gulf Stream)	98/19	11.39	M/S; returned 1946.
	JESSIE TAIT (D)	84/15	5.40	BBV, RDF. TS; returned 1945.
	JEWEL (D)	84/08	1940	M/S; lost 18/5/41.
	JOCELYN (D)	94/15	1940	A/P; returned 1945.
T.56	JOHANNESBURG (S.A.N.) (W) (ex-Suderoy II)	228/25	8.42	M/S; returned 4/46.
FY.924	JOHN & NORA	95/13	12.39	M/S; returned 1945.
FY.1518	JOHN ALFRED	81/09	11.39	M/S, A/P; returned 1945.
	JOHN BAPTISH† (ex-R.N.)	298/18	9.39	M/S; returned 11/39.
FY.536	JOHN CATTLING† (ex-R.N.)	276/18	8.39	M/S; returned 7/45.
Z.149	JOHN FITZGERALD† (ex-R.N.)	235/18	1.40	BDV; returned 1/46.
	JOHN HERD (D)	103/30	1941	Harbour service; returned 1945.
FY.1662	JOHN STEPHEN† (ex-R.N.)	227/20	1.40	M/S; returned 11/45.
	JOHN WATT (D)	84/11	1941	Harbour service; returned 1945.
FY.308	JOHN WILLIAMSON (W) (R.N.N.)	159/12	8.41	M/S; R.H.N. ALFEIOS (1943).
FY.1942	JOHN WILLMENT (D)	101/32	1941	M/S; returned 1944.
	JOSEPH BUTTON† (ex-R.N.)	290/18	8.39	M/S; lost 22/10/40.
FY.1915	J. T. HENDRY (D)	88/08	1940	BBV; returned 1944.
FY.1830	JUNCO	191/17	12.40	M/S, target service; returned 5/46.
FY.752	JUNE ROSE (AD)	96/18	10.39	M/S; returned 5/45.
	JUSTIFIED (D)	93/25	1940	M/S; lost 16/6/42.
FY.736	JUSTIFIER (D)	.../..	12.39	M/S; returned 1/46.
	KAIWAKA (R.N.Z.N.)	169/37	1940	D/L; returned 1946.
T.400	KAPUNI (R.N.Z.N.)	190/09	1941	M/S; returned 1945.

FY.877	KARMOY (R.N.N.) (W) (ex-Globe V)	249/36	4.41	M/S, FIERY CROSS (1944); returned 8/46.
4.148	KASTORIA	307/17	5.40	A/P, M/S; returned 4/46.
	KATHERINE	.../..	3.40	M/S; returned 1946.
	KATHLEEN (AD) (ex-R.N. Breaker)	98/19	11.39	M/S; returned 1943.
FY.112	KELT	455/37	9.39	A/S; sold 1945.
FY.857	KENNYMORE	255/14	11.39	M/S; lost 25/11/40.
	KERYADO	252/20	7.40	M/S; lost 6/3/41.
FY.1877	KIDDAW (D)	86/09	12.39	BBV; returned 7/45.
FY.1524	KINDRED STAR (D)	115/30	12.39	M/S; returned 2/46.
FY.730	KING EMPEROR	246/14	2.40	M/S; store carrier (Y7.14), returned 1/46.
	KING HENRY	162/00	5.40	BGV; lost 13/6/41.
FY.235	KING SOL	468/36	9.39	A/S; returned 12/45.
FY.885	KINGSCOURT‡ (ex-R.N. William Biggs)	203/17	11.39	M/S; returned 9/45.
4.87	KINGS GREY	338/15	8.39	A/P, M/S (FY.502); returned 9/46.
FY.212	KINGSTON AGATE	464/37	9.39	ABV, A/S; returned 1/46.
FY.136	KINGSTON ALALITE	412/33	9.39	A/S; lost 10/11/40.
FY.211	KINGSTON AMBER	467/37	9.39	A/S; returned 2/46.
FY.160	KINGSTON ANDALUSITE	415/34	8.39	A/S; sold 1945.
4.03	KINGSTON BERYL	356/28	9.39	ABV, A/S; lost 25/12/43.
	KINGSTON CAIRNGORM	448/35	9.39	A/S; lost 18/10/40.
FY.214	KINGSTON CEYLONITE	448/35	9.39	A/S, U.S.N. (name unchanged—1942); lost 15/6/42.
FY.236	KINGSTON CHRYSOBERYL	448/35	9.39	A/S; returned 3/45.
FY.184	KINGSTON CHRYSOLITE	448/35	8.39	A/S; sold 1945.
FY.215	KINGSTON CORAL	433/36	9.39	A/S; returned 9/45.
FY.121	KINGSTON CORNELIAN	449/34	8.39	A/S; lost 5/1/40.
FY.216	KINGSTON CRYSTAL	433/36	9.39	A/S; returned 3/45.
FY.217	KINGSTON CYANITE	433/36	9.39	A/S; returned 9/45.
FY.145	KINGSTON GALENA	415/34	8.39	A/S; lost 24/7/40.
4.45	KINGSTON JACINTH	356/29	8.39	ABV; lost 12/1/43.
FY.193	KINGSTON OLIVINE	378/30	8.39	A/S; sold 1945.
4.54	KINGSTON ONYX	357/27	8.39	ABV, A/S; returned 9/44.
4.69	KINGSTON PERIDOT	356/26	8.39	ABV, A/S; returned 12/45.
4.81	KINGSTON SAPPHIRE	356/29	9.39	ABV; lost 5/10/40.
4.31	KINGSTON TOPAZ	357/27	8.39	ABV, A/S; returned 11/45.
4.91	KINGSTON TURQUOISE	356/29	8.39	ABV, A/S; returned 11/45.
	KINGSWAY	211/05	11.39	A/P; returned 1/40.
	KIRITONA (R.N.Z.N.)	136/09	1942	D/G; returned 1946.
FY.174	KIRKELLA	436/36	9.39	A/S; sold 1946.
	KLO (W)	307/37	3.41	A/S; returned 10/46.
T.35	KOMMETJIE (S.A.N.) (W) (ex-Uni 8)	252/30	11.40	M/S; returned 3/46.
	KOPANES	351/15	1940	A/P; lost 19/4/41.
4.297	KORAB I (Polish)	263/38	12.40	Exam.; returned 1946.
FY.79	KOROWA* (R.A.N.) (ex-R.N. Edward McGuire)	324/19	9.39	M/S; returned 1946.
	KOS XVI (W)	258/32	7.40	A/S; lost 24/8/41.
	KOS XXII (W)	353/37	9.40	A/S; lost 2/6/41.
	KOS XXIII (W)	353/37	9.40	A/S; lost 5/41.
T.48	KRUGERSDORP (S.A.N.) (W) (ex-Uni V)	198/23	6.41	M/S; returned 5/46.
FY.692	KUNISHI	303/27	8.39	M/S; sold 4/46.
FY.639	KURD	352/30	1939	M/S; lost 10/7/45.
Z.137	KUROKI	248/09	1.40	BDV; returned 1946.
4.271	KUVERA‡ (ex-R.N.?)	202/19	7.40	A/P; returned 9.45.
FY.712	LACENNIA	348/30	1939	M/S; returned 1945.
4.07	LACERTA	270/11	6.40	A/P, M/S; sold 2/46.
FY.100	LADY BERYL	417/35	9.39	A/S; sold 1945.
Z.226	LADY ELEANOR	324/18	1940	BDV; sold 1/47.
FY.124	LADY ELSA	518/37	9.39	A/S, U.S.N. (name unchanged—1942); sold 1945.
FY.547	LADY ENID	324/18	8.39	M/S; returned 1945.
FY.176	LADY ESTELLE	323/15	1940	A/S; returned 1945.
4.89	LADY HOGARTH	472/37	1939	A/P, A/S; returned 1945.

	LADY LILIAN	581/39	1940	A/S; lost 16/3/41.
FY.283	LADY MADELINE	581/39	1940	A/S; returned 1945.
FY.148	LADY PHILOMENA	417/36	8.39	A/S; returned 10/45.
FY.253	LADY ROSEMARY	472/37	1940	A/S, A/P (4.150); returned 1945.
	LADY SHIRLEY	477/37	1939	A/P; lost 11/12/41.
4.233	LADY STANLEY† (ex-R.N.?)	276/17	1940	A/P; returned 1945.
	LANNER	103/12	11.39	M/S; returned 2/46.
4.315	LAPAGERIA	274/16	9.40	A/P, Fuel tanker; returned 2/46.
	L'APPEL DE LA MER (French)	.../..	8.40	A/P; returned 1945.
T.05	LARSEN (S.A.N.) (ex-A. E. Larsen)	162/24	1.40	M/S; returned 4/46.
FY.172	LARWOOD	452/36	8.39	A/S, lost 25/4/40; salved and German VPG.111.
	LASHER (D)	96/19	1941	Harbour service; returned 2/46.
	L'ATLANTIQUE (French)	659/20	7.40	A/S; returned 1945.
	LAVATERA (D)	84/13	4.40	BBV; returned 1946.
Z.240	LAVEROCK	.../..	5.40	BDV; sold 3/46.
	LEA RIG (D)	.../..	1940	A/P, FOX II (1944); returned 1945.
FY.196	LEEDS UNITED	405/33	9.39	A/S; sold 1945.
	LE FLIBUSTIER (French) (D)	.../..	1940	M/S; returned 1945.
FY.223	LEICESTER CITY	422/34	9.39	A/S; returned 3/46.
	LEMNOS (D)	85/10	1940	Harbour service; returned 1945.
	LE NIVOSE (French)	185/36	1940	A/P; returned 1945.
FY.243	LE TIGER	516/37	12.39	A/S; sold 10/45.
FY.519	LEPHRETO† (ex-R.N. William Symons)	275/17	8.39	M/S, Esso (Y7.17); returned 1945.
	LERINA (D)	71/17	1941	A/P; sold 1946.
FY.103	LEYLAND	452/36	9.39	A/S; lost 25/11/42.
FY.1650	LIBERATOR (ex-Hekla)	354/29	5.40	M/S; returned 1945.
FY.1826	LIBERIA	250/06	1940	M/S; returned 1945.
FY.867	LIBRA (Dutch)	211/12	1940	M/S; returned 1945.
FY.1800	LIBYAN	220/13	1940	M/S, Esso (Y7.18); returned 1945.
FY.940	LICHEN (D)	99/11	11.39	M/S; returned 1945.
FY.798	LIDDOCK‡ (ex-R.N.?)	202/19	3.40	D/L, A/P; returned 1943.
FY.1765	LIGNY† (ex-R.N. Henry Chevallier)	277/18	9.40	M/S; returned 11/45.
	LILIUM (AD) (ex-R.N. Blue Haze)	97/19	1941	D/G; returned 1/46.
	LILY OAK (D)	84/08	1940	A/P; returned 1945.
	LINCOLN CITY	398/33	9.39	A/S; lost 21/2/41.
FY.222	LINCOLNSHIRE	432/36	9.39	A/S; returned 9/45.
	L'ISTRAC	778/07	1939	A/P; lost 11/10/40.
FY.1547	LIZZIE BIRREL (D)	94/13	11.39	M/S; returned 4/46.
	LIZZIE FLETT (D)	88/11	1940	A/P; returned 1944.
	LIZZIE WEST (D)	103/30	1941	A/P; returned 1945.
	LOCH ALSH	385/26	9.40	M/S; lost 30/1/42.
	LOCH ASSATER	210/10	1939	M/S; lost 22/3/40.
4.203	LOCH BLAIR‡ (ex-R.N. James Beagar)	203/17	6.40	A/P; returned 2/46.
FY.688	LOCH BUIE† (ex-R.N. Isaac Arthan)	277/19	8.39	M/S; returned 3/46.
	LOCH DOON	534/37	8.39	M/S; lost 25/12/39.
FY.704	LOCH ERIBOL	352/29	9.39	M/S; lost 12/10/45.
FY.896	LOCH ESK	209/12	11.39	M/S; returned 1943.
4.97	LOCH HOPE	274/15	6.40	A/P; returned 12/45.
	LOCH INVER	356/30	5.40	A/P; lost 24/9/40.
Z.123	LOCH LAGGAN	255/30	9.39	BDV; returned 5/45.
FY.642	LOCH LEVEN	357/28	8.39	M/S; returned 2/46.
Z.165	LOCH LONG† (ex-R.N. Timothy Crowley)	277/17	3.40	BDV; sold 2/46.
FY.151	LOCH MELFORT	440/34	8.39	A/S; sold 2/46.
4.229	LOCH MOIDART* (ex-R.N. James Wright)	326/18	6.40	A/P, M/S; returned 1/46.

FY.135	LOCH MONTEITH	531/36	9.39	A/S, S/M Tender; returned 11/45.
	LOCH NAVER† (ex-R.N. Edward Cattelly)	278/19	8.39	M/S; lost 6/5/40.
M.41	LOCH NEVIS‡ (ex-R.N. Patrick Donovan)	272/20	1940	M/L; returned 1944.
FY.175	LOCH OSKAIG	534/37	8.39	A/S; returned 11/45.
FY.1835	LOCH PARK† (ex-R.N. John Brooker)	248/17	6.40	M/S; returned 8/45.
FY.779	LOCH RANNOCK	178/01	1.40	M/S; returned 11/45.
	LOCH SHIN	255/30	9.39	BDV; lost 26/5/40.
FY.199	LOCH TULLA	423/34	9.39	A/S; sold 1/46.
FY.781	LOIS* (ex-R.N. John Appleby)	286/17	2.40	M/S; returned 11/44.
4.169	LOMBARD	272/09	5.40	A/P, M/S; returned 11/45.
	LONGSCAR	215/30	8.39	Exam.; returned 1946.
	LOON	191/14	3.40	BBV, water carrier; returned 12/45.
	LOOS (R.C.N.)	356/18	1940	BGV; returned 1945.
	LORD ANSON (D)	100/27	1940	Harbour service; returned 1945.
FY.694	LORD ASHFIELD	346/29	9.39	M/S; returned 12/45.
FY.220	LORD AUSTIN	473/37	9.39	A/S; lost 24/6/44.
FY.929	LORD BARHAM	92/25	11.39	M/S; returned 10/45.
FY.608	LORD BEACONSFIELD	302/15	8.39	M/S, A/P, M/S; lost 10/45.
	LORD CAVAN (D)	96/15	11.39	MRV; lost 2/6/40.
	LORD CECIL	228/16	11.39	A/P; returned 1/40.
	LORD COLLINGWOOD (D)	116/30	4.40	A/P; returned 1945.
	LORD CURZON (D)	88/17	9.39	Store carrier; returned 2/46.
FY.1774	LORD DARLING	256/14	8.40	M/S, Exam.; returned 11/44.
	LORD DUNWICH (D)	75/11	9.40	Exam.; returned 3/46.
FY.218	LORD ESSENDEN	464/36	9.39	A/S; returned 10/45.
Z.111	LORD GAINFORD* (ex-R.N. Christopher Dixon)	324/18	12.39	BDV; returned 1946.
FY.1593	LORD GREY	346/28	8.39	M/S; returned 3/46.
FY.109	LORD HAILSHAM	445/34	8.39	A/S; lost 27/2/43.
FY.930	LORD HOOD (D)	92/25	11.39	M/S; returned 8/45.
FY.133	LORD HOTHAM	464/36	9.39	A/S; sold 9/45.
	LORD HOWARD (D)	98/17	11.40	A/P; lost 24/12/40.
	LORD HOWE (D)	75/17	11.40	Flare drifter, TS; returned 2/46.
FY.1611	LORD INCHCAPE	338/24	8.39	M/S; returned 1945.
FY.1617	LORD IRWIN	346/28	8.39	M/S; returned 2/46.
FY.1884	LORD KEITH (D)	116/30	9.39	A/P; returned 12/45.
FY.157	LORD LLOYD	396/33	8.39	A/S; sold 1945.
FY.672	LORD MELCHETT	347/29	8.39	M/S; returned 4/46.
FY.219	LORD MIDDLETON	464/36	9.39	A/S; returned 1945.
FY.780	LORD NORTHCLIFFE	228/16	11.39	BBV; returned 11/45.
FY.221	LORD NUFFIELD	466/37	9.39	A/S; returned 12/45.
FY.181	LORD PLENDER	396/33	8.39	A/S; sold 1946.
FY.877	LORD RODNEY (D)	104/28	9.39	M/S; returned 2/46.
	LORD ST. VINCENT (D)	115/29	9.39	A/P, BBV; lost 7/7/41.
	LORD SELBORNE	247/17	6.40	A/P; lost 31/3/41.
FY.115	LORD SNOWDEN	444/34	8.39	A/S; lost 13/4/42.
	LORD STAMP	448/35	8.39	A/S; lost 14/10/40.
FY.163	LORD STANHOPE	448/35	8.39	A/S; returned 11/45.
FY.187	LORD STONEHAVEN	444/34	8.39	A/S; lost 2/10/42.
	LORD SUFFOLK (D)	115/29	12.39	A/P; returned 1943.
FY.170	LORD WAKEFIELD	418/33	8.39	A/S; lost 29/7/44.
	LORINDA	348/28	9.39	M/S; lost 28/8/41.
4.170	LORRAINE† (ex-R.N. Thomas Chambers)	277/17	6.40	A/P, M/S; returned 1/46.
4.207	LOUIS BOTHA	226/16	6.40	A/P; lost 3/44.
FY.1917	LOUISE ET MARIE (French)	265/16	7.40	M/S; returned 1/46.
FY.942	LOVANIA	292/12	6.40	A/P; sold 2/46.
FY.782	LOWTHER	313/15	2.40	M/S; returned 1/46.
FY.298	LOYAL FRIEND (AD) (ex-R.N. Low Tide)	96/19	12.39	A/S: returned 8/45.
FY.1769	LUCIEN GOUJY (French)	150/35	7.40	M/S; lost 21/2/45.
FY.894	LUCIENNE JEANNE† (French) (ex-R.N. Daniel Harrington)	264/17	4.41	M/S; lost 10/41.
	LUDA LADY	234/14	11.39	M/S; lost 22/1/41.

FY.776	LUDA LORD	224/13	11.39	M/S; Store carrier (Y7.34) returned 11/44.
Z.189	LUMINARY (ex-Kingfisher)	.../..	9.40	BDV; returned 12/46.
FY.588	LUNE	310/30	9.39	M/S, WDV (4.416); sold 7/46.
FY.347	LURCHER (W) (ex-Busen 8)	397/28	1941	A/S; returned 1946.
FY.1553	LYDIA LONG	74/18	1940	A/P; returned 1943.
FY.177	LYDIARD (ex-Loyal, ex-Matabele)	440/35	9.39	A/S; sold 2/46.
	M. A. WEST (AD) (ex-R.N. Broil)	96/19	1940	Exam.; lost 14/5/41.
J.136	MAALOY (R.N.N.) (W) (ex-Globe VI)	249/35	4.40	M/S; lost 27/3/44.
FY.784	MADDEN‡ (ex-R.N. William Browning)	237/17	2.40	M/S, WDV; returned 4/46.
	MAGGIE GAULT (D)	91/10	6.40	Harbour service; returned 4/45.
	MAIDA (D) (ex-Chestnut)	107/14	11.39	M/S; lost 16/3/40.
FY.1597	MAJESTY (D)	.../..	3.40	M/S, A/P; returned 9/46.
FY.796	MALACOLITE† (ex-R.N. Richard Bagley)	248/17	8.39	M/S; returned 9/45.
FY.1837	MANDAL (R.N.N.) (W) (ex-Kos XIV)	258/32	7.40	M/S; returned 1946.
FY.333	MANOR	314/13	8.39	A/S; lost 9/7/42.
FY.104	MAN O'WAR	517/36	8.39	A/S; sold 1945.
	MANX PRINCE	221/10	12/39	M/S; lost 28/11/40.
FY.777	MARANO	245/16	11.39	M/S; returned 1/45.
	MARCEL PIERRE (French) (D)	.../..	7.40	A/P; returned 1945.
	MARCIA (D)	.../..	3.40	BBV; returned 1944.
	MARCONI	322/16	2.40	M/S; lost 20/9/41.
FY.1508	MARE	.../..	11.39	M/S; returned 10/45.
FY.665	MARETTA	350/29	9.39	M/S; returned 11/45.
FY.981	MARGARET HIDE (D)	161/29	11.39	M/S; returned 4/45.
FY.802	MARGARET ROSE	348/12	5.40	M/S; returned 1946.
4.67	MARIA (ex-August Wreidt)	372/29	5.41	WDV; sold 1950.
FY.895	MARIA ELIZABETH (Dutch) (D)	164/29	1940	M/S, Esso; returned 1945
FY.1785	MARIA R. OMMERING (Dutch)	216/14	1940	M/S; returned 2/46.
FY.1567	MARIE ELENA (D)	.../..	8.40	M/S; returned 1944.
Z.238	MARIE LOUISE† (Belgian) (ex-R.N. TR.18)	258/18	8.40	BDV; returned 1/46.
Z.233	MARIS STELLA (French)	285/07	7.40	BGV; returned 1945.
	MARIS STELLA (Belgian) (D)	120/12	7.40	A/P; returned 1945.
FY.1777	MARJORIE M. HASTIE	244/30	6.40	M/S; returned 1945.
FY.714	MARSONA† (ex-R.N. James Christopher)	276/18	10.39	M/S; lost 4/8/40.
FY.1935	MARY A. HASTIE	244/30	11.39	M/S, A/P; returned 1945.
	MARY A. PURDY‡ (ex-R.N. Thomas Haggerty)	202/18	2.40	BBV; returned 10/44.
Z.57	MARY CAM (R.A.N.)‡ (ex-R.N. John Fisser)	202/18	1941	BDV; returned 1946.
FY.501	MARY HERD (D)	96/19	5.40	Water carrier; returned 10/45.
FY.1659	MARY J. MASSON	.../..	5.40	MWU; returned 1946.
	MARY STURGEON (D)	.../..	3.40	A/P; returned 1945.
	MARY SWANSTON (D)	96/20	10.39	Harbour service; returned 10/45.
	MARY WATT (D)	.../18	1941	Harbour service; returned 1946.
Z.147	MARY WHITE	271/35	1.40	BDV; returned 2/46.
Z.138	MASONA	297/15	12.39	BDV; scrapped 6/47.
B.078	MASSABIELLE (Belgian) (D)	110/35	9.40	ASR; returned 1945.
FY.350	MASTIFF (W) (ex-Busen 9)	384/29	1941	A/S; returned 1945.
	MATHILDE SIMONNE (Belgian) (D)	88/31	10.40	A/P, MWU; returned 4/46.
	MEANDER (R.C.N.) (D)	60/34	1940	A/P; returned 1946.

	MEDOC (French)	.../..	1940	A/P; returned 1945.
	MELBOURNE	466/36	9.39	A/S; lost 22/5/40.
	MEMENTO (D)	.../..	1940	M/S; returned 1945.
FY.953	MERBREEZE	120/31	11.39	M/S; returned 1946.
FY.1836	MEROR	250/05	9.40	M/S; lost 3/10/43.
FY.816	MEWSLADE	275/16	3.40	M/S; returned 4/46.
	M. H. BUCHAN (D)	101/17	1940	Harbour service; returned 1946.
FY.943	M. H. STEPHENS	94/18	11.39	Exam. Fire float; returned 12/44.
FY.567	MICHAEL GRIFFITH† (ex-R.N.)	282/18	8.39	M/S; returned 1/45.
	MIDAS (D)	89/10	2.40	Flare drifter, BBV; lost 3/2/41.
4.431	MIKASA	274/15	12.39	A/P; returned 10/44.
FY.128	MILDENHALL	466/36	9.39	A/S; French L'AJACC IENNE (1939).
FY.564	MILFORD COUNTESS† (ex-R.N. Charles Legg)	275/19	8.39	M/S; returned 4/46.
FY.613	MILFORD DUCHESS† (ex-R.N. James McGill)	275/19	8.39	M/S; returned 12/44.
Z.125	MILFORD DUKE† (ex-R.N. James Dinton)	277/18	8.39	BDV; returned 11/45
	MILFORD EARL† (ex-R.N. Andrew Apsley)	290/19	8.39	M/S; lost 8/12/41.
FY.1573	MILFORD KING† (ex-R.N. Valentine Bower)	275/17	12.39	M/S, Store carrier (Y7.36); returned 11/45.
FY.614	MILFORD PRINCE† (ex-R.N. Thomas Allen)	278/20	8.39	M/S; returned 12/45.
FY.616	MILFORD PRINCESS	301/24	9.39	M/S; returned 9/45.
FY.615	MILFORD QUEEN† (ex-R.N. William Browis)	280/17	8.39	M/S; returned 12/45.
	MILL O'BUCKIE (D)	99/14	1941	Harbour service; returned 1945.
	MILLWATER (AD) (ex-R.N. Black Frost)	100/18	6.40	BBV, Exam., A/P; returned 1945.
	MINT (D)	96/12	1941	Water carrier; returned 1946.
FY.1642	MIRABELLE‡ (ex-R.N. Edward Barker)	203/18	11.39	A/P, Esso; lost 17/9/44.
	MIRAGE (AD)	97/18	1940	Harbour service; returned 1943.
4.04	MITRES	250/17	6.40	A/P, salvage vessel; returned 11/45.
	MOED EN WERK (Belgian)	108/31	6.40	D/L; returned 1945.
FY.1697	MOLDE (R.N.N.) (W) (ex-Kos XX)	356/36	7.40	A/S, M/S; returned 1946.
	MONARDA (D)	109/16	11.39	M/S; lost 8/11/41.
FY.677	MONIMIA	374/29	8.39	M/S; returned 11/45.
FY.1728	MONIQUE ANDRE (French)	221/20	7.40	M/S; returned 1/46.
FY.1803	MONIQUE CAMILLE (French)	277/34	8.40	M/S; returned 3/45.
4.171	MONTAMO† (ex-R.N. James Berry)	269/17	1940	A/P, M/S; returned 1945.
T.16	MOOIVLEI (S.A.N.)	252/35	11.39	A/S; returned 3/45.
	MOONLIGHT (D)	100/13	1941	Store carrier; returned 1945.
FY.1863	MOONRISE (ex-Marioute)	.../..	3.40	M/S, BGV (Z.51); sold 5/46.
FY.1922	MOONSHINE (ex-Polo Norte)	344/17	1940	M/S; sold 1/45.
FY.1819	MORAVIA	306/17	6.40	M/S, A/P; lost 14/3/43.
	MORAY‡ (ex-R.N. Henry Jennings)	206/18	1940	D/L, store carrier; lost 13/3/43.
	MORAY ROSE (AD) (ex-R.N. Williwaw)	96/20	1941	Harbour service; returned 1945.
	MORAY VIEW (D)	93/09	3.40	Hospital drifter; returned 2/46.
4.114	MORGAN JONES† (ex-R.N.)	278/18	6.40	A/P; returned 4/45.
	MOSS (R.N.N.) (W) (ex-Gos 1)	274/27	1941	A/S Training; returned 1945.
Z.126	MOUNT ARD	255/31	9.39	BDV; returned 4/45.
FY.684	MOUNT KEEN	254/36	8.39	M/S; returned 4/45.

Left: Trawler Maria was the German Prize August Wreidt.

Below top: A/S Trawler H.M.S. Northern Foam. 1—4 in., 3—20 mm. A.A. (3 × 1). [*I.W.M.*

Centre: A/S Trawler H.M.S. Northern Gem. 1—4 in., 2—.5 in. A.A. (1 × 2), 2—MG. (2 × 1). *Bottom:* A/S Trawler H.M.S. Northern Pride. 1—4 in., 1—20 mm. A.A., 2—.5 in. A.A. (1 × 2), 2—MG. (2 × 1). [*Both I.W.M.*

	MURIEL STEVENS (D)	.../..	1940	BBV; returned 1945.
	MURMANSK	348/29	8.39	M/S; lost 17/6/40.
FY.611	MUROTO	340/30	8.39	M/S; returned 1/44.
	MUSK ROSE (D)	.../..	1941	Exam.; sold 1946.
FY.1784	MYRLAND (R.N.N.)	321/18	4.41	M/S; returned 1946.
FY.654	NAB WYKE	348/30	8.39	M/S; returned 3/46.
FY.1882	NADINE† (French) (ex-R.N.?)	274/19	1940	M/S; returned 1945.
FY.1562	NAIRNSIDE (D)	84/12	1939	M/S, harbour service; returned 1945.
4.104	NAMUR (ex-Emiel Vandervelde)	.../..	5.40	A/P, BDV; returned 1945.
Z.166	NANCY HAGUE	299/11	3.40	BDV; returned 1946.
FY.1725	NARVIK (R.N.N.) (W) (ex-Gos 9)	366/37	10.40	A/S, M/S; returned 1945
Z.244	NATAL II	208/03	11.39	BGV; returned 1945.
T.02	NATALIA (S.A.N.) (W)	238/25	4.40	M/S; returned 6/46.
	NAUTILUS (D)	352/26	1939	D/L; lost 29/5/40.
FY.092	NAUTILUS (R.I.N.)	290/13	1942	M/S, RDF calibrating; returned 1946.
FY.1815	NAZARETH (French)† (ex-R.N. William Carr)	291/18	7.40	M/S; returned 1945.
FY.1722	NEBB (R.N.N.) (W)	250/30	1940	M/S, D/L; returned 1945.
J.104	NEBULA (ex-Vestfold 1)	312/29	1941	M/S; returned 1946.
FY.717	NEGRO	402/32	10.39	M/S; returned 2/45.
FY.259	NEIL MACKAY	266/35	10.39	A/S; returned 1945.
FY.529	NEIL SMITH† (ex-R.N.)	275/17	8.39	M/S; returned 1944.
T.11	NERINE (S.A.N.)	197/25	12.25	M/S; returned 10/44.
FY.1971	NETSUKIS (D)	.../13	11.39	A/P, TRV; returned 4/46.
FY.760	NEW COMET	245/15	11.39	M/S, Store carrier (Y7.21); returned 12/45.
FY.820	NEWHAVEN N.B.	182/09	2.40	M/S; returned 2/45.
	NEWLAND	235/03	5.40	M/S; returned 7/40.
	NEW SPRAY (D)	70/12	1940	BBV; lost 3/1/41.
	NIBLICK† (ex-R.N. Ernest Solvay)	255/17	6.40	A/P, Water carrier, M/S; returned 8/45.
T.40	NIGEL (S.A.N.) (W) (ex-Uni II)	250/30	3.41	M/S; returned 5/46.
FY.1858	NIGHT HAWK	307/15	2.40	M/S; returned 8/46.
Z.113	NIGHT RIDER	327/15	1.40	BDV; sold 2/47.
J.133	NIMBUS (ex-Vestfold II)	312/29	11.41	M/S; returned 2/46.
FY.189	NOBLE NORA (R.N.N.) (W)	160/12	1940	M/S, R.H.N. SPERCHEIOS (1944); lost 3/4/45.
FY.659	NODZU	303/29	9.39	M/S; returned 11/45.
	NOGI	299/23	8.39	M/S; lost 23/6/41.
	NOONDAY (D)	.../..	1941	A/P; returned 1945.
	NOONTIDE (AD) (ex-R.N.)	98/18	1940	Target service; returned 1946.
	NORA NIVEN	163/07	10.42	D/L; returned 2/44.
Z.162	NORBREEZE (AD) (ex-R.N. Outline)	96/20	10.39	Net-layer; returned 1/46.
FY.1906	NORDHAV II (R.N.N.)	425/13	4.40	M/S; lost 10/3/45.
Z.180	NORDLAND	302/16	2.40	BDV; returned 1946.
	NORFOLK COUNTY	.../..	1941	Target service; returned 1945.
Z.145	NORINA	270/17	1.40	BDV; sold 5/47.
	NORLAN (D)	100/14	1940	BDV; returned 1945.
4.106	NORLAND	302/15	5.40	A/P, M/S (FY.1561) returned 10/45.
	NORMAN WILSON (D)	96/19	11.39	BBV; returned 9/46.
FY.1628	NORSE	351/30	8.39	M/S; returned 11/44.
	NORTH ESK (D)	100/13	10.39	Harbour service; returned 12/45.
	NORTH HAVEN (AD) (ex-R.N. Stormcentre)	100/18	1941	Harbour service; returned 1945.
4.100	NORTH NESS† (ex-R.N. Andrew Sack)	275/17	5.40	A/P; returned 7/46.
FY.548	NORTHCOATES† (ex-R.N. George Corton)	277/19	8.39	M/S; lost 2/12/44.

4.34	NORTHERN CHIEF	655/36	8.39	ABV, A/S U.S.N. (name unchanged—1942); returned 2/46.
FY.146	NORTHERN DAWN	655/36	8.39	A/S U.S.N. (name unchanged—1942); returned 2/46.
4.11	NORTHERN DUKE	655/36	9.39	ABV, A/S U.S.N. (name unchanged—1942); returned 1/46.
4.76	NORTHERN FOAM	655/36	8.39	ABV, A/S; returned 11/45.
FY.194	NORTHERN GEM	655/36	8.39	A/S; returned 11/45.
4.50	NORTHERN GIFT	655/36	9.39	ABV, A/S; returned 10/45.
4.25	NORTHERN ISLES	655/36	8.39	ABV, A/S; lost 19/1/45.
FY.1934	NORTHERN LIGHT (D)	.../..	1940	M/S; returned 1946.
FY.105	NORTHERN PRIDE	655/36	8.39	A/S; returned 11/45.
4.06	NORTHERN PRINCESS	655/36	9.39	ABV, A/S U.S.N. (name unchanged—1942); lost 7/3/42.
4.85	NORTHERN REWARD	655/36	9.39	ABV, A/S U.S.N. (name unchanged—1942); returned 1/46.
4.58	NORTHERN ROVER	655/36	8.39	ABV; lost 11/39.
	NORTHERN SCOT (D)	90/11	1941	Harbour service; returned 1944.
4.41	NORTHERN SKY	655/36	9.39	ABV, A/S; returned 9/45.
FY.129	NORTHERN SPRAY	655/36	9.39	A/S; returned 9/45.
4.18	NORTHERN SUN	655/36	9.39	ABV, A/S; returned 12/45.
FY.153	NORTHERN WAVE	655/36	9.39	A/S; returned 9/45.
Z.103	NORTHLYN* (ex-R.N. Robert Murray)	324/19	10.39	BDV; returned 1/46.
FY.338	NORTHMAN	192/11	7.40	A/S; returned 3/46.
FY.795	NORTHWARD HO‡ (ex-R.N. James Hines)	204/19	11.39	M/S; returned 2/46.
FY.229	NORWICH CITY	541/37	9.39	A/S U.S.N. (name unchanged—1942); returned 4/46.
	NOSS HEAD	.../..	1940	A/P; returned 1945.
4.08	NOTRE DAME D'ETEL (French)	.../..	1940	A/P; returned 1945.
FY.363	NOTRE DAME DE FRANCE (French)	433/30	10.41	A/S; returned 12/45.
	NOTRE DAME DE LOURDES† (French) (ex-R.N. William Cowling)	286/18	1940	Harbour service; returned 1945.
Z.227	NOTRE DAME DE MONTLIGEON (French)	234/99	10.40	BGV; returned 10/45.
FY.250	NOTTS COUNTY	541/38	9.39	A/S; lost 8/3/42.
	NOVICE (French)		8.40	BDV; returned 1945.
	NUEVO CALDAS (D)	106/30	1942	Harbour service; returned 1945.
	NUEVO MATARO	106/30	1942	Harbour service; returned 1945.
	OASIS (ex-Al Suez)	201/98	1940	A/P; sold 1945.
	OAKLEA (D)	.../..	1939	A/P; returned 1946.
	OBTAIN (D)	105/17	2.40	Harbour service; returned 10/45.
FY.810	OCEAN BREEZE (D)	112/27	9.39	M/S; returned 1944.
4.364	OCEAN BRINE	277/14	11.39	A/P; returned 11/44.
Z.143	OCEAN EDDY	231/29	1.40	BDV; returned 2/46.
	OCEAN FISHER‡ (ex-R.N. ?)	205/19	8.39	Exam.; returned 8/45.
FY.1976	OCEAN GAIN (D)	77/15	12.39	MWU; returned 5/46.
FY.1977	OCEAN GUIDE (D)	75/14	12.39	MWU; returned 3/46.
	OCEAN LASSIE (D)	96/19	8.39	A/P; lost 4/6/40.
FY.1504	OCEAN LIFEBUOY (D)	131/29	11.39	M/S; returned 1/46.
FY.1503	OCEAN LUX (D)	125/30	11.39	M/S; returned 9/45.
	OCEAN PEARL (D)	.../..	1940	Harbour service; returned 1945.
	OCEAN PILOT (D)	95/13	9.39	Harbour service; returned 6/46.
FY.1654	OCEAN PIONEER (D)	90/15	1941	MWU; returned 1946.

	OCEAN PRIDE (D)	.../..	1941	A/P; returned 1945.
	OCEAN RANGER	58/07	1941	FAA safety vessel, TRV; returned 1945.
FY.1925	OCEAN RETRIEVER (D)	95/12	4.40	M/S, A/P; lost 22/9/43.
	OCEAN REWARD (D)	95/12	12.39	M/S; lost 28/5/40.
4.64	OCEAN ROVER (ex-R.N. Samuel Green)	384/19	1940	TRV; returned 1945.
FY.911	OCEAN SCOUT	86/13	11.39	M/S, TRV; returned 12/45.
FY.1978	OCEAN SPRAY (D)	82/12	1.40	M/S, harbour service; returned 1/46.
	OCEAN STAR (D)	.../..	1942	KBV; returned 1945.
	OCEAN SUNLIGHT (D)	131/29	11.39	M/S; lost 13/6/40.
Z.163	OCEAN SWELL (AD) (ex-R.N.)	96/20	10.39	Net-layer; returned 8/45.
FY.1947	OCEAN TOILER (D)	98/15	4.40	M/S, A/P; returned 1/46.
FY.1918	OCEAN TREASURE (D)	92/13	5.40	M/S, A/P; returned 3/46.
FY.863	OCEAN VIEW	248/30	2.40	M/S; returned 12/45.
FY.951	OCEAN VIM (D)	125/30	9.39	M/S; returned 3/46.
4.80	OCEAN'S GIFT (Belgian) (D)	91/07	7.40	A/P, harbour service; returned 3/46.
T.25	ODBERG (S.A.N.) (W)	351/36	4.41	A/S; returned 6/46.
FY.803	OGANO† (ex-R.N. Hugh Black)	265/17	5.40	M/S; returned 7/44.
FY.561	OHM	302/15	8.39	M/S; returned 12/45.
	OKAPI (W) (ex-A.N.5)	246/29	10.40	A/P; returned 12/45.
Z.146	OKINO	311/17	1.40	BDV; returned 12/45.
FY.907	OKSOY (R.N.N.) (W) (ex-Pol VI)	254/35	8.41	M/S, CYCLONE (1944); R.H.N. PINIEOS (1945), lost 24/10/45.
FY.660	OKU	303/29	8.39	M/S; returned 2/45.
	OLAF I (R.N.N.)	.../..	1941	KBV; returned 1945.
FY.926	OLIVAE (D)	107/15	11.39	M/S; returned 11/45.
	OLIVE BRANCH	.../..	1941	Harbour service; returned 1945.
FY.76	OLIVE CAM† (R.A.N.) (ex-R.N.?)	289/20	9.39	M/S; returned 1945.
FY.1946	OLIVE TREE (AD)	96/18	1940	M/S, A/P; returned 1945.
	OLIVINE (D) (ex-Coreopsis)	.../..	9.39	Harbour service; returned 12/45.
FY.154	OLVINA	425/34	8.39	A/S; returned 12/45.
FY.1586	OLYMPIA	261/17	12.39	M/S; returned 10/45.
FY.983	ONE ACCORD (D)	102/27	11.39	M/S; returned 1946.
FY.761	ONETOS	217/13	11.39	M/S, WDV; returned 1/46.
FY.887	ONWARD	209/05	11.39	M/S; returned 11/44.
T.08	OOSTEWAL (S.A.N.)	179/26	10.39	M/S; returned 5/46.
Z.235	OPHIR	213/06	1941	BDV; returned 194.
FY.178	ORIENTAL STAR	427/34	9.39	A/S; French LA SETOISE (1939).
FY.1897	ORIZABA	233/08	8.40	M/S, Esso (Y7.23); returned 12/44.
FY.782	ORMONDE	250/06	11.39	M/S; lost 16/2/41.
	ORNEN III (R.N.N.)	251/30	1.40	M/S; returned 12/45.
FY.1780	ORPHEUS	228/05	6.40	M/S; returned 1/46.
FY.909	ORVICTO	226/16	4.40	D/L, A/P; returned 10/45.
	ORYX (W) (ex-Hval I)	223/27	7.40	A/P, GEMSBUCK (1944); returned 1946.
FY.580	OSAKO† (ex-R.N. John Brennan)	260/18	2.40	M/S; returned 12/45.
	OSCAR ANGELE (Belgian) (D)	.../..	1940	A/P; returned 1945.
FY.737	OSTA	230/15	11.39	M/S, BBV; returned 11/44.
	OSWALDIAN	249/17	5.40	M/S; lost 4/8/40.
FY.783	OTHELLO	201/07	11.39	M/S, BDV; lost 11/4/41.
FY.1566	OUR BAIRNS† (ex-R.N. James Sibbald)	275/17	12.39	M/S, target service; returned 3/46.
FY.1883	OUR KATE (D)	79/10	3.40	M/S, BBV; returned 1945.
Y7.25	OUTPOST (ex-Vidette)	240/05	3.43	Esso; returned 4/45.
	OVERDALE WYKE	338/34	1940	M/S; returned 1945.
FY.984	OVERFALL (AD) (ex-R.N.)	97/18	11.39	M/S, target service; returned 10/45.
4.101	OYSTERMOUTH CASTLE	283/13	5.40	A/P, M/S; returned 1/46.

A/P Trawler H.M.S. Ocean Brine. 1—12 pdr., 1—20 mm. A.A., 2—MG. (2 × 1—HG.). [*I.W.M.*

Left: M/S Drifter H.M.S. Ocean Vim. 2—MG. (2 × 1—HG.). [*I.W.M.*

Below: S.A.N. M/S Whaler Seskern. 3—20 mm. A.A. (3 × 1), 2—MG. (2 × 1—HG.).

J.80	PACKICE (W) (ex-Vestfold III)	273/27	11.41	M/S; returned 9/44.
Z.215	PANORAMA (ex-Curlew)	180/12	1.40	BDV; sold 3/46.
FY.954	PARAMOUNT	95/11	11.39	M/S; returned 1/46.
	PAS DE LOUP II (French)	.../..	1940	BBV; returned 1945.
	PATRICIA CAM (R.A.N.)	.../..	1941	M/S; lost 22/1/43.
4.326	PATRIE (French)	754/20	8.40	A/P; returned 5/45.
4.102	PATTI	339/29	5.40	A/P, M/S; returned 1/46.
FY.257	PAUL RYKENS	266/35	11.39	A/S; returned 12/45.
	PAX (French) (D)	.../..	1940	M/S, D/L; returned 1945.
	PAXTON (D)	92/11	11.39	Flare drifter; lost 28/5/40.
FY.242	PAYNTER	472/37	1939	A/S; returned 1945.
	PEACEMAKER (D)	.../..	5.40	A/P; returned 1945.
Z.164	PECHEUR (D)	99/14	10.39	N/L; returned 7/45.
4.450	PEGGY NUTTEN	193/07	2.40	A/P, BBV, Esso; returned 11/44.
FY.1821	PEKEN	228/07	7.40	M/S; returned 8/45.
4.103	PELAGOS† (ex-R.N. Charles Donelly)	277/18	5.40	A/P, M/S; returned 8/45.
	PELTON	358/25	1939	M/S; lost 24/12/40.
FY.108	PENTLAND FIRTH	485/34	8.39	A/S U.S.N. (name unchanged—1942); lost 19/9/42.
FY.1714	PERDRANT (French)	.../..	8.40	M/S; returned 1945.
	PERFECTIVE (D)	.../35	1941	KBV; returned 1945.
	PERIDOT (ex-Manchester City)	398/33	8.39	A/S; lost 15/3/40.
FY.1624	PERILIA (AD) (ex-Stormwrack)	98/18	11.39	M/S; returned 2/46.
FY.537	PETER CAREY† (ex-R.N.)	280/19	8.39	M/S; returned 9/45.
FY.260	PETER HENDRICKS	266/35	11.39	A/S; returned 2/46.
FY.869	PHASE (D)	96/19	10.39	M/S; returned 2/46.
	PHILIPPE‡ (ex-R.N. Peter Dobbin)	203/18	4.40	D/L, A/P; returned 1/46.
	PHINEAS BEARD† (ex-R.N.)	278/18	8.39	M/S; lost 8/12/41.
4.141	PHRONTIS	288/11	5.40	A/P; returned 1/46.
	PHYLLIS (R.N.Z.N.)	158/12	1942	D/L; returned 1944.
Z.114	PHYLLISIA* (ex-R.N. Samuel Jameson)	324/18	12.39	BDV Portuguese (name unchanged—1943–45); returned 7/46.
	PHYLLIS ROSE (D)	88/09	4.40	A/P; returned 11/45.
FY.132	PICT	462/36	8.39	A/S; sold 1945.
FY.628	PICTON CASTLE	307/28	8.39	M/S; returned 12/45.
FY.1944	PIERRE ANDRE* (French) (ex-R.N. Robert Cahill)	307/20	7.40	M/S; returned 1/46.
	PIERRE DESCELLIERS (French)	153/33	8.40	A/P, BDV; lost 13/8/42.
FY.1805	PIERRE GUSTAVE (French)	218/32	8.40	M/S; returned 3/46.
	PILOT STAR (AD) (ex-R.N. Drizzle)	96/19	11.39	Harbour service; returned 1946.
FY.1791	PITSTRUAN‡ (ex-R.N. Jonathan Bazino)	211/30	5.40	M/S, Esso; returned 11/44.
FY.738	PLAYMATES (D)	93/25	10.39	M/S; returned 10/45.
	PLOUGASTEL (French)	156/12	1940	Mine-watching; returned 1945.
	PLOUGH (D)	95/12	1941	Harbour service; returned 1945.
Z.303	PLOUGH BOY (D)	102/12	11.39	BDV; scrapped 7/46.
FY.1512	PLUMER (D)	113/19	11.39	M/S, harbour service; returned 7/45.
FY.1869	POINTER	198/06	1.40	M/S; returned 12/45.
FY.630	POINTZ CASTLE	283/14	8.39	M/S; returned 4/45.
	POL V (R.N.N.) (W)	221/25	1940	M/S; returned 1946.
	POL VII (R.N.N.) (W)	338/36	1940	M/S; returned 1946.
	POL X (R.N.N.) (W)	354/37	1940	M/S; returned 1946.
FY.1688	POLAR 5 (R.N.N.) (W)	278/31	3.40	M/S; sold 9/46.
FY.1871	POLAR 6 (R.N.N.) (W)	263/25	3.40	M/S; sold 4/46.
	POLLY JOHNSON† (ex-R.N. John Aikenhead)	290/18	8.39	M/S; lost 29/5/40.
FY.1852	PORTIA (ex-Unitia)	296/13	5.40	M/S; returned 1/46.

	POSEIDON (D)	96/15	1941	Exam.; returned 1945.
FY.1750	POST BOY (ex-Le Royal)	316/41	1940	M/S; returned 7/46.
	POUQUOIS PAS (French) (D)	.../..	1940	A/P; returned 1945.
FY.874	POWIS CASTLE	275/16	2.40	M/S; returned 4/45.
	PRE-EMINENT (D)	96/18	1941	Harbour service; returned 1946.
4.370	PRESENT HELP (D)	82/11	1941	S/M Tender; returned 1945.
	PRESIDENT BRIAND (French)	213/32	1940	M/S; M.O.W.T. 1943.
	PRESIDENT HERRIOT (French) (D)	.../..	1940	A/P; returned 1944.
FY.230	PRESTON NORTH END	419/34	9.39	A/S; returned 1945.
T.59	PRETORIA (S.A.N.) (W) (ex-R.N. Collie, ex-Busen 10)	374/30	1.42	A/S; returned 11/45.
	PRIDE O'MORAY (D)	50/09	1941	Harbour service; returned 1945.
	PRIME (D)	101/14	1941	Harbour service; returned 1945.
	PRIMEVERE (D)	100/14	1941	Harbour service; returned 1946.
	PRIMORDIAL (D)	100/	1941	Harbour service; returned 1945.
Z.172	PRINCE DE LIEGE (Belgian)	324/26	9.40	BDV; returned 1945.
FY.998	PRINCE LEO	218/13	6.40	M/S, BBV; returned 1945.
FY.876	PRINCESS MARY	225/14	1940	M/S; returned 1945.
	PRINCIPAL (D)	91/08	1940	A/P; returned 1945.
	PROGRESS (D)	.../..	1940	Harbour service; returned 1945.
	PROMOTIVE (D)	78/08	10.39	A/P; lost 23/12/39.
FY.1538	PROSPECTS AHEAD (AD) (ex-R.N. Glint)	95/19	12.39	M/S; returned 1/46.
T.43	PROTEA (S.A.N.) (W) (ex-Terje VII)	335/36	6.41	M/S; returned 12/46.
	PYROPE	295/32	8.39	M/S; lost 12/8/40.
Y7.43	QUERCIA	288/12	8.42	Esso, A/P (4.336); returned 12/45.
	QUEST (R.N.N.)	214/17	11.40	Harbour service; returned 10/45.
FY.1776	QUIET WATERS (D)	117/31	9.39	Mine-watching, target service; returned 2/46.
FY.1658	QUINTIA (D)	90/14	5.40	MWU; returned 7/46.
FY.1984	RACHEL FLETT (D)	91/14	12.39	Harbour service; returned 1/46.
FY.511	RADNOR CASTLE† (ex-R.N. William Chaseman)	275/17	8.39	M/S; scrapped 5/47.
4.142	RAETIA	295/12	8.39	A/P, Esso (Y7.26); returned 2/46.
FY.631	RAGLAN CASTLE† (ex-R.N. George Greeves)	280/19	8.39	M/S, A/P; sold 9/47.
	RAHMAN (W)	209/26	1940	M/S; lost 1/3/42.
FY.1920	RAINSTORM (W) (ex-Busen 6)	266/28	10.41	M/S; returned 11/45.
	RALCO	228/12	10.39	A/P; returned 1/40.
T.12	RANDFONTEIN (S.A.N.) (W) (ex-Pol I)	205/26	9.41	M/S; returned 4/46.
FY.1878	RATAPIKO	247/12	7.40	M/S; returned 12/45.
4.99	RAYMOND (Belgian)	131/30	8.40	BBV, target service; returned 11/45.
FY.785	RAYMONT	226/16	11.39	M/S; returned 3/46.
	RAY OF HOPE (D)	98/25	1939	M/S; lost 10/12/39.
	RAYON D'OR (R.C.N.)	342/12	1940	M/S; returned 1945.
FY.602	REBOUNDO	278/20	9.39	M/S; returned 12/45.
	RECEPTIVE (D)	86/13	4.40	M/S; lost 3/7/41.
	RECOIL (ex-Blankenburg)	344/38	5.40	A/S; lost 28/9/40.
FY.786	RECONO	248/16	11.39	M/S; returned 7/45.
	RECORDO	230/10	10.39	A/P; returned 1/40.
FY.900	RED GAUNTLET	338/30	8.39	M/S; lost 5/8/43.
FY.1554	RED SKY (D)	94/18	11.39	M/S, Exam.; returned 3/46.
	REED (D)	99/11	11.39	A/P, M/S; lost 7/11/40.
4.213	REFLECT (D)	78/08	2.41	Exam.; returned 3/45.

	REFORMO	242/99	1941	Harbour service; returned 1946.
FY.945	REFRACTION (AD) (ex-R.N.)	93/19	11.39	M/S; returned 3/45.
FY.830	REFUNDO	258/17	11.39	M/S; lost 18/12/40.
FY.180	REGAL	409/33	9.39	A/S; sold 1945.
FY.831	REGARDO	248/15	11.39	M/S, Esso (Y7.33); returned 1945.
FY.1794	REHEARO† (ex-R.N. John Burlingham)	266/17	9.40	M/S; returned 12/45.
FY.1979	REIDS	92/18	12.39	D/L, A/P; returned 12/45.
FY.134	REIGHTON WYKE	465/37	8.39	A/S; returned 12/45.
FY.343	REINE DES FLOTS (French)	608/23	10.40	A/S; returned 1946.
FY.843	RELONZO	245/14	11.39	M/S; lost 20/1/41.
FY.875	REMEXO	231/12	11.39	M/S; returned 12/45.
	REMILLO† (ex-R.N. Robert Betson)	266/17	4.40	D/L, A/P; lost 27/2/41.
	RENAISSANCE (Belgian) (D)	104/14	1940	A/P; returned 1945.
FY.1520	RENASCENT (D)	100/26	11.39	M/S; returned 1/46.
	RENE (D)	.../..	1.40	Harbour service; returned 5/46.
FY.893	RENZO	230/13	11.39	M/S; returned 10/45.
	REPORTO	230/08	10.39	A/P; returned 1/40.
	RESISTANCE (Belgian) (D)	.../..	8.40	A/P; returned 1945.
	RESMILO	258/17	9.40	M/S; lost 20/6/41.
FY.821	RESOLVO	231/13	11.39	M/S; lost 12/10/40.
	RESOUND (French) (ex-Echo)	.../..	8.40	M/S; returned 1/46.
FY.822	RESPARKO	248/16	11.39	M/S; lost 20/8/40.
FY.1900	RESTART (D)	.../..	10.40	A/P; returned 5/46.
	RESTORE (D)	87/11	5.40	BBV; returned 1945.
FY.834	RESTRIVO	245/14	11.39	M/S; returned 1/45.
	RESURGE (AD) (ex-R.N. Surge)	.../..	1941	Harbour service; returned 7/46.
FY.838	RETAKO	245/14	11.39	M/S; returned 1945.
FY.261	RETRIEVER (French) (ex-Urania)	869/30	1.41	A/S; returned 7/46.
FY.839	RETURNO	245/14	11.39	M/S, Esso (Y7.27); returned 1945.
FY.778	REVELLO	230/08	11.39	M/S; returned 1944.
FY.1990	REVERBERATION (AD) (ex-R.N.)	97/19	11.39	A/P; returned 2/45.
4.429	RIANO	212/06	4.44	A/P; returned 10/44.
	RIANT (AD) (ex-R.N. Green Sea)	95/19	11.39	A/P; lost 25/1/40.
	RICHARD BENNETT‡ (S.A.N.) (ex-R.N.)	227/17	9.39	M/S; returned 5/40.
FY.530	RICHARD CROFTS† (ex-R.N.)	290/18	8.39	M/S; returned 8/45.
	RIFSNES	431/32	8.39	M/S; lost 20/5/40.
FY.1540	RIG (D)	96/11	12.39	M/S, A/P; returned 11/45.
FY.604	RIGHTO† (ex-R.N.)	278/20	9.39	M/S, D/L; returned 11/44.
4.451	RIGOLETTO	212/06	4.40	BBV, Esso; returned 7/45.
FY.1542	RIME (AD) (ex-R.N.)	93/19	12.39	M/S; returned 11/45.
	RINOVIA	429/31	8.39	M/S; lost 2/11/40.
	RISING SEA (AD) (ex-R.N.)	97/18	1941	Harbour service; returned 1945.
4.302	RISKATO	248/15	6.40	A/P; returned 5/46.
FY.203	RISOR (R.N.N.) (W) (ex-Kos V)	248/29	7.40	A/S, ASR; returned 1945.
	RISTANGO	178/13	6.40	BGV; lost 14/11/40.
Z.160	RIVER ANNAN‡ (ex-R.N. George Castle)	204/19	11.39	BGV; returned 11/45.
	RIVER CLYDE† (ex-R.N. Richard Gundy)	276/19	8.39	M/S; lost 5/8/40.
4.161	RIVER ESK‡ (ex-R.N. William Bond)	203/18	6.40	A/P; returned 7/45.
	RIVER GARRY‡ (ex-R.N. John Cope)	203/18	8.39	Exam.; returned 7/45.

4.51	RIVER LEVEN‡ (ex-R.N. John Edsworth)	202/18	8.39	Exam., Esso; returned 3/45
4.246	RIVER LOSSIE‡ (ex-R.N. Arthur Herwin)	203/20	6.40	A/P; returned 2/45.
FY.1643	RIVER SPEY‡ (ex-R.N. David Conn)	202/18	4.40	D/L, A/P, M/S; returned 11/44.
	RIVIERE	226/16	4.40	BBV; returned 11/44.
	ROBERT BOWEN† (ex-R.N.)	290/18	8.39	M/S; lost 9/2/40.
FY.771	ROBERT HASTIE	210/12	11.39	D/L, A/P, ASR; returned 1/46.
FY.687	ROBERT STROUD	219/30	8.39	M/S; returned 4/46.
T.06	ROBINSON (S.A.N.) (ex-C. P. Robinson)	196/27	6.40	M/S; returned 4/46.
FY.1844	ROCKALL (Belgian)	114/30	7.40	M/S; returned 7/44.
	ROCHEBONNE	258/13	2.40	M/S; lost 7/4/41.
FY.1718	ROCHE VELEN‡ (French) (ex-R.N. William Hutchinson)	208/18	7.40	M/S; returned 12/45.
FY.840	RODINO	230/13	11.39	M/S; lost 24/7/40.
	ROGER BLONDE (Belgian)	.../..	1940	BDV; returned 1944.
	ROGER ROBERT (Belgian)	97/22	10.40	A/P; returned 9/45.
FY.1831	ROLLS ROYCE	238/06	7.40	M/S; returned 1/46.
FY.1995	ROMANY ROSE (D)	88/24	12.39	A/P, harbour service; 9/45.
T.14	RONDEVLEI (S.A.N.) (W) (ex-Hektor I)	247/29	6.40	M/S; returned 5/46.
FY.841	RONSO	248/15	11.39	M/S, Esso (Y7.29); returned 3/46.
T.57	ROODEPOORT (S.A.N.) (W) (ex-Hektor VI)	315/29	1.42	M/S; returned 2/46.
FY.1626	ROSA (D)	83/08	4.40	M/S; lost 11/9/43.
	ROSA ARTHUR (Belgian) (D)	114/36	10.40	A/P, exam.; returned 9/45.
	ROSEACRE (AD) (ex-R.N. Sheet Lightning)	92/18	9.39	Harbour service; returned 4/45.
FY.944	ROSEBUD (D)	100/07	1.40	M/S; returned 1945.
	ROSEDEN (D)	.../..	1.40	A/P; returned 1945.
FY.1888	ROSE EMMA (D)	92/12	12.39	M/S, BBV; returned 5/45.
FY.967	ROSE HAUGH (D)	92/18	11.39	MWU; returned 4/46.
FY.740	ROSE HILDA (D)	116/30	8.39	M/S; returned 4/46.
	ROSEMONDE (French)	364/10	7.40	M/S; lost 22/1/42.
FY.1577	ROSETTE (ex-Rose)	218/11	7.40	M/S; returned 11/45.
FY.562	ROSE OF ENGLAND	222/09	11.39	M/S; returned 1945.
FY.1578	ROSE VALLEY (AD) (ex-R.N. Silt)	100/18	10.39	Contraband control; lost 16/12/43.
FY.934	ROSS ARD (D)	92/11	11.39	M/S; returned 10/44.
FY.1822	ROTHERSLADE† (ex-R.N. John Kidd)	276/17	6.40	M/S; returned 5/46.
FY.1741	ROTTERDAM	231/16	1941	M/S; returned 5/46.
Z.191	ROULE (French)	.../..	1940	BDV; returned 1945.
	ROWAN TREE (D)	91/17	1.40	M/S; lost 21/11/41.
4.456	ROXANO	228/07	11.39	BBV, Esso; returned 5/45.
FY.835	ROYALLIEU	211/07	11.39	M/S; returned 11/45.
FY.825	ROYALO	248/16	11.39	M/S; lost 1/9/40.
FY.1704	ROYDUR (W)	174/11	9.39	M/S; returned 11/44.
	RUBENS (Belgian)	320/37	8.40	A/S; lost 13/2/41.
FY.528	RUDILAIS† (ex-R.N. ?)	282/20	9.39	M/S; returned 12/45.
4.162	RUGBY	205/00	5.40	A/P, M/S, Esso (Y7.30) returned 5/46.
FY.750	RUNSWICK BAY	349/29	8.39	M/S; returned 7/46.
	RUTLANDSHIRE	458/36	9.39	A/S; lost 20/4/40.
FY.152	ST. ACHILLEUS	484/34	8.39	A/S; lost 31/5/40.
FY.176	ST. AMANDUS	400/33	8.39	A/S; French LA CANCALAISE (1939).
FY.111	ST. ANDRONICUS	398/33	8.39	A/S; French LALORIENTAISE (1939); lost 6/44.
	ST. APOLLO	580/40	2.40	A/S; lost 22/11/41.
FY.135	ST. ARCADIUS	399/34	8.39	A/S; French LA NANTAISE (1939); lost 8/7/45.
FY.183	ST. ATTALUS	399/34	8.39	A/S; French LA HAVRAISE (1939); lost 27/11/42; salved and lost 9/6/44.

FY.234	ST. CATHAN	565/36	9.39	A/S; U.S.N. (name unchanged—1942); lost 11/4/42.
Z.104	ST. CELESTIN	352/25	9.39	BDV; returned 11/45.
	ST. DONATS	349/24	8.39	M/S; lost 1/3/41.
	ST. ELOI (R.C.N.)	357/17	1941	BGV; returned 1946.
FY.240	ST. ELSTAN	564/37	9.39	A/S; returned 12/45.
	ST. GORAN	565/36	9.39	A/S; lost 3/5/40.
	ST. JOHN BERCHMANS (D) (Belgian)	114/35	8.40	A/P; returned 1945.
FY.264	ST. KENAN	565/36	9.39	A/S; returned 2/46.
FY.276	ST. LOMAN	565/36	9.39	A/S U.S.N. (name unchanged—1942); returned 7/46.
FY.753	ST. MELANTE	358/27	8.39	M/S; returned 8/45.
FY.725	ST. MINVER* (ex-R.N. John Collins)	325/19	12.39	M/S, Esso; sold 5/46
4.139	ST. NECTAN	565/36	5.40	A/P, A/S; returned 4/46.
FY.1599	ST. OLIVE	234/14	3.40	M/S; returned 11/45.
4.105	ST. WISTAN	564/37	5.40	A/P, A/S; returned 5/46.
FY.280	ST. ZENO	608/40	3.40	A/S; U.S.N. (name unchanged—1942); sold 5/46.
4.254	SABINA‡ (ex-R.N. Charles Doyle)	202/19	7.40	A/P; returned 9/44.
FY.1903	SAHRA (W)	355/36	10.41	M/S; returned 1/46.
	SAILOR KING (D)	.../..	1940	MRV, BDV (Z.45); returned 1945.
FY.1623	SALPA (AD) (ex-R.N. Nadir)	99/18	1940	M/S; returned 1946.
4.457	SALVINI	226/16	4.40	BBV, Esso; returned 1945.
	SAMBHUR (W) (ex A.N. 1)	223/26	11.40	A/P; lost 5/5/42.
FY.95	SAMUEL BENBOW‡ (R.A.N.) (ex-R.N.)	122/18	9.40	M/S; returned 1946.
FY.598	SANDRINGHAM	254/30	8.39	M/S; returned 7/46.
FY.699	SANDSTORM (W) (ex-Vestfold VII)	312/25	11.41	M/S; returned 11/44.
4.160	SANGARIUS	211/15	4.40	A/P; returned 4/46.
FY.901	SANSON	231/07	11.39	M/S, Esso (Y7.31); returned 9/46.
	SANSONETTE	212/16	11.39	A/P; returned 1/40.
FY.1986	SANTA (W)	355/36	10.41	M/S; lost 23/11/43.
FY.159	SAON	386/33	8.39	A/S; sold 1945.
	SARAH A. PURDY‡ (ex-R.N. John Moss)	202/19	2.40	BBV; returned 11/44.
FY.968	SARAH HIDE	162/21	11.39	M/S, A/P; returned 1/46.
Z.139	SARBA	315/13	11.39	BDV; returned 7/46.
FY.572	SARGON	297/13	8.39	M/S; returned 7/45.
	SARKA (W)	355/36	10.41	M/S; sold 1946.
FY.1753	SARNA (W)	268/30	3.40	M/S; lost 25/2/41.
FY.1849	SARONTA	316/17	6.40	M/S; returned 12/45.
4.05	SARPEDON	331/16	6.40	A/P, M/S; returned 7/45.
FY.828	SASEBO	308/28	8.39	M/S; returned 2/46.
	SATA	340/31	8.39	M/S; returned 12/45.
FY.1734	SATSA	355/36	10.41	M/S; returned 12/45.
FY.823	SATURN	230/16	11.39	M/S, Esso (Y7.37); returned 12/45.
	SATURNUS	200/35	1940	BBV; lost 1/5/41.
FY.1726	SAURIAN	219/16	6.40	M/S, A/P; returned 11/45.
	SAUVEUR DU MONDE (French)	.../..	8.40	A/P; returned 1945.
FY.629	SAWFLY (ex-Tenby Castle)	307/28	8.39	M/S; returned 10/45.
	SAXONIA	197/00	11.39	A/P; returned 1/40.
FY.258	SCALBY WYKE	443/35	10.39	A/S; returned 10/45.
	SCARLET THREAD (D)	96/19	9.39	Harbour service; returned 9/46.
FY.1913	SCARRON	296/13	6.40	M/S; returned 12/45.
Z.183	SCOMBER	321/14	5.40	BDV; sold 2/47.
	SCOTCH THISTLE (D)	84/13	11.39	MRV; lost 7/10/40.
FY.245	SCOTTISH	558/37	10.39	A/S; returned 1945.

FY.1627	SCOURGE (D) (ex-Lea Rig)	83/08	11.39	M/S, SKYROCKET (1943) returned 5/46.
	SEAFARER (D)		1940	A/P; returned 1945.
FY.969	SEA HOLLY (D)	95/18	11.39	M/S; returned 6/46.
	SEA KING	321/16	8.39	M/S; lost 9/10/40.
FY.107	SEALYHAM (W) (ex-Terje 5)	335/36	4.40	A/S; returned 6/45.
FY.1640	SEA MIST (ex-Duncan)	324/17	2.40	M/S; returned 12/45.
Z.115	SEA MONARCH	329/15	1.40	BDV; returned 6/46.
4.166	SEDDON	296/16	6.40	A/P, M/S (FY.1993); returned 2/46.
	SEDOCK‡ (ex-R.N. Patrick Devine)	202/20	11.39	A/P; returned 2/40.
FY.122	SEDGEFLY (ex-Norman)	520/39	9.39	A/S; lost 16/12/39.
	SEDULOUS (D)	100/12	5.40	BBV, Exam.; returned 10/45.
T.52	SEKSERN (S.A.N.) (W)	249/30	10.40	M/S; returned 4/46.
4.38	SEMLA (W)	217/24	11.41	M/S, A/S; returned 3/46.
FY.726	SEMNOS	216/14	11.39	D/L, A/P; returned 10/45.
FY.327	SENATEUR DUHAMEL (French)	913/27	1.41	A/S U.S.N. (name unchanged—1942); lost 6/5/42.
	SERAPION	195/00	11.39	A/P; returned 1/40.
FY.883	SETHON	295/16	6.40	M/S; returned 10/45.
FY.339	SETTER (W) (ex-Terje 4)	335/36	6.40	A/S; returned 10/45.
Z.140	SETTSU	301/24	1.40	BDV; returned 1946.
FY.1652	SEVRA (W)	253/29	3.40	M/S; lost 6/11/40.
FY.768	SHAMROCK	184/00	11.39	DGV; returned 12/44.
FY.1587	SHANDWICK	166/12	1.40	D/L, M/S; returned 11/45.
4.143	SHELDON	288/12	5.40	A/P, Esso (Y7.38); returned 12/44.
FY.698	SHEPHERD LAD (D)	100/25	8.39	M/S, harbour service; returned 4/46.
FY.1724	SHERA (W)	253/29	3.40	M/S Russian (1942); lost 9/3/42.
FY.1788	SHERATON	283/07	6.40	M/S; returned 9/44.
FY.1664	SHIKA (W)	251/29	3.40	M/S Russian (1942).
FY.1694	SHILA	189/26	2.40	D/L, target service; returned 3/46.
	SHIPMATES (D)	82/11	11.39	Flare drifter; lost 14/11/40.
FY.700	SHOOTING STAR (W) (ex-Vestfold VI)	312/25	11.41	M/S; returned 1946.
FY.1696	SHOVA (W)	180/12	3.40	D/L, target service; sold 3/46.
FY.1702	SHUSA (W)	251/29	3.40	M/S Russian (1942); lost 20/11/42.
FY.669	SICYON	344/30	9.39	M/S; returned 7/46.
T.39	SIDNEY SMITH (S.A.N.) (ex-Southern Sky)	250/29	1940	M/S, PARKTOWN (i) (1942); lost 21/6/42.
FY.1692	SIESTA (ex Arthur Rose)	208/24	1940	M/S, Esso ADELPHI (1944); returned 1945.
FY.324	SIGFRA (W)	356/37	12.41	A/S; sold 3/46.
FY.1709	SIGNA (W)	190/26	2.40	D/L; returned 2/45.
	SIGNAL (R.C.N.)	.../..	9.39	M/S; returned 1944.
Z.116	SILANIAN	366/30	1.40	BDV; returned 12/45.
	SILICIA	250/13	8.39	M/S; lost 8/5/41.
FY.301	SILJA (W)	251/29	3.40	M/S Russian (1942); returned 3/47.
FY.1742	SILVA (W)	221/24	2.40	M/S, traffic control; returned 1945.
FY.733	SILVER CREST (D)	94/28	10.39	M/S, FAA safety vessel; returned 2/45.
FY.1629	SILVER DAWN (D)	85/25	10.39	M/S; returned 10/45.
	SILVER DYKE	.../..	11.39	A/P; returned 1/40.
	SILVER PRINCE (D)	108/13	1940	Harbour service, SKIRMISHER (1941); returned 1945.
FY.946	SILVER SEAS (D)	117/31	11.39	M/S; returned 8/44.
FY.1989	SILVER SKY (D)	96/19	12.39	Exam.; returned 2/46.
FY.970	SILVER SPRAY (D)	.../..	11.39	M/S; returned.

FY.321	SIMBRA (W)	356/37	12.41	A/S; sold 9/46.
4.278	SIMMERSON	248/13	7.40	A/P; returned 6/46.
FY.545	SIMPSON	261/17	6.40	M/S; returned 12/45.
FY.120	SINDONIS	440/34	9.39	A/S; lost 29/5/41.
	SIOUX (French)	.../..	8.40	BGV, INDIAN (1944); returned 1945.
	SIR E. P. WILLS	162/37	9.39	Exam.; returned 8/45.
FY.622	SIR JOHN LISTER† (ex-R.N. Peter Killen)	281/19	9.39	M/S; returned 4/45.
FY.1700	SIRRA (W)	251/29	3.40	M/S; returned 4/46.
	SISAPON	326/28	9.39	M/S; lost 12/6/40.
	SKUDD 3 (W)	245/29	11.40	M/S; lost 27/8/41.
FY.1792	SKUDD 4 (W)	247/29	11.40	M/S, SPATE (1944); returned 3/45.
FY.1806	SKUDD 5 (W)	265/29	11.40	M/S, SURGE (1944); returned 3/45.
FY.1676	SKUDD 6 (W	323/29	7.40	M/S, SLEET (1944); returned 1945.
Y7.28	SLEBECH	222/08	12.39	Esso; returned 1/46.
FY.1773	SLUGA (W)	251/29	3.40	M/S; returned 4/46.
T.15	SMALVLEI (S.A.N.) (W) (ex-Hektor II)	247/29	6.40	A/S; returned 5/46.
FY.575	SNAKEFLY (ex-Fane)	310/30	9.39	M/L; returned 10/45.
FY.1589	SNAP	.../..	1940	D/L; returned 1945.
FY.331	SOBKRA (W)	433/37	1941	A/S; returned 1945.
T.22	SOETVLEI (S.A.N.) (W) (ex-Hektor III)	233/29	7.40	M/S; returned 6/46.
FY.1755	SOIKA (W)	313/25	4.40	M/S; returned 10/45.
	SOJOURNER (D)	.../..	1941	A/P; returned 1945.
	SOLOMON	357/28	8.39	M/S; lost 1/4/42.
FY.601	SOLON	348/31	11.39	M/S; returned 1/46.
FY.937	SOLSTICE (AD) (ex-R.N.)	99/18	12.39	M/S, S/M tender; returned 9/46.
FY.334	SOLVRA (W)	433/37	1941	A/S; returned 1945.
FY.345	SONDRA (W)	433/37	12.41	A/S; returned 10/45.
T.44	SONNEBLOM (S.A.N.) (W) (ex-Terje 8)	335/36	1941	M/S; returned 11/46.
FY.513	SORANUS	250/06	10.40	M/S; returned 10/45.
FY.342	SORSRA (W)	433/37	12.41	A/S; returned 9/46.
	SOTRA (W)	313/25	9.39	M/S; lost 29/1/42.
	SOUBRETTE‡ (ex-R.N. Samuel Gasby)	199/20	8.40	M/S; returned 4/45.
4.140	SOUTHCOATES† (ex-R.N. Samuel Drake)	276/18	6.40	A/P; returned 11/45.
T.28	SOUTHERN BARRIER (S.A.N.) (W)	314/36	10.40	M/S; returned 5/46.
FY.318	SOUTHERN BREEZE (W)	344/36	3.40	A/S; returned 1/46.
FY.304	SOUTHERN CHIEF (W)	295/26	3.40	A/S; sold 2/46.
FY.1790	SOUTHERN FIELD (W)	250/29	3.40	M/S; returned 4/46.
T.26	SOUTHERN FLOE (S.A.N.) (W)	344/36	3.40	A/S; lost 11/2/41.
FY.332	SOUTHERN FLOWER (W)	328/28	3.40	A/S; lost 3/3/45.
FY.1796	SOUTHERN FOAM (W)	295/26	3.40	M/S; returned 1/46.
K.247	SOUTHERN GEM (W)	593/37	3.40	A/S; returned 4/45.
T.29	SOUTHERN ISLE (S.A.N.) (W)	314/36	3.40	A/S; returned 5/46.
T.27	SOUTHERN MAID (S.A.N.) (W)	314/36	3.40	A/S; returned 5/46.
K.249	SOUTHERN PRIDE (W)	582/36	3.40	A/S; lost 16/6/44.
T.30	SOUTHERN SEA (S.A.N.) (W)	314/36	3.40	A/S; returned 5/46.
FY.326	SOUTHERN SHORE (W)	328/28	3.40	A/S; returned 1/46.
FY.323	SOUTHERN SPRAY (W)	319/25	3.40	A/S; returned 11/45.
FY.329	SOUTHERN STAR (W)	340/30	3.40	A/S; returned 1/46.
FY.325	SOUTHERN WAVE (W)	320/25	3.40	A/S; returned 12/45.
	SOUTHWARD HO‡ (ex-R.N.?)	204/19	1944	Esso; returned 1945.
FY.144	SPANIARD	455/37	9.39	A/S; lost 5/12/42.
FY.348	SPANIEL (W) (ex-Terje 1)	335/36	4.40	A/S; returned 4/45.
	SPARSHOLT	127/15	1940	Mooring vessel; lost 13/3/42.
	SPECTRUM (D)	97/18	9.39	Harbour service; returned 8/45.
	SPERANZA (D)	86/11	12.39	A/P; returned 8/46.
	SPESAUREA (D)	.../..	1940	Harbour service; returned 1945.

A/S Trawler H.M.S. Stella Pegasi. 1—12 pdr. A.A., 2—.5 in. A.A. (1 × 2), 2—MG. (2 × 1). [I.W.M.

Left: A/S Trawler H.M.S. Stoke City. 1—4 in., 3—20 mm. A.A. (3 × 1). [I.W.M.

M/S Trawler H.M.S. Wardour. 1—12 pdr. A.A., 2—.5 in. A.A. (1 × 2), 2—MG. (2 × 1). [I.W.M.

	SPESMELIOR (D)	96/19	10.39	Harbour service; returned 4/46.
FY.249	SPHENE (ex-Avanturine, ex-Mendip)	412/34	8.39	A/S; returned 4/45.
	SPIDER (ex-Francisco Antonio Quarto)	.../..	1943	MWU; sold 1946.
FY.1717	SPINA (W)	190/26	2.40	D/L; returned 3/45.
FY.309	SPOSA (W)	316/26	4.40	A/S; returned 4/45.
FY.1654	SPINDRIFT (ex-Polaris)	926/..	1941	A/S TS, M/L; SAN (1946), SKILPAD (1951).
T.38	SPRINGS (S.A.N.) (W) (ex-Uni I)	249/30	11.40	M/S; returned 5/46.
FY.168	SPURS	398/33	9.39	A/S; sold 1945.
J.51	SQUALL (W) (ex-Vestfold X)	299/35	11.41	D/L; returned 1946.
FY.192	STAFNES	456/36	9.39	A/S; sold 1945.
Z.108	STALBERG	358/29	12.39	BDV; returned 1945.
T.60	STANDERTON (S.A.N.) (W) (ex-Helier I)	357/36	10.40	A/S; returned 2/46.
	STAR XVI (R.C.N.) (W)	249/30	10.41	M/S; returned 11/45.
FY.1630	STARLIGHT RAY (D)	94/18	11.39	M/S, Exam., S/M tender; returned 1946.
FY.1678	STAR OF BRITAIN	228/08	6.40	M/S, Esso (Y7.39); returned 11/45.
	STAR OF DEVERON	220/15	11.39	M/S; lost 30/9/41.
T.42	STAR OF FREEDOM	226/17	12.39	Store carrier; sold 7/46.
	STAR OF HOPE	56/02	1939	A/P; returned 1945.
	STAR OF LIBERTY‡ (ex-R.N. John Callaghan)	205/17	9.40	Exam.; returned 1/46.
FY.683	STAR OF ORKNEY	273/36	8.39	M/S; returned 9/46.
FY.1668	STAR OF PENTLAND	239/15	1.40	M/S; returned 5/46.
Z.105	STAR OF THE REALM* (ex-Nordstjörnan, ex-R.N. William Westernburgh)	293/17	1.40	BDV; sold 5/46.
FY.1590	STAR OF THE WAVE	234/17	2.40	M/S; returned 5/46.
FY.1591	STAUNCH (ex-Bengal)	211/05	11.39	M/S, Esso; returned 11/44.
	STAUNTON	283/08	5.40	A/P; lost 28/7/40.
T.36	STEENBERG (S.A.N.) (W) (ex-Southern Barrier)	250/29	11.40	M/S; returned 5/46.
FY.1887	STEFA (W)	253/29	3.40	M/S Russian (1942–46); returned 5/47.
FY.248	STELLA CANOPUS	418/36	10.39	A/S; returned 11/45.
FY.107	STELLA CAPELLA	440/37	9.39	A/S; lost 11/3/42.
FY.352	STELLA CARINA	440/36	5.40	A/S; returned 5/45.
FY.131	STELLA DORADO	416/35	9.39	A/S; lost 1/6/40.
FY.706	STELLA LEONIS	345/28	9.40	M/S, D/L; returned 5/45.
	STELLA ORION	417/35	9.39	M/S; lost 11/11/40.
FY.155	STELLA PEGASI	441/35	9.39	A/S; returned 4/45.
4.258	STELLA POLARIS	498/36	5.40	A/P, A/S U.S.N. (name unchanged—1942); returned 10/45.
FY.657	STELLA RIGEL	358/26	9.39	M/S, D/L; returned 7/45.
	STELLA SIRIUS	404/34	9.39	A/S; lost 25/9/40.
T.37	STELLENBERG (S.A.N.) (W) (ex-Southern Cloud)	250/29	11.40	M/S; returned 5/46.
FY.1706	STERNUS (D)	93/25	10.39	M/S; returned 4/45.
FY.303	STINA (W)	251/28	3.40	M/S; returned 2/46.
FY.232	STOKE CITY	422/35	9.39	A/S; returned 1945.
FY.596	STONEFLY (ex-Malayan)	238/30	8.39	M/S; returned 9/45.
FY.307	STORA (W)	341/29	6.40	A/S; returned 3/47.
FY.1807	STORMCENTRE* (ex-Estrella do Norte, ex-R.N. Daniel Munro)	356/19	1940	M/S; sold 8/46.
FY.1572	STORMWRACK (W) (ex-Busen 4)	266/25	4.42	M/S; returned 11/45.
	STRATHALLADALE	199/08	1944	Esso; returned 1945.
	STRATHAVON	202/06	12.40	BBV; returned 11/45.
	STRATHBEG		12.39	Harbour service; returned 4/46.
	STRATHBORVE	216/30	8.40	M/S; lost 6/9/41.
FY.1810	STRATHDERRY	193/11	2.40	M/S, A/P; returned 1/46.

FY.1813	STRATHDEVON	212/15	1.40	M/S, A/P; returned 1/46.
4.199	STRATHELLA	210/13	7.40	A/P; returned 1945.
4.379	STRATHELLIOT	211/15	1.40	A/P; returned 1/46.
FY.1632	STRATHGARRY	202/24	4.40	D/L, A/P; returned 12/45.
FY.1638	STRATHMAREE	210/14	11.39	D/L, A/P; returned 11/45.
	STRATHMARTIN	210/14	1944	Esso; returned 1945.
FY.1648	STRATHRANNOCH‡ (ex-R.N. James Bashford)	202/19	4.40	M/S, A/P, mooring vessel; returned 7/45.
Z.161	STRATHSPEY	202/06	11.39	BGV; returned 1/46.
FY.1941	STRATHUGIE	210/14	1.40	M/S; returned 9/45.
FY.1782	STRENUOUS (D)	166/04	1940	M/S, harbour service; returned 1945.
FY.1829	STREPHON	250/13	8.40	M/S; returned 2/46.
FY.922	STRIVE	102/12	11.39	M/S; returned 12/45.
	STURDEE‡ (ex-R.N. Michael Brion)	202/19	11.39	A/P; returned 1/40.
FY.1595	STURTON	251/20	8.39	M/S, Esso; returned 10/44.
T.55	SUDEROY I (S.A.N.) (W)	220/25	1941	M/S, PARKTOWN (ii) (1942); returned 4/46.
	SUDEROY IV (R.C.N.) (W)	254/30	8.40	M/S; returned 11/45.
	SUDEROY V (R.C.N.) (W)	252/30	8.40	M/S; returned 11/45.
	SUDEROY VI (R.C.N.) (W)	254/29	8.40	M/S; returned 11/45.
	SUDEROY VII (W)	363/39	....	
	SUBLIME	86/03	7.40	Harbour service; returned 11/45.
FY.1767	SUKHA (W)	251/29	3.40	M/S; returned 11/45.
FY.1874	SULLA (W)	251/28	1940	M/S, Russian (1942); lost 3/42.
FY.618	SUMA	302/27	8.39	M/S; returned 3/46.
FY.297	SUMBA (W)	251/29	1940	M/S, Russian (1942-46); returned 3/47.
	SUMMER ROSE (AD) (ex-R.N. Sternwave)	96/19	1940	A/P; lost 13/10/40.
FY.1927	SUNBURST (ex-Estrella d'Alva)	329/09	1940	M/S; sold 1946.
FY.763	SUNLIGHT‡ (ex-R.N. Thomas Graham)	203/18	11.39	M/S, WDV; returned 2/46.
FY.300	SUNNYSIDE GIRL (AD) (ex-R.N. Northern Lights)	98/19	12.39	A/S; returned 2/46.
Z.203	SUNRISE (ex-Emilia Primero)	421/19	8.40	BDV; sold 1946.
FY.1876	SUNSPOT (ex-St. Clair)	255/04	6.40	M/S; returned 1945.
FY.1997	SUPPORTER	88/14	12.39	Harbour service; lost 5/11/44.
FY.1834	SUREAXE (ex-R.N.)	185/07	8.42	Target service; returned 11/45.
	SUSARION	261/17	6.40	A/P; lost 7/5/41.
	SUZETTE‡ (ex-R.N. Edward Grey)	199/20	11.39	A/P; returned 2/40.
	SUSSEX COUNTY (D)	83/08	11.39	A/P; returned 4/45.
	SUSTAIN (D)	93/08	1941	Harbour service; returned 1946.
4.174	SUTHERNESS	269/15	6.40	A/P, M/S (FY.1563); returned 9/45.
FY.1707	SVANA (W)	268/30	4.40	M/S; lost 8/4/42.
FY.294	SVEGA (W)	253/29	3.40	M/S; Russian (1942).
	SVERRE (R.N.N.)	.../..	1940	KBV; returned 1945.
FY.359	SVOLVAER (R.N.N.) (W) (ex-Kos I)	258/29	7.40	A/S; returned 1945.
FY.1880	SWAN II	239/02	4.40	M/S, Boiler-cleaning ship; returned 4/45.
FY.1817	SWANSEA CASTLE	256/12	7.40	M/S; returned 2/46.
T.09	SWARTBERG (S.A.N.)	220/23	9.39	M/S; returned 5/46.
FY.971	SWEET PROMISE (AD) (ex-R.N. St. Elmos Light)	94/19	11.39	M/S; returned 11/45.
FY.927	SWIFT WING (D)	98/12	11.39	M/S; returned 4/46.
	SWIRL (D)	.../..	1942	A/P; returned 1945.
FY.1802	SWONA (W)	313/25	4.40	M/S; returned 3/46.
T.33	SYDOSLANDET (S.A.N.) (W)	258/35	1940	A/S; lost 6/4/42.
FY.1732	SYRIAN* (R.N.N.)	298/19	4.40	M/S; returned 1/46.
	SYVERN	307/37	1940	A/S; lost 27/5/41.

FY.787	TAIPO	225/16	11.39	M/S, Esso; returned 11/44.
	TAKLA (R.C.N.)	.../..	9.39	M/S; returned 1945.
FY.643	TAMORA† (ex-R.N. William Loft)	275/20	8.39	M/S; returned 3/46.
4.263	TARANA (French)	347/32	8.40	A/P; returned 1945.
FY.915	TARTAN	202/12	11.39	D/L, A/P, M/S; returned 7/45.
FY.1799	TARTARIN (French)	228/31	8.40	M/S; returned 3/45.
Z.229	TEAL	.../..	8.40	BDV; sold 3/46.
FY.525	TEHANA	333/29	8.39	M/S, WDV (4.418); returned 3/46.
FY.247	TEKOURA	368/29	10.39	A/S; returned 8/45.
FY.527	TEROMA† (ex-R.N. Isaac Heath)	276/19	8.39	M/S; returned 3/45.
4.110	TERVANI	409/30	6.40	A/P, M/S; lost 7/2/43.
FY.526	TEWARA	335/30	8.39	M/S; returned 6/46.
	TEXAS† (ex-R.N.)	301/19	1940	M/S; lost 19/7/44.
FY.1963	THAW (AD)	95/19	12.39	M/S, A/P; returned 2/46.
	THE BOYS (D)	92/14	11.39	Flare drifter, A/P; lost 14/11/40.
FY.285	THE PROVOST	.../..	1940	A/S; returned 1945.
FY.1530	THE ROMAN	224/09	12.39	M/S, Esso (Y7.5); returned 8/46.
FY.889	THE TOWER‡ (ex-R.N. Thomas Dennison)	201/19	11.39	BBV; returned 2/45.
Z.127	THE WAY	263/31	9.39	BDV; returned 7/45.
FY.522	THEIR MERIT	275/18	8.39	M/S; returned 11/45.
FY.1980	THERMOPYLAE (D)	84/13	12.39	M/S, A/P; returned 4/46.
	THISTLE (D)	79/04	4.40	Exam.; lost 8/5/41.
FY.552	THOMAS ALTOFT† (ex-R.N.)	290/19	8.39	M/S; returned 4/46.
FY.553	THOMAS BARTLETT† (ex-R.N.)	290/18	11.39	M/S; lost 28/5/40.
	THOMAS CONNOLLY† (ex-R.N.)	290/18	11.39	BDV; lost 17/12/40.
	THOMAS CURRELL (R.N.Z.N.) (ex-R.N.)	205/19	8.39	M/S; returned 11/45.
FY.520	THOMAS LEEDS† (ex-R.N.)	276/19	8.39	M/S; returned 11/45.
FY.1541	THOMSONS (D)	91/07	11.39	M/S, harbour service; returned 2/46.
	THORA (Dutch) (D)	37/30	6.40	BBV; lost 26/4/43.
	THORBRYN (W)	305/36	5.41	A/S; lost 19/8/41.
	THORGRIM (W)	305/36	5.41	A/S; lost 8/4/42.
FY.179	THORNWICK BAY	437/36	8.39	A/S; sold 4/45.
FY.1905	THORODD (R.N.N.) (W)	422/19	4.40	M/S; returned 8/45.
	THORVARD (R.N.N.) (W)	249/30	4.40	M/S; returned 1946.
FY.918	THREE KINGS (D)	98/12	11.39	M/S; returned 9/44.
FY.1523	THRIFTY	139/16	12.39	M/S; returned 4/46.
	THRUSH	92/07	11.39	Harbour service, AMBITION (1944); returned 4/46.
	THUNDERSTONE	225/13	4.40	BBV; returned 4/46.
FY.106	THURINGIA	396/33	8.39	A/S; lost 28/5/40.
	TILBURY NESS† (ex-R.N. Joseph Barratt)	279/18	9.39	M/S; lost 1/11/40.
FY.939	TILLY DUFF (D)	94/19	11.39	M/S; returned 8/46.
4.294	TIRADE (ex-Transportador)	209/99	5.42	A/P; sold 3/46.
FY.593	TOCSIN (ex-Libra)	211/12	11.39	M/S, Esso; returned 9/45.
FY.1965	TOKEN (D)	89/14	1940	M/S; lost 23/12/41.
FY.788	TOKYO II	221/06	10.39	M/S, Esso (Y7.40); returned 1946.
J.137	TONGKOL (R.A.N.)	297/26	9.39	M/S; returned 1945.
	TORBAY II (D)	83/10	1940	A/P; lost 1/11/40.
T.58	TORDONN (S.A.N.)	314/25	1941	A/S; returned 5/46.
	TOREADOR (ex-Sambur)	.../..	1940	BBV; returned 1945.
FY.1740	TORNADO (ex-El Menzalah)	308/17	4.40	M/S; sold 4/46.
FY.1705	TORTEAU (French)	.../..	1940	M/S, BGV; returned 1945.

FY.1610	TOUCHSTONE	173/07	1940	M/S; returned 1945.
	TRADEWIND (AD)	94/19	1940	BBV, harbour service; returned 1945.
	TRANG (W)	205/12	1940	M/S; lost 14/2/42.
	TRANIO† (ex-R.N. George Clarke)	275/18	10.39	M/S; lost 26/6/41.
FY.920	TRANQUIL	294/12	2.40	M/S; lost 16/6/42.
	TRANSVAAL	250/16	1940	A/P, M/S, Esso; (Y7.45); lost 18/11/44.
FY.305	TRANSVAALIA (R.N.N.) (W)	160/12	1941	M/S, R. H. N. EVROTUS (1943); returned 1946.
T.51	TREERN (S.A.N.) (W)	247/29	1941	M/S; lost 12/1/45.
FY.532	T. R. FERRENS† (ex-R.N. Edward Collingwood)	279/18	8.39	M/S; returned 4/45
	TRIPLE ALLIANCE (D)	87/24	11.39	Harbour service; returned 7/46.
4.201	TRITELIA	210/16	11.39	A/P; returned 7/45.
FY.973	TRITONIA (D)	115/30	11.39	M/S; returned 1/46.
	TRITON	230/07	12.39	A/P, Esso (Y7.42); returned 1945.
	TRIUMPH (D)	90/07	5.40	BBV, S/M tender; returned 1945.
Z.218	TROJAN	141/98	1940	BGV; returned 1945.
FY.702	TROMOY (i) (R.N.N.) (W) (ex-Pol IV)	240/26	11.40	M/S, CLOUDBURST (1944); returned 1946.
FY.1987	TROPHY (D)	83/11	11.39	BBV; returned 1/46.
FY.1536	TROUP AHEAD (D)	86/13	12.39	M/S; returned 7/46.
	TRUE ACCORD (D)	92/21	12.39	A/P; lost 26/12/40.
FY.1952	TRUE FRIEND (D)	88/09	10.40	M/S, A/P; returned 2/46.
FY.1653	TRUE REWARD	.../..	1940	MWU; returned 2/46.
FY.351	TRUST (AD)	97/18	1940	A/S; returned 1945.
	TRUSTFUL (D)	95/07	12.39	Harbour service; returned 1/46.
	TRUSTY STAR (D)	96/20	1940	M/S; lost 10/6/42.
	TUIRANGI (R.N.Z.N.)	114/08	1942	M/S; returned 1946.
FY.850	TUMBY‡ (ex-R.N. John Haile)	204/18	11.39	D/L, A/P, M/S; returned 4/45.
Z.128	TUNISIAN	238/30	10.39	BDV; lost 9/7/42.
FY.130	TURCOMAN	455/37	8.39	A/S; sold 1945.
T.61	TURFFONTEIN (S.A.N.) (W) (ex-Vestfold VIII)	355/36	1941	A/S; returned 3/45.
FY.1507	TWEENWAYS (D)	92/20	11.39	M/S; returned 3/45.
	TWINKLING STAR (D)	95/20	9.39	BDV; returned 10/45.
FY.1703	TYPHOON* (ex-Syrian, ex-R.N. Thomas Thresher)	324/18	6.40	M/S; returned 5/45.
	TYRIE (D)	93/08	1941	Exam., PUNGENT (1943); returned 1945.
	UBERTY (D)	93/12	11.39	M/S; lost 8/5/41.
	UBERUS (D)	92/18	12.39	M/S; lost 11/1/41.
4.430	UGIEBANK	205/13	11.39	A/P, Esso; returned 1945.
FY.1966	UGIE BRAE (D)	88/15	1940	MWU; returned 1946.
	UGIE VALE (AD)	95/19	11.39	Harbour service; returned 10/44.
FY.1720	UIVER (Dutch)	200/02	7.40	M/S, BDV; returned 11/45.
	ULLSTEIN (R.N.N.) (D)	.../..	1941	KBV; returned 1945.
4.185	UMBRIEL	.../..	1940	A/P; returned 1945.
FY.956	UNICITY (AD) (ex-R.N. Bubble)	96/19	12.39	M/S; scrapped 10/43.
	UNISON (D)	79/10	1940	Harbour service, HARMONY (1943); returned 1945.
	UNITED (D)	.../..	1940	Harbour service; returned 1945.
FY.855	UNITED BOYS (D)	95/13	11.39	M/S; returned 9/45.
FY.1564	UTILISE (D)	94/18	12.39	M/S; returned 3/46.
FY.1969	UT PROSIM (D)	91/25	11.39	Flare drifter, A/P; lost 2/3/43.
FY.1924	UTVAER (R.N.N.)	171/14	8.40	M/S; returned 1945.

	VAILLANT (French)	916/21	8.40	A/P, BGV; returned 1945.
FY.905	VALDORA	251/16	11.39	M/S; lost 12/1/40.
FY.814	VALESCA	188/16	11.39	M/S, WDV; returned 12/45.
FY.872	VALMONT	245/16	11.39	M/S; returned 11/45.
FY.106	VAN DYCK (Belgian)	352/26	2.41	A/S; returned 11/45.
FY.330	VAN OOST (Belgian)	352/26	7.40	A/S; returned 11/45.
	VAN ORLEY (Belgian)	352/27	3.41	A/S; lost 4/5/41.
FY.1625	VARANGA	361/29	8.39	M/S; returned 11/45.
FY.1613	VARANIS	258/10	12.39	M/S; returned 11/45.
FY.1930	VARDO (R.N.N.) (ex-Kos XVIII)	252/13	7.40	M/S; returned 12/45.
FY.185	VASCAMA	447/35	9.39	A/S, ABV, Portuguese P.6 (1943–44); sold 4/45.
	VELIA	290/14	5.40	/ ; lost 19/10/40.
	VENOSTA (R.C.N.)	316/17	12.39	M/S, BGV; returned 1945.
FY.1754	VENTOSE (French)	185/36	8.40	M/S, Exam.; returned 7/44.
	VERCHERES (R.C.N.)	157/01	1939	M/S; lost 9/5/43.
T.62	VEREENIGING (S.A.N.) (W) (ex-Vestfold IX)	355/36	1941	A/S; returned 3/45.
FY.1603	VERNAL (AD) (ex-R.N.)	98/19	11.39	M/S, TRV; scrapped 1/46.
	VERS LE DESTIN (French)	.../..	8.40	A/P; returned 1945.
	VESTFJIORD (R.N.N.)	.../..	1940	A/P; returned 1945.
FY.244	VICTRIX	472/37	9.39	A/S; returned 12/45.
	VICEREINE (ex-Viceroy)	.../..	1942	TRV; returned 1945.
FY.114	VICTORIAN	447/35	8.39	A/S; sold 1946.
4.33	VIDONIA	276/07	6.40	A/P, Esso (Y7.12); lost 6/10/44.
FY.1710	VIERGE DE LOURDES (French)	154/17	7.40	M/S; returned 1/46.
	VIERNOE (R.C.N.)	273/14	1939	BGV; returned 1945.
	VIGILANT	139/02	6.40	BBV; returned 1945.
	VIGILANT (D)	.../..	1940	A/P, mine-watching; returned 1945.
4.01	VIGRA	184/99	1941	Ferry service; returned 1945.
FY.1781	VIKINGBANK (Dutch)	335/27	1940	M/S; returned 1945.
4.252	VIKING DEEPS	226/16	6.40	A/P; returned 11/44.
U.78	VIKINGS (French)	1150/35	1940	A/S; returned 1945.
Z.118	VILDA	358/29	1.40	BDV; returned 9/46.
	VILLAGE BELLE (D)	.../..	1940	A/P, harbour service; returned 1945.
FY.1711	VINDELICIA	248/13	6.40	A/P, Esso (Y7.5); returned 12/45.
	VINE (D)	77/04	6.40	BBV; returned 1945.
FY.1526	VIOLET FLOWERS	90/14	11.39	M/S; returned 1945.
FY.1531	VIREO	192/12	12.39	M/S; returned 11/43.
FY.138	VISENDA	455/37	8.39	A/S; returned 2/46.
FY.238	VIVIANA	452/36	10.39	A/S; returned 5/46.
FY.286	VIZALMA	608/40	6.40	A/S; sold 12/45.
	WALKERDALE (D)	99/11	1.40	Harbour service; returned 9/45.
FY.832	WALLENA	225/14	11.39	M/S; returned 11/45.
FY.866	WALWYNS CASTLE	255/16	2.40	M/S; returned 3/46.
FY.581	WARDOUR	335/11	8.39	M/S; returned 4/46.
FY.582	WAR DUKE	246/17	11.39	M/S; returned 12/44.
FY.292	WAR STAR	226/14	1940	A/S, Esso; returned 2/46.
FY.906	WAR WING	226/15	11.39	M/S; returned 1/46.
	WARLAND	214/13	4.40	A/P; lost 18/2/42.
FY.182	WARWICK DEEPING	445/34	9.39	A/S; lost 12/10/40.
FY.113	WARWICKSHIRE	466/36	8.39	A/S; lost 30/4/40.
	WASHINGTON	209/09	11.39	M/S; lost 6/12/39.
	WATCHWORD (D)	.../..	1942	KBV; returned 1945.
FY.681	WATERFLY (ex-Walpole)	387/31	9.39	M/S; lost 17/9/42.
FY.703	WAVEFLOWER	368/29	9.39	M/S; lost 21/10/40.
	WEAZEL (ex-Nubia)	196/03	11.39	A/P; lost 10/41.
FY.1609	WELBECK* (ex-R.N. ?)	324/17	6.40	M/S; returned 1/46.
	WELCOME (Belgian) (D)	.../..	1940	BBV; returned 1944.
FY.1521	WELCOME HOME (D)	104/25	11.39	M/S; returned 1945.

FY.137	WELLARD	514/37	8.39	A/S, U.S.N. (name unchanged—1942); sold 1945.
FY.652	WELLSBACH (ex-Welsbach)	369/30	8.39	M/S; returned 9/45.
	WELWYN	.../..	1940	TRV; returned 1945.
FY.161	WESTELLA	413/34	9.39	A/S; lost 2/6/40.
FY.1588	WEST HAVEN (D)	90/10	12.39	M/S; returned 9/45.
	WEST HOLME	152/18	1941	Harbour service; returned 12/46.
Z.154	WESTLYN	284/14	1940	BDV; sold 5/47.
	WHIPPET (W) (ex-Kos XXI)	353/37	1.41	A/S; lost 4/10/41.
T.07	WHYTOCK (S.A.N.) (ex-Charles Whytock)	166/24	2.40	M/S; returned 6/46.
FY.1583	WIGAN	275/16	1940	M/S; returned 1945.
FY.1584	WILLA	.../..	1940	D/L; returned 1945.
FY.1727	WILLIAM BELL† (ex-R.N.)	290/18	6.40	M/S; returned 2/46.
4.112	WILLIAM BRADY† (ex-R.N.)	290/18	6.40	A/P; returned 2/46.
	WILLIAM BUNCE† (ex-R.N.)	275/17	9.39	M/S; returned 1/40.
Z.142	WILLIAM CALDWELL† (ex-R.N.)	290/18	1.40	BDV; sold 12/46.
FY.535	WILLIAM CALE† (ex-R.N.)	276/17	8.39	M/S; returned 7/45.
FY.554	WILLIAM HALLETT‡ (ex-R.N.)	202/19	11.39	M/S; lost 13/12/39.
	WILLIAM HANBURY‡ (ex-R.N.)	203/18	11.39	A/P; returned 1/40.
Z.129	WILLIAM HANNAM† (ex-R.N.)	270/19	10.39	BDV; returned 4/46.
	WILLIAM H. HASTIE	229/16	8.40	Exam., salvage vessel; returned 7/45.
FY.1665	WILLIAM MANNEL† (ex-R.N.)	276/17	6.40	M/S; returned 11/45.
	WILLIAM PURDY	194/14	2.40	BBV; returned 10/45.
J.122	WILLIAM SCORESBY	326/26	1939	M/S; returned 1/47.
FY.806 / FY.1585	WILLIAM STEPHENS‡ (ex-R.N. Joseph Annison)	235/17	11.39	M/S; lost 25/10/43.
4.460	WILLIAM STROUD	214/14	3.44	Esso; returned 3/45.
	WILLIAM WESNEY	364/30	9.39	M/S; lost 7/11/40.
	WILLIAM WILSON (D)	118/29	1940	Hospital drifter; returned 1945.
FY.947	WILLING BOYS	138/30	11.39	M/S; returned 8/46.
	WILSON LINE (D)	116/32	1940	Hospital drifter; returned 1945.
	WINCHAT (D)	.../..	1941	Harbour service; returned 1945.
FY.1932	WINDSOR LAD (D)	.../..	1940	M/S; returned 1945.
	WINDWARD (D)	.../..	8.39	M/S; returned.
FY.574	WINDWARD HO† (ex-R.N.)	263/20	10.39	M/S; returned 1945.
FY.770	WITHAM‡ (ex-R.N. Stephen Kenny)	205/19	11.39	M/S, Esso; returned 11/44.
FY.1637	WITHERNSEA	257/18	11.39	M/S; sold 3/46.
FY.233	WOLBOROUGH	459/37	9.39	A/S; sold 8/45.
FY.158	WOLVES	422/34	8.39	A/S; returned 10/45.
	WOODS‡ (ex-R.N. James Brodigan)	203/18	11.39	A/P; returned 1/40.
	WRANGLER (ex-Triton)	230/07	8.42	M/S; returned.
	WYDALE	102/17	3.40	Exam.; returned 3/46.
FY.1862	WYOMING	302/15	6.40	M/S; lost 20/5/44.
Z.198	WYRE	295/11	6.40	BDV; returned 8/45.
	XMAS EVE (AD) (ex-R.N. Vapour)	95/20	1941	Harbour service; returned 1945.
	XMAS MORN (AD)	89/14	1941	Harbour service; returned 1945.
	XMAS ROSE	96/18	11.39	A/P; lost 21/11/40.

Right: M/S Whaler. I—3 pdr. [*I.W.M.*

FY.1894	YASHIMA	303/29	8.39	M/S; returned 4/46.
	YELLOW HAMMER	217/27	4.41	A/S target carrier, mobile workshop; returned 4/46.
FY.829	YEZO	301/24	11.39	M/S, WDV; returned 6/46.
FY.1937	YMUIDEN (Dutch)	194/99	1940	M/S; returned 4/46.
FY.110	YORK CITY	398/33	8.39	A/S; sold 11/45.
FY.1972	YORKSHIRE LASS (D)	111/20	11.39	M/S, RDF tender; returned 5/46.
FY.1912	YOUNG ALFRED (D)	85/11	11.39	BBV; returned 9/46.
FY.919	YOUNG CLIFF (D)	96/25	11.39	MRV; returned 6/46.
	YOUNG ERNIE (D)	88/24	12.39	A/P; lost 18/4/41.
	YOUNG FISHERMAN (D)	95/14	6.40	A/P; lost 29/11/40.
FY.975	YOUNG JACOB (D)	99/14	11.39	M/S; returned 1/46.
FY.278	YOUNG JOHN (D)	100/14	1939	MWU; returned 1/46.
	YOUNG MUN (D)	90/11	1939	A/P, BRONTOSAURUS (1942); returned 1946.
	YOUNG SID (D)	100/12	5.40	A/P; lost 10/8/40.
4.339	YTHAN BRAES	268/17	8.42	A/P, Water carrier (Y7.41); returned 2/46.
FY.1814	ZAREBA (ex-Ellena)	257/21	8.40	M/S; returned 11/44.
	ZEEMEEUW (Belgian)	200/37	1940	A/P; lost 21/9/43.

DEPLOYMENT

Generally speaking the larger and faster trawlers and whalers were fitted out as A/S vessels and the older vessels as minesweepers and patrol craft. A/S groups, usually of five vessels, were formed in September, 1939, but M/S groups, consisting of four vessels, were not formed until 1940.

Dispositions—September, 1939

Home Fleet:	15 drifters (fleet tenders).
Portsmouth:	1st A/S group (5 trawlers), 8 M/S trawlers, 3 trawlers (2 for disposal), 1 drifter.
The Nore:	6th flotilla (4 trawlers), 8 M/S trawlers, 1 trawler (base ship).
Western Approaches:	2nd A/S group (3 trawlers), 2 M/S trawlers, 1 trawler (for disposal).
Rosyth:	3rd A/S group (3 trawlers), 4 M/S trawlers.
Mediterranean Fleet:	4th A/S group (5 trawlers), 2 trawlers, 4 drifters.
South Atlantic:	2 M/S trawlers.
Dominion Navies:	7 M/S trawlers.
Fitting Out:	140 A/S trawlers (28 groups), 98 M/S trawlers.

Dispositions—May, 1940

Western Approaches:	23 A/S, 32 M/S and 39 miscellaneous vessels.
Portsmouth:	9 A/S and 28 M/S vessels.
Dover:	12 A/S, 27 M/S and 19 miscellaneous vessels.
The Nore:	19 A/S, 202 M/S, 30 barrage balloon and 33 miscellaneous vessels.

Rosyth:	65 A/S, 131 M/S, 15 barrage balloon and 46 miscellaneous vessels.
Orkney and Shetlands	25 A/S, 20 M/S, 10 barrage balloon, 18 armed boarding and 23 miscellaneous vessels.
Gibraltar:	5 A/S and 2 M/S vessels.
Mediterranean:	12 A/S and 8 M/S vessels.
South Atlantic:	5 A/S and 6 M/S vessels.
Royal Canadian Navy:	5 M/S vessels.
Royal Australian and New Zealand Navies:	7 M/S vessels.
Fitting Out:	20 A/S, 94 M/S, 32 barrage balloon and 20 miscellaneous vessels.

Dispositions—May, 1944

Western Approaches:	33 A/S, 1 A/S-M/S, 37 M/S, 117 A/P and miscellaneous vessels and 12 BDV's.
Plymouth:	28 A/S, 16 A/S-M/S, 63 M/S, 32 A/P and miscellaneous vessels and 8 BDV's.
Portsmouth:	28 A/S, 28 A/S-M/S, 24 M/S, 25 A/P and miscellaneous vessels and 15 BDV's.
Dover:	11 M/S, 4 A/P and miscellaneous vessels and 1 BDV.
The Nore:	7 A/S, 177 M/S, 11 barrage balloon, 54 A/P and miscellaneous vessels and 9 BDV's.
Rosyth:	10 A/S, 10 A/S-M/S, 60 M/S, 52 fuel carrying, 54 A/P and miscellaneous vessels and 10 BDV's.
Orkney and Shetlands:	36 A/S, 17 A/S-M/S, 9 M/S, 15 barrage balloon, 108 A/P and miscellaneous vessels and 12 BDV's.
Iceland:	12 A/S, 4 A/S-M/S, 24 A/P and miscellaneous vessels and 3 BDV's.
Western Atlantic:	8 M/S and 2 A/P vessels.
Royal Canadian Navy [Atlantic]:	6 A/S-M/S, 11 M/S vessels and 2 BDV's.
[Pacific]:	1 BDV.
Gibraltar:	10 A/S, 4 A/S-M/S, 1 A/P vessels and 1 BDV.
Azores:	8 A/S and 1 A/P vessels.
Western Mediterranean:	8 A/S-M/S and 3 A/P vessels.
Central Mediterranean:	17 A/S, 37 A/S-M/S, 16 M/S and 3 A/P vessels.
Eastern Mediterranean:	13 A/S, 11 A/S-M/S, 27 M/S vessels and 3 BDV's.
West Africa:	13 A/S, 7 A/S-M/S, 6 M/S, 3 A/P and miscellaneous vessels.
South Atlantic:	22 A/S and 2 M/S vessels.
South African Navy:	19 A/S and 37 M/S vessels.
Eastern Fleet:	15 A/S, 15 A/S-M/S, 14 M/S, 1 A/P vessels and 2 BDV's.
Royal Indian Navy:	13 A/S-M/S and 1 M/S vessels.
Royal Australian Navy:	7 M/S, 1 A/P vessels and 1 BDV.
Royal New Zealand Navy:	12 A/S-M/S, 17 M/S vessels and 3 BDV's.

PENNANT NUMBERS

The flag superior worn by trawlers, drifters and whalers largely followed the system adopted for other auxiliary vessels and was generally indicative of their duties.

The South African Navy originally allocated the pennant numbers T.01-T.62 to their requisitioned vessels thus duplicating numbers already borne by Royal Naval vessels. This was altered in 1944 by re-numbering the South African vessels: those with the numbers T.01-T.21 had 500 added, T.22-T.28 had 440 added and the remainder 400 added.

The following list indicates the main flag superiors worn by trawlers, drifters and whalers during the war years:—

Flag B:	Air-sea rescue vessels.
Flag J:	R.N. D/L, R.A.N. and R.C.N. M/S trawlers, R.N.N. M/S whalers.
Flag K:	Some R.N. A/S whalers.
Flag M:	Controlled M/L trawlers.
Flag T:	R.N. naval A/S-M/S trawlers, S.A.N. A/S and M/S trawlers and whalers.
Flag U:	Some A/S trawlers.
Flag Y:	Fuel, store and water carrying vessels.
Flag Z:	Boom defence, boom gate and N/L vessels, naval drifters (*see Note 1*).
Flag 4:	A/P, balloon barrage, torpedo recovery, wreck dispersal, wreck locating, examination service and armed boarding vessels. Some A/S and M/S vessels.
FY Pendant:	A/S, M/S, D/L, de-gaussing, mine wiping and mine recovery vessels. Some air-sea rescue, A/P, balloon barrage and armed boarding vessels.

Note 1: Formerly wore the FY pendant up to 1940.

PART SEVEN

Coastal Forces

The R.H.N. T.3 was requisitioned by the Royal Navy and entered service as MTB.69.
[*Courtesy, Vosper Ltd.*

THE DEVELOPMENT OF COASTAL FORCES

DESPITE the pioneer work undertaken by CMB's and ML's in the First World War coastal forces lapsed " between the wars " until 1935. In the meanwhile design and development did not greatly advance in the U.K. because an apparently disinterested Admiralty was, in reality, hampered by lack of funds. But in 1935 the first orders were placed, with the British Power Boat Co., for MTB's of the hard chine form. Although this form was more resistful at cruising speeds, and slightly slower at full speed, than the stepped CMB it was better able to maintain speed in a head sea and was not dependent on delicate trim to obtain optimum results.

The first MTB's proved successful and weatherly craft but with the inherent defect that the only lightweight power unit available—the petrol motor—exposed them to the hazard of fire and explosion: under which difficulties they laboured throughout the ensuing hostilities. Progress was such that, by 1938, the two firms most concerned, British Power Boat and Vosper, had built hard chine MTB's as private speculations and competition was intense to secure Admiralty contracts. The issue was finally decided in favour of Vosper but undaunted British Power Boat shipped their private venture (P.V.) boat across to the United States to participate in an MTB design contest sponsored by the United States Navy. Here their P.V. boat met with greater success and was incorporated into the U.S. Navy as PT.9 and accepted as a prototype on which to base further development. A second P.V. boat was shipped over to Canada in 1939 and became the Royal Canadian Navy CMTB.1, while the first steps were also taken to establish the Canadian Power Boat Co. in Montreal.

The possibility of enemy submarines operating in the English Channel, and adjacent coastal waters, had not been overlooked and resulted in British Power Boat producing the MA/SB: a twin-screw version of their triple-screw MTB with less speed and torpedoes sacrificed for A/S weapons. Still adhering to the hard chine form British Power Boat also produced a DCMB, to provide target practice under realistic conditions, and a fast MMS. But this latter had been anticipated by Thornycroft who had, a little earlier, completed two round bilge craft for the Admiralty of less speed but which proved most efficient 'sweepers.

In the meantime a modest programme of Vosper MTB's had been embarked on and the Fairmile company had proposed a scheme for building prefabricated, hard chine ML's for patrol and escort duties which, they rightly considered, would be required in large numbers should the worsening political situation result in hostilities. The Admiralty recognised the merits of the proposal and a small number of orders were put in hand. Enterprise was not lacking and the field widened when White embarked on a hydrofoil MTB, and Swan, Hunter & Wigham Richardson on a large, steel-hulled MTB powered with diesel engines.

Thus in the four short years prior to the outbreak of war the nucleus of coastal forces had been created with design mainly centred on the MTB, the MA/SB, and the ML, and actual conflict was to prove the stern testing ground.

In the German E-boat the British MTB was opposed to a tough opponent. The E-boat was larger, and consequently carried a heavier gun armament; it was diesel-engined and thus less liable to catch fire and explode if its fuel tanks were penetrated; and it presented a low silhouette difficult to pick up on a dark night. This latter attribute in pre-RDF days, which relied on visual sighting, was no mean advantage. For attack the MTB needed more guns or, better still, an MGB to engage with gunfire E-boats screening a squadron of heavy warships or a convoy while they went in with the torpedo. No such craft as an MGB then existed, but as enemy submarines were keeping relatively clear of coastal waters, the MA/SB's found themselves under-employed and were available for conversion to MGB's. Although there was the inevitable difficulties over providing them with suitable guns this was ultimately achieved and the MTB and MGB developed as complementary arms of offence. In September, 1943, by which time considerable development had been effected in both types, MTB's and MGB's were merged as a single type by the simple expedient of providing the former with greater gun power and adding torpedo tubes to the latter. If, with the profound advantage of hindsight, this would appear an obvious combination of duties giving greater operational flexibility it is only fair to note that such a marriage could not have been achieved much earlier until sufficient experience, obtained neither cheaply or hurriedly, had been gained to evaluate requirements and production difficulties mastered.

A certain amount of experimental work was also expended on small MTB's of a size that could be carried by sea-going vessels but the limitations of their size did not result in this line of development being actively pursued. One was in fact (MTB.105) embarked on the special service vessel FIDELITY but with her torpedoes removed and asdic installed. She floated off after the FIDELITY was sunk but eventually foundered as the weather worsened.

By 1942 it was well realised that there was a limit to which the existing short MTB could be loaded and to meet operational requirements for a more powerfully armed and seaworthy craft designs were prepared for a long boat to serve as a fresh basis for development. Initially, round bilge form craft were built and from this the *quasi* hard chine Fairmile " **D** " was evolved. By the end of the war this type carried a formidable array of light guns supplemented by four torpedo tubes but sacrificed some speed in the process. Thereafter, although short boats continued to be built, there was an increasing preference for the long boats—a policy which was surprisingly reversed in immediate post-war development.

Both MTB's and MGB's had frequently been denied the tactical advantage of surprise by the noise of their unsilenced main engines. They were later effectively silenced but in the interim there had been built a class of large, round bilge form SGB's which could move swiftly and silently into attack. But they possessed two great disadvantages: their steam turbine machinery proved extremely vulnerable to the lightest gunfire and, steel built, their construction could only be undertaken at the expense of destroyers. No less than sixty SGB's were originally envisaged, but only nine were finally ordered and seven actually built. With the sides of their machinery spaces later encased in ¾ in. armour, and their armament considerably augmented, the SGB's suffered the inevitable loss of speed which rather negatived their positive qualities.

Although the original ("**A**" type) ML's had come up to design requirements certain obvious improvements suggested themselves which led the Admiralty to prepare a round bilge design which was turned over to the Fairmile organisation to implement. This resulted in the ubiquitous " **B** " type ML which could do practically everything and go practically anywhere. Owing to a critical shortage of engines a twin-screw system was adopted which resulted in some loss of speed but enabled some 50% more craft to be placed in service. Later, a brief return was made to the earlier triple-screw hard chine type, with some modifications, to rapidly meet a demand for more MGB's.

Another successful Admiralty design was the round bilge HDML for patrol work in estuarial and coastal waters. It was of simple construction which enabled it to be built in yards abroad, not all of which possessed the facilities available in the U.K., was easily maintained, and was a most sea-kindly craft. Capable of a wide range of employment it was in demand in every theatre of operations.

The MMS was the direct result of a weapon and counter weapon: the magnetic mine, which required a non-magnetic 'sweeper, and the LL sweep which permitted such a vessel to be of modest dimensions. The design details and construction was entrusted to Richards Ironworks who, despite their incongruous title, were wooden boat builders of wide experience. It was considerably larger than the pre-war MMS, which had only been designed with a view to sweeping contact mines, was capable of world-wide employment and possessed the rugged reliability so essential to its arduous task. The U.S. Navy similarly developed the BYMS which was equally outstandingly successful. The MFV's were built as tenders to serve the large number of naval bases and anchorages which had come into being as a result of global war. For the Normandy invasion some of the larger MFV's were fitted as LL 'sweepers.

Practically all the craft listed herein were built during the duration of the war and formed a coastal force of considerable size which played a major role in keeping open, and moving, Allied sea communications. Their importance far exceeded their size and they were a considerable part of that combination of arms by which sea power is exercised. With very few exceptions they were of wooden construction and so utilised the building capacity of many boat yards, in both the U.K. and abroad, which could not otherwise have been kept fully employed. Their rapid removal from the active list after the cessation of hostilities was inevitable as, except for training, there was little peacetime requirement for them.

Four Vosper 60 ft. MTBs were ordered by the R.N.N., of which only Nos. 5 and 6 were delivered. Nos. 7 and 8 were acquired by the R.N. as their Nos. 71 and 72. They were twin screw boats armed with 2—18 in. T.T. [*I.W.M.*

MOTOR TORPEDO BOATS

B.P.B. type: Nos. 1–12, 14–19.

Displacement: 22 tons.
Dimensions: $60\frac{1}{4} \times 13\frac{1}{4} \times 2\frac{3}{4}$ ft.
Machinery: 3-shaft Napier petrol motors, B.H.P. 1,800/1,500 = 33/29 knots.
Armament: 8—.303 in. (2 × 4) M.G's; 2—18 in. torpedoes.
Complement: 9.
War losses: *1939* No. 6; *1940* Nos. 15, 16, 17; *1941* Nos. 7 (ex-13), 8, 9, 10, 11, 12.

Notes.—Built 1936–39. Nos. 1, 7, 19 were ex-Nos. 7, 13, 1 respectively. Nos. 1 (ex-No. 7), 2, 3, 4, 5, 19 (ex-No. 1) became MAC. 1, 2, 3, 4, 5, 6 (1940/1) and Nos. 14 & 18 became CT.9 & 10 (1942).

Vosper type: Nos. 20–23, 29 & 30.

Displacement: $35\frac{3}{4}$ tons.
Dimensions: $70 \times 14\frac{3}{4} \times 3\frac{1}{4}/5$ ft.
Machinery: 3-shaft Isotta-Fraschini petrol motors, B.H.P. 3,600/3,450 = 42/40 knots.
Armament: 4—.5 in. (2 × 2) M.G's; 2—21 in. T.T.
Complement: 10.
War losses: *1942* Nos. 29 & 30.

Notes.—Built 1939–40. Nos. 20, 21 & 23 were sold to the R. Roum. N. in 1940 and Nos. 29 & 30 were replacement boats for Nos. 20 & 21.

Thornycroft type: Nos. 24, 25 & 28.

Displacement: 37 tons.
Dimensions: $72 \times 16\frac{1}{2} \times 3\frac{3}{4}$ ft.
Machinery: 3-shaft Isotta-Fraschini petrol motors, B.H.P. 3,600/3,450 = 42/40 knots.
Armament: 4—.5 in. (2 × 2) M.G's; 2—21 in. T.T.
Complement: 10.
War loss: *1941* No. 28.

Notes.—Built 1939–40. No.28 was replacement boat for No. 23 (sold). Six similar boats (Nos. M. 1—6) were built for the Irish Naval Service 1939–42.

Thornycroft type: Nos. 26 & 27.

Displacement: $13\frac{3}{4}$ tons.
Dimensions: $55 \times 11 \times 3\frac{1}{4}$ ft.
Machinery: 2-shaft Thornycroft petrol motors, B.H.P. 1,200 = 40 knots.
Armament: 2—.303 in. (2 × 1) M.G's; 2—18 in. torpedoes.
Complement: 5.
War losses: *1941* Nos. 26 & 27.

Notes.—Built 1938 and were acquired from the Chinese Navy.

MTB.01 as completed with quadruple M.Gs. in cockpits forward and aft before they were moved to wing positions abreast the bridge. The torpedo troughs are shown extended over the stern from where the torpedoes were launched tail first.

MTB.34 was an early Vosper boat armed with two 21 in. T.T., a twin .5 in. M.G. abaft the bridge and two single .303 in. M.Gs. before it. In 1943 she was converted into the target boat CT.23. [*I.W.M.*

MTB.48 belonged to the initial group of White boats. The bow is slightly scalloped to provide a clear run for the torpedoes. [*I.W.M.*

Vosper type: Nos. 31–40, 57–66.

Displacement: $39\frac{3}{4}$ tons.
Dimensions: 70 × $14\frac{3}{4}$ × $3\frac{1}{4}$/5 ft.
Machinery: 3-shaft Isotta-Fraschini petrol motors, B.H.P. 3,600/3,450 = 40/38 knots except Nos. 35 up Hall Scott petrol motors, B.H.P. 1,800 = 25 knots.
Armament: 2—.5 in. (1 × 2) M.G's, 4—.303 in. (2 × 2) M.G's; 2—21 in. T.T.
Complement: 12.
War losses: *1940* Nos. 33, 37, 39, 40; *1943* Nos. 61, 63, 64.

Notes.—Built 1940–42. Nos. 57–66 had 1—20 mm. or 4—303 in. (1 × 4) added aft, an additional 2—.5 in. (1 × 2) amidships and 2—.303 in. (2 × 1) fwd. No. 61 had T.T. removed and 3—20 mm. (3 × 1) added when adapted as an MGB. Hall-Scott engines installed owing to shortage of Isotta-Fraschini engines and most were subsequently re-engined with Packard petrol motors when they became available. Nos. 31, 32 & 34 became CT.22, 24 & 23 respectively (1943).

White type: Nos. 41–48, 201–212, 246–257.

Displacement: 33 tons (*Nos. 41–48*), 38½ tons (*Nos. 201–212*), 41 tons (*Nos. 246–257*).
Dimensions: 73 × 18 × 2¾/5½ ft.
Machinery: 3-shaft Sterling petrol motors, B.H.P. 3,360 = 39¾/33¼ knots.
Armament: 2—.5 in. (1 × 2) M.G's, 2—.303 in. (2 × 1) M.G's; 2—21 in. T.T.
Complement: 12.
War losses: *1941* No. 41; *1942* Nos. 43, 44, 47, 201; *1944* R.N.N. AREND (ex-No. 203) 248; *1945* No. 255.

Notes.—Built 1940–43.

Thornycroft type: Nos. 49–56.

Displacement: 52 tons.
Dimensions: 75½ × 16½ × 2¼/5½ ft.
Machinery: 2-shaft Thornycroft petrol motors (two per shaft), B.H.P. 2,600 = 29 knots.
Armament: 2—.5 in. (1 × 2) M.G's, 2—.303 in. (2 × 1) M.G's; 2—21 in. T.T.
Complement: 12.

Notes.—Built 1941 and were converted into target towing launches for the War Office and re-named MEGGIDO, MENIN, MESSINES, MARNE, MONS, MONTAUBAN, MORVAL, NABLUS respectively.

Thornycroft type: Nos. 67, 68, 213–217, 327–331.

Displacement: 17 tons.
Dimensions: 55 × 11 × 3¼ ft.
Machinery: 2-shaft Thornycroft petrol motors, B.H.P. 1,200 = 40 knots.
Armament: 4—.303 in. (2 × 2) M.G's; 2—18 in. torpedoes.
Complement: 5.
War losses: *1941* Nos. 67, 68, 213, 214, 216, 217; *1942* No. 215.

Notes.—Built 1940–41. Nos. 67 & 68 were building for the Finnish Navy and Nos. 327–331 for the Philippine Navy when acquired by the R.N.

Vosper type: Nos. 69, 70, 218–221.

Displacement: 32 tons (*Nos. 69 & 70*); 35 tons (*Nos. 218–221*).
Dimensions: 70 × 14¾ × 3¼/5 ft.
Machinery: 2-shaft Isotta-Fraschini petrol motors, B.H.P. 2,300 = 27½ knots.
Armament: 10—.303 in. (2 × 4 & 2 × 1) M.G's; 2—21 in. T.T.
Complement: 10.
War losses: *1942* Nos. 218 & 220.

Notes.—Built 1940–41. Nos. 69 & 70 were building for the R.H.N. as T.3 & T.4 when acquired by the R.N. The R.H.N. then placed orders for T.3—T.6 which were again taken over by the R.N. after Greece had been overrun. Designed for three engines but only two installed to provide spares for Isotta-Fraschini-engined boats.

Vosper type: Nos. 71 & 72.

Displacement: 25 tons.
Dimensions: 60 × 15 × 3½ ft.
Machinery: 2-shaft Isotta-Fraschini petrol motors, B.H.P. 2,200 = 35 knots.
Armament: 2—.5 in. (1 × 2) M.G's; 2—18 in. T.T.
Complement: 10.

Notes.—Built 1940. Were two of four MTB's building for the R.N.N. The first pair (Nos. 5 & 6) were delivered to the R.N.N. and lost in their service, while the latter pair (Nos. 7 & 8) were taken over by the R.N.

Above: MTB.80 belonged to the first group of Vosper boats which adopted Packard petrol motors after the supply of Isotta-Fraschini engines from Italy had ceased. [*I.W.M.*

Below: MTB.97 belonged to the Vosper 1940 type and was armed with 2—21 in. torpedo tubes and a twin .5 in. M.G. aft. [*I.W.M.*

Vosper type: Nos. 73–98.

Displacement: 47 tons.
Dimensions: $72\frac{1}{2} \times 19\frac{1}{4} \times 2\frac{3}{4}/5\frac{1}{2}$ ft.
Machinery: 3-shaft Packard petrol motors, B.H.P. 4,050/3,600 = 40/38 knots.
Armament: 2—.5 in. (1 × 2) M.G's, 4—.303 in. (2 × 2) M.G's; 2—21 in. T.T.
Complement: 12.
War losses: *1941* No. 80; *1942* Nos. 74 & 87; *1943* Nos. 73 & 77; *1944* No. 93.

Notes.—Built 1941–42. Nos. 90, 91, 92, 94, 96, 98 were loaned to the French Navy.

Experimental type: No. 100 (ex-MMS.51).

Built 1938 and generally similar to MTB.1 except twin-screw: converted into an MTB in 1939.

Experimental type: No. 101.

Displacement: 22 tons.
Dimensions: $67\frac{1}{4} \times 14\frac{1}{2} \times 3$ ft.
Machinery: 3-shaft Isotta-Fraschini petrol motors, B.H.P. 3,450/3,000 = 42/36 knots.
Armament: 2—20 mm. (2 × 1) guns; 2—21 in. T.T.
Complement: 10.

Notes.—Built 1939 and was a hydrofoil: lost 1942 through hydrofoil failure.

Experimental type: No. 102.

Displacement: 32 tons.
Dimensions: $68 \times 14\frac{3}{4} \times 3\frac{1}{4}$ ft.
Machinery: 3-shaft Isotta-Fraschini petrol motors, B.H.P. 3,450/3,000 = $43\frac{3}{4}/35\frac{1}{2}$ knots.
Armament: 1—20 mm. gun; 2— 21 in. T.T.
Complement: 10.

Notes.—Built 1937 as a private speculation and was originally fitted with a bow T.T. in the hull and a re-load carried on deck.

Experimental type: No. 103.

Built 1940 as a stepped boat in which it was intended to fit specially high-powered Isotta-Fraschini petrol motors, but these were never delivered and she was completed as the target boat CT.05.

Experimental types: Nos. 104–107.

Built 1940 and of varying types. No. 104 had a length of 50 ft., Nos. 105 & 106 were of 9 tons and $45\frac{3}{4}$ ft. and No. 107 was of $44\frac{1}{4}$ ft. *War losses: 1940* No. 106; *1943* No. 105.

Experimental type: No. 108.

A 45-ft. hydroplane lost incomplete in 1940.

Above: The Vosper private speculation boat, later taken into service as MTB.102, running trials. She was then fitted with a bow-firing torpedo tube whose upper casing is visible on the fore deck and carried a re-load abaft the wheelhouse. A 20 mm. gun was later shipped abaft the mast (to port) and sided torpedo tubes, angled 10° out from the centre line, abreast the bridge, replaced the earlier arrangement. [*Courtesy, Vosper & Co.*

Below: MTB.238 was armed with two 21 in. T.T., a 20 mm. gun forward, twin .5 in. M.G. aft, and two rocket flare projectors fitted at the fore end of the tubes. AW, SW, and IFF RDF have been added. [*I.W.M.*

Experimental type: No. 109.

Ca. 17 tons: 41 × 11 × $2\frac{3}{4}$ ft.: was never an operational unit.

Vosper type: Nos. 222–245.

Displacement: 47 tons.
Dimensions: $72\frac{1}{2}$ × $19\frac{1}{4}$ × $2\frac{3}{4}$/$5\frac{1}{2}$ ft.
Machinery: 3-shaft Packard petrol motors, B.H.P. 4,050/3,600 = $39\frac{1}{2}$/34 knots.
Armament: 1—20 mm., 2—.5 in. (1 × 2) M.G's; 2—21 in. T.T.
Complement: 13.
War losses: *1942* No. 237; *1943* Nos. R.Neth.N. SPERWER ex-No. 222), 230; *1944* No. 241; *1945* Nos. 242, 243.

Notes.—Built 1942. Nos. 227 & 239 were loaned to the French Navy, and Nos. 222, 229, 231, 235, 236, 240 to the R.Neth.N. and re-named SPERWER (i), GIER, STROMVOGEL, SPERWER (ii), HAVIK, BUIZERD. Nos. 242–245 were replacement boats for Nos. 33, 37, 39, 40 (lost incomplete).

B.P.B. type: No. 258.

Displacement: 30 tons.
Dimensions: 70 × 20 × 4 ft.
Machinery: 3-shaft Rolls-Royce petrol motors, B.H.P. 3,300/3,000 = $44\frac{1}{2}$/40 knots.
Armament: 4—.5 in. (2 × 2) M.G's; 4—18 in. T.T.
Complement: 12.

Notes.—Built 1939 as a private speculation but not taken over by the R.N. and became U.S.N. PT.9 and was used as prototype of PT boat development. Subsequently made available to the R.N. under *Lend/Lease* in 1941.

Elco type: Nos. 259–268.

Displacement: 32 tons.
Dimensions: 70 × 20 × 4 ft.
Machinery: 3-shaft Packard petrol motors, B.H.P. 4,050/3,600 = 45/40 knots.
Armament: 4—.5 in. (2 × 2) M.G's; 4—18 in. T.T.
Complement: 12.
War losses: *1942* No. 259; *1943* Nos. 262, 264, 267; *1945* No. 261.

Notes.—Built 1940. Ex-U.S.N. PT.10–19 made available to R.N. under *Lend/Lease* 1941–42. No. 267 temporarily adapted to carry 4 mines.

U.S. Navy types: Nos. 269–274.

These were U.S.N. PT.5–8, 3, 4 respectively which were made available to the R.N. in 1941 under *Lend/Lease* but never came into operational service. PT.6 was the second boat of this number, the first having been sold earlier to the R.N. and became MGB.68. PT.7 & 8 were of aluminium construction and the latter was, in the final outcome, retained by the U.S.N. as their YP.110. PT.3 & 4 were 25-ton boats with a length of 59 ft.; PT.5 & 6 were 34-ton boats with a length 81 ft.; and PT.7 & 8 were also of this size.

Vosper type: Nos. 275–306, 363–378, 396–411.

Displacement: 37 tons.
Dimensions: $72\frac{1}{2}$ (oa) × $19\frac{1}{4}$ × $2/6\frac{1}{4}$ ft.
Machinery: 3-shaft Packard petrol motors, B.H.P. 4,050/3,600 = $39\frac{1}{2}$/35 knots.
Armament: 1—20 mm., 2—.5 in. (1 × 2) M.G's; 2—21 in. T.T.
Complement: 13.
War losses: *1943* Nos. 284, 285, 288; *1944* Nos. 287, 371, 372.

Notes.—Built 1942–44. Ex-U.S.N. BPT.21–28, 49–52, 29–48 (MTB.275–306); BPT.53–68 (MTB.363–378); and PT.384–399 (MTB.396–411) made available to the R.N. on completion under *Lend/Lease.* Nos. 363–370 were transferred to Russia in 1943 together with U.S.N. PT.400–449 and 661–730 which were also of Vosper design. Twin 20 mm. replaced twin .5 in. M.G's in most.

Elco type: Nos. 307–326.

Displacement: 45 tons.
Dimensions: 77 (oa) × 20 × $5\frac{1}{2}$ ft.
Machinery: 3-shaft Packard petrol motors, B.H.P. 4,050/3,600 = 45/40 knots.
Armament: 1—20 mm 4—.5 in. (1 × 2 & 2 × 1) M.G's; 2—21 in. T.T.
Complement: 12.
War losses: *1942* No. 308. 310, 312, 314; *1943* Nos. 311, 316.

Notes.—Built 1942. Ex-U.S.N., BTP.1–8 (ex-PT.49–56) and 9–20 (ex-PT.57–68, ex-PTC.25–36) made available to the R.N. on completion under *Lend/Lease* except PT.59–68 which were retained by the U.S.N. No. 314 was captured and became the German R.A. 10 (lost 30/4/43).

B.P.B. type: Nos. 332–343.

Displacement: 32 tons.
Dimensions: 70 × 20 × 4 ft.
Machinery: 3-shaft Packard petrol motors, B.H.P. 4,050 = 45/40 knots.
Armament: 4—.5 in. (2 × 2) M.G's; 4—18 in. T.T.
Complement: 12.
War loss: *1942* No. 338.

Notes.—Built 1941. Ex-R.C.N. and transferred to the R.N. in 1941. Modelled on private speculation B.P.B. 70-ft. MTB shipped to Canada in 1939, commissioned by the R.C.N. in 1940 as CMTB.1, and used for training. Sixteen similar boats (TM.22–37) were built for the R.Neth.N. by Canadian Power Boat (first eight) and Fyff's Shipyard (N.Y., U.S.A.—second eight) in 1942. Of these TM.23, 24, 25, 27 were lost in 1943; TM.31 in 1944; and TM.32, 35, 36, 37 were transferred to the U.S.N. as PT.368–371.

Experimental types: Nos. 344–346.

Built 1943. Stepped boats, No. 344 was 60 ft. long and Nos. 345 & 346 45 ft. All were twin-screw and powered by Thornycroft petrol motors of B.H.P. 1,200 for speeds of *ca*. 40 knots, and were armed with two 18 in. torpedoes.

Vosper type: Nos. 347–362.

Displacement: $44\frac{3}{4}$ tons.
Dimensions: $72\frac{1}{2}$ × $19\frac{1}{4}$ × $2\frac{3}{4}/5\frac{1}{2}$ ft.
Machinery: 3-shaft Packard petrol motors, B.H.P. 4,050/3,600 = $39\frac{1}{2}$/35 knots.
Armament: 1—20 mm., 2—.5 in. (1 × 2), 4—.303 in. (2 × 2) M.G's; 2—21 in. T.T.
Complement: 12.
War losses: *1943* Nos. 356, 357; *1944* Nos. 347, 352, 360.

Notes.—Built 1943. In some boats a single 20 mm. gun replaced the twin .5 in. M.G's aft and others had a 1 pdr. in place of the fwd. 20 mm. gun. No. 361 became target boat CT.36 in 1944.

Above: MTB.252 was a White boat armed with 2—21 in. T.T. and a twin .5 in. M.G.
[*Courtesy, J. Samuel White & Co. Ltd.*

Below: MTB.376 was an American built Vosper ex-BPT.66. Later most of this class had the power-operated twin .5 in. M.G. aft replaced by a manual twin 20 mm. mounting. [*I.W.M.*

MTB.378 showing twin 20 mm. guns aft in lieu of the former .5 in. M.Gs. Note the conspicuous R/T whip aerial fitted to the port wing of the bridge. [I.W.M.

Above: MTB.315 was one of the *Lend/Lease* boats, built by the Electric Boat Co., Bayonne, N.J., whose design was based on the 70 ft. British Power Boat built as a private speculation and sold to the U.S.N. in 1939. She was armed with twin .5 in. M.Gs. abaft the bridge; two single .5 in. M.Gs. on the fore-deck; a 20 mm. gun aft and 2—21 in. T.T. [*I.W.M.*

Below: The Vosper MTB.356, slipped for overhaul. [*I.W.M.*

Above: MTB.381 belonged to the flush-decked Vosper (1943) type with heavier torpedo armament and a manually operated twin 20 mm. mounting forward.

Below: MTB.422, here seen passing wrecks at Livorno, was the former U.S.N. PT.92 of the Higgins type. She was armed with a 40 mm. gun aft, a 20 mm. gun amidships, two twin .5 in. M.Gs. abreast the bridge, and 2—21 in. T.T [*I.W.M.*

Experimental prototype: No. 379.

Prototype for and generally similar to Nos. 380–395 following. Introduced heavier torpedo armament, manual twin 20 mm. mounting and flush-decked Vosper design.

Vosper type: Nos. 380–395.

Displacement: 44½ tons.
Dimensions: 73 (oa) × 19½ × 2¾/5½ ft.
Machinery: 3-shaft Packard petrol motors, B.H.P. 4,050/3,600 = 39½/34 knots.
Armament: 2—20 mm. (1 × 2), 2—.5 in. (2 × 1) M.G's, 4—.303 in. (2 × 2) M.G's; 4—18 in. T.T.
Complement: 13.

Notes.—Built 1944. Nos. 381 & 383 became target boats in 1946.

B.P.B. type: Nos. 412–418.

Displacement: 46 tons.
Dimensions: 71¾ (oa) × 20¾ × 5 ft.
Machinery: 3-shaft Packard petrol motors, B.H.P. 3,600 = 39 knots.
Armament: 1—2 pdr., 2—20 mm. (1 × 2), 4—.303 in. (2 × 2) M.G's; 2—18 in. T.T.
Complement: 17.
War losses: *1944* Nos. 412, 417.

Notes.—Built 1942. Ex-MGB.74–81 group. No.418 transferred to R.Neth.N. 1944.

Higgins type: Nos. 419–423.

Displacement: 35 tons.
Dimensions: 78¼ (pp) 81 (oa) × 20 × 6 ft.
Machinery: 3-shaft Packard petrol motors, B.H.P. 4,050 = 40 knots.
Armament: 1—40 mm., 1—20 mm., 4—.5 in. (2 × 2) M.G's; 2—21 in. T.T
Complement: 12.

Notes.—Built 1942. Ex-U.S.N. PT.88, 90,92, 94 made available to the R.N. in 1943 under *Lend/Lease* PT.93 was also transferred but was converted into a target towing boat.

White type: Nos. 424–429.

Displacement: 46¾ tons.
Dimensions: 73 × 18 × 2¾/5½ ft.
Machinery: 3-shaft Sterling petrol motors, B.H.P. 3,360 = 39¾/33¼ knots.
Armament: 1—6 pdr., 2—20 mm. (1 × 2), 4—.303 in. (2 × 2) M.G's; 2—18 in. T.T.
Complement: 17.

Notes.—Built 1944. Became Polish S.5–10 on completion.

B.P.B. type: Nos. 430–432, 434–500, 502–509, 519–522.

Displacement: 37 tons (to *No. 457*), 41 tons (to *No. 492*), 44 tons (*No. 493* up).
Dimensions: 71¾ × 20¾ × 5¾ ft.
Machinery: 3-shaft Packard petrol motors, B.H.P. 3,600 (to *No. 457*) or 4,050 (*No. 458* up) = 39 knots.

MTBs.447 (*above*) and 449 (*below*) are former British Power Boat MGBs re-classed as MTBs. although still lacking torpedo tubes. They were armed with a power-operated 2 pdr. gun forward, a power-operated twin 20 mm. mounting aft, and two twin .303 in. M.Gs. abreast the bridge. [*Both I.W.M.*

Above: MTB.476 was a former British Power Boat MGB reclassed as an MTB. Two 18 in. T.T. have been added and a power-operated 6 pdr. gun replaced the 2 pdr. fitted in earlier boats. [*I.W.M.*

Below: The mercantile GAY VIKING was the former MTB.506 converted for running the blockade to Sweden. She was armed with a single 20 mm. A.A. gun forward and aft and two twin M.Gs. abreast the bridge. [*Courtesy, Camper & Nicholson*

Armament: 1—2 pdr. (to *No. 457*) or 6 pdr. (*No. 458* up), 2—20 mm. (1 × 2), 4—.303 in. (2 × 2) M.G's; 2—18 in. T.T.
Complement: 17.
War losses: *1944* Nos. 430, 434, 448, 460, 463; *1945* Nos. 438, 444, 459, 461, 462, 465, 466, 493, 494.

Notes.—Built 1942–45. Ex-MGB.107–176 and extension of that class. Nos. 436, 437, 453 were transferred to the R.Neth.N. in 1943 and Nos. 459–466, 485, 486, 491 to R.C.N. in 1944. Nos. 481 & 490 became target boats CT.48 & 49 in 1946.

B.P.B. type: No. 433.

Ex-MGB.46 (ex-MA/SB.46, ex-R.Neth.N. TM.51) re-numbered: see under MGB's for details.

Experimental prototype: No. 501.

Built 1942 and completed as an MGB.

Experimental prototype: No. 510.

Built 1943 and completed as an MGB.

Camper & Nicholson type: Nos. 511–518.

Built 1944–46 as interchangable MTB/MGB and listed as latter.

Vosper type: Nos. 523–537.

Displacement: $48\frac{3}{4}$ tons.
Dimensions: $72\frac{1}{2} \times 19\frac{1}{2} \times 5\frac{1}{2}$ ft.
Machinery: 3-shaft Packard petrol motors, B.H.P. 4,050 = 40/38 knots.
Armament: 1—6 pdr., 2—20 mm. (1 × 2), 4—.303 in. (2 × 2) M.G's; 2—21 in. T.T.
Complement: 13.

Notes.—Built 1944–45. Nos. 531 & 537 were completed as target boats CT.44 & 45 and Nos. 534, 535, 536 were cancelled.

Experimental prototype: No. 538.

Displacement: 36 tons.
Dimensions: 68 (pp) $74\frac{1}{2}$ (oa) × $20\frac{1}{4}$ × 6 ft.
Machinery: 3-shaft Packard Petrol motors, B.H.P. 4,050 = 40/31 knots.
Armament: (as *MTB*) 2—20 mm. (1 × 2) guns; 4—18 in. T.T.: (as *MGB*) 1—4.5 in., 2—20 mm. (1 × 2) guns.
Complement: 15.

Notes.—Built 1948. Completed as MGB and then re-numbered MTB.1601.

Experimental prototype: No. 539.

Displacement: 43 tons.
Dimensions: 72 (pp) $75\frac{1}{4}$ (oa) × $19\frac{3}{4}$ × $5\frac{1}{2}$ ft.
Machinery: 3-shaft Packard petrol motors, B.H.P. 4,050 = 42/35 knots.
Armament: 1—6 pdr., 1—20 mm. guns; 4—18 in. T.T.
Complement: 16.

Notes.—Built 1950. **Dark** class prototype and of alloy construction. Re-numbered MTB.1602.

No. 523 belonged to the Vosper (1944) type which adopted power operated guns fore and aft, with a resulting decrease in torpedo armament, to fill the dual MTB/MGB role.

Fairmile " D " type: Nos. 601–800.

Displacement: 90 tons (*as MGB*), 95 tons (*as MTB*), 105 tons (*MGB/MTB*).
Dimensions: 110 (wl) 115 (oa) × 21¼ × 5 ft.
Machinery: 4-shaft Packard petrol motors, B.H.P. 5,000 = 31/27½ knots (*MGB's & MTB's*), 29/26 knots (*MGB/MTB*).
Armament: 1—2 pdr., 2—20 mm. (1 × 2), 4—.5 in. (2 × 2) M.G's, 4—.303 in. (2 × 2) M.G's; 2—21 in. T.T. (*MTB's only*).
Complement: 14 (*MBG & MTB*), 30 (*MGB/MTB*).
War losses: *1942* No. 601; *1943* Nos. 606, 622, 626 (R.N.N.), 631 (R.N.N.) 636, 639, 641, 644, 648, 665, 669, 686; *1944* Nos. 640, 657, 663, 666, 671, 672, 681, 707, 708, 732, 734, 782; *1945* Nos. 605, 635, 655, 690, 697, 705, 710, 712, 715 (R.N.N.), 776, 789, 791, 798.

Notes.—Built 1942–44. Although designed as combined MGB/MTB Nos. 601–695 were completed without T.T. and classed as MGB's. Some later had a 6 pdr. added aft which replaced the twin 20 mm. which was re-sited amidships, while others shipped 2—21 in. T.T. All later had their armament increased to 2—6 pdr. (2 × 1), 2—20 mm. (1 × 2), 4—5 in. (2 × 2) M.G's, 4—.303 in. (2 × 2) M.G's. 4—18 in. T.T. Twenty-nine were completed to a modified design (see below) and a further forty were converted to LRRC for intended Pacific operations of the R.A.F. Nos. 726, 727, 735, 736, 743–746, 748, 797 were transferred to the R.C.N. in 1944.

Modified Fairmile " D " class: Nos. 5001–5029.

Built 1944. Details as above except armed with 2—6 pdr. (2 × 1), 2—20 mm. (1 × 2) guns and 2—21 in. T.T. Nos. 5004, 5006, 5011, 5012, 5014, 5016–5019, 5022–5029 were either cancelled or completed as part of the total of forty LRRC for the R.A.F. (see above). The sole war loss was No. 5001 in 1945.

BUILDERS (MTB's built in the U.K.).

Austins (*East Ham*): Nos. 745, 773, 798, 5012.
Berthon Boat (*Lymington*): Nos. 93, 94, 232, 233, 234, 235.
Boat Construction Co. (*Falmouth*): Nos. 635, 650, 659.
British Power Boat (*Hythe*): Nos. 1–12, 14–19, 100, 258, 412–418, 430–500, 502–509, 519–522.
Brooke Marine (*Lowestoft*): Nos. 611, 622, 639, 660, 681, 695, 711, 729, 762, 5023 (ex-785).
Camper & Nicholson (*Gosport*): Nos. 29, 30, 236, 237, 238, 239.
Collins (*Lowestoft*): Nos. 740, 783.
Dickie (*Bangor*): Nos. 604, 620, 638, 647, 671, 679, 714, 717, 726, 750, 771, 777, 5010, 5024.
Dickie (*Tarbert*): Nos. 615, 629, 664.
Dorset Yacht (*Hamworthy*): Nos. 619, 624, 633, 648, 662, 666, 685, 699, 713, 732, 752, 778, 800.
J. Hall (*Glampton*): Nos. 612, 613, 645, 652.
Harland & Wolff (*Belfast*): Nos. 87–92, 350, 355–359.
P. K. Harris (*Appledore*): Nos. 618, 627, 642, 665, 687, 702, 723, 757, 788, 5021.
Wm. King (*Burnham-on-Crouch*): Nos. 609, 631, 667.
Kris Cruisers (*Isleworth*): Nos. 602, 632, 666.
Lady Bee (*Southwick*): Nos. 654.
H. McLean (*Renfrew*): Nos. 222–228.
McGruer (*Clynder*): Nos. 109, 229, 230, 231.
Morgan Giles (*Teignmouth*): Nos. 86, 95, 96, 240, 241, 360, 361, 362.
Wm. Osborne (*Littlehampton*): Nos. 605, 616, 617, 634, 655, 663, 700, 710, 728, 748, 749, 787, 795, 5005, 5020.

Above: MGB.673 belonged to the Fairmile " **D** " class of combined MGB/MTB but lacking torpedo tubes was classed as an MGB. She was armed with a 6 pdr. gun aft, a power-operated 2 pdr. forward, a power-operated twin 20 mm. mounting amidships, two twin .5 in. M.Gs. abreast the fore end of the bridge and twin .303 in. M.Gs. in each wing of the bridge. [*I.W.M.*

Below: ASRL.007 was a former Fairmile " **D** " MGB/MTB converted into a long range rescue craft for the R.A.F. and defensively armed with three single 20 mm. guns. [*I.W.M.*

Risdon Beazley (Northam): Nos. 646, 649.
Leo. A. Robinson (Lowestoft): No. 770.
Alex. Robertson (Sandbank): Nos. 625, 630, 637, 653, 661, 675, 691, 718, 731, 758.
Jas. A. Silver (Rosneath): Nos. 607, 608, 621, 636.
Sussex Sbdg. (Shoreham): No. 774.
Thomson & Balfour (Bo'ness): Nos. 641, 668.
Thornycroft (Hampton): Nos. 24–28, 49–56, 67, 68, 104–107, 213–217, 327–331, 344–346.
Saunders Roe (Angelsey): No. 539.
Tough Bros. (Teddington): Nos. 601, 603, 626, 644, 651, 673, 674, 703.
J. W. & A. Upham (Brixham): Nos. 628, 658.
Vosper (Portsmouth): Nos. 20–23, 31–40, 57–66, 69–85, 97, 98, 102, 103, 108, 218–228, 242–245, 379–395, 523–538.
(Portchester): Nos. 347, 348, 349.
(Wivenhoe): Nos. 351, 352, 353, 354.
Wallasea Bay Yacht Stn.: Nos. 606, 623, 640, 656.
White (Cowes): Nos. 41–48, 101, 201–212, 246–257, 424–429.
Woodnutt (St. Helen's): Nos. 610, 614, 643, 657, 684, 697, 715, 730, 759, 799, 5001, 5014, 5028.
Builders unknown: Nos. 40K, 669, 670, 672, 676–678, 680, 682, 683, 686, 688–690, 692–694, 696, 698, 701, 704–709, 712, 716, 719–722, 724, 725, 727, 733–739, 741–744, 746, 747, 751, 753–756, 760, 761, 763–769, 772, 775, 776, 779, 781, 782, 784, 786, 789–794, 796, 797, 5002–5004, 5006–5009, 5011, 5013, 5015–5019, 5022, 5025–5027, 5029.

BUILDERS (MTB's built abroad).

Annapolis Yacht Yard: Nos. 275–282, 303–306, 363–378.
Canadian Power Boat (Montreal): Nos. 332–343.
Electric Boat Co. (Bayonne): Nos. 259–268, 307–326.
Fisher Boat Works (Detroit): Nos. 273, 274.
Harbour Boat Bldg. (Terminal Island): Nos. 297–302.
Herreshoff Mfg. Co. (Bristol): Nos. 283–290.
Higgins (New Orleans): Nos. 269, 270, 419–423.
Robert Jacob (City Island): Nos. 291–296, 396–411.
Philadelphia Navy Yard: Nos. 271, 272.

SUMMARY OF MTB TYPES.

Nos.	
1–12	British Power Boat
14–19	British Power Boat
20–23	Vosper
24–28	Thornycroft
29–40	Vosper
41–48	White
49–56	Thornycroft
57–66	Vosper
67–68	Thornycroft
69–98	Vosper
100	British Power Boat
101	White

Nos.	
102–103	Vosper
104–107	Thornycroft
108	Vosper
109	Denny
201–212	White
213–217	Thornycroft
218–245	Vosper
246–257	White
258	British Power Boat
259–268	Elco
269–274	U.S. Navy
275–306	Vosper (built U.S.A.)

307–326	Elco	424–429	White
327–331	Thornycroft	430–500	British Power Boat
332–343	British Power Boat	501	See under MGB's
344–346	Thornycroft	502–509	British Power Boat
347–362	Vosper	510–518	See under MGB's
363–378	Vosper (built U.S.A.)	519–522	British Power Boat
379–395	Vosper	523–538	Vosper
396–411	Vosper (built U.S.A.)	539	Saunders Roe
412–418	British Power Boat	601–800	Fairmile " D "
419–423	Higgins	5001–5029	Modified Fairmile " D "

MOTOR ANTI-SUBMARINE BOATS

B.P.B. type: Nos. 1–5.

Displacement: 19 tons except *No. 1* 18 tons.
Dimensions: $60\frac{1}{4} \times 13\frac{1}{4} \times 2\frac{3}{4}$ ft.
Machinery: 2-shaft Napier petrol motors, B.H.P. 1,000 = 25 knots.
Armament: 2—.303 in. (2 × 1) M.G's.
Complement: 9.
War loss: *1941* No. 3.

Notes.—Built 1938–39. Nos. 1, 2, 4, 5 were converted into ASR's. in 1941 and the last became CT.08 in 1942.

B.P.B. type: Nos. 6–21.

Displacement: 23 tons.
Dimensions: 70 × 20 × 4 ft.
Machinery: 2-shaft Napier petrol motors, B.H.P. 1,000 = 23 knots.
Armament: 8—.303 in. (2 × 4) M.G's.
Complement: 9.

Notes.—Built 1939–40. Were all converted to MGB's in 1940. No. 21 subsequently became CT.25 in 1945.

B.P.B. type: Nos. 22–39, 49.

Displacement: 20 tons.
Dimensions: $63 \times 15 \times 4\frac{1}{4}$ ft.
Machinery: 2-shaft Napier petrol motors, B.H.P. 1,000 = 25 knots.
Armament: 2—.303 in. (1 × 2) M.G's.
Complement: 9.
War loss: *1941* No. 30.

Notes.—Built 1941. All were converted into ASR's 1941–42.

B.P.B. type: Nos. 40–45.

Were ex-R.N.N. Nos. 1–4 and ex-R.Sw.N. Nos. T.1 & 2 MTB's requisitioned by the R.N. originally for conversion to MA/SB's but eventually completed as MGB's. Nos. 44 & 45 became the Polish S.2 & 3 in 1944.

Above: MA/SB.1 was the prototype vessel of her class and was generally similar to the early B.P.B. MTBs. except that she was only twin-screw and sacrificed guns and torpedoes for A/S weapons.
[*British Power Boat Co.*

Below: MA/SB.5 was later converted into an ASR craft. [*R. Perkins*

B.P.B. type: No. 46.

Was the ex-R.Neth.N. TM.51 requisitioned by the R.N. originally for conversion to an MA/SB but eventually completed as an MGB.

White type: Nos. 47 & 48.

Displacement: 39 tons.
Dimensions: 75 × 16½ × 4½ ft.
Machinery: 3-shaft Isotta-Fraschini petrol motors, B.H.P. 3,450 = 42/38 knots.
Armament: 8—.303 in. (2 × 4) M.Gs.
Complement: 9.

Notes.—Were two ex-Polish MA/SB's requisitioned by the R.N. and completed as MGB's. No. 48 became the Polish S.1 in 1944.

B.P.B. type: Nos. 50–67.

Were all ex-French MA/SB's taken over by the R.N. and completed as MGB's.

Higgins type: No. 68.

Made available to the R.N. under *Lend/Lease* and completed as an MGB.

Higgins type: Nos. 69–73.

Were the ex-Finnish RB.1–5 made available to the R.N. under *Lend/Lease* and completed as MGB's.

B.P.B. type: Nos. 74–97.

Ordered in 1941 but all were cancelled. Nos. 74–93 were subsequently allocated to MGB's but Nos. 94–97 were not used again.

SUBMARINE CHASERS

French Navy type: CH.5–16.

Displacement: 107 tons.
Dimensions: 116½ (pp) 121¾ (oa) × 17½ × 6½ ft.
Machinery: 2-shaft Diesel motors, B.H.P. 1,130 = 16 knots.
Armament: 1—75 mm., 1—2 pdr., 2—20 mm. (2 × 1), 4—.403 in. (2 × 2) M.G's.
Complement: 28.
War losses: *1940* CH.6, CH.7, CH.9, CH.16; *1942* RENNES (ex-CH.8); *1943* CARENTAN (ex-CH.5).

Notes.—Built 1939–40. Steel hull. CH.5, 8, 10–15 were renamed CARENTAN, RENNES, BAYONNE, BOULOGNE, BENODET, CALAIS, DIELETTE, PAIMPOL in 1941. Manned by British, French and Polish crews.

Above: M.A/S.Bs. fitting out. Similar to the early British Power Boat Co.'s MTBs, they carried depth charges in racks aft instead of torpedoes and had twin, not triple, screws. [*I.W.M.*

Below: The submarine chaser DIELETTE was manned by the R.N. and was the former French *Chasseur* CH.14. She has a French 75 mm. gun forward; a 2 pdr. A.A. gun aft; two single 20 mm. guns on the bridge and two M.Gs. abaft the funnel. [*I.W.M.*

French Navy type: CH.41–43.

Displacement: 126 tons.
Dimensions: 116½ (pp) 122¾ (oa) × 17½ × 8 ft.
Machinery: 2-shaft Diesel motors, B.H.P. 1,130 = 16 knots.
Armament: 1—75 mm., 1—2 pdr., 2—20 mm. (2 × 1), 4—.303 in. (2 × 2) M.G's.
Complement: 29.

Notes.—Built 1940. Wooden hull. Were re-named AUDIERNE, LARMOR, LEVANDOU respectively in 1941.

BUILDERS.

Fge. & Ch. de la Mediterranée: CH.5–8.
At. & Ch. de France: CH.9–12.
Ch. Worms: CH.13–16
Ch. Normandie (Fecamp): CH.41–43

MOTOR GUN BOATS

B.P.B. type: Nos. 6–21.

Displacement: 31 tons.
Dimensions: 70 × 20 × 4 ft.
Machinery: 2-shaft Napier petrol motors, B.H.P. 1,000 = 23 knots.
Armament: 1—2 pdr. or 1—20 mm. or 4—.303 in. (1 × 4) M.G's, 4—.5 in. (2 × 2) M.G's.
Complement: 10.
War losses: *1941* No. 12; *1942* Nos. 18, 19; *1944* No. 17.

Notes.—Built 1940. Ex-M.A/S.Bs converted in 1940. No. 21 became CT.25 in 1943 and Nos. 8 & 16 were relegated to harbour service in 1945, the latter as a workshop.

B.P.B. type: Nos. 40–45.

Displacement: 24 tons.
Dimensions: 63 × 15 × 4¼ ft.
Machinery: 2-shaft Rolls-Royce petrol motors, B.H.P. 2,200 = 40/36 knots.
Armament: 1—2 pdr., 4—.5 in. (2 × 2) M.G's.
Complement: 10.

Notes.—Built 1940. Ex-M.A/S.Bs.

B.P.B. type: No. 46.

Displacement: 32/37 tons.
Dimensions: 70 × 20 × 4¼ ft.
Machinery: 3-shaft Rolls-Royce petrol motors, B.H.P. 3,300/3,000 = 42½/39 knots.
Armament: 1—2 pdr., 4—.5 in. (2 × 2) M.G's.
Complement: 9.

Notes.—Built 1940. Ex-M.A/S.B.

Above: MGB.13, after conversion from an M.A/S.B. armed with one 20 mm. aft; two twin .5 in. M.Gs. abreast and two single .303 in. M.Gs. abaft the bridge.

Below: MGB.61 was a former British Power Boat M.A/S.B. building for the French Navy, which was acquired by the R.N. and converted into an MGB. She was armed with a 20 mm. gun aft and two twin .5 in. M.Gs. with wide arcs of fire forward. [*I.W.M.*

White type: Nos. 47 & 48.

Displacement: 39 tons.
Dimensions: 70 × 16½ × 4½ ft.
Machinery: 3-shaft Isotta-Fraschini petrol motors, B.H.P. 3,450 = 42/38 knots.
Armament: 1—20 mm., 4—.5 in. (2 × 2), 4—.303 in. (2 × 2) M.Gs.
Complement: 12.

Notes.—Built 1940. Ex-M.A/S.Bs.

B.P.B. type: Nos. 50–67.

Displacement: 28 tons.
Dimensions: 70 × 20 × 4 ft.
Machinery: 3-shaft Rolls-Royce petrol motors, B.H.P. 3,300 = 40/36 knots.
Armament: 1—20 mm. or 4—.303 in. (1 × 4) M.G's, 4—.5 in. (2 × 2), 4—.303 in. (2 × 2) M.Gs.
Complement: 12.
War losses: *1941* No. 62; *1943* No. 64.

Notes.—Built 1940–41. Ex-M.A/S.Bs.

Higgins type: No. 68.

Displacement: 34 tons.
Dimensions: 81 × 20 × 5½ ft.
Machinery: 3-shaft Packard petrol motors, B.H.P. 3,750 = 40/35 knots.
Armament: 1—20 mm., 6—.5 in. (2 × 2 & 2 × 1) M.G's.
Complement: 14.

Notes.—Built and transferred to the R.N. 1940 from U.S.N. (ex-PT.6 (i)).

Higgins type: Nos. 69–73.

Displacement: 30 tons.
Dimensions: 69¼ × 19 × 4½ ft.
Machinery: 3-shaft Hall-Scott petrol motors, B.H.P. 1,500 = 27 knots.
Armament: 1—20 mm., 4—.5 in. (2 × 2) M.G's.
Complement: 12.

Notes.—Built 1940 and transferred to the R.N. from the U.S.N. (ex-Finnish RB.1–5).

British Power Boat type: Nos. 74–81.

Displacement: 47 tons.
Dimensions: 71¾ (oa) × 20¾ × 5 ft.
Machinery: 3-shaft Packard petrol motors, B.H.P. 4,050/3,600 = 40/35 knots.
Armament: 1—2 pdr., 2—20 mm. (1 × 2), 4—.303 in. (2 × 2) M.G's.
Complement: 12
War losses: *1942* Nos. 76, 78; *1943* No. 79.

Notes.—Built 1942. First MGB's designed as such. 2—18 in. T.T. were added in 1943 when they were converted to MTB's.

Above: MGB.75 belonged to the first group of British Power Boats MGBs. designed as such. Her power-operated guns comprised a 2 pdr. forward and a twin 20 mm. aft. [*I.W.M.*

Below: MGB.100 was a Higgins *Lend/Lease* Craft, armed with a 20 mm. gun aft and two twin .5 in. M.Gs. abaft the bridge. [*I.W.M.*

Elco type: Nos. 82–93.

Displacement: 45 tons.
Dimensions: 77 × 20 × 5½ ft.
Machinery: 3-shaft Packard petrol motors, B.H.P. 4,050 = 40/35 knots.
Armament: 1—20 mm., 4—.5 in. (2 × 2) M.G's.
Complement: 12.
War losses: *1941* Nos. 90, 92.

Notes.—Built 1941. Ex-U.S.N. STC.1–12 (ex-PTC.1–12) made available to R.N. in 1941 under *Lend/Lease*. First four originally classed as MA/SB's but by the time the remainder were transferred they had all been reclassified as MGB's.

French type: Nos. 98 & 99.

Were conversions from two French MTB's, towed to U.K. after French capitulation in 1940, and acquired by the R.N. No. 98 was lost in 1941 and No. 99 in 1945.

Higgins type: Nos. 100–106.

Displacement: 30 tons.
Dimensions: 69¼ × 19 × 4½ ft.
Machinery: 3-shaft Hall-Scott petrol motors, B.H.P. 1,500 = 27 knots.
Armament: 1—20 mm., 4—.5 in. (2 × 2) M.G's.
Complement: 12.

Notes.—Built 1941. Laid down in U.S.A. as Finnish RB.6–12 and made over to R.N. under *Lend/Lease* in 1941.

B.P.B. type: Nos. 107–176.

Displacement: 37 tons.
Dimensions: 71¾ (oa) × 20½ × 3/5¾ ft.
Machinery: 3-shaft Packard petrol motors, B.H.P. 4,050 = 42/36½ knots.
Armament: 1—2 pdr., 2—20 mm. (1 × 2), 4—.303 in. (2 × 2) M.G's.
Complement: 12.
War losses: *1943* Nos. 109 & 110.

Notes.—Built 1942. 2—18 in. T.T. were added when converted to MTB's in 1943. Some were so altered while building.

Higgins type: Nos. 177–192.

Displacement: 46 tons.
Dimensions: 78 (pp) 81¼ (oa) × 20 × 5¾ ft.
Machinery: 3-shaft Packard petrol motors, B.H.P. 4,050 = 42/36 knots.
Armament: 2—20 mm. (2 × 1), 4—.5 in. (2 × 2) M.G's, 4—.303 in. (2 × 2) M.G's.
Complement: 12.

Notes.—Built 1942. Ex-U.S.N. PT.206, 214, 215, 216, 201, 204, 207, 208, 209, 211, 213, 217, 203, 205, 210, 212 respectively made available to the R.N. in 1944 under *Lend/Lease*. Nos. 181–188 were transferred to the R.Y.N. in 1945 and Nos. 189, 190, 192, 180 became CT.40, 41, 42, 43 respectively.

Fairmile "C" type: Nos. 312–335.

Displacement: 72 tons.
Dimensions: 110 (oa) × 17½ × 5/6¼ ft.
Machinery: 3-shaft Hall-Scott petrol motors, B.H.P. 2,700 = 26½/23½ knots.

Above: MGB.107 was a British Power Boat craft with power operated guns fore and aft.

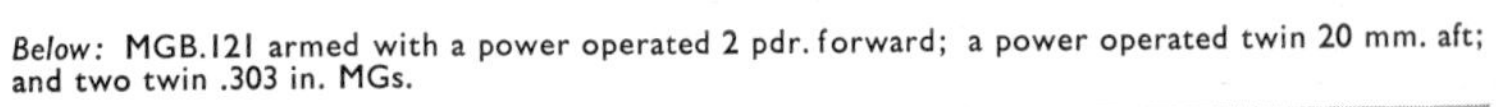

Below: MGB.121 armed with a power operated 2 pdr. forward; a power operated twin 20 mm. aft; and two twin .303 in. MGs.

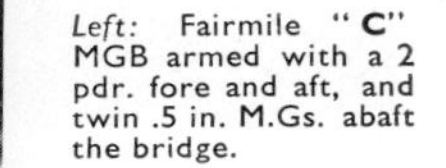

Left: Fairmile "**C**" MGB armed with a 2 pdr. fore and aft, and twin .5 in. M.Gs. abaft the bridge.

Right: MGB.328 belonged to the Fairmile "**C**" class which were armed with a power-operated 2 pdr. gun forward; a manual Rolls-Royce 2 pdr. aft; two twin .5 in. M.Gs. abaft the bridge, and two twin .303 in. M.Gs in the bridge wings. [*I.W.M.*

MGB.601 was the prototype of the Fairmile "**D**" class and was armed with a 2 pdr. forward; a twin 20 mm. aft; two twin .5 in. M.Gs. before the bridge and twin .303 in. M.Gs. in each bridge wing.
[*Courtesy, Tough Bros.*

Armament: 2—2 pdr. (2 × 1), 4—.5 in. (2 × 2) M.G's, 4—.303 in. (2 × 2) M.G's.
Complement: 16.
War losses: *1942* Nos. 314, 328, 335; *1944* Nos. 313, 326.

Notes.—Built 1941. Modifications of Fairmile "**A**" type with supercharged engines for greater speed and heavier gun armament but no A/S weapons. Later re-armed with 2—2 pdr. (2 × 1) and 6—20 mm. (3 × 2) guns.

Experimental prototype: No. 501.

Displacement: 95 tons.
Dimensions: 110 (wl) 117 (oa) × 19½ × 3¾/4½ ft.
Machinery: 3-shaft Packard petrol motors, B.H.P. 3,750 = 32/29 knots.
Armament: 1—2 pdr., 1—20 mm., 4—.5 in. (2 × 2) M.G's; 2—21 in. T.T.
Complement: 21.

Notes.—Built 1942 and became a war loss in the same year. Combination MTB and MA/SB designed to carry 1—3 in., 1—2 pdr. guns & 2—21 in. T.T. but completed as an MGB.

Camper & Nicholson type: Nos. 502–509.

Displacement: 95 tons.
Dimensions: 117 (oa) × 20¼ × 3¾/4¼ ft.
Machinery: 3-shaft Davey Paxman diesel engines, B.H.P. 3,000 except *No. 509* Packard petrol motors B.H.P. 4,050 = 30/27 knots.
Armament: 1—2 pdr., 4—.5 in. (2 × 2) M.G's, 4—.303 in. (2 × 2) M.G's; 2—21 in. T.T.
Complement: 21.
War losses: *1943* MASTER STANDFAST (ex-MGB.508); *1944* GAY VIKING (ex-MGB.506); *1945* Nos. 2002 (ex-No.502), 2007 (ex-No.507).

Notes.—Built 1942. Ex-Turkish and only Nos. 502, 503 & 509 were completed as MGB's while the remainder (Nos. 504–508) were completed as mercantile blockade runners and were named HOPEWELL, NONSUCH, GAY VIKING, GAY CORSAIR, and MASTER STANDFAST. They were armed with 2—20 mm. (1 × 2) and 4—.303 in. (2 × 2) M.G's, could carry 45 tons of cargo, and were capable of 23/20 knots. The MGBs were later re-armed with 1—6 pdr., 1—2 pdr., 2—20 mm. (1 × 2), 4—.5 in. (2 × 1) M.G's, 4—.303 in. (2 × 2) M.G's and were re-numbered Nos. 2002–2009.

Experimental type: No. 510.

Displacement: 75 tons.
Dimensions: 100½ × 19 × 5½ ft.
Machinery: 4-shaft Packard petrol motors, B.H.P. 5,000 = 35 knots.
Armament: 1—6 pdr., 2—20 mm. (1 × 2), 4—.303 in. (2 × 2) M.G's; 2—18 in. T.T.
Complement: 20.

Notes.—Built 1943.

Camper & Nicholson type: Nos. 511–518.

Displacement: 115 tons.
Dimensions: 117 (oa) × 22¼ × 3¾/4¼ ft.
Machinery: 3-shaft Packard petrol motors, B.H.P. 4,050 = 31/26 knots.
Armament: 2—6 pdr. (2 × 1), 4—20 mm. (1 × 2 & 2 × 1) guns; 4—18 in. T.T.
Complement: 30.

Notes.—Built 1944.

MGB.510, an experimental prototype built by Vospers and generally similar to the Camper & Nicholson long boats. She was armed with a 6 pdr. forward; a twin 20 mm. aft; and two twin .303 in. M.Gs. abreast the bridge—all power operated—and two 18 in. T.T. *I.W.M.*

MGB.673 was a later Fairmile " **D** " in which a 6 pdr. gun had replaced the twin 20 mm. mounting aft and the latter re-sited on the coach roof abaft the bridge. Although the bow is scalloped for torpedo tubes, none were in fact fitted, until No. 696. [*Courtesy, Tough Bros.*

The armament of SGBs was very varied. SGB.9 is shown here mounting a 3 in. gun aft; three single 2 pdr. in forward, aft and amidships positions; a 20 mm. bowchaser and two further single 20 mm. in the bridge wings; two twin .5 in. M.Gs. before the bridge; and a single 21 in. torpedo tube abreast the funnel on either side.

Fairmile "F" type: No. 2001.

Displacement:
Dimensions:
Machinery: 4-shaft Bristol petrol motors, B.H.P. 7,000 = 36 knots.
Notes.—Built 1943.

BUILDERS (MA/SB's and MGB's).

Aldous Successors (Brightlingsea): Nos. 318, 329.
British Power Boat (Hythe): Nos. 1–39, 40–46, 49, 50–67, 74–81, 107–176.
Brooke Marine (Lowestoft): No. 319.
Camper & Nicholson (Gosport): Nos. 501, 504–506, 511–518.
(Northam): Nos. 502, 503, 507–509.
Curtis (Looe): No. 325.
Dickie (Bangor): Nos. 314, 322, 334, 335.
Electric Boat Co. (Groton): Nos. 82–93.
Higgins (New Orleans): Nos. 68–73, 100–106, 177–192.
Kris Cruisers (Isleworth): Nos. 323, 2001.
Lady Bee (Southwick): No. 328.
Jas. Miller (St. Monance): No. 313
Wm. Osborne (Littlehampton): No. 320.
Alex. Robertson (Sandbank): Nos. 315, 317.
Jas. Silver (Rosneath): Nos. 321, 326, 332.
Tough Bros. (Teddington): Nos. 316, 330, 331.
Vosper (Portsmouth): No. 510.
White (Cowes): Nos. 47, 48.
Woodnutt (St. Helen's): Nos. 312, 324, 333.
France: Nos. 98, 99.
(Southampton): No. 327.

SUMMARY OF MA/SB AND MGB TYPES.

Nos.	
1–46	British Power Boat
47–48	White
49–67	British Power Boat
68–73	Higgins
74–81	British Power Boat
82–93	Elco
98–99	Ex-French MTB's
100–106	Higgins
107–176	British Power Boat
177–192	Higgins
312–335	Fairmile "C"
501–509	Camper & Nicholson
510	Vosper
511–518	Camper & Nicholson
2001	Fairmile "F"

STEAM GUN BOATS

Denny type: Nos. 1–9.

Displacement: 165 tons.
Dimensions: 137¾ (pp) 145¼ (oa) × 20 × 5½ ft.
Machinery: 2-shaft geared Turbines, S.H.P. 8,000 except Nos. 7–9 S.H.P. 7,200 = 35 knots.,
Armament: 2—2 pdr. (2 × 1), 4—.5 in. (2 × 2) M.G's; 2—21 in. T.T.
Complement: 27.

Notes.—As their steam machinery proved vulnerable to MG fire ¾ in. armour plate was fitted to the sides of the boiler and engine rooms. Their armament was considerably added to and finally consisted of 1—3 in., 2—6 pdr., (2 × 1), 6— 20 mm. (3 × 2) guns & 2—21 in. T.T. This raised their complement to 34 and, together with armour, their displacement to 260 tons with a consequent reduction in speed to 30 knots.

Above: ML.100, here seen fitting out, was the first ML to be built and belonged to the Fairmile "**A**" class. [*I.W.M.*

Below: ML.103 shows the Fairmile "**A**" class as completed armed with a 3 pdr. gun aft and three twin .303 in. M.Gs.—one before and two abaft the bridge. [*I.W.M.*

P. No.	Name	Builder	Launched	Fate
S.301	SGB.1	Thornycroft		Cancelled.
S.302	SGB.2	Thornycroft		Cancelled.
S.303	SGB.3	Yarrow	28. 9.41	GREY SEAL (1944).
S.304	SGB.4	Yarrow	25. 9.41	GREY FOX (1944).
S.305	SGB.5	Hawthorn Leslie	27. 8.41	GREY OWL (1944).
S.306	SGB.6	Hawthorn Leslie	17.11.41	GREY SHARK (1944).
S.307	SGB.7	Denny	25. 9.41	Lost 19/6/42.
S.308	SGB.8	Denny	3.11.41	GREY WOLF (1944).
S.309	SGB.9	White	14. 2.42	GREY GOOSE (1944).

All engined by Metropolitan-Vickers.

MOTOR LAUNCHES

Fairmile "A" class: Nos. 100–111.

Displacement: 57 tons.
Dimensions: 110 (oa) × $17\frac{1}{2}$ × $4\frac{1}{2}/6\frac{1}{2}$ ft.
Machinery: 3-shaft Hall-Scott petrol motors, B.H.P. 1,800 = 25/22 knots.
Armament: 1—3 pdr., 2—.303 in. (2 × 1) M.G's. *Complement:* 16.

War losses: *1940* Nos. 109, 111; *1942* No. 103; *1943* No. 108.

Notes.—Built 1940. Converted to minelayers 1942 and re-armed with 1—3 pdr., 3—20 mm. (1 × 2 & 1 × 1) guns and fitted to carry 9 moored or 6 ground mines.

Fairmile "B" class: 112–311, 336–500, 511–600, 801–933, 4001–4004, 050–129 (ex-Nos. 001–080).

Displacement: 65 tons (to No. 123), 73 tons (from No. 124).
Dimensions: 112 (oa) × $18\frac{1}{4}$ × $3\frac{3}{4}/4\frac{3}{4}$ ft.
Machinery: 2-shaft Hall-Scott petrol motors, B.H.P. 1,200 = 20/$16\frac{3}{4}$ knots.
Armament: 1—3 pdr., 2—.303 in. (2 × 1) M.G's. *Complement:* 16.
War losses: *1940* No. 127; *1941* Nos. 144, 219, 288; *1942* Nos. 129, 130, 132, 156, 160, 169, 177, 192, 242, 262, 267, 268, 270, 298, 301, 306, 310, 311, 339, 352, 353, 362, 363, 364, 365, 372, 373, 374, 375, 376, 377, 388, 389, 432, 433, 434, 435, 446, 447, 457; *1943* Nos. 126, 133, 251, 358, 579, 835; *1944* Nos. 147, 210, 216, 258, 265, 287, 385, 387, 389, 430, 443, 444, 562, 563, 819, 870, 916; *1945* Nos. 183, 230, 460, 466, 558, 591, 891, 905.

Notes.—Built 1940–44. Nos. 492–500 and 511–553 were completed as rescue motor launches (RML's) and were armed with 1—2 pdr., 1—20 mm., 4—.303 in. (2 × 2) M.G's. 1—6 pdr. was added aft in some units but generally later craft had 1—40 mm./2 pdr., 2—20 mm. (2 × 1) guns. Fifty of the earliest craft were fitted with 2—21 in. T.T. (ex-U.S.N. destroyers) for anti-invasion duties in 1940, but they were later removed. A few were fitted as minesweepers with special light sweeps and some temporarily adapted for minelaying. A number were transferred to the War Office as ambulance launches (WOAL's) in 1944 and some were specially equipped as navigation leaders for the Normandy invasion in the same year. Nos. 050–129 were for the R.C.N.; Nos. 390, 391, 412–423, 436–441 for the R.I.N.; Nos. 400–411 for the R.N.Z.N.; Nos. 424–431, 801–827 for the R.A.N.; and Nos. 829–832, 846–857 for the S.A.N. Nos. 052, 062, 063, 123, 244–247, 266, 271, 302 were transferred to the French Navy 1943–44 and re-named GALANTRY, LANGLADE, COLOMBIER, St. RONAN, Ved. 101, St. GUENOLE, St. YVES, St. ALAIN, Ved. 103, Ved. 102, Ved. 104. Eight ML's were built for the U.S.N. as S.C. 1466–73 by Le Blanc Sbdg. No. 310 was salved and became the I.J.N. SUKEI No. 12 and No. 306 the German R.A.9 (lost 16/8/44).

Above: ML.106 shows the Fairmile " **A** " class as converted to minelayers with the funnel removed, the 3 pdr. shifted forward and replaced aft by a twin 20 mm. mounting. There is a twin .303 in. M.G. abaft the bridge (later replaced by a single 20 mm. gun) and six ground mines are carried amidships. [*I.W.M.*

Below: Fairmile "**A**" ML, modified as a minelayer and armed with a 3 pdr. forward; twin .5 in. M.G.s aft and two twin .303 in. M.Gs abaft the bridge. [*Admiralty*

Above: ML.145 has a single 20 mm. aft instead of the M.Gs. in earlier " **B** " type MLs. [*I.W.M.*

Below: ML.188 shows the variation in armament of the " **B** " class MLs. and is fitted with a Rolls-Royce 2 pdr. aft. [*I.W.M.*

BUILDERS (Craft built in the U.K.).

Aldous Successors (*Brightlingsea*): Nos. 138, 170, 206, 225, 278, 301, 463, 492, 519, 559.
Austin's (*East Ham*): Nos. 227, 287, 450, 482, 514, 542 549, 570, 925, 933.
Boat Construction Co. (*Falmouth*): Nos. 137, 164, 187, 226, 261, 271, 336, 446, 471, 491.
Brooke Marine (*Oulton Broad*): Nos. 103, 114, 127, 142, 147, 186, 211, 230, 248, 270, 281, 290, 344, 443, 527, 562.
Cardnell Bros. (*Maylandsea*): Nos. 215, 288, 461, 534.
Collins (*Lowestoft*): Nos. 180, 262, 341, 479, 515, 541, 569, 926.
Curtis (*Looe*): Nos. 123, 130, 131, 139, 140, 143, 145, 146, 161, 172, 173, 241, 242, 249, 250, 251, 256, 257, 276 (*Par*), 280, 295, 307, 308, 458, 465, 480, 481, 490, 493, 513, 521, 525, 530, 533 566, 568.
Dickie (*Bangor*): Nos. 104, 122, 162, 183, 212, 235, 460, 500, 537, 565.
Dickie (*Tarbert*): Nos. 124, 188, 217, 234, 337.
Diesel Constructors (*Isleworth*): No. 345.
H. M. Dockyard (*Sheerness*): Nos. 150, 151, 245, 246.
Doig (*Grimsby*): Nos. 125, 222, 286, 464, 512.
Dorset Yacht (*Hamworthy*): Nos. 135, 144, 189, 229, 258, 268, 293, 296, 298, 462.
Harris (*Appledore*): Nos. 128, 152, 184, 233, 263, 279, 304, 451.
Itchenor Shipyard: Nos. 132, 191, 282, 466, 524, 558, 913.
Johnson & Jago (*Leigh-on-Sea*): Nos. 194, 207, 264, 274, 305, 342, 457, 469, 486, 487, 522, 532, 543, 548, 564, 572, 575, 577, 580, 581, 584, 587, 590, 593, 597, 901, 903, 907, 909, 911, 915, 918, 923.
Wm. King (*Burnham-on-Crouch*): 169, 221, 266, 302.
Kris Cruisers (*Isleworth*): No. 165, 214.
Lady Bee (*Southwick*): No. 117.
Mashford Bros. (*Cremyll*): Nos. 129, 141, 213, 255, 292, 452.
Jas. Miller (*St. Monance*): Nos. 108, 126, 159, 196, 203, 303, 346, 483, 489, 518, 529, 546, 552, 573, 574, 578, 579, 585, 586, 592, 598, 902, 904, 910, 914, 919, 924, 928.
Wm. Osborne (*Littlehampton*): Nos. 109, 174, 210, 219, 273, 291.
H. J. Percival (*Horning*): Nos. 153, 193, 244, 283, 447, 470, 523, 531, 567, 917.
Alex. Robertson (*Sandbank*): Nos. 136, 160, 197, 223, 238, 454.
Leo. Robinson (*Oulton Broad*): Nos. 163, 178, 182, 259, 340 (*Tewkesbury*), 528.
J. Sadd (*Maldon*): Nos. 181, 253, 294, 456, 517.
Jas. Silver (*Rosneath*): Nos. 200, 201, 232, 284.
Solent Shipyard (*Sarisbury Green*): Nos. 134, 176, 190, 239, 267, 285, 306, 459, 472, 526, 563.
Southampton Steam Joinery: No. 252.
Sussex Sbdg. (*Shoreham*): Nos. 133, 148, 202, 216, 231, 299, 488, 496.
Jas. Taylor (*Chertsey*): Nos. 185, 205, 209, 442, 453, 520, 571, 576, 588, 905, 906, 908, 922.
Thomson & Balfour (*Bo'ness*): Nos. 240, 275, 478, 494.
Thornycroft (*Hampton*): Nos. 157, 195, 260, 343.
Tough Bros. (*Teddington*): Nos. 113, 171, 199, 220, 228, 448.
J. W. & A. Upham (*Brixham*): Nos. 166, 167, 179, 236, 237, 247, 254, 277, 297, 309, 445, 511.
Wallasea Bay Yacht Stn.: Nos. 224, 272, 289, 339.
Wm. Weatherhead (*Cockenzie*): Nos. 168, 218, 243, 269, 300, 455, 473, 495, 516, 535.
Woodnutt (*St. Helen's*): Nos. 100, 102, 112, 155, 198. (*Portsmouth*): No. 149, (*Dumbarton*): Nos. 121, 154, 175. (*Rochford*): No. 156, 177.

ML.340 was armed with a 40 mm. gun forward, two single 20 mm. guns aft, and two twin .303 in. M.Gs. on the bridge. She is shown off Skiathos carrying British troops. [I.W.M.

Above: RML.529 was modified as a rescue launch and has a cabin amidships for survivors. She was armed with a 2 pdr. gun forward, a 20 mm. gun aft, and two twin .303 in. M.Gs. abaft the bridge. She is here seen flying the Royal Standard with H.M. King George VI embarked. [*I.W.M.*

Below: One of the Fairmile " **B** " ML's converted into an ambulance launch for the War Office. [*I.W.M.*

(*Southampton*): Nos. 158, 192, 208, 265, 338, 449, 467, 468, 497.
(*Northam*): Nos. 204, 498, 499.
Builders unknown: Nos. 101, 105–107, 110, 111, 115, 116, 118, 119, 120, 347, 444, 484, 485, 536, 538, 539, 540, 544, 545, 547, 550, 551, 553, 554, 555, 556, 557, 560, 561, 582, 583, 589, 591, 594, 595, 596, 599, 600, 912, 916, 920, 921, 927, 929, 930, 931, 932.

BUILDERS (Craft built abroad).

Anglo-American Nile Tourist Co. (*Cairo*): Nos. 360, 361, 386, 387, 835, 836.
Assoc. Boat Bldr. (*Auckland*): Nos. 403, 404, 405, 406.
Bailey (*Auckland*): Nos. 400, 401, 402.
Belmont Dock (*Jamaica*): Nos. 378, 379, 422, 423, 858, 859.
A. C. Benson (*Vancouver*): Nos. 068, 069, 128, 129.
C. L. Burland (*Bermuda*): Nos. 368, 369, 370, 371.
Burn & Co. (*Calcutta*): No. 441.
Thos. Cook (*Cairo*): Nos. 384, 385.
Garden Reach (*Calcutta*): Nos. 412, 413, 414, 415, 418, 439, 440, 477.
Greavette Boats (*Gravenhurst*): Nos. 054, 055, 056, 077, 078, 089, 090, 091, 114.
Green Point Boatyard (*Sydney*): Nos. 424, 425, 426, 427, 428, 429, 430, 431, 801, 802, 803, 804, 805, 806, 807, 808, 809, 810, 811, 812.
Grew Boats (*Penatanguishene*): Nos. 072, 073, 098, 099, 100, 106, 107, 117.
Halvorsen (*Sydney*): Nos. 813, 814, 817, 818, 819, 820, 821, 822, 823, 824, 825.
Hunter Boats (*Orillia*): Nos. 060. 061, 085, 092, 093, 109, 116.
Indian General Nav. & Rly. Co. (*Calcutta*): Nos. 438, 474, 475.
Le Blanc Sbdg. (*Weymouth*): Nos. 064, 065, 083, 084, 111, 120, 121.
Louw & Halvorsen (*Capetown*): Nos. 383, 829, 830, 831, 832, 846, 847, 854, 855.
MacCraft (*Sarnia*): Nos. 062, 063, 101, 102, 103, 104, 105, 115.
Midland Boat Works: Nos. 050, 051, 081, 082, 094, 095, 108, 118.
Minette Shields (*Bracebridge*): Nos. 057, 058, 059, 074, 075, 076, 096, 097, 110, 119.
H. Mohatta (*Karachi*): Nos. 843, 844, 845.
Rangoon Dockyard: contracts transferred to Calcutta.
Shipbuilding Ltd. (*Auckland*): Nos. 407, 408, 409.
Star Shipyard (*New Westminster*): Nos. 070, 071, 125, 126, 127.
Singapore Harbour Board: Nos. 310, 311, 432, 433.
Taikoo Dock (*Hong Kong*): Nos. 376, 377, 434, 435.
Task Rly. & Port Service (*Dar-es-Salaam*): Nos. 366, 367, 833, 834.
J. J. Taylor (*Toronto*): Nos. 052, 053, 079, 080, 086, 088, 112, 113.
Vancouver Shipyard: Nos. 066, 067, 122, 123, 124.
Voss Ltd. (*Auckland*): Nos. 410, 411.
(*Singapore*): Nos. 362,363, 364, 365, 372, 373, 374, 375, 388, 389.
(*Alexandria*): Nos. 348, 349, 350, 351, 352, 353, 354, 355, 356, 357, 358, 359, 837, 838, 889, 840, 841, 842, 860, 861, 862, 863, 864, 865, 866, 867, 868, 869, 870, 871.
(*Bombay*): Nos. 390, 391, 420, 421,
(*Calcutta*): Nos. 416, 417, 419, 436 & 437 (both ex-Rangoon), 476.
(*East London*): Nos. 848, 849, 850, 851, 856, 857,
(*Knysna*): Nos. 852, 853.
(*East Africa*): Nos. 4001, 4002, 4003, 4004,
Norman Wright (*Brisbane*): Nos. 815, 816, 826, 827.
Builders unknown: Nos. 380, 381, 382, 392, 393, 394, 395, 396, 397, 398, 399, 828, 872, 873, 874, 875, 876, 877, 878, 879, 880, 881, 882, 883, 884, 885, 886, 887, 888, 889, 890, 891, 892, 893, 894, 895, 896, 897, 898, 899, 900.

Summary of Fairmile Construction.

Nos.		Nos.	
100–111	" A " class ML's	554–600	" B " class ML's
112–311	" B " class ML's	601–800	" D " class MGB/MTB
312–335	" C " class MGB's	801–933	" B " class ML's
336–491	" B " class ML's	2001	" F " class MGB
492–500	" B " class RML's	4001–4004	" B " class ML's
511–553	" B " class RML's	5001–5029	Mod. " D " MGB/MTB.

HARBOUR DEFENCE MOTOR LAUNCHES

Admiralty type: Nos. 1001–1600.

Displacement: 46/54 tons.
Dimensions: 70 (pp) 72 (oa) × 15 × $4\frac{1}{4}/5\frac{1}{2}$ ft.
Machinery: 2-shaft Gardner diesel motors, B.H.P. 300; or Gleniffer diesel motors, H.B.P. 320; or Thornycroft diesel motors, B.H.P. 260 = $11\frac{1}{2}$ knots.
Armament: 1—1 pdr., 4—.303 in. (2 × 2) M.G's. *Complement:* 10.
War losses: *1941* Nos. 1003, 1011, 1030, 1037; *1942* Nos. 1039, 1062, 1063, 1069, 1090, 1092, 1093, 1094, 1095, 1096, 1097, 1102, 1103, 1104, 1153, 1167, 1168, 1169, 1170, 1213, 1214, 1215, 1216, 1217, 1218, 1219, 1220; *1943* Nos. 1015, 1054, 1100, 1101, 1121, 1154, 1157, 1212, 1244, 1289, 1388; *1944* Nos. 1019, 1057, 1060, 1083, 1119, 1147, 1179, 1227, 1259, 1380, 1381; *1945* Nos. 1163, 1226, 1417.

Notes.—Built 1940–44. 1—20 mm. was added aft in most and some also had the 1 pdr. fwd. replaced by a 20 mm. gun. Nos. 1009–1020 and 1261–1268 were for the R.I.N.; Nos. 1183–1194 and 1348–1351 were for the R.N.Z.N.; Nos. 1321–1329, 1340–1347 and 1352–1359 were for the R.A.N.; and Nos. 1197–1208 for the S.A.N. Twenty-six were transferred to the French Navy between 1943–44 and were variously re-numbered between VP.1–63.

BUILDERS (HDML's built in the U.K.).

Anderson, Rigden & Perkins (*Whitstable*): Nos. 1009, 1010, 1146, 1147, 1233, 1234, 1273, 1274, 1275, 1382, 1383, 1403, 1404, 1479, 1480.
Berthon Boat (*Lymington*): Nos. 1013, 1014, 1025, 1026, 1031, 1032, 1037, 1038, 1046, 1047, 1125–1128, 1237–1240, 1255–1260, 1372, 1373, 1390–1393, 1413, 1414, 1465–1468, 1483.
Wm. Blackmore (*Bideford*): Nos. 1015, 1016, 1065, 1066, 1083, 1084, 1150–1153, 1231, 1232, 1300–1303, 1376–1379.
Graham Bunn (*Wroxham*): Nos. 1019, 1020, 1036, 1054, 1055, 1154, 1155, 1308, 1309, 1310.
Bute Slip Lock (*Port Bannatyne*): Nos. 1156, 1157, 1279, 1280.
E. F. Elkins (*Christchurch*): Nos. 1080, 1162, 1163, 1398, 1399.
Harland & Wolff (*Belfast*): Nos. 1017, 1018, 1034, 1035, 1092–1095.
D. Hillyard (*Littlehampton*): Nos. 1005, 1006, 1044, 1056, 1057, 1158, 1159, 1235, 1236, 1269–1272, 1401.
Lady Bee (*Southwick*): Nos. 1001, 1002.
McGruer (*Clynder*): Nos. 1029, 1030, 1048–1050, 1229, 1230, 1296–1299, 1380, 1381.
McLean (*Renfrew*): Nos. 1076–1079, 1241–1244, 1394, 1395, 1407, 1408, 1476, 1477, 1478.
A. H. Moody (*Swannick Shore*): Nos. 1067, 1068, 1148, 1149, 1221, 1222, 1276, 1277, 1278.

Morgan Giles (*Teignmouth*): Nos. 1039, 1051, 1052, 1053.
Alfred Mylne (*Port Bannatyne*): Nos. 1027, 1028.
R. A. Newman (*Hamworthy*): Nos. 1011, 1012 1040,–1043, 1044, 1209, 1210, 1225, 1226, 1249,–1254, 1384, 1385, 1386, 1387, 1590.
Leo. Robinson (*Lowestoft*): Nos. 1021, 1022, 1075, 1137, 1138, 1247, 1248, 1396, 1397. (*Tewkesbury*): Nos. 1073, 1074, 1139, 1245, 1246.
Sittingbourne Sbdg.: Nos. 1023, 1024, 1071, 1072, 1160, 1161, 1227, 1228, 1281, 1282, 1388, 1389.
Sussex Sbdg. (*Shoreham*): Nos. 1121–1124, 1223, 1224, 1292, 1293, 1294, 1295.
Thornycroft (*Hampton*): Nos. 1129–1136, 1211, 1212, 1283–1291.
Watercraft (*East Molesey*): Nos. 1003, 1004, 1069, 1070, 1164-1166.
Herbert Woods (*Potter Heigham*): Nos. 1142–1145, 1304–1307.
(*Shoreham*): Nos. 1007, 1008, 1085–1087.
(*Poole*): Nos. 1033, 1045, 1064, 1081, 1082, 1140, 1141.
(*Yarmouth*): Nos. 1058, 1059, 1060, 1061.
(*Southampton*): Nos. 1067, 1068.
(*Dumbarton*): Nos. 1088, 1089.
(*Wooton, I.O.W.*): Nos. 1090, 1091.
Builders unknown: Nos. 1401, 1402, 1405, 1406, 1461, 1462, 1469, 1484, 1485, 1501–1589, 1591–1600.

BUILDERS (HDML's built abroad).

Ackerman Boat Works (*Azusa*): Nos. 1348, 1349, 1350, 1351.
African Marine & General Eng. (*Mombasa*): Nos. 1105–1108, 1195, 1196.
Dodge Boat Works (*Newport News*): Nos. 1171–1182, 1364–1367.
Elscot Boats (*City Island*): Nos. 1356, 1357, 1358, 1359.
Everett Marine Rly. (*Washington*): Nos. 1187, 1188, 1189, 1190.
Freeport Port Shipyard (*Long Island*): Nos. 1352, 1353, 1354, 1355.
Garden Reach (*Calcutta*): Nos. 1115, 1120.
Grays Hbr. Shpg. (*Aberdeen*): Nos. 1191, 1192, 1193, 1194.
Hooghly Dock & Eng. (*Calcutta*): Nos. 1112, 1113.
Irrawadi Flotilla Co. (*Rangoon*): Nos. 1100, 1101, 1102, 1103.
E. Jack (*Launceston*): Nos. 1325, 1326, 1329.
Wm. Edgar John (*Rye*): Nos. 1360, 1361, 1362, 1363.
Chas. P. Leek (*New Jersey*): Nos. 1338, 1339.
MacFarlane (*Adelaide*): Nos. 1323, 1324, 1328.
Madden & Lewis (*Sausalito*): Nos. 1183, 1184, 1185, 1186.
H. Mohatta (*Karachi*): Nos. 1109, 1110, 1111, 1265, 1266, 1267.
Frederick Nichol (*Durban*): Nos. 1098, 1099, 1197–1202, 1330–1337.
Pehara Land Co. (*Alexandria*): Nos. 1315–1320.
Purdon & Featherstone (*Hobart*): Nos. 1321, 1322, 1327.
Rangoon Dockyard: No. 1104.
Spradbrow (*Durban*): Nos. 1203, 1204.
L. S. Thorsen (*Ellesworth*): Nos. 1340, 1341, 1342, 1343.
Truscott Boat & Dock Co. (*St. Joseph*): Nos. 1344, 1345, 1346, 1347.
Walker, Son & Co. (*Colombo*): Nos. 1205, 1206, 1207, 1208.
(*Singapore*): Nos. 1062, 1063, 1096, 1097, 1167-1170.
(*Calcutta*): Nos. 1118, 1119.
(*Bombay*): Nos. 1114, 1116, 1117, 1261–1264, 1268.
(*Ceylon*): Nos. 1311, 1312, 1313, 1314.
Builders unknown: Nos. 1213–1220, 1368–1371, 1374, 1375, 1409–1412, 1415–1460, 1463, 1464, 1470–1475, 1481, 1482, 1486–1500.

Left: HDML.1130 is shown with only her forward gun mounted. [*Courtesy, John I. Thornycroft & Co.*

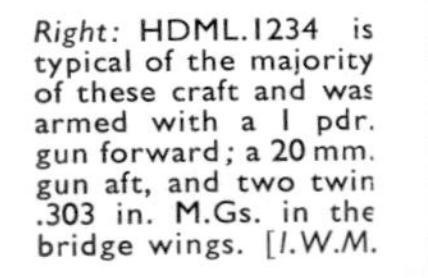

Right: HDML.1234 is typical of the majority of these craft and was armed with a 1 pdr. gun forward; a 20 mm. gun aft, and two twin .303 in. M.Gs. in the bridge wings. [*I.W.M.*

HDML.1383 has a 20 mm. gun forward as well as aft. [I.W.M.

ANTI-SUBMARINE LAUNCHES

Admiralty type: Nos. 1–20.

These were ex-HDML's specially fitted out for the Normandy invasion to counter the midget submarines and manned torpedoes expected to be used against the invasion shipping off the beaches. In addition, many MTB's landed their torpedo tubes and shipped depth charge racks for the same purpose but were not re-classed.

FAST DESPATCH BOATS

Various types: Nos. 1–81.

There is no information on Nos. 1–40, which may have been specially built, but Nos. 41–81 were conversions from HDML's.

MOTOR MINESWEEPERS

Thornycroft type: Nos. 1 & 2.

Displacement: 32 tons.
Dimensions: 75 × 14¼ × 5 ft.
Machinery: 3-shaft Thornycroft petrol motors, B.H.P. 1,500 = 15 knots.
Armament: Nil.
Complement: 11.

Notes.—Built 1937. Became Turkish KAVAK and CANAK respectively in 1939.

Admiralty type: Nos. 1–118, 123–313, COQUITLAM (J.364), CRANBROOK (J.372), DAERWOOD (J.357), KALAMALKA (J.395), LA VALLÉE (J.371), LLEWELLYN (J.278), LLOYD GEORGE (J.279), REVELSTOKE (J.373), ROSSLAND (J.358), ST. JOSEPH (J.359).

Displacement: 165 tons.
Dimensions: 105 (pp) 119 (oa) × 23 × 9½ ft.
Machinery: 1-shaft Diesel motors, B.H.P. 500 = 11 knots.
Armament: 2—.5 in. (1 × 2) M.G's.
Complement: 20.
War losses: *1941* Nos. 39, 95, 96, 123, 124; *1942* Nos. 51, 52, 93, 94, 125, 126, 127, 128, 161, 162, 163, 164, 166, 174, 180; *1943* Nos. 3, 70, 89; *1944* Nos. 8, 55, 101, 117, 170, 229, 257, 278; *1945* Nos. 68, 168, 248.

Notes.—Built 1940–44. Nos. 129, 130, 131, 132, 154 were for the R.I.N. and all named vessels for the R.C.N. A few of the earliest units had a single 20 mm. gun mounted right aft but this was later removed. Nos. 73, 138, 226, 227, 231 were transferred to the R.Neth.N. in 1942–43; Nos. 90, 203, 212 to Russia and Nos. 9, 49, 116, 118, 133, 134, 147 to France 1943–44; No. 144 to the R.H.N. in 1944; and Nos. 43, 75, 79, 112, 182, 187, 188, 189, 193 to Belgium in 1944–45. Nos. 141, 142, 238, 239, 240, 241 were re-named BURFIN, COTTEL, FICHOT, JUDE, QUIRPON, St. BARBE in 1944 as danlayers. Nos. 145, 146, 148, 152, 153, 155–160, 194, 195, 208, 210, 235, 258, 259, 262, 264, 273, 299, 306 were cancelled.

Above: MMS.12 was armed only with a twin .5 in. M.G. mounting. She had no projecting wings to her bridge and an armour-plated conning position was placed abaft the bridge to starboard. [*I.W.M.*

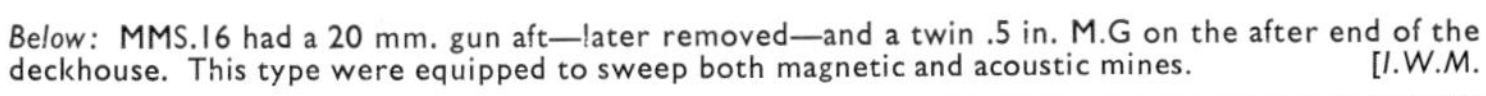

Below: MMS.16 had a 20 mm. gun aft—later removed—and a twin .5 in. M.G on the after end of the deckhouse. This type were equipped to sweep both magnetic and acoustic mines. [*I.W.M.*

Above: Besides the twin .5 in. M.G. mounting aft MMS.192 had twin .303 in. M.Gs. in the projecting bridge wings and the belting was carried over the whole length of the hull. [*I.W.M.*

Below: The MMS ODERIN was one of four vessels building in Newfoundland and requisitioned by the Royal Navy. [*I.W.M.*

Requisitioned craft: Nos. 119–122.

Displacement: (216 tons *gross*).
Dimensions: 116 (pp) 130 (oa) × 26 × 10 ft.
Machinery: 1-shaft Diesel motors, B.H.P. 275 = 9 knots.
Armament: 2—.303 in. (2 × 1) M.G's. *Complement:* 18.

Notes.—Built 1941–42. Were re-named EMBERLEY, ODERIN, MARTICOT, MERASHEEN as dan-layers in 1942.

Admiralty type: Nos. 1001–1090, ALDER LAKE (J.480), ASH LAKE (J.481), BEECH LAKE (J.482), BIRCH LAKE (J.483), CEDAR LAKE (J.484), CHERRY LAKE (J.485), ELM LAKE (J.486), FIR LAKE (J.487), HICKORY LAKE (J.488), LARCH LAKE (J.489). MAPLE LAKE (J.490), OAK LAKE (J.491), PINE LAKE, (J.492), POPLAR LAKE, (J.493), SPRUCE LAKE (J.494), WILLOW LAKE (J.495).

Displacement: 255 tons.
Dimensions: 126 (pp) 139¾ (oa) × 26 × 10½ ft.
Machinery: 1-shaft Diesel motor, B.H.P. 500 = 10 knots.
Armament: 2—20 mm. (2 × 1) guns. *Complement:* 21.
War losses: *1944* No. 1019; *1946* No. 1016.

Notes.—Built 1943–45. All named vessels were for R.C.N. and were transferred to Russia on completion. Nos. 1029, 1071, 1072, 1073, ASHLAKE, BIRCH LAKE, CHERRY LAKE, FIR LAKE, MAPLE LAKE, OAK LAKE were cancelled. Nos. 1005 & 1023 were transferred to Russia in 1944; Nos. 1014, 1022, 1025, 1026, 1043, 1044, 1046, 1074, 1082 to the R.Neth.N. in 1943–44; and Nos. 1085 & 1086 to the R.N.N. in 1944.

BUILDERS (MMS's built in U.K.).

Adams & Stockman (*Brixham*): No. 6.
Camper & Nicholson (*Gosport*): Nos. 1001, 1002.
Clapson & Sons (*Barton-on-Humber*): Nos. 50, 135, 181, 263, 280, 305.
Frank Curtis (*Looe*): Nos. 24, 25, 27, 42, 43.
(*Par*): Nos. 26, 28, 74, 75, 139, 140, 149, 150, 167, 168, 169, 170, 204, 205, 224, 225, 226, 227, 228, 268, 269, 270, 271, 282, 285, 286, 292, 293, 294, 295, 296, 297, 298, 1032, 1033, 1034, 1040, 1078, 1079, 1080.
(*Totnes*): Nos. 171, 172, 203, 207, 220, 221, 264, 265, 266, 267, 284, 290, 291, 1035, 1036, 1075, 1076, 1077, 1088.
J. S. Doig (*Grimsby*): Nos. 116, 117, 118, 179, 206, 229, 1022, 1026, 1042, 1081, 1082.
J. L. Bolson (*Poole*): Nos. 46, 58, 202, 233, 234, 281, 304.
East Anglian Constructors (*Oulton Broad*): Nos. 71, 72, 73, 1005, 1007, 1008, 1027, 1046, 1074, 1085, 1086, 1089.
George Forbes (*Peterhead*): Nos. 2, 20, 79, 80, 81, 184, 185, 209, 230, 1013, 1045.
J. & G. Forbes (*Sandhaven*): Nos. 12, 33, 59, 60, 190, 208.
P. K. Harris (*Appledore*): Nos. 9, 38, 92, 165, 183, 210, 1014, 1031.
Herd & McKenzie (*Buckie*): Nos. 4, 21, 53, 54, 192, 193, 211, 235, 260, 1015, 1016, 1047.
Humphrey & Smith (*Grimsby*): Nos. 180, 212, 213, 1023, 1025, 1043.
Husband Yacht Yard (*Marchwood*): Nos. 7, 22, 23, 65, 66, 67, 137, 138, 262, 309.

R. Irvin (Peterhead): Nos. 3, 55, 136, 186, 187, 278, 299, 302, 308.
John Morris (Gosport): Nos. 5, 49, 89, 90, 91, 109, 110, 111, 112, 274, 287, 288, 289.
MacDuff Eng. & Sbdg.: Nos. 13, 32, 61, 62, 191, 214, 232, 275, 276.
Philip & Sons (Dartmouth): Nos. 88, 175, 216, 300, 1030, 1090.
Walter Reekie (St. Monance): Nos. 14, 63, 182, 217, 260.
(Anstruther): Nos. 31, 64, 1018, 1041.
Richards Ironworks (Lowestoft): Nos. 1, 8, 19, 39, 40, 41, 44, 45, 68, 69, 70, 76, 77, 78, 176, 177, 178, 1006, 1037, 1038.
Rowhedge Ironworks: Nos. 36, 37, 1084.
Thornycroft (Hampton): Nos. 1, 2.
J. W. & A. Upham (Brixham): Nos. 47, 48, 173, 174, 218, 231, 272, 283, 303, 1019, 1020, 1029.
Wilson Noble (Fraserburgh): Nos. 10, 11, 18, 34, 35, 56, 57, 133, 134, 188, 189, 215, 219, 277, 301, 306, 307, 1017, 1021, 1024, 1048, 1049.
Wivenhoe Shipyard: Nos. 15, 16, 17, 82, 83, 84, 85, 86, 87, 113, 114, 115, 236, 237, 1009, 1010, 1011, 1012, 1028, 1044, 1083. *(Milford Haven):* No. 1039. *(Glasgow):* No. 279. *(Southampton):* Nos. 29, 30, 1003, 1004.
Builders unknown: Nos. 261, 262, 264, 273, 1087.

BUILDERS (MMS's built abroad).

A. C. Benson (Vancouver): KALAMALKA, LA VALLÉE.
Belmont Dk. (Kingston): Nos. 222, 223.
Brunton & Co. (Cochin): Nos. 129, 130, 131, 132.
Clare Sbdg. (Metaghan): Nos. 196, 197, 198, 199, 242, 243, 244, 245, 246, 247, 1050, 1051, 1052, 1053, 1054, 1055, 1056, MAPLE LAKE, OAK LAKE.
Colombo Port Commissioners: Nos. 143, 144, 145.
Colomby Cargo Boat Despatch Co.: No. 146.
Fairbanks Morse (Montreal): No. 1069.
Grew Boats (Penatanguishene): HICKORY LAKE, LARCH LAKE.
Irrawadi Flotilla Co. (Rangoon): Nos. 152, 153.
Le Blanc Sbdg. (Weymouth): Nos. 105, 106, 252, 253.
MacCraft (Sarnia): ELM LAKE, FIR LAKE.
Midland Boat Works: ALDER LAKE, ASH LAKE.
Newcastle Sbdg.: COQUITLAM, St. JOSEPH, WILLOW LAKE.
Rangoon Dockyard: No. 147.
Royal Bodden (Grand Cayman): Nos. 258, 259.
Shelburne Sbdg.: Nos. 200, 248, 249.
Star Shipyard (New Westminster): CRANBROOK, REVELSTOKE, POPLAR LAKE, SPRUCE LAKE.
Symonetty Shipyard (Nassau): Nos. 194, 195.
Steers Ltd. (St. John's): Nos. 141, 142, 238, 239, 240, 241.
Pt. Carling Boat Works: BIRCH LAKE, PINE LAKE.
Wagstaff & Hatfield (Port Greville): Nos. 99, 100, 101, 102, 103, 104, 201, 250, 251, 1063, 1064.
Ch. Mar. de St. Laurent: Nos. 254, 255, LLEWELLYN, LLOYD GEORGE.
J. J. Taylor (Toronto): CEDAR LAKE, CHERRY LAKE.
Vancouver Shipyard: DAERWOOD, ROSSLAND, BEECH LAKE.
Vaughan Sbdg. (Fredericton): Nos. 256, 257, 1070.
(Singapore): Nos. 51, 52, 93, 94, 125, 126, 127, 128, 166.
(Hong Kong): Nos. 95, 96, 123, 124.
(Cochin): Nos. 97, 98, 151, 157, 160.

(*Port Quebec*): Nos. 107, 108, 254, 255.
(*Newfoundland*): Nos. 119, 120, 121, 122.
(*Coconada*): No. 154.
(*Mandapan*): No. 148, 155.
(*Rangoon*): Nos. 156, 158, 159, 161, 162, 163, 164.
(*Beirut*): Nos. 310, 313.
(*Tel Aviv*): Nos. 311, 312.
(*Canada*): Nos. 1057, 1058, 1059, 1060, 1061, 1062, 1065, 1066, 1067, 1068, 1071, 1072, 1073.

U.S. Navy type: Nos. 2001–2080, 2137, 2141, 2142, 2148–2150, 2152–2157, 2161, 2162, 2167, 2168, 2171–2175, 2181, 2182, 2186-2191, 2194, 2197, 2202–2214, 2217, 2221, 2223, 2225, 2226, 2229, 2230, 2232–2234, 2236, 2240, 2244, 2246, 2252–2254, 2256–2258, 2261, 2264, 2277–2280, 2282, 2284.

Displacement: 207 tons (*Nos. 2001–2080*), 215 tons (*Nos. 2137 up*).
Dimensions: 130 (pp) 135½ (oa) × 24½ × 6 ft.
Machinery: 2-shaft General Motors diesel motors, B.H.P. 1,000 = 14 knots.
Armament: 1—3 in. A.A., 2—20 mm. (2 × 1) guns. *Complement:* 30.
War losses: *1943* No. 2019; *1944* Nos. 2022, 2030, 2055, R.H.N. KASSOS (ex-No. 2074), 2077, R.H.N. KOS (ex-No. 2191); *1945* No. 2053.

Notes.—Built 1942–44. Ex-U.S.N. BYMS.1–80, ex-YMS.137 up and were made available to the R.N. under *Lend/Lease* on completion. The first series (Nos. 2001–2080) had two funnels which were combined in a single casing in the second series (Nos. 2137 up). Missing nos. in the second series were retained by the U.S.N. 2000 was added to original nos. in 1943 to prevent confusion with MMS's Nos. 2033, 2054, 2056, 2065, 2066, 2067, 2068, 2074, 2186, 2229 were transferred to the R.H.N. and were re-named KALYMOS, GYMS.2054, PAXOI, GYMS.2065, GYMS.2066, GYMS.2067, LEFKAS, KASSOS, GYMS.2186, GYMS.2229.

BUILDERS (BYMS's built in U.S.A.).

Assoc. Car & Foundry (*Wilmington*): Nos. 2001, 2002, 2003, 2004, 2031, 2032, 2033, 2034, 2035, 2036.
Assoc. Sbdrs. (*Seattle*): Nos. 2009, 2010, 2011, 2012, 2013, 2014.
Astoria Marine Con.: Nos. 2137, 2141, 2142.
Ballard Marine Rly. (*Seattle*): Nos. 2025, 2026, 2027, 2028.
Barbour Boats (*New Bern*): Nos. 2029, 2030, 2037, 2038, 2039, 2040, 2041, 2042.
Bellingham Marine Rly.: Nos. 2017, 2018, 2019, 2020.
Berger Boat (*Manitowoc*): Nos. 2155, 2156, 2157, 2161, 2162.
Campbell Machinery (*San Diego*): Nos. 2152, 2153, 2154.
Dachel Carter (*Benton Hbr.*): Nos. 2015, 2016, 2167, 2168.
Gibbs Gas Engine (*Jackson*): Nos. 2043, 2044, 2045, 2046, 2047, 2048, 2049, 2050, 2051, 2052, 2053, 2054.
H. C. Grebe (*Chicago*): Nos. 2171, 2172, 2173, 2174, 2175, 2181, 2182, 2279, 2280.
Greenport Basin (*Long Island*): Nos. 2186, 2187, 2188, 2189, 2190, 2191, 2194.
C. Hiltebrant D.D. (*Kingston*): Nos. 2197, 2202, 2203, 2204, 2205, 2206.
Robert Jacob (*City Island*): Nos. 2207, 2208, 2209, 2210, 2211, 2212, 2213, 2214.
J. M. Martinac Sbdg. (*Tacoma*): Nos. 2217, 2221, 2277, 2278.
Mojean & Erikson (*Tacoma*): Nos. 2223, 2225.

Above: MMS.1017 was armed with two single 20 mm. guns mounted forward and aft. [*I.W.M.*

Below: BYMS.2022 belonged to the earlier group of coastal minesweepers which the Royal Navy received under *Lend/Lease.* [*P. A. Vicary*

F. J. Sample (Boothby): Nos. 2226, 2229, 2230, 2232, 2233, 2234.
San Diego Marine Con.: Nos. 2148, 2149, 2150, 2282, 2284.
Seattle Sbdg. & D.D.: Nos. 2021, 2022, 2023, 2024.
South Coast (Newport Beach): Nos. 2261, 2264.
Stadium Yacht Basin (Cleveland): Nos. 2236, 2240.
Tacoma Boat Bldg.: Nos. 2244, 2246.
Weaver Shipyard (Orange): Nos. 2252, 2253, 2254, 2256, 2257, 2258.
Westerguard Boat Works (Biloxi): Nos. 2055, 2056, 2057, 2058, 2059, 2060, 2061, 2062, 2063, 2064.
Wheeler Sbdg. (Whitestone): Nos. 2005, 2006, 2007, 2008, 2065, 2066, 2067, 2068, 2069, 2070, 2071, 2072, 2073, 2074, 2075, 2076, 2077, 2078, 2079, 2080.

MOTOR FISHING VESSELS

Admiralty type: Nos. 1–442.

Displacement: 50 tons.
Dimensions: 61½ (pp) 64½ (oa) × 17¾ × 4¼/7 ft.
Machinery: 1-shaft Kelvin diesel motor, B.H.P. 88 = 8½ knots; or Gray diesel motor, B.H.P. 106 = 8¾ knots; or Widdop or Lister diesel motor, B.H.P. 120 = 9 knots.
Armament: 1—.303 in. M.G. *Complement:* 6.
War losses: *1944* Nos. 70 & 117.

Hired craft: Nos. 501–520.

These were all requisitioned vessels, fitted out in 1942 and sold or returned in 1946. Original names, as far as known, are given below:—

MFV.505 (ex-Florence U), MFV.506 (ex-Gardner M), MFV.508 (ex-Hommura), MFV.509 (ex-Howe Sound II), MFV.511 (ex-Matsue I), MFV.512 (ex-Matsue II), MFV.513 (ex-Ozaki II), MFV.514 (ex-S.A.), MFV.516 (ex-T.M.B.I.), MFV.517 (ex-Viola Y), MFV.518 (ex-Y.W. II).

Admiralty type: Nos. 601–995.

Displacement: 28½ tons.
Dimensions: 45 (pp) 49¾ (oa) × 15¼/16¼ × 3¼/5¼ ft.
Machinery: 1-shaft Atlantic diesel or Chrysler petrol motor, B.H.P. 60 = 7½ knots.
Armament: 1—.303 in. M.G. *Complement:* 4.

Admiralty type: Nos. 1001–1258.

Displacement: 114 tons.
Dimensions: 69¼ (pp) 75½ (oa) × 19¾ × 5½/9½ ft.
Machinery: 1-shaft Lister diesel motor, B.H.P. 160 = 8½ knots.
Armament: 1—.303 in. M.G. *Complement:* 9.
War loss: *1944* No. 1032.

Above: BYMS.2189 was one of the later group and had both her diesel engine exhausts brought up into a single casing. [*P. A. Vicary*

Below: MFV.31, fitted with sails for her 2,000 mile voyage. [*I.W.M.*

Admiralty type: Nos. 1501–1610.

Displacement: 200 tons.
Dimensions: 90 (pp) 97¼ (oa) × 22¼ × 5½/11 ft.
Machinery: 1-shaft Crossley diesel motor, B.H.P. 240 = 9¼ knots.
Armament: 1—.303 in. M.G. *Complement:* 11.

BUILDERS.

Philips, Anderson (Granton): Nos. 179, 180, 204, 205, 270, 271.
Anderson, Rigden & Perkins (Whitstable): Nos. 21, 22, 57, 58, 101–104, 230, 231, 283, 284.
J. Adams & Sons (Gourock): Nos. 655, 656.
Berthon Boat (Lymington): Nos. 1223, 1224, 1225, 1226, 1229, 1230.
J. L. Bolson & Sons (Poole): Nos. 435–442.
Brooke Marine (Lowestoft): Nos. 35–40, 95–100, 325, 326, 461–463.
G. L. Burland (Hamilton, Bermuda): Nos. 601–608.
Cardnell Bros. (Maylandsea): Nos. 657–660.
D. R. M. Carnie (Leith): Nos. 617–620.
Clapson & Sons (Barton-on-Humber): Nos. 1004–1006.
Collins (Lowestoft): Nos. 816, 817.
Frank Curtis (Looe): Nos. 27–30, 32, 34, 65-88.
(Mevagissey): Nos. 31, 33.
(Par): Nos. 1513–1524.
(Totnes): Nos. 1525–1536.
A. M. Dickie (Bangor): Nos. 307–312, 866, 867, 868, 869.
J. S. Doig (Grimsby): Nos. 1051, 1058, 1102, 1103, 1115–1118, 1173, 1174, 1199, 1206, 1221, 1222, 1242.
Dorset Yacht (Hamworthy): Nos. 698, 699, 726, 727, 734, 735.
East Anglian Constructors (Oulton Broad): Nos. 23–26, 1555–1560, 1573–1579, 1581.
Exe Joinery Works (Exeter): Nos. 151–156.
George Forbes (Peterhead): Nos. 1021, 1022, 1026, 1076–1078, 1093–1096, 1131–1134, 1161, 1162, 1191.
J. & G. Forbes (Sandhaven): Nos. 8, 157, 158, 1035–1038, 1081, 1082, 1085, 1086, 1089, 1090, 1121–1126, 1184–1188, 1211.
P. K. Harris (Appledore): Nos. 1011–1014.
Herd & McKenzie (Buckie): Nos. 1043–1046, 1087, 1088, 1151–1154, 1209.
Humphrey & Smith (Grimsby): Nos. 1031–1034, 1067, 1068, 1100, 1155–1158, 1169–1172, 1177–1180, 1227, 1228.
Husband Yacht Yard (Marchwood): Nos. 129–134, 159, 160, 236–241, 1061, 1062, 1149, 1150, 1201, 1202.
Richard Irvin (Peterhead): Nos. 1018–1020, 1052, 1074, 1075, 1097, 1098, 1105–1108, 1193, 1194, 1218, 1219, 1233, 1234.
Johnson & Jago (Leigh-on-Sea): Nos. 49–52, 125–128, 200, 201, 313, 314.
Jones Slip (Buckie): Nos. 7, 105–108.
Kris Cruisers (Isleworth): Nos. 59, 60, 135–140.
J. J. Lawrence (Leith): Nos. 621–632.
MacDuff Eng. & Sbdg. Co. (MacDuff): Nos. 1039–1042, 1143–1146.
Mashford Bros. (Cremyll): Nos. 15, 16, 41–44, 89–94, 198, 199, 274, 275, 294.
J. Martin (Granton): Nos. 609–616.
Jas. Miller (St. Monance): Nos. 803, 804, 807, 808.
G. A. Mitchell (Mevagissey): Nos. 651–654.
Morgan Giles (Teignmouth): Nos. 315, 316.

Above: MFV.33, was also fitted with sails for her 2,000 mile voyage, and was equipped with a WT set. [*I.W.M.*

Below: MFV.517 (ex-Viola Y) was one of the commercial craft requisitioned by the R.N. Note detached wheelhouse from deckhouse, a practice not followed by naval built MFVs. [*I.W.M.*

John Morris & Co. (Gosport): Nos. 113–124.
New Medway S.P. Co. (Rochester): Nos. 645–650.
Frederick Nicholl (Durban, South Africa): Nos. 141–150.
James Noble (Fraserburgh): Nos. 1001–1003, 1015–1017, 1053, 1079, 1080, 1091, 1092, 1139–1142, 1189, 1190, 1213.
G. Overy (Oulton Broad): Nos. 9–12, 109–112, 181–184, 317.
Charles Pearson (Hull): Nos. 633–638.
Philip & Son (Dartmouth): Nos. 1083, 1084, 1135–1138, 1175, 1176, 1207, 1208, 1239, 1240.
Walter Reekie (Anstruther): Nos. 1104, 1110, 1111, 1113, 1163, 1164, 1166, 1196.
(St. Monance): Nos. 3, 4, 1027–1030, 1109, 1112, 1114, 1165, 1195.
Richards Ironworks (Lowestoft): Nos. 1501–1512, 1567–1572, 1580, 1582–1585, 1607.
Leo. Robinson (Lowestoft): Nos. 877–880.
Rowhedge Ironworks: Nos. 1561–1566.
J. Sadd (Maldon): Nos. 1, 2, 45–48, 282.
J. W. & A. Upham (Brixham): Nos. 1007–1010, 1203, 1204, 1205.
D. W. Williams (Aberyswith): Nos. 639–644.
Wilson, Noble & Co. (Fraserburgh): Nos. 1054, 1127–1130, 1215–1217.
Wivenhoe Shyd.: Nos. 1537–1546.
Yorkshire Yacht Building (Bridlington): Nos. 53–56, 61–64.

SUMMARY OF MFV CONSTRUCTION

WHERE BUILT	ORDERED	CANCELLED	COMPLETED
U.K. South Africa Australia	261 85 96	23 6 71	238 79 25
Nos. 1–442	442	100	342
U.K. South Africa Bermuda E'ern. Med.	263 19 12 20	46 19 2 20	217 — 10 —
Nos. 601–995	314	87	227
U.K.	227	18	209
Nos. 1001–1258	227	18	209
U.K.	100	28	72
Nos. 1501–1610	100	28	72

Notes.—Among those cancelled were Nos. 95–100, 284, 308–312, 314, 317–326, 461–463, 1147.

COASTAL TRANSPORTS

U.S. Navy type: FT.1–30.

Displacement: 238 tons.
Dimensions: 103 (pp) 110 (oa) × 21¼ × 11 ft.

Machinery: 1-shaft diesel motors, B.H.P. 400 = 10 knots.
Armament: 4 20 mm. (4 × 1) guns.
Complement: 20.

Notes.—Built 1943. Ex-U.S.N. APC.51–56, 58–61, 65, 66, 71, 72, 75–79, 57, 62–64, 67–70, 73, 74, 97 respectively and made available to the R.N. under *Lend/Lease* on completion. FT.11–13, 15, 24, 28 were transferred to the R.H.N. and re-named ANKHIALOS, DISTOMON, KALAVRYTA, VELESTINON, ELASSON, LEKHOVON. FT.5, 7, 16 were re-named TENDERFOOT, ASTRAVAL, TENDERHEART in 1944.

BUILDERS.

Camden Sbdg.: FT.7–10, 21–23.
Bristol Yacht: FT.13, 14, 28, 29.
Hogdon Bros. ( ): FT.11, 12, 24–27.
H. G. Marr (*Damariscotta*)*:* FT.5, 6, 20.
Noank Sbdg.: FT.30.
W. A. Robinson (*Ipswich, Mass.*)*:* FT.15–19.
Warren Boats ( ): FT.1–4.

MOTOR ATTENDANT CRAFT

P. No.	Name	Fate
J.142	MAC.1 (ex-MTB.1, ex-MTB.7)	Target boat CT.01 (1942)
J.150	MAC.2 (ex-MTB.2)	Target boat CT.07 (1942)
J.163	MAC.3 (ex-MTB.3)	Target boat CT.03 (1942)
J.171	MAC.4 (ex-MTB.4)	Target boat CT.04 (1942)
J.185	MAC.5 (ex-MTB.5)	Lost 26/12/40
J.196	MAC.6 (ex-MTB.19, ex-MTB.1)	Target boat CT.06 (1942)
J.177	MAC.7 (ex-MTB.40K)	

Notes.—MAC.1, 2, 6, were ASR's in 1941 (Pennant Nos. B.034, B.030, B.047 respectively).

TARGET SERVICE BOATS

B.P.B. type: DCMB.72.

Built 1939. A 57-ft. twin screw craft with a speed of 30 knots.

Converted 1942: CT.01–11.

CT.01	(ex-MAC.1, ex-MTB.1, ex-MTB.7)	CT.07	(ex-MAC.2, ex-MTB.2)
CT.02	(ex-DCMB.72)	CT.08	(ex-MA/SB.5)
CT.03	(ex-MAC.3, ex-MTB.3)	CT.09	(ex-MTB.14)
CT.04	(ex-MAC.4, ex-MTB.4)	CT.10	(ex-MTB.18)
CT.05	(ex-MTB.103)	CT.11	(ex-MTB.100)
CT.06	(ex-MAC.6, ex-MTB.19, ex-MTB.1)		

Completed 1943: CT.12–19.

Converted 1943: CT.20–36.

CT.20	(ex-HSL.112)	CT.26	(ex- ?)	CT.31	(ex-TM.28)
CT.21	(ex-HSL.115)	CT.27	(ex- ?)	CT.32	(ex-TM.29)
CT.22	(ex-HSL. ?)	CT.28	(ex- ?)	CT.33	(ex-TM.30)
CT.23	(ex-MTB.34)	CT.29	(ex- ?)	CT.34	(ex- ?)
CT.24	(ex-MTB.32)	CT.30	(ex- ?)	CT.35	(ex- ?)
CT.25	(ex-MGB.21)			CT.36	(ex-MTB.361)

Converted 1944: CT.38–43.

CT.38	(ex-MTB.353)	CT.40	(ex-MGB.189)	CT.42	(ex-MGB.192)
CT.39	(ex-MTB.354)	CT.41	(ex-MGB.190)	CT.43	(ex-MGB.180)

Converted 1945: CT.44–49.

CT.44	(ex-MTB.531)	CT.46	(ex- ?)	CT.48	(ex-MTB.481)
CT.45	(ex-MTB.537)	CT.47	(ex- ?)	CT.49	(ex-MTB.490)

Notes.—Two *Lend/Lease* craft, PT.93 & 198 (both Higgins), were transferred to the R.N. from the U.S.N. as *target towers* in 1943. CT.31–33 were ex-R. Neth. N. MTBs.

SUBSIDIARY SERVICES

Harbour service: MGB.8.
Workshop: MGB.16.
Store carriers: MGB.13, 56, MTB.629.
High speed target: MGB.21, MTB.353, 354.
Target towing: MGB.60, 65, 91, 325, ex-PT.93, ex-PT.198, MTB.69, 70, 358, 359, 362.
Accommodation: MTB.685.
Air/Sea Rescue: MTB.682, 683, 684, 687, 744.

TORPEDO RECOVERY VESSELS

Admiralty type: TRV.1–8.

Displacement: 235 tons.
Dimensions: 95 (pp) 103 (oa) × $20\frac{3}{4}$ × 6 ft.
Machinery: 1-shaft Widdop diesel motor, B.H.P. 300 = $9\frac{1}{2}$ knots.
Armament: 1—20 mm. gun.
Complement: 12.

Notes.—Built 1945–47. In addition, there was a large number of twin-screw motor boats classed as TRV's.

BUILDERS.

G. L. Watson (Gainsborough): TRV.1, 5, 6, 7, 8.
Rowhedge Ironworks: TRV.2, 4.
Richards Ironworks (Lowestoft): TRV.3.

MISCELLANEOUS CRAFT

Thornycroft type: PAHLAWAN, PANGLIMA, PENINGAT, PANJI.

Displacement: 60 tons.
Dimensions: 76½ (oa) × 13½ × 4¾ ft.
Machinery: 3-shaft Thornycroft petrol & diesel motors, B.H.P. 780 = 16 knots.
Armament: 1—3 pdr., 1—.303 in. M.G. *Complement:* 10.

Notes.—Built 1939 for the Straits Settlements R.N.V.R. PENINGAT became a war loss in 1942 and the remainder were re-named ML.1102–1104 and were manned by the Burma R.N.V.R.

Vosper type: BLOODHOUND.

Displacement: 35 tons.
Dimensions: 68 × 19 × 3 ft.
Machinery: 2-shaft Lorraine-Orion petrol motors, B.H.P. 1,600 = 25 knots.
Armament: 1—21 in. T.T. *Complement:* 6.

Notes.—Built 1937 as a tender for the VERNON establishment.

Hired craft: KALAN (FY.008.)

Was a yacht, modelled on the 60-ft. British Power Boat MTB, which served as a base tender for ML training.

Experimental type: TARRET.

Was a steel built 100-ft. MTB powered by two Davey Paxman diesel motors for a speed of 30 knots, and completed in 1940. She entered service as an MA/SB and was later used for training.

Captured craft: Ex-MAS.452.

Was an Italian MTB captured in 1941 and officially referred to as XMAS!

Admiralty type: PAMELA & UNA

40 tons: 52 (oa) × 13 × 2¼ ft.: 3-shaft Ford petrol motors, B.H.P. 195-10 knots: 1-40 mm., 1-20 mm., 4—.303 in. (2×2) M.Gs.

Notes.—Built 1945 by the Royal Engineers on Chindwin River to assist in military operations in Burma. Two others, one of which had been laid down, were cancelled.

BUILDERS:

Cantieri Baglietto (Varazze): MAS.452.
British Power Boat (Hythe): KALAN.
Swan Hunter & Wigham Richardson (Wallsend): TARRET.
Thornycroft (Singapore): PAHLAWAN, PANGLIMA, PENINGAT, PANJI.
Vosper (Portsmouth): BLOODHOUND.

PENNANT NUMBERS

The following flag superiors were worn followed by the boat number:—

MTB's:	Flag V	HDML's:	Flag Q (see *Note 1*)
CMB's:	Flag S	MMS's:	FY pennant (see *Note 3*)
MA/SB's:	Flag S	MFV's:	FY pennant
MGB's:	Flag S	MAC's:	Flag J
SGB's:	Flag S (see *Note 2*)	DCMB:	Flag P
ML's:	Flag Q	CT's:	Flag P

Note 1: HDML.1001–1099 used Q.01–Q.99.
Note 2: Later changed to flag 8.
Note 3: R.C.N. MMS's used flag J.

DEPLOYMENT

Soon after the outbreak of the war, dispositions were as follows:
Home Waters: MA/SB's 1 to 5; MTB's 22, 40K, 100 and 102.
Mediterranean: 1st. MTB Flotilla (MTB's 1 to 5 & 14 to 19).
China: 2nd MTB Flotilla (MTB's 7 to 12, 26, 27).

The 1st MTB Flotilla left the Mediterranean early in 1940 and was based on Harwich, and until Italy entered the war, the only Coastal Forces craft in the Mediterranean was MA/SB No. 2.

Coastal Forces

Some idea of the growth of Coastal Forces can be obtained by glancing through the dispositions for January 1945.
[By this time, the ML flotillas numbered from 60 to 69 comprised Rescue Motor Launches (RMLs), and those from 101 upwards, comprised Harbour Defence Motor Launches (HDMLs)].

Plymouth Command
(Ports westward from Dartmouth):
5 MTB's; 4th & 10th ML Flotillas (18 boats); 6 ML's unallocated; 63rd Flotilla (8 RML's); 103rd Flotilla (8 HDML's).

W. Approaches Command
(West Coast Ports from Swansea to N.W. Scotland and including N. Ireland):
20 MTB's; 1 MA/SB; 2 MGB's; 16th & 18th ML Flotillas (8 boats); 5 ML's unallocated; 65th Flotilla (8 RML's); 105th Flotilla (6 HDML's).

Portsmouth Command
(South coast Portland to Newhaven):
12th, 23rd, 66th MTB Flotillas (21 boats); 17 MTB's unallocated; 15th MGB Flotilla (6 boats); 5 MGBs. unallocated; 1st SGB Flotilla (6 boats); 2nd, 7th, 20th, 23rd ML Flotillas (34 boats); 61st Flotilla (8 RML's); 105th, 138th, 149th, 150th, 152nd Flotillas (34 HDML's) ; 3 HDML's unallocated.

French & Belgian Coast: 11th ML Flotilla (9 boats).
Dover Command: 9th, 51st MTB Flotillas (11 boats); 50th, 52nd ML Flotillas (8 boats).

Nore Command
(East coast, Sheerness to Grimsby):
1st, 3rd, 4th, 8th, 11th, 21st, 22nd, 29th, 30th, 31st, 32nd, 33rd, 35th, 50th, 52nd, 53rd, 55th, 58th, 63rd, 64th, 65th, 67th MTB Flotillas (198 boats); 12 MTB's unallocated; 2 MGB's; 1st, 5th, 6th, 15th, 19th, 21st, 32nd, 33rd, 51st ML Flotillas (70 boats); 60th Flotilla (8 RML's); 68th Flotilla (10 RML's); 151st, 153rd, 154th, 155th Flotillas (22 HDML's).

Rosyth Command
(East coast, North Shields to Scapa Flow and Iceland):
54th MTB Flotilla (15 boats); 1 MA/SB; 8 RML's; 106th, 107th, 109th ML Flotillas (16 HDML's).

Mediterranean: 7th, 10th, 19th, 20th, 24th, 27th, 28th, 59th MTB Flotillas (60 boats); 56th, 57th, 60th MTB/MGB Flotillas (10 MTB's & 10 MGB's); 45th MGB Flotilla (4 boats); 4 MGB's unallocated; 3rd, 8th, 9th, 22nd, 24th, 25th, 28th, 29th, 31st, 41st, 42nd, 43rd, 44th ML Flotillas (88 boats); 101st, 102nd, 111th, 113th, 114th, 117th, 134th, 139th, 140th, 141st, 142nd, Flotillas (84 HDML's).

West Africa Command
(Dakar and ports in British W. Africa):
12th, 17th, 26th, 27th ML Flotillas (23 boats); 104th, 108th, 123rd Flotillas (23 HDML's).

South Atlantic Command
(Cape and Durban):
119th, 135th ML Flotillas (11 HDML's); 6 HDMLS unallocated.

East Indies
(East Africa, India, Ceylon and R.I.N.):
16th, 17th MTB Flotillas (20 boats); 13th, 14th, 34th, 36th to 40th, 45th, 49th, 55th, 56th, 59th ML Flotillas (98 boats); 107th, 110th, 112th, 120th, 121st, 122nd, 130th, 136th, 137th, 145th, 146th Flotillas (67 HDML's).

South West Pacific
(R.A.N. and R.N.Z.N.):
80th, 81st ML Flotillas (12 boats); 124th, 125th, 127th, 128th, 129th, 131st, 132nd, 133rd Flotillas (44 HDML's); 33 HDML's unallocated.

R.C.N. (Pacific Coast): 75th ML Flotilla (9 boats).

R.C.N. (Atlantic Coast): 70th to 73rd, 76th to 79th, 82nd ML Flotillas (61 boats).

W. Atlantic Command
(Bermuda & Trinidad):
30th, 47th ML Flotillas (18 boats); 116th, 118th Flotillas (14 HDML's).

Reserve Fleet
(Home Ports):
43 MTB's; 19 MGB's; 15 MA/SB's.

Motor Minesweepers

Only three of these were in service in September 1939, but by the time the war ended this number had grown to more than 400.

Their dispositions for January 1945 were as follows:

Plymouth Command: 101st & 142nd M/S Flotillas (16 MMS's); 6 MMS's unallocated.

W. Approaches Command: 107th, 109th, & 141st Flotillas (9 MMS's); 180th & 181st Flotillas (12 BYMS's).

Portsmouth Command: 106th, 115th & 135th Flotillas (24 MMS's).

French & Belgian Coasts: 104th, 118th, 119th, 143rd & 147th Flotillas (40 MMS's); 159th, 167th & 168th Flotillas (22 BYMS's).

Dover Command: 113th, 144th & 204th Flotillas (24 MMS's); 169th Flotilla (7 BYMS's).

Nore Command: 102nd, 110th, 117th, 131st, 132nd, 138th, 201st, 202nd, 203rd, 206th & 207th Flotillas (86 MMS's); 150th, 157th, 163rd, 165th & 170th Flotillas (40 BYMS's); 197th, 198th & 199th M/S Groups (15 MFV's).

Rosyth Command: 116th, 137th, 145th & 205th Flotillas (23 MMS's); 3 MMS's. unallocated.

Mediterranean: 103rd, 105th, 108th, 111th, 114th & 120th Flotillas (35 MMS's); 151st, 152nd, 153rd, 156th, 160th & 162nd Flotillas (34 BYMS's); 251st Flotilla (15 ZZ Craft).

W. Africa Command: 154th & 164th Flotillas (4 BYMS's).

E. Indies: 122nd Flotilla (8 MMS's); 9 MMS's unallocated; 151st (part), 152nd (part), 161st & 166th Flotillas (23 BYMS's).

R.C.N. Pacific: 8 MMS's.

R.C.N. Atlantic: 2 MMS's.

Notes.—For the various ports under each " Command ", see the dispositions for Coastal Forces.

The coastal transport FT.22, was armed with four 20 mm. guns and belonged to a group of vessels loaned to the R.N. from the U.S.N. [*Courtesy, U.S. Navy*

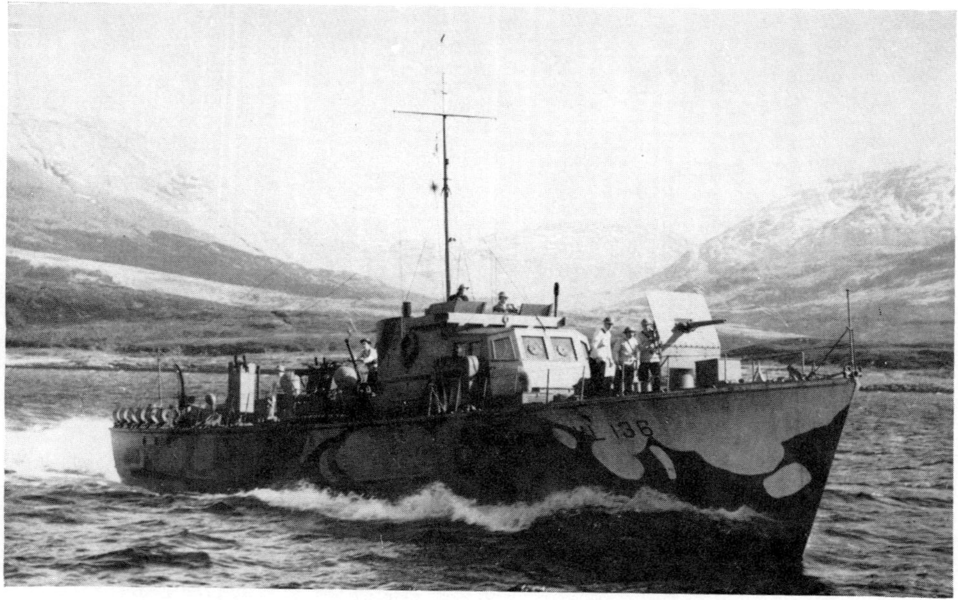

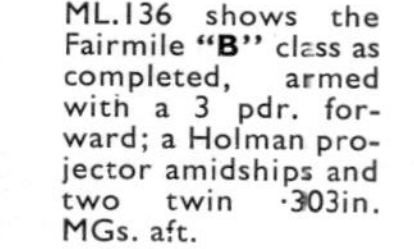

ML.136 shows the Fairmile **"B"** class as completed, armed with a 3 pdr. forward; a Holman projector amidships and two twin ·303in. MGs. aft.

[*I.W.M.*

PART EIGHT

Landing Craft

The Sicilian landings, 1943. In the foreground (from left to right) the boom carrier Leonian, the LSI(S) Prince Baudouin, the LSI(H) Ulster Monarch, and the LSI(M) Queen Emma and, in the background the aircraft carrier H.M.S. Indomitable, the cruiser H.M.S. Orion and the battleship H.M.S. Rodney. [*P. A. Vicary*

The first landings in North Africa, 1942. Loading an LCV off Oran. [I.W.M.

DEVELOPMENT OF LANDING SHIPS & LANDING CRAFTS

BOTH landing ships and landing craft had a common object: that of transporting military forces and their equipment overseas and putting them ashore on a stretch of open, enemy coast. Later, as invasion progressed and ports and harbours were captured, the need for them would decline as their work could then be undertaken by merchant ships; but initially, to secure a beachhead, landing craft were indispensable to an invading army.

The original distinction between landing ships and landing craft were that the former were capable of making a sea passage on their own bottoms, while the latter would have to be transported to the invasion area and put into the sea. As landing craft grew in size many were able to make passages on the open sea.

Landing ships and landing craft each fell into three main groups. Both types were designed to carry (a) military personnel and, (b) military equipment; the third group of landing *ships* was mainly composed of vessels designed to transport landing craft plus a few specialised vessels, while the third group of landing *craft* was principally made up of support craft together with a smaller number of specialised craft. Whereas all basic types of landing craft were designed to beach, this did not apply to landing ships where only those designed to carry equipment were able to do so. This latter group, and all landing craft, were specially designed and built during the war years while the remaining landing ships, except the LSDs, were either naval or mercantile conversions.

Only the following landing craft prototypes had been built, or laid down before the outbreak of the Second World War, *viz:—*

Admiralty type: MLC.1
16 tons: 40 × 12 × 1¼ ft.: Hotchkiss jet propulsion, 4¾ knots.

Notes:—Built 1926 by White. Could carry a 100 troops.

Admiralty type: MLC.10
20/32 tons: 40 (pp) 42½ (oa) × 12 × 1½ ft.: Gill jet propulsion, 5 knots.

Notes:—Built 1929 by Rowhedge Ironworks. Could carry either 1 @ 12t. tank or 100 troops.

Fleming type: MLC.50
8 tons: 35 (pp) 37 (oa) × 9½ × 1½ ft.: 2-shaft petrol motors, B.H.P. 130 = 10 knots.

Notes:—Built 1939 of alloy construction. Later modified as prototype support craft.

Thornycroft type: MLC.51
Built 1939 and generally similar to MLC.50 but of wooden construction and had ¼ in. protective plating. Later modified as prototype support craft.

From these prototypes stemmed the earliest landing craft. MLC.1 although originally built as a personnel carrier had the design requirements enlarged with MLC.10 to accommodate a 12-ton tank. This resulted in the MLC (1) which adopted screw propulsion for higher speed and was put into series production in 1939. Similarly, experience gained with MLC.50 and 51, which were not entirely satisfactory on trials, resulted in the Admiralty designed ALC, whose design was largely based on the Thornycroft craft, also being put into series production in 1939. Both the MLC and the ALC were intended to be transported shipboard to the selected theatre of operations and met basic military requirements for craft that could land a tank or a platoon of troops. If this would appear somewhat meagre preparations for the forthcoming struggle it is only fair to point out that pre-war British planning did not envisage large scale invasions of enemy held territory, where such landings would be stiffly opposed, but only to meet the general requirement outlined above.

Later, in 1942, these and other landing craft built in the intervening years, had their letter designations reversed and then became known as LCMs, LCAs, etc., and this latter form, which was preserved post-war, has been used throughout. Unless otherwise stated all craft are of steel construction: wood only being used for the smaller craft designed to carry personnel and derivations thereof.

LANDING SHIPS INFANTRY (LSI)

THE LSIs were all mercantile conversions and were graded, according to size, into LSI (L), LSI (M), LSI (S), and LSI (H). The bulk of invading forces were carried in them to the beachhead, when they were then transferred to the embarked LCAs for the final run-in. LSIs were indispensable when the shore-to-shore distances involved were long (such as in Pacific operations) but for shorter distances (as in the European landings) a proportion of the invading forces, depending on requirements, could be carried over in minor landing craft which could then beach direct: but for the economical movement of large bodies of troops the LSI gave the best return.

The LSI (L)s were adapted from intermediate passenger and cargo liners with a good turn of speed and were capable of serving anywhere. The largest uniform group were the twelve Maritime Commission C1-S-AY1 type received under *Lend/Lease* but the three **Glens** were the most battleworthy conversions although considerably mutilated in the process. The LSI (M)s and LSI (S)s had been built for commercial operation in sheltered waters and had to be strengthened and made more sea-worthy for world-wide use. They were fast ships but their troop capacity was proportionally small. Whereas nearly all the LSIs carried their LCAs under gravity davits it was impractical to fit these davits into some small LSIs. Their LCAs were consequently carried under projecting spurs and they were classed as LSI (H)s.

The sole disadvantage of the gravity davits were that they could only accommodate a single LCA, and this led to the development of luffing davits, connected by a cross beam at their heads, which could handle three LCAs. Their application was limited to LSI (L)s and only the three **Glens** were so fitted.

For large scale operations large and intermediate liners were temporarily fitted out as LSIs but remained mercantile manned and were operated by the M.O.W.T.

LSI (L)

P.No.	Name	Builder Hull: engine	Launched	Fate

Displacement: 8,108 tons *gross*.
Dimensions: $430\frac{1}{2}$ (pp) 448 (oa) × $60\frac{1}{4}$ × 25 ft.
Machinery: 2-shaft Diesel motors, B.H.P. 10,000 = $15\frac{1}{2}$ knots.

P.No.	Name	Builder	Launched	Fate
F.95	WESTRALIA (R.A.N.)	Harland & Wolff (Govan)	25. 4.29	Ex-A.M.C.; returned 1946.

Notes:—Converted 1943 and could carry 933 troops.

Displacement: 9,890 tons *gross:*
Dimensions: $471\frac{1}{4}$ (pp) $486\frac{1}{2}$ (oa) × $64\frac{1}{4}$ × 27 ft.
Machinery: 2-shaft geared Turbines, S.H.P. 12,000 = 17 knots.
Armament: 1—6 in., 1—12 pdr. A.A., 12—20 mm. A.A. (12 × 1) guns.
Complement: 297.

P.No.	Name	Builder	Launched	Fate
F.132	KEREN (ex-R.N. Hydra, ex-Kenya)	Stephen	27. 8.30	Returned 8/48.
F.128	KARANJA	Stephen	18.12.30	Ex-A.B.V.; lost 12/11/42.

Notes:—Converted 1942 and could carry 1,500 troops, two LCMs, two LCP(L)s, ten LCP(S)s, one LCS(M), and nine LCAs.

Displacement: 10,856 tons *gross*.
Dimensions: $463\frac{1}{2}$ (pp) 482 (oa) × $66\frac{1}{4}$ × 24 ft.
Machinery: 2-shaft Diesel motors, B.H.P. 10,000 = 16 knots.

Armament: 1—12 pdr. A.A., 6—40 mm. A.A. (6 × 1), 8—20 mm. A.A. (8 × 1) guns.
Complement: 350.

F.48	MANOORA (R.A.N.)	Stephen: Kincaid	25.10.34	Ex-A.M.C.; returned 1946.

Notes:—Converted 1942 and could carry 1,228 troops, four LCM(l)s, and eight LCAs.

Displacement: 10,985 tons *gross*.
Dimensions: 460 (pp) 478 (oa) × 66¼ × 24¼ ft.
Machinery: 2-shaft Diesel motors, B.H.P. 10,000 = 17 knots.
Armament: 1—4 in., 2—12 pdr. A.A. (2 × 1), 10—20 mm. A.A. (10 × 1) guns.
Complement: 350.

F.23	KANIMBLA (R.A.N.)	Harland & Wolff	12.12.35	Ex-A.M.C.; returned 1951.

Notes:—Converted 1943 and could carry 1,381 troops, and ten LCAs.

Displacement: 9,800 tons *gross*.
Dimensions: 475 (pp) 507 (oa) × 66½ × 30½ ft.
Machinery: 2-shaft Diesel motors, B.H.P. 12,000 = 18 knots.
Armament: 6—4 in. A.A. (3 × 2), 4—2 pdr. A.A. (4 × 1), 8—20 mm. A.A. (8 × 1) except GLENGYLE 8—2 pdr. A.A. (2 × 4), 12—20 mm. A.A. (12 × 1) guns.
Complement: 523.

4.250	GLENEARN (9,784 t.g.)	Caledon: Burmeister & Wain	29. 6.38	Returned 1946.
4.196	GLENGYLE (9,919 t.g.)	Caledon	18. 7.39	Returned 1946.
4.256	GLENROY (9,809 t.g.)	Scotts: Burmeister & Wain	15. 8.38	Returned 1946.

Notes:—Together with sister ship BRECONSHIRE were requisitioned as commissioned transports in 1939 and converted to LSI(L)s in 1941. Could carry 1,087 troops (697 in GLENGYLE), three LCMs, and twenty-four LCAs. Other sister ships taken over were the escort carrier ACTIVITY (ex-Telemachus) and the German raider MEERSBERG (ex-Glengarry) which was captured incomplete at Copenhagen.

Displacement: 5,319 tons *gross*.
Dimensions: 400 (pp) 414¾ (oa) × 52 × 25¼ ft.
Machinery: 1-shaft Reciprocating (VTE), N.H.P. 912 = 14 knots.

F.120	EL HIND	Lithgows: Kincaid	14. 4.38	Lost 14/4/44.

Displacement: 7,250 tons *gross*.
Dimensions: 457 (pp) 487¾ (oa) × 62¾ × 24¼ ft.
Machinery: 2-shaft Reciprocating (VTE) and exhaust geared turbine, I.H.P. 8,300 = 17 knots.

Left: The Karanja was converted from an ABV to an LSI(L) and was armed with a 6 in. and a 12 pdr. A.A. gun on the poop. She carried two LCM(I).s on deck forward and LCA's. along either side. [*I.W.M.*

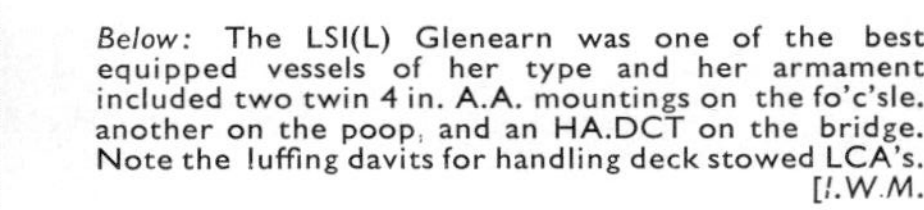

Below: The LSI(L) Glenearn was one of the best equipped vessels of her type and her armament included two twin 4 in. A.A. mountings on the fo'c'sle. another on the poop, and an HA.DCT on the bridge. Note the luffing davits for handling deck stowed LCA's. [*I.W.M.*

Armament: 1—4 in., 1—12 pdr. A.A., 1—40 mm. A.A., 10—20 mm. A.A. (10 × 1) guns.
Complement: 300.

4.420	LAMONT (ex-Clan Lamont)	Greenock: Kincaid	23. 3.39	ARD PATRICK (1945); returned 1946.

Notes:—Converted 1942 and could carry 800, troops, two LCP(S)s, and eighteen LCAs. Sister ship to aircraft transports ATHENE (ex-Clan Brodie), ENGADINE (ex-Clan Buchanan), and depot ship BONAVENTURE (ex-Clan Davidson).

Displacement: 12,864 tons.
Dimensions: 425 (pp) 450¼ (oa) × 61¼ × 25 ft.
Machinery: 1-shaft Diesel motor, B.H.P. 4,320 = 15 knots.

4.422	PAMPAS (ii) (ex-Parramatta)	Harland & Wolff	. .43	PERSIMMON (1944); returned 8/46.

Notes:—Converted while completing and could carry 700 troops, one LCM, and eighteen LCAs.

U.S. Maritime Commission C1-S-AY1 type

Displacement: 11,650 tons.
Dimensions: 396¼ (pp) 417¾ (oa) × 60 × 25½ ft.
Machinery: 1-shaft geared Turbines, S.H.P. 4,400 = 14 knots.
Armament: 1—4 in., 1—12 pdr. A.A., 12—20 mm. A.A. (12 × 1) guns.
Complement: 250.

Notes:—Made available to the MOWT under *Lend/Lease* on completion and were given *Empire* names and served as mercantile LSI(L)s. Transfered to the R.N. in 1944 when most were renamed.

F.184	EMPIRE ANVIL (ex-Cape Argos)	Consolidated Steel Corp.	14.10.43	ROCKSAND (1944); returned MOWT 6/46.
F.170	EMPIRE ARQUEBUS (ex-Cape St. Vincent)	,,	16.11.43	CICERO (1945), mercantile AL SUDAN (1946).
F.161	EMPIRE BATTLE-AXE (ex-Cape Berkley)	,,	12. 7.43	DONOVAN (1946); returned MOWT 1946
F.163	EMPIRE BROAD-SWORD (ex-Cape Marshall)	,,	16. 8.43	Lost 2/7/44.
F.183	EMPIRE CROSS-BOW (ex-Cape Washington)	,,	30.11.43	SAINFOIN (1944); returned MOWT 9/46.
F.162	EMPIRE CUTLASS (ex-Cape Compass)	,,	29. 7.43	SANSOVINO (1945); returned MOWT 6/46.
F.123	EMPIRE GAUNTLET (ex-Cape Comorin)	,,	23.11.43	SEFTON (1944); returned MOWT 9/46.
F.160	EMPIRE HALBERD (ex-Cape Gregory)	,,	24. 7.43	SILVIO (1944); returned MOWT 1945.
F.	EMPIRE JAVELIN (ex-Cape Lobos)	,,	25.10.43	Lost 28/12/44.
F.	EMPIRE LANCE (ex-Cape) Pine	,,	28. 8.43	SIR HUGO (1945); returned MOWT 1945.

Left: Unmistakably a former Clan liner, the LSI(L) Lamont was later re-named Ard Patrick. She was armed with a 12 pdr. A.A. gun on the fo'c'sle and a 4 in. and 40 mm. A.A. guns aft on the poop. Her LCA's were double banked along the sides or stowed on deck. [*I.W.M.*

Right: The LSI(L) Empire Mace belonged to a group of twelve vessels made available to the R.N. under *Lend/Lease.* [*I.W.M.*

F.171	EMPIRE MACE (ex-Cape St. Roque)	Consolidated Steel Corp.	8. 9.43	GALITEEMORE (1945); mercantile MISR (1946).
F.	EMPIRE RAPIER (ex-Cape Turner)	,,	21. 9.43	Returned 1946.
F.172	EMPIRE SPEARHEAD (ex-Cape Girardeau)	,,	7.11.43	Returned 1946.

The following mercantile LSI (L)s were temporarily fitted out between 1942–44 for specific operations, a few on more than one occasion, but were not generally kept long in this role.

Name	Gross tonnage/ year built
ANDES	25,800/39
ASCANIA*	14,013/25
BARPETA	3,194/14
BATORY (Polish)	14,287/36
BRITANNIC	26,943/30
CANTON*	15,784/38
CAPETOWN CASTLE	27,000/38
CHESHIRE*	10,552/27
CIRCASIA*	11,136/37
DERBYSHIRE*	11,660/35
DEVONSHIRE	11,100/39
DILWARA	11,080/36
DUCHESS OF BEDFORD	20,123/28
DUCHESS OF RICHMOND	20,027/28 20,121/29
DUCHESS OF YORK	
DUNERA	11,162/37
DURBAN CASTLE	17,388/38
EMPIRE NIGER (ex-Frauenfels)	7,487/20
EMPIRE PRIDE	9,248/41
EMPIRE TUGELA (ex-Wartenfels)	6,181/21
EMPRESS OF SCOTLAND (ex-Empress of Japan)	26,032/30
ETTERICK	11,279/38
LANCASHIRE	9,557/17

Name	Gross tonnage/ year built
LLANGIBBY CASTLE	11,951/29
LLANSTEPHAN CASTLE	11,299/14
MAURETANIA	35,739/39
MONOWAI* (ex-Razmak)	10,852/25
MONARCH OF BERMUDA	22,424/31
ORION	23,371/35
ORONTES	20,097/29
OTRANTO	20,026/25
PAMPAS (i) (lost 26/3/42)	5,415/41
REINA DEL PACIFICO	17,702/31
RUYS (Netherlands)	14,155/37
SOBIESKI (Polish)	11,030/39
STIRLING CASTLE	25,550/36
STRATHAIRD	22,281/32
STRATHEDEN	23,722/37
STRATHMORE	23,428/35
STRATHNAVER	22,283/31
TEGELBERG (Netherlands)	14,150/37
VICEROY OF INDIA	19,627/29
WARWICK CASTLE	20,107/30
WINCHESTER CASTLE	20,012/30
WORCESTERSHIRE*	11,402/31

* ex-A.M.Cs.

LSI (M)

Displacement: 6,890 tons *gross*.
Dimensions: 366¼ (pp) 385 (oa) × 57 × 18½ ft.

Above: The Monowai was a mercantile LSI(L) and was armed with a 4 in. and two 12 pdr. A.A. guns aft, two 2 pdr. A.A. (2 × 1) before the bridge, two 40 mm. A.A. abreast the fore-funnel, eight 20 mm. A.A. (8 × 1), and eight RP's. (2 × 4). Her LCA's were double banked along each side. [*I.W.M.*

Below: The mercantile LSI(L) Tegelberg was a former Netherlands liner. [*I.W.M.*

Above: The Prince David was converted from an AMC to an LSI(M) and was fitted with two LCM(1)s. and six LCAs. under gravity davits. She was armed with a twin 4 in. A.A. mounting (controlled by an HA.DCT on the bridge), a single 40 mm. A.A. gun forward, and six 20 mm. A.A (6 × 1) abaft the bridge. [*I.W.M.*

Below: The LSI(M) Queen Emma carried two LCM(1)s. and six LCAs. under davits, 372 troops, and was armed with two 12 pdr. A.A., two 2 pdr. A.A., and four 20 mm. A.A. guns. [*P. A. Vicary*

Machinery: 2-shaft geared Turbines, S.H.P. 19,500 = $22\frac{1}{4}$ knots.
Armament: 2—4 in. A.A. (1 × 2), 1—40 mm. A.A., 6—20 mm. A.A. (6 × 1) guns. *Complement:* 200

F.89	PRINCE DAVID	Cammell Laird	12. 2.30	Mercantile CHARLTON MONARCH (1948).
F.70	PRINCE HENRY	Cammell Laird	17. 1.30	Mercantile EMPIRE PARKSTONE (1946).

Notes:—Ex-A.M.C. converted in 1943 and could carry 444 troops, two LCM(l)s, or LCM(3)s, one LCS(M), and five LCP(L)s., or LCAs.

Displacement: 4,136 tons *gross.*
Dimensions: $350\frac{1}{4}$ (pp) 380 (oa) × $47\frac{1}{4}$ × 15 ft.
Machinery: 2-shaft Diesel motors, B.H.P. 12,700 = 23 knots.
Armament: 2—12 pdr. A.A. (2 × 1), 2—2 pdr. A.A. (2 × 1), 6—20 mm. A.A. (6 × 1) guns. *Complement* 227.

4.44	PRINCESS BEATRIX	de Schelde	25. 3.39	Returned 4/46.
4.180	QUEEN EMMA (ex-Koningin Emma)	de Schelde	14. 1.39	Returned 4/46.

Notes:—Converted 1942 and could carry 372 troops, two LCM(l)s, and six LCAs, or LCS(M)s.

LSI (S)

Displacement: 2,950 tons *gross.*
Dimensions: 347 (pp) $359\frac{1}{2}$ (oa) × $46\frac{1}{4}$ × 13 ft.
Machinery: 2-shaft geared Turbines, S.H.P. 15,400 = 24 knots.
Armament: 2—12 pdr. A.A. (2 × 1), 2—2 pdr. A.A. (2 × 1), 6—20 mm. A.A. (6 × 1) guns. *Complement:* 207.

4.120	PRINCE CHARLES	Cockerill	28. 6.30	Returned 2/45.
4.251	PRINCE LEOPOLD	Cockerill	19.11.29	Lost 29/7/44.
4.226	PRINSES ASTRID	Cockerill	20. 7.29	Returned 4/46.
4.238	PRINSES JOSEPHINE CHARLOTTE	Cockerill	12. 3.30	Returned 1945.

Notes:—Converted 1941 and could carry 250 troops and eight LCP(L)s, or LCS(M)s or LCAs.

Displacement: 3,219 tons *gross.*
Dimensions: 360 (pp) 370 (oa) × 46 × 14 ft.
Machinery: 2-shaft Diesel motors, B.H.P. 17,000 = 23 knots.
Armament: 2—12 pdr. A.A. (2 × 1), 2—2 pdr. A.A. (2 × 1), 6—20 mm. A.A. (6 × 1) guns. *Complement:* 200.

4.88	PRINCE BAUDOUIN	Cockerill	16. 9.33	Returned 1945.

Notes:—Converted 1942 and could carry 196 troops, and eight LCAs.

The LSI(S) Prinses Josephine Charlotte was one of the smaller Belgian Channel packets and was equipped with eight LCAs. and could carry 250 troops. [I.W.M.

Displacement: 2,938 tons *gross*.
Dimensions: 360 (pp) 370 (oa) × 46 × 13¾ ft.
Machinery: 2-shaft Diesel motors, B.H.P. 17,000 = 23 knots.
Armament: 2—12 pdr. A.A. (2 × 1), 2—2 pdr. A.A. (2 × 1), 6—20 mm. A.A. (6 × 1) guns.
Complement: 200.

4.35	PRINS ALBERT PRINCE PHILLIPE	Cockerill Cockerill	23. 4.37 29. 9.39	Returned 4/46. Lost 15/7/41.

Notes:—Converted 1941 and could carry 196 and 250 troops respectively, and eight LCAs.

The following mercantile LSI (S)s were fitted out in 1943

P.No.	Name	Gross tonnage/ year built
4.413	AMSTERDAM	4,220/30
4.419	PRINCESS MARGARET	2,552/31

LSI (H)

Displacement: 1,929 tons *gross*.
Dimensions: 316 (pp) 323 (oa) × 41 × 15¾d. ft.
Machinery: 3-shaft Turbines, S.H.P. 11,000 = 22 knots.

4.21	LAIRDS ISLE (ex-Riviera)	Denny	1. 4.11	Returned 1945.

Notes:—Ex-T.S., ex-A.B.V., converted 1944.

Displacement: 1,952 tons *gross*.
Dimensions: 282¼ (pp) 291½ (oa) × 40 × 13¼ ft.
Machinery: 2-shaft geared Turbines, S.H.P. 5,838 = 18 knots.
Armament: 6—20 mm. A.A. (6 × 1) guns.
Complement: 120.

4.255	ST. HELIER	Clydebank	26. 3.25	Returned 1945.

Notes:—Converted 1942 and could carry 180 troops and six LCAs.

Displacement: 2,701 tons *gross*.
Dimensions: 329½ (pp) 337 (oa) × 45 × 17½d. ft.
Machinery: 2-shaft geared Turbines, S.H.P. 8,000 = 23½ knots.

4.262	ISLE OF THANET	Denny	23. 4.25	Returned 1945.

Notes:—Ex-F.A.A. target ship, converted 1943.

Displacement: 2,294 tons *gross*.
Dimensions: 297¾ (pp) 306 (oa) × 38¾ × 15¾d. ft.
Machinery: 2-shaft geared Turbines, S.H.P. 15,000 = 21 knots.
Armament: 1—12 pdr. A.A., 4—20 mm. A.A. (4 × 1) guns.
Complement: 119

4.249	BRIGADIER (ex-Worthing)	Denny	3. 5.28	Returned 1946.

Notes:—Ex-F.A.A. target ship, converted 1942 and could carry 180 troops and six LCAs.

Left: The LSI(H) St. Helier in common with all the smaller LSIs. to which gravity or luffings davits could not be fitted carried her LCAs. under radial davits, or projecting spurs in some vessels, with no mechanical means of hoisting or lowering. She was only lightly armed with six 20 mm. A.A. guns (6 × 1) sited before the bridge, abaft the funnel, and aft on the poop. [*I.W.M.*

Right: The LSI(H) Ulster Monarch carried her LCAs under projecting spurs and was armed with two 2 pdr. A.A. (2 × 1) guns on the fo'c'sle, four 20 mm. A.A. (4 × 1) along the boat deck, and a 12 pdr. A.A. on the poop. [*I.W.M.*

Displacement: 3,791 tons *gross*.
Dimensions: 346 (pp) 359 (oa) × 46¼ × 15½ ft.
Machinery: 2-shaft Diesel motors, B.H.P. 6,350 = 18 knots.
Armament: 1—12 pdr. A.A., 2—2 pdr. A.A. (2 × 1), 4—20 mm. A.A. (4 × 1) guns.
Complement: 130.

F.69	ULSTER MONARCH	Harland & Wolff	24. 1.29	Returned 10/45.

Notes:—Converted 1942 and could carry 580 troops, six LCAs and 150 t.d.w.

Displacement: 2,143 tons *gross*.
Dimensions: 296½ (pp) 306 (oa) × 42 × 14¼ ft.
Machinery: 2-shaft geared Turbines, S.H.P. 5,500 = 19½ knots

4.245	ISLE OF GUERNSEY	Denny	17.12.29	Returned 1945.

Notes:—Converted 1944.

Displacement: 3,743 tons *gross*.
Dimensions: 339¼ (pp) 358 (oa) × 52¼ × 18d. ft.
Machinery: 2-shaft geared Turbines, S.H.P. 10,000 = 21 knots.
Armament: 1—12 pdr. A.A., 8—20 mm. A.A. (8 × 1) guns.
Complement: 120.

4,400	DUKE OF WELLINGTON (ex-Duke of York)	Harland & Wolff	7. 3.35	Returned 1945.

Notes:—Converted 1942 and could carry 250 troops and ten LCAs.

Displacement: 3,250 tons *gross*.
Dimensions: 328 (pp) 339½ (oa) × 47¾ × 14 ft.
Machinery: 2-shaft Diesel motors, B.H.P. 7,500 = 16 knots.
Armament: 1—12 pdr. A.A., ROYAL SCOTSMAN 4/ROYAL ULSTERMAN 5—20 mm A.A. (4/5 × 1) guns.
Complement: 236.

F.115	ROYAL SCOTSMAN (3,288 t.g.)	Harland & Wolff	11. 3.36	Returned 1945.
F.63	ROYAL ULSTERMAN (3,244 t.g.)	Harland & Wolff	10. 3.36	Returned 1945.

Notes:—Converted 1942 and could carry 830 troops, six LCAs, and 100 t.d.w.

Displacement: 4,178 tons *gross*.
Dimensions: 336½ (pp) 347½ (oa) × 50 × 12½ ft.
Machinery: 2-shaft geared Turbines, S.H.P. 11,000 = 22 knots.
Armament: 1—12 pdr. A.A., 4—20 mm. A.A. (4 × 1) guns.
Complement: 146.

4.283	INVICTA	Denny	14.12.39.	Returned M.O.W.T.12/45.

Notes:—Requisitioned while building and could carry 250 troops and six LCAs.

Above: The LSI(H) Duke of Wellington had special tripod davits from which her LCAs. were hung. Note SW.RDF on the foremast. [*I.W.M.*

Below: The LSI(H) Royal Scotsman was also fitted with projecting spurs as a result of her high free-board amidships. [*I.W.M.*

The following mercantile LSI(H)s were fitted out between 1942–43:—

P.No.	Name	Gross tonnage/ year built	P.No.	Name	Gross tonnage/ year built
4.412	BEN-MY-CHREE	2,586/27	4.248	MAID OF ORLEANS	2,386/18
4.96	BIARRITZ *	2,388/15	4.127	MECKLEN-BURG	2,907/22
4.107	CANTERBURY *	2,910/29	4.414	PRINCESS MAUD	2,883/34
4.42	DUKE OF ARGYLL	3,814/28	4.108	VICTORIA	1,641/07
4.421	DUKE OF ROTHESAY	3,812/28	4.423	VIKING (ex-R.N. Vindex, ex-Viking)	1,957/05
4.95	LADY OF MAN	3,104/30			

* Ex-F.A.A. target ships.

LANDING SHIP CARRIERS

FOR any large scale landing the build-up of stores and equipment ashore would be limited by the number of LCMs. available. Most LSI (L)s. carried one or two LCMs., hoisted out by derricks, but the numbers were clearly inadequate and means, therefore, had to be devised of transporting LCMs. to the beachhead. There was no time, in the first instance, to build special ships for this purpose and conversions were made from available merchant ships to LSSs., LSGs., and LSCs. until specifically built LSDs., were made available.

The LSSs., were adopted from two train ferries and carried three rows of LCMs. on the deck, which were launched from the centre row through a chute cut into the stern. LCMs., in the wing rows were first hauled forward, to where an athwartship trolley traversed them to the centre row, and were then hauled aft for launching. Although intended to transport LCMs., they were, in fact used to carry all types of minor landing craft. For the European landings a locomotive bridge was added aft and their capability extended to include the carriage of locomotives and rolling stock, as well as landing craft. Three R.F.A. tankers were selected for conversion to LCGs., and carried their LCMs. in three rows on deck, before and abaft the amidships bridge structure. A travelling gantry crane, with hinged booms extending well outboard, was set athwartships at each station and could plumb any of the three rows of LCMs. and carry them overside for lowering into the water. The LCMs., were stowed on deck rollers and were shifted longitudinally, to positions under the gantries, by means of whips. Although intended to serve in the dual role of tankers and landing craft carriers they were ultimately used exclusively for the latter role as its importance increased. One later sacrificed its oil carrying capacity entirely and was converted for the carriage of fresh water. The LSCs. were simple adaptations from standard heavy lift ships with the LCMs. deck-stowed and handled by the jumbo derricks. They were mercantile manned and operated by the MOWT.

The final outcome of LSCs. were the specially built LSDs. They were envisaged at a time when the LCTs. were well established but when the LSTs. were in the early stages of development and did not appear, at that stage, suitable for large scale production. Whereas the LCTs., for short hauls, could cope with the bulk of heavy military equipment it was considered that they themselves would have to be transported in a fully sea-going vessel to widen their spheres of activity. The size and weight of a loaded LCT., however, presented problems

The LSS Daffodil had a shute cut into her stern from which landing craft were launched. Her bridge and superstructure were arranged portal fashion over a long well deck which ran nearly the whole length of the hull. [*I.W.M.*

in launching and recovery which were impossible to meet unless they were locked in and out from a dock like structure. Therefore, as suggested by their designation, the LSDs. were basically self-propelled floating docks with a ship-shape bow added, the stern closed in by a gate, and the bridge and accommodation arranged portal fashion across the dock walls at the fore end. The dock walls were mainly taken up with ballast tanks (for flooding down), together with the necessary machinery and storage spaces, while the entire deep, cellular double bottom were given over to bunkers and further ballast tanks. Originally designed to stow two of the largest LCTs., they were never in fact used in this role as, by the time they were completed, the difficulties experienced with LST design had been most successfully overcome. They were, however, most advantageously employed as carriers for both major and minor landing craft and could, of course, also be used as mobile floating docks in which small craft repairs, could be affected.

The only other LSCs. were the LSTs. themselves. At the time they were ordered the Royal Navy was receiving large deliveries of LCT(5)s., from the United States, which could either be shipped in three parts as deck cargo on merchant ships or carried complete on deck by an LST: this latter being one of their design requirements. By listing the LST to *ca.* 11 degrees the LCT(5) was launched broadside into the water, a simple and commendable arrangement. As the theatre of operations moved from Europe to the Far East the LSTs. were alternatively fitted to carry seven LCM(7)s. which were stowed athwartships on deck and similarly launched by listing. They were hoisted in by a specially fitted heavy derrick, winched forward on trolleys, and then jacked down.

LSS

Displacement: 2,680 tons *gross.*
Dimensions: 350½ (pp) 363½ (oa) × 58¾ × 11 ft.
Machinery: 2-shaft Reciprocating (VTE), I.H.P. 3,000 = 11 knots.
Armament: 4—2 pdr. A.A. (4 × 1), 5—20 mm. A.A. (5 × 1) guns.
Complement: 200.

F.101	DAFFODIL (ex-Train Ferry No. 2)	Armstrongs: Wallsend	12. 9.17	Lost 18/3/45.
F.90	PRINCESS IRIS (ex-Train Ferry No. 1)	Armstrongs: Wallsend	3. 8.17	Mercantile ESSEX FERRY (1946), ESSEX FERRY II (1956); scrapped Grays 1957.

Notes:—Converted 1941 and could carry thirteen LCM(1)s. or nine LCM(3)s. and 105 troops.

LSG

Displacement: 16,750 tons.
Dimensions: 460 except ENNERDALE 462½ (pp) 483 (oa) × 59¼ × 26½ ft.
Machinery: 1-shaft Diesel motor, B.H.P. 3,500 except ENNERDALE Reciprocating (VTE), I.H.P. 3,000 = 12½ knots.
Armament: 1—4.7 in., 1—12 pdr., A.A. 4 except DERWENTDALE 5—20 mm. A.A. (4/5 × 1) guns.
Complement: 40.

X.14	DERWENTDALE	Harland & Wolff	12. 4.41	Mercantile IRVINGDALE I (1960).

Above: In this view of the LSG Derwentdale the projecting arms of the gantry before the bridge are turned-up in the housed position while the arms of the after gantry are down and extended well over the side. [*I.W.M.*

Below: Looking aft along the dock of the LSD Eastway showing eight M.F.Vs. being transported. [*I.W.M.*

X.51	DEWDALE	Cammell Laird	7. 2.41	Scrapped Antwerp 23/12/59.
X.73	ENNERDALE	Swan Hunter	. 1.41	Scrapped Faslane 14/4/59.

Notes:—Converted while building and could carry fifteen LCM(l)s., and 215 troops.

LSC

Displacement: 14,500 tons.
Dimensions: 416 (pp) 433½ (oa) × 66¾ × 26½ ft.
Machinery: 1-shaft Diesel motors, B.H.P. 2,500 = 11 knots.
Armament: 1—4 in., 1—12 pdr. A.A., 6—20 mm. A.A. (6 × 1) guns.
Complement: 40.

	EMPIRE CHARMAIN (7,513 t.g.)	V.A.(Barrow): Doxford	25.11.42	Mercantile VERCHARMAIN (1951).
	EMPIRE ELAINE (7,513 t.g.)	V.A.(Barrow): Doxford	30. 7.42	Mercantile JOHN LYRAS (1947).

Notes:—Adapted while building and could carry twenty-one LCM(l)s, and 295 troops.

LSD

Displacement: 4,270/7,930 tons.
Dimensions: 454 (pp) 457¾ (oa) × 72¼ × 17 ft.
Machinery: 2-shaft geared Turbines, S.H.P. 7,000 = 16 knots.
Armament: 1—3 in. D.P., 4—2 pdr. A.A. (4 × 1), 16—20 mm. A.A. (16 × 1) guns.
Complement: 290.

F.130	EASTWAY (ex-Battleaxe, ex-LSD. 9, ex-USN BAPM. 1)	Newport News	21. 5.34	Returned U.S.N. 5/47, R.H.N. NAFKRATOUSSA (1953).
F.140	HIGHWAY (ex-Claymore, ex-LSD 10, ex-USN BAPM. 2)	Newport News	19. 7.43	Returned U.S.N. 4/46.
F.142	NORTHWAY (ex-Cutlass, ex-LSD. 11, ex-USN BAPM. 3)	Newport News	18.11.43	Returned U.S.N. 1/47.
F.143	OCEANWAY (ex-Dagger, ex-LSD. 12, ex-USN BAPM. 4)	Newport News	29.12.43	Returned U.S.N. 1947.
F.144	PORTWAY (ex-Spear, ex-LSD. 13, ex-USN BAPM. 5)	Newport News	11. 4.44	Retained as U.S.N. CASA GRANDE.
F.145	SWASHWAY (ex-Sword, ex-LSD. 14, ex-USN BAPM. 6)	Newport News	10. 5.44	Retained as U.S.N. RUSHMORE.

F.146	WATERWAY (ex-LSD. 15, ex-USN BAPM. 7)	Newport News	25. 5.44	Retained as U.S.N. SHADWELL.

Notes:—Made available to the R.N. under *Lend/Lease* on completion. Could carry two loaded LCT(3)s. or LCT(4)s. or three loaded LCT(5)s. or thirty-six loaded LCM(3)s. or 1,500 t.d.w. and 263 troops.

LANDING SHIPS TANK (LST)

THE demands for the first LSTs. were placed in 1940 when requirements were made for ships that could land tanks direct onto a beach anywhere in the world. This presented the difficulty of shallow draught ocean-going ships: an unhappy combination at any time. The problem was tackled in two ways; first by converting suitable mercantile tonnage, and secondly by designing, and laying down, a small class of special vessels—even before any experience had been obtained with the first group.

Three medium-sized tankers, built to pass over the restrictive bars of Lake Maracaibo, were selected for conversion because of their shallow draught. Even then their draught was such that they still required an articulated bow ramp to cover the stretch of water from ship to shore but they clearly indicated the feasability of LSTs. Historically they were the first LSTs., a fact not without passing interest, but they possessed too many inherent disadvantages to be regarded as a prototype for the future. The over-riding feature of the naval designed vessels was that their speed was considerably increased as the speed of the mercantile conversions was considered inadequate. But the bluff bow, associated with any type of ramped landing ship, was not conducive to speed and these LSTs. were, therefore, given a finer ship-shaped entry. This increased their draught and they required a complicated, extending ramp—over a 100 ft. long—to bridge the gap from ship to shallow water. In the absence of any actual experience it was thought that the ships would prove very vulnerable in action and alternative arrangements were therefore provided for landing tanks through side ports into LCTs., or by a 40-ton crane on to a jetty. In fact, opinion on LSTs. was so sceptical that provision was made to adopt them to either tankers or for the carriage of cased aircraft.

When it was later realised that a very large number of LSTs. would be required for the European invasion and the recovery of overseas territory occupied by the enemy, a compromise was sought between the LST(1)s. and the LCTs. The former were over elaborate, not wholly satisfactory, nor could they be mass produced; while the latter were quite unable to undertake prolonged, ocean passages although they had considerably exceeded expectations as regards seaworthiness. An Admiralty plan for an Atlantic TLC was then outlined to the United States Navy and thereafter they proceeded, in partnership with the Royal Navy, to produce the ubiquitous LST(2)—now elevated from a craft to a ship—which met both production and seakeeping requirements. Diesel engined, with the machinery placed well aft, they had the virtue of shallow draught and a simple, hinged ramp in the bows. For ocean passages they could be ballasted down to a deeper draught and their all-welded construction stood up to the rigours of their service. In common with the LST(1)s. they kedged themselves back into deeper water after beaching and discharging their load.

Although the LST(2)s. fully met operational requirements their production was entirely in American hands. As the result of a difference of opinion over their allocation the Royal Navy found itself short of LSTs. and were therefore compelled to embark on a small programme of their own but to a modified design—the LST(3)s—in view of certain limitations. No American diesel engines were available and there was also a lack of welding facilities in the British and Canadian yards which were to build them. The only machinery readily available were the standard steam reciprocating engines installed in the corvettes and frigates and these, together with a large amount of riveting, resulted in larger, heavier, and consequently deeper draught LSTs. without any increase in the military load. The end of hostilities halted this programme by which time over two-thirds of them had been built.

LST

Displacement: 4,890 and 4,800 tons *gross* respectively.
Dimensions: $365\frac{1}{4}$ (pp) $382\frac{1}{2}$ (oa) × 64 × $4\frac{1}{4}$/15 ft.
Machinery: 2-shaft Reciprocating (VTE), I.H.P. 3,000 = 12 knots.
Armament: 2—4 in. smoke mortars, 4—2 pdr. A.A. (4 × 1), 6—20 mm. A.A. (6 × 1) guns.
Complement: 98.

F.110	BACHAQUERO	Furness Sbdg: N. E. Marine	7. 5.37	Returned 1945.
F.117	MISOA	Furness Sbdg: N. E. Marine	22. 6.37	Returned 1945.

Notes:—Converted 1941 and could carry two LCM(I)s., 22 at 25t., or 18 at 30t. tanks or 33 at 3t. lorries, and 217 troops.

Displacement: 3,952 tons *gross*.
Dimensions: 350 (pp) $362\frac{3}{4}$ (oa) × $60\frac{1}{4}$ × $4\frac{1}{4}$/15 ft
Machinery: 2-shaft Reciprocating (VTE), I.H.P. 1,800 = $10\frac{1}{2}$ knots.
Armament: 2—4 in. smoke mortars, 4—2 pdr. A.A. (4 × 1), 6—20 mm. A.A. (6 × 1) guns.
Complement: 98.

F.125	TASAJERA	Furness Sbdg: N. E. Marine	3. 3.38	Returned 1945.

Notes:—Converted 1941 and could carry two LCM(I)s., 22 at 25t. or 18 at 30t. tanks or 33 at 3t lorries, and 217 troops.

LST (1)

Displacement: 3,616/5,410 tons
Dimensions: 390 (pp) 400 (oa) × 49 × $5\frac{1}{2}$/$14\frac{3}{4}$ ft.
Machinery: 2-shaft geared Turbines, S.H.P. 7,000 = 17 knots.
Armament: 2—4 in. smoke mortars, 4—2 pdr. A.A. (4 × 1), 8—20 mm. A.A. (8 × 1) guns.
Complement: 169.

F.121	BOXER	Harland & Wolff	12.12.42	F.D.S. (1944), RDF. TS (1947); scrapped Barrow 5/12/58.
F.127	BRUIZER	Harland & Wolff	24.10.42	F.D.S. (1944), mercantile LILLA (1947), SILVER STAR (19..).

Above: The LSD Highway was armed with a 3 in. A.A. gun forward, four 2 pdr. A A. guns (not mounted in photograph—two abreast the bridge and two aft), and sixteen 20 mm. A.A. guns (four before and six abaft the bridge and six aft). [*U.S. Navy Official*

Below: The LST Bachaquero was converted from a shallow draught tanker and is shown beached with the bow doors open and the ramp about to be lowered. [*I.W.M.*

F.131	THRUSTER	Harland & Wolff	24. 9.42	F.D.S. (1944), R. Neth. N. PELIKAAN (1947).

Notes:—Funnel offset to starboard to provide clear tank deck and could carry 13 at 30t. tanks, 27 at 3t. lorries, and 193 troops.

LST (2)

U.S. Navy type: Nos. 2–5, 8–13, 62–65, 76, 77, 79, 80, 157, 159–165, 173, 178, 180, 198–200, 214–217, 280, 289, 301–305, 307–309, 311, 315, 319–324, 326, 331, 336, 337, 346, 347, 351, 352, 358, 360–369, 371, 373, 380–383, 385, 386, 394, 401–430, 538, 1021.

Displacement: 1,625 tons except *last two* 1,652/2,160 tons.
Dimensions: 000 (pp) 327¾ (oa) × 50 × 3/9½ ft.
Machinery: 2-shaft Diesel motors, B.H.P. 1,800 = 10 knots.
Armament: 1—12 pdr. A.A., 6—20 mm. A.A. (6 × 1) guns.
Complement: 86.
War losses: *1943* Nos. 79, 414, 429; *1944* Nos. 216, 305, 362, 407, 411, 418, 420, 422; *1945* Nos. 80, 178, 364; *1946* Nos. 199, 405.

Notes:—Built 1942-45 and made available to the R.N. under *Lend/Lease* on completion. Could carry 18 at 30t. tanks, 1 LCT(5) or 27 at 3t. lorries and 8 jeeps, and 177 troops. Three were converted to FDTs. (Nos. 13, 216, 217) and six to LSEs. (Nos. 215, 360, 402, 425 and two more).

BUILDERS:

Dravo Corp: Nos. 2–5, 8–13.
Jeffersonville Bt. & Mach. Co.: Nos. 62–65, 76, 77, 79, 80.
Missouri Valley Bridge & Iron Co.: Nos. 157, 159–165, 173, 178, 180, 538.
Chicago Bridge & Iron Co.: Nos. 198–200, 214–217, 237–239.
American Bridge (   ): Nos. 280, 289.
Boston Navy Yd.: Nos. 301–305, 307–309.
New York Navy Yd: Nos. 311, 315.
Philadelphia Navy Yd: Nos. 319–324, 326, 331.
Norfolk Navy Yd: Nos. 336, 337, 346, 347, 351, 352.
Charleston Navy Yd: Nos, 358, 360.
Bethlehem (Fore River): Nos. 361–369, 371, 373, 380–382, 1021.
(*Fairfield*)*:* Nos. 401–430.
Newport News: Nos. 383, 385, 386, 394.

LST (3)

Admiralty type: Nos. 3001–3045, 3501–3571.
Displacement: 2,256/3,065 tons.
Dimensions: 330 (pp) 345¾ (oa) × 54 × 4½/11½ ft.
Machinery: 2-shaft Reciprocating (VTE), I.H.P. 5,500 = 13 knots.
Armament: *Nos. 3001* up 10—20 mm. A.A. (4 × 2 & 2 × 1) guns; *Nos. 3501* up 4—40 mm. A.A. (2 × 2), 6—20 mm. A.A. (2 × 2 & 2 × 1) guns. *Complement:* 104.

Notes:—Could carry 15 at 40t. or 27 at 25t tanks, one LCT(5) or seven LCM(7) or 14 at 3t. lorries and 168 troops. Nos. 3005, 3034, 3045, 3526-3531, 3533, 3535-3571 were cancelled and Nos. 3004, 3018 3023, 3030, 3032 and 3039 were completed as mercantile. No. 3012 and 3013 were converted to LSHs. and renamed LST(Q) 1 and 2, and Nos. 3043 and 3044 were fitted as LSCs.

The LST(1) Thruster was the first of the specially designed LSTs. and had the funnel offset to starboard. She is here armed with ten 20 mm. A.A. (10 × 1) guns disposed four forward, two in the bridge wings, and four aft. [I.W.M.

A U.S. Navy LST(2) beached with bow doors open and ramp down. They only differed from LST (2) supplied to the Royal Navy by having two LCRs. under davits forward, and in armament details. [I.W.M.

LST(3). 3033 was British built and was compelled to adopt steam propulsion as no suitable diesel engines were available. Note chocks for an LCT(5) on foredeck. [I.W.M.

(a) British built *Engined N.E. Marine

Number	Builder Hull: Engines	Launched	Fate
3001	V.A. (Tyne): Hicks, Hargreaves	15. 1.45	W.D. FREDERICK CLOVER (1946).
3002	V.A. (Tyne)	9. 4.45	R.H.N. ALIAKMON (1947).
3003	V.A. (Tyne)	8. 6.45	ANZIO (1947).
3004	V.A. (Tyne): Markham	30. 7.45	Completed mercantile RIO TEJO (1950), SAO JOAQUIM (1951).
3005	V.A. (Tyne)		Scrapped incomplete Barrow 1945.
3006	Harland & Wolff: Lobnitz	. .44	TROMSO (1947), mercantile EMPIRE GANNET (1956).
3007	Harland & Wolff: Worthington Simpson	. .44	R.H.N. AXIOS (1947); for disposal.
3008	Harland & Wolff	. .44	Scrapped Sydney 4/6/50.
3009	Harland & Wolff	. .44	W.D. REGINALD KERR (1946).
3010	Harland & Wolff	. .44	ATTACKER (1947), mercantile EMPIRE CYMRIC (1954).
3011	Harland & Wolff	. .44	AVENGER (1948), R.I.N. MAGAR (1951).
3012	Harland & Wolff	. .44	LST(Q).1 (1945), BEN NEVIS (1947); for disposal.
3013	Harland & Wolff	. .44	LST(Q).2 (1945), BEN LOMOND (1947); scrapped Grays 21/3/60.
3014	Barclay Curle	11.11.44	Scrapped Sydney 4/6/50.
3015	Barclay Curle	16. 3.45	BATTLER (1947), mercantile EMPIRE PUFFIN (1956), barge (1960).
3016	Hawthorn Leslie*	14.12.44	DIEPPE (1947).
3017	Hawthorn Leslie*	18.11.44	R.A.N. TARAKAN (1949); scrapped Sydney 12/3/54.
3018	Hawthorn Leslie: Clark	12. 6.45	Completed mercantile RIO MINHO (1949), SAO PEDRO (1955).
3019	Swan Hunter	4. 9.44	VAAGSO (1947); scrapped Faslane 12/59.
3020	Swan Hunter	31.10.44	R.H.N. ALFIOS (1947); for disposal.
3021	Lithgows: Kincaid	23.10.44	W.D. CHARLES McLEOD (1946).
3022	Lithgows: Kincaid	26. 1.45	Scrapped Sydney 4/6/50.
3023	Lithgows: Kincaid	13. 6.45	Completed mercantile RIO GUADIANA (1949), SAO PAULO (1955).
3024	Smiths Dock	15.10.44	W.D. MAXWELL BRANDER (1946).
3025	Smiths Dock	14. 1.45	BRUIZER (1947), scrapped 1954.
3026	Blyth Sbdg.: Walker Bros.	30.10.44	CHARGER (1946), mercantile EMPIRE NORDIC (1955).
3027	Blyth Sbdg.	26. 1.45	LOFOTEN (1947).
3028	Stephen: Fullerton, Hodgarth & Barclay	16.11.44	W.D. SNOWDEN SMITH (1946); scrapped Spezia 14/1/61.
3029	Stephen	12. 1.45	CHASER (1947), scrapped Spezia 28/3/62.
3030	Hall Russell	12. 6.45	Completed mercantile CLUPEA (1947)
3031	Hall Russell		For disposal.

3032	Connel: Rowan	. .45	Completed mercantile RIO MONDEGO (1950), SAO SEBASTIAO (1956).
3033	Pickersgill: Clark	. .45	Mercantile EMPIRE SHEARWATER (1956).
3034	Pickersgill	. .45	Cancelled.
3035	Denny	24.10.44	R.A.N. LAE (1949); wrecked 3/11/56.
3036	Ailsa Sbdg.	20.11.44	PUNCHER (1947); scrapped Ghent 4/6/61.
3037	Fairfield: Rankin & Blackmore	30. 1.45	W.D. EVAN GIBB (1946); scrapped Italy 1963
3038	Fairfield: Blairs	14. 3.45	FIGHTER (1947); mercantile EMPIRE GREBE (1956).
3039	Fairfield: Rankin & Blackmore	27. 6.45	Completed mercantile RIO DUORO (1951), SAN BERNADO (1957.)
3040	Fairfield	. .45	Scrapped Hayle 17/1/49.
3041	Harland & Wolff (Govan): Fletcher	31.10.44	Mercantile EMPIRE DORIC (1954); scrapped Port Glasgow 13/1/60.
3042	Harland & Wolff (Govan): Lobnitz	31. 1.45	HUNTER (1947); mercantile EMPIRE CURLEW (1956); scrapped Italy 1962
3043	Scotts	27. 4.45	MESSINA (1947).
3044	V.A. (Barrow)	29. 7.45	NARVIK (1947).
3045	V.A. (Barrow)	24.10.45	Cancelled

(b) Canadian Built

3501	Canadian Vickers	24. 8.44	R.A.N. LABUAN (1949); scrapped Japan 11/56.
3502	Canadian Vickers	31. 8.44	R.H.N. STRYMON (1947); scrapped Spezia 10/7/62.
3503	Canadian Vickers	12.10.44	R.H.N. ACHELOOS (1947).
3504	Canadian Vickers	3.11.44	PURSUER (1947), mercantile EMPIRE TERN (1956).
3505	Canadian Vickers	23.11.44	RAVAGER (1947); for disposal
3506	Canadian Vickers	2.12.44	R.H.N. PINIOS (1947).
3507	Davie Sbdg.: C.P. Rly.	28.10.44	Mercantile EMPIRE GAELIC (1954); RJEV (1962).
3508	Davie Sbdg.	30.10.44	SEARCHER (1947); scrapped Milford Haven 20/6/49
3509	Davie Sbdg.: C.P. Rly.	27.11.44	W.D. HUMPHRYE GALE (1956); scrapped Genoa 10/1/61.
3510	Davie Sbdg. C.P. Rly.	28.11.44	SLINGER (1947), mercantile EMPIRE KITTIWAKE (1956).
3511	Davie Sbdg.	29.11.44	Completed Marine Industries; REGGIO (1947); scrapped Grays 12/8/60.
3512	Davie Sbdg.: C.P. Rly.	25. 4.45	Mercantile EMPIRE CELTIC (1954); for disposal.
3513	Davie Sbdg.	26. 4.45	SALERNO (1947).
3514	Canadian Yarrow	. .44	SMITER (1947); wrecked 25/4/49.
3515	Canadian Yarrow	. .45	STALKER (1947).
3516	Canadian Yarrow	. .45	STRIKER (1947).
3517	Canadian Yarrow: Dominion Bridge	. .45	St. NAZAIRE (1947), mercantile EMPIRE SKUA (1956).
3518	Canadian Vickers	6. 4.45	SULVA (1947); scrapped Graus 8/9/60.

3519	Canadian Vickers	20. 4.45	Mercantile EMPIRE BALTIC (1954); scrapped Spezia 10/7 62.
3520	Canadian Vickers	1. 5.45	THRUSTER (1947); mercantile EMPIRE PETREL (1956).
3521	Canadian Vickers	27. 7.45	Scuttled off Halifax 2/46.
3522	Davie Sbdg.	9. 6.45	TRACKER (1947).
3523	Davie Sbdg.: C.P. Rly.	9. 7.45	TROUNCER (1947); mercantile EMPIRE GULL (1956).
3524	Davie Sbdg.: C.P. Rly.	25. 7.45	TRUMPETER (1947), mercantile EMPIRE FULMAR (1956).
3525	Davie Sbdg.: C.P. Rly.	29. 8.45	WALCHEREN (1947), mercantile EMPIRE GUILLEMOT (1956).
3526	United Shpyd.		Cancelled.
3527	United Shpyd.		Cancelled.
3528	United Shpyd.		Cancelled.
3529	United Shpyd.		Cancelled.
3530			Cancelled.
3531			Cancelled.
3532			ZEEBRUGGE (1947); for disposal.
3533			Cancelled.
3534	Canadian Yarrow: Dominion Bridge	. .45	Mercantile EMPIRE CEDRIC (19. .); scrapped Ghent 16/9/60.
3535	Canadian Yarrow		Cancelled.
3536	Canadian Vickers		Cancelled.
3537	Canadian Vickers	11. 8.45	Completed dumb barge M.I.L. 463.

LANDING SHIPS HEADQUARTERS (LSH)

THE importance of maintaining communications with the large numbers of military units involved in a large scale invasion, until a G.H.Q. was established ashore, cannot be overstressed. In fact it would not be overstating the case to say that successs or failure, in operations of these sorts, was largely dependent on the maintenance of this communication link. This resulted in LSHs. which were extensively fitted with communications equipment by which the naval and military commanders could exercise control and co-relate the activities, of their many small and dispersed units. The LSH(L)s., were all mercantile conversions but the LSH(S)s. were naval flotilla vessels and were less elaborately equipped.

LSH (L)

Displacement: 11,250 tons.
Dimensions: 420 (pp) 442 (oa) × 56¼ × 23¾ ft.
Machinery: 1-shaft Reciprocating (VTE) & exhaust Turbine, I.H.P. 5,200 = 14 knots.
Armament: 1—6 in., 1—12 pdr. A.A., 2—2 pdr. A.A. (2 × 1), 11—20 mm A.A. (11 × 1) guns.
Complement: 313.

F.22	HILARY	Cammell Laird	17. 4.31	Returned 1946.

Notes:—Ex-O.B.V. converted in 1943. Later re-armed with 1—12 pdr. A.A., 16—2 pdr. A.A.(4 × 4), 13—20 mm. A.A. (6 × 2 & 2 × 1) guns and could carry six LCP(L)s. and 378 troops

The Bulolo was converted from an AMC to a LSH(L), was extensively fitted with communications equipment, and displayed a wide array of aerials. [I.W.M.

Displacement: 9,111 tons.
Dimensions: 399 (pp) 412½ (oa) × 58¼ × 21½ ft.
Machinery: 2-shaft Diesel motors, B.H.P. 6,130 = 15 knots.
Armament: 4—4 in. A.A. (2 × 2), 5—40 mm. A.A. (5 × 1), 14—20 mm. A.A. (14 × 1) guns.
Complement: 264.

F.82	BULOLO	Barclay Curle: Kincaid	31. 5.38	Returned 12/46.

Notes:—Ex-A.M.C. converted in 1942 and could carry six LCP(L)s. and 258 troops.

Displacement: 5,850 tons.
Dimensions: 342¾ (pp) 375½ (oa) × 51¾ × 20¼ ft.
Machinery: 2-shaft-Diesel motors B.H.P. 5,720 = 17 knots.
Armament: 1—12 pdr. A.A., 2—2 pdr. A.A. (2 × 1), 14—20 mm. A.A. (4 × 2 & 6 × 1) guns.
Complement: 284.

F.43	LARGS (ex-Charles Plumier)	Ch. & At. de Provence	. .38	Returned 1945

Notes:—Ex-O.B.V. converted in 1942 and could carry four LCP(L)s. and 110 troops.

Displacement: 12,786 tons.
Dimensions: 486 (pp) 515½ (oa) × 62¼ × 22 ft.
Machinery: 2-shaft geared Turbines, S.H.P. 9,750 = 16 knots.
Armament: 4—4 in. A.A. (2 × 2), 20—20 mm. A.A. (8 × 2 & 4 × 1) guns.
Complement: 300.

F.168	LOTHIAN (ex-City of Edinburgh)	Cammell Laird	14. 4.38	Returned 1946.

Notes:—Converted 1944.

LSH (S)

The following naval vessels were temporarily fitted out as LSH(S) between 1943–45:—
Hunt class (*type III*) escort destroyers: ALBRIGHTON, GOATHLAND.
Captain class frigates: DACRES, KINGSMILL, LAWFORD.
River class frigates: CHELMER, EXE, MEON, NITH, WAVENEY.
River gunboat: LOCUST.
Notes:—Details of these vessels will be found under their respective class headings in Parts 2, 3 and 4.

LANDING SHIPS FIGHTER DIRECTION (LSF)

ANOTHER requisite for a successful invasion was to secure local air superiority over the beachheads. The provision of fighter aircraft was largely the concern of the R.A.F. but the effective control had to be exercised at the scene of operations. Consequently requisitioned mercantile tonnage were fitted out as LSFs. with AW.RDF., air plots, R/T communications with aircraft, etc., so that enemy air counter attacks against the invading forces could be detected, plotted and the defending fighter aircraft vectored to an intercepting position. Although major naval vessels (capital ships, cruisers, and aircraft carriers) were equipped for this role they could neither be spared or risked close inshore for this duty. The LSFs. were supplemented by three LST(1)s. and three LST(2)s. similarly converted to FDTs.

LSF

Displacement: 2,957 tons *gross*.
Dimensions: 321½ (pp) 330 (oa) × 43 × 18 ft.
Machinery: 2-shaft geared Turbines, S.H.P. 9,000 = 21 knots.
Armament: 2—12 pdr. A.A. (2 × 1).

4.209	ANTWERP	Clydebank	25.10.19	Returned 1945.

Notes:—Ex-convoy escort converted in 1944.

Displacement: 4,686 tons.
Dimensions: 346 (pp) 359 (oa) × 46¼ × 16¼ ft.
Machinery: 2-shaft Diesel motors, B.H.P. 6,350 = 18 knots.
Armament: 6—4 in. A.A. (3 × 2), 8—2 pdr. A.A. (2 × 4), 8—20 mm. A.A. (4 × 2) guns.

F.118	ULSTER QUEEN	Harland & Wolff	28. 3.29	Returned 4/46.

Notes:—Ex-Auxiliary anti-aircraft vessels converted in 1943. Sister ship ULSTER MONARCH was converted to LSI(H).

Displacement: 4,540 tons.
Dimensions: 295½ (pp) 306½ (oa) × 45 × 17½ ft.
Machinery: 1-shaft Diesel motors, B.H.P. 2,640 = 16¼ knots.
Armament: 6—4 in. A.A. (3 × 2), 8—2 pdr. A.A. (2 × 4), 4—20 mm. A.A. (4 × 1), 2—.5 in. A.A. (2 × 1) guns.

F.98	PALOMARES	Doxford	20.10.37	Returned 4/46.

Notes:—Ex-Auxiliary anti-aircraft vessel converted in 1943.

Displacement: 5,000 tons.
Dimensions: 304¾ (pp) 315 (oa) × 44¼ × 19¾ ft.
Machinery: 1-shaft Reciprocating (VTE), I.H.P. 1,900 = 12¾ knots.
Armament: 24—20 mm. A.A. (9 × 2 & 6 × 1) guns.

D.17	STUART PRINCE	Smiths Dock	9. 3.40	Mercantile FORT HAMILTON (1951).

Notes:—Converted in 1943.

FDT: Nos. 13, 216, 217.

LST(2) converted by R.N. to serve as fighter direction tenders and armed with 1—12 pdr. A.A. and 12—20 mm. A.A. (6 × 2) guns. Bow doors welded up, hatch covered with amour plate, and pig iron ballast on main deck served as armour over offices fitted in tank deck. Offices added included: general communications office; transmitting room; R/T receiving room; RDF receiving room; two VHF fighter directing offices; GC.1 office; beacon office; bridge plotting office; bridge conning station; filter room; air control room; storeroom; workshop and four additional generators. No. 216 was lost in 1944 and the remaining pair returned to the U.S.N. in 2/46.

FDT: BOXER, BRUIZER, THRUSTER

LST(1) converted to serve as fighter detection ships. See under LSTs., for details. Re-armed with 8—2 pdr. A.A. (2 × 4), 8—20 mm. A.A. (8 × 1) guns.

LANDING SHIPS EMERGENCY REPAIR (LSE)

BY the very nature of their employment, landing craft of all types were subject to damage both by rough usage and from enemy fire. The earliest large scale landings in North Africa had indicated that wastage among landing craft would be beyond replacement production unless beached and damaged craft, which would otherwise be abandoned, were salvaged. They only had to be sufficiently patched up to return either to their parent ship, or to a repair base, where more permanent repairs would be effected. This led to an emergency repair organisation, equipped to undertake basic repairs to hull, engines, shafts, propellers and rudders, carried in LSEs. specially equipped for the purpose.

LSE: Nos. 1, 2, 50–53 (Ex-LST (2) 425, 215, 360, 402).
These were former LST(2)s. completed in 1944–45 as emergency repair ships.

LSE: ADVENTURE

Former cruiser minelayer converted to an emergency repair ship in 1944. See Part 1 for further details.

MINOR LANDING CRAFT

THIS group covers craft designed to carry military personnel, of which only one type were developed to carry a single vehicle and, with the exception of the LCIs., could all be hoisted by the standard davits fitted on H.M. Ships and mercantile adaptations.

The LCAs. were developed from the pre-war MLC. 50 and 51. They had ¾in. armour along the sides, a ¼in. deck over the machine room, bullet proof side decks abreast the troop space, a bullet proof shelter for the cox'un, and a bullet proof bulkhead forward. The earliest craft had the cox'uns' shelter placed aft but this was soon moved forward, to the starboard side, and the corresponding position to port was fitted with M.Gs. Troops disembarked over a bow ramp and sufficient buoyant material was built-in to support the craft if swamped.

The LCP(M)s. were based on the Northumberland coble and were thought to be more suitable for operations of exposed and rocky coasts. Their single screw was completely enclosed in a tunnel and disembarkation was affected by two portable ladders over the bows and by two fixed ladders on the stern.

The LCP(1) and (2) were small, wooden craft which could be carried under a destroyer's davits. The Mk. I were dumb craft intended to be towed by the Mk. II, which were powered and, together with the LCP(M)s. were built more with raiding in mind than for invasion purposes.

The LCP(S)s. were second flight craft designed to supplement the LCAs. after the latter had made the initial landings under fire and a beachhead had

Above: The LSF Stuart Prince was exceptionally well equipped with AW.RDF and R/T for her fighter direction duties. [*I.W.M.*

Below: The Boxer was converted from an LST(1) to an LSF. She needed four masts to carry her RDF aerials and aircraft homing beacons, and had eight 2 pdr. A.A. (2 × 4) guns added forward. [*I.W.M.*

been established. Disembarkation was by portable ladders placed over the bows. Except for those fitted out as hospital craft they were never ultimately used for this role and were utilised as general purpose harbour craft. They were succeeded by the larger and faster LCUs., also for landings not under enemy fire.

For Far Eastern operations, over shallow water or through swamps where propellors would easily foul, the air-screw propelled LCWs., were designed, with a folding bow ramp, but never came into operational service.

The LCP(L) was a modification of a standard motor boat built by Higgins of New Orleans. They were only lightly armoured, with three $\frac{1}{4}$-inch transverse bulkheads, but fast and could be driven ashore at speed so that no special disembarking arrangements were provided, the troops simply jumping off from the bows onto the beach. Later, a bow ramp was added to decrease disembarking time and those so altered were designated LCP(R). Both types were armed with bow mounted M.Gs. The next step was to widen the bow ramp so that a small vehicle—such as a 1-ton truck or a Bren gun carrier—could be carried as an alternative to troops. This necessitated moving the helm, controls and engines right aft, placing the cox'un in an exposed position on the stern, and both armour and armament had to be dropped. The resulting craft were classed as LCVs. The final step was to combine the most desirable features of the LCP(R) and LCV into a single craft. This resulted in the LCVP which had a full width ramp and was able to carry a 3-ton lorry, was armoured on the sides and on the bow ramp with $\frac{1}{4}$-inch plate, was armed with M.Gs. placed aft, and provided the cox'un with some measure of protection by placing the helm and controls within the troop space on the port side aft. They proved most satisfactory in service and possessed a versatility not common for such small craft.

Early in 1942 requirements were made for a craft able to carry 200 fully equipped troops at a speed of 17 knots and also able to beach. Investigation showed that such craft would have to be steel built, to keep within draught limitations, but as the U.K. shipbuilding capacity was already fully extended at this stage the plans were turned over to the United States Navy whom, in a short time, produced the LCI(L). Although the first proposals that they cross the Atlantic on their own bottoms were only tentatively put forward they successfully made the passage unescorted and generally surprised everybody with their weatherly qualities. From then on they always proceeded independently and were quite safe if handled with seamanlike care. Because of the shortage of steel only 2-inch plastic armour was given to the bridge, wheelhouse and gun pits and the armament of four 20 mm. A.A. guns, although light by American standards was considered adequate by the Royal Navy. The hull was of shipshape form and the bow scarphed to accommodate two gangways for disembarkation but later craft built for the United States Navy reverted to the bow ramp. Innovations introduced were variable pitch propellors and two engines per shaft mounted in tandem.

As the steel-built LCI(L)s. could not be built in the U.K. staff requirements were reduced to permit a wooden craft that could, and design details were entrusted to the Fairmile organisation who arranged for their prefabricated construction. The hull sides, bridge, and gun positions were protected by $\frac{1}{4}$-inch armour laid as scales; the troop spaces were completely enclosed; and disembarkation was by four brows over the stem.

Many of the above craft were adopted for other duties than carrying troops. LCAs. were converted to LCA(HR) to explode minefields in the path of invading forces, LCA(OC) to clear foreshore obstructions, and LCA(FT) when flame throwing equipment was added. As mentioned earlier, some LCP(S)s. were altered to ambulance craft to ferry the wounded to other landing craft converted to LCCSs. and to the hospital ships. Many other landing ships and landing craft, when returning empty to the U.K. during the European landings, were similarly employed. LCNs. were adapted from LCP(L)s. equipped with additional navigation equipment to act as lead-in or survey craft for the initial waves of assault craft, and some LCVs., fitted with light sweeps, became LCV(M/S)s. for minesweeping in the beachhead areas, while others equipped for emergency repairs became LCEs. LCHs. were converted from LCI(L)s. to provide command and communication facilities close inshore and some Fairmile "**B**" MLs. exercised control functions over the large number of craft converging onto the beaches. One LCI(L) was fitted out with Press facilities for the Normandy landings and other LCIs. were equipped with CSA to lay smoke screens or adapted for store carrying.

LCA: Nos. 1–2030.

Displacement: 9/11 (*earlier craft*), 13½ (*later craft*) tons.
Dimensions: 38¾ (pp) 41½ (oa) × 10 × 1/2¼ ft.
Machinery: 2-shaft Ford petrol motors, B.H.P. 130 = 10/6 knots
Armament: 2—2 in. mortars, 3—.303 in. (1 × 2 & 2 × 1) M.Gs.
Complement: 4.
War losses: *1940* Nos. 1, 2, 4, 6, 8, 11, 14–16, 18; *1941* Nos. 28, 31, 32, 38, 39, 45, 48, 49, 51, 60, 63, 64, 70, 75, 79–81, 87, 105, 113, 119, 121; *1942* Nos. 35, 37, 52, 55, 92, 94, 97, 102, 128, 135, 138, 153, 166, 167, 169, 176, 187–189, 192, 193, 196, 209, 211, 214, 215, 218, 219, 221, 227, 235, 237, 239, 244, 245, 247, 251, 259–262, 266, 269, 271, 284, 286, 287, 301, 307, 309, 310, 314, 317, 321, 375, 423, 436, 447, 451; *1943* Nos, 78, 212, 222, 272, 312, 316, 446, 505, 545, 553, 645, 646, 675, 723, 813; *1944* Nos. 33, 54, 56, 59, 69, 107, 130, 146, 149, 171, 182, 208, 226, 248, 254, 279, 289, 303, 320, 323, 326, 337, 339, 341, 347, 349, 350, 352, 360, 364, 367, 382, 383, 387, 394, 398, 400, 401, 409, 417, 418, 424, 428, 431, 433, 434, 440, 442, 458, 459, 462, 463, 476, 485, 487, 492, 494, 496, 503, 509, 518–520, 522, 525, 526, 530, 535, 540, 551, 552, 566, 573, 577, 579, 581, 584, 586, 588–590, 592–594, 611, 613, 614, 623, 625, 637, 642, 649–652, 655, 661, 664, 665, 673, 683, 691, 692, 696, 697, 704, 705, 710, 713, 717, 721, 722, 725, 726, 729, 731, 738, 748, 750, 753, 761, 768, 775, 779, 780, 783, 788, 790–792, 795–797, 803, 808–810, 812, 814, 815, 817, 821, 825, 827, 831, 835, 843, 845, 848, 849, 853, 857, 859, 860, 865, 867, 869–871, 879, 881, 886, 900, 903, 908, 911, 913, 914, 918–920, 929, 933, 946, 949, 958, 978, 984, 998–1000, 1005, 1008, 1013, 1016, 1018, 1021, 1024, 1026–1028, 1030, 1034, 1050, 1057–1059, 1063, 1068, 1069, 1074, 1079, 1082, 1086, 1088, 1091, 1093, 1096, 1125, 1129, 1131, 1132, 1137, 1138, 1143, 1144, 1146, 1149–1151, 1155, 1156, 1188, 1213, 1215, 1216, 1251–1253, 1256, 1260, 1304, 1338–1341, 1343, 1372, 1378, 1379, 1381–1383, 1393; *1945* Nos. 841, 1112, 1153, 1161, 1329, 1346, 1396, 1433, 1472, 1591.

Notes:—Built 1940–44. Wooden construction to Thornycroft design. Armoured conning position was moved from aft in earlier boats to starboard side forward in later craft. Could carry 35 troops or 800lb. equipment.

LCA (FT): Nos.

These were converted LCAs. fitted with flame throwing equipment to act in close support of troops at the beach head.

LCA (HR): Nos.

These were converted LCAs. with strengthened hull frames, designed to explode minefields in the path of an assault landing for which purpose they were armed with 24 mortars in four rows of six. *War losses 1944* Nos. 183, 258, 671, 672, 678, 689, 690, 802, 811, 965, 1072.

LCA (OC): Nos.

These were converted LCAs. equipped for clearing beach obstructions and the sole war loss was No. 1211 in 1945.

Notes:—Neither LCA(FT), LCA(HR), or LCA(OC) were re-numbered but retained their original LCA number with the distinguishing suffixes (FT), (HR), or (OC).

LCP (M): Nos. 1–61.

Displacement: 4½/7½ tons.
Dimensions: 39 (oa) × 10 × 2 ft.
Machinery: 1-shaft Scribbs Ford petrol motor, B.H.P. 65 = 7½ knots.
Armament: 1—.303 in. M.G.
Complement: 3
War losses: *1943* Nos. 14 & 17.

Notes:—Built 1941. Wooden construction. Could carry 20 troops.

LCP (1): Nos.

Displacement: 1 ton.
Dimensions: 20 × 6 × 1¼ ft.
Machinery: Dumb.
Complement: 2.

Notes:—Built 1941-42. Wooden construction. Could carry 18 troops and be towed at 5½ knots by LCP(2).

LCP (2): Nos. 1001–1200.

Displacement: 2/3¾ tons.
Dimensions: 25½ × 6¼ × 1½ ft.
Machinery: 1-shaft Ford petrol engine, B.H.P. 65 = 10 knots.
Complement: 3.
War losses: *1945* Nos. 1021, 1110, 1113.

Notes:—Built 1941-42. Wooden construction. Could carry 18 troops.

LCP (S): Nos. 1–220.

Displacement: 3/5½ tons.
Dimensions: 28½ (pp) 30 (oa) × 8¾ × 1¾ ft.
Machinery: 1-shaft Chrysler petrol motor, B.H.P. 65 = 8 knots.
Armament: 1—.303 in. M.G.
Complement: 3.
War losses: *1943* No. 116; *1944* Nos. 1, 9, 25, 50, 60, 61, 73, 74, 76, 101, 129, 135, 136, 137, 183.

Notes:—Built 1942-43. Wooden construction to Aldous design. Could carry 25 troops.

LCH: Nos. 221–300.

Adapted from LCP (S) and could carry six stretcher cases and ten walking wounded.

LCP (U): Nos. 1–

10-ton boats of wooden construction used for landings not under fire and for general utility purposes. Had a speed of 12 knots, a complement of 4, and could carry 30 troops.

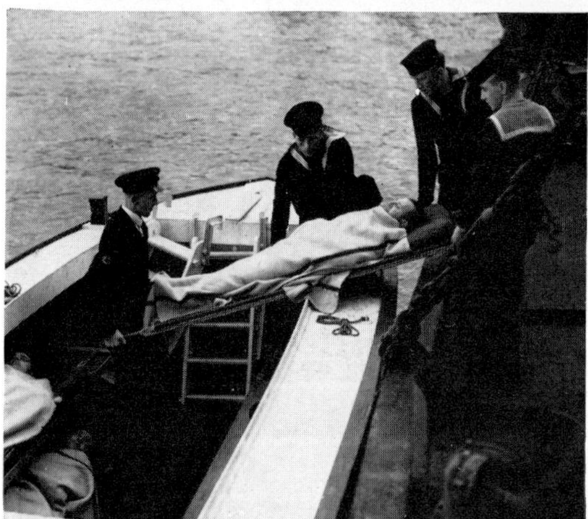

Above: LCA. 365 was one of the later craft of this type in which the cox'un's position was moved from aft to the starboard side forward. [*I.W.M.*

Right: A LCP(S) fitted out as an ambulance launch. [*I.W.M.*

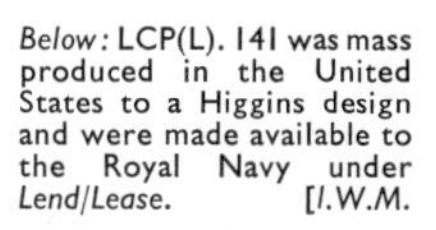

Below: LCP(L). 141 was mass produced in the United States to a Higgins design and were made available to the Royal Navy under *Lend/Lease.* [*I.W.M.*

LCW: Nos.

Designed for Far Eastern operations to operate in shallow water or over swamps and was air-screw propelled. 10-ton craft with a speed of 10 knots, and could carry 35 troops or 5t. d.w.

LCP (L): Nos. 1–400, 501–600, 701–800.

Displacement: 6½/10¾ tons.
Dimensions: 36¾ (oa) × 10¾ × 2½/3½ ft.
Machinery: 1-shaft Hall Scott petrol motor, B.H.P. 250 or Kermath petrol motor, B.H.P. 225 or Gray diesel motor, B.H.P. 225 = 10/8 knots.
Armament: 1—.303 in. M.G.
Complement: 3.
War losses: *1940* No. 30; *1941* Nos. 24, 25, 26, 27, 38, 59, 63, 71, 82, 107, 108, 109, 193, 194; *1942* Nos. 29, 36, 42, 45, 57, 64, 65, 81, 83, 93, 117, 138, 157, 164, 174, 180, 181, 182, 183, 184, 185, 209, 210, 212, 507, 543, 544, 550, 560, 562, 565, 566, 568, 573, 575, 576, 759; *1943* Nos. 17, 80, 87, 106, 126, 136, 203, 204, 205, 206, 276, 277, 316, 325; *1944* Nos. 7, 8, 13, 14, 18, 21, 22, 23, 40, 51, 52, 66, 84, 85, 88, 97, 98, 110, 121, 127, 132, 133, 134, 137, 139, 145, 146, 149, 152, 162, 163, 170, 175, 176, 187, 189, 197, 198, 199, 200, 208, 229, 230, 231, 232, 233, 235, 238, 239, 241, 242, 246, 247, 263, 267, 269, 272, 280, 282, 285, 286, 287, 289, 293, 294, 298, 299, 300, 302, 303, 304, 305, 308, 309, 310, 312, 323, 348, 356, 360, 367, 373, 528, 540, 541, 556, 577, 760; *1945* Nos. 11, 344, 378, 764.

Notes:—Built 1940-42. Wooden construction. Higgins design and made available to R.N. under *Lend/Lease*. Could carry 25 troops or 3½t. d.w.

LCP (R): Nos. 501–1100.

Displacement: 6½/10¾ tons.
Dimensions: 36¾ (oa) × 10¾ × 2½/3½ ft.
Machinery: 1-shaft Kermath petrol motor, B.H.P. 225, or Buda diesel motor, B.H.P. 105 or Gray diesel motor, B.H.P. 225 = 10/8 knots.
Armament: 2—.303 in. (2 × 1) M.Gs.
Complement: 3.
War losses: *1942* Nos. 578, 603, 617, 620, 622, 629, 721, 783, 794, 837, 850, 858, 901, 909, 1008, 1009, 1012, 1029, 1036; *1943* Nos. 613, 661, 673, 680, 684, 685, 689, 692, 693, 727, 753, 769, 771, 780, 782, 795, 879, 1019, 1035; *1944* Nos. 584, 614, 616, 634, 640, 643, 652, 663, 669, 683, 723, 735, 781, 805, 806, 824, 844, 854, 866, 867, 894, 895, 896, 905, 912, 913, 966, 970, 971, 978, 982, 987, 989, 991, 993, 995, 999, 1011, 1023, 1026; *1945* Nos. 707, 738, 832, 840, 965, 979, 1018.

Notes:—Built 1942-43. Wooden constuction. Higgins design and made available to the R.N. under *Lend/Lease*. Could carry 30 troops or 3½t. d.w.

LCV: Nos. 501–600, 701–900.

Displacement: 7/11 tons.
Dimensions: 36¼ (oa) × 10¾ × 1½/3 ft.
Machinery: 1-shaft Hall Scott petrol motor, B.H.P. 250 or Gray diesel motor, B.H.P. 225 = 9 knots.
Armament: 1—.303 in. M.G.
Complement: 3.

No. 829 was one of the LCVs. adapted for minesweeping and is displaying the 'sweepers day signal. The LCVs. had the cox'un in an exposed position right aft which was changed in the later LCVPs. to a more sheltered position within the hull, see above. [*I.W.M.*

The LCVP was developed from the LCP(L) by the inclusion of a full width bow ramp and the cox'un's position moved aft to the port side. [*I.W.M.*

LCI(L). 98, one of the outstandingly successful craft, mass produced in the U.S.A. and made available to the Royal Navy under *Lend/Lease.* [*I.W.M.*

War losses: *1942* Nos. 579, 597, 752, 754, 798; *1943* Nos. 584, 825; *1944* Nos. 719, 801, 894; *1945* Nos. 802, 814.

Notes:—Built 1942. Wooden construction. Made available to the R.N. under *Lend/Lease*. Could carry one Bren gun carrier or 1 at 1t. lorry or 4½t. d.w. or 36 troops.

LCVP: Nos. 1001–1400.

Displacement: 8/11½ tons.
Dimensions: 36 (oa) × 10½ × 2/3 ft.
Machinery: 1-shaft Hall Scott petrol motor, B.H.P. 250 or Gray diesel motor B.H.P. 225 = 9 knots.
Armament: 2—.303 in. (2 × 1) M.Gs. *Complement:* 3.
War losses: *1943* No. 1040; *1944* Nos. 1016, 1029, 1031, 1033, 1044, 1045, 1046, 1049, 1054, 1056, 1062, 1065, 1066, 1084, 1088, 1093, 1098, 1101, 1102, 1103, 1104, 1106, 1111, 1114, 1117, 1120, 1121, 1122, 1124, 1129, 1132, 1133, 1139, 1146, 1153, 1155, 1157, 1159, 1165, 1170, 1171, 1172, 1184, 1188, 1199, 1201, 1204, 1211, 1216, 1218, 1228, 1242, 1245, 1246, 1248, 1249, 1251, 1255, 1260, 1262, 1264, 1288; *1945* Nos. 1167, 1191, 1358.

Notes:—Built 1943. Wooden construction. Made available to the R.N. under *Lend/Lease*. Could carry 1 at 3t. lorry or 3½t. d.w. or 36 troops. LCP(L), LCP(R), LCV and LCVP were numbered consecutively from Nos. 1-1400 but without clear lines of demarcation where one type stopped and another started. Nos. 1-1400 were used by LCP(L); 501-600 by LCP(L), LCP(R), and LCV; Nos. 601-700 by LCP(R); Nos. 701-800 by LCP(L), LCP(R), and LCV; Nos. 801-900 by LCP(R) and LCV; Nos. 901-1,000 by LCP(R); Nos. 1001-1100 by LCP(R) and LCPV; and Nos. 1101-1400 by LCVP.

LCN: Nos.

These were conversions from LCP (L)s. and were fitted with extra navigational equipment to act as lead-in craft for the initial waves of assault craft.

LCP (Survey): Nos. 154 etc.

LCP(L)s. equipped for inshore survey work on the assault beaches. Sole war loss was No. 154 in 1944.

LCC: Nos.

These were converted Fairmile **"B"** MLs. which acted as navigational leaders and control craft for groups of landing craft. They either accompanied those landing craft large enough to make the passage to the invasion beaches on their own bottoms or awaited, at selected points, to lead-in the smaller landing craft which had to be transported. The smaller LCN performed a similar function but herself had to be transported except for very short passages.

LCE: Nos. 1 up

These were converted LCVs. equipped for the salvage and repair of minor landing craft in the beach area. On a loaded displacement of 10 tons they carried, in addition to their crew of 4, two motor mechanics, two shipwrights, one wireman and one stoker and were equipped with a Coston line gun, salvage pump, 80-lb., anchor, fire-fighting gear and a foam tank, engine spares, and spare planking and sheeting. *War losses:* *1943* Nos. 1 & 9; *1944* Nos. 5, 14, 15, 21.

LCV (M/S): Nos. 829, etc.

LCVs. fitted with light sweeps for minesweeping close inshore on assault beaches.

LCI (L): Nos. 3–16, 33, 35, 75, 97–136, 161–187, 193 209–218, 229, 231, 238–318, 374–391, 411, 487–496, 498–502, 505, 507–512, 537.

Displacement: 234/384 tons.
Dimensions: 150 (pp) 158½ (oa) × 23¼ × 4¾/6½ ft.

Machinery: 2-shaft General Motors diesel motors, B.H.P. 1,440 = 14 knots.
Armament: 4—20 mm. (4 × 1), 2—.303 in. (2 × 1) M.Gs.
Complement: 24.
War losses: *1943* Nos. 7, 107, 162, 309; *1944* Nos. 99, 102, 105, 132, 273.

Notes:—Built 1942-43. Ex-U.S.N. craft made available to the R.N. under *Lend/Lease*. Could carry 188 troops, except No. 537 210 troops, or 75t. d.w. Thirty were transferred to the R.C.N. and twenty converted into LCH. No. 101 was fitted out with Press facilities in 1944.

LCH: Nos. 100, 185, 243, 317, etc.

Were adapted from LCI(L)s. from which they were practically indistinguishable except for rigging details, to act as communications H.Qs., for groups of landing craft. *War loss: 1944* No. 185.

LCI (S): Nos. 501–600.

Displacement: 63/110 tons.
Dimensions: 100 (pp) 105 (oa) × 21½ × 3¼/3¾ ft.
Machinery: 2-shaft Hall Scott petrol motors, B.H.P. 1,140 = 14½ knots.
Armament: 2—20 mm. A.A. (2 × 1), 2—.303 in. (2 × 1) M.Gs.
Complement: 17.
War losses: *1944* Nos. 511, 512, 517, 524, 531, 532, 537, 540.

Notes:—Built 1943. Fairmile " **H** " type of wooden construction. Could carry 102 troops.

LCI(S). 501 on trials. Fairmile H type infantry landing craft were armoured and lightly armed; they proved very efficient during the invasion of France. [*Courtesy, Tough Bros.*

BUILDERS (Minor Landing Craft)

Allonson (Preston): LCP(M) 28–31.

A. R. C. Marine (Littlehampton):

Arbuthnott & Sons (Montrose):

Austin's (East Ham): LCP(S) 251, 257, 260; LCI(S). 507.

E. Ayling & Sons (Putney):

E. Bacon & Co. (Grimsby):

W. Bates & Son (Chertsey):

Bathurst (Tewkesbury):

Beeley & Sleight (Grimsby):

H. C. Benham (Horning):

Berthon Boat (Lymington): LCA 14–18, 53–56, 129–131; LCP(S) 41–70; LCH 243–252.

Bristol Boatbuilding:

Brooke Marine (Lowestoft): LCI(S) 512–515, 534, 538, 539.

J. Bushnell (Wargrave): LCP(M) 14–21, 32–41.

Calcutta Port Commissioners: LCA 2023–2030.

Cambridge Welding Co. (Hanwell): LCP(S) 186–200.

Cochin Hbr. Board: LCA 2001–2008.

M. Condron (Weymouth):

Consolidated Steel Corp. (Orange): LCI(L) 75, 97–136.

Cosens & Co. (Weymouth):

F. J. Deacon (Burlesdon):

Diamond Boatbuilding Co. (Cardiff):

J. W. Dixon & Sons (Exmouth):

East Kent Sbdg. & Eng. (Whitstable):

S. Elliott (   ): LCA 956.

Education Supply Services (London):

Edward (Kenley): LCP(S) 131–180.

Federal Sbdg. (Port Newark): LCI(L) 161–187, 193.

Fellows & Co. (Great Yarmouth):

J. E. Fletcher (Oulton Broad):

Garden Reach (Calcutta): LCA 322–331, 338–356, 2009–2016.

W. H. Gaze & Sons (Roehampton): LCP(S) 71–100, 201–220.

Hampton & Sons (Battersea):

Harris Lebus (London):

Harrison (Amble): LCP(M) 1–5.

A. C. Head (Greenock):

Higgins (New Orleans): LCP(L); LCP(R); LCV; LCVP.

Humphries & Sons (Parkstone):

J. James & Co. (Brightlingsea):

Johnson Bros. (*Peterhead*):

Kaygee Contracts (*Twickenham*):

C. F. Kearly (*Chiswick*):

R. D. Lambie (*Wallsend*):

E. C. Lansdowne (*Wroxham*):

Lavers & Co. (*Dartmouth*):

Geo. Lawley (*Neponset*): LCI(L) 209–218, 229, 231, 238, 374-391, 411.

C. H. Lewis & Sons (*Exmouth*):

Luke Bros. (*Hamble*):

A. Malcolm (*Port Bannatyne*):

Mann, Egerton & Co. (*Norwich*).

J. B. Marr (*Twickenham*):

Jas. Mears (*Twickenham*):

Menzies & Co. (*Leith*):

Minter (*Putney*): LCP(S) 21–40.

Chas. Morris (*Rye*):

Morris & Leavett (*Beaumaris*):

D. Monro & Son (*Blairmore*):

McNicoll Bros. (*Maryhill*):

New York Sbdg: LCI(L) 3–16, 33, 35.

Parkstone Joinery: LCP(S) 1–20.

R. J. Perkins (*Whitstable*):

Pleasure Craft Co. (*Lowestoft*): LCI(S) 520, 532.

P. D. S. Poole (*Parkstone*):

Jack Powles (*Wroxham*):

Leo A. Robinson (*Oulton Broad*): LCI(S) 511, 533.

Robsons Boatbuilders (*South Shields*):

Rodgeman Pomphrett (*Plymouth*): LCP(M) 6–13, 52–61.

Rose Street Foundry & Engine Co. (*Inverness*):

D. E. Scarr (*Goole & Hessle*):

K. R. Skentlebury (Plymouth):

Solent Shyd. (Sarisbury Green): LCI(S) 506.

Southern Rly. (Eastleigh): LCP(S) 101–130.

Thornycroft (Hampton): 3 × LCA; 5 × LCP(M); LCP(S) 181–185.

Timbercraft Ltd: (Rhu):

W. J. Todd (Weymouth):

Todd, Eyrie & Barber (New Jersey): LCI(L) 239–318, 487–496, 498–502, 505, 507–512, 537.

Tollesbury Yt. & Bt. Bldr.:

Tough Bros. (Teddington): LCI(S) 501, 525.

Underwood (South Benfleet): LCP(M) 22–27, 42–51.

United Trading Corp. (Calcutta): LCA. 2017–2022.

Walton Yt. Wks. (Shepperton):

Warren's New Holland Shyd.:

Western Marine Craft (Pwhllheli):

Willoughby (Plymouth):

Wood & Davidson (Aberdeen):

LANDING CRAFT MECHANISED (LCM)

AT the outbreak of war the only craft possessed by the Royal Navy that could land a tank were the LCM(1)s. which were then building. These craft were essentially powered pontoons with bullet proof bulwarks and propelled by twin screws. The cox'un was placed in a bullet proof position right aft, at the level of the tank deck, and consequently had rather restricted vision forward.

The LCM(2)s. were Higgin's prototypes adapted from shallow draught river tugs for the United States Marine Corp. Thereafter, they evinced little interest until sighted by a British naval mission in the United States who realised that, with a little modification, they could be altered to carry a 30-ton tank: double the load of an LCM(1). This resulted in the LCM(3), which was mass produced in the United States and transferred to the Royal Navy in large numbers under *Lend/Lease*. They were slightly larger than the LCM(1) and the after end of the tank deck was plated over and the cox'un placed there in a small, bullet proof shelter where his all-round vision was greatly increased. But while the riveted LCM(1) could be hoisted with her tank load the welded LCM(3) could not and the earlier model continued in production for some time.

The LCM(4) and LCM(5) were variants of the LCM(3) and were experimental types of which only a very few were ever built. The LCM(6) was an LCM(3) lengthened by a 6-foot section amidships to take a 34-ton tank and were only used in the United States Navy. To take an even heavier tank, and also with Far Eastern operations in mind, the Royal Navy developed the LCM(7) which was generally similar to the LCM(6). The final stage was reached with the

LCM(8), again used only by the United States Navy, which could accommodate a 55-ton tank.

Whereas the the earliest LCMs. built in the U.K. were constructed in the traditional yards, they were urgently required for other naval work and LCM construction was, therefore, soon switched to structural firms that could undertake the work. The Great Western Railway (Swindon) and the Southern Railway (Eastleigh) built large numbers of LCMs. and developed a technique, quite different from the traditional yards, for their construction which was passed on to the other firms that became involved in their construction.

LCM (1): Nos. 1–500, 4001–4100.

Displacement: 21/36 tons.
Dimensions: 44¾ (pp) 48½ (oa) × 14 × 2½/3½ ft.
Machinery: 2-shaft Thornycroft or Chrysler petrol motors, B.H.P. 120 = 7½ knots.
Armament: 2—.303 in. (1 × 2) M.Gs.
Complement: 6.
War losses: *1940* Nos. 10, 11, 12, 14, 15, 17, 18, 19, 20, 22; *1941* Nos. 1, 32, 55, 67, 82, 95, 96, 97, 103, 106, 107, 108; *1942* Nos. 23, 24, 25, 31, 34, 38, 45, 46, 51, 53, 56, 63, 64, 65, 69, 72, 73, 84, 89, 90, 93, 98, 110, 113, 119, 120, 122, 135, 137, 139, 140, 145, 146, 147, 148, 153, 161, 169, 186; *1943* Nos. 26, 33, 58, 61, 80, 181, 232; *1944* Nos. 76, 91, 127, 128, 131, 138, 165, 168, 180, 182, 183, 191, 192, 203, 207, 209, 212, 215, 216, 218, 219, 226, 229, 231, 234, 241, 243, 251, 254, 263, 272, 277, 279, 281, 282, 285, 288, 295, 316, 319, 324, 327, 329, 330, 335, 337, 338, 340, 345, 346, 348, 355, 357, 367, 377, 382, 383, 408, 409, 419, 421, 424, 425, 443, 444, 466; *1945* Nos. 136, 270, 339, 354, 359, 422, 493.

Notes:—Built 1940-44. Thornycroft design. Could carry 1 at 16t. tank or 6 jeeps or 100 troops and be hoisted with the load on board.

LCM (2): Nos.

Displacement: 21/51 tons.
Dimensions: 00 (pp) 45 (oa) × 14 × 3 ft.
Machinery: 2-shaft Kermath petrol motors, B.H.P. 200 = 7½ knots.
Armament: 2—.303 in. (1 × 2) M.Gs.
Complement: 4.

Notes:—Built 1941. Higgins design adapted from shallow draught river tugs. Twelve were built but do not appear to have come into operational service with the R.N.

LCM (3): Nos. 501–650, 900–1400.

Displacement: 22/52 tons.
Dimensions: 00 (pp) 50 (oa) × 14 × 3½/4½ ft.
Machinery: 2-shaft Diesel motors, B.H.P. 220/450 = 8½/11 knots.
Armament: 2—.303 in. (1 × 2) M.Gs.
Complement: 3.
War losses: *1942* Nos. 501, 508, 509, 510, 516, 518, 519, 520, 522, 523, 528, 532, 537, 539, 543, 547, 551, 555, 556, 558, 564, 567, 569, 571, 572, 574, 581, 584, 590, 592, 593, 595, 596, 606, 609, 611, 613, 620, 624, 632, 634, 635, 636; *1943* Nos. 545, 583, 938, 1044, 1165, 1182; *1944* Nos. 525, 527, 531, 534, 535, 540, 558, 559, 568, 577, 587, 588, 591, 618, 623, 627, 628, 631, 640, 641, 650, 907, 908, 910, 929, 930, 1022, 1029, 1045, 1053, 1059, 1062, 1064, 1071,

1083, 1088, 1098, 1101, 1108, 1115, 1120, 1123, 1127, 1128, 1130, 1139, 1145, 1146, 1161, 1171, 1173, 1175, 1189, 1197, 1200, 1204, 1205, 1207, 1208, 1212, 1220, 1221, 1227, 1232, 1233, 1240, 1244, 1278, 1282, 1293, 1297, 1313, 1314, 1373, 1378, 1380, 1381, 1397; *1945* Nos. 1011, 1092, 1131, 1185, 1319, 1327.

Notes:—Built 1942-44. Higgins design and made available to R.N. under *Lend/Lease*. Could carry 1 at 30t. tank or 60 troops or 30t. d.w.

LCM (4): Nos.

Were British variants of LCM(3) and only a few were built.

LCM (5): Nos.

Were British variants of LCM(3) and only a few were built.

LCM (6):

Displacement: 25/59 tons.
Dimensions: 000 (pp) 56 (oa) × 14 × 3½/4½ ft.
Machinery: 2-shaft Diesel motors, B.H.P. 450 = 9/11 knots.
Complement: 4.

Notes:—Higgins type LCM(3) with the hull lengthened 6 ft. amidships and not used in R.N. and could carry 1 at 34t. or 120 troops.

LCM (7): Nos. 7001–7150.

Displacement: 28/63 tons.
Dimensions: 57¾ (pp) 60¼ (oa) × 16 × 3¾/3¾ ft.
Machinery: 2-shaft Diesel motors, B.H.P. 290 = 9¾ knots.
Armament: 2—.303 in. (1 × 2) M.Gs.
Complement: 6.

Notes:—Built 1943-44. Thornycroft design. Could carry 1 at 35/40t. tank.

LCM (8):

Displacement: 60/115 tons.
Dimensions: 73¾ (oa) × 21 × 5¼ ft.
Machinery: 2-shaft Diesel motors, B.H.P. 650 = 9 knots
Complement: 8.

Notes:—Not used in R.N. and could carry 1 at 55t. tank.

BUILDERS (LCMs.)

Aldous Successors (*Brightlingsea*): LCM(1).
D. Badcock (*Greenwich*): LCM(1).
H. Balfour (*Fife*): LCM(1).
Cammell Laird (*Birkenhead*): LCM(I) 79–86, 131–134.
Clydebank: LCM(1) 103–110.
Danks (*Birmingham*): LCM(1).
Fairfield (*Govan*): LCM(1) 87–94, 135–138.
Fraser & Fraser (*Bromley-by-Bow*): LCM(1).
G.W.R. (*Swindon*): LCM(1) 151–162 and 28 more.
J. Harker (*Knottingley*): LCM(1).
Hawthorn Leslie (*Hebburn*): LCM(1) 115–118.
Higgins (*New Orleans*): LCM(2) : LCM(3).
Chas. Hill (*Bristol*): LCM(7) 7111–7123.
Humphrey & Grey (*Greenwich*): LCM(1).
Markham (*Chesterfield*): LCM(1).
Millen Bros. ( ): LCM(7).

Left: LCM(3). 528 was mass produced in the United States and was made available to the Royal Navy under *Lend/Lease*. The upper half of the bow ramp was of sparred construction to aid the forward vision of the cox'un. [*I.W.M.*

Right: LCM(7). 7174 belonged to the final mark of LCM produced for the Royal Navy during the war years. [*I.W.M.*

H. McLean (Renfrew): LCM(1) 33–38, 185–194, 365–370, 493–498, 4026-4031; LCM(7) 7099–7104.
Penarth Pontoon Slipway: LCM(0).
Port Talbot D. D. : LCM(1).
Prince of Wales D. D. (Swansea): LCM(1).
Retford Metal Works (Barking): LCM(1).
Scotts Sbdg. & Eng. (Glasgow): 3 × LCM(4)
Scottish Motor Traction (Edinburgh): LCM(7).
S.R. (Eastleigh): LCM(1).
Stephen (Linthouse): 4 × LCM (1).
Swan Hunter & Wigham Richardson (Hebburn): LCM(1) 67–78, 104–107.
John Thompson Watertube Boilers (   ): LCM(7).
Thornycroft (Woolston): 5 × LCM(1); 1 × LCM(7).
Tilbury Contracting & Dredging (Greenwich): LCM(7).
Towler & Sons (London): LCM(1).
V.A. (Tyne): LCM(1) 59–66.
Vosper (Portsmouth): LCM(1).
Jos. H. Westwood (Millwall): LCM(1).
White (Cowes): LCM(1) 123–126.

LANDING CRAFT TANK (LCT)

THE LCTs. were a natural upward development from the LCMs. Whereas the latter had to be transported to the beach area and could only carry a single tank, the scheme envisaged with the LCTs. was a craft to make an open sea passage and carry three of the heaviest tanks (40 tons) then contemplated.

The LCT(1)s. were built in the traditional shipyards and set the pattern for future construction. They had a long tank deck amidships, of cellular construction, with severely angled end sections. A hinged ramp was fitted forward and the bridge, engine room, and accommodation arranged aft. The tank deck was closed by doors at its fore end but was only covered by tarpaulins spread over steel bar supports. The tanks embarked were otherwise protected from the weather by a deep side, also of cellular construction, topped by a bulwark and these wing compartments were used for petrol storage, stores and bathrooms. There was an armoured wheelhouse over which was placed an open bridge and, abaft this, the deck was extended to the side to accommodate a single 2-pdr. A.A. gun in each wing. As their shallow draught made them difficult to manoeuvre they were given twin rudders and screws but were frequently prone to "take charge". They had to be handled with a heavy hand and leeway was best applied in multiples of 25°. They could be dismantled into four sections for transhipment as deck cargo if required.

The LCT(2)s. were generally similar but were given a slightly increased beam to raise the deadweight capacity, and three screws which fractionally improved the speed. With this group the first orders started to be spread among the structural steel firms to release the traditional shipbuilders for other essential work which only they could undertake. The later units of this class were also fitted with diesel instead of petrol engines which aided performance.

Demands for still increased deadweight resulted in the LCT(3)s. which again reverted to twin screws for simplified construction, and they had a 32 ft. section added amidships. This increased the number of sections to five when dismantled for transhipment. The prototype was obtained by adding this further section to an LCT(1) then building and the increased length proved quite satisfactory and, if anything, slightly raised the speed. Most of this group were built by the structural steel firms and smaller shipyards but a second series

Above: Two LCT(2)s under construction clearly showing the cellular form of bottom and wing tanks. [*Courtesy, Stockton Construction Co. Ltd.*

Below: An LCT(2) completing. Note hatch bars covering tank deck and armament of two .303 in. (2 × 1) M.Gs. [*Courtesy, Stockton Construction Co. Ltd.*

was undertaken, later in the war, by the traditional yards which again adopted petrol engines of much increased power.

A need for even more, and larger, craft of this type produced the LCT(4)s. Their construction was given over entirely to the structural steel firms and the design modified to suit their facilities. A flimsier form of construction was adopted; the beam further increased, to improve the deadweight, which resulted in a loss of speed; and all armament and armour was sacrificed. Although satisfactory from a purely functional view, they were later strengthened and armed, and those eventually destined for the Far East were further strengthened to make the passage out. In spite of their flimsy construction they were able to withstand considerable damage and stress and one unit entered harbour towing its disintegrated bow section astern!

LCT(5)s. reversed one of the original LCT conceptions, that of being able to make an open sea passage, as it was only intended to operate between ship and shore and was of reduced size. The reduction in size was only resorted to as an alternative to speed production, and the design was prepared concurrently with that for LST(2)s. whose specifications included that they could carry a complete LCT(5) on deck. For transhipment as deck cargo the LCT(5)s. were built in three sections and a large number were delivered in this way from the United States, where they were all built, and joined together afloat. From the LCT(5) the United States Navy developed the LCT(6), which was ramped at either end to facilitate loading from an LST and discharging on to a beach, and the LCT(7) which also adopted the double-ended arrangement but with more ship-shape lines to improve seaworthiness and speed.

The final stage was reached with the LCT(8)s. which were specially designed to meet operational requirements in the Far East and with them LCTs. passed from sea-going to fully ocean-going craft. Although the tank deck still remained open it was enclosed forward by a considerably heightened bow section fitted with a power operated ramp and bow doors. The poop was lengthened to provide more engine room and accommodation space and the after superstructure made more substantial. The engine power was doubled by fitting two diesel engines in tandem to each shaft and the speed increased to 12½ knots. Troop accommodation was also provided for the embarked tank crews and there was little doubt of the ability of these craft to make prolonged passages and keep the seas. Like so many Far Eastern projects their construction was arrested by the sudden end of hostilities when only a very few had been completed of which none served operationally. Compared with the rugged and simple LCT(1) the LCT(8)s. were far more complicated but sacrificed nothing in strength, still adhering to the cellular form for bottom and sides which had served the earlier craft so well. Their improved amenities for the crew were criticised in some quarters but, perhaps, overlooked the point that, with the earlier landing craft, combined operations had been mainly confined to the Mediterranean and North European areas where the amenities which did not exist aboard could be found ashore. But for the contemplated Far Eastern theatre there were no shore amenities and the crew would, perforce, be compelled to live aboard. The modicum of comfort provided only considered the vital human factor that no warship, of any type, can be efficiently operated without a fit and healthy crew. Perhaps the fairer comparison would be that the LCT(8)s. were not over elaborate in their amenities for the crew, but that the crew amenities provided in earlier craft were plainly primitive.

Such versatile craft as LCTs. naturally leant themselves to adaptation for other duties. The Mk. II, III, IV were converted into LCFs., LCG(L)s. and LCT(R)s.; while others were fitted out to carry locomotives and rolling stock; as hospital carriers; for emergency repair work; for clearing harbour obstruction;

Above: Bow view of LCT(2). 130, beached with the ramp down. Note two 20 mm. A.A. guns aft in bridge wings and method of covering tank hold by hatch bars and tarpaulins. [*I.W.M.*

Above and Below: Broadside views of LCT(2). 131 and 144. [*Courtesy, Stockton Construction Co., Ltd.*

as floating generator stations with a capacity of 2,000 kW., and as salvage craft when rigged with 50-ton sheerlegs.

The **"Z"** lighters were not used operationally but in harbours and anchorages for providing a ship-to-shore service with tanks, armoured vehicles, motor transports, etc. They were prefabricated in Indian shipyards and assembled in the Mediterranean where they were exclusively employed. Modelled on the military **"A"** lighters they were no more than powered pontoons, although fitted with a bow ramp, and it was not intended that they be used outside of port limits.

LCT (1): Nos. 1–99.

Displacement: 226/372 tons.
Dimensions: 135 (pp) 151¼ (oa) × 29 × 3/5¾ ft.
Machinery: 2-shaft Hall-Scott petrol motors, B.H.P. 1,000 = 10 knots.
Armament: 2—2 pdr. (2 × 1) guns.
Complement: 12.
War Losses: *1941* Nos. 1, 2, 5, 6, 7, 8, 10, 11, 12, 14, 15, 16, 19, 20; *1943* No. 3.

Notes:—Built 1940-41. Could carry 3 at 40t. or 6 at 20t. tanks. Craft were transportable in four sections. No. 3 was later salved and became NSC(L). 94.

LCT (2): Nos. 100–299.

Displacement: 296/453 tons.
Dimensions: 143 (pp) 160 (oa) × 31 × 3¾/7 ft.
Machinery: 3-shaft Napier petrol motors, B.H.P. 1,050 = 10½ knots (*earlier craft*) or Davey Paxman diesel motors, B.H.P. 1,380 = 11 knots (*later craft*).
Armament: 2—2 pdr. (2 × 1) or 2—20 mm. (2 × 1) guns.
Complement: 12.
War losses: *1941* Nos. 102, 103, 105, 109, 110, 143; *1942* Nos. 119, 120, 121, 124, 126, 145, 150, 155, 159; *1943* Nos. 106, 107, 115; *1944* No. 129.

Notes:—Built 1942-43. Could carry 3 at 40t. or 7 at 20t. tanks.

LCT (3): Nos. 300–499 (*first series*), 7001–7150 (*second series*).

Displacement: 350/640 (*first series*), 625 (*second series*) tons.
Dimensions: 175 (pp) 190¾ (oa) × 31 × 3¾/7 ft.
Machinery: 2-shaft Davy Paxman diesel motors, B.H.P. 920 = 10½ knots (*first series*) or Stirling petrol motors, B.H.P. 2,000 = 11½ knots (*second series*).
Armament: 2—2 pdr. (2 × 1) or 2—20 mm. (2 × 1) guns.
Complement: 12.
War losses: *1943* Nos. 326, 329, 332, 333, 343, 353, 358, 381, 385, 391, 395, 403, 418; *1944* Nos. 328, 375, 377, 387, 390, 427, 480, 488, 491, 494, 7011, 7014, 7015, 7057, 7064, 7089; *1945* Nos. 357, 492.

Notes:—Built 1941-42 (*first series*) & 1943-44 (*second series*). Could carry 5 at 40t. or 11 at 30t tanks or 10 at 3t. lorries or 300t. d.w. Were adapted from LCT(2) with 32 ft. section added amidships.

LCT (4): Nos. 500–1364.

Displacement: 200/586 tons.
Dimensions: 171 (pp) 187¼ (oa) × 38¾ × 3¾/4¼ ft.
Machinery: 2-shaft Davey Paxman diesel motors, B.H.P. 920 = 10 knots.

Above: A stern view of LCT(2). 162 showing the severely angled lines at the stern and at the turn of the bilge, the three shaft arrangement of the screws, and the single rudder. She is shown *below* running trials. [*Courtesy, Redpath, Brown & Co. Ltd.*

Armament:	Nil.
Complement:	12.
War losses:	*1943* Nos. 547, 553, 572, 583, 618, 621, 624, 626; *1944* Nos. 511, 524, 589, 609, 631, 689, 715, 750, 757, 789, 809, 839, 875, 886, 901, 936, 943, 947, 967, 976, 1022, 1023, 1029, 1039, 1045, 1074, 1076, 1092, 1133, 1171; *1945* No. 1238.

Notes:—Built 1942-45. Could carry 6 at 40t. or 9 at 30t. tanks or 12 at 3t. lorries or 300t. d.w. or be used as netlayers. Earlier units were unarmed and of flimsy construction but 2—20 mm. (2 × 1) guns were later added and the hull strengthened. For Far Eastern service they were further strengthened and the displacement rose to 611 tons.

LCT (5): Nos. 2002, 2004–2006, 2008–2014, 2037–2057, 2073–2079, 2119–2124, 2130, 2131, 2135, 2138, 2150, 2186–2194, 2225–2236, 2238–2240, 2243, 2246, 2261–2267, 2269, 2270, 2272, 2273, 2275, 2281–2287, 2289, 2291, 2292, 2295–2297, 2301–2304, 2306, 2307, 2308–2310, 2312, 2313, 2331, 2334–2339, 2341, 2343–2345, 2361, 2363, 2398, 2399, 2402, 2420–2430, 2432, 2433, 2435–2442, 2444, 2445, 2450, 2453–2455, 2461, 2477–2480, 2483–2485, 2487, 2488, 2490, 2491, 2498–2500.

Displacement:	143/311 tons.
Dimensions:	112¼ (pp) 117½ (oa) × 32¾ × 3/4½ ft.
Machinery:	3-shaft Gray diesel motors, B.H.P. 675 = 8 knots.
Armament:	2—20 mm. (2 × 1) guns.
Complement:	13.
War losses:	*1942* Nos. 2006, 2054, 2187, 2190, 2192, 2281, 2284, 2312; *1943* Nos. 2231, 2239, 2267, 2335, 2341, 2344, 2398, 2480; *1944* Nos. 2039, 2049, 2229, 2263, 2273, 2301, 2307, 2331, 2402, 2428, 2454, 2461, 2498.

Notes:—Built 1942-43. Ex-U.S.N. craft made available to the R.N. under *Lend/Lease* and had 2000 added to their original U.S.N. numbers. Could carry 3 at 50t. or 4 at 40t. or 5 at 30t. tanks or 9 at 3t. lorries or 150t. d.w. Were transportable in three sections of which five sections or one complete LCT(5) could be carried on an LST (2).

LCT (6): Nos. 2627 & 2628.

Displacement:	143/310 tons.
Dimensions:	112¼ (pp) 120 (oa) × 32¾ × 3½/4 ft.
Machinery:	2-shaft Gray diesel motors, B.H.P. 675 = 8 knots.
Armament:	2—20 mm. (2 × 1) guns.
Complement:	13.

Notes:—Built 1943. LCT(5) modified to permit bow or stern loading and with ramps at either end and the bridge offset to starboard. Twenty-one were provisionally to be made available to the R.N. under *Lend/Lease* but only the two above appear to have been delivered.

LCT (7):

Displacement:	513/900 tons.
Dimensions:	190 (pp) 203½ (oa) × 34½ × 3½/7 ft.
Machinery:	2-shaft General Motors or Fairbanks-Morse diesel motors, B.H.P. 2,800 = 13½ knots.
Armament:	6—20 mm. (6 × 1) guns.
Complement:	52.

Notes:—An improved U.S.N. version of the LCT(5) which retained the double-ended arrangement with the more ship-shape lines and better speed. Could carry 3 at 40t. or 5 at 30t. tanks and 54 troops. These craft were later re-classed as LSMs. in the U.S.N. and none ever served in the R.N.

Above: LCT(3). 398 was armed with two 2 pdr. A.A. guns and this type were lengthened editions of the LCT(1). [*I.W.M.*

Below: View from the bridge of the tank deck of an LCT(4). [*I.W.M.*

LCT(4). 1195 after being launched at the Warrenpoint shipyard.

Above: LCT(5). 2296 belonged to a group that was made available to the Royal Navy under *Lend/Lease* when 2000 was added to their original U.S.N. numbers. They were armed with two 20 mm. A.A. (2 × 1) guns and were diminutives of earlier marks of LCTs. [*I.W.M.*

Below: LCT(8). 4064 belonged to the final group of LCTs. and had a raised fo'c'sle to improve seaworthiness and adopted the bow doors fitted in LSTs. [*Courtesy, Redpath, Brown & Co. Ltd.*

LCT (8): Nos. 4001–4200.

Displacement: 657/895 tons.
Dimensions: 225 (pp) 231¼ (oa) × 39 × 3¾/5 ft.
Machinery: 2-shaft Davy Paxman diesel motors (two per shaft), B.H.P. 1,840 = 12½ knots.
Armament: 4—20 mm. (4 × 1) guns. *Complement:* 22.

Notes:—Built 1945-47. Thornycroft designed for Far Eastern service. Could carry 8 at 30t. tanks or 13 at 3t. lorries or 350t. d.w. and 42 troops.

" Z " Lighters: Nos. 1–60.

Displacement: 360/455 tons.
Dimensions: 134 (pp) 145 (oa) × 30 × 2¼/4 ft.
Machinery: 2-shaft Gray diesel motors, B.H.P. 200 (*earlier units*)/240 (*later units*) = 7½ knots.
Armament: Nil. *Complement:* 7.

Notes:—Built 1943-44. Design adapted from War Office "**A**" lighters. Could carry 6 at 15t. tanks or 9 at 3t. lorries or 95t. water.

BUILDERS (LCTs.)

Alcock, Ashdown (*Bombay*): 8 × "**Z**".
Sir Wm. Arrol (*Meadowside*): LCT(2) 149–152; LCT(3) 302–304, 360–365, 392–399, 403–407, 422–444, 461–464, 473–480, 7014–7017, 7122–7125; LCT(4) 500–504, 506, 656, 920, 921, 1108, 1109; LCT(8) 4064.
(*Alloa*): LCT(4) 849–864, 878–891, 1092–1099, 1162–1169, 1315–1320, 1329–1336, 1357–1364; LCT(8) 4037–4048, 4136–4147.
W. Badger (*East Smithfield*): LCT(4) 726–730 and 3 more.
Bison Sbdg. Corp. (*North Tonowanda*): LCT(5) 2186–2194; LCT(6) 2627, 2628.
Burn R Co. (*Calcutta*): 8 × " **Z** " (Z.6 (completed Hooghly)).
Cammell Laird (*Birkenhead*): LCT(1) 5, 6, 23, 24; LCT (2) 111, 112; LCT(3) 7043–7050.
Clydebank: LCT(1) 13, 14, 27, 28.
Decatur Iron & Steel: LCT(5) 2331, 2334–2339, 2341, 2343–2345.
Doxford (*Sunderland*): 2 × LCT(0).
Darby Products (*Kansas City*): LCT(5) 2281–2287, 2289, 2291, 2292, 2295–2297.
Fairfield (*Chepstow*): LCT(4) 599, 1000 and 59 more;
(*Govan*): 4 × LCT(0).
Alex Findlay (*Old Kilpatrick*): 5 × LCT(2); LCT(3) 802–809, and 30 more; 123 × LCT(4); 4 × LCT(8).
Furness Sbdg. (*Haverton*): LCT(3), 7101–7104.
Garden Reach (*Calcutta*): 14 × " **Z** " (Z.302–309, 319–321).
General Steam Nav. Co. (*Deptford*): LCT(2) 129; LCT(3) 335, 336, 341.
Green & Silley Weir (*Blackwell*): LCT(4) 723, 735–739 and 10 more.
Harland & Wolff (*Belfast*): 4 × LCT(4).
(*North Woolwich*): LCT (3) 903 and 11 more.
Hawthorn Leslie (*Hebburn*): LCT(1) 17, 18, 29, 30; LCT(3) 7069–7074.
Chas. Hill (*Bristol*): LCT(3) 7096.
Hooghly Dock & Eng. (*Calcutta*): 4 × " **Z** " (Z.1, Z.2, Z.13, Z.14).
Indian General Nav. Co. (*Calcutta*): 11 × " **Z** ".
Jones & Laughlin Steel Corp. (*Pittsburg*): LCT(5) 2073–2079.
Kansas City Structual Steel Co.: LCT(5) 2037–2057.
Lagan Construction Co. (*Belfast*): LCT(0).
Lobnitz (*Renfrew*): LCT(2).
Manchester D. D. Co. (*Runcorn*): LCT(0).
Manitowoc Sbdg. Corp.: LCT(5) 2002, 2004-2006, 2008–2014.

Missouri Valley Bridge & Iron: LCT(5) 2261–2267, 2269, 2270, 2272, 2273, 2275.
H. Mohatta (Karachi): 4 × "Z".
Motherwell Bridge & Eng. (Meadowside): LCT(4) 602–608, 781–789, 1041, 1346 and 39 more.
Mount Vernon Bridge Co. (Ironton): LCT(5), 2361, 2363, 2398, 2399.
MacLellan (Glasgow): 4 × LCT(2); 6 × LCT(3); LCT(4) 525, 668, 683, 881, 1048 and 72 more; 2 × LCT(8).
Omaha Steel Works: LCT(5) 2301–2304, 2306–2310, 2312, 2313.
New York Sbdg. (Camden): LCT(5) 2402, 2420–2430, 2432, 2433, 2435–2442, 2444, 2445, 2450, 2453–2455, 2461, 2477–2480, 2483–2485, 2487, 2488, 2490, 2491, 2498–2500.
Pickersgill (Sunderland): 6 × LCT(1).
Pidgeon Thomas Iron Co. (Memphis): LCT(5) 2225–2236, 2238–2243, 2246.
Jas Pollock (Faversham): LCT(2) 148; LCT(3) 350.
Quincy Barge Bldr.: LCT(5) 2119–2124, 2130, 2131, 2135, 2138, 2150.
Redpath Brown (Meadowside): LCT(2) 162–164; LCT(3) 308, 309, 376–379, 408–419, 445–460, 465–472, 7006–7013, 7018–7033, 7118–7121.
(Edinburgh): LCT(3) 404.
J. Russell & Co. (London): LCT(3); LCT(4) 637, 890–902.
Scotts (Greenock): LCT(1) 15, 16; LCT(3) 420.
Short Bros. (Sunderland): 1 × LCT(1).
Smiths Dock (Middlesbrough): LCT(3) 7051–7056.
Stephen (Linthouse): 2 × LCT (1).
Stockton Construction Co.:* LCT(2) 131–141, 143–147, 169–171; LCT(3) 300, 301, 327–332, 342–349, 353–359; LCT(4) 558–588, 613–616, 629–636, 639–641, 664, 665, 667, 669–682, 873–880, 922–935, 1006–1037, 1080–1091, 1100–1105, 1144–1157, 1211–1216, 1218–1224, 1275–1280, 1337; LCT(8) 4001–4006, 4027.
Swan, Hunter & Wigham Richardson (Wallsend): LCT(3) 7097–7100.
Tees Side Bridge & Eng. (Middlesbrough): LCT(2); LCT (3) 386; LCT(4) 555, 704–711, 720, 721, 762, 1072, 1120–1128 and 8 more.
Thornycroft (Woolston): 1 × LCT(3).
Tilbury Dredging & Contracting Co. (Greenwich): LCT(4).
V.A. (Tyne): LCT(1) 3, 4; LCT(2) ; LCT(4)
Warrenpoint (Co. Down): LCT(4) 1195.

LANDING CRAFT SUPPORT

THE need for support craft was early realised and was taken up pre-war when the prototype LCAs. (MLC 50 and MLC 51) were converted into BSCs. The basic idea was that both assault and support craft should have the same hulls, with the former carrying the troops and running-in under the close cover of the latter, which would be armed. Consequently, a proportion of the production LCAs. were armed with a 4-inch smoke mortar and two, single .5-inch M.Gs. mounted in the troop well and were classed as LCS(M)(1)s. They were protected by ¼-inch armour along the sides, a bullet proof shelter for the cox'un, and a bullet proof plate on deck, between the engines, to shield the motor mechanic. They were followed by the LCS(M)(2)s. which were similarly armed and armoured except that the M.Gs. were placed in a twin, power-operated mounting in a super-firing position abaft the cox'un's shelter. Both types suffered from the limitations of using a basically unaltered LCA hull form designed to beach, which they were not required to do. The LCS(M)(3)s. were, therefore, designed with a more ship-shape hull form and adjusted trim while retaining the same armament, and continued in production to the end of the war.

* Was a consortium formed by Cleveland Bridge & Eng. Co., Head Wrighton & Co., South Durham Steel & Iron Co., and Whessoe Ltd.

Following the introduction of the LCS(M)s. came the suggestion for HSCs. capable of countering tanks present in the beach area and of a size that could be hoisted out by a landing ships derricks. These were known as LCS(L)(1)s. and were provided with a tank type turret and gun as the most suitable anti-tank armament. They were, virtually, wooden floating and armoured tanks as opposed to their automotive counterparts ashore but the scale of protection was meagre and limited to thinly armoured sides ($\frac{3}{4}$-inch) and deck ($\frac{1}{4}$-inch) and bullet proof plating to the cox'un's shelter ($\frac{1}{2}$-inch) and gun positions ($\frac{1}{4}$-inch). They were armed with a 2-pdr. Besa gun in a Daimler turret forward, a 4-inch smoke mortar amidships abaft the cox'un's shelter, and a twin .5-inch M.G. mounting aft. They were not outstandingly successful in their designed role, too much having been attempted on the displacement, and did not remain long in production. However, as the need to counter tanks still remained a problem, the type was not completely abandoned but the weight restrictions were lifted. This enabled ten LCI(S)s. to be converted into LCS(L)(2)s. on the same general principles as the earlier craft except that a 6-pdr. replaced the 2-pdr. gun forward and two 20 mm. A.A. guns the smoke mortar amidships which was re-sited well forward, before the turret.

One result of the experience gained in the evacuation of Crete was the danger to which invading forces were exposed by aerial counter attack and the necessity for BPCs. in the absence of sufficient, or timely, air cover. In addition to increasing the A.A. armament of landing craft the need was felt for special A.A. landing craft. Two LCT(2)s. were accordingly converted into prototype LCF(2)s. and were respectively armed with heavy and light A.A. armaments, as opinion was divided as to which was most suitable. LCF(2)1. was a formidable small craft armed with two, twin 4-inch A.A. mountings, separated by blast screens on the tank deck, and controlled by an R.D.F. fitted HA.DCT on the bridge. A single 20 mm. A.A. gun in each bridge wing, and another right forward, completed the armament. LCF(2)2. adopted a uniformly light A.A. armament and had eight single 2-pdr. guns along the tank deck and four 20 mm. guns equally disposed for and aft. The latter armament was finally preferred and was mounted in the first group of LCF(3)s. but was modified for the second group and the LCF(4)s. by replacing four 2-pdr. by an equal number of 20 mm. guns.

The LCG(L)s. were introduced to engage the fixed shore defences expected to be encountered in coastal areas suitable for large scale landings from the sea. Although such targets were normally the commitment of pre-invasion bombardments by fleet units, there was always the possibility that some would escape destruction and would have to be dealt with, on the spot, when landings were mounted. Also, for small scale operations, fleet units may not be available for bombardment purposes. Following the success of LCF(2)1 the LCG(L)(3)s. were converted from LCT(3)s. and armed with two 4.7-inch guns ex-destroyers and three/five 20 mm. A.A. guns in wing positions before (not in all) and abaft the bridge and right forward. The gun crews were formed by Royal Marines and the craft were protected by $\frac{3}{8}$-inch armour on deck and sides and over the magazines. They proved most successful and a number of LCT(4)s. were more elaborately converted to LCG(L)(4)s. with a more ship-shape bow form, the after 4.7-inch gun made superfiring, all single 20 mm. replaced by twin mountings and two further wing positions added amidships, a simple pedestal director was placed on the bridge (also ex-destroyer), and the protection over vitals was increased to 1 to 2 inches of armour.

Developed at the same time as the LCG(L)s. were the LCT(R)s. These were simple conversions from LCT(2)s. and LCT(3)s. by the provision of a false deck over the tank space on which were placed nests of six rocket projectors fixed in bearing and elevation. This meant that LCT(R)s. had to be manoeuvred to an exact firing position off the beaches which, considering the vagaries of wind, tide, and the craft themselves (and the belonged to a group notorious for their idiosyncrasies in handling), was only achieved with difficulty in practice. Having made the desired position they could effectively saturate a beach area of 750 × 160 yards with a most impressive and morale boosting performance. A complete reload of rockets, for all projectors, was stowed under deck but took some time to effect and they were thus limited to two full discharges and a relatively short period at the beach heads. While undoubtedly more effective than the LCG(L)s. they lacked their mobility and endurance and the celerity with which they could answer demands from the shore for fire support.

The overall success of the LCG(L)s. largely inspired the LCG(M)s. which were specially designed and built to engage tanks and pill boxes ashore on near equal terms, and also incorporated a military requirement that fire power from Army type weapons should be available from the first moment of the initial assault. This meant, in its simplest terms, putting military guns into a ship sufficiently large to make an open sea passage which, by special flooding arrangements, could then ground as an off-shore gun platform. They were protected by ⅜-inch to ½-inch armour and were armed with two 17-pdr. or 25-pdr. gun/howitzers, mounted in turrets *en echelon* on the foredeck, and two 20 mm. A.A. guns abaft the bridge. By the time the first LCG(M)s. were completed the main European landings were over and later units were modified, for Far Eastern service, with less protection but increased armament and the special flooding arrangements omitted.

As the LCG(M)s. with their ship-shape hull forms, proved such better seaboats than the LCTs. they were considered superior alternatives to the LCT(R)s. if armed with rockets instead of guns. Classed LCS(R)s. for this new role only the prototype was completed before the sudden end of hostilities and they were deprived of the opportunity to show their merit.

From the design point of view the support craft were, by far, the most interesting among the family of landing craft and their conception and design all things considered, was of the highest order. They unhesitatingly closed the beaches to render all possible support to the troops ashore and deservedly won high praise from all quarters.

LCS (M) (1): Nos. 1–24.

Displacement: 9/10½ tons.
Dimensions: 38¾ (pp) 41½ (oa) × 10 × 2 ft.
Machinery: 2-shaft Ford petrol motors, B.H.P. 130 = 10 knots.
Armament: 1—4in., smoke mortar, 2—.5 in. (2 × 1) M.Gs.
Complement: 11.
War losses: *1941* No. 1; *1942* Nos. 4, 6, 9, 11, 14, 15, 18, 19, 22; *1943* Nos. 16, 17, 23.

Notes:—Conversions from LCAs.

LCS (M) (2): Nos. 25–40.

Displacement: 10½/12½ tons.
Dimensions: 38¾ (pp) 41½ (oa) × 10 × 2 ft.
Machinery: 2-shaft Ford petrol motors, B.H.P. 130 = 10 knots.
Armament: 1—4 in., smoke mortar, 2—.5 in. (1 × 2) M.Gs
Complement: 11.
War losses: *1942* No. 28; *1945* No. 30.

Notes:—Conversions from LCAa.

LCS (M) (3): Nos. 41–120.

Displacement: 11½/13¼ tons.

Dimensions: 38¾ (pp) 41¾ (oa) × 10 × 2 ft.
Machinery: 2-shaft Ford petrol motors, B.H.P. 130 = 10 knots.
Armament: 1—4 in. smoke mortar, 2—.5 in. (1 × 2), 2—.303 in. (2 × 1) M.G.
Complement: 11.
War losses: *1944* Nos. 42, 46, 47, 49, 54, 59, 69, 75, 76, 80, 81, 83, 91, 99, 101, 103, 108, 114; *1945* No. 148.

Notes:—Built 1942-43. Wooden construction.

LCS (L) (1): Nos. 1–250.

Displacement: 20/24½ tons.
Dimensions: 45(pp) 47 (oa) × 12½ × 2/4 ft.
Machinery: 2-shaft Gray diesel motors, B.H.P. 330 = 10¾ knots.
Armament: 1—4 in. smoke mortar, 1—2 pdr., 2—.5 in. A.A. (1 × 2), 2—.303 in. A.A. (2 × 1) M.Gs.
Complement: 13.
War losses: *1943* No. 201.

Notes:—Built 1943-44. Thornycroft design of wooden construction.

LCS (L) (2): Nos. 251–260.

Displacement: 84/112 tons.
Dimensions: 000 (pp) 105 (oa) × 21½ × 2¼/3¼ ft.
Machinery: 2-shaft Hall Scott petrol motors, B.H.P. 1,140 = 14½ knots.
Armament: 1—4 in. smoke mortar, 1—6 pdr., 2—20 mm. A.A. (2 × 1), 2—.5 in. A.A. (1 × 2) M.Gs.
Complement: 25.
War losses: *1944* Nos. 252, 256, 258.

Notes:—Conversions from LCI(S).

LCF (2): Nos. 1 & 2.

Displacement: 539 tons.
Dimensions: 143 (pp) 160 (oa) × 31 × 3¾/7 ft.
Machinery: 3-shaft Davey Paxman diesel motors, B.H.P. 1,380 = 11 knots.
Armament: 4—4 in. A.A. (2 × 2), 3—20 mm. A.A. (3 × 1) guns (*No. 1*) or 8—2 pdr. A.A. (8 × 1), 4—20 mm. A.A. (4 × 1) guns (*No. 2*).
Complement: 74 (*No. 1*) or 67 (*No. 2*).
War losses: *1942* No. 2; *1944* No. 1.

Notes:—Conversions from LCT(2), subsequently re-classed as LCF(L).

LCF (3): Nos. 3–6 (*first group*), 7–18 (*second group*).

Displacement: 470 tons.
Dimensions: 175 (pp) 190¾ (oa) × 31 × 3¾/7 ft.
Machinery: 2-shaft Davey Paxman diesel motors, B.H.P. 920 = 11 knots.
Armament: 8—2 pdr. A.A. (8 × 1), 4—20 mm. A.A. (4 × 1) guns (*first group*); or 4—2 pdr. A.A. (4 × 1), 8—20 mm. A.A. (8 × 1) guns (*second group*).
Complement: 62 (*first group*) or 66 (*second group*).
War losses: *1943* No. 13; *1944* No. 15.

Notes:—Conversions from LCT(3), subsequently re-classed as LCF(L).

LCF (4): Nos. 19–46.

Displacement: 415 tons.
Dimensions: 171 (pp) 187¼ (oa) × 38¾ × 3½/4½ ft.

Above: LCS(M)(3). 47 was modelled on the LCA hull but with a ship-shape bow and was armed with a 4 in. smoke mortar forward and a twin .5 in. M.G. mounting. Note armoured sides and conning position. [*I.W.M.*

Below: LCS(L)(2). 253 was converted from an LCI(S) and was armed with a 6 pdr. gun, two 20 mm. A.A. (2 × 1) amidships and two .5 in. M.Gs. (1 × 2) aft. In addition, a 4 in. smoke mortar was countersunk before the turret. [*H. T. Percival*

LCF(4). 32 was converted from an LCT(4) and was armed with four 2 pdr. (4 × 1) and eight 20 mm. (8 × 1) A.A. guns and proved a most useful craft. [I.W.M.

Left: LCG(L). 939 converted from an LCT(4), armed with two 4.7 in. (2 × 1) and seven 20 mm. A.A. (7 × 1) guns. The single 20 mm. were later replaced by twin manual mountings in most of this type. [I.W.M.

Below: LCG(L). 13, here seen making smoke, was converted from an LCT(3) and was armed with easy recognisable ex-destroyer 4.7 in. guns. [I.W.M.

Machinery: 2-shaft Davey Paxman diesel motors, B.H.P. 920 = 11 knots.
Armament: 4—2 pdr. A.A. (4 × 1), 8—20 mm. A.A. (8 × 1) guns.
Complement: 66. *War losses:* 1944 Nos. 31, 37, 38.
Notes:—Conversions from LCT(4), subsequently re-classed as LCF(L).

LCG (L) (3): Nos. 1–30.

Displacement: 491 tons.
Dimensions: 175 (pp) 190¾ (oa) × 31 × 3¾/7 ft.
Machinery: 2-shaft Davey Paxman diesel motors, B.H.P. 920 = 10 knots.
Armament: 2—4.7 in. (2 × 1), 3/5—20 mm. A.A. (3/5 × 1) guns.
Complement: 47. *War losses:* *1943* Nos. 15 & 16; *1944* Nos. 1 & 2.
Notes:—Conversions from LCT(3) armed with ex-destroyer guns.

LCG (L) (4): Nos. 680, 681, 687, 764, 831, 939, 1007, 1062, etc.

Displacement: 570 tons.
Dimensions: 171 (pp) 185½ (oa) × 38¾ × 3¾/4½ ft.
Machinery: 2-shaft Davey Paxman diesel motors, B.H.P. 920 =10 knots.
Armament: 2—4.7 in. (2 × 1), 10/14—20 mm. A.A. (5/7 × 2) guns.
Complement: 48. *War losses:* *1944* Nos. 764, 831, 1062.
Notes:—Conversions from LCT(4) armed with ex-destroyer guns.

LCT (R): Nos. 334, 425, 452, 457, 460, 473, 1064, 1405, etc.

Conversions from LCT(2) and LCT(3) which could rapidly revert to LCTs. and were consequently not renumbered. Fitted with false decks on which LCT(2) mounted 792—5 in. rockets (132 × 6 and LCT(3) 1,080—5 in. rockets (180 ×6) which were electrically fired in 24 salvoes at a fixed range of 3,500 yards saturating a beach area of 750 × 160 yards with a density of one rocket per 100 sq. yd. Either H.E., C.S.A., or incendiary heads could be fitted to the rockets. *War loss: 1944* No. 457.

LCS (R): Nos. 1–30.

The success of the LCT(R)s. led to the suggestion that future conversions be made from the more seaworthy LCG(M)s. However, with building capacity fully extended, it was only possible to complete rocket-armed LCG(M)s., which were classed as LCS(R)s., at the expense of their gun-armed contemporaries. A limited number of such conversions were put in hand but only the prototype craft was completed before the termination of hostilities.

LCG (M) (1): Nos. 101–200.

Displacement: 270/381 tons.
Dimensions: 0000 (pp) 154½ (oa) × 22¼ × 6 ft.
Machinery: 2-shaft Davey Paxman diesel motors, B.H.P. 920/1,000 = 13½/11¾ knots.
Armament: 2—17 pdr. or 25 pdr. (2 × 1), 2—20 mm. A.A. (2 × 1) guns.
Complement: 31/35. *War losses:* *1944* Nos. 101 & 102.
Notes:—Built 1944. Clydebank design.

LCG (2): Nos. 501–524

Were LCG(M)(1)s. modified for Far Eastern service with increased armament, reduced protection and flooding arrangements omitted. None entered service.

BUILDERS (Support landing craft).

Sir Wm. Arrol (*Meadowside*)*:* LCF(3) 15, 16; LCG(L)(3) 1; LCT(R) 460, 473; LCG(M)(1) 143–150; LCG(M)(2) 513–524 and 8 more.

Left: Another view of LCG(L). 939 converted from an LCT(4). [*I.W.M.*

Below: LCT(R). 334, converted from an LCT(3), armed with two 20 mm. A.A. guns in addition to rockets, she was also fitted with SB.RDF to aid position fixing. [*I.W.M.*

Above: LCG(M). 177 was armed with two 25 pdr. Army pattern guns in turrets mounted *en echelon* on the foc's'le and two 20 mm. A.A. (2 × 1) guns abaft the bridge. [*Courtesy, Stockton Construction Co. Ltd.*

Right: Bow view of LCG(M). 176 while fitting out. [*Courtesy, Stockton Construction Co. Ltd.*

Austins (*East Ham*): LCS(L)(2) 251.
Berthon Boat (*Lymington*): LCS(M)(1) 23, 24.
Brooke Marine (*Lowestoft*): LCS(L)(2) 255.
Denny (*Dunbarton*): LCG(L)(4) 687.
Dickie (*Bangor*): LCS(L)(2) 254.
Alex. Finlay (*Motherwell*): LCF(4) 19 and 2 more; 15 × LCG(L); 4 × LCT(R).
Fleming & Ferguson (*Paisley*): LCG(L)(3) 26.
General Steam Navigation Co. (*Deptford*): LCG(M) 120, 187; LCF(3) 9, 10.
H. T. Percival (*Horning*): LCS(L) 253, 259.
Jas. Pollock (*Faversham*): LCF(3) 11.
Redpath Brown (*Meadowside*): LCF(3) 17, 18.
J. Russell (*London*): LCF(3) 7, 8.
Solent Shyd. (*Sarisbury Green*): LCS(L) 252, 258.
Stockton Construction Co.: LCG(M)(1) 175–190; LCF(3) 13, 14; LCF(4) 35; LCG(L)(3) 3; LCS(R) 25–29.
Tees Side Bridge & Eng. (*Middlesbrough*): LCF(3) 1, 2 (both completed *Palmers, Hebburn*), 3; LCF(4) 38; LCG(L)(3) 2; LCG(M)(1) 124, 127; LCS (R) 5, 10.
Thornycroft (*Woolston*): 24 × LCS(M).
Tilbury Dredging & Contracting (*Greenwich*): LCF(3) 12.

LANDING BARGES

ALTHOUGH the production of landing craft reached a high level and, at times, the highest priority, numbers were always slightly below requirements. To meet this deficiency a large number of commercial swim barges were requisitioned for the European landings and played a valuable role in the ensuing operations.

The barges (LBs.) originally taken up were not structurally altered, at first, but were later ramped (LBRs.). A proportion of the LBRs. were subsequently powered and re-classed as either LBV(1)s., for those remaining dumb, or LBV(2) for those barges that were engined. The groups were not individually numbered, nor were they of uniform size, and were used to ferry vehicles and military equipment from the landing ships to the beach.

The LBOs. and LBWs. were also a collective group, powered, and fitted with two cylindrical tanks for the bulk carriage of fuel or water. The LBEs. were ramped and powered and carried a workshop lorry which they could, if required, put ashore. The LBKs. had a large galley built over the hatch while the hold below was used to store provisions. They were powered and could so proceed independently over the whole beach area and keep the troops and the crews of minor landing craft fed.

The LBFs. and LBGs. both carried Army pattern guns, on wheeled mountings which could be used in support of the troops until they were required ashore. As both types were ramped and powered they could be beached and their guns landed. The troops embarked as gun crews fought their weapons both afloat and ashore.

The barges used were of a variety of types but fell into three main groups of *ca.* 100t., 150t., or 200t. d.w. Their conversions were kept simple and, except for the LBFs., and LBGs., they were armed with a single or twin M.Gs. They proved an excellent substitute for landing craft but were too large to be handled by anything other than a heavy derrick.

LB: Nos. 1–500*.

Dumb swim barges of 150t. d.w. and 200t. d.w. *War losses: 1942* (150t.) Nos. 332 & 362 (200t.) No. 382.

* All four groups were collectively numbered.

LBR: Nos. 1–500.*

Dumb swim barges of 100t. d.w. and 150t. d.w. fitted with stern ramp. *War losses: 1944* (100t.) Nos. 43, 65, 83; *1945* (150t.) Nos. 59 & 114.

LBV (1): Nos. 1–500*.

Dumb swim barges of 100t. (*ca.* 70 × 18 × 5 ft.), and 150t. d.w. (*ca.* 78 × 20 × 5 ft.), fitted with stern ramp and generally armed with 1—.303 in. M.G. *War losses: 1944* Nos. 3, 16, 19, 20, 27, 28, 49, 51, 52, 61, 67, 83, 84, 94, 95, 103, 116, 121, 122, 136, 149, 154, 175, 209, 214, 229, 266, 267, 367, 497; *1945* Nos. 1, 5, 9, 11, 31, 35, 42, 65, 72, 73, 75, 76, 99, 118, 211, 212.

LBV (2): Nos. 1–500*.

Swim barges of 200t. d.w. (*ca.* 82 × 23 × 5 ft.) fitted with stern ramp, powered by 2-shaft Chrysler petrol motors, B.H.P. 130 = 6/5 knots, and generally armed with 2—.303 in. (1 × 2) M.Gs. *War losses: 1944* Nos. 172, 176, 206, 232; *1945* Nos. 132, 137, 140, 152, 157, 170.

LBO: Nos. 1–100†.

Swim barges of 150t. and 200t. d.w. fitted with two tanks, powered by 2-shaft Chrysler petrol motors, B.H.P. 130 = 6/5 knots, and generally armed with 2—.303 in. (1 × 2) M.Gs. *War losses: 1944* (150t.) Nos. 4, 10, 30, 73 (200t.) Nos. 46, 50, 53, 56, 84, 87; *1945* (150t.) Nos. 11, 17, 21, 24, 26, 77, 82, 92, 95 (200t.) Nos. 13, 37, 63, 69, 88, 96.

LBW: Nos. 1–100†.

Swim barges of 150t. and 200t. d.w. fitted as LBOs. *War losses: 1944* (150t.) Nos. 7, 11, 14 (200t.) No. 15; *1945* (150t.) Nos. 1 & 6.

LBE: Nos. 1–60.

Swim barges of 150t. and 200t. d.w. fitted with stern ramp, powered by 2-shaft Chrysler petrol motors, B.H.P. 130 = 6 knots, and generally armed with 1—20 mm. A.A. gun. Carried a 3t. workshop lorry fitted with lathe, drill, two benches, and self contained generator and welding equipment, or a crawler crane. *War losses: 1944* Nos. 8, 17, 25, 26, 27, 57, 60; *1945* Nos. 12, 30, 32, 33, 34. *Complement:* 18/24.

LBK: Nos. 1 up

Swim barges of 150t. d.w., powered by 2-shaft Chrysler petrol motors, B.H.P. 130 = 6 knots, and fitted and stored to feed 900 troops for one week. *Complement:* 25. *War loss: 1945* No. 8.

LBF: Nos. 1 up

Swim barges powered by 2-shaft Chrysler petrol motors, B.H.P. 300 = 7 knots, and armed with 2—40 mm. A.A. (2 × 1 on army wheeled mountings), 2—20 mm. A.A. (2 × 1) or 4—.303 in. A.A. (2 × 2) M.Gs. *Complement:* 6 plus 16 troops.

LBG: Nos. 1 up

Swim barges powered by 2-shaft Chrysler petrol motors, B.H.P. 300 = 7 knots, and armed with 2—25 pdr. (2 × 1 on Army mountings), 2—20 mm. A.A. (2 × 1) guns. *Complement:* 6 plus 16 troops.

---

* All four groups were collectively numbered.
† Both groups were collectively numbered.

Above: An LBR fitted with a stern ramp and conning position aft and armed with an MG. forward. [*I.W.M.*

Below: LBV(L) 44 was one of the larger (200t. d.w.), powered barges fitted with a stern ramp and a twin MG. mounting forward. [*I.W.M.*

Above: An LBO showing tank fitted in the hold. [*I.W.M.*

Below: LBK.1 providing food for landing craft crews. [*I.W.M.*

MISCELLANEOUS AUXILIARIES

(a) Accommodation ships (not commissioned as H.M. Ships)

P.No.	Name	Gross tonnage/ year built	Requi- sitioned	Fate
	ALBERT C. FIELD	1,764/23	1942	Returned M.O.W.T. 1944; lost 18/6/44
	DUCHESS OF ROTHESAY	338/94	1943	Ex-P.M.S.; returned 1946.
	EAGLESCLIFF HALL	1,900/28	1942	Returned 1945.
	HANTONIA	1,560/11	1942	Returned 1945.
	NORTHLAND	1,255/29	1943	Returned 1944.
	PAUL EMILE JAVERY	2,471/26	1942	Returned 1945.
	PRESIDENT WARFIELD	4,273/28	1943	Returned 1944.
	SOUTHLAND	3,117/08	1943	Returned 1944.
	TROUBADOR	1,245/24	1942	Ex-A/S yacht; sold 1947.

Notes:—NORTHLAND, SOUTHLAND and PRESIDENT WARFIELD were made available to the R.N. under *Lend/Lease*.

(b) Special service and training ships:

	ALICE	527/30	1943	Ex-A/S yacht; returned 1945.
	ATALANTA	463/06	1942	Returned 1945.
	CACOUNA	202/32	1943	Ex-escort yacht; returned 1946.
	JUDITH	000/00	1942	Returned 1945.
	PING WO (R.A.N.)	3,105/22	1943	Water carrier (1944); returned 1946.
	St. ADRIAN	388/27	1943	Sold 1945.
	SISTER ANNE	250/29	1942	Ex-accommodation yacht; returned 1945.
	THALABA (ex-Atlantis)	223/26	1943	Ex-M/S yacht; returned 1946.
	YING CHOW	1,992/05	1942	Base ship 1945; returned 1945.

DEPLOYMENT OF LANDING SHIPS AND CRAFT—May, 1944

FORCE G LSH(L) Bulolo (flag)

Assault group G.1 (*Weymouth*): LSH(S) Nith; LSI(L) Empire Arquebus, Empire Crossbow, Empire Spearhead, Glenroy.

Assault group G.2 (*Weymouth*): LSH(S) Kingsmill; LSI(L) Empire Lance, Empire Mace, Empire Rapier.

Assault Group G.3 (*Weymouth*): LSH(S) Albrighton; LSI(L) Empire Halberd.
Unattached: LSD Northway; LSE Adventure, No. 2.

FORCE J LSH(L) Hilary

Assault group J.1 (*Exbury*): LSH(S) Lawford; LSI(L) Llangibby Castle; LSI(M) Queen Emma; LSI(H) Biarritz, Canterbury, Duke of Argyll, Invicta, Isle of Thanet, Lairds Isle, Mecklenburgh, Ulster Monarch.
Assault group J.2 (*Southampton*): LSH(S) Waveney; LSI(L) Monowai; LSI(H) Brigadier, Duke of Wellington, Isle of Guernsey, Lady of Mann, St. Helier.
Assault group J.3 (*Cowes*): LSH(L) Royal Ulsterman; LST Tasajera & 8 LST(2)s.
Assault group J.4 (*Southampton*): LSI(M) Prince David, Prince Henry; LSI(S) Amsterdam, Prins Albert, Prinses Astrid, Prince Baudouin, Prince Charles, Prinses Josephine Charlotte, Prince Leopold, Princess Margaret; LSI(H) Maid of Orleans, Princes Maud, Victoria.
Unattached: LSI(L) Lamont; FDT Nos. 13, 216, 217.

FORCE L

Assault group L.1 (*Southwold*): LST Bachaquero, Misoa.

FORCE O

LSI(L) Empire Anvil, Empire Javelin.

FORCE S LSH(L) Largs

Assault group S.1 (*Portsmouth*): LSH(S) Locust; LST 9 LST(2)s.
Assault group S.2 (*Newhaven*): LSH(S) Goathland.
Assault group S.3 (*Portsmouth*): LSH(S) Dacres; LSI(L) Empire Battleaxe, Empire Broadsword, Empire Cutlass, Glenearn.

FORCE U

LSI(L) Empire Gauntlett.

Fitting out (in U.K.): LSI(L) Pampas (ii); LSI(H) Royal Ulsterman; LSH(L) Lothian; LSS Daffodil, Princess Iris; LSC Empire Charmain; LSD Eastway; LSE No. 1 (on passage to U.K.).
Mediterranean: LSI(L) Ascania, Batory, Circassia, Derbyshire, Empire Pride, Keren, Glengyle, Sobieski, Winchester Castle; LSI(M) Prinses Beatrix; LSI(H) Royal Scotsman; LSG Derwentdale, Dewdale, Ennerdale; LSD Highway, Oceanway; LST 8 LST(2)s.; LSF Antwerp, Boxer, Bruizer, Palomares, Stuart Prince, Thruster, Ulster Queen.
East Indies: LSI(L) Barpeta; LSC Empire Elaine.
Australia: LSI(L) Kanimbla, Manoora, Westralia.

ABBREVIATIONS

A.A. anti-aircraft
A.B.V. armed boarding vessel
ALC assault landing craft, later LCA
AM ocean minesweeper (U.S.N.)
A.M.C. armed merchant cruiser
A.M.S. auxiliary minesweeper
A/P auxiliary patrol
A.P.V. auxiliary patrol vessel
AR repair ship (U.S.N.)
ARS salvage vessel (U.S.N.)
A/S anti-submarine
ASL anti-submarine launch
A.S.R. air/sea rescue
AT fleet tug (U.S.N.)
ATR rescue tug (U.S.N.)
Aux. auxiliary
A.W. air warning

B & P Boulton & Paul turret(s)
B.B.V. balloon barrage vessel
B.D.V. boom defence vessel
B.G.V. boom gate vessel
B.H.P. brake horse power
BPC beach protection craft
B.S. base ship
BSC beach support craft, later LCS(S)
B.V. barrage vessel (dumb)
BYMS motor minesweeper (U.S.N. designation)

C.A.M. catapult merchant ship
C.F. coastal forces
CMB coastal motor boat
C.R.S. convoy rescue ship
C.S.V. coastal salvage vessel
CT control & target boat
C.V. cable vessel

d depth (*not draught*)
DC diagonal compound
DCMB distant control motor boat
D/G de-gaussing
D.G.V. de-gaussing vessel
D/L danlayer
D/P de-perming
D.P.V. de-perming vessel
D.S. depot ship
DTE diagonal triple expansion
d.w. deadweight (tons)

Esso fuel carrying trawler
Exam. examination service

F.D. flight deck
F.D.B. fast despatch boat
F.D.S. fighter direction ship
F.P.B. fishery protection vessel
F.R.S. fishery research vessel
FY fishery pennant
F.D.T. fighter direction tender

G/B gunboat
G.V. gate vessel (dumb)

HA.DCT high angle director control tower
HDML harbour defence motor launch
H.D.P.C. harbour defence patrol craft
H.G. Hotchkiss machine gun
HMC & E Customs & Excise
H.Q.S. headquarters ship
HSC heavy support craft, later LCS(L)
H.S.L. high speed launch (R.A.F.)

I.H.P. indicated horse power
in. inch

KVB kite balloon vessel

LB landing barge
LBE landing barge, emergency repair
LBF landing barge, flak
LBG landing barge, gun
LBK landing barge, kitchen
LBO landing barge, oiler

LBR	landing barge, ramped
LBV (1)	landing barge, vehicle, Mk. I
LBV (2)	landing barge, vehicle, Mk. II
LBW	landing barge, water
LCA	landing craft, assault
LCA (FT)	landing craft, assault, flame thrower
LCA (HR)	landing craft, assault, hedgerow
LCA (OC)	landing craft, assault, obstruction clearance
LCC	landing craft, control
LCCS	landing craft, casualty clearing station
LCE	landing craft, emergency repair
LCF (2)	landing craft, flak, Mk. II, later LCF (L)
LCF (3)	landing craft, flak, Mk. III, later LCF (L)
LCF (4)	landing craft, flak, Mk. IV, later LCF (L)
LCF (L)	landing craft, flak, large
LCG (L) (3)	landing craft, gun, large, Mk. III
LCG (L) (4)	landing craft, gun, large, Mk. IV
LCG (M) (1)	landing craft, gun, medium, Mk. I
LCH	landing craft, hospital or headquarters
LCI (L)	landing craft, infantry, large
LCI (S)	landing craft, infantry, small
LCI (Press)	landing craft, infantry, Press
LCI (Smoke)	landing craft, infantry, smoke
LCI (Stores)	landing craft, infantry, stores
LCM (1)	landing craft, mechanised, Mk. I
LCM (2)	landing craft, mechanised, Mk. II
LCM (3)	landing craft, mechanised, Mk. III
LCM (4)	landing craft, mechanised, Mk. IV
LCM (5)	landing craft, mechanised, Mk. V
LCM (6)	landing craft, mechanised, Mk. VI
LCM (7)	landing craft, mechanised, Mk. VII
LCM (8)	landing craft, mechanised, Mk. VIII
LCM (Smoke)	landing craft, mechanised, smoke
LCN	landing craft, navigation leader
LCP (1)	landing craft, personnel, Mk. I
LCP (2)	landing craft, personnel, Mk. II
LCP (L)	landing craft, personnel, large
LCP (M)	landing craft, personnel, medium
LCP (R)	landing craft, personnel, ramped
LCP (S)	landing craft, personnel, small
LCP (Sy)	landing craft, personnel, supply
LCQ	landing craft, administration
LCS (L) (1)	landing craft, support, large, Mk. I
LCS (L) (2)	landing craft, support, large, Mk. II
LCS (M) (1)	landing craft, support, medium, Mk. I
LCS (M) (2)	landing craft, support, medium, Mk. II
LCS (M) (3)	landing craft, support, medium, Mk. III
LCS (R)	landing craft, support, rocket
LCT (1)	landing craft, tank, Mk. I
LCT (2)	landing craft, tank, Mk. II
LCT (3)	landing craft, tank, Mk. III
LCT (4)	landing craft, tank, Mk. IV
LCT (5)	landing craft, tank, Mk. V
LCT (6)	landing craft, tank, Mk. VI
LCT (7)	landing craft, tank, Mk. VII
LCT (8)	landing craft, tank, Mk. VIII
LCT (CB)	landing craft, tank, concrete breaker
LCT (E)	landing craft, tank, emergency repair

LCT (H)	landing craft, tank, hospital
LCT (HE)	landing craft, tank
LCT (Loco)	landing craft, tank, locomotive
LCT (R) (2)	landing craft, tank, rocket, Mk. II
LCT (R) (3)	landing craft, tank, rocket, Mk. III
LCT (SV)	landing craft, tank, salvage
LCU	landing craft, utility
LCV	landing craft, vehicle
LCV (M/S)	landing craft, vehicle, minesweeping
LCVP	landing craft, vehicle/personnel
LCW	landing craft, air propelled
LG	Lewis machine gun
LRRC	Long range rescue craft (R.A.F.)
LSC	landing ship, carrier
LSD	landing ship, dock
LSE	landing ship, emergency repair
LSF	landing ship, fighter direction
LSG	landing ship, gantry
LSH (L)	landing ship, headquarters, large
LSH (S)	landing ship, headquarters, small
LSI (H)	landing ship, infantry, hand hoisting
LSI (L)	landing ship, infantry, large
LSI (M)	landing ship, infantry, medium
LSI (S)	landing ship, infantry, small
LSS	landing ship, stern chute
LST (1)	landing ship, tank, Mk. I
LST (2)	landing ship, tank, Mk. II
LST (3)	landing ship, tank, Mk. III
MAC	motor attendant craft
M.A.C.	merchant aircraft carrier
M & RS	maintenance and repair ship
MA/SB	motor anti-submarine boat
MD	mine destructor
M.F.V.	motor fishing vessel
MG (or M)	machine gun
MGB	motor gun boat
ML	motor launch
M/L	minelayer
MLC	mechanised landing craft later LCM
mm.	millimetre
MMS	motor minesweeper
M.R.V.	mine recovery vessel
M/S	minesweeper
M.S.	maintenance ship
M.V.	mooring vessel
M.W.U.	mobile wiping unit, part of the de-gaussing service
M.O.W.T.	Ministry of War Transport
N.H.P.	nominal horse power
N/L	netlayer
(oa)	overall
O.B.V.	ocean boarding vessel
O.S.V.	ocean salvage vessel
pdr.	pounder
P.M.S.	paddle minesweeper
(pp)	perpendicular length
PT	motor torpedo boat (U.S.N. designation)
PTC	motor anti-submarine boat (U.S.N. designation)
R.A.N.	Royal Australian Navy
R.C.N.	Royal Canadian Navy
R.D.F.	radar
R.H.N.	Royal Hellenic Navy
R.E.A.N.	Royal East African Navy
R.I.N.	Royal Indian Navy (now partitioned as Indian & Pakistan Navies)
RML	rescue motor launch
R.N.	Royal Navy
R.Neth.N.	Royal Netherlands Navy
R.N.N.	Royal Norwegian Navy
R.N.Z.N.	Royal New Zealand Navy
R.P.	rocket projector
R.P.N.	Royal Pakistan Navy
R.S.	repair ship
S.A.N.	South African Navy
S.G.B.	steam gun boat
S.H.P.	shaft horse power
S.V.	surveying vessel

T.C.C.	tank cleaning vessel	**VG**	Vickers machine gun
TLC	tank landing craft (later LTC)	**VQE**	vertical quadruple expansion
T.R.V.	torpedo recovery vessel	**VTE**	vertical triple expansion
T.S.	training ship	**W.D.V.**	wreck dispersal vessel
T.T.	torpedo tube	**W.O.A.L.**	war office ambulance launch
U.S.N.	United States Navy	**YN**	boom defence vessel (U.S.N.)
VC	vertical compound	**YT**	harbour tug (U.S.N.)

(**Note:** Vessels allocated to the R.N. under *Lend/Lease* had the prefix B).

INDEX

A

Accommodation ships, base and, 352
    yachts, 330
Admiralty drifters, 407
Aircraft carriers, 52, 56
    ,, merchant, 255
    transports, 260
Amenities ships, 355
American coastal escort patrol sloops, ex., 248
    destroyer escort frigates, ex., 242
    escort sloops (coastguard cutters), ex., 240
    frigates, ex., 247
    minesweeping sloops, ex., 241
    submarines, ex., 152
Anti-aircraft guardships, 295
    vessels, auxiliary
        (coastal), 285
        (seagoing), 280
    submarine boats, motor, 507
        ,, launches, 534
        ,, yachts, 322
Armed boarding vessels, 278
    merchant cruisers, 265
        ,, ,, deployment, 274
    yachts, 322
Attendant craft, motor, 546
Auxiliary anti-aircraft vessels
        ,, (coastal), 285
        ,, (seagoing), 280
    minelayers, 306
    minesweepers, 300
    netlayers, 357
    patrol vessels, 297

B

Barges, landing, 624
Barrage balloon vessels, 280
Base and accommodation ships, 352
Base ships, controlled minelayer, 312
Battlecruisers, 18
Battleships, 15
Boarding vessels, armed, 278
    ocean, 276
Boom carriers, 356, 357
    defence vessels, 360
British destroyer deployment, 133
        development from 1918, 95
    submarine deployment, 156
        development from 1918, 135

C

Cable vessels, 316, 318
Capital ships, 13, 20
    fleet distribution, 74, 75
Carriers, aircraft, 52, 56
    merchant aircraft, 255
    boom, 356, 357
    escort, 255
    landing ship, 571
    seaplane, 56
Chasers, submarine, 509
Coastal escort patrol sloops, ex. American, 248
    escorts, war construction, 162
        ,, ,, modifications, 163
    forces, deployment, 549
        ,, development of, 483
    minelayers, 308
    ocean and, escort sloops, 160
    salvage vessels, 390
    transports, 545
Coastguard cutters, ex. American escort sloops, 240
Controlled minelayer base ships, 312
    minelayers, 310
Convoy escorts, 279
    rescue ships, 396
Corvettes, 201
    war construction, 162
    modifications, 163
Cruiser minelayers, 50

Cruisers, 25
armed merchant, 265
,, ,, deployment, 274

D

Defence motor launches, harbour, 530
vessels, boom, 360
,, harbour, 355
Deployment—armed merchant cruiser, 274
coastal forces, 549
destroyers, British, 133
drifters, 480
escort vessels, 250
landing craft and ships, 628
sloops, 250
submarines, 156
trawlers, 480
whalers, 480
Depot and repair ships, 333
Despatch boats, fast, 534
Destroyer, British deployment, 133
,, development of, from 1918, 95
escort frigates, ex. American, 242
Destroyers, 98
escort, 126
ex. French, 132
ex. R.Neth.N., 133
the old, 79
Destructor vessels, mine, 304
Development of coastal forces, 483
landing ships and craft, 555
Dispersal vessels, wreck location and, 394
Drifters, Admiralty, 407
deployment, 479
naval, 403, 405, 412
requisitioned, 433

E

Emergency repair landing ships, 587
Enemy submarines, ex., 153
Escort carriers, 255
destroyers, 126
,, ex. American frigates, 242
ex. American coastal, sloops (coastguard cutters), 240
ocean and coastal, sloops, 160
sloops, 165
Escorts, coastal, war construction, 162
,, ,, modifications, 163
convoy, 279
ex. American coastal patrol, 248
war construction, 162
war modifications, 163

F

Fast despatch boats, 534
Fighter direction, landing ships, 585
Fishing vessels, motor, 541
Fleet distribution, capital ships, 74, 75
French destroyers, ex., 132
Frigates, 225
ex. American, 247
,, ,, destroyer escort, 242
war construction, 162
war modifications, 163

G

Gate vessels, 357
Guardships, anti-aircraft, 295
Gunboats, motor, 511
river, 312
steam 521

H

Harbour defence motor launches, 355, 530
,, vessels, 355
Headquarters landing ships, 583

I

Infantry, landing ships, 556
Introduction, 6

L

Landing barges, 624
craft, mechanised, 599
,, minor, 587
,, support, 614
,, tank, 603
ship, carriers, 571
ships and craft, deployment of, 628
,, ,, ,, development of, 555
,, emergency repair, 587
,, fighter direction, 585
,, headquarters, 583
,, infantry, 556
,, tank, 576
Launches, anti-submarine, 534
harbour defence motor, 355, 530
motor, 523
Location, wreck and dispersal vessels, 394

M

Mechanised landing craft, 599
Merchant aircraft carriers, 255
cruisers, armed, 265
,, ,, deployment, 274
Mine destructor vessels, 304
Minelayers, 162, 305
auxiliary, 306
coastal, 308, 310
controlled, 310
,, base ships, 312
cruiser, 50
observation, 312
Minesweepers, 161
auxiliary, 300
Minesweepers, motor, 534, 550
paddle, 302
war construction, 162
war modifications, 163
Minesweeping, ex. American, sloops, 241
sloops, 174
yachts, 324
Minor landing craft, 587
Miscellaneous auxiliaries (Part 8), 628
service yachts, 327
vessels (Part 5), 397
(Part 7), 548
Monitors, 24
Mooring vessels, 357, 359
Motor, anti-submarine, boats, 507
attendant craft, 546
fishing vessels, 541
gunboats, 511
launches, 523
,, harbour defence, 530
minesweepers, 534, 550
torpedo boats, 486

N

Naval trawlers and drifters, 403, 405, 412
Neth., R.N., destroyers, ex., 133
Netlayers, 356
auxiliary, 356, 357

O

Observation minelayers, 312
Ocean and coastal escort sloops, 160
boarding vessels, 276
salvage vessels, 389
Old destroyers, the, 79, 81

P

Paddle minesweepers, 302
Patrol sloops, 199

Patrol vessels, auxiliary, 297
Purchased trawlers and whalers, 409
Pennant numbers—auxiliary fighting vessels, 330
,, support vessels, 399
coastal forces, 549
corvettes, 165
destroyers, 80
drifters, 480
frigates, 165
sloops, 165
submarines, 156
trawlers, 480
whalers, 480

R

Recovery vessels, torpedo, 547
Repair landing ships, emergency, 587
ships, depot and, 333
Requisitioned trawlers, whalers and drifters, 433
Rescue ships, convoy, 396
River gunboats, 312

S

Salvage vessels, 366
,, coastal, 390
,, ocean, 389
Seaplane carriers, 56
Service boats, target, 546
Sloops, 159
deployment, 250
escort, 165
ex. American coastal escort, patrol, 248
,, ,, escort (coastguard cutters), 240
,, ,, minesweeping, 241
minesweeping, 174
ocean and coastal escorts, 160
patrol, 199
Special service vessels, 278
Steam gunboats, 521
Submarine, British, deployment, 156
,, development of, from 1918, 135
chasers, 509
Submarines, 136
ex. American, 152
ex. enemy, 153
ex. Turkish, 153
Subsidiary services, 547
Support landing craft, 614
Surveying vessels, 316, 317

T

Tank landing craft, 603
,, ships, 576
Target service boats, 546
Torpedo boats, motor, 486
recovery vessels, 547
Transports, aircraft, 260
coastal, 545
Trawlers, deployment, 479
naval, 403, 405, 412
purchased, 409
requisitioned, 433
Tugs, 366, 367
Turkish submarines, ex., 153

W

War construction, coastal escorts, 162
,, corvettes, 162
,, escorts, 162
,, frigates, 162
,, minesweepers, 162
modifications, coastal escorts, 163
,, corvettes, 163
,, escorts, 163
,, frigates, 163
,, minesweepers, 163
Warships of World War II, 11
Whalers, deployment, 479
requisitioned, 433
purchased, 409
Wreck location and dispersal vessels, 394

X

" X " craft, 155

Y

Yachts, accommodation, 330
anti-submarine, 322
armed, 322
minesweeping, 324
miscellaneous service, 327